P9-DGB-897

ULISYS

Basic Craft Techniques

BASIC CRAFT TECHNIQUES

By Tommy Karlén

CHARTWELL BOOKS INC.
Published by
CHARTWELL BOOKS INC.
a division of
BOOK SALES, INC.
110 Enterprise Avenue
Secaucus, N.J. 07094

ISBN 0–87749–419–3
LCCCN 72–10492

Published in 1973 by Drake Publishers, Inc.
381 Park Avenue, South
New York, N.Y. 10016

Printed in the United States of America

CONTENTS

LIST OF TABLES

CHAPTER 1

INTRODUCTION

1–3. General

a. The earliest works of art are prehistoric. The caveman decorated his caves and fashioned his weapons. We know this from relics, archeological discoveries, and the writings of the earliest historians. Later, artists decorated mud-plaster walls with simple drawings and watercolor paints or engraved or cut designs in stone walls and then painted them. Thus, crafts began because people had an innate desire to beautify their homes and surroundings. These people were limited as to tools and materials, so each article made had to be functional. The colors were soft because they were derived from plants and earth pigments. This original art used common objects (flowers, birds, trees, human figures) as motifs, but some intellectuals developed geometric designs. Surprisingly, some of the oldest designs known to man are still favorites today.

b. The ideal way of working would be to develop original designs; however, this requires creative genius or extensive experience in the field. Few people can meet either criteria. But there is an alternative—one that can be learned easily and is suited to the normal individual. This can be copying or adapting designs to an-other shape or character; *for example,* a small object in a large design can be used as the dominant unit in a new element.

c. The object of the craftsman is to create some useful or decorative piece out of commonplace materials. He finds the greatest pleasure in the exercise of creativity. The procedures given have been carefully studied and the student should be warned that haphazard departure from these procedures may result in a loss of quality. Products, however, should not be measured by monetary values but by what the creating has meant to the student. Once a student has achieved his goal, he will feel a satisfaction that will far exceed any possible monetary gain.

d. The student must be shown that each material has its own characteristics, personality, and limitations. For this reason, this manual does not present a set of rigid rules and regulations but gives hints and examples so that each patient can develop his own resources. It is also important that he be well informed about tools, as no one can turn out really satisfactory work without knowledge of both tools and materials.

CHAPTER 2

ART AND DESIGN

Section I. DESIGN

2–1. General

Good design and good workmanship are the basic qualities of beautiful and satisfying craftsmanship. As considered here, design includes both the form and the decoration of the piece. The inherent differences in the materials and their response in each of the crafts greatly influence the design of each medium. The slender lines possible with silver, for instance, are not appropriate for ceramics. The realism possible with oil painting cannot be achieved in stencil painting. The craftsman must be familiar with the form and design appropriate to each material and work with the possibilities and within the limitations of the materials he is using. Much of the selection of form and design is, and should be, the choice of the craftsman; much can be done to teach good design to the patients quickly and to guide them to use it. Examples of good design through pictures, samples, and literature will often influence selection, as will appropriate suggestions.

2–2. Form

Objects have form or shape. All forms are variations and combinations of the four basic shapes: the sphere, the cone, the cube, and the cylinder (fig. 2–1). Most objects are created to serve a function. For good design, the requirements of the function must be incorporated into the shape. For instance, a pitcher must be designed not only to be pleasing, but it must have a spout which pours well; it must be of an appropriate size for what it is designed to pour; and provision must be made for an easy, secure, and well-balanced grasp of the pitcher. The same principle of design, combined with function, can be applied to weaving. A baby blanket, for instance, must be warm, yet of a lightweight material. The plan or design should also include the use of fine wool rather than of cotton warp or rug wool.

2–3. Design

When the form (or the plan for it) is complete, additional decoration called applied design can be added to enrich the form. The design does not alter the form, yet it must be planned to suit the form and the material used. Good design should be so clearly related to the basic form that it seems to be a part of it. Design includes line, space, proportion, and color. A well-done design can impart a feeling to the observer. Examples of building blocks of design are given in this manual. Some are familiar to everyone; others may not be so obvious. Consideration of all of them, however, may be of some help, both

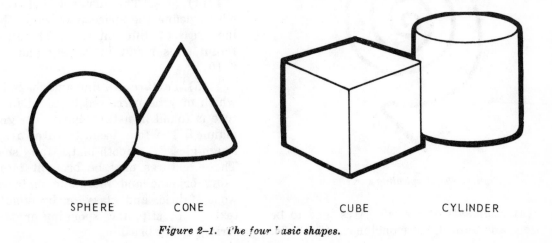

SPHERE   CONE   CUBE   CYLINDER

Figure 2–1. The four basic shapes.

in actually designing and in finding a new appreciation of the work of others.

a. Elements of Design. The following elements of design may be a guide in planning design:

(1) *Line.* The basic lines are straight and curved, but there are many variations. Lines can express moods and qualities.

(*a*) *Straight lines.* These suggest rigidity, precision, hardness, dignity, or strength (fig. 2–2).

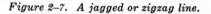

Figure 2–2. A straight line.

(*b*) *Slightly curved lines.* Femininity, lightness, continuity, gracefulness, and softness are indicated by slightly curved lines (fig. 2–3).

Figure 2–3. A slightly curved line.

(*c*) *Curved lines.* Lines which change directions rapidly are active and forceful (fig. 2–4).

Figure 2–4. A curved line.

(*d*) *Spiraling curves.* These are dynamic lines which may typify growing things (fig. 2–5).

Figure 2–5. A spiraling curve.

(*e*) *Segments of a circle.* Arcs tend to be repetitious and unified, but monotonous (fig. 2–6).

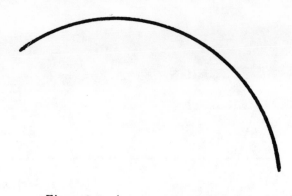

Figure 2–6. A segment or arc of a circle.

(*f*) *Jagged or zigzag lines.* These lines are disquieting and tend to show nervousness or excitement. They can denote conflict or battle (fig. 2–7).

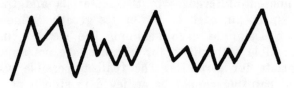

Figure 2–7. A jagged or zigzag line.

(2) *Directions.* In a design, the direction of the line imparts a feeling.

(*a*) *Horizontal.* These lines tend to be restful, quiet, and passive (fig. 2–8).

(*b*) *Vertical.* Severity, uprightness, strength, dignity, and the feeling of soaring are expressed here (fig. 2–8).

(*c*) *Oblique.* This line usually needs the support of a line at right angles to it. It expresses movement, action, and excitement (fig. 2–8).

(3) *Shape.* Shape is a series of lines of different directions defining an area. This area may be round, square, triangular, or another shape (fig. 2–9).

(4) *Size.* The distance between the lines which define the space may vary, thereby making areas of different sizes. These areas of different sizes result in variety and interest (fig. 2–10).

(5) *Texture.* All line and shape have texture which may be perceived by sight or touch. Texture is found in nature, but in design it must be planned. The four basic textures are rough-mat, rough-glossy, smooth-mat, and smooth-glossy. These textures may be brought into design by using organic and inorganic materials such as wood, fabric, and glass, or by simulating these textures by stippling, sponging or daubing, spattering, or dry brushing.

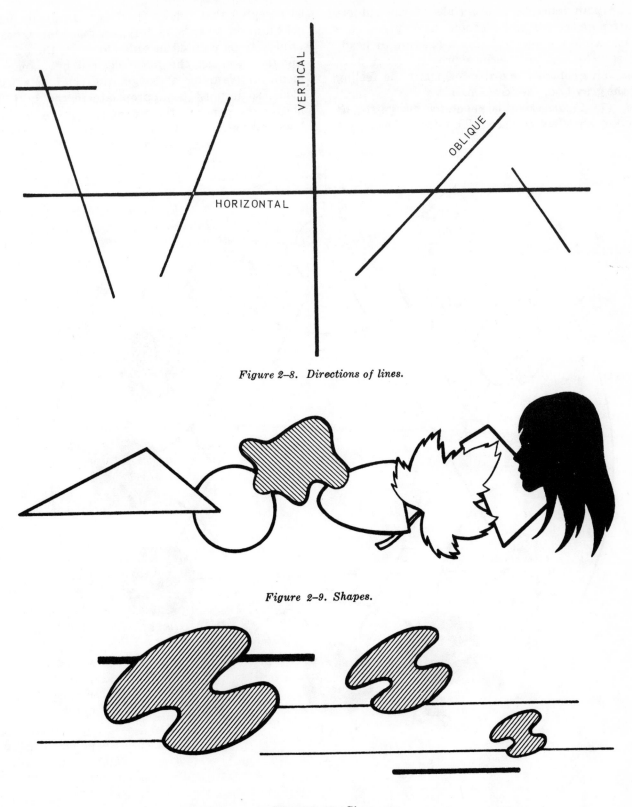

Figure 2–8. Directions of lines.

Figure 2–9. Shapes.

Figure 2–10. Size.

(6) *Value*. Value refers to the amount of lightness or darkness. The values used in a design impart a feeling to the observer. If the contrast between the darkest and the lightest values is great, the feeling is stimulating and cheerful. If there is little value contrast in the design, the feeling is more dignified or perhaps depressed. In planning a design, then, the mood set by the

value plan must be appropriate to the subject matter. A circus scene should have great contrast, while a scene depicting a meeting of heads of state to decide a serious problem must have less value contrast in order to impart the feeling of the gravity of the occasion.

(7) *Color.* Color is generally recognized as having an effect on mood. This theory has been so accepted that color experts are available for consultation when a factory, an office, or a hospital is to be painted in order to select the coloring that will set the mood desired by management. In planning a design, the color sets the mood, so it must be appropriate to the subject matter. In general, the warm colors (reds, yellows, oranges, and browns) are the ones which

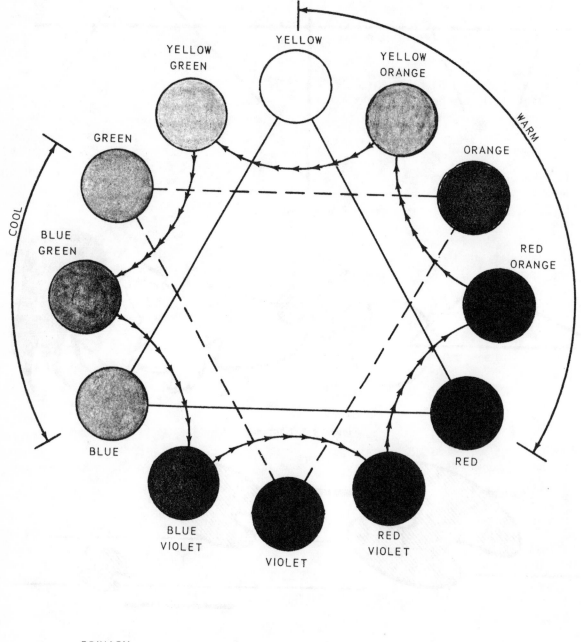

Figure 2–11. Color wheel.

stand out from their backgrounds and are positive, aggressive, and stimulating (fig. 2–11); the cool colors (greens, blues, and violets) tend more to recede into the background; they are retiring, aloof, and more negative. White reflects light, whereas black absorbs light. Some specific colors or hues and the feeling they each impart are listed below:

- Red—greatest power of attraction; most popular; exciting, danger, courage, sex.
- Yellow—least popular; bright, sun, gay, lively; darker greenish yellows—sickness, cowardice, treachery.
- Blue—tranquil, serene, hope, sincerity.
- Purple—stately, pompous, rich, royalty.
- Green—restful, faith, freshness, youth.
- White—delicacy, airiness, purity, truth, truce.
- Black—depressing, solemn, death, evil.

This world would be a bizarre place if the three primary colors were all that were available (fig. 2–11). Mixing color is a fascinating skill, but only the very basic principles can be considered here. One theory of mixing colors is diagramed in the color wheel, which is made by bending the spectrum into a closed circle (fig. 2–11).

(a) *Primary colors.* These are the three colors from which all other colors are derived. Unmixed, they have the highest strength and intensity possible—this is referred to as chroma. The three primary colors are—

- red
- yellow
- blue

(b) *Secondary colors.* Mixing two primary colors gives the secondary colors—

- red and yellow—orange
- yellow and blue—green
- blue and red—violet

(c) *Tertiary or intermediate colors.* These are a mixture of one primary and one secondary color—

- red and violet—red violet
- red and orange—red orange
- blue and violet—blue violet
- blue and green—blue green
- yellow and orange—yellow orange
- yellow and green—yellow green

(d) *Neutrals.* Neutrals are black and white and the many grays produced by mixing black and white in different amounts. Neutrals with just a little color added are near neutrals. Mixing a color with a neutral, either black or white, lowers the intensity of the color.

(e) *Grayed color.* When a color is mixed with a color from the opposite side of the color wheel (called its complement), the result is a grayed color. Red and green, for instance, result in a grayed or near-neutral color.

(f) *Tints.* Colors mixed with whites produce a tint. Red mixed with white produces pink.

(g) *Shades.* Colors mixed with black produce shades. Red-orange mixed with black produces brown.

(h) *Broken color mixing.* This is the old and recently revised technique of placing small units of different colors next to each other without mixing them. The result is more alive and intense than is obtained by actually mixing the colors together.

(i) *Color schemes or combinations.* Colors are combined in many ways. Some combinations are almost traditional because of their constant, age-old, and frequent use. Other combinations, less familiar and less comfortable, are dictated by fashion and fad, so they come and go. The designer must be free to use any combinations he wishes in order to impart the message or feeling that he has in mind. Color schemes that may be used in a design or that may serve to suggest other possibilities are shown below:

- *Monochrome.* Only a combination of one color or hue in different tints, tones, and shades is used.
- *Analogous.* One primary color is used with its neighboring secondary and tertiary colors (*for example,* blue with blue-green and green).
- *Complementary.* Only the two colors opposite each other on the color wheel are used in the design (*for example,* red and green).
- *Split complementary.* One color and either one or both of the colors to the right and left of its complement are used (*for example,* red with yellow-green and/or blue-green).
- *Triad.* Three colors which are equidistant apart on the color wheel are used in a design (*for example,* green, violet, and orange).

b. *Principles of Design.* The principles of design are the fundamental laws of relationship or the plans of organization which determine the way the elements of design are combined for certain effects.

(1) *Repetition.* In repetition, the difference

between the units is in their position or placement.

(*a*) *Exact repetition.* One unit is repeated without even a difference of space between units (fig. 2–12). It is monotonous and uninteresting because of absence of variety.

Figure 2–12. Exact repetition.

(*b*) *Varied repetition.* One unit is repeated, but its direction, size, texture, value, and color may be varied (fig. 2–13).

Figure 2–13. Varied repetition.

(*c*) *Alternate repetition.* One unit followed by a second (or more) unit that is different, giving rhythm and variety (fig. 2–14).

Figure 2–14. Alternate repetition.

(*d*) *Number of repetitions.* An odd number of repetitions is more interesting than an even number (fig. 2–15).

(2) *Harmony.* Harmony is the proper relationship of the parts to the whole.

(*a*) *Harmony of elements.* The units are similar in one or more of the design elements (fig. 2–16).

(*b*) *Harmony of function.* Harmony of dissimilar objects is occasioned by their common association together (fig. 2–17).

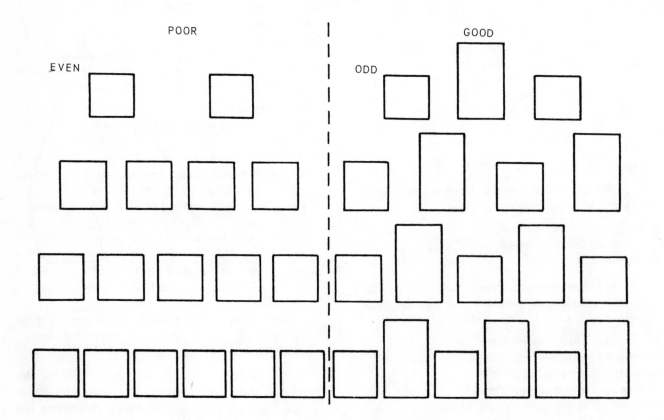

Figure 2–15. Number of repetitions.

12

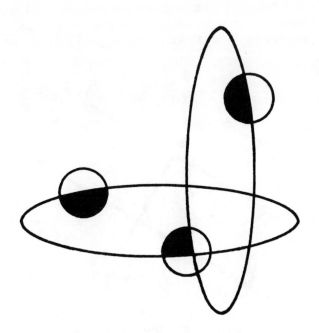

Figure 2–16. Harmony of elements.

Figure 2–18. Harmony of symbolism.

Figure 2–17. Harmony of function.

Figure 2–19. Gradation of sequence.

(c) *Harmony of symbolism.* Harmony occurs also in the symbolism of subject matter; *for example,* a rabbit in a hat conveys the idea of a magician (fig. 2–18).

(3) *Gradation.* This is a type of harmony in which the relationship is one of space and movement rather than of ideas.

(a) *Steps in sequence.* Elements are connected by a series of harmonious steps (fig. 2–19).

(b) *Radiation.* Gradation of directions may be shown by radiation of lines (fig. 2–20).

(4) *Contrast.* Such things as opposing lines, directions, shapes, and colors make contrast in design.

(a) *Discord.* This is complete contrast with no similar design elements. The units are totally unrelated and the result is garish and poor design (fig. 2–21).

(b) *Variety or mild contrast.* Some units

Figure 2-20. Gradation of direction.

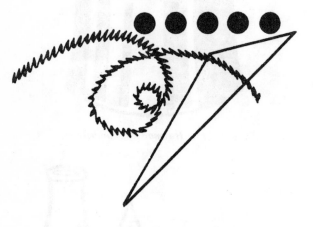

Figure 2-21. Contrast—discord.

have harmonious design elements and others have contrast. This is essential to good design as it stimulates interest and arouses excitement (fig. 2–22).

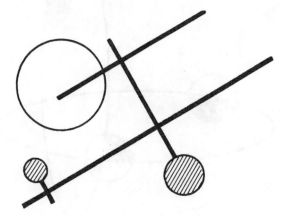

Figure 2–22. Contrast—variety.

(5) *Unity.* This is a oneness and a cohesion of design brought about by the other design principles (repetition, harmony, gradation, variety, dominance, and balance).

(6) *Dominance.* One unit of a design must dominate the other units (fig. 2–23).

(7) *Balance.* The feeling that the designer wishes to give determines the type of balance used.

(a) *Formal or symmetrical balance.* A balance on opposite sides of an axis of one or

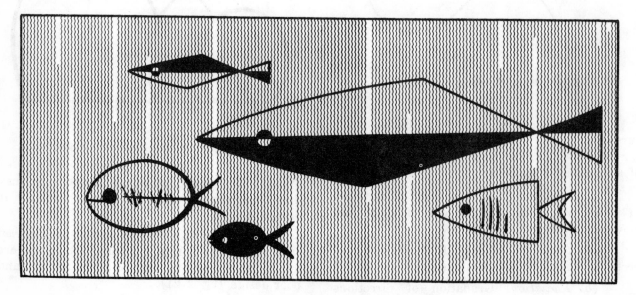

Figure 2-23. Dominance.

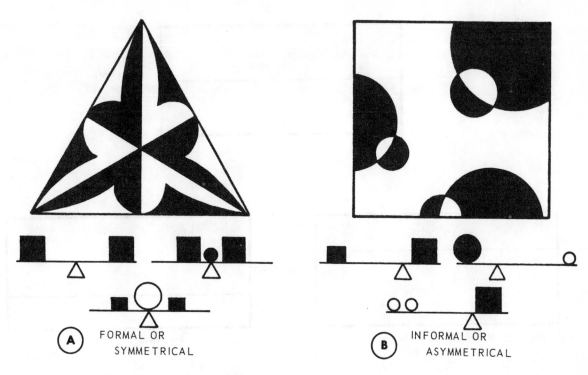

Figure 2–24. Balance.

more units by identical or very similar units. This is classical balance, which is stately, dignified, and serene (A, fig. 2–24).

(b) *Informal or assymmetrical balance.* A balance on opposite sides of an axis of one or more units by dissimilar or contrasting units. This more modern type of balance is informal and less peaceful in feeling, but more interesting (B, fig. 2–24).

(8) *Proportion.* This is a comparison of intervals of length and area which brings about a harmonic relation between parts or different things of the same kind.

(a) *Breaking of a surface.* A good breaking of surface has unit and variety produced by parts which contrast in size and in shape, yet

are related to each other and to the original surface. Although a division at the center is perfect unity, it is monotonous and uninteresting, so halfway points should be avoided (fig. 2–25).

(b) *Horizontal division of an area.* Unequal division of an area can serve to give emphasis in a picture (fig. 2–26).

(c) *Ratios between height and width.* Obvious ratios between height and width, such as 1 to 1 and 2 to 1 are undesirable. Good ratios are 2 to 5, 3 to 8, 7 to 10, etc.

c. *Methods of Design Development.* The basic lines in a(1) above can be developed into motifs or designs in many ways, some of which are suggested to provide a background for further development. *For example,* several different meth-

GOOD

POOR

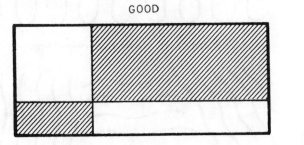

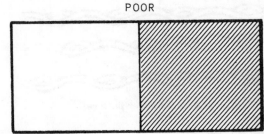

Figure 2–25. Division of surface.

15

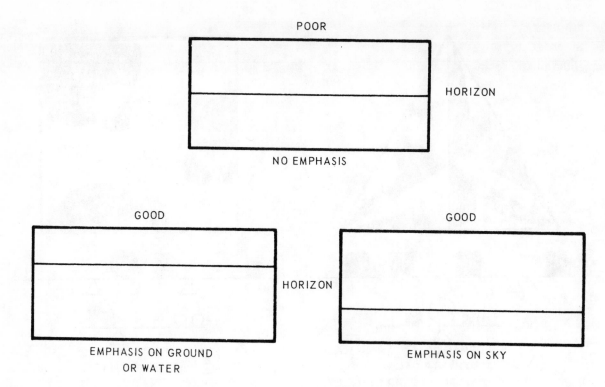

POOR

HORIZON

NO EMPHASIS

GOOD

HORIZON

EMPHASIS ON GROUND
OR WATER

GOOD

EMPHASIS ON SKY

Figure 2–26. Horizontal division of an area.

ods of treating the slightly curved line are shown below. Other lines and simple motifs might respond in as interesting a way to at least some of the methods of treatment.

(1) *Repeat.* The slightly curved line was repeated to form a very simple border design (fig. 2–27). It can also be repeated to make an allover pattern. Here the line has been combined ((2) below) with an arc and repeated laterally and horizontally to form a well-related, allover pattern (fig. 2–28).

(2) *Combine.* Two or more simple elements can be combined to develop an effective design (fig. 2–29).

(3) *Expand.* The curved line is effective in a design if it is expanded (fig. 2–30).

(4) *Condense.* The same element is entirely different when it is condensed (fig. 2–31).

(5) *Change direction.* Changing the direction of the line can be developed into an entirely different border design (fig. 2–32). This could also be made into an allover pattern.

Figure 2–30. Expanded curved line.

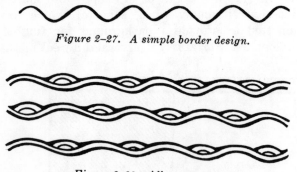

Figure 2–27. A simple border design.

Figure 2–28. Allover pattern.

Figure 2–29. Combining elements.

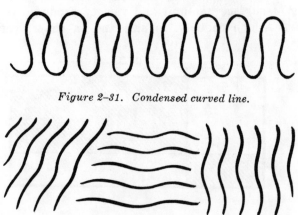

Figure 2–31. Condensed curved line.

Figure 2–32. Changing direction.

d. Interpretation of Design. It is the privilege of the designer to interpret the design as he wishes in order to impart the feeling that he wants people to get from his design. Some of the most common treatments of the same theme are given below:

(1) *Naturalistic.* Record what is seen exactly as it appears in nature without artistic stylization (fig. 2–33).

NATURALISTIC   CONVENTIONAL

ABSTRACT   GEOMETRIC

Figure 2–33. Interpretation.

(2) *Conventional.* In this interpretation, the artist reduces the details, thereby simplifying the naturalistic interpretation (fig. 2–33).

(3) *Abstract.* Here, the motif is reduced to simple shapes and forms, which represent rather than record (fig. 2–33).

(4) *Geometric.* This interpretation is completely angular—without the use of curved lines (fig. 2–33).

Section II. CHARCOAL AND PASTELS

2–4. General

In both charcoal and pastel work, pigment in the form of chalklike materials, is applied to textured paper. The texture of the paper plays an important role in the texture and feeling of the work.

CAUTION

Because of the nature of this medium, the work produces a considerable amount of dust. It is therefore suggested that papers be spread under the working area, that the artist be protected by an all-over apron, and that provisions be made for frequent wiping of the fingers, especially if shading is to be done with the fingers.

2–5. Tools, Equipment, and Supplies

a. Chamois Skin. The chamois skin is used for blending large areas in both pastel and charcoal work.

b. Charcoal. Several types of charcoal are available; inherent in each is a certain softness or hardness or a size which provides textures desired by the artist. A type that is often used is vine charcoal (fig. 2–34). Vine charcoal is not pressed but is in the natural shape of the vine. It is usually softer than pressed and is very fragile to handle. It is available in both large and small sizes.

c. Drawing Board. A drawing board with a smooth surface is important to have when using either pastels or charcoal.

d. Fixative or Fixatif. Because charcoal and pastels are powdery, they must be sprayed with a clear, quick-drying, varnish-based liquid to protect them from rubbing off the paper. Two types of fixatives are used—

(1) Workable fixative dries quickly to a mat finish and may be worked over with charcoal or pastels. It is used to set the work before it is finished.

(2) Spraying with regular fixative is done after the work is completed, to protect the surface from rubbing and from smudges. It cannot be worked over; it is waterproof and crystal clear; and it is available in either gloss or mat finish.

e. Fixative Sprayer. Both charcoal and pastels

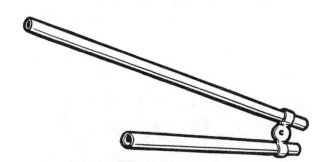

FOLDING ATOMIZER

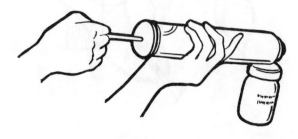

HAND PUMP

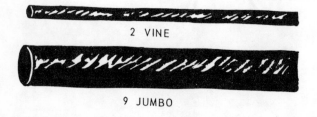

2 VINE

9 JUMBO

Figure 2–34. Vine charcoal.

Figure 2–35. Sprayers.

are sprayed with a material to keep them from smearing. The atomizer (fig. 2–35) is put into the bottom of fixative; blowing into it makes a spray. A different type of sprayer is also shown in figure 2–35. Pressurized cans of fixative are also available.

f. Kneaded Rubber. This soft rubber can be kneaded in the fingers to keep a clean working surface ready to cut out highlights on a drawing.

g. Paper. Several types of paper are used in this work, and some are available in pads as well as in sheets. The choice depends upon the needs of the patients and upon the texture. Newsprint can be used quite successfully for practice work. Following is a list of papers which can be used:

(1) Tinted charcoal.

(2) Suede paper.

(3) Sanded paper in 7–0, 8–0, or 9–0.

h. Pastels. Pastels are usually packaged in sets or single colors in a box of 6 or 12 (fig. 2–36). They are available in different degrees of hardness and in many colors, each with varying percentages of white mixed in the pastel. For use with patients in occupational therapy, it is usually economical to purchase sets of 12 to 30 colors. Then, when necessary, boxes of the most used colors are purchased.

i. Sandpaper Block. A pad of medium sandpaper mounted on wood is used for keeping a point on charcoal, pencils, and pastels (fig. 2–37).

Figure 2–36. Small set of pastels.

Figure 2–37. Sandpaper block.

j. Stumps. Stumps are soft gray paper rolled to form a point to use when blending or shading charcoal or pastels in small areas. They may be double-pointed or single-pointed (fig. 2–38). Stumps may also be made of felt or of leather.

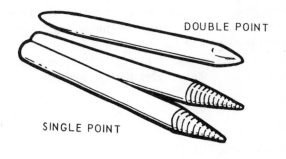

DOUBLE POINT

SINGLE POINT

Figure 2–38. Stumps.

2–6. Using Charcoal

Charcoal is used to plan areas and to sketch in objects in preparation for other drawings. It is also an interesting medium to use in itself. In charcoal work, the subject is viewed as being composed of planes, with light and shadows within the planes. The following steps may be used as a guide in doing charcoal work:

a. With mostly straight lines, divide the area to be used, then sketch in the subject. Use the chamois to erase unwanted lines.

b. Darken the shadowed areas. Do this in two ways—

(1) Draw them in, using a sharpened charcoal stick with medium pressure, stroking in one direction.

(2) Rough the dark areas in with charcoal, then shade with the finger for the large areas and with a stump for the small areas.

c. Use the stumps for softening hard edges or for creating half tones.

d. Use the kneaded eraser to clear the paper of charcoal and thereby pick out the highlights.

2–7. Using Pastels

Pastels are handled in about the same way as charcoal but with the added challenge of color. There are seemingly innumerable colors and variations from which to choose. It is also possible to superimpose one color over another to get subtle shadings. Each artist has his own method of working, but the following steps may be used as a guide:

a. Plan the space by drawing guidelines roughly to get proportions and general form. This drawing is done with charcoal or with a neutral color pastel. Throughout the work, the guidelines must be retained as long as there is a need for them.

b. Start filling in the cloors, using the brighter ones first, as they can be neutralized later. A good policy is to use cool tones for shadows and warm tones in the lighter areas. A color may be altered by working over it with another.

c. Along with the coloring, work with the center of interest to bring it out. An outline of charcoal or browns may be used to emphasize an area. Conform the direction of the stroke to the lines of the object.

d. Blend color with the fingers or a chamois skin in the large areas and with a stump in the smaller areas.

e. Set the color several times with workable fixative. This is done best by spraying at a distance of 20 to 24 inches and using several light coats rather than one heavy one.

f. Step back frequently to appraise the work.

g. Bring out details, outlines, and sharp edges with charcoal or with a finely pointed pastel.

h. When the work is completed, tap the paper to remove loose particles of pastel, then protect the picture with fixatif or frame it, using glass as a covering but with it built up about 1/4 inch from the drawing.

Section III. FINGER PAINTING

2-10. General

Finger painting is perhaps the most fluid, yet the least demanding, means of expression in the art field. Learning to use tools is not a problem; errors are easily erased and an entirely new beginning is provided with a wipe of the hand. The paintings can be framed and used as pictures, or made into book jackets, used to cover wastebaskets, or made into greeting cards or note paper; the larger sheets can even provide interesting paper for wrapping gifts.

2-11. Tools, Supplies, and Equipment

a. Iron. An ordinary iron is used to straighten the paper after the painting is dry.

b. Newspapers. Spread newspapers provide an ideal place for drying the paintings.

c. Paint. Finger paint is a smooth, paste-like water-soluble, nonpoisonous material which comes in a variety of colors (about eight). Sets include finger paint paper, wooden sticks for taking paint from the jars; and small jars of paint in red, yellow, green, blue, brown, and black. It can be purchased in different quantities; the most economical depends upon the quantity of paint used. It is

available in half pint, pint, quart, and gallon sizes. Sometimes it is more economical and more practical to make finger paint. Following are several recipes, including both cooked and uncooked:

(1) *Cooked finger paint.*

(a) 1/2 box laundry starch
1 quart boiling water
1/2 cup talcum powder
1 1/2 cup soapflakes
Oil of wintergreen
Tempera or poster paint

Dissolve the laundry starch in cold water, then add a quart of boiling water to the mixture while stirring it vigorously. Cook the starch and water mixture until it has a glossy appearance. Set it aside to cool. While it is cooling, add 1/2 cup talcum powder and, after the mixture becomes tepid, stir in 1 1/2 cups soapflakes. Add a few drops of oil of wintergreen as a preservative. Pour the finger paint into jars, then add thinned tempera or poster paint for the colors desired.

(b) 1/2 cup laundry starch
Cold water
2 cups boiling water
Food coloring or tempera paint

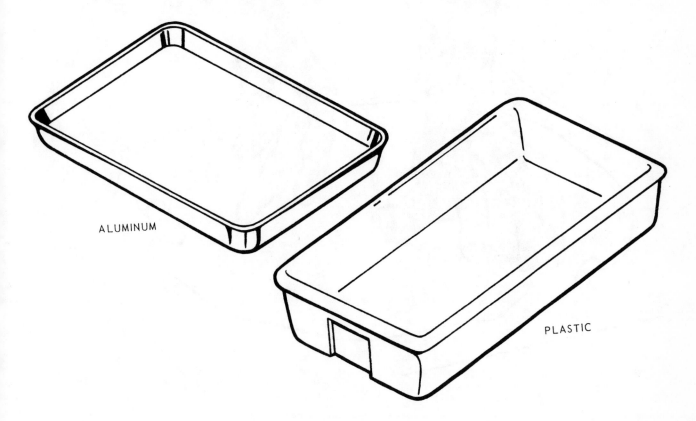

ALUMINUM

PLASTIC

Figure 2-39. Finger paint trays.

Mix the starch with enough cold water to make a thick, smooth paste. Add the boiling water; stirring constantly. Cook until thick and clear—keep stirring. Cool. Add colors. Two tablespoons sodium benzoate will help preserve the paint.

(2) *Uncooked finger paint.*
  (*a*) 3 cups cold water
    1 cup wheat paste (wallpaper paste)
    1 teaspoon dry or liquid tempera

Stir the wheat paste into the cold water, little by little. Add the tempera paint.

  (*b*) Liquid starch
    Dry tempera powder or crumbled chalk
    A little cold water

Use the liquid starch as it comes from the jar. Add a little cold water to aid the spreadability of the starch. Mix in powdered tempera to the color consistency desired.

d. Pans for Water. If there is no sink in the working area, pans of water (fig. 2–39) large enough to pull the 16-inch by 22-inch paper through will be needed. Other pans to hold water for washing the hands will also be used.

e. Paper. Finger-paint paper is strong when wet and has a glossy surface. It is cut in sheets, usually 16 inches by 22 inches, and is available by the sheet, in a package of 100 sheets, or by the ream. White shelf paper is a good substitute for commercial finger paint paper.

f. Rags. These are essential for wiping up paint.

g. Sponge. A sponge is used to clean one color from an area of the paper before another color is added.

h. Spoons. The paint is taken from the jar to the paper with a spoon. Tongue depressors are a good substitute and they do not need to be cleaned.

i. Table. Finger painting should be done on a table with a smooth top which will not be damaged by water. If one is not available, masonite cut larger than the paper is a good substitute.

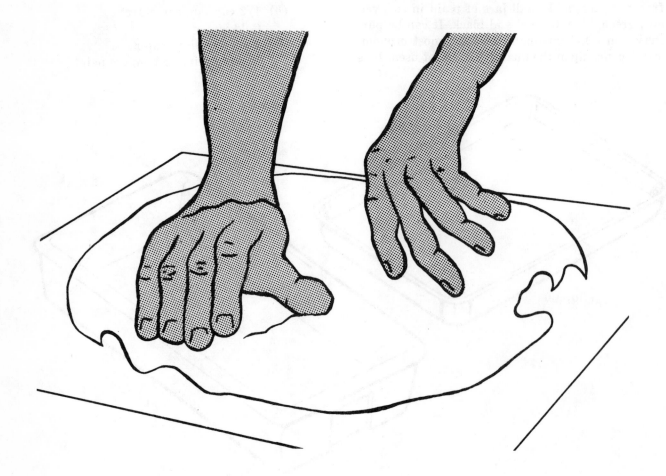

Figure 2–40. Spreading the finger paint.

2–12. Processes

Before any painting is done, the area must be protected from both paint and water. To foster freedom of motion and relaxation, the artist's clothes should also be well protected.

a. Wet the Paper. Run the paper through the water to wet it on both sides. Do not soak the paper as it will lose strength. Lay the wet paper, with the glazed side up, on the working surface. Smooth all air bubbles from under the paper by picking up one end and stroking the paper in the direction of the raised end.

b. Put Paint on the Paper. Put about a heaping teaspoonful of the desired color paint in the center of the wet paper. With the hand, spread the paint over the entire sheet of paper (fig. 2–40), smoothing out any lumps of paint at the same time. In order to cover the edges of the paper with paint, the smoothing might extend over the paper and onto the table at the edge. If the paint begins to get dry, sprinkle on a little clear water and smooth the paint again.

c. Experiment With the Paint. Begin to try the effect of various parts of the hand and arms in the paint. There is no routine or pattern to follow; this is a fluid modality and the artist works as he wishes. Some suggestions to enlarge the scope of effects which can be obtained with this type of painting are listed and illustrated below.

(1) The heel of the hand is used here for pushing the paint around and getting the rhythmic effect. Flower forms can be made by twisting with the heel of the hand (fig. 2–41).

(2) Large leaves can be formed by using an upward stroke with the side of the hand (fig. 2–42).

(3) The little finger and the fingernails give fine detail (fig. 2–43).

(4) The entire forearm may be used for bold, sweeping effects (fig. 2–44).

(5) The clenched fist drawn, twisted, or set on the paint provides additional interesting stro (fig. 2–45).

d. Do a Painting. After thorough exploration has acquainted the artist with the freedom and the possibilities of the modality, he is ready to give attention to composition. The artist should not be bound by realism or meaning necessarily, as just "feeling" can be expressed well with finger painting. When one composition is completed,

Figure 2–41. Using the heel of the hand.

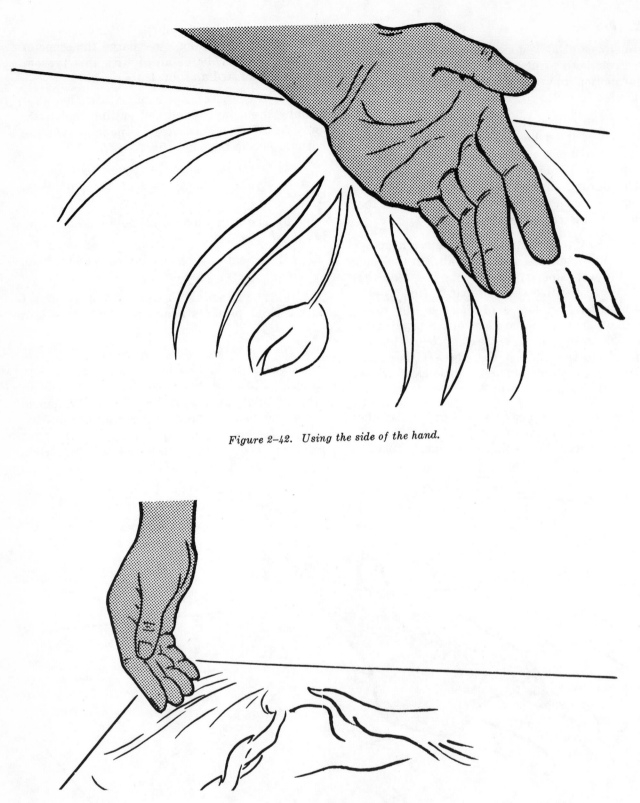

Figure 2-42. Using the side of the hand.

Figure 2-43. Using finger motions for details.

another can be done in the same way, but perhaps with another color of paint.

e. Add Colors. In finger painting, color is secondary to form and shape. It is possible to use several colors in one painting. Blending of colors is done with the hand. To add a new color and keep it clear, put a little of the new color on the table, moisten it, and rub it free from lumps,

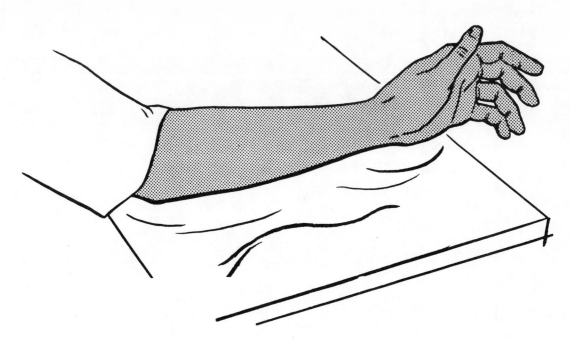

Figure 2–44. Using the entire forearm.

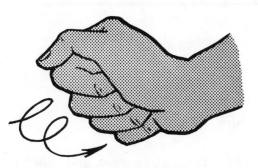

Figure 2–45. Using the fist.

ready for use. Clean the desired spot in the composition by wiping it free of the first color with a rag or sponge, then put the prepared new color in the spot. Proceed then to give the paint the desired form, taking care to keep the background color from mixing with the new color.

f. Finish the Painting. Lift the painting carefully by two corners and peel it from the table or board. Put it on newspaper to dry. After it is thoroughly dry, press it on the reverse side with a hot iron.

Section IV. OILS

2-14. General

Oil has been the basic medium in the art field for over 500 years and there is good reason for this popularity. Oils achieve an unparalleled depth of tone and intensity of color at the start, during the painting, and after completion. Oils dry slowly, so there is time to work and to correct errors before the paint becomes dry. Rewards are obtained from other than the completed painting. Just getting out in the open with a project and a goal is a relaxing change for the person who must work within the confines of a building most of the time. Painting provides a relief from the spectator role and enables the painter to match his ever-developing skills against the complexities of what he sees. Perhaps the greatest intrigue of all is that art is always a pursuit, impossible to catch up with no matter how skilled one becomes.

2-15. Tools, Equipment, and Supplies

a. *Brushes.* Most artists stress the importance of buying the best brushes that one can afford. When purchasing for one's own use, this is recommended. When they are purchased for use in occupational therapy where there is little or no control over how and when they will be cleaned or whether they will be returned, medium-priced student grade brushes seem to be the most serviceable and the most economical. There are many kinds of brushes on the market and each artist soon learns which ones are the best for the type of work he does. Some painters have several brushes of one type and size to use in different colors and thereby save a great deal of wiping and cleaning as they paint. There are two common types of brushes used in oil painting:

(1) *Bristle brushes.* Bristle brushes (fig. 2-47) have rather stiff bristles. The most frequently

used in oil painting are the "brights" which are flat, thin brushes with short hair. The "flat" brush is also flat in shape, but the bristles are longer and thicker. The round bristle brush which comes to a point is used less frequently than the flat ones.

POINTED ROUND SABLE BRUSH

ROUND BRISTLE BRUSH

FLAT "BRIGHT" SABLE BRUSH

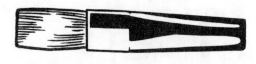

FLAT BRISTLE BRUSH — LONG HAIR — "FLAT"

FLAT BRISTLE BRUSH — SHORT HAIR — "BRIGHT"

BLENDER

Figure 2–47. Actual sizes of recommended bristle brushes.

Figure 2–48. Actual sizes of recommended stable brushes.

(2) *Sable brushes.* Sable brushes are used for oil painting as well as for watercolors. They are made both flat and round (fig. 2–48). Although they are soft, they are somewhat springy and are useful in oil painting for fine detail, for soft brush strokes, and for delicate blending of colors.

(3) *Varnish brush.* A flat 1-inch varnish brush is used to put varnish on the painting. It is obtainable at any paint or hardware store and it does not need to be expensive.

(4) *Brush care.* Good brushes are expen-

SOLVENT SAVER BRUSH WASHER

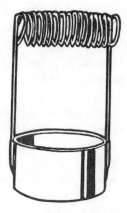

BRUSH WASHER WITH SPIRAL HOLDER FOR BRUSHES

Figure 2–49. Brush washers.

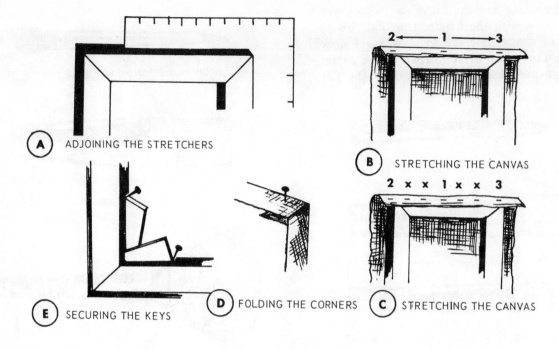

A ADJOINING THE STRETCHERS

B STRETCHING THE CANVAS

2 ← — 1 — → 3

2 x x 1 x x 3

E SECURING THE KEYS

D FOLDING THE CORNERS

C STRETCHING THE CANVAS

Figure 2–50. Stretching the canvas.

sive and they deserve good care. Paint should never be allowed to dry in a brush. To insure proper care, you should—

(a) *Rinse brush while working.* Rinse the brush in a solvent such as turpentine, kerosene, or mineral spirits and wipe it with a rag frequently as you work. The commercial washer in figure 2–49 keeps the brush above the dirty sediment which has settled in the bottom after other cleanings. It also keeps the solvent usable longer. This model can be made at home of two tin cans, with the smaller one cut to about an inch in height and then holes punched down into it. The other washer in figure 2–49 has a spring at the top which holds the brushes in the solvent when they are not being used.

(b) *Clean brushes after use.* After each painting session, insure that the brushes are well cleaned.

- *Paint out excess paint.* Paint out excess paint on newspaper, then rinse well in solvent, working the solvent up near the ferrule, the "heel" of the brush.

- *Wash brush.* Wash it with a mild face soap and in warm water. Work up a lather in the palm of the hand and rub the brush to clean it well. Rinse. Repeat this until the brush shows no trace of color.

- *Shape brush.* Rinse it again, then shape it carefully, and put it away to dry. Never stand a brush on the bristles.

- *Protect from moths.* If the brushes are to be stored over a period of time, take precautions against moths.

b. *Brush Washers.* These were discussed in *a*(4) (*a*) above.

b. *Canvas.* Canvases are available with different textures—rough, smooth, and medium. The selection is up to the artist, based on personal preference and the texture he wishes to have in the painting. Canvas sheets which come in tablet form are inexpensive and good for beginners. Canvas may be purchased already mounted on a rigid surface, or it may be purchased by the yard to be mounted by the artist. The latter method is less expensive and better because it does not warp, but it requires more preparation. The wooden stretchers to which the canvas is usually fastened can be patented strips which are purchased with their corners already mortised and tenoned. Four strips can be assembled to form a rectangular frame of any desired dimension. When the frame is assembled, the canvas is cut to a size 1 inch larger all around than the stretcher (12 by 14 inches for a 10- by 12-inch stretcher). A carpenter's square should be used to check to see if the stretcher strips are correctly alined (A, fig. 2–50). If the stretcher joints are loose, submersion in water will swell the wood and immobilize the joints for some time. Then the canvas is placed on the stretcher, with its face toward the artist, using these steps—

(1) Fasten the canvas on the middle of a stretcher strip with an upholstery tack 3/8 inch long. Pull the canvas in direction 2, (B, fig. 2–50), and place the second tack near the end of a stretcher strip.

(2) Next pull the canvas in direction 3, (B, fig. 2–50), and place the third tack near the opposite end of the stretcher strip.

(3) Fasten the canvas with the remaining tacks placed about 2 inches apart as in C, figure 2–50. Each tack on the illustration is marked with an "X."

(4) Repeat steps 1–3 on the opposite side of the stretcher strip; then on the two remaining strips.

(5) Fold the canvas as shown in D, figure 2–50. Place the keys (small wooded wedges that come with the stretchers) in the grooves on each stretcher strip and hammer them in carefully.

To hold the keys in place, drive a nail in front of each (E, fig. 2–50).

NOTE

When the work is completed, the canvas should be smooth and taut, but it should not be overstrained.

d. Charcoal. Charcoal (sec. II) is used to sketch in spacing and ideas before painting.

e. Easel. Because different types and models of easels are being developed (fig. 2–51), it is wise to look carefully at what is available before one is purchased. If working outdoors is contemplated the easel should be lightweight, folding, and sturdy; the hardware should be rustproof; and the legs should be pointed. Easels of aluminum have been used quite satisfactorily in the past few years. There are many designs; the choice is up to the artist, based on the type of work he does.

SCHOOL EASEL

TABLE EASEL

STUDIO EASEL

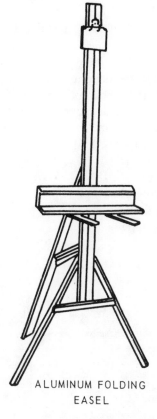

ALUMINUM FOLDING EASEL

Figure 2–51. Types of easels.

f. Paint. In this work, there is no substitute for good quality paint. Not only does good paint look better, but the manner in which it responds enables the artist to do better work and derive more satisfaction from his work. In· addition to the conventional oil paint, an acrylic polymer, resin-based paint will also be considered because of its facility for work with patients.

(1) *Oil base color.* Oil colors are made by mixing pigments (dry colored powders) with a high grade linseed oil. The pigments do not dissolve in the oil, but powerful mechanical grinding disperses them uniformly throughout the oil. Oil paint has a thick creamy consistency as it comes out of the tube. If not altered with a painting medium, it will retain the brush marks when dry. The drying time of oil paints is influenced by the type of paint, the color, the medium used, the thickness of the paint, and the atmospheric conditions. At least a day is required for some, and a week may be required for others.

- Oil colors are put in tubes of different sizes and are sold by the box (table 2–1). The smaller tubes (II or IV) are usually the most economical to buy for use in occupational therapy. However, white is used more than any other one color, so it is usually purchased in larger tubes.

- There are some 70 oil colors on the market. The colors selected depend, in a large measure, not only on the ones with which the artist likes to work, but also upon the subject matter. Here is a list of colors suggested for a basic landscape pallet:

Alizarin crimson
Burnt sienna
Cadmium red light
Cadmium yellow light
French ultramarine
Ivory black
Light red
Viridian
Yellow ochre
Zinc or Titanium white

Table 2–1. Tube Sizes and Quantity in a Box

Tube No.	Size	Number in each box
II	½″ x 2″	6
IV	½″ x 4″	6
VI	¾″ x 3⅛″—Economy size	6
IX	1″ x 4″—Studio tube 1.25 oz	3
X	1″ x 6″	3
XI	1½″ x 6″	1

They can be supplemented at a later time by the following:
Burnt umber
Cadmium orange
Cadmium yellow deep
Cerulean blue
Cobalt blue
Oxide of chromium opaque
Raw sienna

(2) *Acrylic polymer resin paint.* These synthetic paints have become a widely used fine arts medium in the last decade. There are several reasons why they should be considered for use in occupational therapy. Perhaps the most important reason for occupational therapists is that they are water thinned, thereby eliminating the need for turpentine and other painting mediums. Brushes can be cleaned easily in water—but it must be done immediately. They are cheaper than oils and less messy. The paint dries as fast as water does, which is a boon in some ways to the impatient amateur painter. This one paint can be used for a variety of fine arts and craft techniques. It is available in 1 1/8-inch by 5-inch and in 1 1/2-inch by 6 1/4-inch tubes in over 30 colors and at a lower cost than fine oils.

g. Paint Rags. Rags may be obtained from any source. They should be free from loose lint and be absorbent.

h. Palette. Paint is kept ready for the artist and is mixed on the palette (A, fig. 2–52). Some artists prefer a wood palette; others, plastic. The disposable paper palettes have been found quite satisfactory and time-saving in a setting such as is found in occupational therapy. They come in pads of 50 sheets of oilproof, waterproof papers, each of which is torn off of the pad and then destroyed.

i. Palette Cups. These small cups (B, fig. 2–52) slip over the edge of the palette and hold the mixing medium such as oil and turpentine.

j. Palette Knives. There are many types of palette knives (fig. 2–53). Some are for mixing colors on the palette and some are used as a brush in painting. The selection is based on the intended use and the preference of the artist.

k. Painting Mediums. A painting medium is any of several liquids used with oil paints to accelerate or to retard the drying time of the paint. It is wise to use these sparingly as they alter the quality of the paint.

(1) *Turpentine.* "Turp" is probably the most

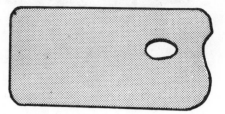

PLASTIC PALETTE

WOOD PALETTE

DISPOSABLE PAPER PALETTE

Ⓐ TYPES OF PALETTES

Figure 2–52Ⓐ. Types of palettes and palette cups.

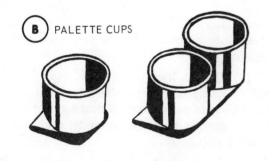

Ⓑ PALETTE CUPS

Figure 2–52Ⓑ. Types of palettes and palette cups.

frequently used medium to cut the consistency of the paint and to speed drying time. Only the pure gum spirits or rectified turpentine should be used. It is available at artist's supply stores rather than at hardware stores.

(2) *Cobalt dryer.* Small amounts added to the paint speed drying time; too much dryer affects the permanence of the paint.

(3) *Linseed oil.* The addition of linseed oil to the paint slows drying time. Too much will make the paint stick and it will yellow after the paint dries.

(4) *Stand oil.* This slows drying time and is also non-yellowing.

(5) *Mixed medium.* To obtain a medium which will give the desired texture and qualities to the paint, several of the media above may be mixed. Some artists prefer a formula of their own; others purchase a mixture already mixed. Some favorite formulas are as follows:

(*a*) 1/3 capal oil varnish
1/3 linseed oil
1/3 turpentine

(*b*) 1/2 turpentine
1/2 linseed oil

(*c*) Oil of capal
Stand oil
Linseed oil

TROWEL SHAPED PALETTE KNIFE

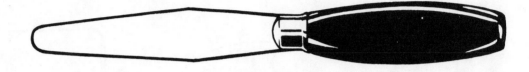

STRAIGHT BLADE PALETTE KNIFE

Figure 2–53. Palette knives.

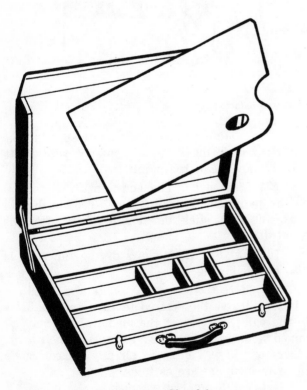

Figure 2–54. Sketch box.

l. Sketch Box. This is another item which is selected according to the needs and the preferences of the artist. There are many types, filled and empty, with different types of palettes, different sizes, partitions, and materials. Some are basic, others have a number of extra features. Figure 2–54 shows a portable sketch box. Some come equipped with detachable legs.

m. Painting Stool. Some artists would rather stand while they work; others like to sit down, at least some of the time. A folding stool is handy to put the sketch box on, if not to sit on.

2–16. Processes

a. Set the Palette. Setting the palette (putting the paint on the palette) is an individual matter. Each artist has his own way—no way is right or wrong. There are some considerations, however, to take into account when a personal method is developed.

(1) Once a handy and comfortable arrangement of paint on the palette has been found, it should be kept consistent so that having a certain hue in a certain place is automatic and no time is wasted looking for it.

(2) Some artists follow the spectrum found in the color wheel when setting up their palette.

(3) Putting side by side the colors which are mixed most frequently is another way to plan a palette.

(4) The time to clean the paint from the palette is also at the discretion of the artist. Some clean it after each use, while others let the paint accumulate until the surface is too full of paint to use and then they clean it.

32

b. Try Out Brushes. Before a picture is started, practice with various brushes and palette knives on a piece of scrap to see how they respond and what they will do. Make thin lines and wide lines; paint in an area with different strokes for different effects. Try first with pure color as it comes from the tube.

c. Try Mixing Paint. Next, try mixing the colors to see how they respond. Mixing colors is an art and a skill based on understanding of the principles involved and experience. Paragraph 2–3a(7) gives a basic theory of mixing colors. For additional information, consult a book on oil painting. After working out step (*b*) above and this step and obtaining some familiarity with the brushes and paint, the beginning painter can then think about painting.

d. Decide What to Paint. The key thought here is to keep it simple. Do not try to paint all that is seen—paint only a small area of it and leave out the details. Outdoors, a tree or a door may be selected. Indoors, a simple still life may be the answer.

e. Sketch in Forms. Roughly sketch the picture over the entire canvas with charcoal. This is just to get the size and placement of the objects. Go over these charcoal lines with a very thin solution of black paint so that the charcoal can be rubbed off. If it is left on, it will "muddy" the color.

f. Paint. Painting should be done in the most comfortable way for each artist. Some hold the brush near the ferrule, some out toward the center. Some people sit, some stand, some hold the palette, some would rather have it on the table. Following, though, are a few suggestions which may be of some help:

(1) A painter should step away occasionally to view the work. This will help to keep the beginner from falling into the trap of overdeveloping one small area, thereby losing the breadth of effect or the meaning of the total picture. Work on the entire canvas as a unit.

(2) Many errors can be corrected by painting over. If, however, in working with an area, it becomes hopeless, scrape off the paint from that area with a palette knife, rub the area with a rag, and start over. Now it is possible to profit from the mistakes made in the first attempt.

(3) It is often helpful for the beginning painter to paint some objects which are distasteful, rather than pleasant, with regard to his taste for subject matter. The task of painting a distasteful subject in itself offers a challenge to the artist and may help to develop a critical eye and more awareness in the artist.

(4) When painting out of doors or when painting natural scenes, it is more realistic to use tints, shades, and subtlety in color rather than brilliant color or color directly from the tube.

(5) A three-dimensional quality can be developed in the painting by using highlights and shadows and by overlapping tints and shades, rather than using dark outlines which are often overworked and tend to hold the picture together.

(6) Perfection should not be the target in painting, but rather enjoyment of the experience with paint. Be patient; skills will develop with practice. Keep your paintings for your own evaluation and constructive criticism from friends.

(7) Plenty of old rags should be kept on hand for cleaning up and for removing paint from wrong areas. Do not paint in your best clothes unless they are well protected by an outer garment such as a smock or an old shirt.

(8) If the tops of the tubes are difficult to unscrew, they may be loosened by heating them with a match. A box of matches should be a part of the artist's equipment.

Section V. STENCILING

2-19. General

a. Stenciling is an ancient process, having been known by the Egyptians as early as 2400 B.C. Today it is a simple, adaptable craft which can be used when a design is to be repeated several times.

b. A stencil is a sheet of thin but strong material from which shapes have been cut so that when it is laid on a surface and color applied, a certain figure is produced.

c. Stenciling may be used for decorating greeting cards, stationery, note paper, posters, place mats, luncheon sets, scarves, chairs, toys, and wastebaskets, to name just a few.

2-20. Tools, Equipment, and Supplies

a. Brushes. Stencil brushes have short, rather thick handles. The bristles are set into a round ferrule and are cut flat at the end, rather than tapered to a point. They are available in several sizes. The selection used depends upon the size of the work being done.

b. Drawing Board. A drawing board with a smooth surface is important.

c. Knife. To cut paper stencils, a thin, sharp knife is essential. A stencil knife is ideal, as is an X-acto knife with a suitable balde (fig. 2-56). If a sharp knife is not available, a new, single-edged razor blade is a good substitute. It is tiring

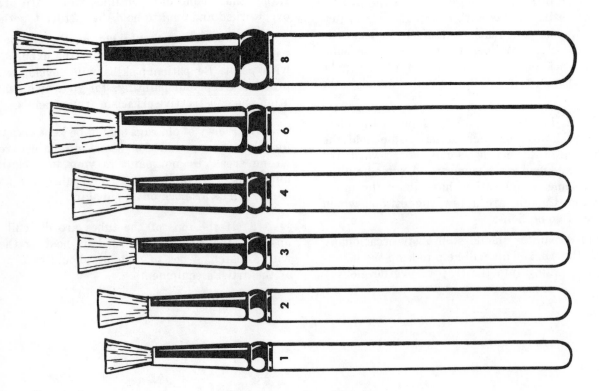

Figure 2-55. Stencil brushes.

STENCIL KNIFE

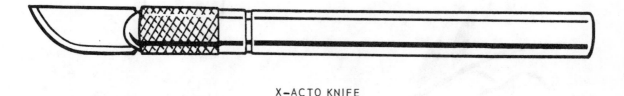

X—ACTO KNIFE

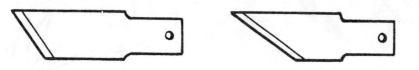

SUITABLE X-ACTO BLADES

Figure 2–56. Knives for cutting stencils.

on the hand, however, if a great deal of cutting is to be done.

d. Material to Stencil. Any smooth surface that will take paint can be stenciled, to include the following suggested materials:

(1) Fabric, such as cotton, linen, rayon, silk, or synthetic fibers which will absorb paint. The fabric should have a smooth weave and should not be fuzzy.

(2) Glass.

(3) Metal.

(4) Paper.

(5) Plastic.

(6) Wood.

e. Pallet. A pallet tray (opaque white trays with depressions) may be used for small amounts of color. For larger amounts, a tile or a piece of glass or plexiglass may be substituted.

f. Pallet Knife. Pallet knives (fig. 2–53) are best for mixing certain types of paint.

g. Paint. The type of paint used depends upon the material used.

(1) Fabric. Textile paint with *extender* to make the paint go farther and *thinner* to thin the paint.

(2) Glass, metal, plastic, wood. Oil paint.

(3) Paper. Watercolor, tempera, or ink.

h. Ruler. A ruler is helpful.

i. Stencil Paper. Several commercial stencil papers of different weights are available on the market. There are also some substitutes for commercial stencil paper which are very satisfactory (3 below).

(1) *Stencil board.* Commercial stencil board is a heavyweight, tough paper which is impervious to water and oil. This material is ideal because it holds up well and, when cut, has clean, sharp edges. It is relatively expensive, however, and is not always available in an occupational therapy clinic.

(2) *Stencil paper.* A strong, transparent, moisture-resistant paper which cuts easily and holds its edge.

(3) *Substitutes.* Substitutes with some of these same qualities include exposed X-ray film, tympan paper, and acetate paper.

j. Square. Include a square with equipment.

k. Tracing Paper. This is for tracing the parts of the design from which the stencil is made.

2–21. Process

Unless readymade stencils are used, the design must be selected, then colored, and the stencil cut before any actual painting can be started.

a. Select a Design. Usually each color in the design requires a separate stencil, which can make stenciling with a number of colors quite complex. As in any new undertaking, it is wise to start with a simple, two-color design (fig. 2–57).

Figure 2–57. Color design.

(1) Select the design and colors.

(2) Line a rectangle around the drawing to serve as a locator for the stencils as they are made.

b. Trace the Design.

(1) On a sheet of tracing paper, trace all of the areas that are to be the same color. In the cor-ner of the tracing, mark the right angle of at least two corners of the rectangle around the design. Thees are registry angles (fig. 2–58).

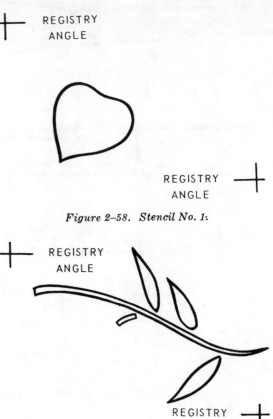

Figure 2–58. Stencil No. 1.

Figure 2–59. Stencil No. 2.

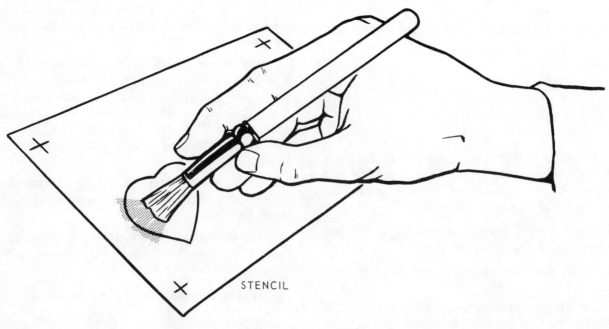

Figure 2–60. Stroking.

(2) Retrace each drawing on stencil paper, using a different sheet of paper for each color. The tracing must include the registry angles.

(3) Repeat steps (1) and (2) above, for each color in the design (fig. 2–59).

c. Cut the Stencil. After the tracings have been made on stencil paper, cut the stencil. To do this, lay the stencil paper on a sheet of Masonite or heavy cardboard and with a sharp knife or a razor blade, cut out the traced areas. The cut lines of the stencil paper must be sharp.

d. Prepare the Background.

NOTE

Steps (1) and (2) below are not used for material other than fabric.

(1) If a washable fabric is being used as background, remove the sizing by washing the material in lukewarm water and mild suds. It must then be dried and ironed.

.(2) Next, stretch the fabric over a firm backing such as the drawing board and hold securely with tacks or with tape.

(3) Decide exactly where the design will be on the background paper, cloth, metal, or wood, and mark registry angles. This can be marked with removable ink or paint, pins, thread, or paper.

e. Paint the Stencil.

(1) Select the stencil for the lightest coler first (fig. 2–58) and place the corner of the stencil paper accurately in the registry mark on the background material. Tack the stencil in place.

(2) Get some paint on the stencil brush, then brush or wipe it nearly dry on a paper towel. If there is too much paint in the brush, it will smear the background.

(3) With the brush held in nearly vertical position, stroke lightly over the opening of the stencil from the outside edge toward the center of the background material (fig. 2–60).

(4) Carefully pull the stencil back from time to time to see how much paint is being deposited on the background material. It is frequently darker than it appears to be.

(5) Shade by stroking more in the area to be darker.

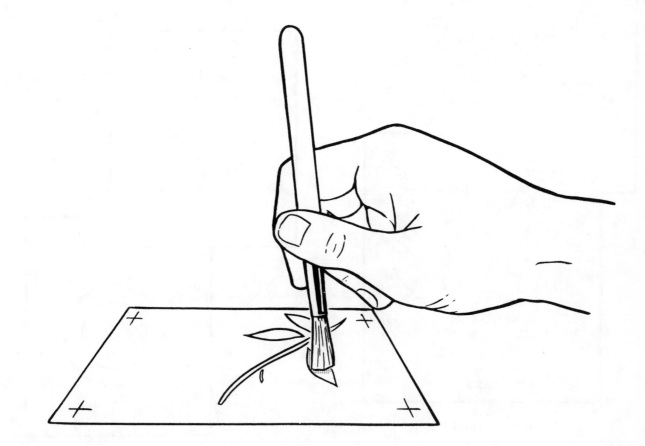

Figure 2–61. Stippling.

(6) To obtain a rounded appearance to the design, make the outer edges of the design darker.

(7) Usually, stroke so as to conform to the direction of the plane being painted.

(8) Use variations if needed. *For example,* it is also possible to hold the brush perpendicular to the stencil and stipple the color on. This is the way to color small areas that are too small to stroke (fig. 2–61). Spattering the color is also an interesting variation. It is especially appropriate to spatter ink on paper. The use of both the positive and the negative parts of the stencil can provide additional variations in stenciling. The positive stencil (A, fig. 2–62) makes a colored figure on the background while the negative stencil (B, fig. 2–62) makes a white figure on a colored background.

f. Set the Color in Cloth. Allow the textile paint to dry for 24 hours, then press the design on the wrong side with a hot iron. Use an iron set to the temperature which corresponds to the background fabric.

g. Correct Mistakes on Cloth. If the cloth is large, many accidents with paint can be prevented by covering the area around the stencil with paper. If a paint spot must be removed near the design, rub the spot carefully with penetrator thinner. If the paint spot is away from the design, rub in extender, let it stand for a few minutes, then wash the area carefully with soap and cold water.

2–22. Design

This medium lends itself to decoration, abstraction, and design, rather than to naturalism. Designs should have well-defined areas, especially for the beginner. As skill develops, more color may be added, along with more intricacy of design. The design must allow for each "hole" to be surrounded by enough stencil paper to hold securely enough to work over it. For instance, a design for the letter "O" must provide some means of support for the inner circle of stencil paper (fig. 2–63).

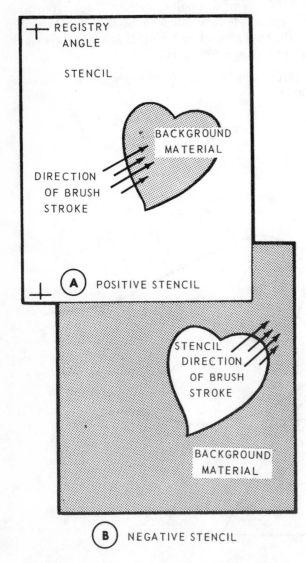

Figure 2–62. Use of positive and negative stencils.

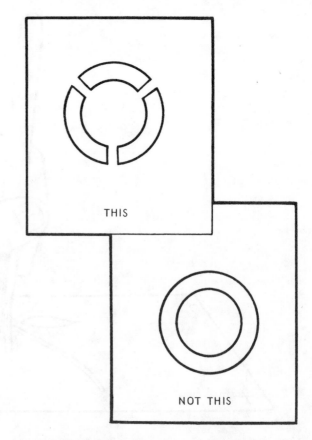

Figure 2–63. Stencil for the letter "O."

Section VI. WATERCOLOR

2-24. General

a. Watercolor is a light, flowing paint which should be applied spontaneously. It is a difficult medium to use because of the speed which must be employed to complete the work while the painting is still wet, and because it is almost impossible to correct errors. Its advantages are that the paint is relatively inexpensive, may be stored in a small area, and is easy to clean up because it is water soluble.

b. Watercolors are classified into two general groups: transparent and opaque. Both types are often used to paint landscapes or still life drawings, though any subject may be chosen. In making signs and posters, the poster paints (opaque) are especially appropriate.

(1) *Transparent watercolors.* Transparent paints allow the white of the paper to show through, giving a fresh, light feeling to the painting. However, this transparency makes it nearly impossible to cover mistakes.

(2) *Opaque watercolor.* Unlike transparent watercolor, the opaque is not affected by the underlying color and thus is more easily handled by the beginner who may wish to cover mistakes. If the opaque paints are used without thinning, a rich texture may be achieved; however, they may also be thinned if more of the feeling of the transparent washes is desired. This thinned opaque paint does not attain as fresh a feeling as the transparent.

2-25. Tools, Equipment, and Supplies

a. *Brushes.* The selection of brushes in figure 2-64 has been recommended for watercolor painting. This great a selection is not at all necessary, however. The No. 3, No. 6, and the 3/4-inch brushes are all that are needed for the work usually done in occupational therapy. The 3/4-inch brush is a work brush for large areas such as sky. The usually valid theory that it is economical to purchase the best brushes available does not apply where brushes are easily lost and are not always left perfectly clean. Medium-priced brushes are usually the most satisfactory and economical under such circumstances. Care in storing brushes by wrapping them in paper keeps the bristles in shape and free from dust.

b. *Drawing Board.* A drawing board with a smooth surface is needed.

c. *Eraser, Art Gum.* This eraser is made from pure gum rubber and is used for safe and quick cleaning of artwork.

d. *Opaque Watercolors.* Opaque watercolors are available in several forms, including egg tempera, casine, acrylic, and poster paints. Only the more commonly available poster paints, commonly termed "tempera," are discussed here. These opaque watercolors are available in ready-mixed form or in powder form. The ready-mixed form saves the chore of mixing, but it will dry out if not used. It is available in sets or by the jar. The powder form stores without damage over a period of time. It is sold in 1-pound cans. Recommended colors are as follows:

Black	Green	Red
Blue	Orange	White
Brown	Purple	Yellow

e. *Transparent Watercolors.* Transparent watercolor paint is available in two forms—

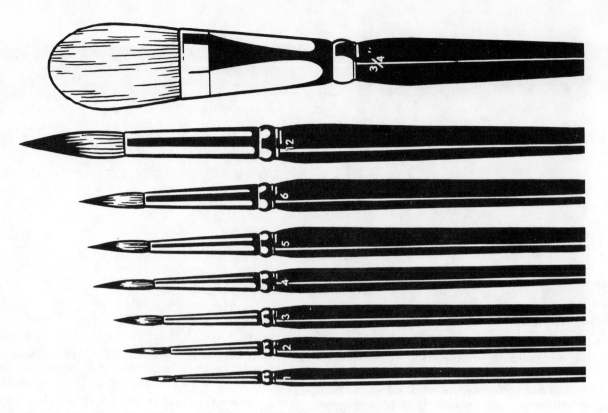

Figure 2–64. Watercolor brushes.

(1) *Watercolor tubes.* Watercolor paint comes in tubes. It can be purchased in sets or by the single tube. Because the paint has a water base, it dries quite rapidly unless the cap is kept tightly closed. The following list are colors which are recommended for starting:

Alizarin crimson   Ivory black
Burnt sienna   Lemon yellow
Cadmium red   Monastral blue

Ultramarine blue   Yellow ochre
Veridian

(2) *Semimoist watercolor.* These sets are available in different sizes. The half-pan in figure 2–65 has 8 colors: the whole pan has 16. This is a convenient way to take watercolors to the ward. It is also easy for the patients to handle. Replacement pans are available for any of the colors, but they are usually sold by the dozen.

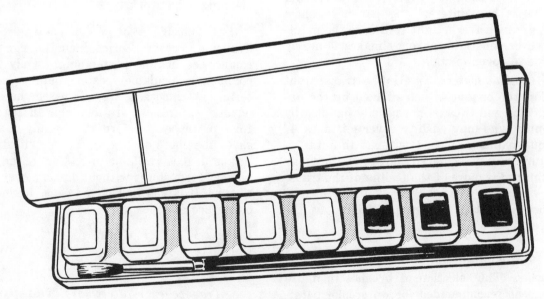

Figure 2–65. Semimoist watercolor paint set.

f. Pallet Tray. These are opaque white trays with depressions designed for mixing colors. A smaller but similar tray is made into the lid of the semimoist watercolor box.

g. Paper. Watercolor paper is available in different grades, textures, sizes, and prices. It can be purchased by the sheet or in tablets. The budget, the type, and the number of patients, as well as personal preference, are considered when slection is made. A durable paper which is made to resist wrinkles even after it is wet should be used. It is good to have a selection of cold press paper, which is suitable for large free paintings, and hot press paper, which is smoother and is used for more detailed work. However, a rough paper is better for transparent watercolors. If large sheets of paper are purchased, they can be halved or quartered to provide the best size for the patient. Paper must be stored out flat, however, rather than rolled. Illustration board is usually used with opaque paint for such things as posters and signs.

h. Tape, 2-Inch, Gummed. This is used to hold the paper on the board while it is drying.

i. Sponge, Elephant Ear. This soft sponge is sometimes used to put wash on large areas.

j. Water Jar. Any jars will do to hold water for cleaning and rinsing out brushes.

2–26. Using Transparent Watercolor

a. Stretching Paper. All papers except the very heavy 300- and 400-pound papers must be stretched before painting. This stretching prevents uneven wrinkling and buckling of the paper.

(1) *Preparing watercolor paper.*

(a) Soak the paper in water for 1–3 minutes.

(b) Lift one side of the paper by its corners and allow the water to drain.

(c) Lay the paper flat on the drawing board so that no air bubbles form beneath the paper.

(d) Blot off the excess water with a clean rag or sponge.

(e) Tape the paper tightly on the drawing board, with four strips of gummed tape, each strip 2 inches longer than the sides of the paper.

(f) Allow the paper to dry as it is taped to the board.

(2) *Preparing illustration board.*

(a) Moisten both sides of the board with a sponge.

(b) Place the board on a clean, hard surface under weights.

(c) Allow the board to dry.

b. Transparent Watercolor Painting. Choose simple subjects for this type of painting. Start over again if the work does not go as it should Some corrections can be made, but do not lose the brilliance of white paper. An interesting additional technique is the use of pen and ink applied over a watercolor wash to outline or accent figures.

(1) Sketch the subject lightly in outline on prepared paper.

(2) Wet the paper and paint onto it before it dries if a soft blended effect is desired. To obtain sharper lines, use drier paper.

(3) Dip brush in water and mix pool of color as needed on pallet. Test the color on a piece of scrap paper before using. Add more water to lighten the value.

(4) Begin painting by flowing on light colors first, using 3/4-inch flat scale brush or elephant ear sponge for washing in large areas. Use color generously, keeping light areas warm (yellow, red, orange, and brown) and shadows cool (green, blue, purple).

(5) Apply the intermediate values next over the dry or damp underpainting.

(6) Apply dark values, outlines, and accents last. Use a No. 12 round sable brush for shadows and small areas.

c. Framing the Picture. In framing a watercolor, the picture is covered with glass to protect the surface from dust and dirt. Watercolors sent to exhibititions must be framed and under glass. In framing, a mat to surround the picture is cut from a strong mat board. The mat may be white or may be painted a discreet neutral tint. A large margin of 4 to 5 inches should be allowed on an average-size painting, though a narrower mat will look better if the frame is to be wide. The mat should be about 1/2 inch wider on the bottom than on the sides or top. The frame may measure from 1 to 4 inches wide, depending on the size and nature of the picture. The wood may be waxed, stained, or painted.

2–27. Opaque Watercolors—Poster Paints

a. Sketch the subject lightly on heavy paper or illustration board.

b. Follow the instructions for transparent watercolors, but remember that the paint is opaque, so it is not affected by the underlying surface in the same manner as the transparent.

c. Use white paint to lighten the color value, though a semitransparent wash may be made by adding water to the opaque paint.

d. Achieve texture through the application of several layers of paint or by the addition of ingredients such as sand or asbestos.

CHAPTER 3

CERAMICS

3–1. Introduction

a. General Definition.

(1) Ceramics is the general term used to describe the art of making things from clay, which is pliable or plastic in the natural state but which, upon exposure to high temperature, becomes hard and durable. Clay is a simple, formless material with little value until the potter, in processing, shaping, and decorating, changes it into a useful or beautiful object of worth. This art has been going on through the centuries and even with the inventions of science, clay remains a challenge. There is still the suspense of firing the kiln and awaiting either the pang of disappointment or the thrill of success. Either result serves as a challenge to greater effort.

(2) The field of ceramics includes a wide variety of industrial produtcs such as bricks, tile, and insulators, but in occupational therapy, ceramics is confined generally to objects such as tableware, decorative knickknacks, jewelry, and sculpture.

b. Definition of Terms. The following terms are pertinent to the field of ceramics.

(1) *Armature.* A form used to support a piece while it is being modeled.

(2) *Bat.* A slab of plaster or fired clay used to work on or to dry moist clay.

(3) *Bisque or biscuit ware.* Clay which has been fired without glaze.

(4) *Blunging.* The process of mixing clay in a blunger, which is a huge mixing machine with rotating paddles.

(5) *Bone dry.* Clay which is thoroughly air-dried but not kiln fired.

(6) *Ceramics.* The art of producing clay products.

(7) *Clay.* Material from which ceramic pieces are formed. The word is generally applied to the natural state without processing.

(8) *Coil.* A rope-shaped piece of clay.

(9) *Crackle.* Deliberate crazing of glaze for effect.

(10) *Crazing.* Minute cracks in the glaze.

(11) *Deflocculants.* The addition of sodium carbonate or sodium silicate to clay to reduce thc amount of water necessary to make it pourable. Used in making slip.

(12) *Dry footing.* Removing the glaze from the foot or from the bottom of a piece so it can be fired in a kiln without the use of stilts.

(13) *Earthenware.* Low-fired pottery (under 2,000° F), usually red or tan in color.

(14) *Engobe.* A thin layer of slip, usually colored, used for decorating clay body.

(15) *Fettling.* The act of removing the seams from a cast piece.

(16) *Glaze.* A liquid mash of finely ground minerals applied to the surface of green or bisque ware. After the glaze dries, it is fired in the kiln, which results in a glossy, glass-like covering over the clay.

(17) *Green ware.* Clay pieces which have not been fired. Moistening could return clay to the plastic state.

(18) *Grog.* Clay which has been fired and ground; used in clay bodies to reduce shrinkage, to give a rough texture, and to prevent warping.

(19) *Key.* Rolls of plastic clay used to hold pieces on the wheel.

(20) *Kiln.* An oven or furnace used to fire ceramic products.

(21) *Kiln wash.* A solution of refractory material painted on the floor and shelves of kilns to keep glaze from sticking.

(22) *Knead.* A method of working clay with the fingers or the heel of the hand to obtain a uniform consistency. Also a method of wedging.

(23) *Leather hard.* Clay which is still moist enough to be carved or burnished easily but is too dry to be plastic.

(24) *Modeling wheel or bench whirler.* A small wheel revolved by hand. Originally used for decorating and banding pottery. Also used in hand building to obtain symmetry.

(25) *Mold.* A hollow form or pattern usually made of plaster of paris and used for casting or pressing clay into a definite shape.

(26) *Overglaze.* Colors applied and fired at a low heat after the piece has been glazed.

(27) *Rib.* A wood base or metal tool used to refine shapes being thrown on a potter's wheel.

(28) *Plasticity.* The capacity of yielding to pressure and of holding the form given by that pressure. A quality of clay.

(29) *Pyrometric cones.* Pyramids made from clay and auxiliary fluxes used as an indicator of heat within the kiln. The composition of the cone determines the melting point.

(30) *Slurry.* Thick slip used frequently for gluing two pieces of clay together.

(31) *Sgraffito.* A form of decoration in which the clay body is covered with a coating of contrasting color. The design is cut through the first layer to the contrasting body.

(32) *Shrinkage.* Contraction of a clay piece due to evaporation and expulsion of water during drying and firing.

(33) *Sizing.* Application of a coating to prevent two pieces, usually plaster, from sticking together.

(34) *Slip.* Liquid clay, the consistency of thick cream, used for casting, for slip painting, or for sticking clay parts together.

(35) *Slip-casting.* The process of pouring slip into a mold in which it is shaped.

(36) *Sprig decoration.* Wafer-thin bits of clay formed into decorative shapes to be applied on green ware.

(37) *Stacking.* Placing shaped pieces in the kiln for firing.

(38) *Stilts.* Refractory material upon which pottery is placed in the kiln during firing to prevent the flowing glaze from sticking to the kiln furniture.

(39) *Template.* An outline or pattern used to shape the profile of a piece.

(40) *Throwing.* Shaping pottery on the wheel.

(41) *Turning.* Trimming down the shape on a lathe or wheel when the clay is leather hard in order to perfect the shape.

(42) *Underglaze.* Colored decoration applied on green ware or on bisque ware before the glaze is applied.

(43) *Warping.* Loss of the original shape of a piece as a result of uneven drying and/or firing.

(44) *Wedging.* Cutting, pounding, slapping, and kneading clay to obtain a uniform texture and to remove all air pockets.

(45) *Wedging board.* A wood- or plaster-covered surface used for wedging clay.

(46) *Wheel.* A vertical lathe used by potters for throwing and turning pottery.

3–2. Forms of Clay

Clay is a mixture of aluminum, silicon, and chemically combined water which, in most instances, contains various impurities which impart special characteristics. Common clays are kaolin, ball clay, fire clay, stoneware, and common (or red) clay. Most of the ceramic clays used today have been compounded to suit specific requirements and may be purchased in the dry state, in moist form, or as casting slip.

a. Dry Clay. When purchasing clay, more clay per pound is obtained by buying the dry form rather than the moist, as the water is included in the weight of the moist clay. Dry clay must be mixed with water before it is used. To mix clay, use a rustproof container and add the clay to the water rather than the water to the clay. Small amounts can be mixed in a plastic bag (fig. 3–1). It is best to allow any clay mixture to stand at least 12 hours before using, as the plasticity of the clay seems to improve with this aging process. It must then be well wedged. The advantages of using dry clay are—

(1) It is less expensive.

(2) It is sometimes therapeutic for patients to mix the clay.

(3) Only the amount that is needed can be mixed, thereby solving the problem of storing moist clay.

b. Moist Clay. Although moist clay is more expensive than dry clay, it is ready to use with little preparation. In some circumstances, this convenience is well worth the cost. To be usable, it must be kept moist in damp boxes or in plastic bags. If it becomes too hard to work easily, a number of thin holes should be poke through

Figure 3–1. Mixing clay in a plastic bag.

the clay to within an inch of the bottom. Water is poured over the clay and it is left to stand. Then it must be mixed, kneaded, and wedged to distribute the water evenly throughout.

c. Slip. This is a mixture of clay and water For casting, chemicals known as deflocculants (sodium silicate and soda ash) are added. With a deflocculant, more clay can be suspended in a given amount of water. Casting slip can be made from dry or moist clay, which is less expensive than purchasing slip by the gallon. The balance of clay, water, and deflocculant is delicate, however, and varies with each type of clay. If this balance is not correct, casting is difficult or impossible. It is sometimes economical to purchase slip as such to insure more satisfying and rewarding work. Slip without the defloccu-lant is used as a mending material to join two pieces of plastic or leather-hard clay; it should be the same clay as the piece being mended. Clay is sometimes called slurry when used in this way. Slip is also used in decorating. Slip may be reconstituted if not fired and should be strained through a fine sieve to remove foreign bodies.

3–3. Types of Clay

Following is a listing of various types of clay used in hand forming. Of those listed, Indian

red and white talc seem to be the most commonly used.

a. Nonfiring Clays. Clays which harden without being fired. These clays are suggested for areas where kilns are not available.

(1) *Mexican pottery clay.* When no kiln is available, this red clay is used because of its self-hardening qualities. The clay is prepared in moist form and can be shaped by any hand method or thrown on the potter's wheel. When dry, the clay is hard and durable, but is not waterproof. Show-card colors or tempera paints are used for decorating; then a clear protective coating is applied. The coating may be shellac, varnish, or one of the commercial products made for this purpose. This is only a protective coating and it will not waterproof the piece. This clay is available in moist form only.

(2) *Modeling clay.* This is an oil-base, non-toxic, nonhardening clay available under a number of different trade names. The texture is fine and smooth, and it is commercially available by the pound in soft or in strong, bright colors. It can be modeled or carved, it retains fine detail, and it is not affected by such things as temperature changes or humidity.

(3) *Oven-baked clay.* All modeling techniques may be employed with this clay. When the piece is completed and dry, it is placed in a regular kitchen oven and baked at 250°–305° F for 20 minutes, then cooled slowly. The piece will be gray in color. It will also be hard and permanent, but not waterproof. For decorating, tempera paints or show-card colors and a clear, portective coating are used, but the coating will not waterproof the piece. This clay comes in moist, ready-to-use form.

(4) *Self-hardening clay.* This is a red clay which requires no firing in the kiln. When the piece is completed and is air dried, it becomes strong and durable. Decorating is done with show-card colors or tempera paints, which are covered with a clean protective coating such as shellac, varnish, or one of the commercial products made for this purpose. These finishes do not waterproof the piece. This clay is available in moist form only.

b. Kiln-Fired Clays.

(1) *Indian red clay.* [Cones 06 or 05 (1859° or 1904° F)] This is a favorite clay, perhaps because it is plastic and is excellent for all forms

of hand modeling. However, it has more of a tendency to shrink and warp than do some other clays. It is a rich red color both before and after firing, which forms the basis for many interesting decorating effects with different glazes and sgraffito designs. The clay is available in dry, in moist, and in slip form.

(2) *Jordan clay.* [Cones 06 or 2 (1859° or 2129° F)] This is a fine working clay which is light pink buff color after it has been fired. It can be used for modeling of all kinds, including throwing, but it is particularly good for slip casting. It comes only in dry and moist forms.

(3) *Monmouth.* [Cones 06 or 2 (1859° or 2129° F)] One of the smoothest working clays on the market, it is excellent for all hand-forming methods and for throwing. It is available only in moist form and is a medium buff color after firing.

(4) *Porcelain clay.* [Cones 3 or 6 (2138° or 2246° F)] Before planning to work with porcelain, check to see if the kiln is made to fire porcelain clay to maturity. Also check to see that the glazes will not burn out at these high temperatures. The modeling formula for this clay is recommended for wheel throwing, for sculpture, and for all other methods of hand forming. It has a smooth plastic quality and is light gray before firing, but the bisque is white. This formula is available in both moist and dry form. Porcelain casting slip is made in white, black, pink, peach, blue, aqua, green, and yellow. These colors can be contrasted in decorating or combined for interesting effects.

(5) *Stoneware.* [Cones 4 or 8 (2174° or 2300° F)] Before planning to work with this clay, check to see if the kiln is made to fire at temperatures high enough to mature stoneware. Also see that the glazes will not burn out at these temperatures. Stoneware is made from natural clays, usually combined to produce a plastic workable clay for modeling and throwing. Because of the chemical makeup and the high firing temperature, the bisque will hold water if it is fired to full maturity. Since the bisque is waterproof and attractive in color, unique effects can be obtained by partial glazing, with slip trailing, and with underglaze decoration. This clay is available only in dry and moist forms.

(6) *Terra cotta.* [Cones 06 or 5 (1859° or 2201° F)] Rough-textured and outdoor pieces such as tiles, planters, and lamps are usually made from this clay, which is red and buff clays

mixed with more grogg than other clays contain. As a result, there is little cracking, shrinking, or warping, and it lends itself well to the forming of large pieces.

(7) *White talc.* [Cones 06 or 05 (1859° or 1904° F)] This clay is versatile, so it is used for hand forming, throwing, and slip casting. It is gray-white before it is fired, but the bisque is intensely white. Decorating colors and transparent glazes retain their true color and brilliance on this bisque, a quality desired by many ceramists. It is available in dry and moist forms, as well as in slip.

3–4. Ceramic Tools and Equipment

a. Tools.

(1) *Bamboo brushes.* These brushes (fig. 3–2) are used to apply underglaze.

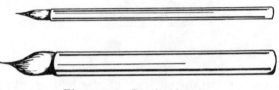

Figure 3–2. Bamboo brushes.

(2) *Calipers, wooden.* Calipers (fig. 3–3) are used to measure outside diameters when turning on a potter's wheel.

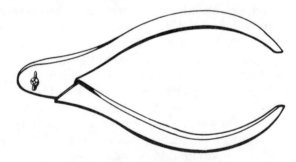

Figure 3–3. Calipers.

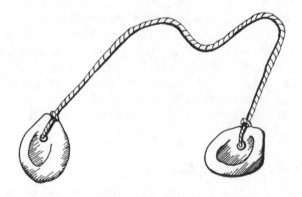

Figure 3–4. Clay pull.

Figure 3-5. Fettling knife.

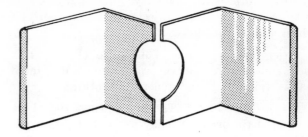

Figure 3-7. Metal lifters.

Figure 3-6. Glaze brush.

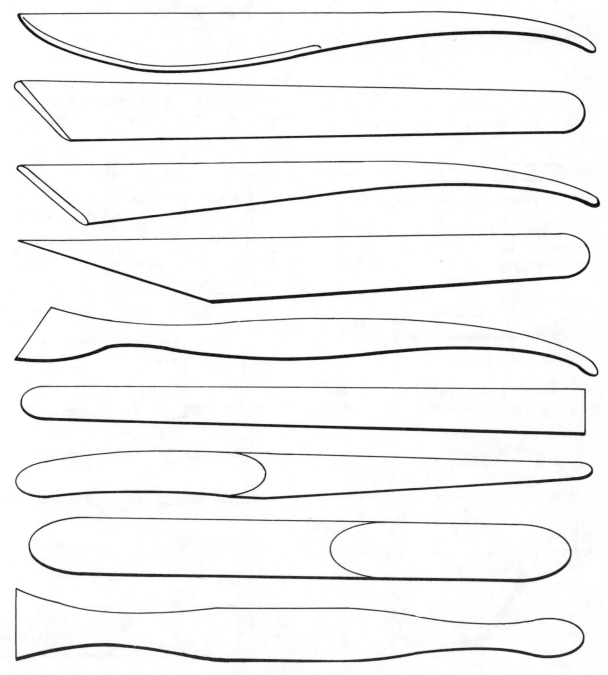

Figure 3-8. Wood modeling tools.

(3) *Clay pull.* The clay pull (fig. 3-4) is used to cut finished projects from the potter's wheel and to cut clay.

(4) *Fettling knife.* This knife (fig. 3-5) is used for cleaning green ware, removing mold marks, trimming, and general smoothing.

(5) *Glaze brush.* The glaze brush (fig. 3-6) is a soft-hair brush, usually camel hair, approximately 3/4 to 1 inch wide, used for applying glaze.

(6) *Metal lifters.* These lifters (fig. 3-7) are used as an aid in lifting projects from the potter's wheel.

(7) *Modeling tools, wooden.* Modeling tools (fig. 3-8) are used in shaping or modeling clay objects.

(8) *Needlepoint or lace tool.* This tool (fig. 3-9) is used for trimming and crosshatching during various methods of construction such as the slab method or throwing.

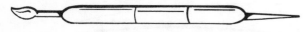

Figure 3-9. Needlepoint or lace tool.

(9) *Sgraffito and cleanup tool.* This tool (fig. 3-10) is used to incise a design in green ware, to smooth rough spots, or to trim seams left by molds.

Figure 3-10. Sgraffito and cleanup tool.

(10) *Sponge, elephant ear.* This is a fine-grain sponge (fig. 3-11) used to smooth green

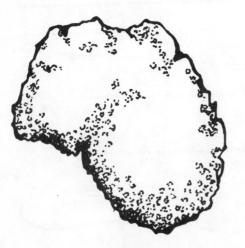

Figure 3-11. Elephant ear sponge.

ware, remove excess water, and moisten leather-hard clay projects before glazing.

(11) *Slip tracer or trailer.* This is a tool (fig. 3-12) used in decorating with slip. It is filled with slip and slowly squeezed to expel slip, thereby leaving a trail or decoration.

Figure 3-12. Slip tracer or trailer.

(12) *Throwing ribs, wooden.* These throwing ribs (fig. 3-13) are an aid used in shaping and raising a cylinder on the potter's wheel.

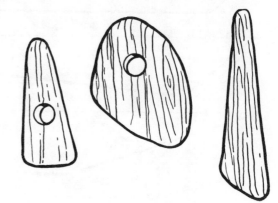

Figure 3-13. Wooden throwing ribs.

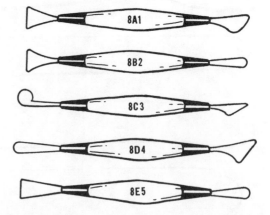

Figure 3-14. Double-wire end or loop tools.

Figure 3-15. Rolling pin (wooden).

(13) *Double-wire end or loop tools.* These tools (fig. 3–14) are used to remove excess clay in modeling, throwing, and sculpturing.

(14) *Rolling pin, wooden.* The rolling pin (fig. 3–15) is used for rolling clay flat in preparation for the slab method of clay construction.

b. *Ceramic equipment.*

(1) *Bat.* A bat (fig. 3–16) is a flat slab of

Figure 3–17. Cross section of damp box.

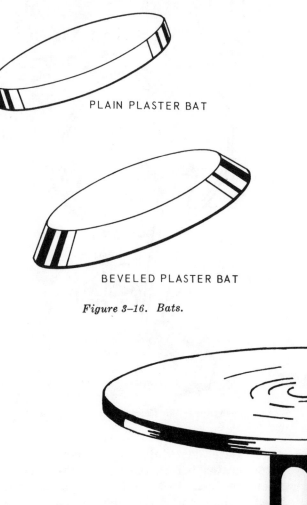

Figure 3–16. Bats.

Figure 3–18. Decorating wheel.

plaster or bisque used when modeling or throwing clay. It is also used to dry out clay.

(2) *Damp box.* A damp box (fig. 3–17) is a storage area with extremely high humidity, designed to keep clay from drying. It must have a rust-proof lining and a tight-fitting door and be equipped with shelves which are open to allow for circulation of moisture throughout the box. It is usually available where ceramics are sold or it can be made—an old ice box is ideal. A large plaster slab at the bottom of the box may be kept water-soaked to maintain the humidity in the box.

(3) *Decorating wheel.* The decorating wheel (fig. 3–18) usually has an 8-inch wheel head marked with concentric circles. It rotates on ball bearings and is used when modeling, sculpturing, banding, spraying, and decorating. When the wheel is transported, it must be picked up by the base, as the wheel will separate from the base.

(4) *Goggles, safety.* Goggles are used to protect the eyes when grinding and spraying ceramic glaze.

(5) *Grinder.* The grinder (fig. 3–19) is hand operated. (It is clamped to the table or workbench and has a fine carborundum wheel attached.) It is used to remove irregularities from the foot of bisque ware and dripping or stilt marks from glazed ware.

(6) *Kiln, electric.* Figure A, 3–20 is a top-loading kiln, and figure B, 3–20 is a side-loading kiln. These ovens are designed to reach temperatures necessary to fire clay to its maturity.

(7) *Mortar and pestle.* The mortar and pestle (fig. 3–21) are used for mixing and grinding glazes.

(8) *Pitcher.* A pitcher (fig. 3–22) is used to pour strained slip into molds.

(9) *Pyrometer, electric.* A pyrometer (fig. 3–23) installed on a kiln indicates firing chamber temperatures. This is an electronic and mechanical device and should be used in conjunction with a pyrometric cone for safe, sure firings.

(10) *Spray gun and air compressor.* The spray gun contains the glaze or englobes to be applied and the compressor (fig. 3–24) supplies the proper supply of air to spray. A 45-pound air pressure is recommended. The compressor should be equipped with a safety pressure valve to prevent pressure build-up from going too high.

(11) *Spray booth.* The spray booth is equipped with an electric exhaust fan (fig. 3–25) that

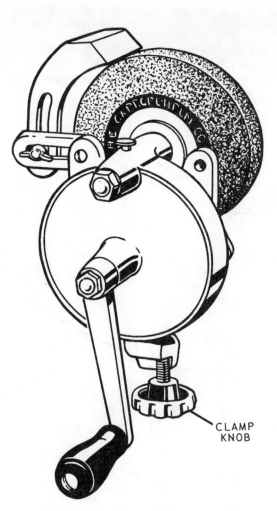

Figure 3–19. Clamp knob hand grinder.

CLAMP KNOB

pulls glaze dust into a fireproof impregnated filter located before the fan at the back of the booth or box. A decorating wheel is generally used to hold the ware when being sprayed, so that it may be rotated for an even coating of glaze.

(12) *Potter's wheels.* Figure A, 3–26 is a foot-powered (kick) wheel and figure B, 3–26 is an electric-powered wheel. Some electric wheels have a 2-speed control; others have a rheostat for variable speeds. All are used for turning cylindrical shapes of ceramic materials.

(13) *Protective spray mask.* This mask (fig. 3–27) is used to prevent inhalation of glass or glaze during spraying procedures.

(14) *Kiln shelves.* Kiln shelves are thin but strong shelves (fig. 3–28) with crescent-shaped notches to facilitate quick heat diffusion. They are made of a silicon carbide, a refractory ma-

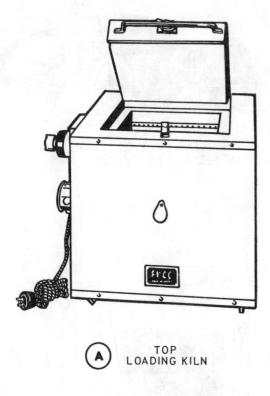

TOP
LOADING KILN

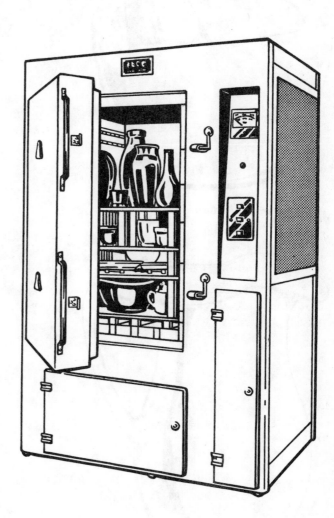

B
SIDE
LOADING KILN

Figure 3–20. Electric kilns.

Figure 3-21. Mortar and pestle.

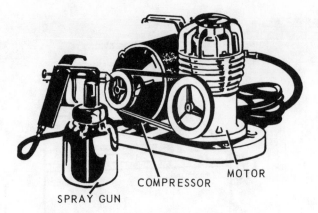

SPRAY GUN   COMPRESSOR   MOTOR

Figure 3-24. Spray gun and air compressor.

Figure 3-22. Pitcher.

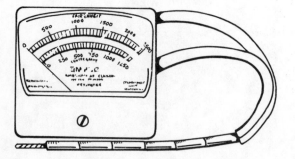

Figure 3-23. Pyrometer.

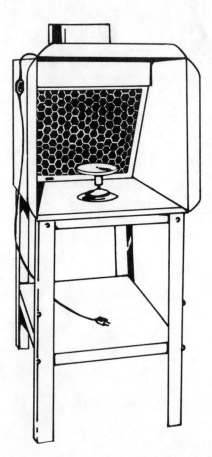

Figure 3-25. Spray booth with exhaust fan.

terial. These shelves are placed in a firing chamber and ceramic ware is stacked on them. The top of each kiln shelf must be coated with kiln wash.

(15) *Shelf supports.* Shelf supports (fig. 3-28) are used in the firing chamber of a kiln to prop, support, or space kiln shelves when stacking ceramic ware in the kiln.

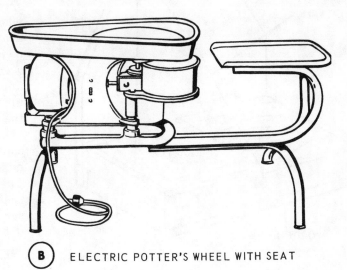

(A) KICK WHEEL

(B) ELECTRIC POTTER'S WHEEL WITH SEAT

Figure 3-26. Potter's wheels.

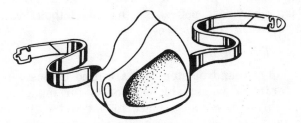

Figure 3-27. Protective spray mask.

(16) *Wedging board.* Clay is wedged on a wedging board (fig. 3-29). If the clay is too moist, the plaster part is used; if the moisture content is right, the wooden part is used in the wedging. The wooden areas of a wedging board are covered with a water-resistant lacquer. The fine steel wire, which is for cutting clay, is held taut by a turn buckle, and the absorbent plaster section should be smooth.

3-5. Plaster of Paris

Molds, wedging boards, and bats for sculpturing and for throwing are made from plaster of paris. Because of this extensive use, one of the first things a ceramist must learn is to mix and to form plaster. Plaster of paris is a gypsum rock that has been specially heated to remove the moisture. The heating process reduces the rock to a soft material which is easily crushed into a fine white powder. This powder has an affinity for water; when it is mixed with water, it sets

or crystallizes once more into a hard, white solid state.

a. Mixing Plaster. When mixing plaster, both water and plaster must be measured accurately. The correct proportion for making molds is 2 3/4

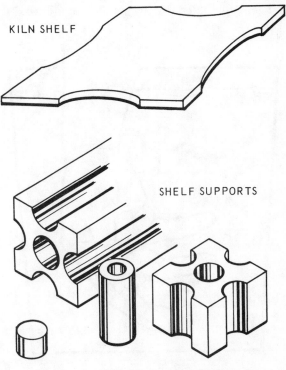

KILN SHELF

SHELF SUPPORTS

Figure 3-28. Kiln shelf and shelf supports.

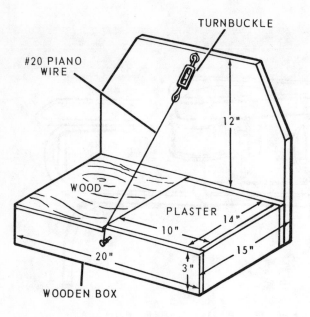

Figure 3-29. Wedging board.

pounds of plaster to 1 quart of water. A greater proportion of plaster produces a mix which is too hard or dense, and not sufficiently absorbent for molds. A smaller proportion produces a weak substance which crumbles easily. In mixing, the water is measured first and put in a pail or bowl, then the plaster is weighed and sprinkled into the water. (If the plaster is sprinkled into the water rather than being poured in, there is less likelihood of it lumping.) When all of the plaster has been sprinkled in, it should be allowed to

slake or set for 2 minutes. This slaking period is important, for if the plaster is stirred too soon, it will form lumps. After slaking, stirring should be done by hand in such a way that the whole mass is agitated and the air bubbles are drawn out. If a pail or deep bowl is used, a method of stirring is to put the hand palm upward on the bottom of the pail and wiggle the fingers vigorously so that the plaster is forced up to the top (fig. 3-30). In a small container, the mixture should be stirred so that the fingers rub the bottom of the container. Stirring should continue for 2 to 3 minutes after the plaster is mixed, or until the plaster begins to thicken. The plaster is ready to pour when the mixture is thick enough so that a finger drawn over the surface leaves a slight trace. Shortly after this, it begins to set.

b. Pouring. Plaster must be poured slowly and quickly, but smoothly without any splashing, so that no air bubbles are trapped and no vacant spaces are formed. It is good to work on a table which can be jarred or vibrated right after the plaster has been poured so that air bubbles can be forced to the surface.

c. Plaster Bats.

(1) Round plaster bats are used extensively in ceramics as movable platforms for modeling and throwing or as a place to put wet clay for drying. To make them, a pie tin about 6 to 8 inches in diameter can be used. Oil or vaseline is rubbed on the pan, but all excess is wiped off before pouring plaster. More than enough plaster should be poured in the pan and, as it begins to

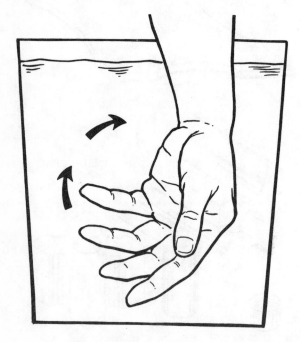

Figure 3-30. Stirring plaster.

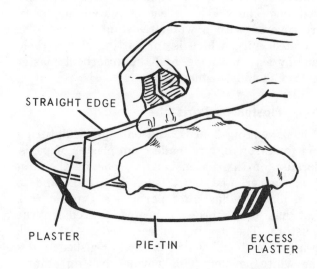

Figure 3-31. Leveling the top of a plaster bat.

set, it should be jarred to release any air bubbles; a straightedge or ruler should be drawn across the top to level it, as shown in figure 3–31; then it must be jiggled a bit to get the surface smooth again.

(2) Removable plaster bats are frequently used on the potters' wheel as a base for throwing. It is possible to purchase a special throwing headset (fig. 3–32) which also serves as a mold for making bats. This head consists of a recessed aluminum wheel head which replaces the regular head on the wheel and an aluminum mold for casting plaster bats. When a piece is thrown on a bat in the recessed head, both the piece and the bat may be removed and set aside for drying without having to remove the piece from the bat. Another bat can be placed in the recess and the wheel is ready for use again immediately.

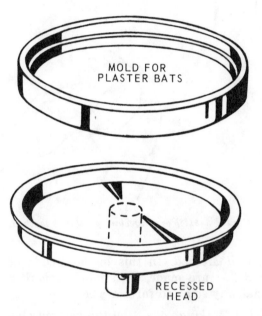

Figure 3–32. Special throwing headset.

d. Drying plaster. Freshly made plaster feels warm and moist as it sets or becomes firm. As it begins to dry, it feels cool and damp. This coolness is present until the plaster is completely dry. To test for dryness, the plaster is held to the cheek. When it no longer feels cool, it is dry. Drying may take from two to six days, depending upon the thickness of the piece and the atmospheric conditions. To hasten the drying process, the plaster can be placed near a *warm* radiator, but not on it, lest the plaster get hot enough to weaken and crumble.

e. Sizing. Plaster may be poured onto moist clay or a clean sheet of glass; when it hardens it will separate from the other material without sticking. If it is poured onto another piece of plaster, however, it will stick. To prevent sticking, soap sizing is used. An easy way of preparing sizing is to put a cake of soap in the bottom of a gallon jar, fill the jar with hot water, cover it and shake it vigorously, then let it stand overnight. The next day there will be a thick layer at the bottom of the jar and a clear liquid at the top. The clear liquid at the top is used for the sizing. When all the clear liquid has been used, hot water is added to the layer at the bottom; it is then shaken vigorously and left to stand overnight. Sizing must be applied to the plaster in several successive applications, each of which is thoroughly wiped off after application. The first application should be very thin so it will soak into the plaster. Sizing may be applied with a soft brush and wiped off with a sponge, or a sponge may be used for both operations.

3–6. Clay

Clay is one of the most plastic, responsive materials that the craftman has at his command. Even the degree of plasticity is easily controlled by the water content of the clay. Clay, as it comes from the ground, is essentially without worth or form; the skill of the potter is the sole determinate of its shape and worth. The shapeless, formless lump of clay has certain inherent qualities which are unyielding to change. In working with clay, the ceramist must respect these qualities or his work is doomed to failure. The methods of forming clay in the following paragraphs have been developed throughout the years. They exploit the plastic qualities, yet stay within the rather stringent limits set by the properties of the clay.

3–7. Preparing the Clay

Clay must be well wedged and pliable before a project is started. Wedging removes the air bubbles which are one cause of pieces exploding in the kiln, and it gives the clay an even texture throughout. While wedging, it is also possible to alter the moisture content. To wedge the lump of clay, hold it in both hands and push it through the wire on the wedging board so that it is cut in two. On the cut surface there will probably be air spaces (A, fig. 3–33). To force the air out of the clay, *throw* one of the two pieces of clay onto the surface of the wedging board, *cut part away*, then throw the other piece of the clay on the first piece in the same manner. The two pieces will land one on top of the other and form one lump of clay. Pick us this lump and again cut it in two on the wire and throw the two pieces on the board, one on top of the other as before. Repeat these steps 20 to 25 times, then check to see if all air bubbles are out of the clay (B, fig. 3–33). If they are not, continue wedging until the clay is *entirely* free of air. The dry plaster half of the board will absorb some of the moisture from the clay. This can be prevented by tacking canvas over the plaster or over the wooden half of the board and wedging on the canvas. More moisture can be added to the clay by poking holes and adding water, then kneading the clay and wedging it.

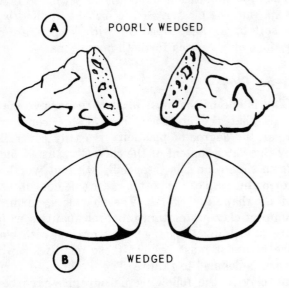

Figure 3–33. Wedged clay.

3–8. Methods of Forming Clay

There are innumerable methods of forming clay, both in the commercial field and in methods considered to be handcrafted. Those methods most practical for use in occupational therapy are the following:

a. Pinch Pot. This is one of the most simple methods of forming clay. Frequently the beginner is asked to start with a pinch-pot piece to get the "feel" of the clay, to know how it responds and what it will do. The hands are the only tools used to form the clay in the pinch-pot method.

(1) Take a piece of wedged clay approximately the size of an orange.

(2) Press the thumb into the center of the ball to within about 1/2 inch from the bottom.

(3) Keep one hand cupped around the ball and rotate it as the thumb of the other hand presses the sides into an even wall about 1/2 inch thick (fig. 3–34). If the clay begins to crack or pull apart, it is too dry. Add a little water by dipping the fingers in water, then continue the forming motions.

(4) When the wall is even, smooth the top or open edges and flatten the bottom so it will set evenly, then put the piece aside to dry.

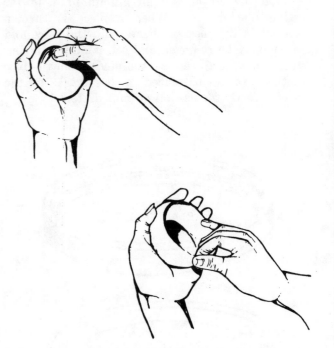

Figure 3–34. Forming clay, pinch-pot method.

b. Coil Method. In this method, coils of clay (fig. 3–35) are made, then joined together in a special way so as to form a piece.

(1) *Making coils.* Roll the wedged clay on a flat surface. This is done by taking a ball of clay about the size of a golf ball and rolling it with the palms of the hands back and forth on the flat surface until it is a smooth, round coil. Start to roll the coil in the center and roll toward the ends. There should be no cracks in the coils, as cracks will trap air and result in an exploded piece. If the coil cracks when it is bent, the clay is too dry, so water must be added. Coils should usually range from 3/8 inch in diameter for small articles to 1 inch in diameter for large pieces. The coils should be used as soon as they are made or they should be covered with plastic, because they dry quickly if left in the open.

(2) *Shaping.* As a guide in shaping the ob-

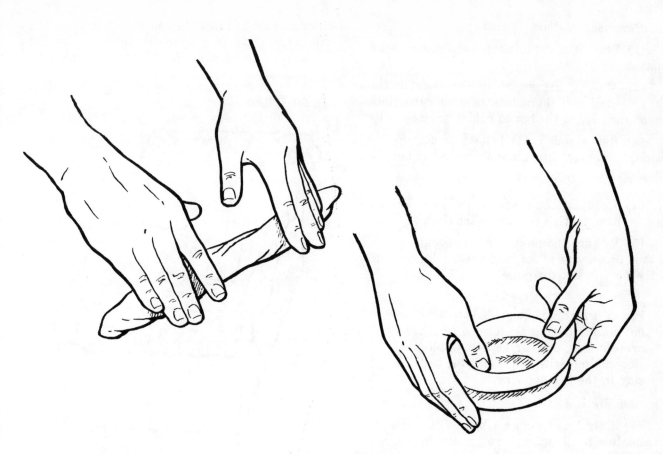

Figure 3–35. Coil method.

ject to be made, make a profile drawing and from it cut a cardboard template. This method is used for the more complex shapes, but for simple forms like cylinders and ovals, the template is not necessary. If a certain size piece is desired, it is advantageous to make the template one tenth larger than the finished product to allow for the loss in size due to shrinkage of clay.

(3) *Adding the base and coils.* Prepare the base of the piece by rolling a ball of clay with a rolling pin between two 1/2-inch wooden strips. Cut the desired shape of the base from this 1/2-inch thick slab of clay and place on a plaster bat. Rough up the top edge of the base where the coil is to be placed with a tool or with the edge of a piece of screening, then coat the rough area with slip. Treat the first coil similarly and apply to the base. Move the two pieces of clay back and forth, then press them firmly together. Continue to add coils in this manner, placing one on top of the other. When the article is about half completed, it is wise to stop and smooth all joints, both inside and out. After this has been done, apply more coils until the proper height and shape are attained. The walls can then be smoothed until they are of uniform thickness.

If a template is used, it should be compared frequently to maintain the proper contour. Apply the last coil to the top, and taper or bevel the end of the coil so as to form a smooth ending. Smooth the entire surface and edge of the piece with a damp sponge to make the surface more smooth in appearance.

c. Clay Hump Mold.

(1) Make a mold by shaping a high hump of moist clay. All sides of the hump should slope toward the top, with no undercuts. Cover the hump with several layers of moist cheesecloth.

(2) Place a fresh clay slab (*e*(1) below) 1/4 inch, 3/8 inch, or 1/2 inch thick over the mold and shape to form with the hand. Smooth the clay slab with a wet sponge and flexible scraper.

(3) Trim around the edge of the clay with a fettling knife and smooth the edges with a sponge.

(4) When the piece is dry enough to retain its shape (called leather hard), remove it from the mold. Smooth the edges with a sponge and flatten the bottom with a metal scraper or add clay legs to keep it from rocking.

d. Hammock Method.

(1) Stretch a damp cloth loosely across an empty box.

(2) Make a depression in the cloth to the shape desired and thumbtack or staple the cloth around the edge of the box to hold it in place.

(3) Roll a slab (*e*(1) below) of clay to the desired thickness and place it in the hammock (fig. 3–36).

(4) Readjust the shape of the hammock, if need be, by adjusting tension of the cloth.

(5) Be sure the piece is deep enough to hold what it was designed for, and avoid folds in cloth as they will mark the piece.

NOTE

Pieces which are too shallow tend to flatten out during the bisque firing. To prevent this, prop areas that would possibly flatten with stilts or with balls of clay in the bisque firing.

e. Slab Method.

(1) Knead and wedge a ball of clay the approximate size needed and roll it out into a slab (fig. 3–37), using a pair of sticks. One stick is put on each side of the clay to hold the rolling pin up so the clay will be the desired thickness. The

sticks may be 1/4 inch, 3/8 inch, 1/2 inch, or 3/4 inch thick, depending upon the thickness needed for the piece to be made. Because clay shrinks, the

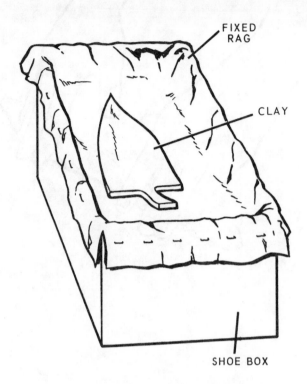

Figure 3–36. Hammock method.

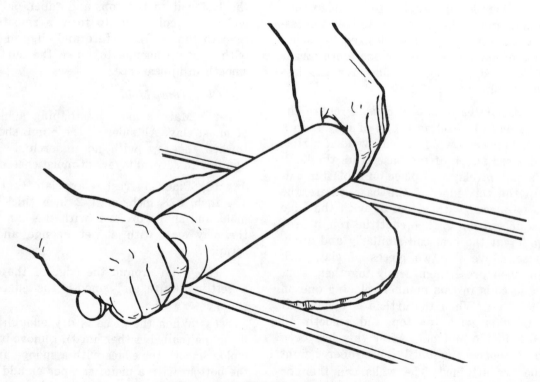

Figure 3–37. Making a clay slab.

wet clay must be thicker than is desired for the finished product.

(2) Cut a pattern from paper to the shape selected, allowing for the thickness of the clay. Lay the pattern on the clay slab (fig. 3–38) and cut out around it with a fettling knife.

Figure 3–38. Cutting slab to pattern.

(3) Assemble the cut sections on a canvas or on a smooth plywood surface. Clay slip is used as an adhesive in joining the slabs. Rough the surface to be joined with a sharp pointed tool, apply slip, and put the pieces together. Settle each piece in with a little back-and-forth motion, then press them together.

(4) To strengthen the joints, press 1/8-inch coils of clay along the edges and corners (fig. 3–39), use a wooden stick to press the coils into the corners, and smooth them with a finger dipped in water.

f. Throwing. Throwing on the potter's wheel is the ultimate of the potter's skill. It is considered by many to be the most interesting and satisfying method of forming caly. To throw well requires patience and practice, but the rewards are well worth the effort. Each ceramist develops his own methods which suit him best. As a result, there are nearly as many throwing techniques as there are ceramists who throw. The steps and suggestions given herein are fundamental principles from which the student's own skill and methods may be developed.

(1) *Hints for throwing.*

(a) Because the head of the wheel turns counter-clockwise, place the right hand outside of the form and the left hand inside. In this way, the clay is turning away from the fingertips, mak-

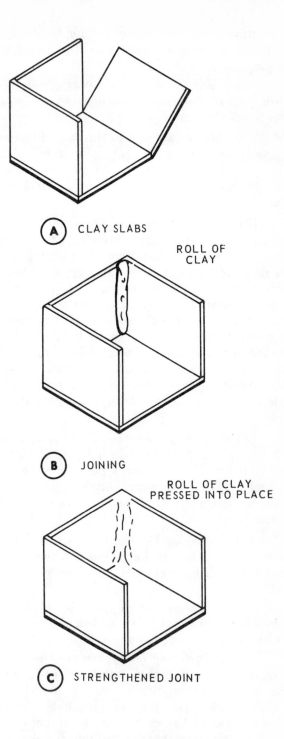

Figure 3–39. Strengthening the joints.

ing it less likely that they will dig in and puncture or pull the piece being shaped.

(b) Use the hands as a unit. One of the most important things to note throughout the entire throwing process is that the hands are usually used as a unit, with one braced against the other. If this is not done, the pressure easily becomes uneven on the piece, throwing if off center.

This practice is very important for the beginner to follow as he is developing skill and becoming acquainted with the clay.

(c) Keep the hands always wet while throwing. If they become too dry, the clay will be pulled off the center.

(d) Keep water out of the base of the piece being thrown. If this is not done, it will absorb into the piece, which will then lose strength. To get the water out of the base, use a damp elephant ear sponge.

(2) *Preparing the clay.* The condition of the clay is important to good throwing. If the clay is sticky to touch, it is too moist and wedging should be done on dry plaster. If cracks appear when the finger is pressed into the clay ball, it is too dry and water must be added during wedging. The clay must be completely wedged for throwing, for air pockets in the clay can throw the piece off center. After the clay is thoroughly wedged, it is formed into a round ball. The amount of clay in the ball determines the size of the thrown piece. A piece the size of a large orange is a good starting size.

(3) *Preparing the wheel.* If the piece is to be thrown directly on the wheel head, be sure the metal is dry. If a bat is used, put it in place on the wheel head and dampen it a little. A pan of water and a sponge are kept within easy reach while throwing.

(4) *Throwing.* The steps below should be followed in making a simple piece. They must be mastered before more elaborate throwing can be accomplished.

(a) *Tossing the clay on the wheel.* Start the wheel moving and toss the ball of clay onto the wheel as near the center as possible (fig. 3–40).

(b) *Centering or mastering the clay.* Dip the hands in water, then stabilize the upper arms by pressing them firmly against the rib cage. With the wheel turning rapidly, hold the hands firmly against the clay with the thumbs riding on top, and force the clay ball into the shape of a cone (fig. 3–41). Then, force the clay down again by pushing the top of the cone gently (fig. 3–42). Repeat this several times to center the clay on the wheel and condition the clay. As this is done, the clay and the hands may become too dry and cause a dragging. When this happens, dip the hands in water again.

(c) *Opening the clay.* With the arms still braced and with fast speed on the wheel, hold the hands against the side of the clay with the

Figure 3–40. Tossing the clay.

Figure 3–41. Centering the clay.

thumbs braced (fig. 3–43). Gradually push the tips of the thumbs down in the center of the clay to make an impression in the top of the clay. When the depression has been made to within about 1/2 inch of the bat, keep the left hand in place against the outside of the clay and move the right hand over to enlarge the opening made by the thumbs.

(d) *Raising the cylinder.* Press the knuckle of the right index finger against the outside of the

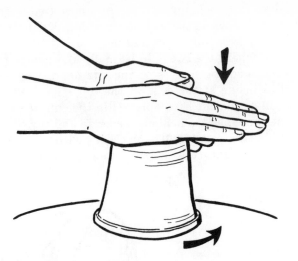

Figure 3-42. Pushing the clay down.

Figure 3-44. Raising the cylinder.

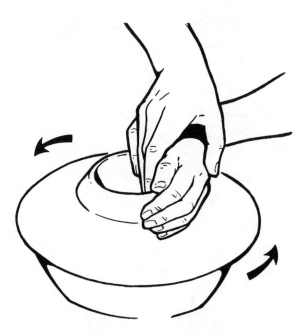

Figure 3-43. Opening the clay.

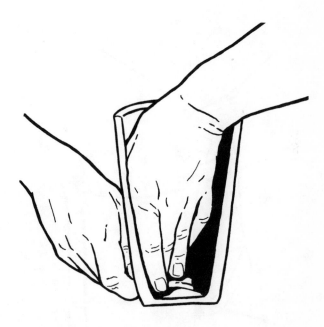

Figure 3-45. Raising a cone (cross section).

clay and press the left index finger outward against the inside of the clay wall. Keep the thumb of the left hand braced against the back of the right hand. Start at the bottom of the cylinder, then slowly and evenly bring the two hands straight up together, pulling the clay into a cylinder (figs. 3-44 and 3-45). A beginner may not be able to raise the cylinder completely at one time, so the raising step may have to be repeated until the cylinder is raised as far as desired.

(e) *Choking in.* To make the cylinder taller and narrower, hold the heels of the hands together and, with the fingers, squeeze in evenly around the cylinder, constricting it to the more narrow shape

(fig. 3-46). Squeezing too hard or too rapidly when choking will make the cylinder twist. After the cylinder is choked, it can be raised more by repeating the raising process to make a taller cylinder with a thinner wall. Of course, the cylinder must be left sufficiently large to get the left hand into it.

Figure 3–46. Choking in.

(f) *Shaping.* Shaping is making bulges and indentations in the cylinder. Have the fingers of the left hand pressing the cylinder out from the inside and the right hand supporting the clay from the outside, or the right hand pressing the cylinder in to make it smaller in places. While shaping, lock the thumbs for support (fig. 3–47).

edge. If this happens, cut the uneven edge from the piece while the wheel is turning. Hold a knife or a needlepoint tool against the outside of the cone where the cut is to be made and gently push it toward the fingers of the left hand, which are held inside of the cone at the top (fig. 3–48). As soon as the cut is complete, flip the cut ring off of the piece as it is held on the knife and the fingers. After the top is cut, smooth it with the fingers and then carefully with a sponge.

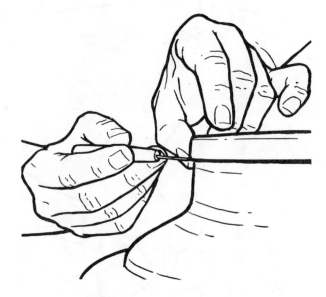

Figure 3–48. Cutting the top.

Figure 3–47. Shaping the cylinder.

(g) *Finishing the edge.* Skilled ceramists can make a piece with an even top edge, but beginner's work often comes out with an uneven top

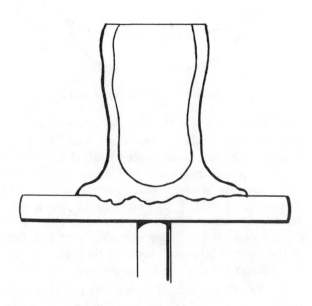

Figure 3–49. Cross section showing clay left at base of piece.

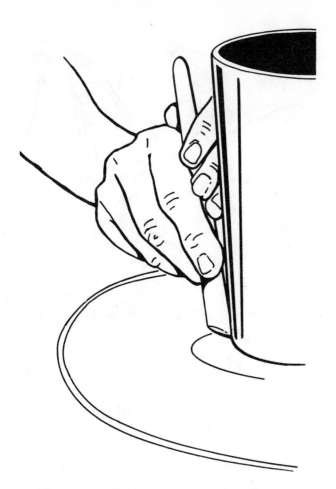

Figure 3–50. Trimming bottom with wooden tool.

Figure 3–52. Lifting the thrown piece with metal lifters.

Figure 3–53. Lifting the thrown piece by hand.

Figure 3–51. Cutting the cylinder from the wheel.

(h) *Removing excess water.* Remove any excess water collected in the bottom of the cone from time to time with a damp sponge. If it is allowed to collect, it will soak into the clay and weaken the bottom of the piece.

(i) *Cleaning the base.* After shaping, there is usually excess clay left on the wheel at the base of the piece (fig. 3–49). While the wheel is turning, remove this with a wooden tool such as a modeling tool (fig. 3–50). Take care that the tool does not dig into the base of the piece or scratch the bat.

(j) *Removing the piece.* If the piece has been thrown on a plaster bat which is not needed in the immediate future, remove the bat with the piece on it to the damp box to start the drying process. Usually by the next day the piece will have dried enough to break away from the bat.

By that time it is almost leather hard and can be removed easily by hand. This is the recommended method because it is the safest. However, if the piece must be removed from the bat, cut it from

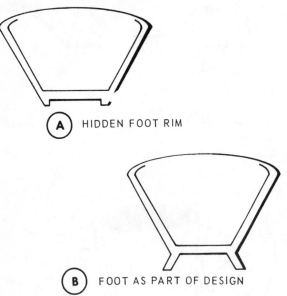

Figure 3-54. *The foot.*

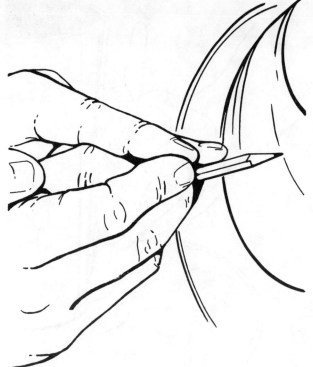

Figure 3-55. *Testing for centering.*

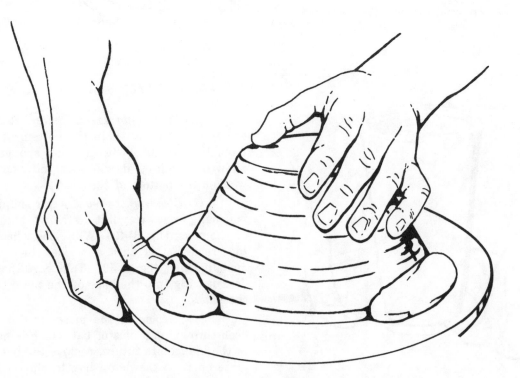

Figure 3-56. *Using clay keys to secure piece.*

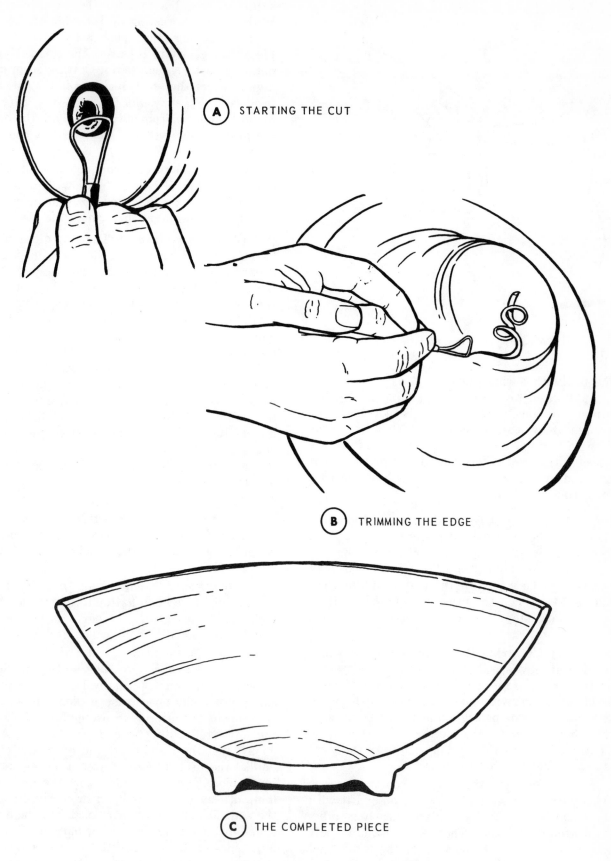

A STARTING THE CUT

B TRIMMING THE EDGE

C THE COMPLETED PIECE

Figure 3–57. Turning the foot on a thrown piece.

Figure 3–58. Forming the spout.

the bat with a clay pull (fig. 3–51) by holding the pull close to the bat and pulling gently but firmly. Obviously, if the pull is not held low enough, the piece will be cut from its base, or the base will be too thin. Remove the piece from the wheel with metal lifters (fig. 3–52) or remove it by hand by using the extra strength of the base for lifting (fig. 3–53).

(5) *Turning the foot.* Turning is trimming clay from the leather-hard pieces to form a foot. The more carefully done ceramic pieces have a small ridge of clay called a "foot." The foot may or may not be a part of the design of the piece (fig. 3–54). When the piece has dried to a firm, leather-hard stage, invert it on the wheel head for turning.

(a) *Centering the piece.* With the wheel turning at slow speed and the piece upside down on the wheel, use a pencil to check for centering. Hold the pencil with the point close to the piece (fig. 3–55). If the pencil bumps at one point, stop the wheel and move the piece away just a little. Continue this checking and moving until the piece is exactly centered on the wheel.

(b) *Securing the piece.* When the piece is exactly centered, secure it to the head or bat with three clay keys (fig. 3–56) placed nearly equidistant around the piece. These keys should be soft enough to hold to the surface of the wheel and form easily around the edge of the piece.

(c) After the thrown piece is centered and

secure, turn out a foot for the piece to rest on. With the hands resting on the edge of the wheel or on a turning stick, push a loop tool into the piece very gently to cut away the excess clay and obtain a foot (A, fig. 3–57). Cutting several thin layers rather than one thick one is the safest and produces the best results (B, fig. 3–57). Care must be taken to keep from cutting through the base of the piece. C, figure 3–57 illustrates the completed piece.

(d) If the piece is completed, set it aside to dry thoroughly. It is wise to allow it to dry some of the time in the inverted position to maintain even moisture content throughout the piece.

(6) *Forming a spout.* The only difference between a shaped cone and a pitcher is a spout and a handle. Both additions are easy to do and they increase the versatility of what the potter can turn out. If a spout is to be formed, leave a little extra thickness at the top of the piece. Stop the wheel from turning, but while the piece is still on the wheel and the clay is very plastic, form the spout. Wet the hands and press the first two fingers of the left hand against the outside of the piece at the top edge (fig. 3–58), and with the index finger of the right hand placed behind these fingers and on the inside of the piece, pull the clay out between the fingers of the left hand. The clay must be pulled and stretched very gently. The marks left by the fingers can be obliterated with a damp sponge.

(7) *Making a handle.* After the thrown piece has dried for an hour or two so it will hold its shape a little, apply the handle, which can be either rolled or pulled.

(a) *Rolled handle.* Make a rolled handle from a coil of clay and flatten it. Cut it then to the right length, rough up the surfaces of the piece and on the handle, and attach it with slip or slurry.

(b) *Pulled handle.* The pulled handle has a better shape and it usually looks more professional. To make one, grasp a "longish" lump of clay, about the size of an orange, and hold it in the left hand with one end protruding (A, fig. 3–59). Wet the right hand and gradually pull or "milk" the protruding end into a somewhat flattened piece, tapering down from the size of the lump of clay in the left hand to nearly a point at the end. The clay must be coaxed into the desired shape by squeezing—a pulling motion (B, fig. 3–59) repeated throughout the length a dozen or more times. When the clay is thin enough for a handle, it will be very pliable. Turn the clay up

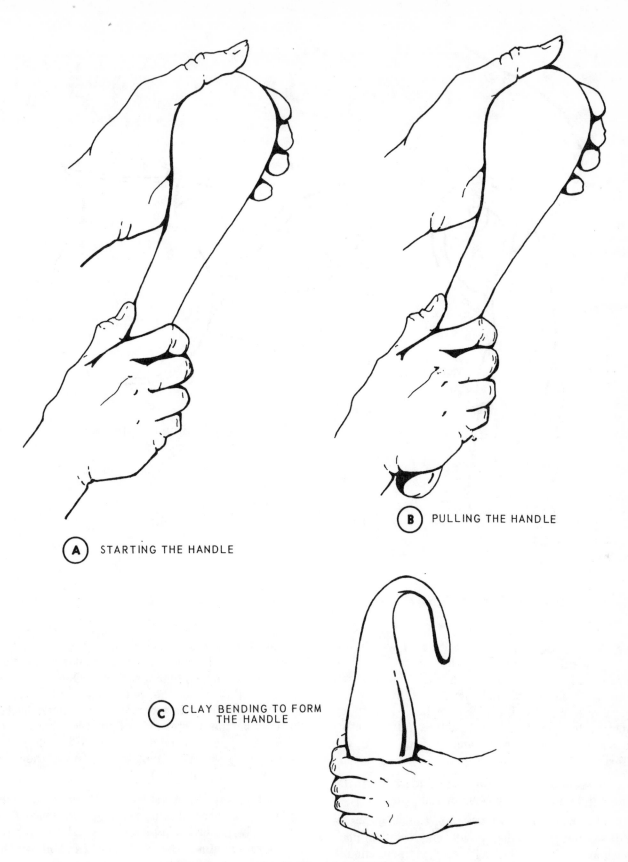

A. STARTING THE HANDLE

B. PULLING THE HANDLE

C. CLAY BENDING TO FORM THE HANDLE

Figure 3–59①. Pulling a handle (sheet 1 of 2).

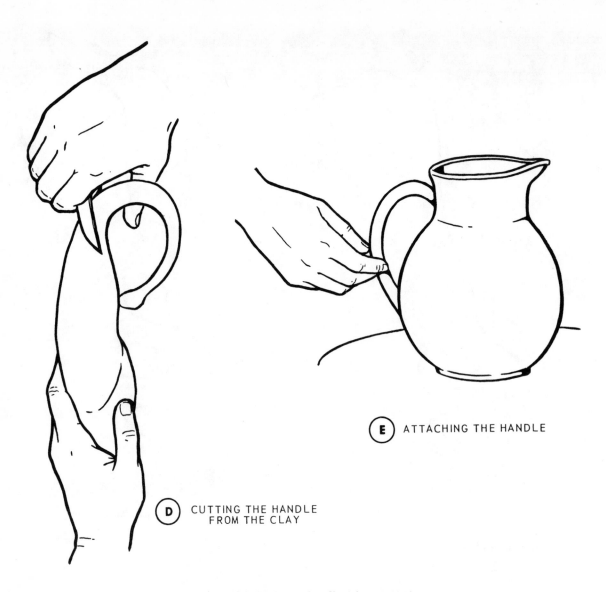

D CUTTING THE HANDLE
FROM THE CLAY

E ATTACHING THE HANDLE

Figure 3–59②. Pulling a handle (sheet 2 of 2).

and the clay tail will bend of its own weight in-to a graceful loop (C, fig. 3–59). Set it aside to harden for 2 or 3 hours. When the clay is set, trim it (D, fig. 3–59) and then attach to the piece (E, fig. 3–59). Pulling a handle is a skill which must be developed through practice, but the better shape on a nicely thrown piece is well worth the effort.

g. Sculpturing. The true test of artistic crafts-manship in clay is with ceramic sculpture.

(1) *Preparation of the clay.* Consider first a suitable clay for modeling. The clay must be plas-tic enough to be worked with ease, yet firm enough to hold up under its own weight. Most modeling clays are firm enough for small pieces (6 inches or

so) but for very large pieces, an armature must be used. For good modeling or sculpturing, the clay must be of the right consistency. One test is to press the thumb into the wedged clay. If the clay is sticky to touch, it is too moist and should be re-wedged on the plaster side of the wedging board. If cracks appear in the depression of the clay ball, add a little water to moisten the clay, then re-wedge the clay thoroughly.

(2) *Three dimensions in shaping.* In con-structing a piece of sculpture, be concerned first with only general shaping: establish the broad masses and values first, and detail can follow. The general shape should be slightly larger than the desired finished size to allow for size lost in

shrinkage and in carving clay off to form the piece. Rotate the piece and view it from various angles as work progresses, for sculpturing embodies three dimensions. It is frequently helpful to work on a decorating wheel which provides for easy turning of the piece.

(3) *Steps in sculpturing.* Small bulky sculptured pieces to approximately 6 inches tall are

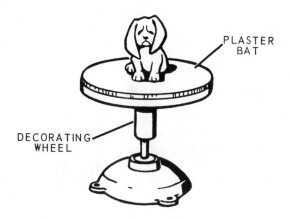

Figure 3–60. Sculpture without armature.

usually sturdy enough to support their own weight and do not need an armature for added support (fig. 3–60). Basic directions for modeling with and without an armature are listed below.

(a) *Without armature.* To do a small basic project, shape well-wedged clay into a ball approximately the size of an orange (A, fig. 3–61), then squeeze and press it with both hands (B, fig. 3–61) and slowly shape into a simple rhythmic shape (C, fig. 3–61). From this point, the figure or shape of the piece is left to the imagination and dexterity of the sculptor, who is free to model the clay into anything he desires, such as an animal, bust, bowl, or abstract figure. Sculpturing is done mainly with the hands, aided with a few modeling tools. The piece must be hollowed out (fig. 3–62) to have a wall 1/4 inch to 1/2 inch thick, to speed drying and to keep it from exploding during the firing process.

(b) *With armatures.* Pieces requiring armatures are generally busts or action poses of figures. In some shapes, the clay cannot support its own weight. *For example,* with a slender body and in a figure with the arms reaching outward, the body and arms will have to be supported dur-

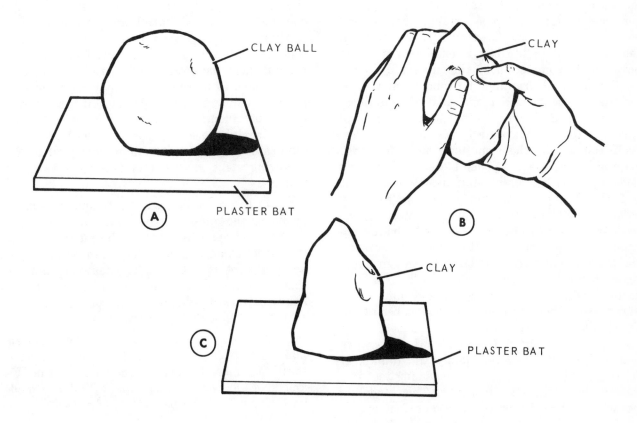

Figure 3–61. Starting a small sculptured piece.

¼" TO ½" THICK

HOLLOWED AREA

Figure 3–62. Hollowed sculptured piece.

ing the modeling, or the clay will collapse. For this type of sculpturing, use an armature of pipe and wire such as that in figure 3–63. The armature may be a simple upright piece of wood or the more complicated wire and pipe arrangement. It can also be a plastic bag filled with sand and then tied. The sand in the bag is excellent; it is removed upon completion of the project by opening the bag and draining the sand, then removing the plastic bag. For the sake of simplification, doing a bust over a sandbag armature will be considered. In this project, most techniques are used: the use of the armature; hand forming; shaping by the use of wooden blocks, mallets, and modeling tools. The first step in modeling a bust is to form an appropriate amount of wedged clay around the upright piece of wood containing the sandbag on the armature. Then, with hands opposing one another, press the clay into roughly the desired shape (fig. 3–64). After rough shaping with the hands, use wooden blocks or a mallet for pushing or pounding the clay into shape (fig. 3–65). When the roughing cut has been completed and the large masses are shaped, more modeling detail begins (A, fig. 3–66). This work is done with the fingers, mainly the thumb. If the thumb becomes weary, the modeling tool is a good replacement (B, fig. 3–66). This modeling tool with its broad, slightly curved surface is useful for pressing on additional lumps of clay to build up form. The next step is the final detail

and finishing of surfaces, and a wire loop tool in various shapes is useful for removing excess clay, for example, around the eyes and the nose (C, fig. 3–66). This sculpturing and shading may take days or even weeks to complete. When it is not being worked on, it must be kept moist with wet towels and plastic. Upon completion, smooth the surface with a damp sponge and set the piece aside to dry slowly and evenly to leather hard. Then remove the armature by untying the string or binding holding the sand and removing the wooden post and plastic bag. Let the piece dry thoroughly and evenly until it is bone dry and is ready to fire.

3–9. Mold Making and Slip Casting

Mold making and slip casting are discussed together because in practice they are inseparable. The molds into which clay slip is poured are made of plaster of paris. Utmost care must be taken in making molds in order to have good results in the process of slip casting.

a. Mold Making. Depending upon the shape of the piece being reproduced, molds may be simple one-piece molds, or they may be very complex with many pieces fitting together. The beginner should attempt to reproduce a simple shape, one that requires no more than a two-piece mold. A shape with undercuts requires a mold which separates laterally. It can be reproduced in a two-piece mold if the bottom is flat, rather than footed. A shape to be reproduced may be made from plaster, it may be modeled from oil-base clay, or it may be taken from a readymade piece. Because of the shrinkage of clay, a mold will produce a duplicate a little smaller than the original. The following steps are used in making a two-piece mold:

(1) *Cut a template.* Cut a template to fit the profile of the piece exactly. To do this, draw center lines on opposite sides of the model, dividing the model exactly in half. This can be done with a try square (fig. 3–67). The template must fit this marked line. The template may be cut from heavy cardboard, which is then coated with three coates of shellac and sized with soap.

(2) *Embed the modeling clay.* Lay the template on soft clay, then put the model in place so that it is embedded exactly to the centerline. Fill any space between the template and the model with clay to secure a perfect fit. (fig. 3–68).

(3) *Make a plug to form the opening.* Out of clay, make a plug to fit 1/2 inch beyond the top

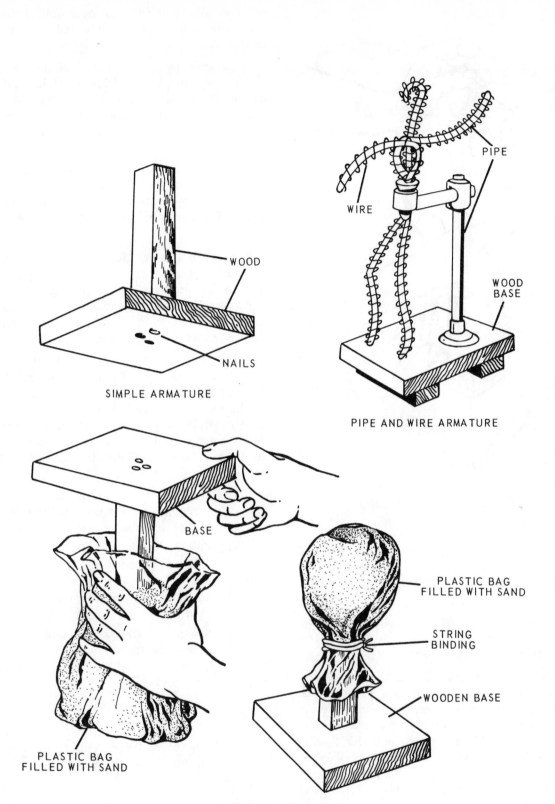

WOOD

NAILS

SIMPLE ARMATURE

PIPE

WIRE

WOOD
BASE

PIPE AND WIRE ARMATURE

BASE

PLASTIC BAG
FILLED WITH SAND

STRING
BINDING

WOODEN BASE

PLASTIC BAG
FILLED WITH SAND

SAND BAG ARMATURE

Figure 3–63. Three types of armatures.

Figure 3–64. Rough shaping of clay.

rim of the mold. Pouring will be easier if the plug is a little larger at the top, as the slip must be poured in and drained out of the opening left by the plug.

(4) *Size the model.* After the plug is in place, size the model, set the casting box around the clay, and size the box (para 3–5e).

(5) *Make a casting box.* A simple, adjustable frame for casting rectangular shapes is made from four pieces of 3/4-inch lumber about 6 inches wide and 15 inches long. Each piece of lumber has a piece of strap iron screwed to one end (fig. 3–69). There, the four pieces of wood fit together to make a box of any size up to 15 inches square. Four wedges are used to hold them tightly while the plaster is poured.

(6) *Pour plaster.* Mix enough plaster to fill nearly the remaining space in the casting box and pour the plaster (para 3–5b) into the box.

(7) *Prepare for second half.* When the plas-

ter has set, turn the box over and remove the clay backing and the template, but keep the model in the mold.

(8) *Pour the second half.* Put another plug of clay at the top of the model; cut notches in the first half of the mold (two on one side and one on the other side); size the mold, the model, and the casting box; then pour the second half of the mold.

(9) *Finish the mold.* After the plaster sets, remove the box and the plug and gently separate the two halves of the mold. The mold is completed (fig. 3–70) and can be used when it is thoroughly dry.

b. Care of Molds. Molds require care because plaster is not a sturdy material and any scratch or nick in the plaster will be reproduced in the casting. If molds are dried thoroughly after each use, they work more satisfactorily because the absorption of water is more rapid.

(1) After the molds are used, clean them. It is easier, and best for the mold, to clean the clay off before it hardens. The clay can be taken off of the outside of mold with a fettling knife, but care must be taken not to scratch the mold. A damp sponge or kidney shape rubber is an excellent tool to use for cleaning a mold as neither will scratch the surface.

(2) Wipe the working surface with a damp (not wet) sponge. If this does not remove all of the clay, rub gently with an old nylon stocking.

(3) Dry the mold as rapidly as possible so that it will be ready to use again. It will dry more rapidly if it is left unassembled. It must not be heated over 120 °F, as plaster does not stand up at higher temperatures.

(4) When the parts of the mold are completely dry, assemble them, using rubber bands to hold them together, and store the mold where it will not get bumped.

NOTE

Molds do wear out after repeated use, but good care is very important in prolonging their usefulness.

c. Slip Casting. The fundamental principles which make this process possible are interesting. Plaster is porous and it absorbs water quite rapidly. As the water from the slip is absorbed, the clay suspended in the water is deposited on the surface of the plaster. When this deposit of clay is sufficiently thick, the remaining slip is poured

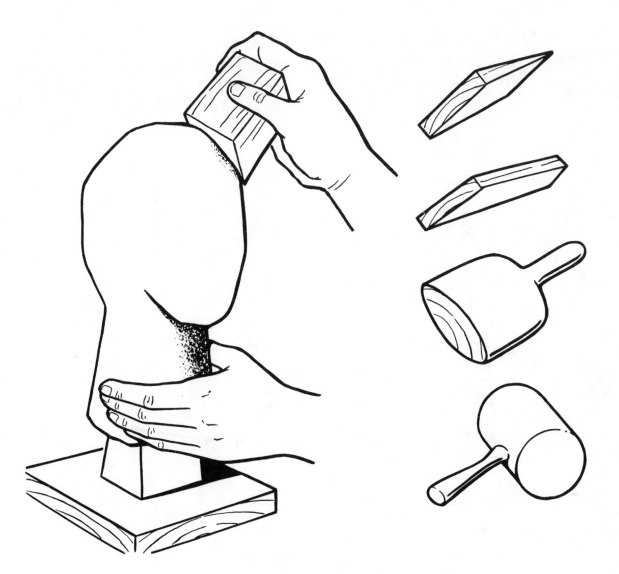

Figure 3–65. Rough shaping of clay with block of wood.

from the center of the mold so that no more deposit is made. Absorption and evaporation serve to remove the water from the deposit until the volume of the deposit lessens and it becomes smaller in size and therefore pulls away from the plaster. The following steps are used in slip casting:

(1) *Prepare the mold.* When the mold is thoroughly dry, it is ready for slip casting. A mold can be held together in one of several ways; perhaps the most satisfactory is with rubber bands made by cutting slices of an inner tube to a width of 3/4 inch or 1 inch.

(2) *Prepare the slip.* Make the prepared slip ready for use by mixing it well and straining it so there will be no lumps. Put the slip in a container which will hold enough to fill the mold.

(3) *Pour the slip.* Pour a steady stream of slip into the center of the mold until the slip is level with the top of the mold. Tap the mold a little with the hand so that any air bubbles will come to the top.

(4) *Keep mold full.* As water is absorbed by the plaster, the level of the slip in the mold will go down, so add more slip to keep the mold full to the top of the waste rim.

(5) *Test for thickness.* The longer the slip stays in the mold, the thicker the sides of the piece being molded will be. It is not possible to guess accurately how long the slip should remain in the mold, because the consistency of the slip, the dryness of the mold, and the humidity in the

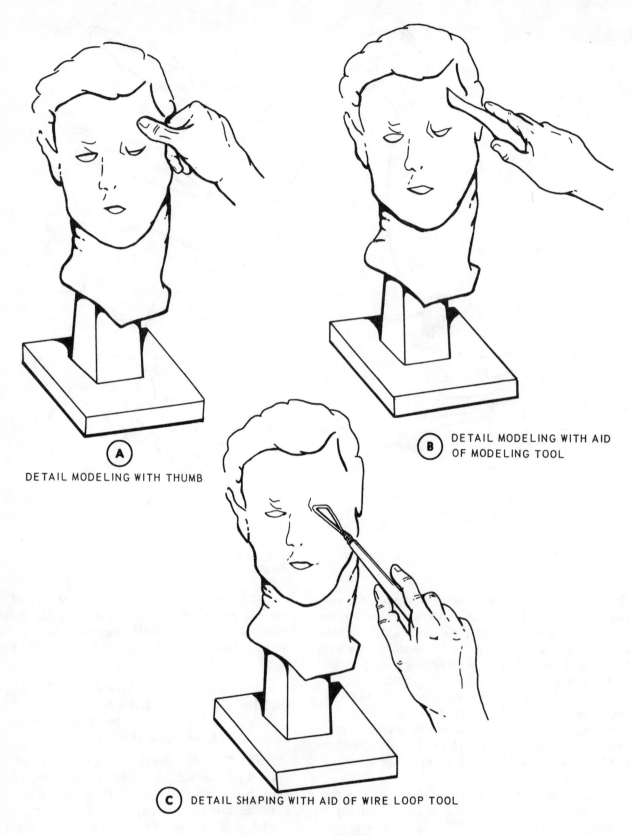

A DETAIL MODELING WITH THUMB

B DETAIL MODELING WITH AID OF MODELING TOOL

C DETAIL SHAPING WITH AID OF WIRE LOOP TOOL

Figure 3–66. Detailed modeling.

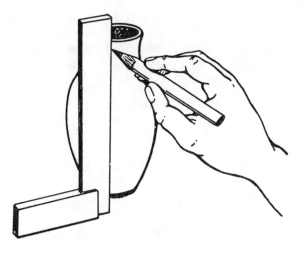

Figure 3–67. Marking the centerline.

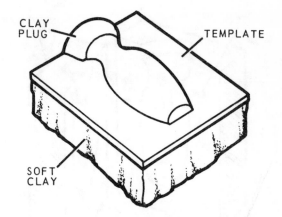

Figure 3–68. Model, template, and plug in place.

air all have a bearing on how rapidly the water is absorbed by the plaster. To determine the thickness of the deposit, cut into the deposit on the waste rim which was formed on the mold by the plug of clay. Continue checking in a different spot each time until the deposit of clay is of the desired thickness.

(6) *Pour the slip.* The liquid slip must be poured from the center of the mold. To do this, take the mold in two hands and, while holding it over a bowl or pitcher, pour it while rotating it with a slow, steady motion until the mold is nearly upside down. Hold it for a few minutes (do *not* shake it) until most of the slip has run out, then rest it on two sticks of different height, which are placed over the bowl (fig. 3–71). Tip the mold during the final draining to prevent drops of slip from forming on the bottom of the mold. If a mug with a handle is being drained, it is often advis-

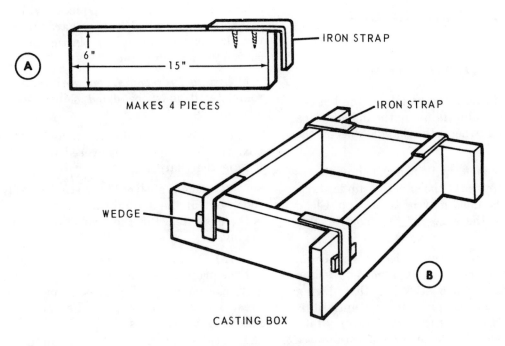

Figure 3–69. Aline the box.

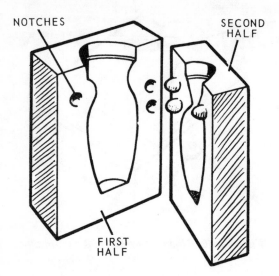

Figure 3-70. Finished mold.

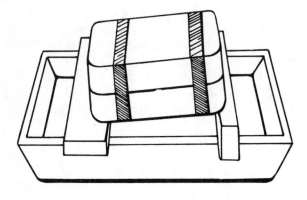

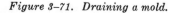

Figure 3-71. Draining a mold.

able to let it drain with the handle at the bottom so that the drained slip will fill up the indentations otherwise formed where the handle meets the mold.

(7) *Turn the mold up.* When the shine disappears from the surface of the slip, the slip is starting to dry and the mold may be turned up. Clean off the slip from the edges of the mold at this time.

(8) *Dry.* As the casting dries, it will begin to pull away from the mold. It is good to loosen carefully any part which sticks so that drying will be even. Allow the piece to dry until it is largely pulled away from the mold. This may take an hour or two. Cut the waste rim off of the piece and put it with the scrap slip to be reclaimed.

(9) *Remove casting from mold.* The best time to remove the piece from the mold is determined from experience mainly. It must be sufficiently dry to maintain its shape out of the mold. Remove one half of the mold first and let the piece dry in the other half a little longer before removing it.

(10) *Trim.* While the casting is leather hard, scrape off the seam marks with a fettling knife and smooth them with a damp elephant ear sponge. Smooth the top rim also by rubbing it over a piece of sandpaper or glass which is on the flat table top. Smooth the edge with an elephant ear sponge and set the piece aside to dry.

3-10. Storage and Drying of Clay and Projects

a. Storage of Clay. For clay to stay plastic and workable, it must be kept moist.

(1) Unshaped clay is stored in a rust-proof container with a tight-fitting cover. A large crock with a lid is excellent. For temporary storage, clay can be wrapped in wet cloth and kept in a plastic bag.

(2) Projects which have been started and are to be worked on again can be carefully wrapped in wet cloths, slipped into a plastic bag, and stored in the damp box. If they are not worked on for several days, the cloths may have to be dampened again. Work stored in the damp box must be kept covered with a wet cloth if it is to remain plastic. Uncovered, pieces will gradually dry to what is called leather hard. In this state, the clay is too dry to be plastic but it can be carved without chipping.

b. Drying Projects. When work on a project is complete, it must be dried slowly, evenly, and thoroughly.

(1) Drying should be started in the damp box. Leave the piece uncovered in the box until it is leather hard.

(2) Open shelves in a comfortably warm room, out of the sunlight and away from drafts, is the next step. Put the project on them to finish drying.

(3) Drying must take place evenly throughout the project lest the difference in volume of the clay, caused by greater loss of moisture in one area, makes cracks appear. Be sure to take the following precautions:

(*a*) Since the base of a piece on a solid shelf will dry more slowly than the top, turn the piece ever as often as is necessary to keep the drying even. This is particularly important when making tiles. They must be turned every few hours to keep them from becoming warped.

(b) Use special care with such projects as sculptured pieces, pitchers, and cups which have slender protuberances that dry more rapidly than the piece as a whole. To keep the drying even, hang a small piece of wet cloth over the area which might dry too rapidly. These bits of cloth must be redampened when indicated.

3–11. Surface Coloring and Finishing

a. *Types.*

(1) *Underglaze.* This is a mixture of ceramic materials compounded for use on green or bisque ware. Although pieces decorated with underglaze may be fired and left as bisque, usually a transparent glaze is applied over the entire surface to enhance the appearance, to strengthen the piece, and to waterproof it. The popularity of underglaze decoration stems from the fact that almost any type of design is possible—from the most delicate brush stroke to a solid background of color. Underglazes can be painted, sprayed, sponged, or spattered, with endless variations and combinations possible in each technique. Before the underglaze is applied, it must be stirred thoroughly. It must also be stirred at frequent intervals during use in order to maintain maximum color strength, as the pigments settle to the bottom of the container. Only by trial and error can one determine the exact amount of underglaze to be applied. Underglaze has a water base and will dry in the jar when exposed to air, so it should be stored in an airtight jar. If glaze becomes too thick, the consistency can be restored by adding a little water. Underglazes may be purchased in prepared liquid form, which is ready to use, or in powdered form, to which water is added. If underglazes are to be used in quantity, they are less expensive to purchase in powder form.

(2) *Glaze.* Glaze is a thin coating of glass which fuses to the surface of a clay body during firing. It provides strength and beauty and is impervious to moisture and dirt. Glaze comes in decorative textures and permanent colors, and it provides a cover for underglaze decoration. Different glazes are made to fire at different temperatures; each is indicated on the container.

(a) *Majolica glaze.* These are brilliant, opaque, transparent colors which may be applied to green or to bisque ware. They are available in liquid or in powder form to which water is added.

Glazes will produce a rich, shiny surface which flows slightly and thereby corrects irregularities of the brush application. Crawling, running, and separating of colors are common difficulties with Majolica glaze. These problems can be overcome by proper application of the glaze, by correct handling of the ware, and by controlled firing. Each make of glaze may have a different firing temperature. The recommended cone firing for each glaze is found on the container or it is provided by the distributor.

(b) *Mat glaze.* This glaze fires with a soft dull finish. It is particularly effective on contemporary or traditional shapes with simple lines. Mat glaze flows enough to cover most application defects, but not as much as Majolica glaze. Because of this nonflowing quality, mat glazes are adaptable for some unique types of decorations, both alone and in combination with other glazes. They may be applied by spray, brush, or dipping, as with other glazes. Mat glaze may be purchased in ready-to-use liquid form or in dry powder, to which water is added.

(c) *Crackle glaze.* Crackle glaze is made to craze as it cools. Decorative effects may be obtained from the patterns of the fine lines which develop in the glaze. The crackle is prominent in the light transparent glaze colors, but less apparent in the opaque. Rubbing light- or dark-colored inks into the fine lines accentuates the crackle. This is done after the piece has been removed from the kiln and while it is still warm. Brushing, dipping, and spraying are suitable methods for application of crackle glaze on green ware or bisque ware. The glaze may be purchased in liquid form in various colors.

(d) *Opalescent glaze.* These glazes are so named because, in addition to the gloss, they have an opal or mother-of-pearl quality, rather than the plain color of some other glazes. Opalescent glaze may be used on any fine art clay, but it develops its greatest opalescence and most interesting texture when used over red clays. It is applied on bisque or green ware by brush or by dipping, pouring, or spraying. On red bisque, these glazes should be applied rather heavily. A slow, rather than fast, firing is best.

(e) *Alligator glaze.* No two pieces glazed with alligator glazes are ever alike due to the many variations in texture which occur in firing. Varied mat textures are predominant at low-firing temperatures and gloss textures at higher temperatures, with a mingling of mat and gloss between extremes. A crepe-like texture is characteristic and the entire piece is enriched with warm undertones. It is applied as other glazes and purchased in liquid ready-to-use or in dry powder form.

(f) *Speckle glaze*. This unique glaze has a multicolor speckled finish. Because of the presence of the specks, it is *not suitable for spraying*. Approximately three heavy coats are recommended for application. Speckled glazes are purchased in a variety of colors in liquid form only.

(g) *Wood glaze*. This is a realistic-looking "wood finish" glaze applied rather heavily by a brush in long strokes or with a cloth to green ware or bisque to grain the surface being glazed. Wood glazes are available in liquid form only, in seven different types: hickory, walnut, mahogany, redwood, fruitwood, driftwood, and birch.

(3) *Overglaze*. Overglaze decorations are painted on ceramic pieces which have been glazed and fired. After the overglaze is applied, the piece is allowed to dry, then it is put in the kiln and fired just high enough to allow the glaze to soften slightly so that the colors become locked in the glaze. The correct firing temperature is indicated on the container. During firing, the glaze does not run and one color may be brushed on top of another, so the colors may be blended to get intermediary tones. Overglaze comes in liquid form only in a variety of colors.

(4) *Salt galze*. Salt glazing is an interesting type of glazing which is accomplished entirely in the firing process. This method of glazing was discovered by German potters in the 15th century and it is still done there. It was used in America in the 19th century to produce utilitarian pieces such as crocks, churns, and jugs. Salt-glazed pieces are often decorated with a blue engobe. Green ware is placed in the kiln and fired to maturing temperature of the clay. At that temperature, salt is thrown into the fire box of the kiln. The salt vaporizes in the heat of the kiln and combines with the silica of the clay to form a thin, mat glaze over the pieces in the kiln. A downdraft kiln, open fired, is preferable for salt glazing, but it must be vented into a chimney to prevent the fumes (chlorine gas) from escaping inside the building. This type of glazing is *not* done in an *electric* kiln. After repeated firings, the entire inside of the firing chamber becomes coated with glaze. Most ordinary clays will salt glaze successfully.

(5) *Bisque stains*. Bisque stains are applied to bisque ware that has been fired no higher than cone 06 (a higher temperature will mature the clay so that it will not absorb the stain). The piece is not refired after the stain is applied. Bisque stain is used to decorate items such as figurines, boxes, and wall plaques. It should not be used for items such as cups, bowls, and dishes, as bisque absorbs liquids and the stain is water soluble. Stains of different colors can be mixed like paint; *for example*, blue and yellow can be mixed to make green. Colors of stain are true as they come from the jar and they do not change as fired glazes do. When dry, the stain is bright and lusterless. To get a shiny finish, a spray-fix mat or clear lacquer is applied. Some possibilities of decorating with stain are antiquing and wood-graining.

b. *Glazing Methods.*

(1) *Pouring*. The consistency of the glaze must be controlled in order to have the correct thickness deposited on the piece. Dense bodies absorb little or no water; therefore, the glaze used on more matured clay must be thicker than that used on porous, less-mature pieces.

(a) Pouring is perhaps the most satisfactory method of glazing the inside of hollow pieces such as vases and pitchers. To glaze the inside, pour *more* than enough glaze to cover the area (fig. 3–72), then slowly rotate the piece to deposit the glaze evenly while pouring the excess glaze out and back into the glaze container.

(b) Outside surfaces can be glazed by pouring the glaze over them (fig. 3–73).

(2) *Spraying*. This method is good for glazing large pieces. Spraying tends to deposit a more even coating of glaze, it is faster, and only enough glaze to cover the piece is required. An air compressor, a paint sprayer, a ventilated spray booth, and a revolving table are equipment necessary for spray glazing. The glaze is sprayed by air pressure in a regular paint sprayer at high velocity onto the surface of the bisque ware. Spray gun nozzles differ, so the exact distance cannot be predetermined. If the gun is held too far from the piece, the glaze will dry before it hits the piece and loose, fluffy glaze will be deposited. If the sprayer is held too close to the piece or held too long in one place, the glaze deposit becomes too wet and it will run (fig. 3–74). The person using the sprayer must wear a protective mask to prevent inhalation of glaze which can be harmful after a period of time.

(3) *Dipping*. This method is used for production work because it is possible to obatin an even coating of glaze quickly. For the studio potter, however, its chief disadvantage is the large amount of glaze required. To prevent too heavy a

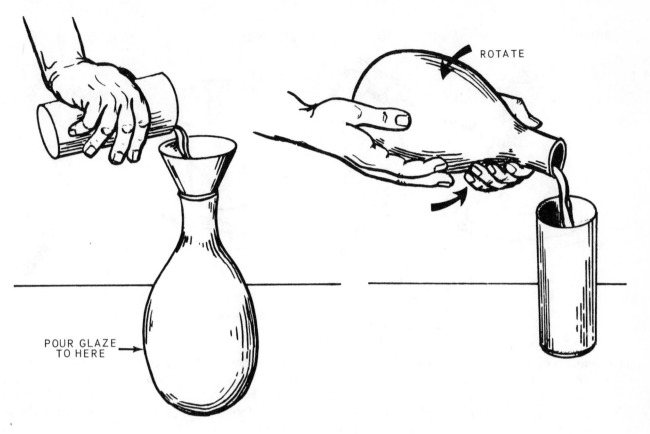

POUR GLAZE
TO HERE

ROTATE

Figure 3–72. Glazing inside of piece.

glaze large and deep enough to cover the entire piece being glazed. Care must be taken to avoid surface air bubbles by dipping the piece slowly into and out of the glaze. After the piece is dipped, it is placed on a screen to drain and dry.

(4) *Brushing method.* The glaze is applied with a flat 1-inch glaze brush. The creamy glaze should be flowed on, rather than brushed. Three layers are usually recommended. The strokes of the second coat are made perpendicular to those of the first and third coats. More care must be taken to insure an even application if nonflowing glaze is used. Brushing has the advantage of requiring only a small amount of glaze.

c. Defects in Glazes. There is always an element of uncertainty in firing glazes. Many things can go wrong, and the source of trouble is sometimes hard to trace. It may lie in the glaze or in the way the ingredients were weighed. There may be faults in applying or in firing. Ninety percent of the defects are due to mechanical error and ten percent to chemical error. A few of the

Figure 3–73. Glazing outside of piece.

coating, the piece must be sponged with a damp sponge, then quickly immersed in a container of

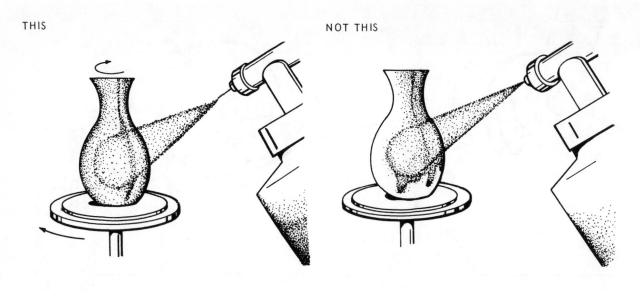

Figure 3-74. Spraying glaze on a piece.

most common glaze defects and some of the things which cause them are listed below.

(1) *Crazing.* When a glaze crazes, it develops tiny cracks over the surface. Sometimes these show immediately after the piece comes out of the kiln, but often they do not appear until several months later. Crazing indicates that the glaze and the body have a different coefficient of expansion. If the ware is fired again at a higher temperature, the crazing will often be corrected.

(2) *Crawling.* The term "crawling" refers to the piece coming out of the kiln with bare spots where the glaze has moved away, exposing the body underneath. Some of the causes of crawling are dust or oil from the fingers on the ware before it was glazed, too heavy application of glaze, underfiring, firing before the glaze was completely dry, or too porous a clay body for the type of glaze used.

(3) *Blistering.* Blisters or craters are formed on the surface of the glaze. Too heavy application of glaze, firing damp glaze, too low firing, or too fast firing will cause blistering.

(4) *Pinholes.* Tiny holes or pits in the glaze are referred to as pinholes. They are often caused by air holes in the clay, especially in cast pieces. Other causes are too rapid firing or too rapid cooling. Painting over a glaze after it has dried may also cause this trouble.

(5) *Running.* Too much flux in the glaze will cause the colors to run. Some underglazes add an extra amount of flux to a glaze, causing certain colors to run more than others. If a clear glaze which has not had all of the impurities removed (is not fritted) is applied over underglaze, it will run.

(6) *Dryness.* Dryness in a glaze is a rough surface, rather than a smooth, glossy one. Underfiring, not enough flux, or not enough glaze put on the piece will cause dryness.

(7) *Shivering.* This term refers to sections of glaze lifting off the piece. It is usually caused by the clay and the glaze not fitting together. Purchasing the glaze and the clay from the same source should eliminate the problem. Another cause of shivering may be too rapid firing or too rapid cooling.

(8) *Discoloration.* Occasionally the glaze does not produce the color that it should. This may be due to the presence of chromium in the kiln, such as in a chromium green underglaze. Odd bits of stray colors are due to careless handling and are called "tramp color."

3-12. Decorating

There are many ways of decorating ceramic pieces in all three forms—green ware, bisque, or glazed. When a piece of clay has not been fired, it is said to be green ware. Green ware is very fragile and will form slip if it contacts water. The firing transforms the green ware into what is known as bisque (or biscuit) ware. Bisque is sufficiently hard and durable to require no processing, but it is rough, dull, and porous. Glazing puts a glasslike coating on the piece which makes it smooth, nonporous, and waterproof.

a. Decoration on Green Ware.

(1) *Carved.* The design can be carved directly into the leather-hard clay as in wood carving. A knife such as a fettling knife is used.

(2) *Liquid rubber (rubber latex).* This can be used in place of wax as a resist material. One of the advantages of rubber is that no bisque firing is required to burn the rubber out, as with wax. The liquid rubber is removed by prying up its edge with a sharp tool and peeling it off. This means that the piece can be glazed and fired in a single operation. If the rubber latex becomes a little thick for the brush work, it can be thinned with diluted ammonia. Also, ammonia is used to clean the brush immediately after use.

(3) *Slip.* Slip is usually applied as a form of decoration in one of the following manners:

(*a*) *Painting.* Colored slip (engobe) is applied to leather-hard clay with a brush.

(*b*) *Slip trailing.* Thick slip is applied to leather-hard clay with a tracing tube or cake decorator. This leaves the design in a ridge of clay, either to match the body or to contrast with it.

(*c*) *Sgraffito.* A thin coat of slip of a contrasting color is applied over the surface of the leather-hard piece. After it dries, a design is scratched through the colored slip to expose the base color beneath.

(*d*) *Mishima.* Leather-hard green ware is incised with a design, and then a slip of a contrasting color is painted over the incising. After the top layer dries, it is scraped off, leaving the slip of a contrasting color in the design.

(*e*) *Airbrush.* Slip decoration is applied by use of stencils and a spray gun. The same effect can be obtained by spattering color slip on the piece instead of spraying it.

(*f*) *Sponge.* Instead of a brush being used to put designs on either green ware or bisque ware, applying the color with a sponge provides a nice change. A sponge is dipped into slip and dabbed on the piece; interesting color combinations as well as textures can be obtained by this method.

(*g*) *Stencils.* The desired pattern is cut out of paper; then color is dabbed on with a sponge to reproduce the design on the ware.

(*h*) *Masks.* This is the reverse of the stencil. A shape is cut out of paper and laid on the ware; then a sponge dipped in engobe is dabbed around the paper mask.

(*i*) *Spatter.* Engobe can be spattered on ware by dipping a stiff bristle brush into the engobe and then drawing a knife blade across the bristles in a direction away from the ware. A different type of spatter can be done with a soft-haired brush. The brush is dipped into the engobe and shaken at the piece.

(4) *Sprig decoration.* Sprig decorations are wafer-thin bits of clay formed into decorative shapes to be applied to formed leather-hard green ware. This method of deocrating was developed by Josiah Wedgewood who used two colors of clay, usually putting very delicate figures of white clay on a background of colored clay. These shapes are usually made in a sprig mold, which is a block of plaster with a depression shaped like the decorative shape in reverse. To use this mold, a ball of clay smaller than a golf ball is flattened out a bit and pressed into the mold. With a spatula, the clay is trimmed off level with the mold, then the formed ornament is carefully lifted out of the mold and applied to the leather-hard green ware with slip (fig. 3–75).

(5) *Stamped or impressed.* Designs can be pressed into soft clay with stamps of metal, wood, bisque, or plaster. Stamps may be purchased or made by the ceramist. Impressing can also be done with a roller which is applied by revolving it on the soft clay.

PLASTER

SPRIG MOLD

PIECE DECORATED WITH A SPRIG

Figure 3–75. Sprig decorating.

(6) *Wax resist.* The design is painted on the piece with liquid wax, then the entire surface of the piece is covered with an engobe. The engobe does not adhere to the wax so that the areas painted with wax will remain the color of the clay piece. During the bisque firing, the wax will burn out and disappear completely. Melted paraffin can be used as the wax, but it must be very hot. It is a little difficult to handle since it cools rapidly when it touches the surface of the piece. The painting will be much easier if a commercial emulsion of liquid paraffin is used. This can be applied without heating and responds to a brush in much the same manner as tempera paint. It is also much easier on brushes than hot paraffin, which eventually causes the hairs to loosen and fall out. The wax-resist emulsion can be washed out of the brush immediately after the brush has been used. If the emulsion hardens in the brush, benzine will be required to remove it.

(7) *Underglaze color.* These are colors designed to be used on green ware or bisque ware and then covered with transparent glaze. The color can be applied by means of a brush, a sponge, a sprayer, or an airbrush. If a brush is used, three coats are usually applied to obtain good coverage and solid color. The colors change very little in firing, so color combinations and blending can be observed as work progresses. The underglaze dries quickly and can be handled without damage.

b. Decorating on Bisque.

(1) *Glazes.* Various colors and effects can be achieved through the use of glazes. Some are transparent, others are opaque. They come commercially prepared in many novelty finishes such as crackle, crystalline, and mat.

(2) *Underglaze colors* (*a*(7) above).

(3) *Underglaze crayon.* A recent development offers interesting effects with a crayon of underglaze color. It is used on bisque and leaves a mark much like a crayon leaves on paper.

c. Decorating on Fired Glaze.

(1) *Overglaze colors.* Such things as tiles, dinnerware, sculpture, and costume jewelry may be highlighted with these colors. They are water soluble and may be mixed for shading. They are applied either by spraying or by brushing and refiring at cone 018–020.

(2) *Gilding.* Gold or platinum color can be penned, brushed, or airbrushed over glaze to highlight and enrich the design. Refiring the piece then to cone 019–017 fuses the metallic material to the glaze.

3–13. Types of Kilns

Essentially, a ceramic kiln is an oven which is designed to reach high temperatures, sometimes up to 2350 ° F. Most kilns are lined with a refractory material called fire brick and are insulated with dead airspace, fuller's earth, asbestos, glass fiber, or vermiculite to keep the heat in the chamber. Kilns may be heated with wood, oil, gas, or electricity, and they are designed so that the heat will circulate throughout the chamber. There are many types of kilns, homemade and commercial, all with both desirable and undesirable features. The selection of a kiln depends upon the cost of fuel in the area, the type and amount of firing to be done, and the personal preference of the ceramist. A brief look at two types of kilns which are *not* commonly used in occupational therapy clinics is given below, plus a more detailed account of the electric kiln which is generally used.

a. Muffle Kiln. A muffle is a chamber made of refractory material in which ceramic pieces are placed for firing. In a muffle kiln (fig. 3–76), the flame circulates between the muffle and the outer wall and leaves through the flue at the top. In some muffle kilns, the flames travel in tubes which are inside of the muffle. The heat is more evenly distributed in this type of kiln because tubes can be put at the back and at the front of the kiln. In these kilns, the pieces being fired are not endangered by coming in contact with the flame; however, they are not economical of fuel (usually oil or gas).

b. Downdraft Kiln. There is no muffle in a downdraft kiln (fig. 3–77), so the flames come in direct contact with the pieces in the kiln. This is all right for bisque pieces, but glazed pieces must be put into saggers or boxes which act as small muffles. Downdraft kilns are economical of heat and they will also reach high temperatures. Wood is frequently used to heat these kilns, which are usually large walk-ins.

c. Electric Kilns. Electric kilns are used extensively in Army occupational therapy clinics because they are clean, easy to operate, and safe; require little space; and do not need a flue; and also because electricity is always available. The source

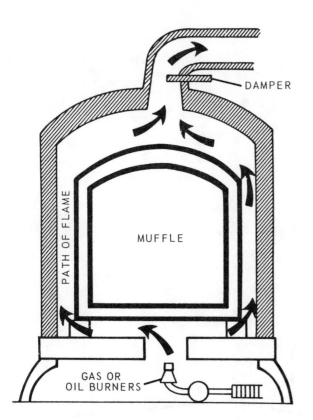

Figure 3-76. Portable muffle kiln.

of heat is electric elements, which are set into grooves of the refractory brick. The elements may be Nichrome, which can be used for temperatures up to 2000° F or Kanthal, which can go as high as 2300° F. Globar, a carborundum compound in the form of a bar, is used if higher temperatures are required. It requires special electrical installation and transformers, but it can be fired up to 2700° F. (This temperature is beyond the needs of most amateurs.) Nichrome elements are statisfactory for the work done in most clinics. Many electric kilns require 220 volts, others use 110 volts, and some models can be ordered with either requirement. The size of electric kilns vary a great deal. If the kiln is small, too much time is required for stacking and unstacking. It if is too large, the patients must wait too long for a firing. A good-sized kiln for the average clinic is 16 inches by 16 inches by 16 inches, or 18 inches by 18 inches by 18 inches. Electric kilns (fig. 3-78) are made to load from the top or from the side. The top-loading kiln is easier to stock, but it cannot be used as an enameling kiln as can the side-loading kiln. With a top loader, it is important to prop the kiln for cooling so that the props are supported on the metal, rather than on the firebrick. When opening and closing a side-loading kiln, care must be taken to keep the firebrick

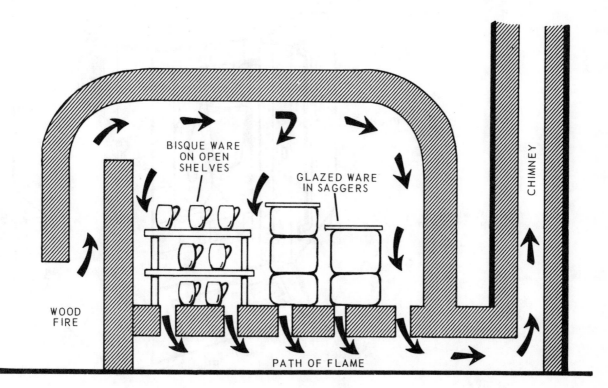

Figure 3-77. Downdraft kiln.

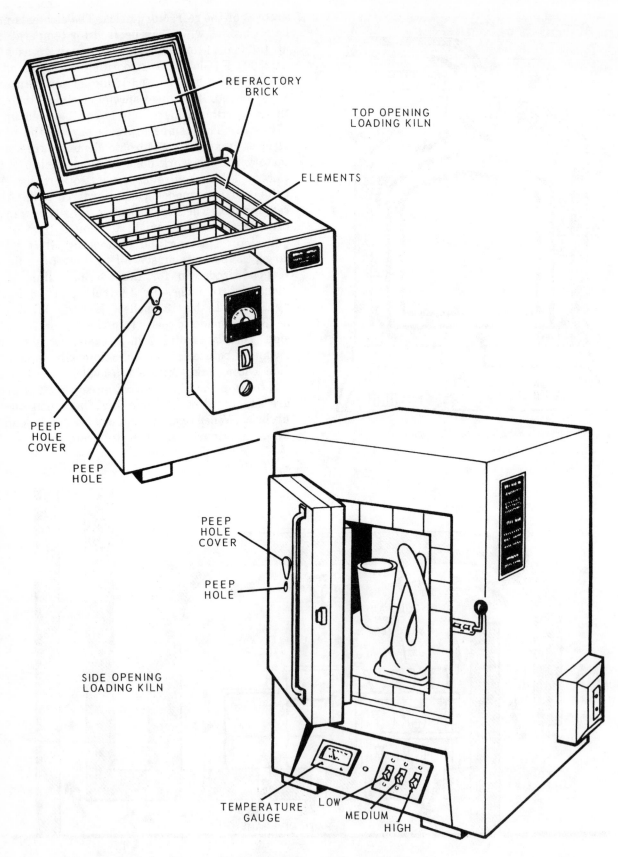

REFRACTORY BRICK

TOP OPENING
LOADING KILN

ELEMENTS

PEEP
HOLE
COVER

PEEP
HOLE

PEEP
HOLE
COVER

PEEP
HOLE

SIDE OPENING
LOADING KILN

TEMPERATURE
GAUGE

LOW

MEDIUM

HIGH

Figure 3–78. Types of kilns (electric).

from chipping. The kiln has a peephole (fig. 3–78) which functions as a vapor exhaust in the first stages of firing and as an observation "window" to check the pyrometric cones in the final stages. In between, the cover may be closed over the hole to prevent loss of heat.

3–14. Using the Kiln

Much of the success of good ceramic work depends on skilled firing of the kiln.

a. Preparing the Kiln. In order that shelves and floor of the kiln are protected from bits of glaze which may drip, they are painted with kiln wash at frequent intervals as needed. Kiln wash is a mixture of flint and china clay which does not fuse during firing so that any glaze which falls on it can be chipped off. Usually kiln wash is sold in powder form, so it must be mixed with water to the consistency of cream. It is then brushed on the floor and the top surface of the kiln shelves with a varnish brush.

NOTE

Do *not* coat the top or the sides of the kiln, or the undersides or edges of the shelves, as the kiln wash may flake off during firing and make ugly blemishes on the glazed pieces.

b. Stacking the Kiln. Stacking the kiln is a real art. First, the pieces must be put in so that they will fire well, then the kiln should be stacked as full as possible for economy; this will also permit more patients to get their pieces sooner. When clay and glaze are purchased, it is usually advisable to select both products that fire at the same temperature; then bisque and glaze firing can be done at the same time. Most ceramic companies consider this in the manufacture, but if products are bought at several places or if other than the standard products are bought, this is a consideration in selection. Shelf supports (fig. 3–79), which come in different lengths, are used to support one shelf over the other so that more pieces can be fired at one time.

(1) *Stacking bisque.* Unequal pressures on bisque pieces that are being fired tend to warp the pieces because, when clay matures, the fluxes melt and become soft until they are cool again. Unglazed pieces can be stacked close together, even on top of each other, but the distribution of weight on each piece must be kept even (fig. 3–80).

(2) *Stacking glazed pieces.* Glaze becomes

Figure 3–79. Shelf support.

molten when it is fired. During this molten state, a glazed piece will stick permanently to anything it touches (fig. 3–81). Because of this, precautions must be taken to prevent sticking.

(*a*) Glaze should be removed from the base of the foot of the piece.

(*b*) If there is no foot and/or if the base needs to be glazed because the piece is to hold liquid (vases, mugs, etc.), it must be supported up and off of the shelf in some way. There are several types and sizes of supports which can be used for different purposes (fig. 3–82). The aim of good stilting is to give adequate support, yet have as little of the glazed surface touching the stilt as possible (fig. 3–83). If the stilt leaves a rough spot in the glaze, it can be smoothed with a metal file or on a grinder.

(*c*) The pieces must be put at least 1/4 inch apart in the kiln and must not be put any closer than 1/4 inch from the kiln shelf supports.

(*d*) The glaze must be sufficiently thick to cover the piece well, but not so thick that it will drip. To prevent one piece from dripping on another, the pieces should be placed in such a way that they will drip on a shelf rather than on other pieces.

(*e*) The volatile gases from some glazes have a tendency to tint other glazes in the kiln. You must know which glazes should be fired separately.

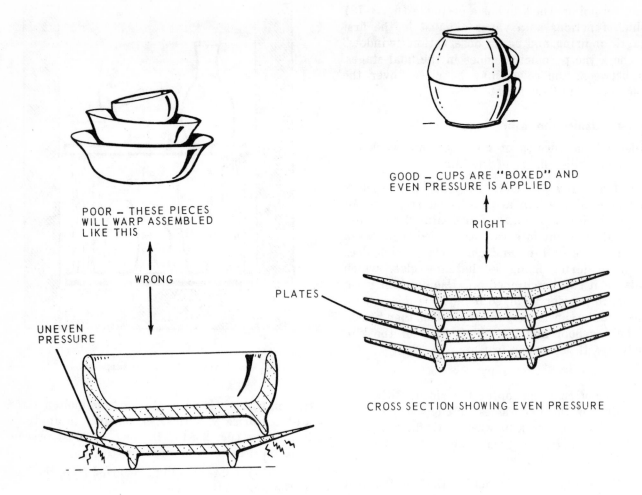

POOR — THESE PIECES
WILL WARP ASSEMBLED
LIKE THIS

WRONG

UNEVEN
PRESSURE

CROSS SECTION SHOWING POOR PLACEMENT.
UNEVEN PRESSURE WILL CRACK OR WARP PLATE.

GOOD — CUPS ARE "BOXED" AND
EVEN PRESSURE IS APPLIED

RIGHT

PLATES

CROSS SECTION SHOWING EVEN PRESSURE

Figure 3–80. Stacking bisque ware.

(3) *General hints on stacking.* A person who has stacked the kiln previously does it more easily and can get more into one load than someone with little experience because he has learned tricks to expedite stacking; *for example:*

(*a*) Put pieces of one size on the same shelf so the shelves can be more efficiently packed.

(*b*) For greater stability of shelves in the kiln, put the flatter pieces at the bottom so the shelves at the bottom do not have to be raised so high.

(*c*) When a large piece or a piece which has a narrow base is stilted, test to see that it is well balanced. Pieces change shape sufficiently during firing sometimes to cause a top-heavy piece to fall. Such an accident not only spoils the piece that falls, but it frequently rearranges the

WRONG — THESE TWO
PIECES WILL FUSE
TOGETHER WHEN
KILN IS FIRED.

Figure 3–81. Stacking glazed pieces.

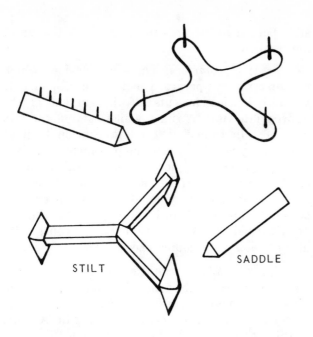

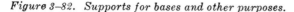

STILT

SADDLE

Figure 3–82. Supports for bases and other purposes.

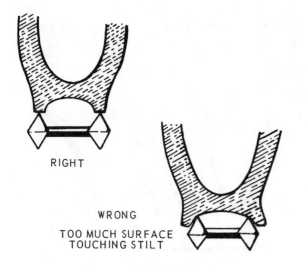

RIGHT

WRONG

TOO MUCH SURFACE
TOUCHING STILT

Figure 3–83. Stilting.

pieces in the kiln sufficiently to spoil many of them, too.

(*d*) If there is any fear that a piece might blow up in the kiln, fire it separately.

(*e*) Be sure that all green ware and glazed pieces are dry before they are put in the kiln. Test them against the cheek. If they feel cool, they are not dry.

(*f*) Stack 1 day, then leave the kiln open overnight so that the pieces can finish drying.

(*g*) As the kiln is heating, keep the peephole open to let moisture escape until a cool glazed piece or a mirror held in front of the peephole does not gather condensed moisture.

(*h*) Stack figurines with the faces pointing

away from the elements which are hotter and may distort the delicate color of the face.

(*i*) Stack pieces at least 1 inch away from the elements.

(*j*) If the piece is from a mold and if the mold does not allow for airholes, put a hole in an inconspicuous place to let the air out.

(*k*) Be sure that pieces over 1 inch thick contain a considerable amount of grog or make them thinner before firing is attempted.

c. Firing the Kiln. After the piece has been successfully shaped, decorated, and put in the kiln, it is not free from possible damage until after it is fired. Firing must be done with accuracy and patience. The accuracy of the firing depends upon measurement of the temperature within the kiln.

(1) *Temperature measurement.* The temperature in the kiln can be measured with pyrometric cones, the most accurate and reliable method; with a kiln sitter, a mechanical-type cutoff which is activated by the bent cone; or with a pyrometer.

(*a*) *Pyrometric cones.* Pyrometric cones are slender clay pyramids made with selected fluxes so that they will start to bend at a certain heat. The temperature at which the cone will bend is indicated by a number impressed into one side at the base of the cone. The lower the number, the lower the temperature at which the cone will bend. Table 3–1 lists cone temperatures, which also indicate the color in the kiln, the effect of that temperature on clay, and the type of object fired at that temperature. This table is only a general indication of what is fired at certain temperatures. Specific temperature and cone information is on the package of glaze or clay, as well as in the catalog from which it was ordered. Cones are available in two sizes. The larger cones are 2 1/2 inches high and have a 1/2-inch base; the smaller ones, which are convenient for small kilns, are 1 1/8 inch high and have a 1/4-inch base. The cones are put in a clay pat, positioned so that the number on the cone faces the worker and the cone angles to the right at about 8 degrees from vertical. A series of three cones is recommended for each firing (fig. 3–84). The center cone is the firing cone and is selected to bend at the temperature at which the ware is to be fired. The warning cone is at the right of the firing cone, positioned so that it will not fall on the other cones. When the warning cone bends, the ceramist knows that the firing cone will bend in a short time. The guard cone indicates whether or not the kiln has been overfired (fig. 3–84). The clay pat will explode and cause damage to the ware in the kiln if the clay is not well wedged, if it is too thick and without grog, and if it is put into the kiln before it is completely dry. Cones are put into the kiln after it is stacked. The pat must be placed so that the cones are easily visible through the peephole, yet so that the cone will not touch a piece when it falls. If there are two peepholes, the pat should be placed at the higher one, as the temperature is higher at the top of the kiln. When starting to work with a new kiln, some potters place cone pots at various places in the kiln to determine where the kiln is the hottest and the coolest in order to plan more effective stacking.

(b) *Kiln sitter or kiln guard.* This is an easily installed mechanical kiln cutoff which is activated when the cone bends. Some of these devices also have timers which can be set to turn off the kiln in the event that the cone does not activate the cutoff. These are quite reliable and inexpensive and are a great help for people who tend to forget the kiln. Because no mechanical device is absolutely foolproof, a kiln should not be fired without pyrometric cones and a respon-

sible person in the area to doublecheck the cutoff mechanism.

(c) *Pyrometers.* These are devices which measure the temperature inside the kiln and, if the kiln is electric, cuts off the current at the appropriate time. A timer which cuts off the kiln at a certain time is a good precaution to have with the pyrometer. Since the pyrometer is a delicate and expensive piece of equipment which is easily thrown out of adjustment, the kiln should never be left alone when it is being fired, and someone must check to be sure that the kiln has been turned off. Most ceramists use cones with a pyrometer as a double check.

(2) *The firing cycle.* Certain changes in the clay take place as the temperature in the kiln increases. To understand these changes is to have better control of what occurs in the kiln. A chart of this cycle in brief is shown in table 3-2.

(a) *Water smoking.* Even though the clay feels dry, it still contains two types of moisture: *atmospheric,* which is from the water in the atmosphere, and *chemically combined water,* which

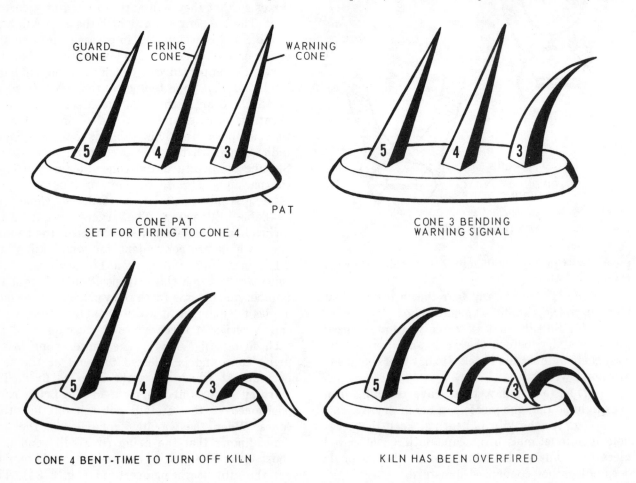

Figure 3-84. Cones set in clay pot for firing.

Table 3–1. Cone Temperatures

Cone	Centi-grade	Fahren-heit	Color of fire	What happens to clay	Type of ware and glazes
15	1435	2615			
14	1400	2552			
13	1350	2462			
12	1335	2435		Porcelain matures	Porcelain
11	1325	2417	White		
10	1305	2381			
9	1285	2345		Stoneware clays mature	China bodies, stoneware, salt glazes
8	1260	2300			
7	1250	2282			
6	1230	2246			
5	1205	2201			
4	1190	2174			
3	1170	2138		Red clays melt	China glazes
2	1165	2129			
1	1160	2120			Semivitreous ware
01	1145	2093	Yellow		
02	1125	2057		Buff clays mature	Earthenware
03	1115	2039			
04	1060	1940		Red clays mature	
05	1040	1904			
06	1015	1859			
07	990	1814			Low-fire earthenware
08	950	1742	Orange		
09	930	1706			Low-fire lead glazes
010	905	1661			
011	895	1643			
012	875	1607	Cherry red		Lustre glazes
013	860	1580			
014	830	1526			
015	805	1481			
016	795	1463			Chrome red glazes
017	770	1418		Organic matter in clay burns out	
018	720	1328	Dull red		
019	660	1220			Overglaze colors enamels
020	650	1202		Dehydration begins	
021	615	1139			
022	605	1121			

is the water in the molecular structure of the clay particles. In the water-smoking period, the atmospheric water leaves the clay. During this time, before the kiln reaches 300° F, the heat should be raised slowly and a way provided for the moisture to escape. Gas-, oil-, and wood-fired kilns have flues through which moisture escapes. When an electric kiln is fired, the door should be left open a crack during this first period and the peephole should also be left open.

(b) *Complete dehydration.* Before the kiln reaches 1000° F, the combined water in the clay leaves. The door is closed to get the temperature up this high, but the peephole is left open until all moisture has escaped.

(c) *Expansion of silica.* At about 1063° F, the silica in the clay begins to expand; this is a critical period for larger pieces which might expand unevenly and break if firing is too rapid.

(d) *Burning of organic matter.* Between 1000° F and 1500° F, the organic matter in the clay burns out. If native red clay is being fired, it is important to increase the temperature slowly during this period.

(e) *Color of kiln (cherry red).* At about 1000° F, the kiln begins to get cherry red and it is possible to see objects in the kiln. This is not true with an electric kiln in which the elements glow and furnish light before this temperature is reached.

(f) *Firing.* The bending temperature of bisque is reached at 1121° F. Beyond 1112° F, the firing of bisque can be speeded up, but glazed pieces must be fired more slowly to prevent the formation of pinholes.

DIAGRAM OF FIRING SCHEDULE

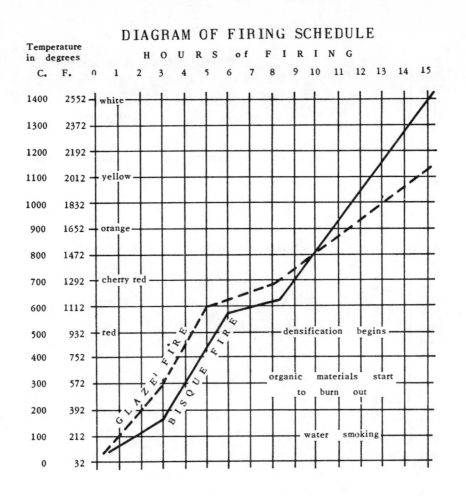

Table 3-2. Diagram of Firing Schedule

(g) *Maturing of ware.* As soon as the kiln reaches maturing temperature for the clay or the glaze being fired, it must be shut off. The damper or the peephole should be left open for about 10 minutes to allow products of combustion to escape.

(h) *Cooling.* The kiln must cool slowly to prevent unwanted crazing and even breakage. Any kiln should cool for at least 24 hours. After that time, the cooling may be hastened by gradually opening the door; *for example,* an inch every 1/2 hour as an estimate. This is called "cracking the kiln." Do *not* remove pieces from the kiln until they can be removed without the protection of gloves.

3-15. Ceramic Design

Form, texture, and decoration in ceramic design are considered as they relate to each other. In this medium, more than in any other, the sense of touch is included with the eyes and the imagination in the enjoyment of a piece. For instance, a drinking mug should be well balanced, comfortable to hold, and easy to drink out of. This quality in ceramics is as important as, and it is dependent upon, the shape, color, and texture of the piece.

a. Form. The four basic forms (fig. 2-1) are seen repeatedly, but with myriads of variations and combinations. Because of the nature of the material, ceramic pieces are not slender and willowy, but rather tend to be more rounded and bulky. One sculptor of note tried to design his pieces so that if they were rolled, no part would break off. This need for more compact roundness does not preclude graceful, clean lines, however.

b. Texture. Texturing of ceramics may be obtained by putting grog in the clay; by using different glazes; by rolling the clay on textured material such as burlap; or by making the surface with a comb, fork, screen edge, ridged paddle, bisque, or stamps, to name just a few. The texturing should be appropriate to the shape and to the intended use of the piece. Deep, narrow grooves in the clay provide interesting texture that is appropriate to a flower pot, for instance, but not to a dinner plate.

c. Decoration. Decoration can be put on the clay with underglazing, slip painting, coils, slip trailing, running glaze, and wax resist; or with scratching into the clay. The decoration should be planned to relate to the shape and to the function of the piece. The Egyptians did this well by planning the decorating to accent the shape of the clay. Small motifs were used at the base and the neck of the urns and larger, more important figures were put along the widest area of the piece. Decoration can accent an area or perhaps break up a plain area; it can be symbolic, pretty, humorous, or abstract; or it can carry a message. (Basic pertinent information on design is covered in chapter 2.)

CHAPTER 4

MOSAICS

4-1. General

Literature on early mosaics is rather meager, so the origin of the art is not clear. Although the earliest evidences of mosaics are found on jewelry, ivory thrones, and temple columns made in 1400 B.C., it is generally conceded that the art had its beginning as floor decoration. It reached its highest development from 1400–1500 B.C., during which time entire church interiors were decorated in this manner. The art is regaining popularity at present, and the methods employed are basically the same as those that were used in the 1600's. Some contemporary projects that are practical to make in an occupational therapy clinic are ash trays, book ends, boxes, coasters, lamp bases, pictures, tabletops, and trivets. Any number of materials can be employed, to include ceramic tile (purchased or handmade), cork, glass, paper, pebbles, plastic, rubber tile, sand, seeds, shells, vinyl tile, and various woods. The use of several of these materials together can result in interesting and often expressive textures.

4-2. Tools and Equipment

a. Brushes. For spreading glue.

b. Mixing Bowl. For mixing large quantities of grout.

c. Mixing Cups. For mixing small quantities of grout. The use of old cans or paper cups will save the time and energy of cleaning containers.

d. Plastic Bags. For keeping material. Kept this way, material is easy to handle and can be identified without labeling. Cutting tile in the bag offers additional protection from flying chips of tile.

e. Putty Knife, Tongue Depressor, or Rubber Kidney. For pushing and smoothing the grout into the cracks between the tiles.

f. Rags. For wiping the hands or for wiping grout from the surface of the tiles.

g. Rolling Pin. For use with a flathead to level tiles after they are set in place.

h. Safety Glasses. For protection of the eyes while cutting tile.

i. Sponge. For wiping grout from the surface of the tiles.

j. Tile Cutters or Nippers. For cutting small pieces of tile and glass to the desired size and shape. Nippers (fig. 4–1) are usually carbide-tipped for extra strength and longevity.

Figure 4–1. Tile cutters or nippers.

k. Tweezers. For planing the pieces. If the pieces of tile are small or the space into which they fit is small, tweezers facilitate planing.

l. Wooden Mallet. For use in combination with a flathead for leveling the tiles after they are set in place (fig. 4–2).

Figure 4-2. Wooden mallet.

4-3. Material

a. Glue is used to hold the mosaic material to the background.

(1) Casein glue or polyvinyl acetate resin emulsion (Elmer's glue) is commonly used where

Figure 4-3. Ceramic tile available in prepatterned sheets.

pieces are to be indoors or in any other place where they will not come in contact with water.

(2) Epoxy glue is used on pieces which will come in contact with dampness.

b. Grout is a prepared mixture to which water is added. It is used to fill in the spaces between the mosaic pieces. It can be colored with grout stain to blend with or to accent the color of the mosaic.

c. Mosaic material can be any one or any combination of the following:

(1) Ceramic tile, which is available in several forms.

(*a*) It can be made from clay and glazed the desired colors.

(*b*) Readymade tiles are packaged in bags and sold by the pound or fraction of a pound.

(*c*) Some tiles are arranged in a pattern and lightly glued to a coarse netting. These are sold by the sheet (fig. 4-3). The sheet is cut to size and is then glued to the mounting surface.

(2) Cork, cut and painted.

(3) Glass, crushed or pieces.

(4) Paper.

(5) Pebbles.

(6) Plastic.

(7) Rubber tiles.

(8) Sand, available in various colors.

(9) Seeds, beans, peas, rice, etc., as well as garden seeds.

(10) Shells.

(11) Vinyl tile.

(12) Woods of different shapes and types. types. The pieces may be painted or finished to preserve the natural finish.

(13) Wax, silicone, or marble polish to protect the grout.

d. Mounting surfaces vary according to what is being made.

(1) Masonite provides a good base for small projects which will not be in contact with moisture. It is used mainly as a base for pictures up to about 10 by 12 inches in size.

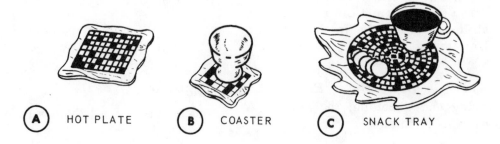

Ⓐ HOT PLATE   Ⓑ COASTER   Ⓒ SNACK TRAY

Figure 4-4. Plywood mountings for mosaics.

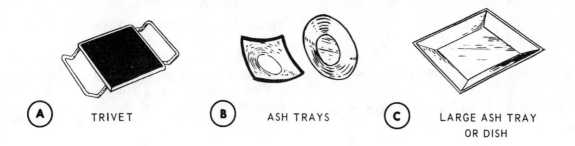

A TRIVET	**B** ASH TRAYS	**C** LARGE ASH TRAY OR DISH

Figure 4–5. Preformed mountings for mosaics.

(2) Plywood (fig. 4–4) of different thicknesses can be used as a mounting surface for projects *larger* than 10 by 12 inches because it does not bend as readily as Masonite.

(*a*) A consideration, however, with a larger piece is to provide for the weight of the plywood, plus the weight of the tile and grout. The thickness of plywood required for various sizes of projects are suggested below.

Figure 4–6. Transfer design to prepared background.

- ¼-inch plywood for projects 3 by 3 feet or less.
- ½-inch plywood for projects 3 by 6 feet or less.
- ¾-inch plywood for projects larger than 3 by 6 feet.

(b) Both the sides and the edges of plywood can be protected from dampness and any resulting warping by coating them with varnish. If this is done, projects which come in contact with a certain amount of moisture can be made with satisfactory results. The mosaic material must be resistant to water, however, and an epoxy-like glue must be used.

(3) Preformed mounting surfaces can be purchased or made (fig. 4–5).

4–4. Design

Simplicity is the keynote to design in this media. There should be a minimum of color and lines as too much detail becomes lost in the texture. Strong contrasts of color help to bring out the design. Geometric and free-form designs are especially good for the beginner as he gets the "feel" of the material and tests what can be done with it.

a. A good way to get a design is to select a motif and repeat it in a variety of ways.

b. Another way is to paint on a large sheet of paper with a brush, using showcard colors.

c. Decorative repetition of geometric designs can be very good.

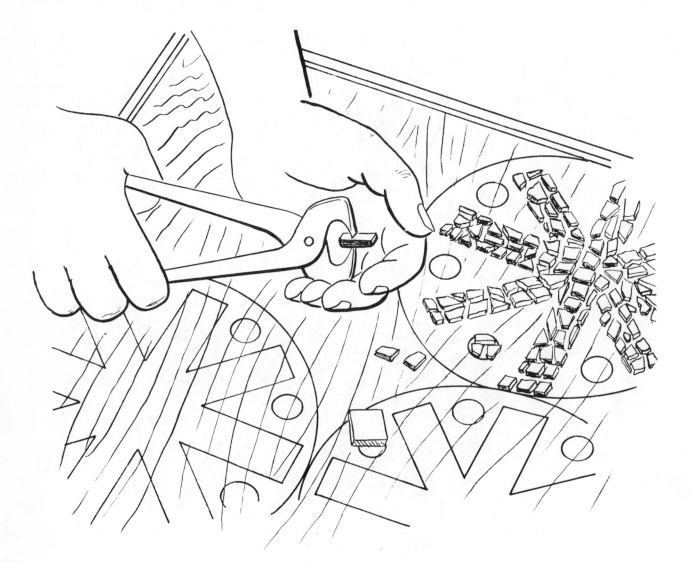

Figure 4–7. Cut tiles of fit into design shapes.

4–5. Procedures

Results can be highly pleasing and the processes involved are not complex if these steps are followed:

a. Plan the design and the colors to be used. Paint, crayon, charcoal, cut paper, or even the tiles themselves can be used in the planning.

b. Transfer the design to the prepared background surface (fig. 4–6).

c. Fit the mosaic pieces into the design. If tiles are used, they may need to be cut with the tile nippers (fig. 4–1) to fit into design shapes (fig. 4–7). Care must be taken to protect the eyes from flying chips of tile by wearing protective glasses or by cutting the tile inside of a plastic bag.

d. Glue pieces individually or spread glue evenly over an area (fig. 4–8). The glue should be thick enough to hold the mosaic pieces securely, yet not thick enough to ooze up between the tiles. The size of the area that should be spread with glue depends upon how fast the glue dries, the size of the pieces, and the agility of the worker. The mosaics must be in place (fig. 4–9) before the glue dries. If grout is to be used, the pieces should be set 1/16 inch to 1/8 inch apart to allow space for grout.

e. Add grout if indicated, after the glue is dry. Some types of mosaic materials such as sand and seeds do not need grout. However, if grout is used, follow this method—

(1) Mix the grout by putting a small amount of water in an appropriate-sized container and add the powdered grout until it is the consistency of heavy cream. If the mosaic is vertical or if it is not framed, make the grout thicker.

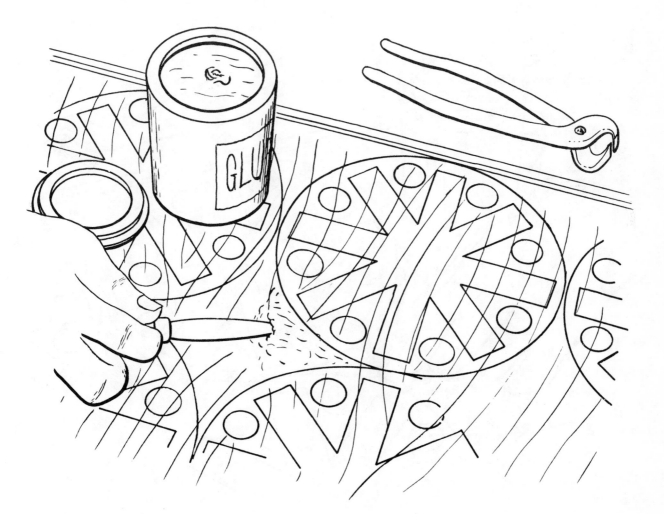

Figure 4–8. Spread an area with glue.

(2) Pour and spread the grout over the surface (fig. 4–10) and rub it into the spaces between the tiles with the hand (fig. 4–11), with a tongue depressor, or with a rubber kidney.

(3) Allow time for the grout to set, then remove it from the surface of the tiles with a dampened sponge, rag, or paper towel (fig. 4–12).

f. Give the surface a final cleaning (fig. 4–13) to insure that all grout is removed from the surface. When the grout is completely dry, apply silicone, marble polish, or wax to protect the grout.

NOTE

If tile is purchased by the sheet, cut the sheet to size and start with *d* above. To fill all areas with tile, some of the tiles may need to be pulled from the netting, cut, and fitted into the empty space.

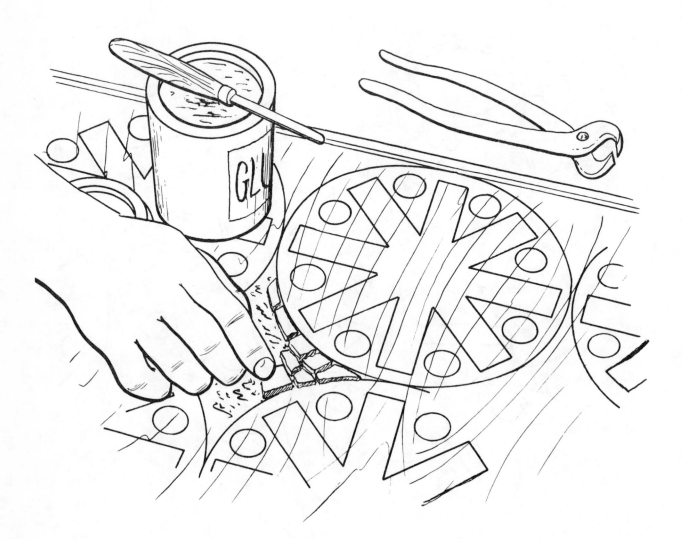

Figure 4–9. Press mosaic pieces in place.

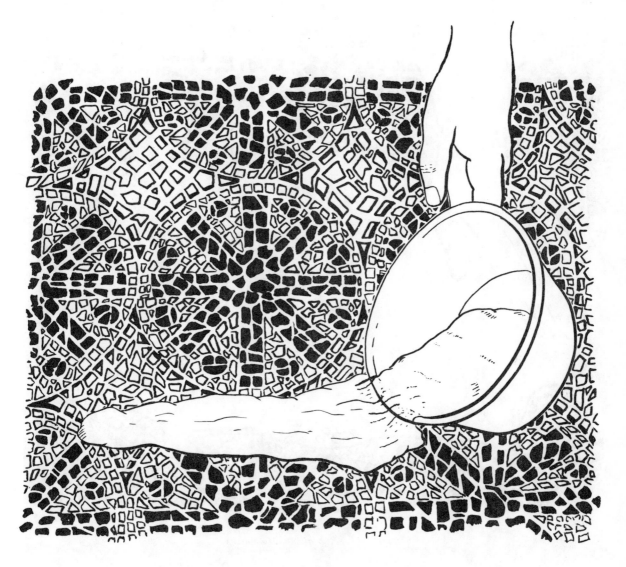

Figure 4–10. Pour prepared grout over surface.

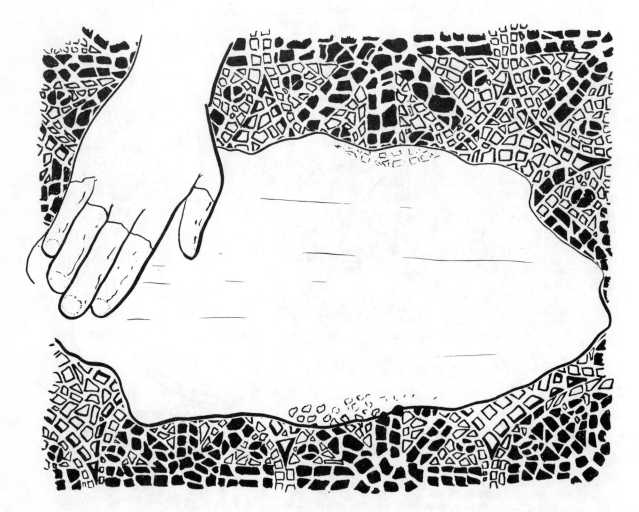

Figure 4–11. Rub grout into spaces.

Figure 4–12. Remove excess grout.

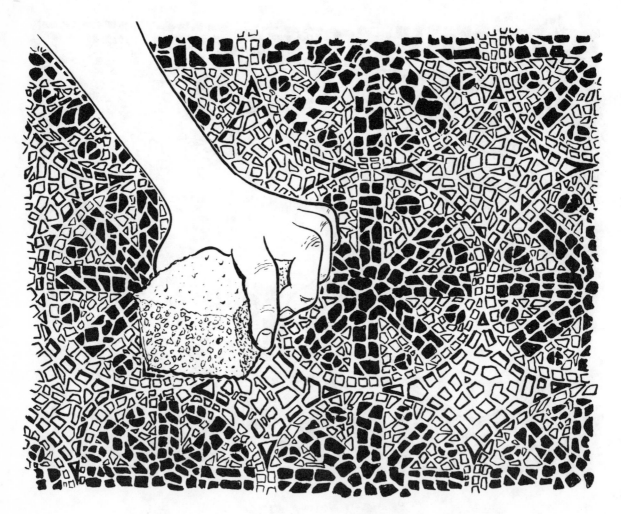

Figure 4–13. Clean surface with damp sponge.

CHAPTER 5

PLASTICS

5–1. Introduction

a. *History of Plastics*. The history of plastics dates back to 1868 and was prompted by a search for a more available material to be used as a substitute for ivory in the production of billiard balls. An American, John Wesley Hyatt, produced a material called Celluloid which, when treated with proper amounts of heat and pressure, became hard and could be molded into desired shapes. Further discoveries were not made until the beginning of the twentieth century when Adolph Spittler, a German, produced a second material which was a casein plastic. In 1909, Dr. Leo Backeland, an American, produced the first synthetic resin, called "Bakelite." Since its founding, numerous types of plastics have been placed on the market. By 1961, approximately 150 companies were producing plastic in the United States, making available about 40 primary plastics, either being commercially produced or being studied in various plants.

b. *Definition*. The word "plastic" can be defined as that which is capable of being molded or modeled. It refers to any nonmetallic substance which can be molded into almost any desirable shape. It generally applies to the synthetic products of chemistry, thus omitting such materials as rubber and glass.

5–2. Classification of Plastics

Plastics may be classified by their physical properties and by their chemical source.

a. *Physical Classification*. Physical classification is based on the reaction of the material to heat.

(1) *Thermoplastic*. This material can be shaped into desired forms under heat and pressure and becomes solid on cooling. It can be softened and remodeled when subjected to the same conditions of heat and pressure.

(2) *Thermosetting*. This material can be shaped into desired form under heat and pressure, but it cannot be remodeled after it becomes solid.

b. *Chemical Classification*. Chemical classification is based on the chemical source. The forty or more plastics now produced generally fall into the following four general groups:

(1) *Cellulose plastics*. These plastics include cellulose nitrate and cellulose acetate. Cellulose nitrate was the first successful thermoplastic, with Celluloid as the oldest example. It is made by treating cotton linters or wood pulp with acids (nitric and sulphuric) in the presence of some catalyst, prior to forming into slabs and baking under pressure. Cellulose acetate is produced in the same manner but uses a different acid (acetate). This method is more advantageous in that it reduces inflammability and is more resistant to sunlight. It also has a greater color range.

(2) *Synthetic resin plastics*. These plastics include the phenolic furfural, phenol formaldehyde, urea formaldehyde, styrene, vinyl, and acrylic plastics. There are several types of *vinyl* plastics which are colorless, tasteless, odorless, and nontoxic. They are thermoplastic and are not affected by alkalis, most acids, and oxidizing agents. Their uses include dentures; watch crystals; records; sealing containers, waterproof and airtight; and shatter-proof windows. The *acrylic* plastics, also thermoplastic, are crystal clear and practically unbreakable. They also come in brilliant opaque colors and have many applications such as road reflectors and models of equipment which display their inner mechanisms. This group consists of the commonly used Lucite and Plexiglas.

(3) *Protein plastics*. These plastics are made from agricultural products such as soy beans, peanuts, milk, and coffee beans. The *casein* plastics are the most common of this group. They are a thermoplastic but have not been as popular here as in Europe. Their thinness incurs warping, which more or less limits their application to such small articles as buttons, buckles, and novelties.

(4) *Natural resin plastics.* Shellac, asphalt, resin, amber, and pitch are included in this group.

5-3. Procurement of Plastics

To insure wise ordering of this rather expensive material, it is important to contact your supply procurement officer, who is responsible for purchasing good materials.

a. Forms of Plastics. Cellulose, acetate, and synthetic resin plastics are available. These come in different forms.

(1) Sheet plastic is made in sheets from 6 by 12 inches to 100 by 120 inches. It is also made from .040 inch to 3 inches thick.

(2) Plastic rods are obtainable from 1/4 inch to 2 inches in diameter and from 12 to 60 inches in length.

(3) Thermosetting plastics which have been molded to different shapes (fig. 5-1) are also on the market. These shapes come in about 12-inch lengths and can be sliced to any thickness, then filed and sanded for finer shaping or polishing.

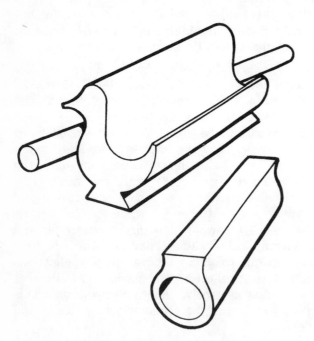

Figure 5-1. Shaped rods of thermosetting plastic.

(4) Special forms can be purchased for specific purposes. Corrugated, ribbed, pebbled, and frosted plastics are examples of what is available.

b. Colors of Plastics. Plastics may be purchased in a wide range of colors, including white, black, and fluorescent. Colors are made in transparent, translucent, and opaque forms; however, the price of colored plastic is slightly more than that of the clear. In sheet form, colored plastic is made in thicknesses of 1/16 to 1/4 inch.

c. Purchase of Plastics. Plastics are purchased by the square inch or the square foot. There is often a discount for large orders, but even then it is quite expensive. Under normal working conditions, it is more feasible to purchase the standard sizes and special shapes as they are listed in the catalogs of the various companies.

5-4. Designing Plastic

a. Design. Like wood and metal, plastic can be formed into an endless variety of shapes and objects. Of the three, plastic is undoubtedly the easiest to form as it lends itself to nearly any shape when it is heated to the proper temperature. In designing plastics, it is usually best to retain the feeling or the natural appearance of the material; do not attempt to make plastic look like wood or any other medium. In this contemporary age, modern designs call for balance and simplicity, not novelty. In design, novelty is usually expressed in such things as in a cutting board so highly decorated that it loses its functional use or in the use of too much miscellaneous materials (twig, flower, rope, etc.) in conjunction with the basic material. All parts of the article designed should have some functional purpose. Carving, veining, and other forms of decorations must be used with care because a poorly designed object cannot be improved by applying decoration. An object that is designed correctly and of good proportion will seldom need decorating. However, along with good design, proportion, and function, it is important to consider the proper choice of material and the purpose for which the material is to be used; for example, Plexiglas should not be chosen to cover a radiator or to be used near stoves as it will burn or bend out of shape.

b. Characteristics.

(1) Plastic ranks high among those materials which resist sagging. Generally, it will sustain considerable stress but when used in the form of large sheets with relatively little support, it has a tendency to sag. This can be prevented by changing the direction of the stresses (fig. 5-2).

(2) The surface of plastic has a very brilliant sheen that is readily and easily polished.

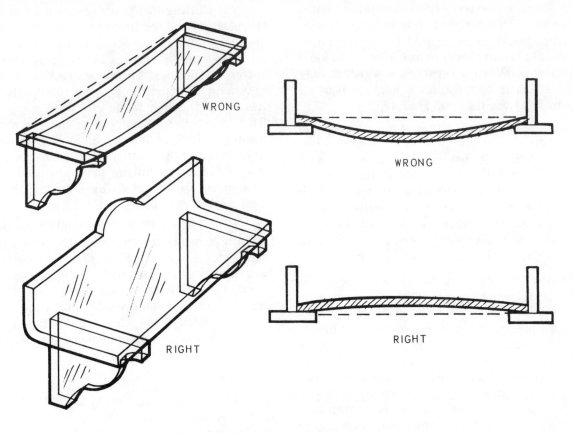

WRONG

WRONG

RIGHT

RIGHT

Figure 5–2. Prevention of sagging of plastic.

The ease with which this material can be finished and polished indicates that it is just as easily scratched or marred through careless use. A plastic article should be so designed that the large areas are not placed where they are scratched in normal use. *For example,* the bottom of a box will scratch badly if feet or legs are not used to raise and support it (fig. 5–3).

(3) The clarity of plastic lends itself to the transmittance of light even through bent pieces of the material. This makes plastic especially adaptable to lighting fixtures which can be decorative as well as functional.

(4) Plastic also has a high refractive power, and because of this, it is best to have designs incorporate the use of sharp corners and flat edges which will reflect the light (fig. 5–4).

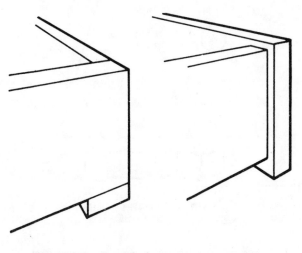

Figure 5–3. Good design prevents scratching.

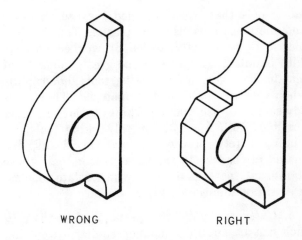

WRONG　　　　RIGHT

Figure 5–4. Designed to reflect light.

(5) Plastic is extremely strong and can withstand considerable stress, but it is not unbreakable. This should be considered in the design of large objects (chairs) and in any attempt to bend sharp corners. When a corner is desired, it may be accomplished by making a joint instead of trying to bend the material sharply.

(6) Plastic is easier than wood or metal to form because it bends to almost any shape when heated properly. It natural appearance should always be retained. However, plastic can be formed and combined with other materials such as wood and metal to achieve attractive results. *For example,* an interesting contrast between clear plastic and wood can be created by laminating the two together.

c. Laying Out the Design. Once a design or pattern has been selected, it should be transferred to the masking paper covering the plastic. It can be put on by marking around it or by tracing it over carbon paper laid on the masking paper. When no pattern or design is used, it is practical to draw freehand or with measuring devices. If the masking paper has been removed from the plastic, it is easily marked and scratched. Therefore, it is preferable to cover the surface with masking tape or to cement the design or pattern directly to the plastic with rubber cement. This protects the surface and permits the paper or tape to be removed without affecting the plastic. It is important to keep masking tape or some covering on the plastic as long as is possible, but it must be removed before gluing and forming. However, designs or patterns can be laid out on the uncovered surface of plastic by using an awl or wax pencil.

5–5. Processing Plastics

Most tools that were designed for use on wood and metal can be used on plastic. This enables plastic to be machine-tooled or worked entirely with handtools. Because of the greater density of plastic, however, woodworking tools dull rapidly when they are used on this material. Thus, it is advisable to use metalworking tools whenever possible. Both wood and metalworking tools, including safety procedures, are specifically discussed in chapter 13. For that reason, only those significant features of tools which relate to plastics will be mentioned here.

a. Cutting. Plastic that is no thicker than ⅛ inch can be cut in a manner similar to cutting paper or cutting window glass.

(1) Cutting like paper can be used only after the plastic has been heated and becomes rubbery. In this state, it can be cut like heavy rubber with scissors, tin snips, a heavy knife, or a paper cutter (guillotine). The more practical manner of obtaining a straight cut, using this method, is to heat only the line to be cut on a strip heater. This avoids the difficulty (encountered when the complete sheet is heated) of having to hold hot, limp plastic while attempting to cut a straight line. When these cutting tools are used, a wider area must be provided for finishing the edges, because the cuts are often rougher and warped.

(2) Cutting like window glass is done by making a deep scratch across the sheet, using a straightedge and a scribe. Then one half is held firmly against the surface of a table with the deep scratch alined over the table edge and the other half is pressed down over the table edge; the plastic will break along the scribed line. However, this method is only recommended for short breaks and thin material.

b. Sawing.

(1) *Handsawing.* Of the many types of handsaws for straight cutting, the most useful is the hollow-ground saw with very little set and eight to ten teeth per inch (fig. 5–5). The most common of these are the hack saw and backsaw. Fine-toothed compass saws, ripsaws, and crosscut saws will produce satisfactory results, but they do have a tendency to chip the plastic. Sawing curves is

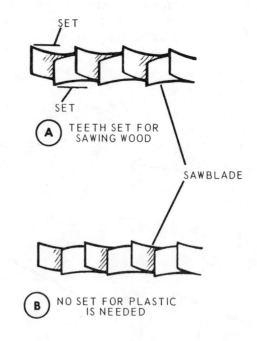

Figure 5–5. Comparison of set of saw teeth.

best accomplished with a fine-tooth coping saw or jeweler's saw. Very narrow blades also give the best results, especially when sawing sharp curves. Regardless of the type of handsaw being used, it should be kept free from kinks, and it should be used with light pressure, since any binding may cause the plastic to crack. It is also important and frequently essential to secure plastic with clamps or jigs when handsawing.

(2) *Power sawing.* The plastics which are commonly used for craft work begin to soften at 140° F. Care must be taken, therefore, when using power tools, to keep the heat of friction from building up to a temperature which will soften the plastic and thereby gum up the tools or cause the tool to stick or "freeze" in the plastic. A lubricant such as oil, wax, or soap is often used on saw blades and drills to cut down heating by reducing friction. In addition, plastic should be fed into power machines more slowly than wood in order to keep friction at a minimum. Any of the power saws (jigsaw, band saw, and circular or table saw) that are used on wood can also be used on plastic.

(a) *Jigsaw.* This is a very excellent tool for cutting curves and making interior cuts, since it saws with a short, thin blade. However, this saw should be used to cut only thin stock. Thicker stock (1/2 inch or over) produces too much heat, which causes the plastic to melt behind the cut and weld back together. Of all the power saws, the jigsaw is the slowest and least dangerous. It is inexpensive to operate, even though the blades break frequently, as they are inexpensive and easy to replace. The blades, approximately 6 inches long, are sized by teeth per inch, with 30 to 60 teeth per inch, which provides excellent cutting of metal, plastic, and other hard material. If the blades break too frequently, this can be partially corrected by running the jigsaw slower or by feeding the plastic more slowly against the blade. Moreover, with approximately one inch of teeth actually cutting, the blades tend to wear. For this reason, it is more feasible to buy the slightly longer blades, so that they may be set higher or lower in the chuck, thereby bringing new teeth into use. The plastic may also be put on wood thick enough to raise it so that new teeth are engaged. Cutting through the wood and plastic also tends to keep thin plastic from breaking. Soap, beeswax, or candle wax applied to the blade reduces friction and also helps to prevent breakage.

(b) *Band saw.* This saw is almost as versatile as the jigsaw, depending on the width of the blade being used. The blades come in sizes from 1/8 inch to 1 inch wide. Those that are 1/8 inch and 3/8 inch wide are the best for plastic. Blades with 6 to 20 teeth per inch are suitable for plastic, but as the plastic increases in thickness, the number of teeth per inch should be lessened. The band saw's long continuous blade cools as it makes it circuit around the wheels, thereby reducing the chance of heating the plastic. To avoid gumming, binding, or breakage, the material should not be fed faster than the blade cuts. Rapid feeding and quick turns are frequent causes of blade breakage in band saws. Especially on sharp curves, the plastic should be occasionally backed up to allow the teeth to ride against the waste side of the plastic, widening the cutting line. This gives the back of the blade more room to swing around the curve (fig. 5–6). A band saw

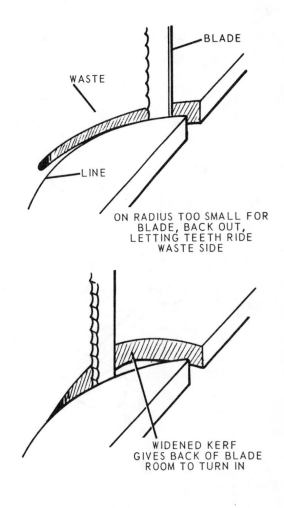

Figure 5–6. *Widening the kerf to facilitate sawing curves.*

produces rather rough edges in plastic which require more extensive finishing.

(c) *Table or circular saw*. This saw is the most dangerous of the power saws. The work must not be pushed past the saw by hand. As in cuttig wood, a push stick should be available for this purpose. Although the table saw is dangerous, its cut is quite smooth so it requires less finishing. A good blade for this type of saw is a hollow-ground blade with no set and 7 to 10 teeth per inch. When using a circular saw, a larger diameter (15 inches to 16 inches) is recommended, since the teeth have more chance to cool during each revolution. However, the diameter of the blade used will depend on the size of the table saw. If a small table saw is available, a 7-inch to 10-inch blade is satisfactory. Heavy material can be cut successfully with a small saw by taking a series of cuts, deepening them at a rate of about ½ inch each time, pulling the plastic away from the blade after each cut to let it cool, then going back to cut another ½ inch.

c. Turning. Plastic may be turned on either a metal or wood turning lathe, but it is best to use a metal lathe because of its rigidity and wide range of performance. (Turning plastic on a wood lathe requires a steady hand, as the density of the plastic increases the vibrations.) The procedure for turning plastic is essentially the same as for turning metal. Turning on a lathe is the only available means for producing parts such as table legs and vases. Because of the skill and experience necessary to operate a lathe, it has been only briefly mentioned here. Information and excellent manuals describing this operation may be obtained from the various manufacturers of lathes.

d. Filing. Files are the tools that erase saw markings and produce semifinished edges on plastic. Coarse wood or metal files can be used for smoothing and shaping rough plastic; medium- or fine-cut files are used for finer smoothing. A 10- to 12-inch, smooth-cut flat file is recommended for rapid smoothing of sawed edges and ends. The half-round and rattail files are useful for inside curves and for enlarging holes; the tri-

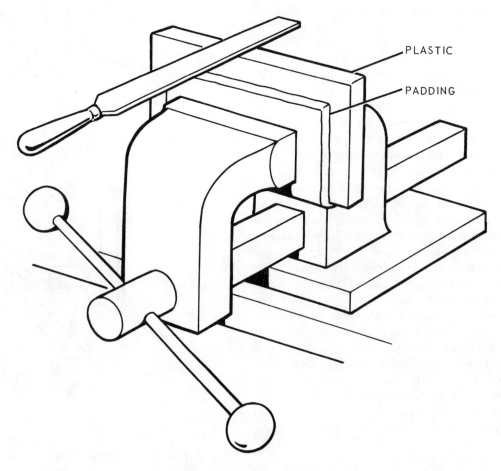

PLASTIC

PADDING

Figure 5–7. Padded vise.

108

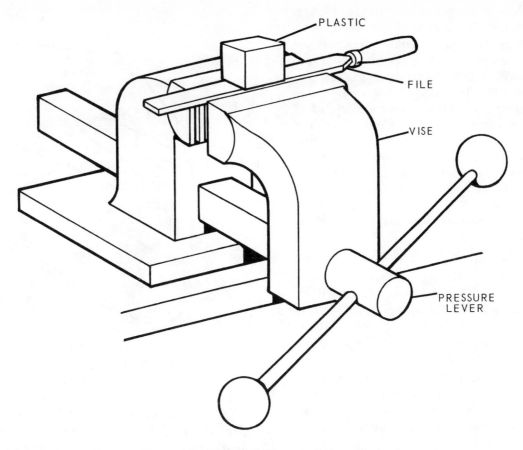

Figure 5–8. Method of filing small pieces of plastic.

angular file fits well in grooves and sharp corners. For very fine work, Swiss-pattern needle files are recommended. It is important to remember that file teeth cut on the forward stroke and therefore filing should be done in one direction. Since filings of metal or other material tend to dull and to stick in the teeth, it is better to reserve a set of files for plastic. If the files are to cut smoothly and rapidly, they should be cleaned frequently with a file card or brush. When plastic is filed, it should always be clamped securely in a padded vise or jig (fig. 5–7). Care must be taken to pad and protect the surfaces of the plastic, because the masking paper is not enough to prevent marring. When filing small pieces of plastic, it is simpler to clamp the file in a vise and rub the piece along the file (fig. 5–8). It is necessary to take out all of the saw marks with the file before starting to use sandpaper.

e. Scraping. This method is even faster than filing and will produce a semipolished edge. The scraper can be made from almost any piece of thin, hard steel, such as an old plane blade, files (fig. 5–9), hack saw blades, cabinet scraper, or a simple piece of rectangular steel. All that is

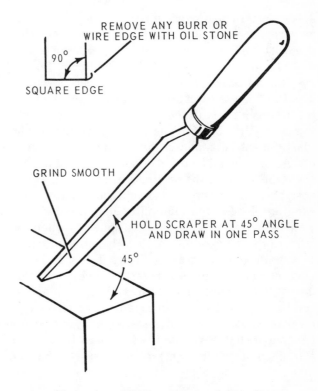

Figure 5–9. Making a scraper from a file.

needed to make a scraper is a square-cut edge. Any burr or wire edge is removed on an oilstone, keeping the edge straight and square. The scraper is held at a 45-degree angle and drawn across the entire edge of the plastic in one pass. Although this method is faster, it has certain disadvantages such as leaving minute defects after buffing and creating riffled or hollow edges. The minute defects can be corrected by simply using fine silicon carbide sandpaper or steel wool before polishing. The riffles and hollow edges occur because more pressure is exerted on the plastic midway than at the ends of the stroke. It is possible to avoid this by not pressing as hard in the center of the piece of plastic.

f. Sanding. Sanding is done to remove the file marks and, if the plastic has been cut close to the line and smoothly with a fine-tooth saw, it will remove the saw marks. The complete process of sanding includes removing the larger scratches with a coarse abrasive and the smaller scratches with finer abrasives.

(1) *Hand sanding.* The same criteria should be followed as for woodworking (ch. 13) in selecting and using the right grade of sandpaper for plastic. You should always begin with the finest grade sandpaper that will remove the scratches and progress to finer abrasives as the scratches are removed. If saw marks or deep file marks are to be removed, begin with No. 3/0 or 4/0 garnet (dry sandpaper). When fine file marks or garnet sandpaper marks are being removed, begin with silicon carbide abrasive paper No. 360 or 400 and progress to even No. 500 to 600 for top results. Silicon-carbide abrasive paper is waterproof and is used wet for sanding plastic. The water acts as a coolant and keeps plastic from stacking up on the abrasive and causing scratches. The plastic must be kept wet during the sanding procedure but should be dried occasionally and held to the light to check the progress of the work. When possible, the sandpaper should be used with a sanding block to eliminate depressions and rounded edges. Best results are obtained when the surface of the sanding block is backed with firm rubber or felt. Just as in filing, it is simpler to rub very small pieces across the sandpaper (fig. 5–10). It is worth mentioning that, in place of sandpaper, steel wool can also be used effectively on plastic. Coarser grades can be substituted for sandpaper, but No. 0000 is often used in place of the silicon-carbide (wet) sandpaper No. 360 or 400.

(2) *Power sanding.*

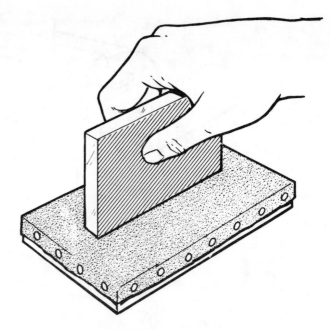

Figure 5–10. Method of sanding small pieces of plastic.

(a) *Disc sander.* The disc sander is an excellent machine for rapid removal of rough saw and file marks, as well as for rounding corners and cutting bevels and chamfers. Keep in mind that the sanding disc cuts faster near the outer edge and slower near its center. It is very dangerous sanding to the right of the center because the counterclockwise rotation of the disc will kick the plastic up off the table (fig. 5–11). The speed of the disc will also cause the edge of the material to burn if it is forced against the disc or if too fine an abrasive is used. For coarse sanding, a No. 1½ garnet paper will quickly remove saw and file marks. Finer sanding can be accomplished by attaching waterproof abrasive paper to the disc, but belt sanders are best for this type of finish. The abrasive is kept wet by applying water with a brush. The sanding table must be dried when the work is finished in order to prevent rusting.

(b) *Belt sander.* The combined use of a belt sander and a disc sander produces excellent results with plastic. This is accomplished by shaping with coarse dry sandpaper on the disc and finishing with a finer wet sandpaper on the belt. The belt sander is excellent for sanding flat surfaces and also has the advantage of being useful for sanding inside curves on its drum or roller (fig. 5–11). Th regular dry belt sander can be adapted for wet sanding by using a

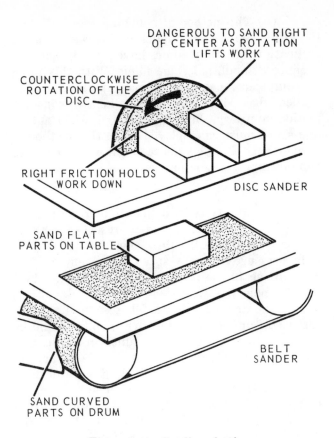

DANGEROUS TO SAND RIGHT OF CENTER AS ROTATION LIFTS WORK

COUNTERCLOCKWISE ROTATION OF THE DISC

RIGHT FRICTION HOLDS WORK DOWN

DISC SANDER

SAND FLAT PARTS ON TABLE

BELT SANDER

SAND CURVED PARTS ON DRUM

Figure 5–11. Sanding plastic.

punched can to drip water onto the belt, with a drip pan underneath and splash guards at the end of the belt. The recommended belt abrasives are No. 180 to give plastic a smooth grade of surface and No. 280 which leaves plastic ready to buff.

g. Polishing. If sanding is done in a careless or hasty manner, the final polishing will reveal the scratches that were not removed. Since this will require that the wet sanding stage be repeated, it is more feasible to do a thorough job of sanding before beginning the buffing procedure. Buffing should bring the edges of the plastic to a high polish.

(1) *Hand polishing.* Buffing by hand with a soft cloth, flannel, or felt is entirely possible, although it is very tedious and slow. When wrapped around a stick or rod and sprinkled with a non-scratch household cleaner, a cloth will provide a fine polish. Other very fine abrasives which lend themselves to hand polishing are toothpowder, fine pumice, and tripoli. The powders are mixed with oil or water, so that they will adhere to the

cloth. Tripoli can be rubbed on a piece of flannel which is secured to a smooth piece of wood. The plastic then is rubbed briskly along the flannel. The final polishing should be completed with a clean, abrasive-free buffer.

(2) *Power polishing.* Power-driven buffing wheels are recommended and are found in most occupational therapy clinics. This method is far less strenuous and considerably faster than hand buffing. The buffing disc or wheel varies in diameter from 1 inch to 18 inches; the diameter utilized will be regulated by the conditions of the individual clinic. Wheels as large as 15 inches in diameter are excellent, but much smaller buffs will give good results. Cloth wheels 6 to 10 inches in diameter are recommended, but this will depend on the motor. The motor should turn a 6-inch buffing wheel at about 2500 rpm. Buffing wheels also vary in the texture of softness. The types most commonly found in the average clinic are cotton and linen. Clean, loosely stitched wheels are soft and they produce excellent results for the very fine buffing. If the wheels are too tightly sewn, the edges are hard. (This can be corrected by cutting the outer rows of stitches and/or holding coarse sandpaper against the wheel to loosen the threads.) One wheel should be reserved for coarse polishing and one for fine polishing. Those wheels used on plastic should not be used on metal or vice versa. Neither should jeweler's rouge or other metal polishing compounds be applied to the buffing wheel used on plastic. Buffing wheel compounds consist of fine abrasives in combination with wax or grease binders and polishing tallow. Both are available in bar or tube form and should be used as recommended by the supply source from which the plastic is purchased. It eliminates having to apply tallow first, then a buffing compound. If tripoli is not available, fine pumice or tooth-powder can be put on a wheel lubricated with vaseline. When a buffing wheel has been used repeatedly, any hardened compound can be removed by running it against a sharp metal edge before applying more compound. Tripoli is applied by holding the bar of tripoli for a few seconds to the edge of the buffing wheel as it is spinning. The edge of the plastic is then held at the edge of the buffing wheel (fig. 5–12). To avoid heating the plastic to the point where it may become pitted or warped, it must be moved back and forth with light but moderate pressure. Pitting or burning are defects that occur only when the buffing is continued too long in one spot or when too much pressure is used. If buffing compound collects on the plastic, it indicates either

111

that there is too much on the wheel or that the piece is being pushed too hard. As the wheel spins, there is a tendency for it to kick down the piece being polished. To avoid this, the operator should stand so that the wheel is running toward him and the plastic is held just beolw the center of the wheel. He should also remember that square edges or corners should not be forced into the wheel and that it is dangerous to use any type of tool rest to support the palstic while buffing.

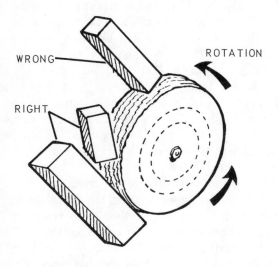

Figure 5–12. Buffing on a wheel.

(3) *Solvent and flame polishing*. These methods are frequently overlooked. A certain degree of skill is needed to accomplish good results, but only a little practice is needed to obtain this skill.

(*a*) The use of solvent is an excellent, quick method of polishing holes and, on specific occasions, the edges of plactic. Rather than the standard method of wet-standing with abrasive paper wrapped on dowels and then buffing with felt-wrapped dowels, a solvent that will dissolve the plastic is poured into the hole. However, the hole must be dry, clean, and free of chips. Alcohol is useful for this purpose because it cleans, dries rapidly, and helps to remove chips. When this has been accomplished, an eye dropper is used to fill the hole with ethylene dichloride. This should be done in a well-ventilated room and away from any flames. The solvent should remain in the hole for only 1 minute and then be poured out. Approximately 24 hours is needed for the plastic to harden again, because the solvent causes the walls of the hole to become spongy. After hardening, the hole is free of nicks and grooves.

(*b*) The method of polishing edges of plastic with a flame is also quick and excelelnt. Most occupational therapy clinics have a torch that will produce a small, pale blue flame. With this piece of equipment, pass the flame rapidly over the sanded edge. The flame must be kept in constant motion, to prevent burning of the plastic. Caution and speed must be employed when this method is used on very thin plastic because it will burn more rapidly than thicker plastic.

h. Drilling.

(1) Ordinary twist drills are used on plastic. When possible, a set should be reserved for this particular purpose. Drilling should be done with light pressure and slow speed to prevent melting and cutting in the hole. To obtain the smoothest possible hole, the walls should be scraped, not cut, during the drilling process. There is a slight difference of opinion on what drill points should be reground to produce the best finish in a hole. One thought is that regrinding is not necessary on drill points under 5/16 inch if light, careful pressure is used. The more common thought seems to be to regrind all drill points used on plastic. It is recommended that the positive rake be ground from the drill point in order to enable the drill to scrape rather than cut into the walls of the hole. The rake (fig. 5–13) can be altered with a file or on the grinder. The common manufactured angle on a drill point is adequate but it can be reduced to 60° to obtain a sharper point, which some prefer (fig. 5–14).

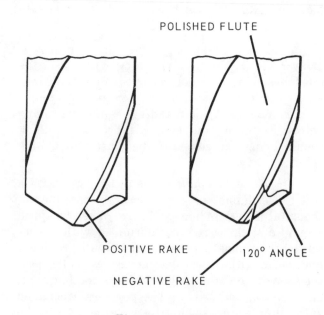

Figure 5–13. Rake.

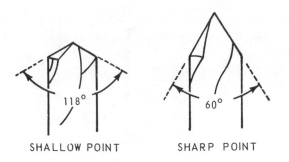

SHALLOW POINT   SHARP POINT

Figure 5–14. Changing the angle of a drill point.

(2) A polished, slow, spiral flute is important in achieving the best possible finish in a hole. It allows the drill to clear the shavings and prevents them from rubbing against the walls of the hole. To begin the drilling process, it is necessary to locate and mark the hole with a sharp scratch awl, because drills tend to skip around on smooth, slick surfaces. However, this mark will only hold the small drills true. Because the point of the big drill is larger than the indentation made by the awl, the hole should first be started with a small drill. Drilling may be accomplished with a hand drill or brace, electric portable drill, or the drill press. Regardless of the method used, the plastic should be firmly held and supported during the process of drilling. Care should be employed to avoid breaking through the opposite side from too much pressure. This will happen frequently with thin stock. To avoid this, back the plastic with a block of wood and lighten the pressure of the drill as it nears completion. When a hand drill or brace is used, avoid working with the plastic in an upright position. If this cannot be avoided, keep in mind that without the wood backing it is easy to crack either the plastic project or the existing hole. The same holds true when using the electric portable drill.

(3) In the use of a drill press, the same general instructions apply; also, smaller drills may be run at faster speeds than larger drills. *For example,* a 1/8-inch drill can be run at an approximate speed of 3000 rpm., while a 1/4-inch drill should be maintained at approximately 1750 rpm., and a 1/2-inch drill at 1000 rpm., or less. Holes which are shallow can be drilled without a lubricant, but deep holes require one. The deep holes may be kept cleaner by keeping the drill moist and reducing friction with either water, soap, or oil; it is also important to remove the bit frequently so that shavings can be cleared away.

(4) Small holes in plastic can also be made by punching thin plastic with a hot needle or brad and withdrawing it quickly before it cools. This method can be used when small screws or fasteners are to be inserted in plastic.

i. Fastening. Plastic cannot be fastened together in the same manner as wood. However, the techniques employed in fastening wood can be adapted for plastic. Frequently, self-tapping, drive, or machine screws are used with plastic (fig. 5–15). In using the self-tapping or drive screws as fasteners, it is necessary to drill a hole slightly smaller than the diameter of the screw. As this screw is driven into the hole, it turns by itself, cutting its own threads. The drive screw may not be removed after it has been inserted. Some authorities feel that the most practical method of fastening is with the machine screw. The procedure for inserting a machine screw is the same as previously mentioned, with the exception of driving the screw with a screwdriver. Wood screws are used to fasten plastic to wood. The shank hole is drilled into the plastic and the pilot hole in the wood. Another method, which is employed to fasten hinges and catches, is to use escutcheon pins or brads as fasteners. A hole is drilled slightly smaller than the pin or brad. As the pin or brad is being pushed into the hole, heat is applied to the head (fig. 5–16). This method can also be used when a hinge-type plastic joint is required. The only alteration is to make the hole in the stationary piece of plastic slightly larger, so that the pin or brad may move freely in the hole. It is also possible to thread plastic doweling with a die and use it in place of a conventional type of screw. Cutting should be done slowly and with a lubricant to keep the plastic from chipping. The die should be backed out slightly when necessary to clear the thread of chips. (Large threads are less likely to break.) A drill hole is then tapped to fit the plastic screw.

j. Grooving. Grooves are used in plastic for recessing panels, for inlaying, and in making picture frames. There are several ways in which they can be cut. A circular saw may be used to cut grooves in plastic just as it is in wood. A hack saw may be used to cut narrow or wide grooves. A single saw kerf will make narrow grooves; for wider ones, as many kerf as necessary are sawed out, side by side, to the desired depth. The groove

SELF-TAPPING   DRIVE

MACHINE

Figure 5–15. Screws used in plastic.

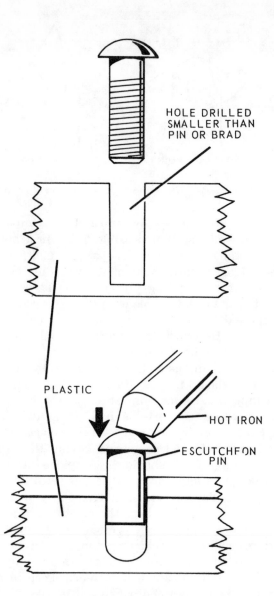

HOLE DRILLED
SMALLER THAN
PIN OR BRAD

PLASTIC

HOT IRON

ESCUTCHEON
PIN

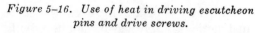

is then smoothed out with a file. Files alone can be used to make grooves, but only where short lengths are required. Grooves can also be made with a chisel. It is necessary to lay out the lines for the groove on the plastic with a sharp awl and steel straightedge. The straightedge is clamped along this layout line. Then the chisel is pulled along the straightedge until the groove is of the desired depth.

k. Forming. Bending plastic is one of the most interesting phases of working with this material. It offers innumerable possibilities in design and requires both knowledge and skill. Any thickness of thermoplastic material can be bent or at least its shape can be changed when it is correctly heated. The thinner the piece, however, the sharper the angle it will take. One-fourth-inch plastic will not take a sharp angle but must be bent in rounding curves. Before plastic is heated, the masking paper must be removed and the plastic thoroughly cleaned. Temperature and heating time vary with the type and thickness of the

Figure 5–16. Use of heat in driving escutcheon pins and drive screws.

(Note. Nick shank of pin with pliers before using.)

plastic. Experience will tell when the piece has reached the right temperature for forming. If the plastic bends but has a springy quality, reheat it; if it handles limply, while holding one end, it is at the proper temperature for forming. Thinner material must also be heated to a higher temperature than thick material since the amount of heat which can be stored is much less than can be stored in thick plastic. However, thick plastic must be heated longer because it takes longer to attain the same temperature throughout. It also takes thick plastic much longer to cool than thin plastic.

(1) The most common method of heating small pieces of plastic is in an oven. This can be done in a plastic kiln especially made for the purpose or in an ordinary kitchen oven. Regardless, any oven used for this purpose should be equipped with a regulator as the recommended temperature for heating plastic is 220° to 300° F.

(2) A strip heater (fig. 5–17) is used to heat only a straight line across a thin piece of plastic in order to bend it at an angle. Strip heaters may be commercially obtained. The plastic is placed over the heating element until it softens. It can then be bent to any desired angle (fig. 5–18). To bend thick plastic, it is necessary to heat both surfaces to the proper temperature.

CAUTION

The plastic must not be placed directly on the heating element as the heat will mar the surface of the plastic.

(3) Other methods for heating small sections of plastic include the use of a hotplate. The part being formed or reformed is held above the plate until it becomes sufficiently hot. A hood over the plate speeds up the heating process; it can be made quite easily from a tin can. Still another method is to use a reflector spotlight on thin plastic. Ordinary water can also be used in forming plastic. The water is heated to the boiling point in a pan large enough to accommo-

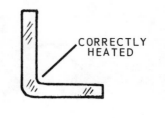

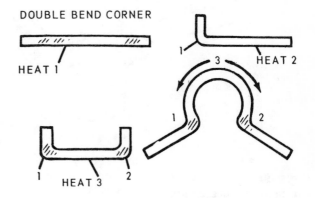

Figure 5–18. Bending plastic.

date the plastic. Once the boiling point has been reached, the water is removed from the heat and left to stand for a minute. The plastic is immersed and left in the water until it becomes sufficiently hot to be formed. This method is adequate for thin, 1/8-inch plastic but not for thicker pieces, because the water cools before the plastic can be evenly heated.

(4) Regardless of the method used in forming, soft gloves should be worn to protect the hands from heat and to prevent the surface of the plastic from being marked. Gloves that are too soft and thin make it difficult to hold the hot plastic while it cools. Two thicknesses of soft gloves will help to alleviate this but thick gloves, when turned inside out, frequently offer a soft surface. As indicated, forming techniques can be performed by simple hand manipulation of the heated plastic. With this technique, it is possible to execute some simple shapes without benefit of molds or jigs. Shapes formed in this manner can be clever and highly artistic but they are difficult to repeat.

(5) Molds or jigs (fig. 5–19) are made to facilitate forming and to make it possible to repeat a certain series of curves in a piece of plastic. Forms for 2-dimensional or 3-dimensional shapes can be made of wood and, with the aid of vises, clamps, or hand pressure, can create in-

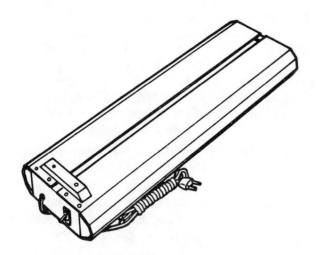

Figure 5–17. Strip heater.

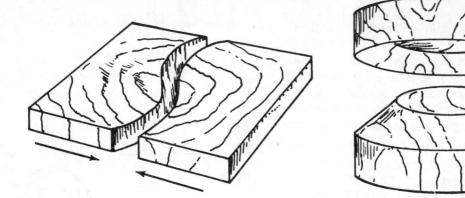

Figure 5-19. Jigs for bending plastic.

teresting results. Either convex or concave forms can be used, or a combination of both.

(6) Well-dried white pine and mahogany are the best woods to use. End grain may mark the plastic and should be avoided unless the mold or jig is covered with a smooth material. The best materials for lining molds or jigs are moleskin (surgical adhesive tape), flannel, or felt. The nap of these cloths helps to prevent imprints of the weave on the soft plastic. The molds or jigs should be free of variations in contour, which cause optical distortion. They should be stored carefully to protect them from denting, chipping, or warping, since such defects will appear in the heated plastic. When plastic is laid over or set into a jig, it should be held in the desired position (fig. 5–20) with wedges, cleats, clamps, or rubber bands, or by hand until the sheet is thoroughly cooled. The cooling time will depend on room temperature as well as on the thickness of the plastic. If the plastic is not thoroughly cooled before it is removed from the form, it will tend to return to its original shape. Plunging the hot plastic into cold water is not recommended as it causes uneven cooling. Another technique of forming is to use rings and plugs (fig. 5–21). To prevent marring of the plastic, the same type of lining is used that was previously mentioned.

l. Cementing. Ordinary adhesive glues or cements used in the woodshop, in the household, or on model airplanes are not recommended for plastic. This type of glue forms an *adhesion* between the cemented surfaces. To get satisfactory results in cementing plastic, it is necessary to achieve a *cohesion* of the cemented surfaces. Cohesive cement is the type that will soften the surfaces of the plastic, allowing the two surfaces or edges to fuse together into a single unit. Cohesion occurs as the solvent evaporates and the plastic begins to harden again as one single bond. There are several types of plastic cement, commonly called plastic solvents. Ethylene dichloride is one that is often used. Methylene dichloride is another that is frequently found in occupational therapy clinics and is somewhat better than other solvents. Both these solvents evaporate rapidly, so the plastic must be preassembled or assembled quickly. Other plastic solvents include chloroform, acetone, and acetic acid. All these solvents are thin and fluid but vary as to speed of action. They are also all toxic and some are inflammable, which requires well-ventilated working areas, away from any flames. For safety reasons, they should all be kept in tightly closed small containers and stored in a metal cabinet; if large quantities are stored, they should be in a metal shed away from the building.

(1) *Joints.* Some of the more common woodworking joints are quite practical for plastic (fig. 5–22). However, wood joints do not require the preparation necessary for plastic joints. For example, the plastic joint has to fit very closely and accurately; clamping devices (fig. 5–23) have to be properly alined; accurate masking of the surfaces is often necessary; and solvent must

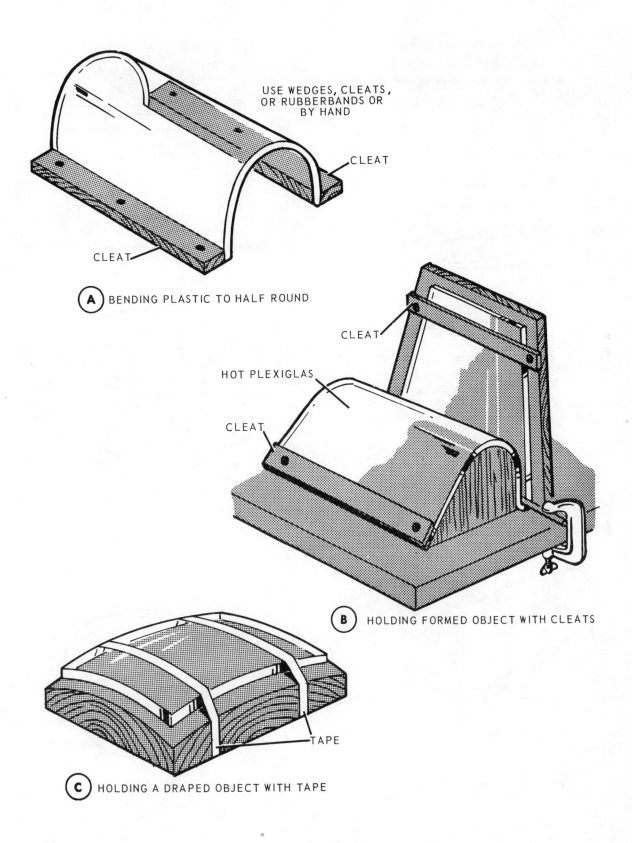

USE WEDGES, CLEATS,
OR RUBBERBANDS OR
BY HAND

CLEAT

CLEAT

A BENDING PLASTIC TO HALF ROUND

CLEAT

HOT PLEXIGLAS

CLEAT

B HOLDING FORMED OBJECT WITH CLEATS

TAPE

C HOLDING A DRAPED OBJECT WITH TAPE

Figure 5–20. Holding plastic in desired position.

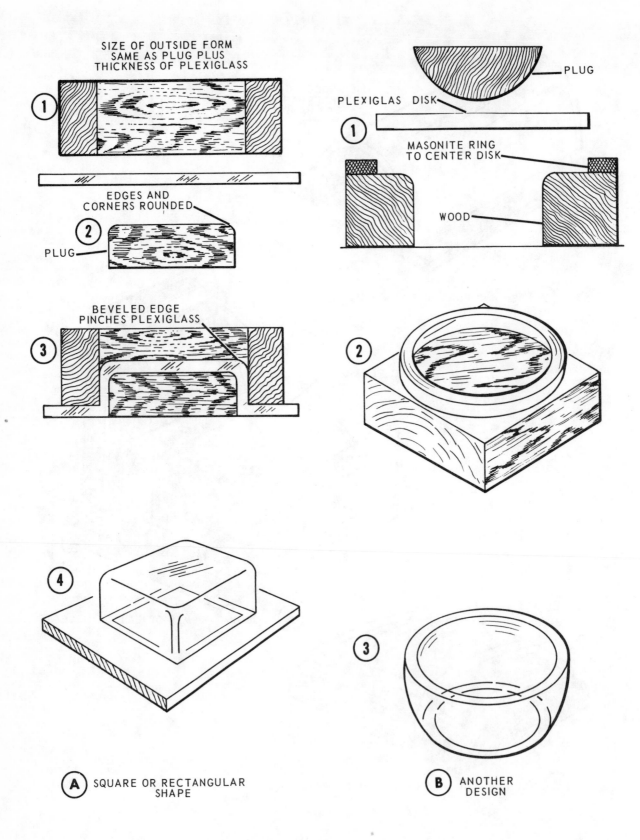

SIZE OF OUTSIDE FORM
SAME AS PLUG PLUS
THICKNESS OF PLEXIGLASS

①

EDGES AND
CORNERS ROUNDED

② PLUG

③ BEVELED EDGE
PINCHES PLEXIGLASS

④

Ⓐ SQUARE OR RECTANGULAR
SHAPE

PLUG

PLEXIGLAS DISK

① MASONITE RING
TO CENTER DISK

WOOD

②

③

Ⓑ ANOTHER
DESIGN

Figure 5–21. Use of plug and ring in forming
plastic.

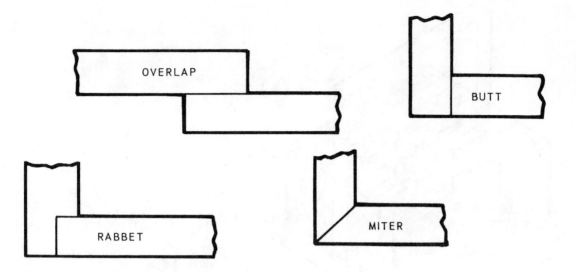

Figure 5–22. Joints used for plastic.

be carefully applied. Some recommend that surfaces which are to be cemented be roughened with sandpaper. Others advise that plastic solvent works just as well on polished surfaces as on sanded surfaces if the surfaces are dry and clean.

NOTE

The accuracy of a joint line is easily checked by putting a film of water on one surface and bringing the two pieces together. If the fit is proper, the water will form an even film along the joint line. Surfaces that are not perfectly flat will need more filing or sanding because the solvent will produce bubbles where the surface is uneven.

(2) *Application.* If any of the various solvents is accidentally dropped on the plastic during the cementing process, it will make a cloudy mark. When that happens, wait until the spot is thoroughly dry, then sand it with a No. 400 to 600 abrasive paper and buff it. Several methods may be used to apply solvents.

(a) *Soak method.* The soak method is used when one of the two pieces to be cemented can be put into the solvent (fig. 5–24). The plastic is placed in the solution to the depth desired. Care must be taken to avoid getting the solvent on any other part of the piece. The amount of solvent used will be determined by how much of the plastic is to be submerged. Generally, brads should be placed in a shallow glass or metal dish

with just enough cement to cover the brads partially, not completely. Usually one of the edges is soaked until it is swollen into a "cushion" by the cement's action. The length of time the plastic is soaked depends upon the desired depth of the cushion and the type of solvent used. The usual time is less than 3 minutes. Soaking time should be sufficient to form a good cushion but short enough to prevent the plastic from becoming too soft. After the cushion has formed, the two surfaces are immediately brought together and uniform pressure is applied along the joint with clamps or jigs. The pressure should be just enough to squeeze out the air bubbles. Too much pressure will squeeze out the solvent and create dry spots. The joint should then be strong and clear after it dries.

(b) *Dip method.* The dip method is similar to the soak method, but one surface is merely dipped into the solution and brought out immediately. The surfaces are then assembled and held with light pressure until they are set and do not pull apart.

(c) *Flow method.* The flow method requires matched, well-fitted surfaces. The cement may be introduced with a brush, eyedropper, or hypodermic needle to the surfaces of the joint and allowed to spread to the balance of the joint area by capillary action.

(d) *Glue method.* The glue method is used where broad areas are to be cemented. This ne-

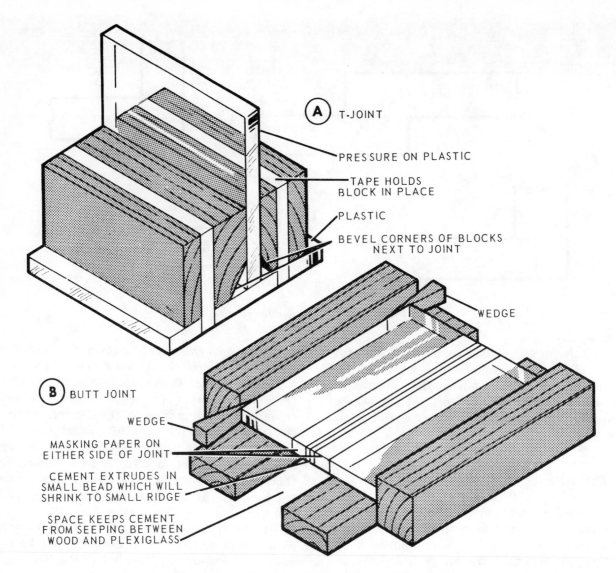

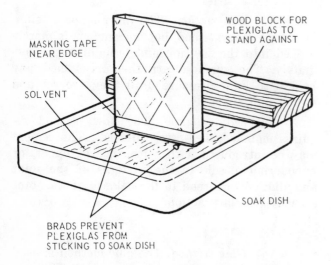

Figure 5-23. Clamping device used for gluing plastic.

Figure 5-24. Soaking plastic in a solvent.

cessitates a slower acting and thicker solution than the straight solvents. The solvents are thickened by adding small plastic chips or shavings to the solvent unitl it is of a syrup-like consistency. These chips or shavings can be made by cutting plastic into small pieces or by using the shavings from plastic which has been drilled or scraped. The mixture can be applied like glue, because the chips or shavings also retard the speed of the solvent's action. With this glue, it is usually necessary to use masking tape around the joint to facilitate removal of excess cement which may be forced from the joint.

(e) *Laminating.* Another method, laminating, is used to laminate layers of plastic or layers of wood and plastic together. The soak method is frequently used in this application, but the glue method can also be used. The pieces being laminated are clamped for approximately 24 hours or until thoroughly dry. In this method, two layers of plastic may be laminated to form a thicker layer; a colored piece of plastic may be laminated between two clear ones; or wood may be laminated to a layer of plastic. In all cases, the plastic cushion must be quite thick and the pieces should be larger than the finished product. This precaution is necessary because the slippery cushion often causes the layers to slide.

(f) *Welding*. The one means of joining plastic without the use of a solvent is by welding. This method is only suitable for the end-to-end type of joint. The end surfaces must be clean and free of dirt or oil. They are heated on a hot plate until they begin to bubble and smoke (approximately 660° F). At this stage, the ends are quickly brought together and held under enough pressure to force out the air bubbles. When done properly, no seam can be detected after the piece is sanded and polished. In an occupational therapy clinic, this method can be used to join various colors of plastic together and, if a large hot plate is available, to enlarge sheets of scrap plastic. It is advisable to experiment before attempting to weld on a large project.

m. Decorating. Simplicity of design is always desirable in plastic, but there are various methods for decorating which must be used with discretion. A few of these, plus combinations of methods will be mentioned briefly.

(1) *Beveling*. Beveling is one of the more common forms of decorating and, if done correctly, will add to the attractiveness, as it makes additional facets for reflecting light. The bevel is polished in the prescribed manner but, in so doing, care must be taken to keep the surface of the bevel from becoming rounded.

(2) *Laminating*. Laminating is an ideal way to affix thin, sparkling bits of metal or glitter, pieces of copper and brass, strips of tinsel, metallic screening, threads, sequins, wire, aluminum foil, bits of cloth cutouts, and other such thin material between two layers of plastic. Both surfaces to be laminated are unmasked and cleaned. The bits of material are laid out in a design on the bottom piece of plastic. The glue method, described previously, is used to apply the thickened solvent to the surface of the top piece. The glue should be distributed evenly and should be thick enough so that the surfaces come into direct contact and do not rest on any of the material that has been inserted. After the glue has been spread, the top piece is turned quickly and applied gently to the bottom piece of plastic. Care must be exercised when pressure is applied, because too much pressure may force the inserted material out of the edges. The piece should be left to dry for 24 hours. In the finishing process, too much pressure from sanding or buffing will create friction and cause the softened inner layer of material to burn out and also allow particles to be forced between the edges of the plastic. Because it sometimes requires a month for the soft inner layer to harden, the best method of finishing the edge is to use methylene dichloride. The solvent is carefully brushed along the edge of the plastic to produce a smooth, clear finish.

(3) *Surface decorating.*

(a) *Glue decorating*. Another decorative method very similar to laminating is to design the surface with fine glitter, powder, or sawdust. The surface on a piece of plastic is frosted or roughened with the round end of a belt sander or coarse sandpaper on a block of wood. The design is then made on the surface, using the syrup-like solvent described in the glue method. The solvent may be used plain; or fine glitter, powder, or sawdust can be mixed in it before pouring. As the solvent is poured, the width of the lines in the design will vary with the manner of pouring. The design must be allowed to set and harden on a flat surface and, if possible, in a dust free room.

(b) *Veining*. Another type of surface design is veining, which is the simplest form of surface decoration. It consists of scratching a design or outline on the polished surface of the plastic with a sharp-pointed awl. These lines can be filled with a quick-drying colored lacquer or with ordinary ink.

(c) *Engraving*. Engraving is a method of scraping a design on a surfce of the plastic with an X-acto knife, with a razor blade, or with fine sandpaper. This produces a frosted effect which can be shaded and made interesting. When used in conjunction with the veining method, the simple outline should be scratched first and then the center of the design scraped.

(d) *Embossing*. Embossing is another method of surface decoration. It is a convenient way to imprint a design in heated plastic. There are any number of objects which will give an interesting texture to the surface. *For example*, some of the materials that can be used for embossing are coarse-textured cloth, common screening, sandpaper, block prints, or embossed metal. The procedure for embossing is to heat the plastic until it is thoroughly soft and press it against the textured material with even pressure until the plastic is cool. When materials such as screening or sandpaper are used on surfaces which are going to be exposed to abrasion, they tend to lessen the usual obvious appearance of the abrasions. Pictures and designs can be embossed in plastic. Wire can be used to outline the picture on a smooth plywood board, burying the wire ends in the back piece. Tin or metal patterns can also be cut and attached to a board for embossing. Uniform pressure over the complete area is important in producing an even texture or design. In embossing, care should be taken to avoid distorting the edges of the plastic while they are warm.

(e) *Surface carving.* Surface carving is a method of cutting designs on the back of clear plastic to different depths. This will produce a 3-dimensional effect. A rotating drill such as a "Moto-tool" or a dental drill is used with various types of burrs. Used dental burrs of various shapes are quite satisfactory (A, fig. 5–25). The work is done from the back surface of the plastic but is to be seen from the front. Surface carving is quite simple to do and requires only a little

practice to produce some rather satisfactory effects. It is suggested, however that some practicing be done on scrap plastic.

(f) *Internal carving.* Internal carving, as the name implies, consists of carving inside a thick piece of plastic with tapered drills. The plastic is held in one hand or in a jeweler's vise and the cutting is watched from the front. The same type of drill is used for internal carving as is used for surface carving. Drill bits (B, fig. 5–25) in sizes from 5/64 to 1/8 inch may be ground to a sharp point or tapered on the end, or may be purchased at a supply house. Dental burrs are always used in combination with the tapered drill. The tools are moved from side to side or back and forth, forming a cavity of the shape desired such as flowers or leaves (fig. 5–26). When the carving is complete, it can be colored with liquid plastic dye applied with a hypodermic needle, eye dropper, or cotton wrapped around a toothpick. The drilled area should be completely cleaned of shavings before being dyed. Of prime importance is the order of drilling and dyeing. *For example,* the center of a flower should be drilled and dyed before the petals are started. After drilling and dyeing the petals, leaves and

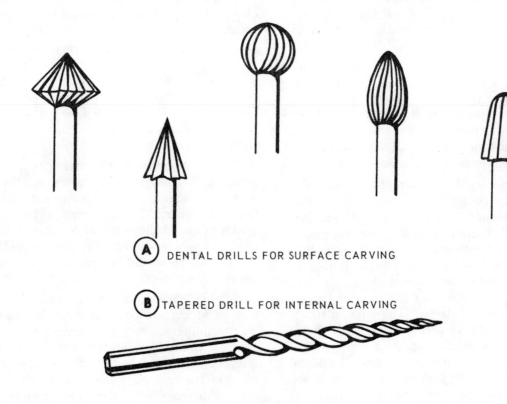

Ⓐ DENTAL DRILLS FOR SURFACE CARVING

Ⓑ TAPERED DRILL FOR INTERNAL CARVING

Figure 5–25. Types of drills used for carving plastic.

stem are done. This sequence keeps each dye within the area where it belongs. After the drilling and dyeing processes have been completed, the cavity is filled with dry dental plaster of paris. Next, the plastic is struck sharply to force the plaster into the tips of the carving. The cavity opening is sealed by placing a few drops of water on the plaster and smoothing it with a knife blade. The entire back surface may then be laminated to a piece of opaque plastic if so desired. The final appearance should be that of an object buried within the plastic.

(g) *Dyeing.* Another method of decorating plastic is with dye. Plastics may be obtained in a wide range of colors, but sometimes a different color is needed. Dyeing plastic is a rather messy job at best. The color fades in time because the dye penetrates only the surface. However, it is fun to play with and patients often enjoy experimenting with it. There are two types of plastic dye: dip dyes and laminating dyes.

• *Dip dyes* are sold in plastic supply houses in several types of powdered dye (which must be prepared before using), as well as in solution ready to use. The powdered dyes are dissolved in a mixture of 60-percent acetone and 40-percent water. First, the dye is dissolved in acetone, then the water is added.

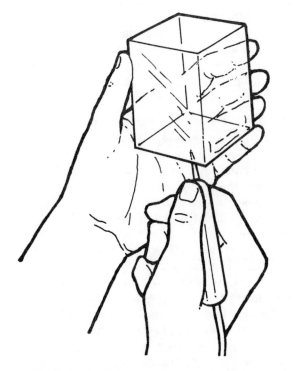

Figure 5–26. Internal carving with a dental drill.

Another very satisfactory dye can be made in the shop by dissolving a package of all-purpose fabric dye in a small amount of hot water. To this solution, add 20-percent acetone, 20-percent isopropyl alcohol, and 60-percent water. As the term "dip dyes" implies, the plastic is immersed or dipped in the dye. It is important to remove all traces of dirt and oil from the plastic before it is dipped, in order to achieve uniform color. The entire piece or area is immersed in the dye, which may be hot or cold, depending upon the type used. The piece should be moved around in the dye to insure even coloring. The darkness of the color depends upon the length of time the piece is in the solution. As the dye does not penetrate the plastic to any depth, the piece must be finished and polished before it is dyed. When the color is dark enough, the piece is removed from the dye and rinsed in cold water; then it is dried and waxed. If a more intense color is desired, it is best to leave the surfaces unpolished. After dipping, the unpolished plastic should be rinsed, dried, and buffed on a dry, clean buffing wheel. Rub dyeing is a method in which cloth is dipped into the plastic dye and rubbed (fig. 5–27) over the surface of the plastic. When the back or rear surface of a bevel is tinted in this manner, it produces an interesting coloring throughout the plastic. Once the tinting has been completed, the surface is rinsed, dried, and waxed. The tint will remain until the surface is buffed.

• *Laminating dye* is a method of adding color to a joint line. The dye is dissolved in a plastic solvent such as methylene dichloride and then it is applied with a brush or hypodermic needle to the surface of the joint. After applying the dye, pressure is applied to force out air bubbles. The piece should be allowed to dry thoroughly before it is buffed. Another method of decorating can be accomplished by using opaque paints. The paint should be viewed through the transparent plastic. Polished surfaces should be painted with oil paints or lacquers, while water paint will adequately cover unpolished or frosted surfaces. The application of paint can be made by painting, by flowing, or by spraying; however, painting will produce brush marks unless care is taken to use an adequate amount. Some feel that the best method of application is spraying or flowing the paint on the plastic. In both dyeing and painting plastic, attention

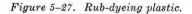
RUB OVER WITH CLOTH
USING PLASTIC DYE

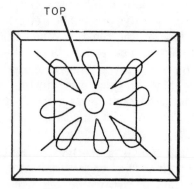
TOP

Figure 5–27. Rub-dyeing plastic.

must be paid to the possibility of it crazing. Crazing is a pattern of tiny fissures within the plastic which occur because of surface strain. This surface sometimes occurs when hot plastic is shaped, leaving invisible strains in the bent piece. It will also occur if too much heat is generated during the machining and finishing operation. For this reason, it is advisable to anneal plastic before dyeing or painting, to prevent the dye or paint from seeping into the fissures. It is also recommended that annealing be performed after dyeing, as well as after machining, after pol-

ishing, and before cementing. Annealing after dyeing prevents the tendency to crazing caused by the dye. To anneal plastic, leave it in a warm place for several hours at a temperature of not more than 130° F. This temperature is enough below that necessary for forming so that it will not alter the shape of the formed piece. Although this precaution may seem unnecessary and some dyeing is done adequately without annealing, there is always the danger of crazing, which should be avoided if possible.

n. Cleaning Plastic. To be attractive, plastic must be cleaned carefully. Care must be taken in the cleaning process to prevent scratching the plastic with an abrasive in either the cleaning compound or in the cloth with which it is rubbed. The best method is to use the hands and plenty of pure soap and water. Even paper toweling will scratch plastic so a soft cloth or chamois should be used to wash and dry plastic. Grease smears and oil cannot be washed off so they must be removed with a cleaning solution which will not dissolve the surface. Chemical solutions that should not be used on plastic are gasoline, concentrated alcohol, benzene, acetone, carbon tetrachloride, fire extinguisher or deicing fluid, lacquer thinner, or glass window cleaning sprays. Soap and water or plain alcohol are the best to use on plastic. After cleaning, the surface can be waxed to improve the appearance and to guard against scratching. There are antistatic waxes on the market which reduce the static charge and decrease dust attraction. Plastic can be sanitized with any one of a number of commercially available compounds based on Hyamine 1622. Strong alkali solutions may also be used.

o. Storage of Plastic. Sheets of plastic should be stored standing on end with the masking paper on. It is convenient to have a rack for storing small quantities, such as would be used in an occupational therapy clinic (fig. 5–28). Partitions are placed so that even when inventory is low, sheets will not be at a sharp angle, which causes sagging or bowing. If a sheet does become bowed, it should be tilted in the opposite direction or laid flat to straighten gradually. Where it is not possible to store sheets on end, flat storage is recommended. It is a good practice to store sheets of similar size and thickness together, then stack (fig. 5–29) the largest sheets on the bottom and the smallest on top to prevent overhanging, which will cause bowing. All tubes and rods, like sheet plastic, should be stored flat or on end. The storage

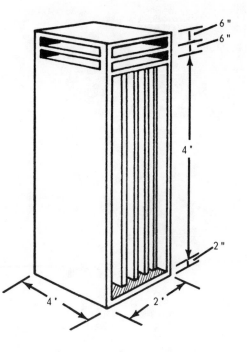

Figure 5–28. Storage rack for plastic.

room should be well ventilated, not over 125° F temperature, and not too dry or too moist. If too much moisture or heat is present, the masking paper will deteriorate or dry out and come loose from the plastic. The room should be away from possible sources of solvent vapors which may attack the surface. Direct sunlight does not harm clear plastic, but it may fade colored pieces.

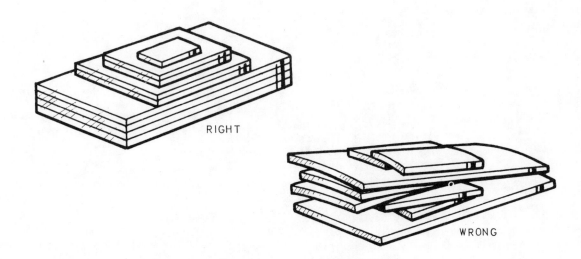

Figure 5–29. Stacking plastic.

CHAPTER 6

METALWORK AND JEWELRY

Section I. COPPER ENAMELING

6-1. Introduction

The first known pieces of enamel on metal are from Greek sculpture of the 5th century B.C. However, as one reads art literature or visits museums, the Byzantine pieces of the 9th to 11th century are generally the first tangible glimpse of this media. As each proceeding generation has passed, significant works of enamel art have been contributed in all schools of the world. Now, techniques have been simplified and manufacturers have provided materials and equipment which allow the amateur to accomplish what was previously done by skilled craftsmen only.

6-2. Glossary

a. Cloisonné. Enameled pieces separated by partitions or "fences" which are usually made of wire.

b. Counter-Enamel. Enameling and firing a copper piece on the back.

c. Dusting. Method of sprinkling enamel on copper through a mesh screen.

d. Enamel. A glassy, colored, opaque substance fused to sufaces of metal, glass, and pottery as ornamental or protective coating. Several types are commonly used—

(1) Opalescent—an enamel with a cloudy or milky appearance similar to that of an opal.

(2) Opaque—solid color enamel that does not permit light to pass through.

(3) Translucent—enamel that lets light pass through but diffuses it so that objects on the other side cannot be distinguished.

(4) Transparent—enamel that lets light pass

through so that objects on the other size can be seen.

e. Enamel Flux. Basic enamel material to which metal oxides are added to form colored enamel.

f. Gauge. Term used to describe the thickness of metal.

g. Gum Tragacanth. Adhering solution; holds enamel to copper before firing.

h. Kiln, Enameling. Small oven for baking enamel.

i. Lumps. Enamel in chunks.

j. Maturing. Firing enamel until it flows and sets.

k. Overfiring. Firing enamel until it becomes overmature or burned out.

l. Pickle. Acid solution used to clean metal.

m. Sgraffito. A method of designing based on scratching through one layer to expose another layer.

n. Sludge. Scrap enamel.

o. Slush colors. Enamels finely ground and suspended in water. Used for painting on enamel.

p. Strings. Enamel in short thread-like pieces.

6-3. Tools, Equipment, and Materials

a. Tools.

(1) Brushes—watercolor brushes; sizes 1, 4, and 6 are recommended for enameling.

(2) File—jeweler's type, for smoothing edges when shaping or finishing.

(3) Pliers—smooth needlenose, the best for shaping wire.

(4) Pointer—sharp awl or dental tool.

(5) Spatula—tool which is sometimes used for applying enamel.

(6) Spider—iron mesh stand (fig. 6–1) for supporting enameled pieces while they are being fired in the kiln. Ceramic stilts with metal points can be substituted.

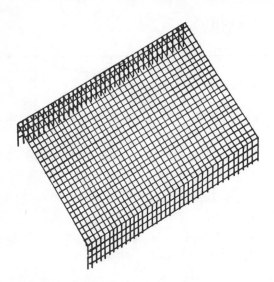

Figure 6–1. Iron mesh spider.

(7) Spreader—any small flat tool.

(8) Tongs—instrument used to lift the spiders in and out of the kiln.

(9) Tweezers (fig. 6–2)—tool used to place lumps or strings in place.

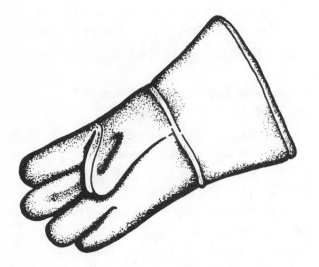

Figure 6–2. Tweezer, bevel point.

Figure 6–3. Asbestos gloves.

b. *Equipment.*

(1) Asbestos gloves—special gloves (fig. 6–3) used to handle pieces being put into and taken out of the kiln.

(2) Asbestos sheets or pads (fig. 6–4)—material placed under the kiln. They also provide a cooling area for enameled pieces.

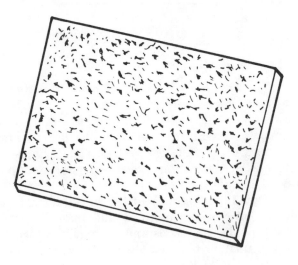

Figure 6–4. Asbestos pad.

(3) Goggles—specially designed glasses (fig. 6–5) to protect the eyes during soldering or buffing.

Figure 6–5. Goggles.

(4) Kiln—a type of oven. If a considerable amount of enameling is done or if the pieces are larger than a small ash tray, it is best to have the larger, more expensive kiln with the temperature indicator (A, fig. 6–6). However, the smaller kiln (B, fig. 6–6), heats faster, is less expensive to purchase and to operate, and is very adequate for

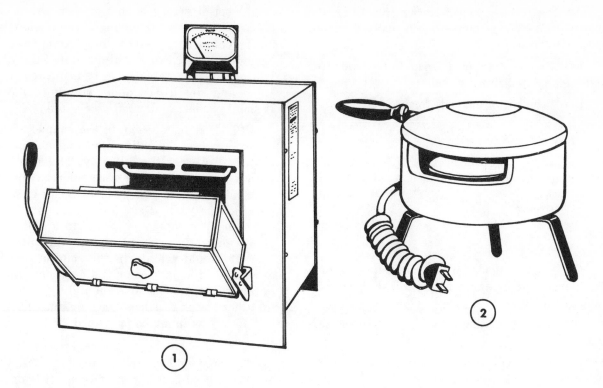

Figure 6–6. Enameling kilns.

small pieces such as jewelry. All kilns must be attended at all times but, because enameling kilns are not usually temperature controlled, watching them is even more important. The kiln must be set on a piece of asbestos sufficiently large to be under the entire kiln and still have room to place iron mesh spiders for cooling. If the kiln is near a wall, the wall must also be protected with asbestos. The smaller kiln heats rapidly and has little, if any, insulation, so extra care must be taken. A pilot light on the switch to indicate when the kiln is on can be helpful in avoiding burns.

(5) Propane torch—a torch used to provide heat to solder findings.

c. *Materials.*

(1) Asphaltum for etching.

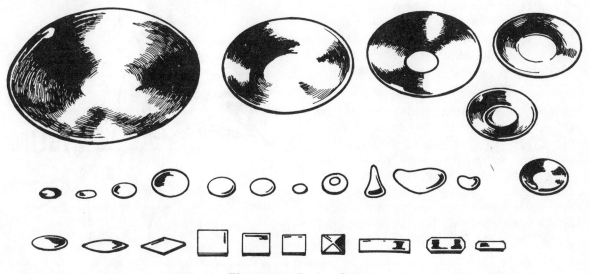

Figure 6–7. Copper shapes.

(2) Copper preshaped forms (fig. 6–7), usually in 16–18 gauge, available in many different shapes and sizes.

(3) Emery cloth, medium and fine grade, for cleaning and polishing metal.

(4) Basic list of enamels for use:

Opaque	Transparent
Red	Flux
Medium blue	Red
White	Yellow
Grey	Green
Black	Dark blue
Chartreuse	Lavender
Light green	Grey
Turquoise	Aqua
Yellow	

(5) Gum tragacanth for adhering enamel. Best purchased in liquid form; 3-in-1 oil can be a substitute.

(6) Jewelry findings for pins, cufflinks, earring backs, etc.

(7) Nitric acid for etching solution and pickling solution.

(8) Paper for use under enamel piece during dusting process. Also for making stencils.

(9) Clean rags for cleaning copper pieces.

(10) Soft solder and flux for soldering jewelry findings or commercial tube solder.

(11) Steel wool, sizes 00 and 1, for cleaning metal.

(12) Wire, silver or copper, about 25 gauge, for colisonné work.

6–4. Processes

It is possible to enamel on many metals: gold, silver, copper, bronze, iron, steel, brass, and aluminum. However, for clinic projects, copper is attractive, less expensive, and is readily available in a variety of forms and shapes. Therefore, copper will be the standard material used in the procedures covered here.

a. *Cleaning Copper.* Careful cleaning of the metal surface is one of the most essential steps in enameling. Every trace of foreign material, including oil from fingerprints, must be removed before the surface can be successfully enameled. To test for oil on the surface, place the piece under running water. If the water does not adhere to the surface but runs freely off, the piece is not clean of oils. There are two methods of cleaning copper before enameling—

(1) The surface is cleaned with fine (00)

steel wool or emery cloth and then wiped free of all foreign matter. To remove the oil left by the steel wool or emery cloth, the piece is rubbed vigorously with a clean rag dipped into vinegar, then baking soda or table salt. It is picked up with tongs and rinsed well under running hot water. It should be left to dry *without wiping*.

(2) If defects occur in the enamel after this cleaning process, pickling the copper may be necessary to prevent the difficulty. This can be done with a relatively harmless commercial pickle called Sparex, or the pickle solution can be made by pouring one part of sulphuric acid into 10 parts of water. The copper is heated to a dull red and, using tongs, it is dropped into the pickle solution. It should remain in the solution until it is clean and is a pink color. Using tongs, the piece is removed from the solution and held under running hot water to rinse. Once again, it should be left to dry without being wiped or touched with the fingers.

b. *Preparing Enamel.* In most clinics, the enamels are used in the ground form. If transparent enamels are cloudy after firing, they can be purified by washing. To do this, place enamel in a jar, fill it with water, and stir. Let the larger pieces of enamel settle out. Pour off the water from the top (save for further refining). Continue to wash the enamel until there is no scum left on the set-

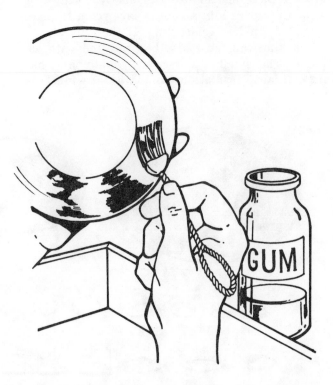

Figure 6–8. Applying gum tragacanth.

tled enamel (five washings are usually sufficient). The enamel can now be dried or used as wet inlay.

c. *Dusting Enamel.* To hold the enamel on the metal surface, liquid gum tragacanth is applied evenly to the entire surface of the piece to be enameled with a brush (fig. 6–8) or by spraying it on (3-in-1 oil can be a substitute for the gum tragacanth). Before the dusting is begun, spread a clean piece of paper on the table and place the copper piece in the center. The paper makes it possible to save the enamel that spills over the edges. Select the jar of enamel to be used, cover the top with a fine wire mesh (80) screen (fig. 6–9), or an old nylon stocking. Dust (sprinkle) the enamel on the copper, first on the edges and then on the rest of the piece until it is covered. Apply the enamel evenly (fig. 6–10) and about 1/32 inch thick. Let the enamel dry. It is possible to hasten drying by placing the piece under a lamp or on top of the warm kiln. Return the clean enamel to the jar (fig. 6–11).

d. *Firing.* The kiln is preheated to 1500 degrees. After the oven reaches this temperature, place the copper piece on a wire spider in the center of the

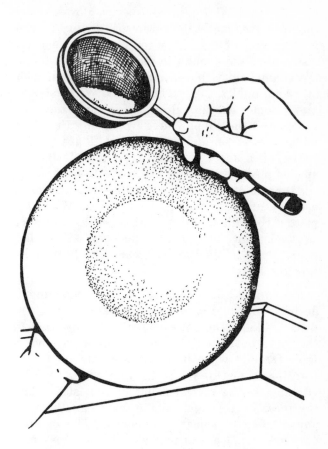

Figure 6–10. Enamel must be applied evenly.

Figure 6-9. Applying enamel with an 80-mesh sieve.

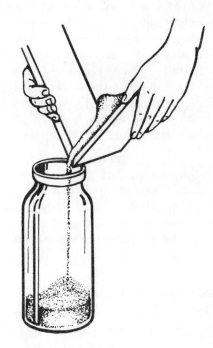

Figure 6-11. Clean enamel returned to storage jar.

131

kiln, using metal tongs and asbestos gloves. Check the piece frequently to prevent overfiring. To prevent cooling of the kiln when checking, open the door only wide enough to see the piece. In firing, the enamel turns black and craterous; then pebbly; and, finally, smooth and shiny. With asbestos gloves, open the kiln door and remove the wire spider and the copper piece by placing the tongs under the screen and lifting it out. Place the hot spider on a sheet of asbestos to cool. If the enameled piece is a flat one and seems to have warped, turn it over on the asbestos sheet and place a heavy metal on top; an iron will do. When the piece is cool, file the edges with a needle or pattern file, and clean the back with steel wool. Metal lacquer can be applied to the cleaned back to maintain the luster.

e. Counter-Enameling. If counter-enameling is desired, it should be done before the front of the piece is done. Dust the enamel onto the back of the piece but when the piece is fired, remove it from the kiln when it is in the pebbly stage (before it has matured). To prevent this side from sticking on the second firing, it is best to place the piece on ceramic stilts rather than the wire spider. If counter-enameling is being done on pins, earrings, etc., leave unenameled the area on which the findings will be soldered.

f. Jewelry Findings. If the piece requires jewelry findings (such as pin, cuff-link back, and earrings), it is best to use soft solder as it requires less heat to melt and it will not melt the enamel. First, clean the findings with steel wool and also clean the spot on the enamel piece where the finding is to be attached. Put some soft solder flux or flux paste on the cleaned area of the enameled piece. Place the finding on the solder and cut some very small pieces of soft solder and lay them along the side of the finding. Slowly heat the piece with a small propane torch until the solder flows.

NOTE
Many commercial soft solders come in tube form. These do not require a flux and are applied like a paste. When heated, they form a sufficient bind for most purposes. Silver soldering can be found in section IV of this chapter.

6–5. Decorative Processes

a. Stenciling. A stencil of the desired design (fig. 6–12) can be cut from paper. Wet the paper before placing it on the enameled piece so it will hold better. Brush gum tragacanth on the exposed

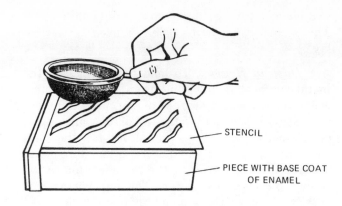

STENCIL

PIECE WITH BASE COAT OF ENAMEL

Figure 6–12. Stenciling.

areas of the piece, then dust a contrasting enamel on over the piece and the stencil. Remove the stencil and refire the piece.

b. Lumps and Strings. These may be purchased in either the opaque or transparent forms. When fired, they fuse with the base coat and appear as dots or lines. Brush the base coat with the gum solution to help hold these pieces in the desired spot during firing.

c. Wet Inlay. This technique is especially useful when enameling in many small areas with a wide variety of colors. Mix the enamel with a gum solution to a paste consistency. Then, apply with a spatula and pack down with a spreader (used dental tools work well). When the piece has been covered and dried, it can be fired.

d. Sgraffito. The name comes from the Italian words that mean "to scratch." Sgraffito work is done on a piece which has a coat of base enamel. Cover this base enamel with gum solution, and dust a contrasting color of enamel on the piece; allow it to dry. Use any pointed or blunt instrument such as a ceramic tool, dental hand instrument, or knife to scratch the design through the unfired layer of enamel to the fired enamel below, then refire the piece. Lines which vary in thickness add to the overall design and it is possible to remove areas of unfired enamel to create shape.

e. Slush Colors. These may be purchased or you may use some of the fine pieces left after washing enamel. Mix with the gum solution until liquid enough that they can be applied with a brush. Combine this technique with sgraffito for very interesting results.

f. Champlevé. This form of decoration combines two metal techniques. First, etch a design into the copper. Cover a piece of copper with asphaltum wherever the metal is not to be etched. Then, place the piece in a nitric acid solution (1 part nitric acid to 2 parts water). Allow the piece to remain until the copper has been etched to about 1/32 inch or for about 2 to 2 1/2 hours. (A needle inserted along the edge will tell the depth.) Then remove the metal and clean with turpentine. Next, inlay wet enamel into the etched areas. Several firings may be necessary to bring the enamel to the same level as the metal.

g. Cloisonné. In this technique, the colors are separated by a "fence," usually of wire (fig. 6–13). The wire should be of a thin gauge (about 25). Bend it with pliers to conform to the desired design. Place the wire on a pre-enameled copper shape which has been covered with gum solution. Next, apply the wet inlay evenly to avoid bubbling. After the enamel has dried, refire the piece. When the piece has cooled, place it under water and rub it with a carborundum stone until the wire reappears. If the piece is dull, it can be refired until glossy.

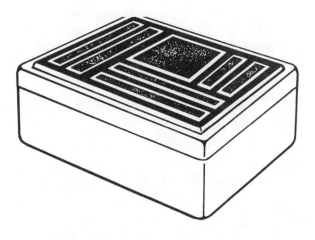

Figure 6–13. Cloisonné cigarette box.

6–6. Design

Almost any method of applying design to a material, such as stenciling, silk screening, and spinning, can be used with enameling. It is a very versatile craft, so the designs are unlimited. Colors placed over or alongside each other change their shade of color or tone. Thus, a transparent over an opaque will produce a new value. However, it is wise to start simply until the techniques are mastered.

6–7. Defects—Causes and Corrections

Almost all defects in enameling are due to careless work habits. Materials and tools must be kept clean, work areas free of litter, and procedures followed carefully.

a. Cracks. There are various causes for cracking; *for example,* enamel may be applied too thickly or transparent glazes may be cooled too suddenly. Cure: Maintain an even layer of enamel, not much over 1/32 inch thick. Counter enamel flat pieces. Always weigh flat pieces when cooling.

b. Steel Wood "Fishhooks." These are a result of poor housekeeping. Fine pieces of steel wool have contaminated the enamel, but they cannot be seen until after the firing. Cure: Clean the metal in a different area from where you apply enamel.

c. Burned-Out Areas. Burned-out areas (fig. 6–14) result when the enamel was applied in an uneven thickness and/or the piece was left in the kiln too long and overfired. Cure: Remove the enamel from the piece in the following manner and start over. Insert the piece in acid to remove the firescale. Reheat the piece and remove from kiln while it is still very hot. Drop it into cold water. The old enamel will usually flake off.

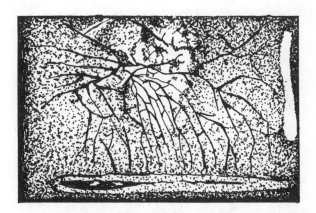

Figure 6–14. Burned-out areas.

d. Craterous Bubbling. Craterous bubbling (fig. 6–15) results when enamel has been placed on the top of a greasy deposit, usually fingerprints. Cure: Always make sure the piece is thoroughly clean. If the bubbling occurs, scrape it away as much as possible, refire, clean, and then reenamel.

e. Firescale. This appears in the form of dull black flecks on the enameled surface (fig. 6–16). Cause is usually contaminated enamel, but it may result from placing an unfired piece that is drying too near a piece that is cooling. Cure: Keep

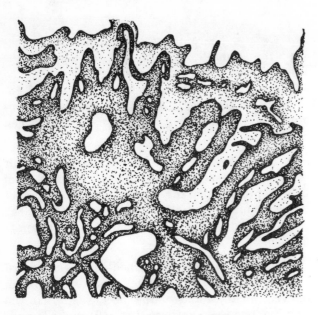

Figure 6-15. Craterous bubbling.

enamel covered, so foreign matter does not get in. Just before firing a dried piece, brush off any foreign matter. Separate drying and cooling areas.

f. "Watermarks." Scummy blobs and rings are a result of uneven application of the gum solution. Cure: Take special care to brush or spray the gum on evenly.

6-8. Safety

"Cleanliness is next to Godliness" is truer for this craft than almost any other. Assure that you have adequate space in which to work, that cleaning areas are separate from enameling areas, that drying and cooling areas are apart, and that tools and equipment are kept clean.

a. If acid solutions are used, make certain, when mixing acid, that *the acid is added to the water,* not the water to acid. If acid spills, wash the part freely with clear water immediately for it will blister or burn the skin and eat clothing. The pickle should be stored in a glass jar with a lid or in a Mason crock jar. Label all jars to avoid misuse.

b. When torch soldering is done or a buffing wheel used to polish the metal, make certain that goggles are always worn.

c. Place the kiln on an asbestos sheet and have other asbestos sheets available to use for the pieces while they are cooling. Check the kiln's wiring periodically. Before purchasing a kiln, be sure that the electrical outlet will carry the load.

d. Wear asbestos gloves when putting pieces in or taking them out of the kiln.

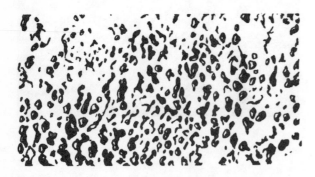

Figure 6-16①. Firescale (sheet 1 of 2).

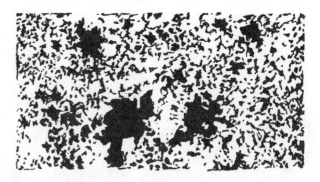

Figure 6-16②. Firescale (sheet 2 of 2).

Section II. COPPER TOOLING

6–10. General

Metal tooling is a well-liked activity, probably because it is so adaptable to the needs of the patient. It can be long term or short term, large or small, simple or complex, all depending upon the type of design selected. The tooled piece can be mounted and used as a picture, it can be put onto bookends, or it can be used to decorate such things as boxes.

6–11. Tools

Although several modeling tools of different shapes can be purchased commercially, the only important one can be made from a 1/4-inch wooden dowel, sharpened to a point at one end and slanted flat and smooth at the other (fig. 6–17). A No. 1 leather modeling tool is also handy for getting into the small, hard-to-get-to areas.

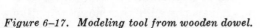

Figure 6–17. Modeling tool from wooden dowel.

6–12. Equipment

Another characteristic which makes copper tooling popular is that little equipment is needed, so it can be done at home or on the ward, as well as in the clinic. A soft but firm surface such as is afforded by a magazine, folded newspaper, or a hard felt pad is needed when stretching the metal. A smooth, hard surface such as Formica or Masonite is used when flattening the background.

6–13. Material

Copper tooling requires little material. Material needed includes—

a. Tracing paper.

b. Masking tape or Scotch tape.

c. Metal foils, which may be obtained in thicknesses ranging from 5/1000 inch to 1/100 inch. Tooling is done on 36–30 gauge metal in copper, brass, aluminum, or jeweler's bronze. Pewter in 26 or 28 gauge can be tooled. Copper foil is most commonly used, perhaps because it stretches easily and has warmth of color. Its best weight for tooling is 36 gauge. It is sold by the lineal foot in rolls 12 inches wide and can be cut to the desired size with scissors.

d. Beeswax, which can be rubbed occasionally onto the wooden tool to make the tool slide more easily over the surface of the metal.

e. A variety of designs that are good to have, ranging from simple designs with large areas for beginners, to complex designs composed of small areas to challenge people who have developed this skill.

f. Plastic molds, if treatment indicates.

6–14. Processes

The processes involved in copper tooling are not complicated. The goal is to stretch the metal in appropriate places as indicated by the design and thereby make a picture in relief. Extreme care must be taken to stretch the metal gradually and with care, so as not to break through the foil. The entire design must be worked, rather than just a small area, to prevent warping. These steps should be followed:

a. Trace Design on Metal. To put the design on metal, first trace it onto tracing paper, then cut the foil to fit the design and fasten the traced design to the metal with masking tape. Trace again, this time with the pointed edge of the tool (fig. 6–17), which is held like a pencil. Exert enough pressure on the tool to make a clear mark, yet not a deep one. When the design is completely traced, remove the tracing paper and masking tape.

b. Tooling. To tool, place the metal face down on a soft but firm surface (a padded board or a magazine), and trace another line beside the original one in all areas to be raised. With the slanted flat part of the tool, begin to gradually push out all the part of the design that is to be raised. Do not concentrate in one area—work the entire design to prevent warping. The higher an area is to be, the more (not the harder) it should be pushed. Frequently turn the copper over and straighten out the background by pressing it down with the same part of the tool but on a smooth, hard surface. For good sharp relief, get right to the edge of the design with the tool. Turn the foil over again on the padded board or magazine and push the design out. Continue pushing out the design from one side and straightening the background from the other until the desired results are obtained. The background can be left plain or it can be textured. One very satisfactory method of obtaining a texture is to place the metal over a piece of coarse sandpaper, window screen, or coarse-grained wood, then rub the metal with a blunt tool such as the slanted end of the dowel. Another slower method of backgrounding is to tap a round-pointed tool lightly and gently into the metal, thus making small dents in the metal.

c. Molds. In certain cases, it is desirable to use the molds that are available at a number of general craft stores. Although they eliminate all originality and expression, as well as most of the skill required in copper tooling, they can be used when a quick, easy, highly successful project is indicated to restore ego and self-confidence. To use these molds, cut the copper to the size of the outside of the mold, tape the edges of the copper around under the edge of the mold, and stretch the copper gently and evenly either over the mold or into the mold. When the copper is well-pushed into the contour of the mold, remove it and proceed as for the more conventional method of tooling.

d. Filling Back of Design. When both the design and the background are tooled, fill in the raised portion of the design in order to keep the design from being pushed in from the front. The filler may be candle wax or base clay, plaster of paris, plastic wood, or any substance that will conform to the shape, then harden.

CAUTION

It has been found that in time the chemicals in some of the oil base "clays" will eat through the copper unless the area which will contact the "clay" is sprayed with plastic spray.

e. Oxidizing. To bring out the design, to highlight and to soften the brightness of copper and brass, oxidize it with a solution of liver of sulphur (sulfurated potash). To make this solution, dissolve one teaspoon of liver of sulphur into a pint of warm water. Clean the metal with steel wool so that it is free from wax and oil from the hands. It is important to clean down in the depressions as that is where it should be the darkest. Paint or swab the warm oxidizing solution over the metal, rinse it with cold water, and let it dry *completely.* When the metal is dry, rub the raised portions gently with steel wool to remove the darkness. The background can also be rubbed to the desired brightness, but the cracks and low places in the picture are left unpolished for contrast.

f. Finishing the Metal. Since the metal will tarnish quickly if it is not protected from the air with some type of a finish, use either metal lacquer, paste wax, or plastic spray.

- Spray or paint a thin coating of lacquer over the entire piece.
- Apply wax easily by warming the metal a bit before applying and polishing the wax.

g. Several Ways to Mount the Tooled Piece.

(1) Attach the tooled sheet to a wooden base with brass or copper escutcheon pins evenly spaced and driven through the metal into the wood. To do this, first pierce the holes with an awl or drive punch, insert the pin, and drive it with a hammer. A nail set used on the head of the pin as it gets near the wood may keep the metal from being marred.

(2) Wrap the metal around the wooden piece and tack it to the wood on the back. When this is done, it may be left open or it may be slipped into a frame.

(3) Cover a piece of wood larger than the metal picture with burlap and then mount the metal with escutcheon pins over that. The texture of the metal in contrast to the burlap is often interesting.

(4) Pour plaster of paris into the back of the

tooled piece. This is another interesting, but not as substantial, way to mount a piece of copper tooling. Allow 3/8 inch of metal to extend beyond the edge of the plaque. Turn this edge up on all four sides to form a shallow pan. Fill this pan with plaster and let it harden. Insert a loop of string or wire into the wet plaster, making a nice firm way to hang the picture.

6–15. Safety

This is a reasonably safe activity; however, the edges of the metal may be rough from cutting. Masking tape over these rough edges prevents injury. It is also wise to use a small piece of leather to protect the hands from the steel wood or to use nylon web scouring pads, which are available through supply.

Section III. METAL FORMING

6–17. General

Metal forming is one of the more noisy, active processes. If the tools and equipment are available for silver, very little else needs to be added in order to do metal forming.

a. Tools.

(1) Ball peen hammer.

(2) Hardwood mallet (fig. 6–18). This mallet has a curved surface at one end of the head and a flat surface at the other end. The curved surface is used for stretching the metal with a minimum amount of marking. The flat surface is used to "true" or flatten an area.

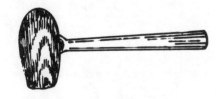

Figure 6–18. Wooden mallet.

b. Equipment.

(1) Molds of wood or aluminum alloy are used to shape the metal.

(a) The wooden forms (fig. 6–19) are made of hard maple. They are good because they keep their shape and they do not mark the metal being formed.

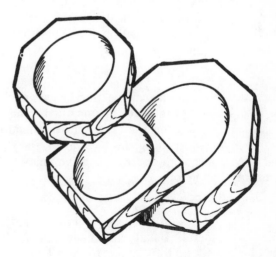

Figure 6–19. Wooden forms.

(b) Molds of different shapes are available made of aluminum alloy. These forms (fig. 6–20) are more varied in shape and a little less expensive, but they tend to mark the metal more than the wood.

Figure 6-20. Aluminum forms.

(2) A heavy canvas bag nearly filled with sand provides a good base into which metal can be shaped. Just push an indentation of the desired size into the sand in the bag, then pound the metal into it. This is especially good when making free-form shapes.

(3) Metal can be annealed with an acetylene torch, a small furnace with a heat-measuring device, or an annealing pan.

c. *Material*. Metal can be purchased in sheets or in disc form; the latter is smoothed, ready for shaping. Considering the time and the amount of waste involved in using sheet material, the ready-cut discs, although more expensive, may be an economy in the long run.

(1) *Aluminum*. This is a relatively soft, inexpensive metal. Usually 18 gauge is used for small projects and 16 gauge for the larger ones. It must be handled with care to prevent breakage.

(2) *Brass*. Possibly because it is harder to shape and it is a little more expensive, brass is used less frequently than copper. It is available in 18 gauge for 6- and 8-inch circles.

(3) *Copper*. Its beauty, malleability, and relatively low price usually makes copper the metal of choice for forming.

(4) *Pewter*. Pewter is also a soft metal which can be marked without having to be annealed. Either 16 or 18 gauge is used. The cost of pewter is such that copper, brass, or aluminum are used more frequently.

(5) *Sterling silver*. The beauty, adaptability, and ease of manipulation make silver the choice of craftsmen.

6-18. Process

A shallow bowl, ash tray, or tray is formed into a mold in the following manner:

a. Center the metal disc over the mold (fig. 6-21).

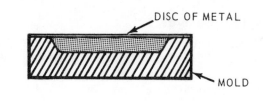

Figure 6-21. *Cross section of disc centered over mold.*

b. Gradually and evenly stretch the metal and depress it into the mold. This is done with the curved surface of the wooden mallet, starting at the outer edge of the metal and working in concentric circles toward the center. Top the metal with glancing blows in overlapping rotation and

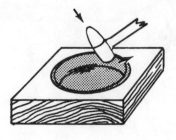

Figure 6-22. *Method of shaping disc in mold.*

turn the mold just a little after each blow (fig. 6–22).

c. If the edge of the piece buckles, true it be tapping it with the flat end of the mallet over a wooden (maple) stake (fig. 6–23).

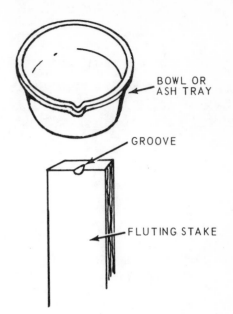

Figure 6–24. Method of fluting edge.

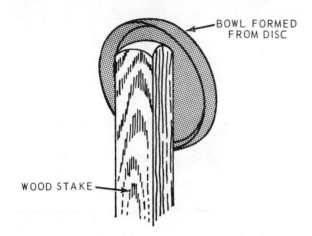

Figure 6–23. Truing edge of bowl.

d. "Planish" to obtain a more perfect shape. This is done with a smooth metal planishing hammer, tapping the piece lightly as it is held over a metal stake.

e. To finish the piece, go over it well with fine steel wool and then with pumice and water. This will provide a mat surface. For a higher luster, use jeweler's rouge for polishing.

6–19. Decoration

There are several ways in which a formed metal piece can be decorated. Only two of these will be considered here.

a. Metal Tapping. With a ball peen hammer and a metal stake, tap the piece lightly so as to cover the surface evenly with small hammer marks. This must be done carefully to preserve the shap-

ing of the piece.

b. Fluting. Use flutings as pure decoration or as a part of a functional design such as one to hold the cigarette on an ash tray. The flutings may be made inward or outward or both. A fluting stake is made with grooves cut to the desired size, then filed and sanded to a smooth surface. The edge of the bowl or ash tray is gently pounded into this groove with a small hammer (fig. 6–24). The flutings may be evenly spaced around the edge or they may be grouped. There are any number of ways in which fluting can be used to form a pleasing design.

6–20. Safety

Precautions are the same as for those for jewelry (para 6–26).

Section IV. SILVER JEWELRY

6-22. General

a. Since ancient times, various materials have been used in the creation of jewelry (wood, seeds, ivory, gem stones, enamels, plastics, and metals). However, the basic material in jewelry making is metal, and the metal that is most commonly used in occupational therapy for the construction of jewelry is sterling silver.

b. Pure silver (fine silver) is the whitest of all metals, has the greatest luster and, second to gold, is the most malleable and ductile metal. Its qualities of malleability (softness) and ductility (plasticity) contribute especially to its popularity since it can be easily bent, hammered, and molded into almost any form. However, pure silver is a little too soft to make durable objects that require lightness and stability of form. For this reason, it is usually alloyed with copper to harden it and to give it strength. An alloy of 92 1/2% fine silver and 7 1/2% copper is called sterling silver. This proportion of metals is fixed by law and any other alloy is not sterling silver. This alloy was determined to be the most desirable since it gives silver the necessary strength and hardness without substantially reducing its best characteristics of malleability and ductility. Copper allows silver to be oxidized (darkening of metal to enrich its surface quality) in controlled ways. However, each alloy of metal reduces the melting point of the original metal. The melting point of fine silver is 1761° F and the melting point of sterling silver is 1640° F. This factor does not interfere with the use of sterling silver in the construction of most jewelry, but it does prevent its decoration by the method known as enameling. Therefore, only fine silver is used in enameling.

c. Sterling silver can be purchased in sheet form in almost any dimension and thickness; in wire form, in round, square, triangular, and half-round; in solid or hollow rods; and in bar or ingot form. The Brown and Sharpe gauge system is used in the United States to measure the thickness of all nonferrous metals (metals which do not contain iron or steel). A piece of wire or a sheet of metal is measured in thickness by inserting it into the numbered slot in the gauge that fits it best; this number is used to describe the thickness of the metal and is referred to as the gauge of the metal. (The smaller the number, the thicker the piece of metal or wire.) Precious metals, to include silver, are weighed by the troy weight system; 12 ounces troy equals 1 pound troy. (Troy weight is a little less than avoirdupois weight, which is the standard of measurement most commonly used in everyday life.) When silver sheet is ordered from the supplier, the length, width, and gauge must be stated; when silver sheet is ordered by weight, the width, gauge, and desired number of ounces must be stated. When silver wire is ordered, the length, gauge, and shape (round, half-round, etc.) must be stated. When wire is ordered by weight, the gauge, shape and desired quantity (ounces) must be stated.

d. Sterling silver can also be purchased in soft or hard form. The soft form (annealed) is the most commonly purchased for clinic use. However, there may be an occasion to purchase spring (hard) silver for use in the construction of money or tie clips. Spring silver is sterling silver that has been reduced several times its original thickness by drawing or rolling. This reduction in thickness makes the silver very hard and very springy. It should not be used in projects requiring a great amount of soldering since heat destroys the springy quality.

e. Sterling silver to be used in an occupational therapy clinic is usually ordered in sheet form and in wire form. These two forms are the most adaptable for general use and the most economical for practical purposes. Silver that is processed to a greater extent (hollow rods, spring silver, etc.) is more expensive. The gauges of sheet silver most frequently ordered are: 16 gauge for such items as rings, belt buckles, and cuff links; 18 and 20 gauge for lightweight pierced designs, earrings, and brooches; and 26 gauge, which is usually ordered if stone setting by the bezel method is done. Many different sizes of wire are used in jewelry. The most commonly used gauges are 16, 18, and 20 round and 8 gauge half-round. Bezel wire with a shoulder is used for setting stones.

6–23. Tools, Equipment, and Materials

a. Basic Tools.

(1) *Brush.* A small, pointed oil or watercolor brush. The brush is dampened with water or flux and is used to put flux on metal for soldering and to place pieces of solder.

(2) *Burnisher, curved.* A handtool used primarily for setting stones in a bezel. The curved burnisher (fig. 6–25) has a wooden handle and a curved steel end which is usually oval-shaped and polished. Care should be taken to not scratch the polished surface of the tool since a rough place

could cause scratches in the silver bezel which would be difficult to remove. If a rough place develops on the tool, it should be polished before being used again.

Figure 6–25. Burnisher, curved.

(3) *Drill, twist.* A hard drill (fig. 6–26) used with the smaller sized metal drills for making a hole in metal. A center punch is used to mark a guide for the drill, as drills tend to slip on the slick metal during the start of the drilling process and may mar the surface of the silver. A drill press may be used to make a hole in the metal; however, since it revolves at a much greater rate of speed than the twist drill, it is difficult to hold the metal as it becomes hot with the increased friction. Holes should be drilled with little pressure; the waste silver coming up from the forming hole should be in a long, thin spiral if properly drilled. Too much pressure can damage the thin drill bit.

Figure 6–26. Drill, twist.

(4) *Drawplate.* A flat, rectangular piece of steel with graduated holes of various shapes (fig. 6–27) used to reduce the diameter or to change the shape of wire. It is also used for the construction of tubing. The holes are funnel-shaped in cross section—larger in the back and smaller in the front. The holes in the drawplate are round, half-round, square, etc.

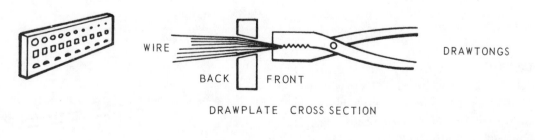

Figure 6–27. Drawplate.

(5) *Drawtongs.* A long, large pair of pliers with serrated jaws (fig. 6–28) used for pulling wire through the drawplate. The wire should be annealed often when being pulled through the drawplate, and beeswax should be used as a lubricant during the pulling.

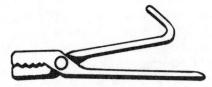

Figure 6–28. Drawtongs.

(6) *Files, general use.* Steel tools used to smooth irregularities in the edge of the metal after it has been sawed or cut. These files (fig. 6–29) are also used for original shaping and are longer and larger than other files which are described in (7) and (8) below. The most useful file sizes are coarse No. 0 flat and smooth No. 2 half-round. When filing, pressure should be applied only on the forward stroke away from the body, since files cut only in this direction. After each forward stroke, the file should be lifted from the metal and returned to its original position before making another stroke. If pressure is applied in both directions, the file becomes clogged and dulled so it is less effective. Files should be cleaned regularly with a file card during use; they should also be cleaned after each use. In filing, the entire length of the file should be used to avoid excessive wear in one spot.

Figure 6–29. File, general.

(7) *Files, neeedle.* Thin, small files, usually 5 1/2 inches in total length with a 2 3/4-inch cutting area, that are used to finish smoothing the edges of metal. They are fairly smooth and are used to remove scratches left by the general files. Swiss files are by far the superior type of file. They are double cut and the coarseness is marked by number. The numbers range from the coarsest (00) to the smoothest (8). American files are usually a single cut file classified by name: rough, bastard, second cut, smooth, and super smooth. Files can be obtained in a variety of shapes: round, square, barrette, half-round crossing, three-corner, knife, equaling, and crochet (fig. 6–30).

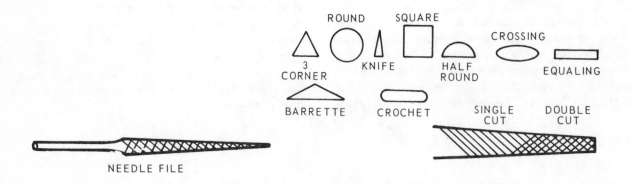

Figure 6–30. Needle files and file shapes.

(8) *Files, riffler.* A thin steel file (fig. 6–31) approximately 5 1/2 inches long, with curved, cutting ends, that is used to smooth rough places in silver which are inaccessible with other files. It is frequently used to file off excesss solder at a joint.

Figure 6–31. File, riffler.

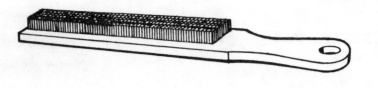

Figure 6–32. File card.

(9) *File card.* A wire brush-like tool (fig. 6–32) used to clean files.

(10) *Gauge, metal.* A measure to determine the thickness of a piece of metal or wire (fig. 6–33).

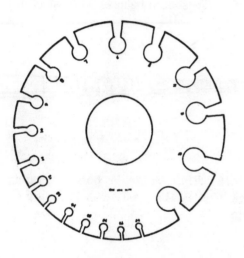

Figure 6–33. Gauge, metal.

(11) *Jeweler's saw frame.* An adjustable 2 ¼ to 4-inch steel frame (fig. 6–34) used with jeweler's saw blades for the purpose of cutting metal. Jeweler's saw blades range in size from No. 8/0 (thinnest) to No. 14 (thickest). Number 0 is generally used in silver-work but, ordinarily speaking, the softer the metal, the coarser (higher numbered) the blade to use.

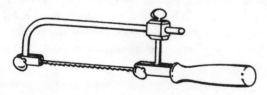

Figure 6–34. Jeweler's saw frame.

(12) *Hammers.* A metal hammer (fig. 6–35) that is used often in metalwork for processing, such as raising, forming, planishing, smoothing, and flattening. Its use in silver jewelry is limited to decorative textures. A metal hammer should never be used to form such objects as rings, since it tends to stretch the silver and to leave surface marks. When hammers are used for flattening or for decorative purposes, the proper blow is a tapping blow using the wrist. Metal that is hammered with a steel hammer should not be struck while placed on a wooden surface; it should be placed on an anvil.

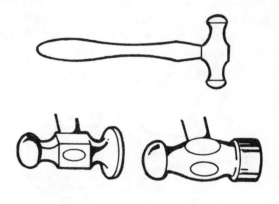

Figure 6–35. Hammers.

(13) *Hack saw.* A large type of frame saw (fig. 6–36) with steel blades that is used in jewelry work to cut thick metal rods, wires, and tubes. The blade is useful also for removing excess jeweler's rouge or tripoli from a buffing wheel and for restoring a flat surface to the buffing wheel.

(14) *Mallet, rawhide.* The tool of choice (fig. 6–37) for flattening or for forming silver jewelry because it does not leave surface marks. The head is made of rolled rawhide. When it is new, it is usually coated with shellac. This coating

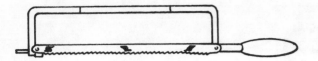

Figure 6-36. Hack saw.

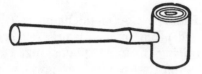

Figure 6-37. Mallet, rawhide.

should be removed before use in order that the soft leather may be exposed. Isopropol alcohol is used to soften the shellac for removal.

(15) *Pliers.* Steel tools used primarily to shape wire and thin metal. There is an assortment of pliers (fig. 6-38) for various types of work. Most jewelry pliers are available in 4-inch, 4 1/2-inch, and 5-inch lengths. End- or side-cutting nippers are almost indispensable in jewelry work; they are used to cut wire. Pliers with smooth gripping jaws are preferred in jewelry work as pliers with serrated jaws mar the surface of silver.

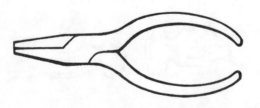

Figure 6-38. Pliers.

(16) *Ring clamp.* A hand-clamp with leather-lined jaws (fig. 6-39) used for holding rings while polishing, filing, or setting stones. The ring is placed between the leather jaws and held in place by forcing a wedge between the opposite jaws. Care must be taken when using the ring-clamp to hold a ring while polishing. If excessive pressure is maintained against the polishing wheel, the resultant frictional heat may damage the leather on the wooden jaws. Fingers may be burned, also, if the ring is removed too quickly from the clamp after polishing.

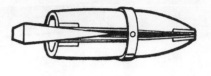

Figure 6-39. Ring clamp.

(17) *Ring mandrel.* A tapered steel rod usually 12 or 14 inches long and circular in shape (fig. 6-40) on which rings and circular bands are formed. It is sometimes marked with sizes and thus substitutes for a ring gauge. It is also useful in stretching a ring that is too small. A rawhide mallet should be used when stretching a ring.

Figure 6-40. Ring mandrel.

(18) *Ring gauge.* A hollow, graduated, long stick (fig. 6-41) used for measuring the size of rings.

Figure 6-41. Ring gauge.

(19) *Ring sizes.* A number of metal rings, each marked with a standard ring size (fig. 6-42), which are slipped on the finger to determine the size of the ring desired.

(20) *Scriber.* A steel tool pointed on both ends with a twisted center portion (fig. 6-43), that is used to scratch a line or design accurately on metal. Care must be exercised in using this tool to mark designs since mistakes cannot be removed easily.

(21) *Sparklighter.* A flint-metal tool with a spark of sufficient size to light the acetylene torch (fig. 6-44). Its advantages are that the torch can

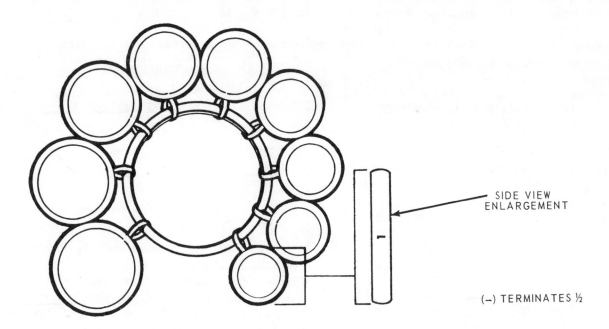

SIDE VIEW
ENLARGEMENT

(—) TERMINATES ½

Figure 6–42. Ring sizes.

Figure 6–43. Scriber.

Figure 6–45. Tongs, copper.

be held with one hand and a light obtained with the other and no matches are around to burst into flame if the flame of the torch gets too close.

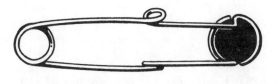

Figure 6–44. Sparklighter.

Figure 6–46. Tweezers, pointed.

(22) *Tongs, copper.* Large copper implements (fig. 6–45) used to lift the project from the pickling solution. Tweezers or tongs of other metals are not used for this purpose as they sometimes leave marks on the project and contaminate the pickling solution, making it ineffective for cleaning purposes.

(23) *Tweezers, pointed.* An implement (fig. 6–46) used for picking up small pieces of silver if delicate work is being done. Tweezers are not used while soldering.

b. Care of Tools. In general, tools should be used for the purpose for which they were designed. A file, for example, should not be used to pry a lid from a can. Tools made of steel (except files) should be cleaned periodically with steel wool or with a wire brush and oiled with a high grade machine oil to prevent rust. Polished tools such as hammers and burnishers should be kept polished. They can be polished in the same manner as silver. Tools will last longer if they are correctly used and maintained.

c. Storage of Tools. Tools in general use should

be kept on a shadow board in a dry place to prevent rust. They should be attached so that they will not fall off of the board if one tool is removed. Small tools such as needle files and drill bits should be kept in a block with holes drilled to fit each file. Files should be placed point down in the block if the block does not have a lid. Storing each tool separately also helps to prevent rust and makes selection of the desired tool easier.

d. Basic Equipment.

(1) *Annnealing pan.* A revolving pan (fig. 6–47), usually 12 to 18 inches in diameter, filled with material to reflect heat. It is used primarily to support the project when annealing or soldering.

Figure 6–47. Annealing pan.

(2) *Anvil.* A steel block (fig. 6–48) on which metal can be formed, bent, flattened, and planished. It is essentially a self-supporting metal stake.

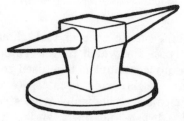

Figure 6–48. Anvil.

(3) *Asbestos block.* A pad of asbestos (fig. 6–49) on which pieces of metal may be soldered; however, it is not as effective as a charcoal block since it does not reflect the heat. Its primary use in clinics is to protect such items as tables from hot tools, projects, and other objects which may be placed there during the soldering process.

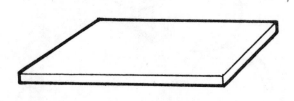

Figure 6–49. Asbestos block.

(4) *Bench vise.* A small vise (fig. 6–50) usually with smooth, adjustable jaws. It attaches to a table and is used for holding metal when filing. If a vise has serrated jaws, they should be covered with leather, cardboard, or with several layers of masking tape to protect the silver and to keep it from being marred.

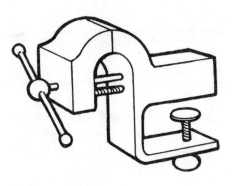

Figure 6–50. Bench vise.

(5) *Bench pin.* A wooden block with a V-notch (fig. 6–51) which is of valuable use in supporting silver while it is being cut with the jeweler's saw.

(6) *Charcoal block.* This block should always be used to support pieces being soldered. It is a small block made of charcoal (fig. 6–52) and is invaluable as an aid in soldering since it reflects the heat on the project. It is also useful in positioning pieces to be soldered as is easily carved to fit the piece.

(7) *Polishing buffs.* Cloth or felt wheels (fig. 6–53) used on a motor (polishing) to shine metal. (Although buffs are also made of other materials

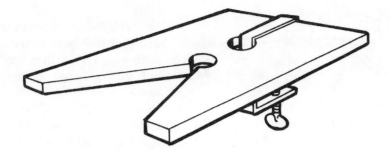

Figure 6–51. Bench pin.

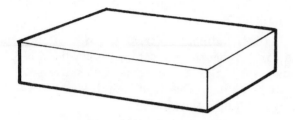

Figure 6–52. Charcoal block.

such as leather, these are rarely used in clinics.) Sometimes they are referred to as polishing wheels and are soft or hard depending upon the closeness of the stitching. (Closely stitched are harder than loosely stitched or unstitched wheels.) The wheels primarily used in polishing silver are 3, 4, or 5 inches in diameter. A different wheel is required with each compound or abrasive used. Periodicallly, these wheels should be cleaned by holding a hack saw blade horizontally and lightly against the wheel—and also below the center line of the wheel—while it is revolving.

(8) *Polishing motor.* A buffing machine (fig.

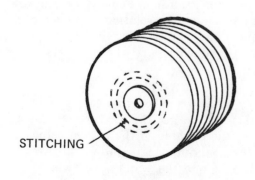

STITCHING

Figure 6–53. Polishing buffs.

6–54) characterized by a motor with two tapered spindles, one on each side, on which the polishing buffs can be attached. There should be a shield covering the area where the wheels are attached. This is used for safety and for ease in cleaning the area.

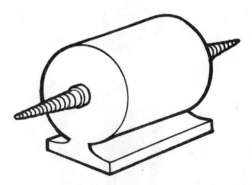

Figure 6–54. Polishing motor.

(9) *Torch, acetylene.* A torch using acetylene as fuel (fig. 6–55) used for soldering or annealing metal. The tank should be well secured so that it cannot move or fall. The valve should be turned on slightly until a hissing sound is heard and then lighted with a spark lighter. The flame used should be light blue and small. The valve should be turned off after each use. (This is the easiest method to obtain the required heat for soldering, although it is not the least expensive.) Other types of torches require an adjustment of the gas and oxygen; therefore, they are not as easy to use as an acetylene torch which requires only one adjustment.

(10) *Cylinder, propane.* A small, easily portable cylinder of propane with a soldering tip (fig. 6–56). It may be purchased if acetylene and a torch are not available as it requires less initial outlay.

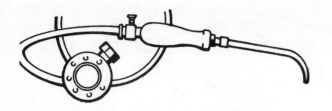

Figure 6–55. Torch, acetylene.

Figure 6–56. Propane cylinder with soldering tip.

e. Basic Materials and Their Use.

(2) *Beeswax.* A wax used as a lubricant when cutting metal with the jeweler's saw, when drawing wire through the drawplate, and when drilling metal.

(2) *Binding wire.* A thin wire made of iron, usually purchased in spool form, used to hold pieces of metal together until they are soldered. Binding wire should not be used unless absolutely necessary since solder may flow over the wire and considerable effort will be expended to remove it. It can also deflect the flame of the torch, making soldering difficult. Binding wire must be removed prior to placing project into cleaning solution, as it will contaminate the solution and discolor the project. Its use should be avoided most of the time.

(3) *Borax.* A substance used as a flux in soldering silver. In powdered form, it can be mixed with water to a thin paste consistency and applied with a brush to the piece to be soldered. It tends to bubble excessively when heated and causes movement of the pieces to be soldered or the solder itself. In an effort to prevent this, the heat must be applied very slowly when using borax.

(4) *Crocus cloth.* A polishing cloth coated with jeweler's rouge and used in the last step of hand polishing.

(5) *Emery cloth.* An abrasive cloth used to remove scratches from metal in the first stages of hand polishing.

(6) *Findings.* A term given to items such as earring backs, pin backs, tie clasps, and cuff-link backs. Silver solder is never used with a plated finding; the heat required to melt the solder will melt the plating.

(7) *Flux.* A substance used to keep the solder and the parts to be joined from oxidizing during the heating process. It keeps the joint clean and aids the flow of the solder. The flux for solft solder is a commercial product in paste form. Glycerin is also sometimes used. The flux for hard solder is borax, potassium floride, or a commercial green liquid, available in 1-ounce to 1-quart bottles, which is used with silver, gold, and copper. For best results, both flux and solder must be kept clean.

(8) *Potassium sulfide or liver of sulphur.* Chemical used to color or to darken silver to enhance the design or the natural beauty of the metal.

(9) *Pickling solution.* A solution to clean metal, usuallly after soldering. It is more effective in a heated form; if there is no heat available to warm it, the metal can be heated and dropped into the pickling solution. For safety purposes, OT clinics often use a solution of Sparex No. 2 as a pickling solution. Otherwise, sulphuric acid (heated), mixed 1 part with 10 parts water, is used.

CAUTION

This is an acid and extreme care should be taken not to get the mixture on the body or the clothing of the person using it. When mixing this solution, always add the acid to the water; otherwise a chemical explosion may occur.

(10) *Pumice powder.* A fine abrasive used to polish metal.

(11) *Jeweler's rouge.* A polish for silver, gold, etc. It is a burnisher, not an abrasive. When used on a buff, it produces the highest luster possible.

(12) *Rubber cement.* A temporary cement used to hold or paste a paper design on silver while the design is being cut out with the jeweler's saw. It is very effective and is easily removed from the silver after use.

(13) *Silver solder or hard solder.* An alloy of silver, copper, and zinc which is used to join pieces of silver (or copper, brass, etc.) together. It produces the strongest joint possible in silver. There are three kinds of hard solder: hard, medium, and easy flow. The melting points range from 1365° F to 1280° F, respectively. In clinics, medium and easy flow silver solder is preferred. Hard flow solder is extremely difficult to use because of the high melting point and is essential only if there are several soldering operations on the same piece.

(14) *Soft solder.* A solder which flows at a relatively low temperature. There are several types—

(*a*) One is an alloy of tin and lead usually used to fasten plated findings to the back of jewelry. The melting point is approximately 340° F and the piece soldered cannot be immediately quenched with water. The solder must cool first and set before the piece can be picked up with tweezers. Since this solder does not provide a strong joint, it should not be used when one is required.

(*b*) There is also a silver-colored soft solder that contains no lead, melts at 350° F, and does not tarnish. It is excellent for soldering findings and enameled pieces, and also might be used on pewter.

(*c*) Solderall is a flux mixed with solder furnished in a lead tube, which squeezes like toothpaste. Very little heat is needed on small pieces, and it is especially good for soldering findings onto enameled pieces.

(15) *Steel wool.* Used in jewelry for polishing and cleaning. Usually the finest grades are used (0–00–000–0000).

(16) *Sulphuric acid.* A pickling agent for silver. It is used to clean the silver. Its use in the clinics should be avoided since it is an acid. The best pickling solution for clinic use is Sparex No. 2.

(17) *Tripoli.* An abrasive compound used to remove fine scratches from silver. It is applied to the buffer while it is revolving. The difficulty resulting from using tripoli in clinics is that patients often will use this compound on a buff intended for jeweler's rouge. Since tripoli does not produce the final luster on silver, its use can be completely avoided by doing more hand polishing. In many instances, this is preferred.

(18) *Scotch stone.* An abrasive, fine stone used to remove small scratches in inaccessible places. It is dipped in water and used like sandpaper. This is the only abrasive that will remove fire scale on sterling silver.

(19) *Yellow ochre powder.* A powder mixed with water to make a paste that is used to coat previously soldered joints if there is danger of joints opening with the heat from soldering another joint. After the soldering is complete, the coating may be removed by soaking the article in water and then scrubbing it with an old toothbrush.

6–24. Processes

a. Transferring a Design to Metal. There are many methods of transferring the design to metal by using such devices as carbon paper or direct drawing with pencil. The most satisfactory method is to draw or trace the design on tracing paper and to cut around this design and glue it directly to the metal with rubber cement. A good joint between the paper and the metal is obtained by coating the metal and the back of the tracing paper design with rubber cement, allowing both to dry until tacky, then smoothing the paper design onto the silver. If other methods are used, the design will have to be scratched into the metal with a scriber; otherwise, the design will rub off the slick metal. The design is always placed as close to the edge of the metal as possible to avoid waste and to allow easy cutting. When a straight-edged piece of silver (square, rectangular) such as a ring band or cuff link is cut, a scriber may be used with the steel square and the lines marked directly on the silver. Wing dividers may also be used if there is a straight edge on the metal to use as a guide.

b. Sawing. Sawing in metal is done with a jeweler's saw frame and jeweler's saw blades. After loosening the jaw nuts on both ends of the frame, the blade is inserted in the top jaw nut and tightened. It is inserted all the way in and positioned so that the teeth of the blade are pointing down toward the handle. The frame handle is pushed toward the top of the frame, the blade is inserted in the lower jaw nut while the frame is on a "bind," and the wing nut (bottom) is tightened. When plucked with the finger, the blade should have a high-pitched tone if it is tight enough. The blade must be tight (taut) as it is very difficult to cut with a blade that is not. When a cut is begun on the edge of sheet metal, a starting groove must first be made for the blade, as it sometimes will stick or slide off the desired cutting line. This groove is made by making a few cuts on the upstroke. This is the only time that there is cutting with the upstroke; all other cuts will be on the downstroke. (The blade teeth point down toward the handle; therefore, silver is cut on the downstroke.) Sawing sheet metal is always done on a V bench pin with the metal horizontal to the vertically moving saw frame. The metal is supported against the saw frame with the fingers, and it is moved with the fingers during the sawing process (fig. 6–57). The actual cutting is done in the sawed-out V area of the bench pin. (The saw should never be forced forward against the silver or downward while moving the saw.) The secret to successful sawing is to use the full length of the blade; to keep the saw straight up and down vertically; and to use smooth, easy, patient strokes. When sawing a curve, the metal is turned with the fingers against the moving blade; when sawing around a corner or a square, the saw is moved in position a few times to allow it to be turned freely at an angle. Beeswax may be used as a lubricant on the saw blade, but excessive

waxing can clog the saw teeth. Saw blades rarely wear out in the clinic; they are usually broken through misuse. To avoid breaking, the blade must never be forced; it must never be tilted right or left, or forward.

c. Filing. The proper way to file is from the tip of the file to the handle with all pressure applied on the forward stroke (fig. 6–58). It is best to file at a diagonal along the entire metal edge with a long, evenly applied stroke. This sliding stroke may be used on straight convex and concave edges. Filing should never be concentrated in one area to remove dents or high places. The entire edge should be filed, as concentration on an irregular spot will only increase the irregularity. The file should be lifted after each forward stroke and returned to its original position; if the file is moved back and forth across the edge, it will become clogged and dulled. The first filing should be done with a coarse file; finer files are then used to remove the scratches left by the coarser files. A flat file is used for straight edges. For concave and convex edges, the best file is a half-round file. Round files may be used for concave edges and for round holes. Work being filed can be held in a bench vise, ring clamp, or in the hand. After an edge has been filed, the resultant burr on the edge of the metal may be removed by sliding the file at an angle to the edge.

d. Stoning. After filing is completed, a scotch stone may be used with water to remove all the

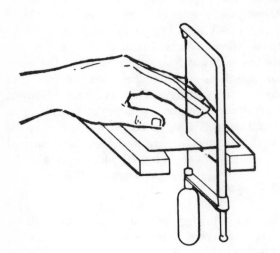

Figure 6–57. Position in sawing.

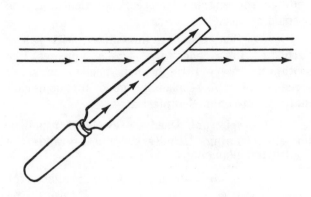

Figure 6–58. Direction of file while filing an edge of metal.

scratches left by files. Water is always used with the scotch stone in order to prevent loose particles of metal from becoming embedded in the stone itself (water washes these particles away from the stone). The stone is rubbed back and forth across the edge or surfaces to be polished. Scotch stones are usually used when the area to be polished is hard to reach. If a piece is well stoned, the polishing time is cut to a minimum.

e. Annealing. This term is applied to the process whereby silver is softened and once again returned to a ductile, malleable state. When silver or any metal is formed, bent, hammered, etc., it will in time become hard and brittle. If annealing is not done at this time, the piece being formed will break. The piece of silver is placed in the annealing pan, the torch is lit, and heat is applied evenly to the whole piece until it becomes a dull red. Next, it is picked up with copper tongs and dropped into the pickling solution or water. It will then be soft and ready for more shaping. Soldering a piece also anneals it. Pieces of work that may require annealing include such things as bracelets and wire to be drawn.

f. Forming. Forming is a term used for the depressing and bending of metal to form a project or a design. Pliers are used to form wire projects, wire designs, bezels, and thin sheet metal (above 20 gauge). A rawhide mallet is used to form such things as heavy wire and sheet metal around a stake, an anvil, a mandrel, etc. Most forming in jewelry making is actually a series of bends. Rings, bracelets, and such are bent around a mandrel; pliers bend wire to the desired shape. When pliers are used to form wire, they should not be squeezed too tightly against the metal or they will dent the wire. When a mallet or hammer is used to form sheet silver, the desirable blow is a tapping motion using only the wrist. When using an anvil or a mandrel, the sheet metal or wire is held securely at its side and the top edge is extended slightly up and over the mandrel. The top edge is tapped lightly until it takes the rounded shape of the mandrel. When this is accomplished and more forming is desired (as with a ring), the remaining metal is extended above the mandrel and the operation repeated until the ring is formed (fig. 6–59). A square bend in sheet metal is obtained by holding the metal flat against the side of an anvil with the part to be bent extending upward. This part is then bent flat against the top of the anvil on a flat surface. The piece can also be held vertically in a vise at the line of the bend; a

mallet is used to tap the protruding metal until the desired bend is produced.

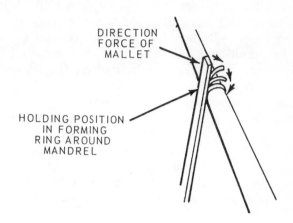

Figure 6–59. Forming on a mandrel.

g. Drawing. This is a process whereby the diameter or shape of the wire may be reduced or changed. A drawplate is placed in a vise (preferably a wood vise). The end of the wire to be drawn is tapered with a file. It is then placed in a hole slightly smaller than its original diameter. The tapered end of the wire is grasped with drawtongs (fig. 6–60) and pulled until the entire length of the wire has been drawn through the hole. It is then annealed and placed into the next smaller hole and the process continued until the desired diameter or shape is obtained. Beeswax may be used as a lubricant to ease the operation. The wire will not only be smaller in diameter, but it will also be longer since it is stretched by this procedure.

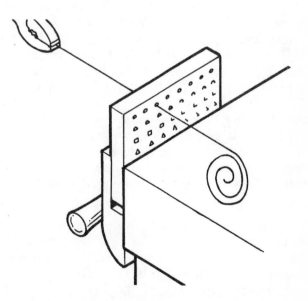

Firure 6–60. Drawing a wire.

h. Chain Construction. A link is made by winding silver wire around in a spiral on a nail, rod, bar (whatever the desired shape). If a nail is used, the end (head) should be sawed off. After a spiral of wire is obtained, a cut is made down the length of the spiral with the jeweler's saw. The result will be many links that are slightly twisted. The links are twisted in the opposite direction until a fitting joint is obtained. They can be linked together and soldered (each link must be soldered) or they can be linked together to form a bracelet or necklace and left unsoldered. If used as a necklace to hold a heavy pendant, they should be soldered (fig. 6–61). These links can be joined together in many different ways to make attractive necklaces and bracelets.

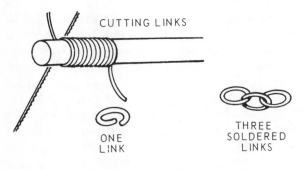

Figure 6–61. Chain construction.

i. Twisting Wire. Twisted wire makes attractive rings, designs in rings, bracelets, cuff links, and earrings. Any number of wires may be twisted together. The wires to be twisted are bent in the middle to form a loop; the cut ends are placed in a vise, preferably with serrated jaws; and a nail or a rod is placed in the loop. If the nail is grasped and pulled to keep the wire taut and, at the same time, turned a number of times, a twisted wire results (fig. 6–62). These twisted wires can, in turn, be soldered together to form wide bracelets, flattened to produce a different effect, or left as they are. However, they must be soldered together in the desired position before they are formed on a mandrel. If the twist is uneven, the tension is not taut enough.

j. Soldering (Hard). Before soldering can be accomplished, the pieces to be joined must fit. The joint must be tight, even, and smooth. Solder will not compensate for irregularities in the surface. The parts of the joint must touch not only in one spot, but along the entire length

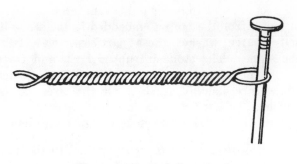

Figure 6–62. Twisting wire.

of the joint. If the joint does not fit, it must be shaped, filed, and bent until it does. The next step after obtaining a properly fitted joint is to clean both the joint and the solder. Solder is cleaned with steel wool; after it is cleaned, it must not be touched, as the oil on the hands will leave a coating of oil on the solder. The parts to be joined can be cleaned with pickle, files, steel wool, or heat. After the joint and the solder are cleaned, flux is applied to all surfaces of the joint. A thin, even coat of flux is sufficient. Solder is then cut into small pieces approximately 1/32 inch square. To do this, cut a fringed edge with scissors; then, holding one finger against the fringed edge, cut across the fringed edge with the scissors (fig. 6–63). The solder will then be in small squares.) Soldering is almost always performed on a charcoal block. The silver pieces are placed on the charcoal. The solder is positioned so that each piece is touching both edges of the joint and spaced not less than 1/8 inch apart. The torch is then lighted with a spark lighter and the flame is adjusted until it is small and blue. The silver piece is gradually heated with a moving, constant flame. As the piece begins to get hot (pink color), the flame is directed to the joint itself. It should be concentrated (fig. 6–64) so as to draw the solder through the joint; solder follows heat so it will flow to the hottest point. After the solder flows, the heat is removed and the project is picked up with copper tongs and dropped into the pickling solution. This will cool and clean the piece. The piece is removed from the pickling solution with the copper tongs and washed with water. If the joint does not hold, it indicates faulty fit, poor fluxing, improper cleaning, or uneven application of heat (fig. 6–65). If the solder "balls up" and does not flow, it is probably dirty or the flux may have been improperly applied. The heat applied may have been inadequate to cause the solder to flow; however, if the silver was a dull red, the heat was adequate.

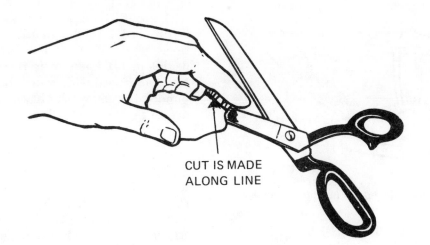

Figure 6–63. Cutting solder.

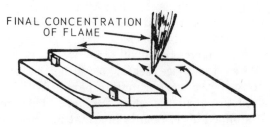

Figure 6–64. Direction of flame in soldering.

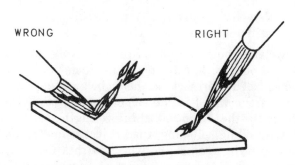

Figure 6–65. Proper distance of torch tip from project.

k. Application of Findings. Although it is best to use sterling silver findings on sterling silver, this is not always possible. When plated findings are used, they should be soft-soldered into place. Silver findings may be soldered with easy-flow silver solder. Soldering silver findings to a project is done in the same manner as other hard soldering. The only variation in technique is that the flame of the torch must not touch the find-

ing. The finding is very small in relation to the size and thickness of the project; therefore, all heat must be applied to the project itself (fig. 6–66). If, by chance, heat is applied to the finding, the solder will flow on the finding instead of under it. This is due to its small size and to the fact that it becomes hot quicker than the thicker project. The bottom of the finding will absorb heat from the project itself. When soldering a finding to a piece, apply the flux only to the bottom of the finding; this may prevent solder from flowing into the mechanism of the finding. When cuff-link backs are soldered into place, the flame must not touch the finding or it may damage the temper of the spring. The spring should be removed if possible. When a pin assembly is soldered into place, the pin stem should not be in position. Heat will anneal the pin stem so it will bend easily and have no spring. The parts of a pin must be in line and be soldered in the middle of the brooch (fig. 6–67). The catch should be on the left side, with the slot in the catch pointing down. The joint should be placed at an angle so that the pin stem will be behind the catch before insertion into the catch. The position of the catch and joint should be marked on the project. After the catch and the joint are soldered, the pin stem is secured into the joint with a rivet wire.

l. Soldering (Soft). Soft solder is a tin lead alloy that melts at approximately 340° F. It does not produce a strong joint and is never used to solder two pieces of silver together. However, some findings such as plated ones require soft soldering. The flux used is a commercial prepara-

153

Figure 6-66. Direction of flame in soldering finding.

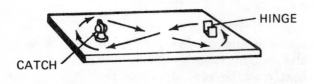

Figure 6-67. Direction of flame in soldering pin clasp and joint.

tion in a thick paste form. Glycerin may be substituted. The back of the piece and the bottom of the finding must be cleaned. The flux is applied to the bottom of the finding; the finding is positioned on the project and some of the flux should stick to the project. Next, the finding is lifted and placed upside down on the charcoal block. A small piece of lead solder is cut and placed on the bottom of the finding. The finding is lightly heated until the solder melts and flows on its bottom. The finding is then turned over with the tweezers and placed in proper position on the flux. Heat is now applied to the back of the silver piece until the solder runs out of the bottom of the finding and is visible in the joint. The flame is then removed and the piece is left to cool until the solder has set. It is then picked up with the tweezers and cooled with water. (Pickle may damage the soft-solder joint.) Soft soldering is always the last soldering to be done in jewelry. It is not recommended for cuff links, pendants, buckles, or any project subject to stress.

m. Oxidation. This is a term given to the darkening or the coloring of metal to enhance the design, to darken areas that cannot be polished, and to enrich the natural beauty of the project. After all the soldering is completed and the piece is cleaned of solder and is scratch free, the entire silver project is oxidized. A small piece of liver of sulphur (1/4 inch) is mashed up and mixed with about 3 ounces of hot water. The silver piece is dropped into the solution and, upon contact, turns black. When it has turned to the desired degree of blackness, it is removed from the solution and rinsed with water. It is rubbed with fine pumice to remove the black from the parts that are to be shiny. If a high gloss is desired, these areas are polished.

n. Polishing. A piece of silver attains a high luster by means of a series of scratches or abrasions which become progressively finer until a shine results. Filing could be considered the first step in polishing. The high areas or the areas where a dark color is not desired (after oxidation) are removed by steel wool or carborundum paper (No. 200). The scratches are made along the length of the piece, always in one direction. These fine scratches will be continued until the piece begins to shine a little. When the piece begins to shine and when there are no cross scratches or deep scratches, No. 400 carborundum paper (or a finer grade of steel wool) is then used. When the piece begins to shine, water is used to wet the carborundum paper, which is then used to polish the piece further. (This process, if stopped here, results in a mat finish which is also desirable.) When the piece appears to have no scratches, it is buffed on the polishing wheel with jeweler's rouge.

NOTE
Jeweler's rouge is not an abrasive and will not remove scratches.

Jeweler's rouge is applied to the revolving wheel —it should be *lightly* touched *occasionally* to the wheel. The project is held below the center line of the wheel in the same position to the heel as with the hand polishing (lengthwise) (fig. 6-68). While polishing, the project is moved from left to right against the wheel, with a little pressure applied, to prevent the wheel from becoming grooved. This occurs when projects are polished in one area or when too much pressure has been applied to the wheel. If jeweler's rouge sticks to the project's surface, it is an indication that too much has been applied to the wheel or that too much pressure has been applied in polishing. When the project has a high luster and does not have any gray (dull) spots or scratches, the polishing is completed. If there are gray spots, they are probably fire scale, a term used to denote oxidation caused by heat. This must be removed with scotch stone before the highest luster can be obtained. After the polishing is completed, the piece is dipped into alcohol or washed with soap and water to remove the traces of jeweler's rouge.

NOTE

Polishing does not have to be done on the polishing wheel; it is possible to obtain a high luster by hand rubbing with crocus cloth.

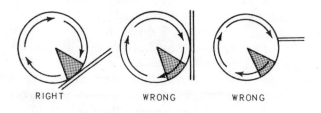

Figure 6–68. Polishing area of wheel and angle of polishing.

6–25. Design

a. A design for silver work must be functional, simple, practical, and adaptable to the materials available and to the project in mind. These are the basic elements of the design.

b. There are numerous methods of obtaining an original design for a project made of silver. Designs may be asymmetrical or symmetrical; abstract (free-form) or geometric (square, round, etc.); or a combination of these shapes. Designs may be obtained by random scribbling or doodling with a pencil (selecting resultant desirable lines or shapes); by ink blotting (dropping ink on paper and folding paper while ink is wet to obtain unusual shapes); by cutting folded paper with scissors; by simplifying forms in nature, such as fish, trees, and leaves; by simplifying man-made objects such as violins; by rearranging and overlapping cutout geometrical shapes; and by other methods. It is desirable to plan a design on paper and then execute the plan into silver after deciding on the process to be used.

c. There are also numerous ways of executing the desired design into silver. Some of these methods, called the decorative processes, are listed below.

(1) *Piercing.* A term given to the process of sawing a hole or a shape within the sheet of metal.

A hole is drilled in the sheet metal with a twist drill and a small bit. A guide for the drill bit is made with a center punch to prevent the drill from slipping on the slick metal. After the hole is drilled, the loosened bottom end of the saw blade is inserted through the hole and secured at the handle of the saw frame. An area of metal is then removed by sawing on a bench pin in the proper manner as previously described. The resultant design is known as a pierced design (fig. 6–69).

Figure 6–69. Pierced design.

(2) *Chasing and repoussé.* Terms referring to the three-dimensional modeling of a design in sheet metal using steel tools. *Chasing* is the term applied to the process of modeling the design from the front side of the sheet metal with blunt, chisel-like tools known as chasing tools. The piece of sheet metal is placed on a bowl filled with pitch and the background or lowered areas of the design are tapped down into the plastic pitch, thereby raising the design areas. *Repoussé* refers to the modeling which is performed on the back of the metal; the design areas are tapped down into the pitch from the back of the metal, thereby raising the design on the front of the metal. Rounded steel tools are used in repoussé; blunt tools are used in chasing. Often the two processes are used interchangeably on the same project. These methods are not often used in a clinic.

(3) *Carving.* A process referring to the removal of part of the surface of the metal, usually with tools known as gravers, to produce a design or a texture. Gravers are rarely used in occupational therapy to perform this process as a great deal of skill is involved in using these sharp tools. However, this decorative process can

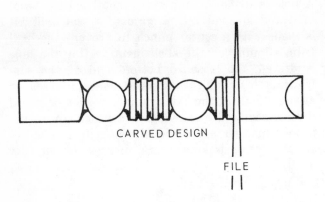

CARVED DESIGN

FILE

Figure 6-70. Using a needle file to shape a design.

also be done with files to form desired lines and shapes in the surface metal, preferably in wire. Carving designs in thick, half-round bracelet wire is a desirable activity for many patients. A guide for the file cuts can be made with a hack saw, jeweler's saw, or with the knife-shaped needle file. After the guidelines are made, needle files can be used to shape the lines into the desired form for the design (fig. 6-70). If the design is to be deeply carved, it is advisable to bend the bracelet before it is carved, as deep carving weakens the metal and it may break in the bending process.

(4) *Wire design.* A process in which wire is used to produce a line design on flat silver (by soldering wire to the sheet silver). It can be shaped into a line design itself and used for such projects as brooches. It can be twisted to form rings, or the twisted wire can be flattened and soldered as a design on sheet metal. There are innumerable ways of using wire in the decorative process (fig. 6-71).

(5) *Etching.* Decorative etching, which consists of painting the design on the metal with an acid-resisting medium (asphaltum) and then submerging the work into an acid solution which will eat all parts not covered with asphaltum. The depth of the etching depends upon the length of time the work is left in the acid and the strength of the solution. One part nitric acid

poured into three to four parts of water is recommended for silver. Etching is not used very often in occupational therapy due to the fact that acid is dangerous to use in a clinic situation. Similar effects may be obtained in jewelry by soldering a pierced design to a piece of flat silver (design area willl be depressed) or by soldering a flat shape such as an initial on another piece of flat metal (design area will be raised).

(6) *Domes.* Domes (hemispheres and spheres) which are made with the dapping die and dapping punches. An annealed piece of metal is placed over a hole of the desired size in the dapping die. A punch is selected that fits into the depression. It is then held above the piece of metal which is above the desired hole. The punch is driven into the hole with a hammer. This forces the silver into the hole, stretching it to fit the shape and resulting in a concave or convex area in the silver. This area is then sawed out of the remaining flat metal to produce a hemisphere (half-dome). If a dome is desired, two hemispheres may be soldered end to end, but a hole must be left to permit air to escape. Hemispheres and spheres are useful in producing three-dimensional designs that reflect light on all sides (fig. 6-72 and 6-73).

(7) *Balls.* Silver balls, which may be used in a design when small, spherical shapes are desired. When completely melted, silver rolls into a ball. Small scrap pieces of flat silver or wire may be used to make balls. The piece should be cleaned and coated with flux. Heat is applied until the piece of silver becomes liquid and forms a ball. Then the heat is removed and the piece is picked

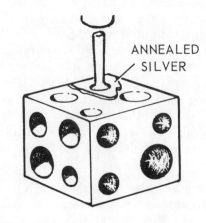

ANNEALED SILVER

Figure 6-72. Forming hemispheres with dapping die and punch.

Figure 6-71. Wire design.

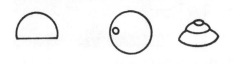

Figure 6-73. Hemispheres.

up with tweezers and dropped into the pickling solution. The resultant ball will have a flat bottom since it will be resting on a flat piece of charcoal. This flat bottom is usually satisfactory as it gives an area where the piece will balance in the soldering process. If a completely round ball is desired, a round hole can be made in the charcoal and the silver melted into the depression. If several balls of the same size are desired, pieces of wire in equal lengths can be melted. Silver balls are made when small spheres are desired; large spheres are made with the dappling die and punch, since weight is a consideration in the construction of a project.

(8) *Fusing.* A decorative process of construction in which various shapes and sizes of scrap silver are melted together with the torch to produce an irregular, free-form piece which may be used independently as a pin or brooch or which can be soldered as a design to another piece.

(9) *Planishing.* In making silver jewelry, a process that is used primarily for decoration through texture. It is also a method of polishing in metalwork. It consists of hammering the metal on a flat anvil with a metal hammer, thereby producing dents in the surface of the silver. Planishing is used to denote background areas of a design or to produce a design through texture.

(10) *Stone setting.* Regularly shaped stones with smooth, sloped, rounded edges (cabochons) and irregularly shaped polished stones (tumbled stones) that are usually used in jewelry making. Stones may be set by the bezel method, by the prong method, or with wire.

(*a*) A bezel setting is usually used to set cabochons (round, oval, square, etc.). A bezel is a thin, silver rim encircling the stone and supported by a base or by the project itself. Thin bezel wire (26 gauge) is used to make a bezel (fig. 6-74). It is wrapped around the bottom edge of the stone and cut with shears at the point of the overlap. The two ends of the wire are soldered together and the resultant rim is soldered to a base or to the project. After all soldering is com-

pleted, the stone is placed into the fixed rim and the top edge of the rim is bent in toward the stone with a burnisher. When the stone is secured and the bezel edge is smooth, the setting is complete. There must be no soldering done after the stone is set since the heat will crack the stone.

(*b*) A prong setting involves soldering small prongs (wire) to a piece of silver or to each other in order to form a fixed support for the stone. The stone is placed in the support and the prongs are bent in toward the stone with a burnisher. This method can be used with irregularly shaped stones.

(*c*) The wire method consists of wrapping the stone with wire in such a manner as to hold the stone. The stone is removed from the wire and the ends of the wire are soldered together, forming a cage. After all soldering is completed, the wire shape is twisted open to allow entry of the stone, and pressed closed so that the stone cannot fall out. This is a stone setting without a base or support (fig. 6-75).

(11) *Combination of silver and wood.* Hardwood such as ebony and walnut can be attached

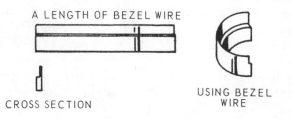

Figure 6-74. Using bezel wire.

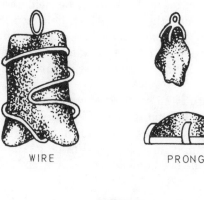

Figure 6-75. Using stone settings.

to silver with bezels, wires, glue, and rivets to form an attractive, contrasting design (fig. 6–76). Silver can also be embedded into the wood to form designs. If the project will be subjected to stress, glue should not be used to join wood and silver. Wood and silver projects are polished and filed in the same manner as a silver project; the finishing is more effective if it is done after the wood and silver have been joined together.

(12) *Enameling.* A process that can be done on sterling silver but not as easily as on copper, because sterling silver begins to break down at 1500° F. It becomes liquid at 1640° F. The method of enameling is the same as for copper but, because of the lower tolerance to heat, it is important to observe the following precautions when enameling on silver:

(*a*) When possible, work on concave surfaces to avoid surface tensions.

(*b*) Plan the design so that only one or two firings are needed.

(*c*) Do not raise the temperature above 1500° F.

6–26. Safety

a. The soldering area for jewelry work should be located in a dark corner of the clinic so that, when metal is being heated, its changing colors can be seen readily. The area should be well ventilated so that poisonous gases resulting from some fluxes can be dispersed. However, the actual soldering area (the flame) should be shielded from direct drafts of air to prevent the flame from blowing and setting something on fire. It is preferable to have asbestos shields surrounding three sides of the annealing pan.

b. When soldering jewelry, a small flame should be used, and it should be held the proper distance from the project. If held too close, it will "pop" and sometimes go out; or the flame end may bend on the project and reflect or bounce off the soldering area and start fires. The torch flame should be shut off after each soldering job has been fully completed. Fires have been started by a flame left unattended. The tank valve should be turned off when the last patient group has left the clinic and the remaining gas should be let out of the hose and dispersed in air.

Figure 6–76. Silver and ebony design.

c. The soldering tank should be secured (preferably against the wall or in an enclosed cabinet) to keep it from being bumped and tipped over. The hoses should be kept out of the way as much as possible to prevent disconnection or damage by bumping.

d. Mandrels and other implements should not be left protruding from a worktable after work is completed. A person walking around the table could be injured. A vise should not be left open for the same reason.

e. Tools should be attached to a tool board in such a manner as to prevent any tool from falling when one tool is selected or when the tool board is accidently bumped. Pointed objects in a tool block such as needle files should be placed handle up in the block to prevent puncture cuts when selecting a tool.

f. Mallet and hammer heads should be checked periodically to see that they are securely attached to the handle. Hammers having damaged heads and handles should be removed from the tool board and should not be used again until they are repaired.

g. While polishing, goggles should be worn to protect the eyes from foreign objects. An apron should be worn to protect clothing from dust resulting from polishing (jeweler's rouge). However, the strings on an apron should be tied behind the boby since a revolving wheel ·can easily catch loose strings. For the same reason, a tie should never be worn while polishing. Since projects held improperly against the wheel are sometimes flung across the room, a protective covering should enclose the polishing wheel. Chains or similar items should not be polished without first being attached to a board. They may become wrapped around the polishing wheel and cause injury to the fingers if they are not firmly attached to a board.

CHAPTER 7

WEAVING

7-2. Glossary of Weaving Terms

a. A general glossary of terms is listed below.

(1) *Apron.* Material, usually canvas, fastened to the cloth beams to which the warp ends are tied.

(2) *Beam, breast.* Top crosspiece at the front of the loom over which the finished cloth passes to the cloth beam.

(3) *Beam, cloth.* The roller at the front of the loom on which the cloth is wound after it is woven.

(4) *Beam, warp.* The beam around which the warp is wound at the back of the loom.

(5) *Beaming the warp.* Rolling the warp onto the warp beam.

(6) *Beater.* The frame which holds the reed and is used to "beat" the weft to its place in the woven piece.

(7) *Beating.* Pulling the beater each time a weft thread is put in, to push it into place in the newly woven cloth.

(8) *Castle top.* Large roller or bar which extends across the side posts and from which the harnesses are hung.

(9) *Chaining.* A method of looping the warp as it is removed from the warping frame or reel.

(10) *Cone.* A shaped core around which threads and light yarns are sometimes wound.

(11) *Cross or lease.* The place where the threads cross at the start of a warp to keep the threads in sequence during threading.

(12) *Dent.* A single space in the reed through which the warp is threaded.

(13) *Draft.* A drawing, usually on squared paper, which indicates the placement of the threads in the harnesses to form a certain pattern.

(14) *Dressing the loom.* The process of preparing and threading the warp for weaving. Also referred to as warping.

(15) *Filler.* Weft thread, usually warp, used for weaving until the gaps between the warp threads are eliminated.

(16) *Gating the loom.* The process of adjusting and alining the parts of the loom.

(17) *Guide plate.* A metal plate which fits into a slot in the back beam and has holes which serve as a guide as the warp threads are pulled toward a section in sectional weaving.

(18) *Guide string.* The first string to be put on a warping frame or beam. It serves as a guide in making the warp.

(19) *Harness.* The heddles, heddle rods, and harness frames.

(20) *Heading.* A band or edging woven, usually in tabby, at the beginning and end of some fabrics.

(21) *Heddle.* A wire, string, or flat piece of thin metal with an eye or slot in the center through which the warp ends are threaded.

(22) *Lams.* Horizontal levers attached to a side post of the loom between the harnesses and threadles. They aid in bringing down the harnesses evenly.

(23) *Lease or cross.* The place where the threads cross at the start of a warp to keep the threads in sequence during threading.

(24) *Lease sticks*. Two thin sticks used to hold the threads in order at the cross or lease.

(25) *Ply*. The number of single strands which are twisted together to form a thread or cord.

(26) *Reed or sley*. The comblike spacing device in the beater which evenly spaces the warp threads and beats the weft in place.

(27) *Reed hook*. The hook used to facilitate threading the warp through the dents of the reed and the eye of the heddle.

(28) *Roller*. Another name for the cloth beam, for the warp beam, or for the top castle bar on which the harnesses are supported.

(29) *Selvage or selvedge*. The edge of the cloth.

(30) *Shed*. The horizontal opening, made by the separation of warp thread, through which the shuttle passes.

(31) *Slot*. Passage of the shuttle through the shed, depositing one weft thread.

(32) *Shuttle*. The stick or boatlike container which holds the weft threads.

(33) *Skein winder or swift*. An adjustable revolving holder to facilitate the winding or unwinding of skeins or yarn.

(34) *Sley or reed*. The comblike spacing device in the beater which evenly spaces the warp threads and beats the weft in place.

(35) *Sleying*. The threading of the warp through the dents of the reed.

(36) *Snitch knot*. A knot frequently used in gaiting the loom.

(37) *Spool rack*. A rack designed to hold a number of tubes of warp while beaming.

(38) *Tabby thread*. The thread inserted between pattern threads.

(39) *Tabby weave*. The plain weave formed by interlacing of single warp and weft threads.

(40) *Tension box*. A device designed to maintain even tension and to guide the warp threads being put on the warp beam.

(41) *Treadles*. Levers used to raise or lower the harnesses on looms. Often referred to as levers on a table loom and pedals on a floor loom.

(42) *Treadling*. Pressing down certain treadles of the loom to raise or lower the attached harness. When done in a prescribed sequence, it makes the pattern in weaving.

(43) *Tying down*. The tying of the warp threads to the apron.

(44) *Warp*. Threads running lengthwise of the loom across wich the weft threads are passed to form cloth.

(45) *Warping*. The process of preparing and threading the warp for weaving. Also referred to as dressing.

(46) *Warping board*. A wooden frame with pegs spaced so that small warps can be wound or made.

(47) *Warping reel*. A revolving open barrel-like frame around which a fairly long warp can be wound or made.

(48) *Weft or woof*. Threads woven horizontally across the warp to form coth.

(49) *Web*. A piece of woven cloth.

(50) *Woof or weft*. Threads woven horizontally across the warp to form cloth.

b. The list above is not intended to be all inclusive. Other weaving terms may occur in books on weaving.

7–3. Equipment

a. Looms

(1) *Table looms.*

(*a*) Two-harness looms (Peacock looms) are light and portable. They are simple an uncomplicated to operate and range in weaving width from 12 to 16 inches (fig. 7–1).

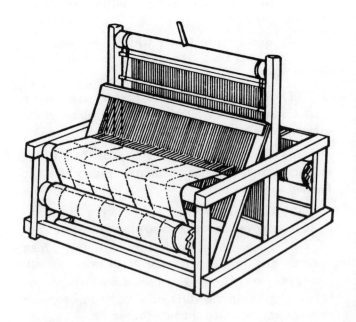

Figure 7–1. Peacock loom.

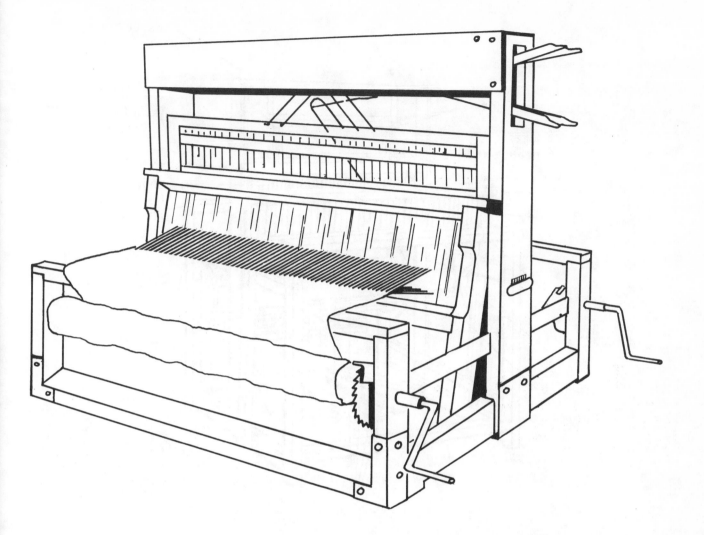

Figure 7-2. Four-harness table loom.

(b) Four-harness table looms are heavier than Peacock looms and are operated by levers which are depressed to change the shed. When purchasing this type of loom, one should look for those that can be easily changed from right-hand treadling to left-hand. The weaving width usually ranges from 16 to 24 inches in looms of this type.

(2) *Floor looms.* Floor looms (fig. 7-3) are commonly available with two or four harnesses. The 4-harness loom is the most versatile as it affords a better range from simple to complex activity. A number of makes of looms are available but basically they are very similar.

b. *Weaving Accessories.*

(1) *Spool rack* (fig. 7-4). Frame with rods to hold spools when winding warp directly onto warp beam.

(2) *Skein winder* (fig. 7-5). Adjustable wheels mounted on frame to hold skeins of yarn for winding—also called a swift.

(3) *Warping frame* (fig. 7-6). Heavy wooden frame with pegs at intervals around which warp is wound. Used mainly when warping table looms.

(4) *Warping reel* (fig. 7-7). Wooden reel with pegs at top and bottom around which warp is wound. Used mainly when warping table looms.

(5) *Tension box or guide plate.* Devices to attach to back beam through which the warp threads are threaded when winding a sectional warp (fig. 7-8). The box enables one person to wind a sectional warp as it guides the threads as well as to keep a correct tension. The guide plate just guides.

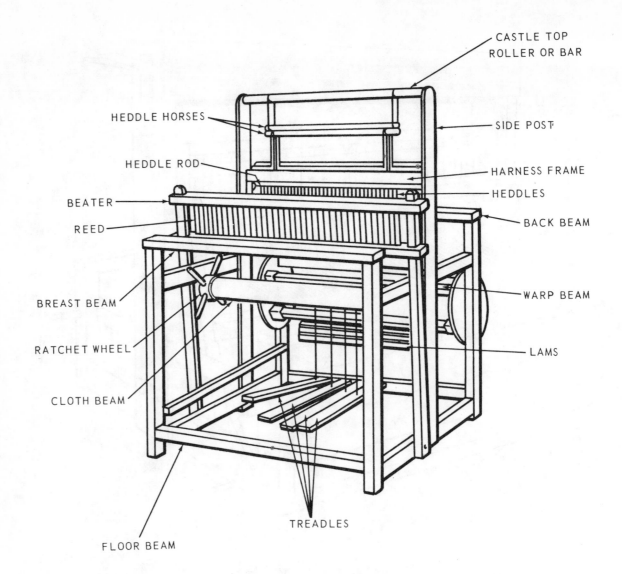

HEDDLE HORSES

HEDDLE ROD

BEATER

REED

BREAST BEAM

RATCHET WHEEL

CLOTH BEAM

FLOOR BEAM

CASTLE TOP
ROLLER OR BAR

SIDE POST

HARNESS FRAME

HEDDLES

BACK BEAM

WARP BEAM

LAMS

TREADLES

Figure 7–3. Floor loom.

(6) *Loom bench* (fig. 7–9). Bench, usually with a hinged cover over a shallow box which holds weaving materials.

(7) *Rug shuttle* (fig. 7–10). A large shuttle used to hold heavy weft and tabby thread for weaving on floor looms.

(8) *Flat shuttle* (fig. 7–11). A flat stick with grooves at the ends for holding light weft threads. Used mainly with table looms.

(9) *Reed hook or sley hook* (fig. 7–12). Slender steel hook used to thread the reed and heddles.

7–4. Weaving Materials

The selection of weight, type of thread, and color of weaving materials depends upon the proposed use of the finished article.

a. Cotton. This material is used extensively in weaving because it is washable, durable, and easy to work with.

(1) Carpet warp is a 4-ply heavy cotton material which may be purchased in 4- or 8-ounce tubes. This material is commonly used for rug warp. Finer cotton material for finer work comes in sizes 20/2, 24/3, etc. The upper part of the fraction refers to the size of the material; the larger the number, the smaller the thread. The lower number refers to the "ply," or the number of strands found in the cross section of the yarn or thread.

(2) It is possible to purchase spools of machine-wound warp which can be slipped onto a rod of the warp beam of the 4-harness table loom. This warp is available in white and in several colors, in fine warp, or in the heavier carpet warp.

162

Figure 7–4. Sppol rack.

Spools of the finer warp have 60 ends apiece, and each strand is 20 yards long. Spools of carpet warp have 30 ends, each 10 yards long. This wound carpet warp is more expensive, and the finer warp is impractical for a busy clinic.

(3) Roving is a 3- or 4-ply soft cotton yarn often used as weft in weaving rugs. It comes in a variety of colors and is usually purchased in 1/4-pound skeins.

(4) A knitting and crochet 4-ply cotton yarn, about the diameter of wool worsted, is frequently used for tabby. It, too, comes in a variety of colors and is purchased in 100-yard skeins, 12 skeins per box.

b. Wool. Four-ply worsted wool is used for afghans and wool scarves. Wool tends to be sticky when used as a warp as it often causes the shed not to be clear. The finer wools are difficult to use for both warp and weft, but they make handsome pieces when used as weft with a cotton warp and tabby.

c. Linen. Linen is nice to use for finger towels, place mats, and dresser scarves. The largest linen

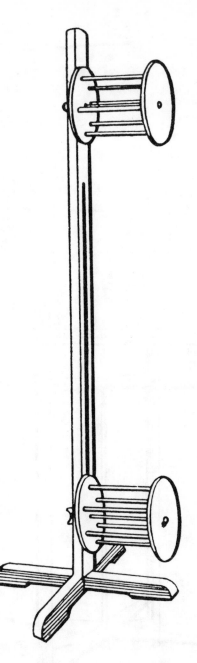

Figure 7–5. Skein winder.

thread is No. 1, the smallest is No. 40/2; therefore, the larger the number, the finer the thread. Linen comes in warp linen and weft linen. Warp linen can be used for both warp and weft; however, weft linen can only be used for weft as it is not strong enough to tolerate the tension of the loom.

d. Synthetics. Nylon and orlon yarns are easier to use for warps than 100 percent wool. Metallic and other novelty materials may be woven to give a dramatic effect. These are only used for weft

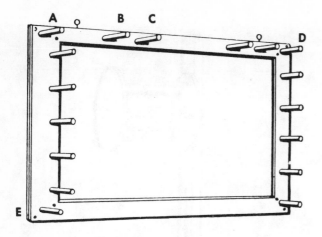

Figure 7-6. Warping frame.

(1) All looms should have loom covers to protect the material from dust.

(2) Cotton and synthetic materials last longer if they are stored in a dry, clean area.

(3) Woolen materials should be protected from moths and should not be packed too tightly. When winding wool yarn from the skein into a ball, a little slack should be allowed to keep the wool from being stretched. Winding the yarn over the fingers, as the ball is held, provides sufficient slack. If a loom has wool warp, the tension should be released when the loom is not in use to keep it from stretching.

7-5. Weaving

There are three basic steps in weaving. First, certain threadles are depressed to form the shed. Second, a weft thread is put into the shed by putting the shuttle through the shed. Third, the beater which pushes the weft thread is pulled into its place in the fabric being woven. Almost endless variations are possible in weaving by putting the warp threads through the dents of the harness in various sequences to make different patterns. By treadling each pattern in different ways, variations of the pattern are possible. Therefore, weaving can be graded from a simple, somewhat mechanical activity to a very complex, absorbing avocation. The techniques and patterns available are so numerous and can be combined in so many ways that people have devoted a lifetime to seeking them out and developing them. Before a loom can be readied for weaving, there must be a plan for warping (or dressing) the loom. First in that plan is the selection of the type of weaving and of the pattern which is to be put on. After a pattern is selected, it usually must be adapted to the loom.

a. Plain or Tabby Weave. This is the simple over-and-under weave (fig. 7-13) such as is done in darning a sock. Only two harnesses are required, but more can be used.

(1) Threading of the 2-harness loom is relatively simple so it can be done quite rapidly and with little chance for error. Weaving patterns are set up on graph paper, with each row representing a harness frame. Row No. 1 represents the harness nearest to the breast beam. The pattern draft is read from right to left so that the first thread of the warp goes into the eye of the first

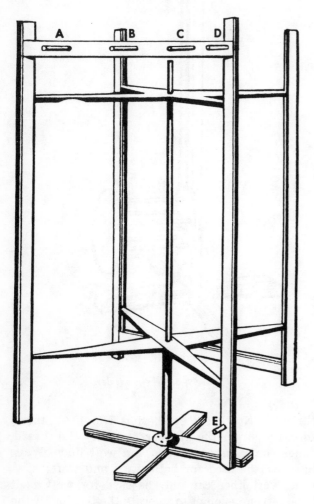

Figure 7-7. Warping reel.

threads as they are uneven, stretch easily, and are not strong.

e. Care and Storage of Equipment Materials.

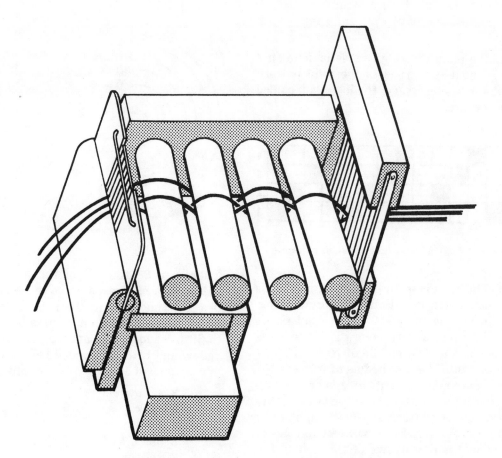

Figure 7-8.   Tension box showing threading.

Figure 7-9.   Loom bench.

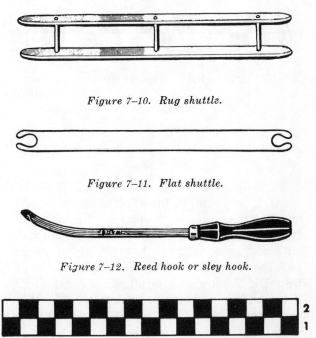

Figure 7-10.   Rug shuttle.

Figure 7-11.   Flat shuttle.

Figure 7-12.   Reed hook or sley hook.

Figure 7-13.   Two-harness plain or tabby pattern.

heddle of harness No. 1. The second thread goes into the eye of the first heddle of harness No. 2. This is continued until all of the warp is threaded.

(2) If the plain or tabby weave is done on a 4-harness loom, it is warped in the twill pattern (fig. 7–14). For tabby weave, the loom is treadled 1–3; 2–4, alternately.

Figure 7–14. Four-harness tabby or twill pattern.

(3) The hounds tooth pattern (fig. 7–15) is one of the interesting variations of plain weaving. The threading is the same 1–2 pattern but use is made of a light and a dark color. The first dark thread is put in the first heddle of harness No. 1 and the second into the first heddle of harness No. 2, etc. Then the first two light threads are threaded in the same manner, and so on. Use two shuttles when weaving this pattern, one with light color weft and one with dark. First, weave two rows of the dark color, then two rows of the light color, continuing in this manner for the desired length.

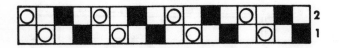

Figure 7–15. Hounds tooth pattern.

(a) When the warp for plaid is being made, it is wound in the selected sequence of colors and the order is maintained throughout the threading of the loom. The plaid pattern must be balanced, however, so that both edges of the cloth look the same. For instance, in the MacLeod plaid below, if the loom were warped as the pattern is listed and using only one repeat, one edge of the cloth would have eight yellow threads and there would be two red threads at the other edge. The pattern is balanced by reversing the sequence of colors in the following manner:

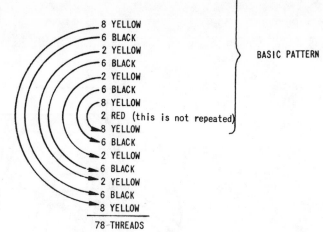

BASIC PATTERN

8 YELLOW
6 BLACK
2 YELLOW
6 BLACK
2 YELLOW
6 BLACK
8 YELLOW
2 RED (this is not repeated)
8 YELLOW
6 BLACK
2 YELLOW
6 BLACK
2 YELLOW
6 BLACK
8 YELLOW

78 THREADS

There are 38 threads in the first repeat of the pattern, 2 red threads in the center, and 38 threads in the second part of the pattern, making a total of 78 threads. The total threads are not enough to fill most looms, so another unit of 2 red and 38 yellow and black are added below, which provides now a warp of 118 threads as follows:

8 yellow
6 black
2 yellow
6 black
2 yellow
6 black
8 yellow
2 red
8 yellow
6 black
2 yellow
6 black
2 yellow
6 black
8 yellow
2 red
8 yellow
6 black
2 yellow
6 black
2 yellow
6 black
8 yellow
118 threads

If more threads are needed, another unit of 4 threads must be added in order to keep the pattern balanced. If the loom will not take 40 more threads, the plaid pattern itself may need to be altered by decreasing, the number of threads

166

throughout the plaid. It then, of course, is not an authentic MacLeod plaid, but rather an adaptation of the MacLeod plaid.

(b) To weave, a shuttle of each color is wound and weaving is done, using the same number and succession of threads which were used in making the warp. For instance, to weave the MacLeod plaid, 8 yellow threads are woven first and the beating of the weft regulated so that a square of yellow is formed in the areas where 8 yellow threads are found in the warp. Six black threads are woven in the same manner. The weft thread is started and ended each time it is used. This is continued until the piece is the desired length.

(c) Following are patterns for some authentic Scotch Tartan plaids:

MacArthur	MacLeod	MacDuff
12 green	8 yellow	20 red
4 black	6 black	5 dark blue
4 green	2 yellow	5 black
12 black	6 black	7 light green
4 green	2 yellow	4 red
4 black	6 black	2 black
12 green	8 yellow	4 red
2 yellow	2 red	
Repeat from top	Repeat from top	Repeat in reverse, starting with 2 black

b. *Twill Weave.* A twill pattern (fig. 7–14) is used frequently in occupational therapy because it is an interesting pattern, it is a step between simple tabby weaving and the more complex patterns, and warping the loom in twill is not difficult. The loom is warped just as it is for 4-harness tabby. Variations can be obtained by treadling in different ways. This can be woven with or without a tabbby thread.

(1) Treadling for plain twill is—
1–2; 2–3; 3–4; 4–1; and repeat, starting at 1–2.

(2) For a herringbone or zigzag pattern, treadle—
1–2; 2–3; 3–4; 4–1; 3–4; 2–3; and repeat, starting at 1–2.

(3) Goose eye is obtained by treadling—
4–1; 3–4; 2–3; 1–2 (repeated the desired number of times) 2–3; 3–4; repeat, starting at 4–1.

c. *Pattern Weaving.* Pattern weaving provides an interesting challenge in selecting a good pattern for the intended use, in fitting the pattern to the loom, and in dressing the looms, as well as the obvious challenge of weaving without error.

(1) Selection of pattern. A small piece, such as a purse, place mat, or dresser scarf, usually is more pleasing if the pattern is small. Bedspreads and rugs look nicer with larger patterns. The size of the pattern is determined by the number of threads in the pattern. For instance, the honeysuckle pattern (fig. 7–16) is 26 threads wide. This is a small pattern and can be repeated several times, even on a small piece. However, some patterns are over 100 threads in length.

Figure 7–16. Honeysuckle pattern.

(2) The number of dents per inch in the reed controls the texture of the cloth. This number is stamped on one end of the reed. If there are only a few dents per inch, the warp threads will be spread far apart and will weave cloth of a coarse texture. If there are more dents per inch, the texture of the cloth will be close and therefore finer. If the reed is coarse and a rather fine cloth is desired, two threads can be put through each dent.

(3) Fitting the pattern to the loom must be done so that the finished piece will be symmetrical. If a rug is to be made on a loom with a reed with 15 dents per inch, 525 threads will be needed to make the rug 35 inches wide (15 x 35 = 525).

(a) If the pattern being considered is 75 threads wide, it will fit exactly.

(b) If the pattern is 60 threads wide, it will be repeated 8 times, but there will be 45 threads left. This will make the piece 32 inches wide. It is possible to add a part of the pattern on each side to accommodate more threads. Care must be taken, though, to make both sides of the piece symmetrical by reversing the addition on one side.

(4) Treadling. When treadling, certain treadles are depressed, which, by their attachment, either raise or lower certain harnesses. The treadling, coupled with the pattern on the loom, determines the woven pattern. Variations in treadling provide variations in the woven pattern. Treadling may be written, for example, as 4–3–1x, then 1–2–6x. The 4–3–1x indicates to the weaver that treadles 4 and 3 are pressed down and the pattern shuttle is put through the shed once. It is then understood that a tabby thread follows the pattern thread in the appropriate tabby treadling. Next, treadles 1–2 are

pressed down and the pattern shuttle is put through the shed, followed by a tabby thread with the appropriate treadling. The number 6 after the 1–2 indicates that 1–2 is repeated six times with a tabby thread between each repeat of the pattern. The treadling for the honeysuckle pattern (fig. 7–17) would be as follows:

        4–3–1x
        3–2–1x
        2–1–1x
        1–4–1x
        4–3–3x
        2–3–3x
        1–2–6x
        2–3–3x
        4–3–3x
        1–4–1x
        1–2–1x
        2–3–1x

If treadling for a pattern is not available it may be woven as "drawn in." This means circling the first two threads on the draft 4 and 3,

then the second and third which would be 3 and 2. Continue in this overlapping manner until the complete repeat is used.

(5) Tabby. In most patterns, a tabby thread is used between each pattern thread to hold the pattern threads in place. Often the tabby is the same weight as a warp thread, or at least is thinner than the pattern thread so that the pattern will dominate. The tabby is wound on a shuttle which is used alternately with the shuttle holding the pattern material. Most patterns are planned so that if the loom is threaded correctly, tabby will be treadled on 1–3 and 2–4. Usually, treadles 1–3 are used when the shuttle is put through the shed from left to right and 2–4 when going from right to left.

7–6. Dressing the loom

This is an involved, precise, often slow process which must be done with care and accuracy. After the weaving patttern has been selected and adapted to the loom, the warp must be made and put on the loom. No matter what make or size

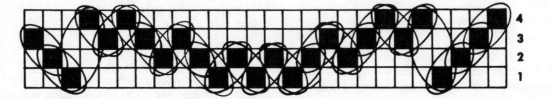

Figure 7–17. Treadling honeysuckle pattern.

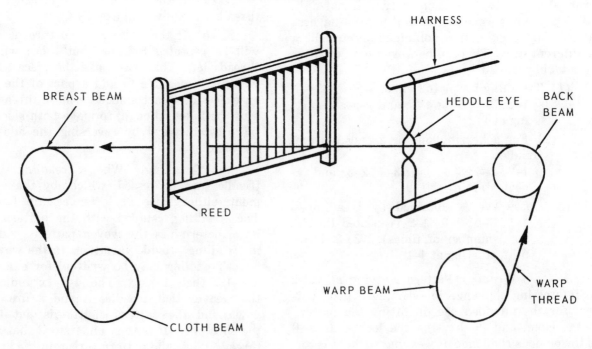

Figure 7–18. Route of each warp thread.

of loom is used or how many threads are in the warp, the aim of dressing the loom is to have each thread follow the route shown in figure 7–18.

a. Use of the Warping Frame and Warping Reel. The process of "making warp" in either the frame or the reel is the same. The frame is used for warp consisting of about 100 threads or less and 10 yards or less in length. The reel is for a 100–300 thread warp, 6 yards to 20 or 25 yards in length. Longer warps are done by sectional beaming. Warp on either the frame or reel is made in the following manner:

(1) Determine the length of the warp and make a guide string the length that the warp is to be, but of a contrasting color.

(2) Tie the guide string on peg A (fig. 7–19); go under B and over C and D.

(3) Continue around enough of the pegs on the frame to end of peg E with the desired warp length. Tie off. On the reel, continue enough revolutions to reach the desired length on peg E and tie off.

(4) Begin the actual warp by tying to peg A and follow the guide string to peg E, then reverse back to peg D—go over it, *under* C, and *over* B, making A cross between pegs B and C.

(5) Continue this procedure until the desired number of threads are wound.

(6) To secure the lease or cross made by the threads between pegs B and C, place lease sticks in the same position as the B and C pegs so that the cross of threads between these pegs is kept in place. The cross helps the warp threads to be tied in or threaded into the loom in the correct sequence. Tie each end of the lease sticks (fig. 7–20①). The cross may also be secured with a string (fig. 7–20②) or with tongue depressors with the ends taped together.

b. Chaining the Warp. The procedure for removing the warp from a warping board or reel is called chaining. Remove the warp from the bottom peg, loop the warp over the hand, pull the section marked 2 (fig. 7–21) through the loop; then through that loop, pull another section of warp; and so on. This is like making a crochet chain using the hand as a crochet hook. Chain

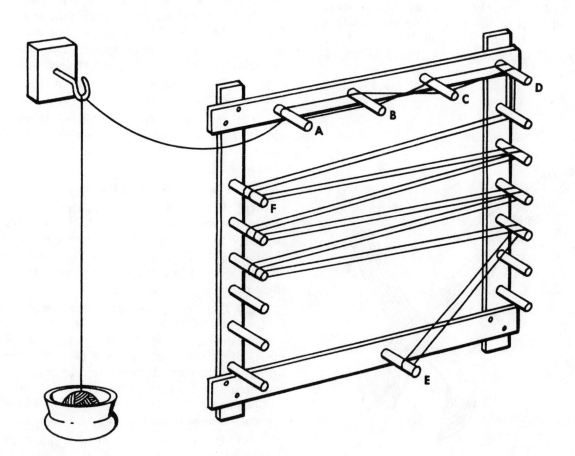

Figure 7–19. A warping frame with warp.

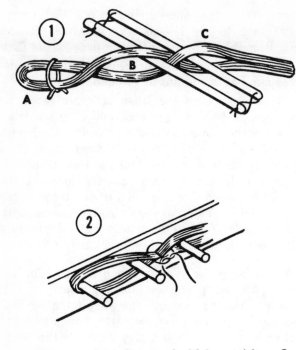

Figure 7-20. *Cross ① secured with lease sticks or ② tied with a string.*

off all the warp on the board up to the lease. Tie the last loop to the remaining warp with a contrasting string. *Do not* pull the end of the warp through the last loop as it will be impossible then to release the chain.

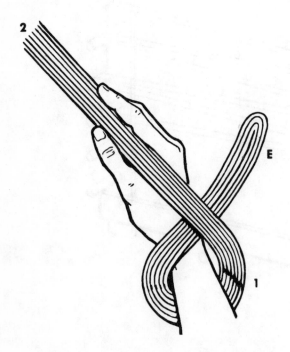

Figure 7-21. *Starting to chain a warp.*

c. Sectional Beaming. This is winding the warp directly from the spools on a spool rack on to the warp beam. It has definite advantages over either of the other methods, especially when winding very long, wide warps. Sectional beaming can be done only on looms equipped with sectional warp beams. Today many looms have these. It is a simple matter to convert the ordinary warp beam into a sectional one, if desired. The sectional warp beam differs from the ordinary beam because it is divided into sections by equally spaced dowels. The sections are made by wooden pegs, usually 4, set equidistant around the beam. The warp lies in these sections instead of being spread evenly along the beam. This method of warping is a distinct time-saver and is most satisfactory if properly done. Perhaps its only disadvantage is that it requires sometimes as many as 40 or 60 spools of warp of one size and color. Unless the weaver plans to weave a number of articles with the same warp, it requires a considerable financial outlay, as the complete spool yardage is not required for a single warping of a loom. The spools may weigh 2 to 8 ounces. Cones cannot be used satisfactorily because of their shape. The warp does not pull off of the cone easily. The procedure for doing sectional beaming is as follows:

(1) Decide upon the width of the article to be woven.

(2) Determine the number of threads required to weave the article, which will be the desired width of the article multiplied by the number of dents per inch.

(3) Find the center of the reed.

(4) From the center, measure to the left along the reed a distance of half the width of the piece to be woven. Measure the same distance to the right. This will center the woven piece on the loom. Place pieces of colored thread in these dents as markers.

(5) Cut two pieces of thread long enough to tie onto the breast beam, pass through the marked dents, and tie onto the warp beam. These pieces of thread must run in a perfectly straight line from the breast beam to the warp beam; they must not angle. These threads mark the sections on the sectional warp beam within which the warp will be wound.

(6) Divide the total number of ends required by the number of sections lying inside the pieces of thread. It may be that one or two

of the sections will require one less or one more thread than the rest of the sections.

NOTE

Looms which come equipped with a sectional warp beam are usually constructed with a roller which is a yard around. Most of these also have a gauge to measure the yardage.

On a converted warp beam, it may be necessary to wind a guide string the lenghh of the warp around the beam. Tnis will give you the number of turns which are needed to wind the warp to the length desired. You should train yourself from the beginning to start and stop the turns at some specified place (as, for instance, when the handle is at the bottom of the turn). The same number of turns should be used to fill all the sections to prevent one section from running out of thread and thereby wasting all of the warp on the other sections.

(7) Place the number of spools needed for each section on the spool rack, with all ends coming from the spools in the same direction, preferably from under the spool. If possible, place spools on every other row on the spool rack and allow thread to pass under the empty rod below. Be careful to do this or to see that it is done or twisting will ensue when the winding begins. Place the spool rack about 4 feet away from the back of the loom.

(8) Place the tension box in position (fig. 7–8). If a tension box is used, thread it as shown, or follow the directions that came with it. Start with the spool on the lower left-hand side of the spool rack and thread the end through the lower left hole in the guide. Continue putting the threads through in rotation from the left side. Be careful to take them in order and to avoid crossing them, for if they are crossed, they will break during the winding. When this process is finished, each thread will be in the same position coming through the plate as the spool is on the spool rack.

NOTE

Fastened to each section on the beam is a tape or cord wo which the warp threads are tied. The tapes or cords not in use should be wound around their section and attached in such a way that they will not flop as the warp is wound.

At this point, it is a good idea to check the direction in which the warp beam should be turned so that the dog will engage correctly in the ratchet wheel to hold the warp at a tension. Some beginners have had the misfortune to turn the warp beam in the wrong direction for the entire winding and others have wound some of the sections in one direction and some in the other. This error complicates things considerably and necessitates rewinding the warp.

(9) After threading all ends from the spool rack through a tension box or through the guide tie them into the loop of tape or cord fastened to the section to be wound first. There is no rule governing which section should be filled first. This is sometimes guided by the colors being used. To prevent undue stress on the warp beam, it is advisable to wind the first section, then the last, alternating back and forth until all sections are filled.

(10) After securely fastening the warp ends to the cord and determining the number of turns, begin the actual winding of the warp onto the beam. Take care to insure that the groups of threads are centered in the section and not piled up near the pegs or in the center. If a very long warp is being wound, it is wise to pound the wound warp gently with a mallet after each 10 to 15 turns to be certain it is not piling up.

(11) After the required number of turns have been made and the first section has been filled, spread a piece of masking tape across the threads while it is still taut. Cut the warp above the tape and secure it to the wound section with another piece of tape. This keeps the threads in the position in which they came from the tension box and were wound around the warp beam.

(12) Untie the cord for the next section, tie the group of warp ends just cut to the loop, and wind the section. Proceed until all sections have been wound. The loom is now ready to be threaded and sleyed, in that order.

d. Sleying the Loom. Sleying the loom is the process of putting the warp threads through the dents of the reed in succession. The reed separates the warp threads evenly and later is used to pack the weft threads in place to make cloth. The process of sleying is standard but, with a chained warp, the threads are sleyed from the front of the loom toward the back before they are put through the heddles. If it is a sectional warp, the warp threads are put through the heddles first on the warp beam at the back of the loom and then through the dents of the reed from the back toward the front of the loom.

(1) If the warp is chained, lay the lease sticks and the warp chain on top of the breast beam of the loom, with the beginning of the warp toward the reed. Place the chain in a box on a chair so it cannot get dirty or make much of a pull on the ends of the warp. Cut through the ends of the loops which were at the beginning of the board.

(2) If the warp is sectional, note that each thread will be in a heddle. Center the warp in the reed and proceed to sley.

(a) *Centering the warp in the reed.* The warp can be the full width of the reed or any width less than this. It should always be as near to the center of the reed as possible. To center the warp, figure the number of dents in the entire reed by multiplying the dents per inch by the length of the reed (exclude the flat pieces at the end). Then figure the number of dents needed for the number of warp threads and subtract this number from the total number of dents. Divide this number by 2 and leave the number of dents obtained empty at each end. Example: If the reed should happen to have 200 dents and there are 160 warp threads which are to be sleyed 2 threads to the dent, 80 dents will be needed. Subtract 80 from 200 leaves 120 dents that will not be used. That means that there will be 60 empty dents on each side.

(b) *Sleying.* Sleying is a very simple process, but it is easy to make mistakes and difficult to correct them, if they are not caught immediately. Too many threads in a dent or a missed dent will make an ugly streak for the full length of the web, so it must be corrected. Most people use a hook for sleying. It should be held with the slotted side down and the threads drawn through the reed with a downward cutting motion. It is easier to sley from right to left for right-handed persons. The first thread or first two threads should be put as they come from the lease stick through the dent on the right where the material is to begin. The next thread is taken from the lease stick and put through the next dent. Threading is easier and time is saved if two people work together. One person stands at the front reed and takes each thread in succession from the lease sticks, first a thread from over the first stick, then a thread from over the second stick, and so on. The other person stands in back of the loom or between the harnesses and the back beam, putting the threading hook through the dent to receive the warp thread; then, as the first person places the thread over the hook, the second person draws it through

to the rear. During sleying, the beater should stand in an upright position between the heddles and the breast beam. It may be fastened in place by cords before the sleying begins or may be anchored by a loop knot tied in the first group of threads sleyed.

e. *Threading the Loop.* Threading is the process of putting the warp threads through the heddles in a sequence to produce the desired pattern. To determine the pattern, see paragraph 7–5.

(1) With a chained warp, the threads have been put through the dents of the reed so that the ends lie behind the reed but in front of the harness. The next step is to thread each one through a heddle in the harness, in the order devised to produce the desired pattern.

(2) The sectional warp is on the warp beam and the threads are secured in order with a tape. The beam is fixed with the ratchet to keep it from turning. With the tape still around the warp, two turns are unwound from the warp beam and the threads are laid in order over the back beam. Keeping the threads in order prevents them from being crossed or twisted, which interferes with smooth weaving. Tension of the warp between the warp beam and the back beam should be maintained, then the threads should be stuck in order to the back beam with tape. The tape at the end of the threads may now be removed. The threads are in order across the back beam and are 1 to 1 1/2 yard long so that they can be threaded through the heddles.

(3) This process is easiest with two people, one in back of the loom choosing the correct thread and the second person at the front of the loom picking out the next heddle on the correct harness. The threading hook is again used with the slot side down.

(4) To avoid and correct mistakes early in threading, it is wise to check at the end of each repeat of pattern or possibly every 10 or 20 threads. One person should read off the pattern while the other checks. Before passing on to the next repeat or group of threads, one should take this particular group and catch them together with a loop knot to keep them from falling out of the heddles.

NOTE

Some patterns require many more heddles on one harness than on another and it is desirable to calculate the number of heddles needed on each harness before the threading is begun.

(5) Any adjustments that are needed should be made at this time. It is far simpler to move heddles before any threading has been done. If there are extra heddles on any harness, these should be divided with half on one side and half on the other side of the harness, or preferably removed from the harness so that the harness will not hang unevenly.

(6) After sleying is complete and any corrections have been made, the apron is pulled over the breast beam. The threads are separated into ten or twelve groups or into as many groups as there are loops or holes in the apron and the groups tied to the apron or rod, starting at the center. The knot is made as in figure 7-22. The tension of the threads should be kept even within the group and the tension of each group should be the same as that of the other groups.

Figure 7-22. Steps in tying warp to apron or rod.

f. Beaming the Warp. Beaming the warp means putting the warp onto the warp beam. This has been described with the sectional warp but not with the chained warp. To get the

chained warp on the warp beam, proceed as follows:

(1) Attach the warp threads to the apron of the warp reel at the back of the loom. To do this, pull the threads through from the back of the harness until they can easily reach the apron. Even them up and divide them into as many sections as there are loops or slits in the apron. Start with those groups at the middle of the apron and tie them through the slits in the apron or to the rod attached to the warp beam.

(2) At the front of the loom, run the fingers through the warp until all tangles in the first 2 feet of warp have been smoothed out. Then roll the warp beam back until the warp begins to roll around the beam. Keeping the tension taut, lay a heavy paper; 3 or 4 thicknesses of newspaper; or, preferably, a narrow, rather flat stick over the row of tied knots so as to true up the warp and prevent an uneven start. The secret of good warping is to keep the warp firm, taut, and even (fig. 7-23).

(3) For this step, get another person to work with you. One of you stands at the back of the loom to wind the warp around the warp beam. The other stands at the front of the loom, pulls out the tangles, and holds the warp taut while it is being wound.

(4) To free the warp of tangles, pull the warp out at the front of the loom. Untangle 2 or 3 feet at a time. Take half of the threads in each hand. Run the fingers through the tangles of the first 3 feet of warp. Keep pulling and

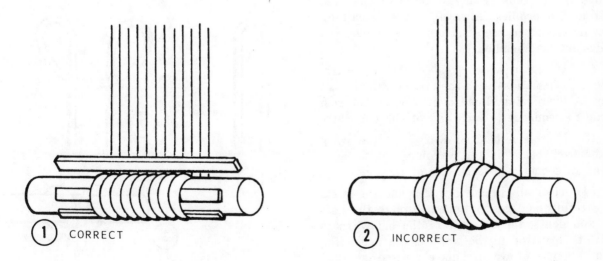

Figure 7-23. Correct and incorrect winding of warp.

combing until the warp is smooth and free from tangles. Shaking the warp vigorously also helps. If the threads are either very fine or have little tensile strength, they will have to be treated very gently during this process. The person at the front of the loom holds the warp with both hands pulling it taut while the other pserson winds up the warp that has been untangled.

CAUTION

The warp must not be allowed to slide through the hands. When new tangles reach the reed, the process must be repeated. Continue to use heavy paper or flat sticks which are longer than the warp is wide under each new round. The sticks should measure 1/8 inch thick and not less than 1/2 inch wide. Their purpose is to prevent a pileup of warp on one part of the beam and to keep all the threads and the tension even.

(5) Continue this process until only 2 feet of ends remain in front of the reed. Untangle this remaining warp, trim it to an even length, separate the ends into as many groups as there are loops in the apron, and tie the groups to the apron (or rod) starting at the center of each end (fig. 7–22).

g. Tying On. Tying on is a short cut which may be employed when rewarping the loom. It should be used with discretion, however, for with this method, any errors in the old warp are carried over to the new. It should therefore be used only if the old warp had no errors or if all errors have been corrected.

(1) When the warp is nearly used, do not remove the threads from the dents of the reed or from the heddles. Always tie the remaining warp in groups to keep it from being pulled out of the dents and heddles.

(2) If the new warp is a chained warp, place the lease sticks with the cross on the breast beam as for sleying. Instead of sleying, tie each thread in sequence to each end of the old warp.

(3) If it is a beamed warp, put the warp on the back beam as for warping and tie each thread in sequence to each end of the old warp.

(4) After all threads are tied and the knots are carefully and gently pulled through the heddles and dents, tie the ends of the old warp to the cloth beam or to the warp beam, depending upon the type of warp. This old warp is called a dummy warp and it saves warp.

h. Gaiting the Loom. Gaiting the loom is adjusting the loom and is usually necessary after the loom is warped.

(1) *Cord used.* The cord used in loom tie-ups should be a woven cord of linen, if possible, and not too heavy. A cord used in upholstry or a heavy varnished cord used in deepsea fishing is suitable, as are the more expensive heavy grades of Jacquard cord.

(2) *Adjustment of harnesses.* The counterbalanced 4-harness loom has a large roller at the top from which are suspended two small rollers or heddle horses. Two long double cords should be attached to the small back roller with two loops attached to the large top roller. The double cords should pass once around the large top roller and be tied into the loops on the small roller by means of the snitch knot (fig. 7–24). The cords should not be nailed to the large roller. The small roller should hang about halfway between the tops of the harness frames and the large roller. When these first ties have been made and the small rollers leveled, they should be tied together to keep them in place. In the same manner, again with the snitch knot, the 4-harness frames should be hung in pairs from the small rollers. The harnesses should hang at the level which permits the warp to pass from the back beam to the breast beam in a straight line. If the warp is deflected upward, the harnesses hang too high. The threads should come through the center of the reed.

(3) *Adjustment to lams.* When the harness have been hung at the correct level, they should be tied to keep them in place while the tieup is made to the lams and treadles.

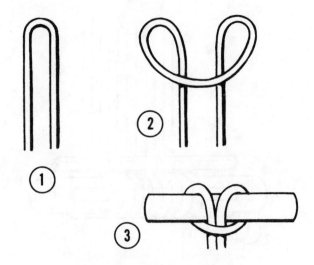

Figure 7–24. Tying a snitch knot.

NOTE

The lams are a set of levers attached to one or the other of the uprights of the loom. They are attached a foot or more below the harnesses and extend across the bank of the treadles. The lams are used to bring down the harnesses evenly. If treadles were attached directly to the harnesses, all treadles except the one at the center would pull down the harnesses at a slant. A cord from the center of each harness frame is attached to the corresponding lam, and the tie is made with the snitch knot. A chain may be used here instead of cord. The lams are given a slight upward slant to keep them from stacking against the outer treadles when the sheds are opened. When they have been adjusted correctly, they are tied together to keep them in position while the tieup to the treadles is being made.

(4) *Treadle tieup.* The correct tieup to the treadles differs with the weave and with the type of loom used. With many weaves, one lam is tied to several treadles. This depends on the tieup given for the pattern and will be indicated with the pattern. The exact height at which the treadles are tied is left to the discretion of the weaver. They must be high enough to open a shed wide enough to permit the easy passage of the shuttle, yet not so high that the weaver's knee hits the apron or the web as he reaches for the treadle. After the height has been decided on, pieces of wood or books are placed under the treadles to keep them in opsition while the snitch knots are tied.

7–7. Weaving Process and Techniques

After the pattern is selected and adapted to the loom, the warp is made, and the loom is threaded, gaited, and checked, the actual weaving can be started.

a. Basic Steps. Although the weaving process is not complex, good weaving requires know-how and skill which can be developed only by practice and attention to details. These steps are basic for all types of weaving.

(1) Depress the levers. These levers may be foot treadles or hand levers or they may require turning the roller on a Peacock loom. The levers change the position of the harnesses which sep-

arate the threads into a shed. If the harnesses are threaded with a pattern, the threads are separated so as to make the pattern.

(2) Put the shuttle through the shed. This deposits a weft or tabby thread between the two layers of warp threads. The newly placed weft thread should be pulled with enough tension to have it lie against the edge warp threads, but it should not pull them together, as this practice will make the woven piece become narrow. If the thread is left at a slant, rather than parallel to the warp, the selvage of the woven piece will be more even.

(3) Pull the beater. The metal pieces of the sley push the weft to the desired place against the outer weft threads.

(4) Repeat from (1) above.

b. Use of Filler. When the warp is tied to the apron, spaces are left between the groups of threads. These spaces are eliminated by weaving, in tabby pattern, with heavy scrap material such as rags or ends of roving. This filler should be left in loops at the selvage edge in order to allow the groups of threads at each edge to spread in both directions. Scrap material is used because the filler is removed after the weaving is completed. The gaps between the bunches of warp threads decrease in size as more of the filler is put in. The filler must continue to be woven until the warp threads are evenly spaced across the loom and the edges are spread out to the same width as that of the reed.

c. Heading. After the filler, the tabby thread is started, and it, too, is woven in plain weave. The resulting fabric is called heading. It provides a firm base for the fringe at the end of the piece or if the piece is to be hemmed, the heading is made larger so that it can be used as turnover in the hem. The heading is not removed so, if the weft has much thickness, it should be started in the conventional manner as in *d* below.

d. Starting of Weft Thread. The thread is untwisted to separate the several strands which make up the weft thread. Then it is split in half for about 2 inches. The shuttle is sent through the shed, and when the split end gets to the first strings on the edge, one part of the split weft is pulled up through the warp threads, and the other part is bent around the first warp string on the edge and then back into the shed (fig. 7–25).

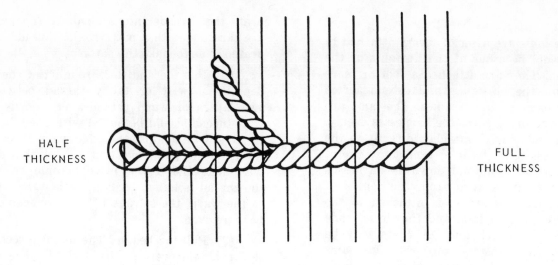

HALF
THICKNESS

FULL
THICKNESS

Figure 7–25. Starting weft.

e. Body. After the heading is complete, the body of the piece is started.

(1) If the woven piece is to be done in plain weave, which does not require the use of a tabby thread, the thread used in the heading is ended as in *h* below, and the weaving thread is begun as in *d* above.

(2) For pattern weaving, the tabby thread is continued as started in the heading, but between each tabby shot a pattern thread is put in, using the treadling selected to make the desired pattern.

f. Techniques of Beating. Different fabrics require different techniques in beating but, no matter what the technique, the beating must be consistent and even in order to produce fine cloth. The beater must be pulled with the same amount of strength each time and must be grasped so as to insure equal pressure on all areas. It may be pulled with both hands on the beater equidistant from the edges or, if pulled with one hand, grasped in the center.

(1) Hand looms with cotton warp often beat better if the beater is used with a gentle snap.

(2) When heavy fabric is made such as that found in rugs, the beater can be pulled back rather hard. For an extra firm beat, the shed is changed and the fabric is beat again before putting the shuttle through in the new shed.

(3) If wool is used, the beating must be *very* gentle—often just the weight of the beater is enough. If the beater is pulled with too much force, the weft packs too tightly and the piece is hard instead of soft, as it should be.

g. Splicing of Weft. During the weaving, new lengths of weft need to be added. Because knots would show if they were woven into the fabric, splicing is done. There are a number of ways to splice, but only one can be considered here. The strands of the weft in the shed of the loom are separated and half of them are cut off at different lengths. The same thing is done with the end of the piece being started. The cut ends in the shed are overlapped and the beater is pulled. If strips of color are being used, the weft of one color should be ended in the last row of that color; then, the new color is started in the next row. Ending the weft is done in the same way as starting.

h. Ending of Weft Thread. When the piece is the desired length (and a pattern is ended), the pattern thread is ended and woven in the same amount of heading as was woven at the start. It is also wise to add more filler to hold the heading in place and keep it from raveling. When all weaving is completed, the tension on the back ratchet wheel is removed, and the woven piece is pulled forward until the end of the weaving reaches the breast beam. All tension on the warp threads must be loosened, including the weight of the woven piece. The warp threads are cut, leaving enough length in the piece to tie for fringe, if that is the plan. Groups of warp coming through the dents of the beater are *immediately* tied together into four or five loose knots against the beater so that they will not be pulled from the beater (fig. 7–26). After the warp is secured against the beater, the rug is untied from the apron.

i. Finishing of Woven Pieces. The proper fin-

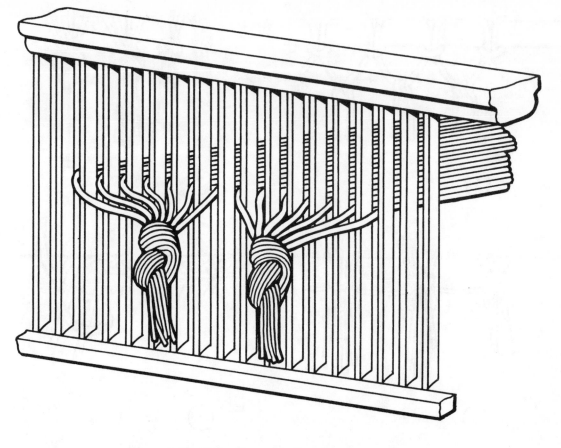

Figure 7-26. Tying the warp after removing weaving.

ishing of woven pieces is an important part of the finished product. The filler is removed from one end either in entirety or in as much as can be tied immediately. Figure 7-27 shows examples of types of knots and fringes which can be used.

j. Correction of Errors. It is unusual to dress a loom without making errors. A loom is not completely warped until it is checked and all errors are corrected. After the loom is warped and the warp is tied down, it is checked by weaving with filler on tabby treadling. In most patterns, the tabby treadling will produce an over-and-under simple weave. If inconsistencies in the simple weave are at regular intervals, they are probably a part of the pattern; if not, they indicate errors in threading. Some of the more common mistakes and ways in which they can be corrected are—

(1) If a group of warp threads become twisted between the back beam and the heddle, it is usually worth the time to remove the twisted ones from the dents and heddles, straighten them out, and rethread them according to the pattern.

(2) Heddles may become crossed if they are

not put on the frame carefully. If it is feasible, the crossed heddles should be slipped off of the frame and uncrossed. If this process would involve too much time, one of the crossed heddles should be cut and removed from the frame.

(3) Threads may be crossed between the heddles and the shed. Both threads must be pulled from the dents and rethreaded correctly. Sometimes several of the warp threads may need to be resleyed to correct the rror.

(4) If there are errors in threading the heddles, it is usually expedient to remove all threads from the beginning of the error and rethread them correctly. This is why it is advisable to check for errors frequently. If a new heddle is needed, see (5) below.

(5) Sometimes a great deal of rethreading can be avoided if a string heddle can be added in a certain place on the harness. To make this, a piece of regular cotton warp string is measured to twice the length of a regular heddle, plus about 4 inches. The string is doubled and hung evenly over the top heddle rod. One knot is tied in the two pieces of string exactly level with the

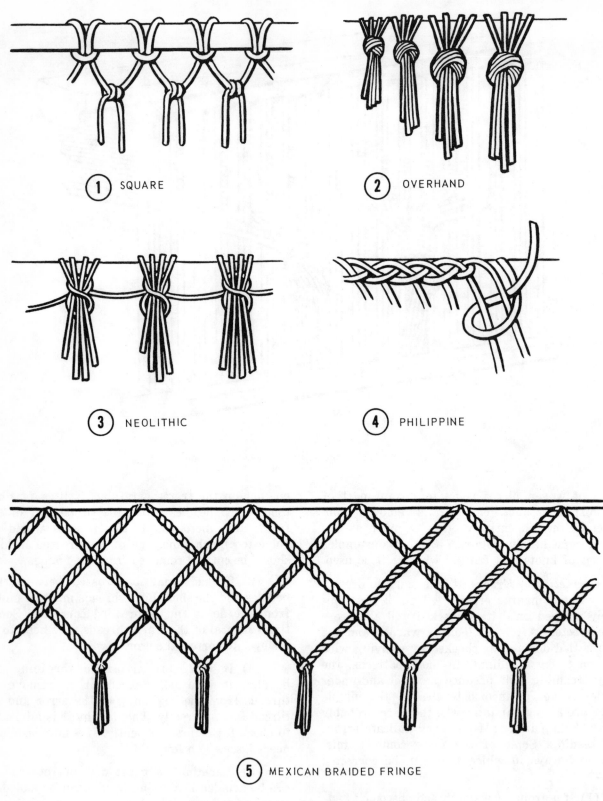

Figure 7-27. Types of knots used for fringes.

top part of the eye of the regular heddle. Another knot is tied in the two pieces of string exactly level with the lower part of the eye of the regular heddle. Then the two pieces of the heddle are tied together under the bottom heddle rod (fig. 7-28).

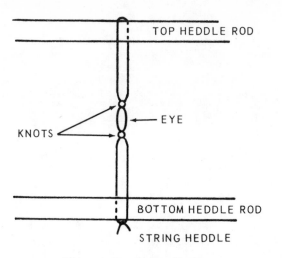

TOP HEDDLE ROD

EYE

KNOTS

BOTTOM HEDDLE ROD

STRING HEDDLE

Figure 7–28. String heddle.

(6) If a dent is left empty while sleying or if two threads (instead of the intended one) are put into a dent, the threads must be resleyed from the error to the nearest edge as the mistake will be noticeable in the weaving.

(7) Broken warp threads are fixed with replacement threads rather than with knots. When a broken warp thread occurs, a matching thread long enough to complete the length of the woven piece is cut. It is threaded through the heddle and beater and pinned down in position on the woven piece. The other end is tied with a bow knot to the end of the broken thread at the back beam. When the bow knot reaches the heddles, it is tied back again to the back beam. This procedure is continued until the web is complete.

CAUTION

Do not break off the broken warp thread.

After the woven piece is removed from the loom, the end of the broken warp thread is rethreaded and included in the warp as it is tied to the apron.

(8) Faulty tension of the warp threads can cause a poor shed and/or uneven weaving. This should not occur if the warp is put on the beam well, if the group of warp threads are tied to the apron with even tension, and if the beating of the piece is done with equal force on all parts of the beater. If many threads become loose while the piece is being woven, they may be made tighter by putting a folded piece of paper between the loose threads and the back beam. After the piece being woven is completed and removed from the loom, the paper should be removed. If the tension is too uneven, the warp may need to be removed from the beam and rewound with more care.

CHAPTER 8

CORD KNOTTING OR MACRAME

8–1. General

a. Cord knotting or macrame is of Arabic origin and has been an art since ancient times. Through the years it seems to have been used most extensively in France, but in recent times, it is finding its way into other countries. Interesting changes in designs have occurred as a result of such travel. There has been a revival of this art with new innovations of color and texture to make unusually interesting and creative wall hangings, decorations, and tote bags.

b. Cord knotting is not difficult to learn for there are just a few basic knots, but the skill of good work lies in making the knots all of the same tension and making each of the heads lie in the desired direction. This skill is the result of practice and careful work. The art of cord knotting is in developing pleasing designs with various knots, colors, and textures.

8–2. Use of Frames or Hooks

Square knotting can be done on a frame or on one of several kinds of hooks.

a. The top of the back piece is separate and is held to the base piece by wingnuts attached to two long bolts inserted from the bottom, which go up through the back and the removable top piece. The bolts extend 3/4 to 1 inch above the top piece in order to hold the wingnuts. The slot between the fixed and movable pieces of the back forms a vise-like arrangement for holding a buckle or for holding a project after it is started. On the top of this removable piece, brads or finishing nails are set in a semioval shape (fig. 8–1). The strands are looped over these brads when pieces are started. Eight or ten cuts 3/4 inch deep and 3/8 inch apart are made with a coping saw in the front upright of the frame. These cuts hold taut the strands or core around which the knot is made, so they must

be of a size to hold the cords firmly. The cord knotting frames must have strong firm joints because of the pull exerted between the front and back uprights. They should also be well sanded and finished with shellac or varnish.

b. Instead of a frame, it is possible to tie the work to a firm object, then secure the strands in a hook of some type, tied around the waist.

(1) The hook may be made of plastic (fig. 8–2) or of wood. The slit must be made so that it will hold two strands of the cord firmly.

(2) Another hook can be made by driving a 20d (4-inch) nail through a wooden block and then bending back the pointed end of the nail to hold the cords. Strings to fasten around the waist are attached to the block which holds the nail in place. The block expedites locating the bent nail. It is possible to bend the point of the nail and tie the strings around the nailhead and then around the waist.

8–3. Materials

Materials for cord knotting are relatively few and inexpensive.

a. Cord used for cord knotting, belts, and purses must have a high twist, be hard, be strong, and must not stretch or be "springy." The finer the cord, the finer, more delicate, and time consuming is the work. The cords most commonly used for this purpose are—

Navy cord
Derry cable cord
Macrame cord
Belfast cord or dreadnaught cord
Sein cord

It is also possible to use strong, high-twist silk, rayon, cotton or linen, but they are rather small, and working with them is tedious. For wall hangings, jute, worsted yarn, mohair yarn, roving, or any material with the desired color and texture is used with interesting results.

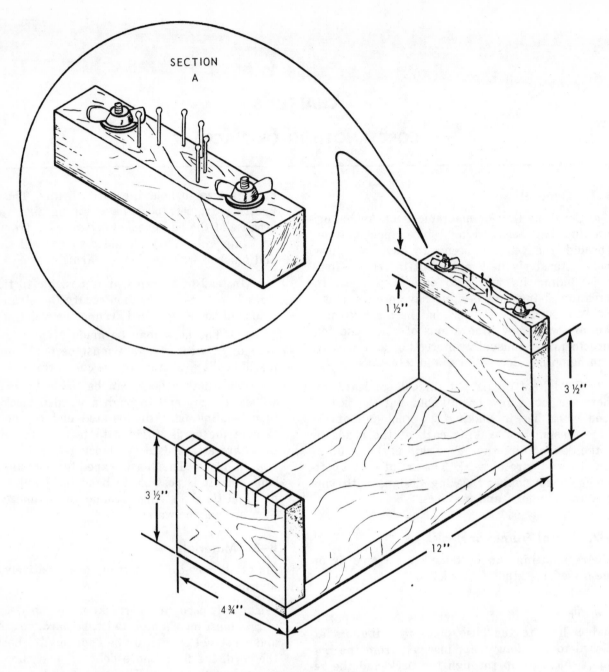

Figure 8–1. Cord knotting frame.

b. Almost any type of buckle can be used if a belt is to be made. They may be nice and handmade of silver or wood, or they may be plain and nickel-finished.

c. If a purse or bag is to be made with a handle, the cords can be fixed to rings, to a purse frame, or to a selected handle.

8–4. Processes

a. It is desirable, especially with a small pro-

ject, to cut the cords sufficiently long to eliminate the need to splice. Because each cord is folded over in the center (middle), it should be eight times as long as the length of the finished project. A 36-inch belt should have 8-yard strands, each of which is coupled to form two 4-yard strands. Because it takes four strands to make a knot, the total number of double strands should be a multiple of four such as 4, 8, 12, 36, and 44. To prevent the long cords from tang-

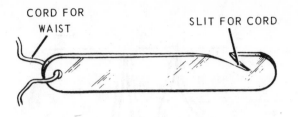

Figure 8-2. Plastic cord knotting hook.

ling, they can be individually wound on shuttles, rolled up and held with elastics, or chained up with a very loose crochet loop. If a patient were working on shoulder or elbow motion, the strand would not be so shortened, as shortening decreases the motion obtained.

b. Starting the project is one of the more complicated and important processes. It may be done in two ways—

(1) Starting may be from a foundation such as a belt buckle, whistle loop, key ring, purse frame, or taut cord. In starting this way, the cords to be knotted are middled and secured to the foundation with a knot. To tie the beginning knot, the loop (formed when the cord was middled) is placed over the foundation and the ends of the cord pulled up under the foundation and through the loop (fig. 8-3). The desired number of strands are knotted to the foundation.

(2) It is possible to start an article which has a pointed end, such as a belt or a cigarette case, at the point, using brads or finishing nails to anchor the strands. To insure a multiple of four in the number of strands, an even number of nails must be used. To do this, two nails are put at the tip of the triangle, two strands are middled and hung over two small nails as shown in figure 8-4. Using the inside strands as the core, a square knot is made with the two outside strands.

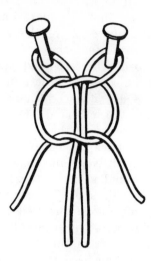

Figure 8-4. Starting at the pointed end.

Figure 8-5. Adding strands to the beginning knot.

A double strand is added on each side over a nail sightly below the square knot just tied. Then, using each double strand and the two adjoining strands, a square knot is made on each side as shown in figure 8-5. After adding each set of double strands, the strands are removed from the nails and the knots pulled up taut to tighten the loop formed by the nailhead. Adding strands are continued until the belt is the desired width, with any square knots that are necessary made in the center of the belt.

c. The basic square knot can be made in two ways. (A skilled person executes both with ease and accuracy.) In the first method, the square knot is made in two movements; in the second, the knot is made in one operation. However, it is best for the beginner to learn these methods in sequence.

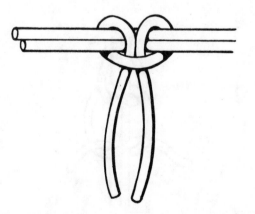

Figure 8-3. Beginning knot.

(1) The half knot, also called the macrame knot, is the basic knot of square knotting. It is tied around the two cords of the warp or core. Four strands are used, the center two being used as the core. The left-hand strand (1) is looped across the core and is left in a horizontal position (fig. 8–6). The right-hand strand (2) is brought over the left-hand (1) on the right-hand side, parallel with the core (fig. 8–7). It is then passed under the core and up through the loop made with No. 1 on the left (fig. 8–8). Both cords are pulled until the knot is tight. This makes the half knot. The square knot consists of two half knots, one tied from the left as shown in figure 8–6 and the other tied in the same manner, but from the right; that is, the right-hand cord, now No. 1, is looped over the core; No. 2 is brought down over No. 1 parallel to the core, then under the core, and up through the loop made with No. 1 on the right (fig. 8–9). Both cords are then pulled up tightly. A series of alternating left-hand knots from a Solomon bar (fig. 8–10). This is the basic knot which is the reason for the name "square knotting." If a series of identical knots are made without alternating left and right, the bar will spiral, forming what is called a twisted or Bannister bar (fig. 8–11).

(2) The second method of tying the square knot is more complicated and difficult to learn, but it is much faster once it is mastered. Four strands are used in this method also, but the entire square knot is tied with one procedure rather than with two. The first step is to take the left-hand cord (1, A, fig. 8–12) up over the two center cords, forming a loop over them. The thumb and index finger are next placed through the loop,

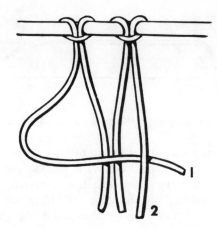

Figure 8–7. Continuing the half knot.

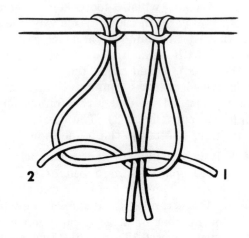

Figure 8–8. Completing the half knot.

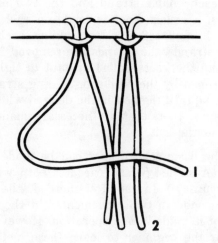

Figure 8–6. Starting the half knot.

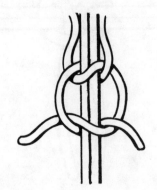

Figure 8–9. Square knot made from two half knots.

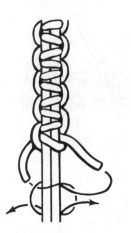

Figure 8–10. Basic square knot in series (Solomon bar).

Figure 8–11. Bannister bar.

and the two ends of this left-hand cord are pulled under the core and up through the loop (B, fig. 8–12). Next, the right-hand strand (2, C, fig. 8–12) is passed through the two loops made in the step above. Strand No. 1 and the loop marked No. 3 in C, figure 8–12 are pulled down and out simultaneously until the work appears as in D, figure 8–12. The first half of the knot is then pulled tightly, followed by the second half. In pulling these knots, it is important to pull them with equal power and with both hands in a corresponding position to the work. If the right hand pulls from a position 6 inches above the work and the left hand is 2 inches below the work, the knots will not be even and the pattern will be distorted.

(3) The square knot is the unit which is repeated to make a fabric. The basic fabric is made with rows of square knots in the following manner, using as many knots as are needed to make the desired project. The first knot is made using the first four strands; the second knot, using the second four strands; and so on, across the row, using all of the strands. To begin the second row, the first two strands are put aside and a row of knots are made using the strands in sequence as was done in the row above. Two untied strands will be left at each end of the row. The third row is a repeat of the first; the fourth, a repeat of the second; etc. (fig. 8–13). To increase the wear of a belt and to improve its appearance, the head of the square knots on the left side of the belt and in the middle should be on the left and the head of the knots on the right side should be on the right. Those on the left are tied by starting with the left strand as directed in (2) above; those on the right side of the belt are tied, using the right strand first. This reverses the knot. It is absolutely essential to do this reversal if two colors are used in a project; otherwise, the pattern of colors will not be corrected. It is preferable, however, to do it with all projects.

(4) With a knowledge of just one more knot, the half hitch, a number of patterns can be developed in conjunction with the basic knot.

(*a*) The half hitch is made by holding one strand out taut and half hitching around it by bringing the knotting strand over the taut strand (fig. 8–14) and down through the loop, drawing it up taut. Two half hitches must be tied with each strand to hold the strands up taut. This operation may be repeated as many times as is desired over the same core, making a corkscrew bar (fig. 8–15).

(*b*) There are several interesting patterns that may be tied by combining the half knot or the square knot with the half hitch. The first of these makes use of two diagonal rows of half hitches. First, the project must be brought to a point. This is done by tying a row of knots, using all strands, followed by a row in which two strands on either edge are not used in the tying, thus making one less knot than in the first row. In the third row, two more strands are left out on both sides, giving one less knot again. The knotting is continued in this way, dropping in each row two more strands on the left and two more on the right until the row is reached where there are only four strands left

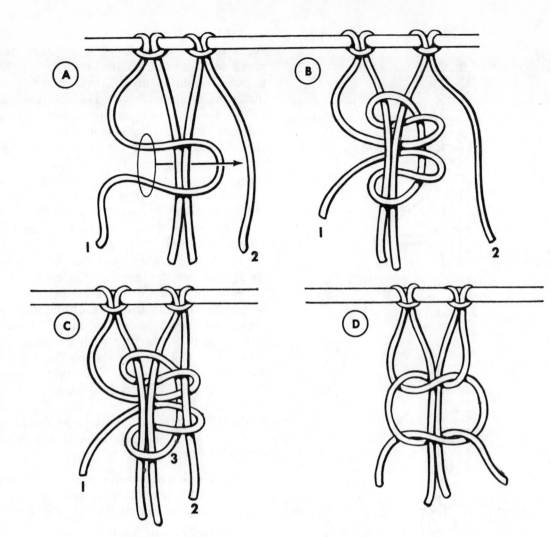

Figure 8–12. *Making a square knot, second method.*

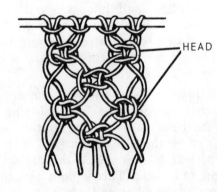

Figure 8–13. *Making fabric of square knots.*

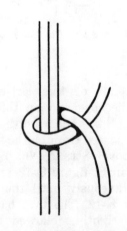

Figure 8–14. *Beginning the half hitch.*

in the center and one knot is tied. The double row of diagonal half hitches may now be tied. The outside left-hand strand must now be grasped and held in a diagonal position in line with the knots just tied and, with each successive strand from the left side to the center, two half hitches are tied over this cord. The half hitches must be drawn close to the other work. Then the outside right-hand strand is grasped and two half hitches are made around it with each strand, including the strand that was brought to the center from

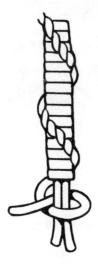

Figure 8–15. Half hitches in a series.

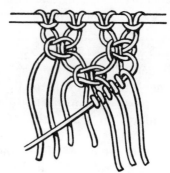

Figure 8–16. Using half hitches as part of design.

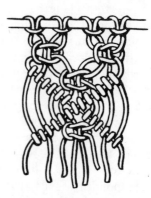

Figure 8–17. Carrying diagonal of half hitches "in".

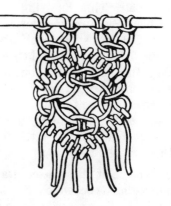

Figure 8–18. Carrying diagonal of half hitches "out.

the opposite side (fig. 8–16). When the first row of· half hitches has been completed from both sides, it should be followed by another, done in the same manner. These diagonals are carried from the center out to the opposite sides, tying two half hithces over them with each cord. If it is desired to fill in the area along the edges between the diagonals with square knots, these must be tied after the diagonals reach the center and before they start out again toward the edge. To complete the pattern, tie square knots between the apex of the diagonals as was done before starting the half hitches (fig. 8–17). This pattern may be done in reverse, starting at the middle and carrying the diagonals out to the edge and back to the middle, then making a diamond and filling it in with square knots (fig. 8–18). Another of these patterns, the twisted or bannister bar (spirals), which consists of a series of half knots all tied from the same side, has been mentioned before. A dozen or so of such half knots tied with each group of four strands makes an attractive pattern (fig. 8–11), or a series of square knots may be tied with each group of four strands. These are called Solomon bars or flats (fig. 8–10). After six or seven of these knots, the cords must again be joined by dropping out two cords on either side of the work and tying with the rest of the cords. In any pattern, strands of different colors often make the piece more attractive and more interesting. Two and sometimes three colors may be used in a knotted project. These colors usually must be evenly distributed in the project to give an attractive design. When colors are used, mistakes become even more noticeable, so

the knotter must be doubly careful about tying each knot from the correct side.

d. If a cord proves too short, it may be spliced while it is being used as the core of a bar. The two ends are raveled, each end is divided into 3 parts and waxed well, and each part is scraped to a taper point. The ends are joined, allowing tips to overlap and the solid part of the cord to overlap slightly. These are twisted to the right and, with a piece of thread the same color as the cord, the ends are whipped. The cord is rolled between two boards and covered with thin spar varnish.

e. The ending can be done in several ways and what is done depends upon the project. Belts are made more frequently in occupational therapy than are most other projects, so ending them will be considered in some detail. Consideration will be given first to a belt started at the point and ended at the buckle. Next, the directions will be for a belt started at the buckle and ended at the point.

(1) After making the belt one inch longer than the desired total length, bring the center of the belt to a point as in figure 8–19. Then take the strands on one side of the point and, working at right angles, square knot with these strands toward the edge (fig. 8–20). Continue the knotting with all strands on this side until the piece is 2 1/3 times as long as the belt is wide. This piece will be the belt loop. Bring the belt loop to a point on the same side as the point in the belt itself (fig. 8–21). Now bring the belt loop around on top of the belt to the other side and, with corresponding cords from the loop and the other half of the point of the belt, tie square knots with *two* strands (no core). There will be half as many square knots as there were cords used in the belt. This knotting joins the belt loop to the belt. Be sure to draw these knots up very tightly. Cut the strands off about 1/4 inch below this knot. Turn the belt loop inside out before putting the belt on the buckle. Apply the buckle by placing the belt loop under the bar of the buckle, sticking the tongue down through the center of the belt, and pulling the belt through the buckle and then back over the top of the belt bar and through the belt loop.

(2) If the belt has been started on the buckle end, it must be ended at the point end. To do this, take the knots down to a point (fig.

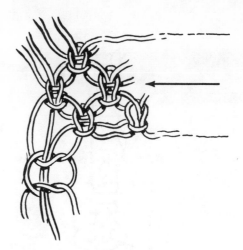

Figure 8–20. Making a keeper.

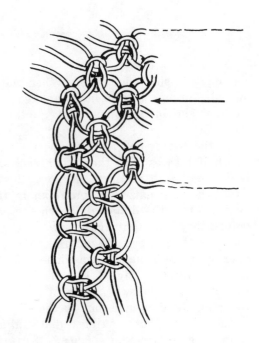

Figure 8–21. Completing the keeper.

8–16) and make two rows of half hitches, both ending in the center, and tie the core strands securely in a square knot. With a large needle, mark each cord back from the end 1/4 to 1/2 inch and cut it off close to the belt. Put shellac over the cut ends to keep them from untwisting or working back. This is a good ending to use for many projects.

8–5. Other Pattern Possibilities

The number of combinations of colors, designs, textures, and projects that are possible to make with cord knotting seem to be limitless.

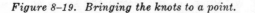

Figure 8–19. Bringing the knots to a point.

CHAPTER 9

BRAIDING AND HOOKED RUGS

Section I. BRAIDING

9–2. Material

Almost any material which is flexible and can be made into strips can be braided. The strands need to be of about the same thickness to keep the braiding even so that the creative aspects of the work come from color combinations. In occupational therapy, gimp of various colors is the material most frequently used for braiding.

9–3. Processes

No matter what type of braiding is done, the tension must be kept even in order to have a nice product.

a. Strands of a length to produce the desired article are cut. The following rule of thumb is useful in estimating the correct length: An average braid is approximately two-thirds the length of the unbraided strips; the unbraided strips should therefore be about one-third longer than the length of the finished product.

b. Securing the strands is important even to braiding. This may be done by tying the ends together, by tying them with a piece of string, or by looping them over a lanyard hook. If the strands must be kept flat, they may be held with tape and paper clips or with a bulldog paper clamp. After the ends are secure, they are attached to some sturdy object or placed in a vise so that even tension can be maintained while braiding.

c. Although there are seemingly endless variations of braiding, most of them can be put into three main groups: flat, round, and square.

(1) *Flat braiding.*

(*a*) Three strand is the most simple type of flat braiding. It may be used for belts or for braiding cloth which is to be used to make rugs or mats. To accomplish this braid, take the right strand 1 (A, fig. 9–1), over strand 2. Then take the left strand 3 over 1. Strand 2 is then taken over 3. These steps are repeated until the braid is the desired length (B, fig. 9–1).

(*b*) Braiding four strands is a somewhat different method from braiding three strands as it incorporates the fundamentals of weaving; that is, the over-under principle. Strand 1 is brought over 2, under 3, over 4 and drawn tightly down next to 4 (A, fig. 9–2). In the next step, strand 2 is brought over 3, under 4, and over 1, as it is in its new position next to 4. Strand 2 is then drawn down next to 1. These steps are continued until the desired length has been braided (B, fig. 9–2).

Figure 9–1. Three-strand braiding.

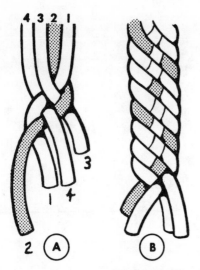

Figure 9-2. Four-strand braiding.

Figure 9-3. Five-strand braiding.

Figure 9-4. Six-strand braiding.

This method may be used for braiding six, seven, or eight strands.

(c) Five-strand braiding is somewhat similar to the four-strand method, except that the braiding is done from both sides. Strand 1 (fig. 9-3), on the right, is brought over 2 and under 3; then from the left, strand 5 is brought over 4 and under 1. Then from the right again, strand 2 is brought over 3 and under 5. Braiding must always be done from one side and then from the other. The outside strand is always taken over one strand and then under one strand. This process is continued until the desired length has been braided.

(d) Six-strand braiding (fig. 9-4) can be done in at least two ways; one of the more interesting is quite similar to three-strand braiding. Use 1, 2, and 3 as a triple strand, 4 as a single strand, and 5 and 6 as a double strand, and braid, using the same method as in three-strand braiding (fig. 9-1). Six strands can also be braided with the method used in four-strand braiding.

(e) Seven-strand braiding is worked from both sides an is quite similar to braiding with five strands. The right strand 1, is brought over 2, and under 3 and 4. The left strand 7 is brought over 6 and under 5 and 1. Next, strand 2 is brought over 3 and under 4 and 7 (fig. 9-5). The outside strand is always taken over one strand and under two.

(f) For nine-strand braiding, the outside strand is always brought over 1, under 2, and over 1. The work is done first from one side, then the other, as is shown in figure 9-6.

(g) In twelve-strand braiding, the high-

Figure 9-5. Seven-strand braiding.

Figure 9-6. Nine-strand braiding.

est strand must be taken around behind the braid, where it goes under three strands, then over three strands.

(*h*) In braiding sixteen strands, the highest strand goes under 4 and over 4.

(2) *Round braiding.* Round braiding can be done with four, six, or eight strands. Four-strand is the most common, probably because it is the simplest and also because generally useful articles such as key chains, zipper pulls, and lanyards are made from it. The heavier braids that are usually used in harnesses or dog leashes can be made using six or eight strands.

(*a*) To accomplish four-strand round braid, two thongs of contrasting colors are inserted through the zipper attachment, lanyard hook, the ring on a whistle or knife, or around a spike which has been driven into a block of wood. The two long strands are arranged so that half of each strand is on each side of the hook. If the colors are arranged with both strands of one color on one side and both strands of the other color on the other side, the diamond pattern will result; whereas if they are arranged alternately, the spiral pattern will result (fig. 9-7). It is this original arrangement (A, fig. 9-8) that makes the difference in pattern, for the braiding is the same for both types. The outer left strand 3 is brought around behind strand 1 and 4, in a clockwise direction, through the space between 3 and 4 at the right. It is then carried back to the left, over strand 1, so that it lies beside strand 4 (B, fig. 9-8). Next, the outer right strand 2 is carried in the same way behind strand 1 and 3, then turned over 3 so it will lie between strand 1 and 3 (C, fig. 9-8). Strand 4 is turned under strand 2 and 3 and carried back to the left over strand 2 so that it will lie beside strand 3 (D, fig. 9-8). In short, working first from the left, then from the right, the outside strand is taken under two and flipped over one. Care must be taken to prevent twisting. This is continued until the desired length has been braided. It is sometimes difficult to start this braid again if it must be left before the knot is completed. When restarting, it is a help to know which outer strand of braid should be used next. To determine this, the crossing of the two strands in front of the work should be observed. If the upper strand in the crossing goes toward the left, the outer right strand is used next. If the upper strand goes toward the right, the outer left strand is used next. Another help in restarting, if the diamond pattern is being done, is to hold the strands so that those of one color are in one

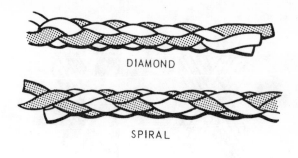

DIAMOND

SPIRAL

Figure 9-7. Four-strand round braid.

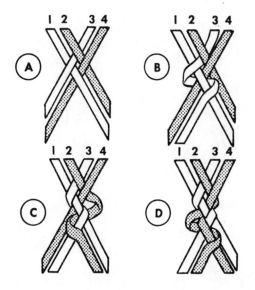

Figure 9-8. Starting the 4-strand round braid.

hand and those of the other color are in the other hand. If the spiral design is being done, one of each color should be in each hand.

(*b*) For six-strand round braiding (fig. 9-9), the strands are arranged and the ends secured as for four-strand braiding (fig. 9-2). Strand 3 is put over 4, under 5, and over 6. Then strands 2 and 1 are woven over and under as indicated. The same weaving is done with strands 4, 5, and 6 until all strands have crossed and are on the other side as in A, figure 9-9. Braiding is started with the outer right strand 3, which is an "over" strand, as after the crossing, it is over 6. Strand 3 is passed across the back and is guided with the right forefinger to keep it from twisting, while it is brought up between 4 and 5 at the left. It is crossed over 5 and under 6, then returned back to the right side (B, fig. 9-9). Next, strand 4 is taken, in the same way, across the back, up between 1 and 2, crossed over 1 and under 3 and back to the left (C, fig. 9-9). Braiding should continue in this manner, using alternately the upper right, then the outer left

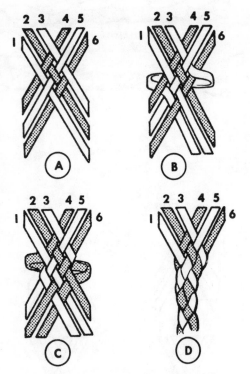

Figure 9–9. Six-strand round braiding.

strands (D, fig. 9–9). Different arrangement of colors at the beginning will produce different effects.

(c) The strands for eight-strand braiding are arranged and secured as in figure 9–10. Strand 4 is put over 5, under 6, over 7, and under 8 (A, fig. 9–10). Strands 3, 2, and 1 are woven as indicated until the cross is made with a woven center, and strands 1–4, which were on the left, have crossed to the right and strands 5–8, which were on the right, are on the left. Braiding starts with the outer right strand 4, which is put across the back and brought out between strands 6 and 7 on the left. It is passed over 7 and under 8 (B, fig. 9–10). Next, the upper left strand 5 is passed across the back and is brought out on the right between strands 1 and 2 and from there, over 1 and under 4 to the left side (C, fig. 9–10). Braiding is continued in the same way until the braid has reached the desired length. Care must be taken to keep the strands from twisting and to pull the work up tightly each time a strand is braided.

(3) *Round or square braiding.* Round or square braiding is usually done with four strands. It is often used to finish off round braiding as for a lanyard slide, but it may also be started with loose cords and done without a core.

(a) For round, four-strand braiding, the

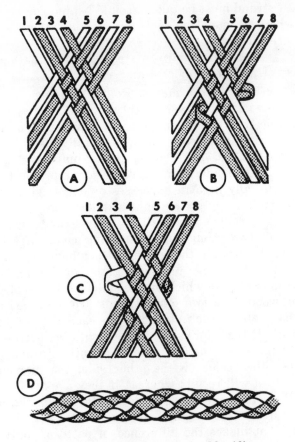

Figure 9–10. Eight-strand round braiding.

strands are middled, then all are clipped or held together at the middle, and are held with the longer strands to be braided, pointing upward (A, fig. 9–11). The steps in making the first row are as follows. Strand 1 is put between strands 2 and 3, leaving a loop (B, fig. 9–11). Strand 2 is put across strand 1 and between 3 and 4 (C, fig. 9–11). Strand 3 is put across strand 2 and between 4 and where strand 1 originated (D, fig. 9–11). Strand 4 is put over strand 3 and under the loop made by strand 1 (E, fig. 9–11). All four strands are pulled up with even tension (F, fig. 9–11). These five steps are repeated until the braid is the desired length and it is finished with a lock knot ((d) below).

(b) Four-strand square braiding is started in the same manner as the round, following steps A through F figure 9–11. Instead of repeating the steps in the same direction as in round braiding, the strands are reversed back on themselves. Strand 4 is placed back over itself and between strands 3 and 2, leaving a loop. Strand 3 is put back over strand 4 and between 2 and 1. Strand 2 is put over 3 and between 1 and 4. Strand 1 is put back over 2 and under the loop left by strand 4. These last steps are con-

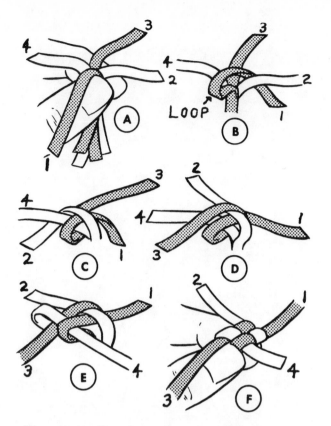

Figure 9–11. Steps in starting a four-strand square braid.

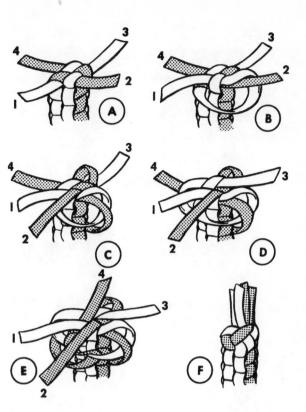

Figure 9–13. A lock knot.

Figure 9–12. Braiding with a core.

tinued until the braid is the desired length, then it is finished with a lock knot ((d) below).

(c) The same process is employed when the braiding is done over some solid core (fig. 9–12), as would be the case if you were making a slip knot over the round braid (fig. 9–11). The braid is formed loosely around the round braid so that it will slide easily. The braiding process is the same, with or without a core.

(d) A lock knot (fig. 9–13) to finish the round or square braiding is made in the following manner. Strand 1 is carried around 2 and is tucked through the loop which holds 2 in place. Strand 2 is carried around 3 and is tucked through the loop which holds 3 in place. The same is done

with 3 and 4. This brings all four strands together in the center of the knot and makes a neatly finished end when they are drawn tightly. The ends may be left about an inch long to form a tassel, or they may be cut off close to the knot.

9–4. Design

Design is brought about by the selection and placement of color in braiding. One design will result if contrasting strands are arranged alternately; another, if they are arranged adjacent to each other. Not only can two colors be used but interesting effects may be obtained with the use of several colors.

Section II. BRAID WEAVING AND TURKISH KNOTTING

9–7. Tools and Equipment

Both braid weaving and Turkish knotting require essentially the same tools and equipment.

b. Portable Braid Weaving Frame. This frame (fig. 9–15) is similar to the loom part of the floor model. The main differences are that the portable one is smaller, lighter in weight, and usually not adjustable. It is made of ¾-inch pine, about 2 inches wide (fig. 9–16). The size is optional. It should be small so as to have it light and manageable, yet large enough to make a nice project. The frame must be well constructed because the pull of the warp tends to twist the frame apart. It is therefore suggested that end lap joints be used in each corner, reinforced with screws or with bolts. The top of the upper crosspiece and the bottom of the lower piece have slits to hold the warp. These slits are about 5/16–3/8 inch deep and about 5/16 inch apart. When cutting these slits, time is saved and a more even warp is assured if the upper and lower pieces are fixed together and sawed at the same time.

c. Shuttle. If a shuttle is needed, the flat one is used (fig. 7–11).

9–8. Materials

Weaving materials (ch. 7) are used in this work. Because both braid weaving and Turkish knotting require so little material, frequently scraps from weaving can be employed effectively.

a. Carpet Warp. This is used to warp these looms, as well as in weaving, to hold the Turkish knots in place.

b. Roving. This is used both in braid weaving and in Turkish knotting.

c. Knitting and Crochet, 4-Ply Cotton Yarn. This can also be used in both modalities in this section. Because these yarns are relatively fine, however, the project may become tedious.

d. Wool, 4-Ply Worsted. This is rather fine and expensive but it can be used for small pieces.

e. Cloth Strips. Strips are cut into 3- to 4-inch widths, both edges are folded into the center of the material, and then the strip is folded in half. This method hides all of the raw edges and makes a sturdy, washable rug.

9–9. Processes

a. Warping. Warping the loom is similar for both types of weaving. For Turkish knotting, there should be an even number of threads in the warp. Because each thread should be doubled or tripled to increase the strength, two or three spools can be used together as the warping is done. A loop is tied in the warp threads and put over the first and second slits on the top crosspiece (fig. 9–17). The warp string is taken down to the bottom crosspiece and put into the first slit, then drawn through the slit and to the back of the board, around the back, and forward through the second slit to the front. Next, it goes back up to the second slit in the upper crosspiece, around the back, through the third slit to the front, and down to the third slit in the

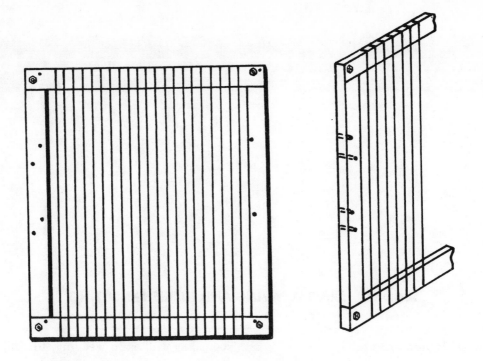

Figure 9–15. Portable braid weaving frame.

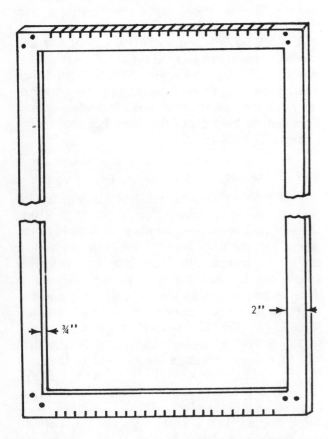

Figure 9–16. Construction of braid weaving frame.

lower crosspiece. This is continued until the warped area is the desired width and the ways string fastened. To keep the starting end even, two or three thin strips of light cardboard are woven into the starting end of the warp. A heading of about six rows of fine material should be woven in at the beginning and at the end of the rug to make it firmer and to have a base for the fringe (fig. 9–20).

b. Braid Weaving. Two ends of weft thread are used in this type of weaving. One of the best of several ways to start is to roll each end of a long piece of the selected weaving material and secure each roll with a rubber band. There should be about 2 feet of the material not rolled.

(1) Weaving. The weft is held at the side of the first warp thread in such a way that one ball is in front of the warp and the other one is behind it. The ball which was to the rear is brought to the front between warp threads 1 and 2. The ball which was in front is pushed to the rear between warp threads 1 and 2. Next, the ball in the front is put to the rear between warp threads 2 and 3, and the ball in the rear comes to the front between the same warp threads. At the same time, the weft is crossed by putting the strand which was under, over the strand which was on top. This crossing (fig. 9–18) re-

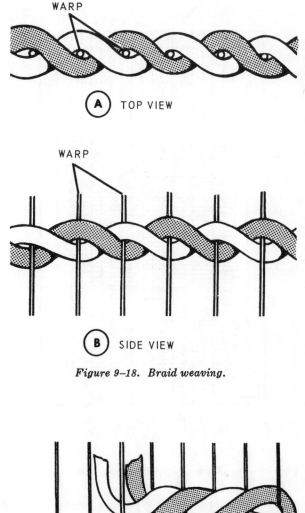

Figure 9–18. Braid weaving.

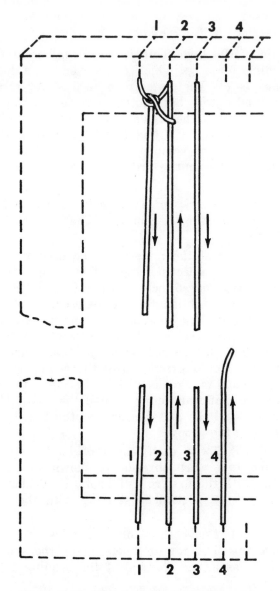

Figure 9–17. Warping a braid weaving frame.

sults in a better looking product as it keeps the warp from showing and the weaving firmer. The steps are continued in this manner to the end of the row.

(2) Subsequent rows. An extra twist of the two weft strands at the ends of the rows reverses the position of the strands so that they cover the warp and produce a pattern visible on a side view (fig. 9–19). The direction of the twist of the strands is reversed in each row, also (fig. 9–19).

(3) Splicing. The same method for splicing is used as is described in paragraph 7–7g. It is not advisable to splice the strands at the same place in the weaving. To prevent this, more weft

Figure 9–19. Diagram showing method of braid weaving.

should be used on one half than in the other when the weaving is started. If this has not been done and the strands end at the same place, one is cut shorter and spliced; then weaving is continued until the longer strand needs to be spliced.

(4) Ending is done in the same manner as starting a weft thread in weaving (para 7–7d).

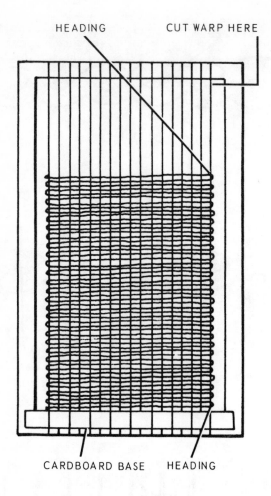

HEADING   CUT WARP HERE

CARDBOARD BASE   HEADING

Figure 9–20. Removing rug.

(5) To remove the piece after it is completed—

(*a*) Cut the warp close to the frame at the end that has the longest warp exposed (fig. 9–20).

(*b*) Pull the looped ends of the warp from the frame and carefully lay the piece on a flat surface.

(*c*) Grasp the first two cut ends and gently pull them until the loop at the far end of the piece just touches the weft. If the first warp thread is a single strand, tie it to the first loop to keep it from pulling out.

(*d*) Tie two adjacent, cut warp threads together in a square knot. The tie should be close to the weft but not tight enough to pull.

(6) Fringe can be added by cutting it and tying it into the loops of warp.

c. Turkish Knotting. Turkish knotting is considered with braid weaving because the same type of loom is used, warping is the same, and similar materials are used for both. In Turkish knotting, however, two types of weaving material are used, usually a lighter one for the tabby and a heavier one for the knots.

(1) Heading. This is very similar to the heading for rugs which are woven on a loom (para 7–7*c*). The material to be used for tabby is wound onto a flat shuttle and the weaving is usually done in the regular tabby, over-and-under weave. Between 1/2 and 1 inch of this heading is used. At the completion of the heading, the weft and the shuttle are left at the end of the row.

(2) Two rows of Turkish knots are tied in after the heading is complete. They are tied as follows:

(*a*) Cut the material to be used for the knots into a selected length. For a very thick shaggy rug, use 5-inch lengths; for less thickness, 4- or 3-inch lengths may be used. To obtain a number of these lengths easily and quickly, cut a board with the outside measurements a little more than the desired length of the strand of material. Cut a groove down the center length deep enough to allow one blade of scissors to slip, with the material wound around the board (fig. 9–21). Wind the material around the board and cut along the groove.

(*b*) Twist each length of knot material around two warp threads as shown in figure 9–22. With the first row of knots, tie a knot on each two warp strands, starting with the first two.

(*c*) Weave three or four rows of tabby above this first row of knots, using the shuttle which was left at the end of the heading ((1) above).

(*d*) Tie in two more rows of Turkish knots. For the first row, skip the first warp thread and tie a knot on threads 2 and 3, 4 and 5, etc., across the row. On the second row, start with the first thread as in the first row.

(*e*) Weave in tabby as in (*c*) above.

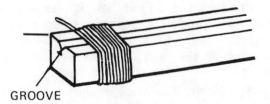

GROOVE

Figure 9–21. Cutting Turkish knot material.

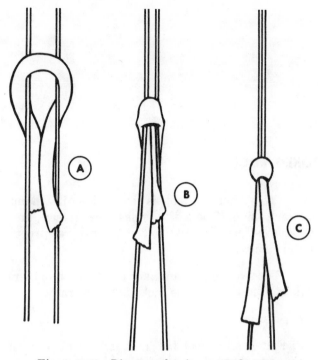

Figure 9–22. Diagram showing method of tying Turkish knot.

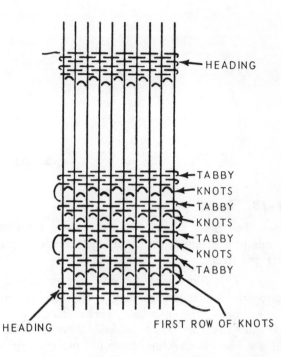

Figure 9–23. Schematic drawing of plan of Turkish knot rug.

(f) Repeat (b) through (e) above until the piece is of sufficient length.

(g) Weave in tabby to match the heading and remove the piece from the loom (b(5) above).

NOTE

Figure 9–23 shows a schematic drawing of a plan for a Turkish knot rug.

9–10. Design

Color, rather than design, produces the best effect in both of these modalities.

a. In braid weaving, stripes of various colors and widths are the most frequently used form of decoration. It is possible to "lay in" design as in weaving. The process can be looked up in a weaving book if a need for it arises.

b. Because of the shaggy quality of the piece, intricate designs do not show up well. It is possible to put in wide stripes, borders, or large geometric designs. In addition, to relieve the monotony of one color, several colors can be alternated, producing a tweed effect. A solid border is nice on this pattern.

Section III. HOOKED RUGS

9–13. Tools

a. Rug hook. There are a number of different kinds of rug hooks on the market, some of which are pictured.

(1) Hooks used to pull the material *up* through the backing (fig. 9–24). When using these hooks, the operator works from the right side of the rug being hooked. These hooks can be used when hooking either old material or new.

(2) Hooks used to push the material *down* through the backing can be used with new material only.

(*a*) When using the hook in figure 9–25, the operator works from the wrong side of the fabric being hooked. Although expert rug hookers frown on this type of a hook, it seems to be easier for men to handle, at least while they are learning the skill.

(*b*) Another hook is grasped with a hand on each side. Then the sides are raised and lowered alternately with a bilateral reciprocal motion (fig. 9–26).

b. Woodworkers hammer or tack hammer. This is used to drive the tacks into the frame.

c. Scissors.

d. Flat head carpet tacks. It is helpful to push each tack through a 1/2-inch tab of leather or cardboard. The material acts as a marker and keeps the head of the tack from going through the burlap. It also facilitates removing the tacks.

9–14. Equipment

The only equipment needed is a rug frame of an appropriate size as described in section XVII, chapter 13.

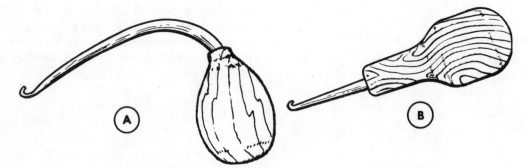

Figure 9–24. Rug hook used to pull material through backing.

Figure 9–25. Rug hook that pushes material through backing.

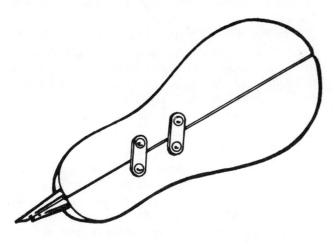

Figure 9–26. Rug hook that is worked bilaterally.

9–15. Material

a. Burlap. Burlap is graded by the weight per yard. Medium weight, which is designed for upholstery work, is the best weight for rug hooking.

    (1) Light weight—6–8 oz/yard.

    (2) Medium weight—10–12 oz/yard.

    (3) Heavy weight—14 oz/yard.

b. Hooking Material.

    (1) Wool yarn. The 4-ply worsted is expensive but is considered by many to be the best of the new, purchased materials. Wool is good for a rug because it is resilient and because it is somewhat resistant to soil. A rug 26 by 30 inches requires about twelve 4-ounce skeins or approximately 48 ounces of 4-ply worsted yarn.

    (2) Cotton knitting or crocheting yarn is available in a variety of colors and makes up into a very acceptable and less expensive rug.

    (3) Cotton or wool material cut into strips was the original material used in making hooked rugs. It is still the material of choice for many rug hookers.

9–16. Planning a Hooked Rug

Four factors combine to make a good hooked rug: design, color, texture, and technique. Although it is preferable to have the student design his own rug, he may not have the inclination, imagination, or the time for this. It is therefore expedient to have several patterns available for selection.

Regardless of who makes the design, the following suggestions may be helpful:

a. Designing. Design is the arrangement of units of various sizes and shapes within an area. The units must be in proportion to the space. Whether the unit be floral, scroll, or abstract, three or four of these units are cut from paper and arranged in various ways on the burlap or on the paper which is to be the pattern.

b. Putting the Design Onto Burlap. When a pleasing arrangement is found, the design is put onto the burlap by drawing around the paper patterns with a crayon. Details such as tendrils, sprays of small leaves, eyes, or fold marks can then be added by freehand drawing. In planning a repeat design or a design with formal balance just one unit is made and then repeated. If the design is made on paper, it is transferred to the burlap with carbon paper or the design is heavily retraced on the back of the paper with a dark wax crayon. The wax is melted onto the burlap by placing the wax traced design on the burlap and ironing the front of the paper.

c. Selecting Colors. The colors used depend upon the size of the rug, as well as what the person prefers, where the rug is to be used, and what other furnishings are to be in the room. Lest the rug be too dominant in the room, it is important to use muted or grayed tones in the large areas and save the more vibrant colors for small accents. Darker earth tones such as browns, tans, greens, and grays are best in an area where there is a great deal of walking over the rug. Lighter background colors can be used more successfully on the second floor, especially in the bedrooms.

d. Planning Texturing. Nice texture of the background is obtained by using different textures of material such as hard tweeds and soft homespuns. The direction of hooking is also an important phase of texturing the background. The outline of the pattern is followed. When about a third of the background space is filled, work starts at the border design and proceeds toward the center until the hooking meets.

9–17. Processes

The selection of design, color, and texture is important to the appearance of the rug. Good techniques of hooking and finishing are important to the wearing qualities of the rug.

a. Tacking Burlap to the Frame. The burlap should be taut, and it should be stretched with even tension across the frame. The burlap is tacked to one end, then stretched and tacked to the opposite end. The same process is followed on the sides. The tacks should be put through a piece of cardboard or leather first, then tacked about 2 inches apart. The raw edge of the burlap should be hemmed or folded under so that it will not ravel during the handling of hooking.

b. Hooking Process. There are two methods of hooking, with the selection depending upon the type of needle being used—

(1) With the hook which pulls the material up through the backing, hold a strip of cloth in the left hand under the burlap, fold it lengthwise between the thumb and index finger, and hold it with the crease toward the operator. With the hook held in the right hand, push it down between the meshes of burlap and pick up the end of the folded material and pull it to the right side. Loop the end of the strip over the index finger of the left hand in order to get the first bit through more easily. As the hook is pushed down, hold the hook away and pull the back of the shank of the hook against the side of the opening nearest the operator. In that way, when the strip is brought up, the hole will be large enough to prevent the barb of the hook from catching in the burlap. Skip two threads of burlap and make a second stitch, repeating the process of the first except that this time a loop is brought up instead of an end. Repeat this process to the end of the cut strip of material. This end of the strip must also be brought up on the right side to keep the loops from pulling out. To start

the second strip, pull it up in the same hole where the end of the last strip is. This locks the stitch and makes a more durable rug. Loops of 1/4 to 3/8 inch are good; they should be arranged in the burlap in the manner shown in figure 9–27. There is a tendency for beginners to pull out a loop or two previously hooked as they bring a new one up. To prevent this, hold the looped ones in place by pressing the fingers of the left hand against the backs of the loops.

(2) To use the hook shown in figure 9–25, thread the yarn down toward the tip of the needle by putting the yarn through the holes, down through the shaft of the needle and out through the hole in the tip of the needle. Leave a 2- or 3-inch tail of yarn projecting from the tip. Working from the back of the canvas, push the needle through the burlap to the place where it is set to stop. Pull the needle back just until the tip comes out of the burlap, then push it down through the next hole. With this method, use every other space, every other row as indicated in figure 9–28. Once again, the finger can be used to hold the loops if such is indicated. If the yarn going into the top of the needle is without tension, there is less tendency for the loops to pull out.

9–18. Finishing the Rug

First, the rug is removed from the frame, then the burlap edge is trimmed if necessary, and turned twice into a hem (fig. 9–29) and pinned in place. The hem is stitched to the backing firmly

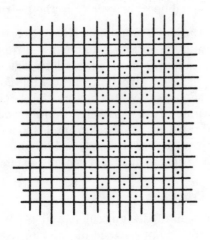

FRONT
OF BURLAP

Figure 9–27. Magnified drawing of burlap backing, showing placement of loops when using the rug hook.

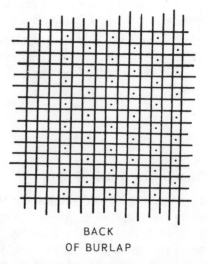

BACK
OF BURLAP

Figure 9–28. Magnified drawing of burlap backing, showing placement of loops when using rug needle.

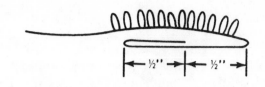

Figure 9–29. Diagram showing method of hemming hooked rug.

with heavy carpet or button thread. Another way is to baste the hem (double just once) before hooking, then hooking through the hem to hold it in place; this involves moving the rug on the frame several times. It is also advisable to spray or paint the back of the rug with rug backing which helps to keep the loops from pulling and to keep the rug from slipping on the floor.

CHAPTER 10

HUCK TOWELING, RAKE KNITTING, AND NEEDLEWORK

Section I. HUCK TOWELING OR SWEDISH WEAVING

10–1. General

Such crafts as huck toweling, Swedish weaving, and huck weaving all refer to a type of embroidery work which is done on cloth of a special weave called huck. In this weave, there is a pair of vertical longer threads woven at regular intervals across the fabric. They are arranged as are bricks from row to one-half row (fig. 10–1). Embroidery strands or yarns of various colors are slipped under the pairs of threads in various sequences to form interesting patterns. The decorative strands do not go through the material, so they do not show on the reverse side. A number of articles can be decorated, to include aprons, bibs, curtains, draperies, dresser scarves, knitting · bags, napkins, place mats, purses, skirts, tablecloths, and towels. Although this is a type of embroidery, the process is highly structured and the designs are sufficiently geometric and masculine to render this an activity which appeals to many men.

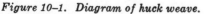

Figure 10–1. Diagram of huck weave.

10–2. Tools and Equipment

The tools and equipment needed for huck toweling are few and easily obtainable.

a. Embroidery floss. Either pearl cotton or 6-strand floss is used for articles which will need to be laundered frequently.

b. Huck fabric.

  (1) *Cotton.* Available in 17-, 36-, and 51-inch widths and in a variety of colors. This is less expensive than linen huck and the pairs of threads are easier to see.

  (2) *Linen.* Available in 14- and 17-inch widths in several colors. Good quality linen combined with handwork makes very nice towels, dresser scarves, and place mats.

c. Needles.

  (1) Blunt-pointed tapestry needles, used for slipping under the pairs of threads in the huck.

  (2) Sharp sewing needles, needed for sewing through the material as in hems.

d. Huck patterns. Available at—

  (1) *McCall's Treasury of Needlecraft,* Simon and Schuster, Inc., New York, N.Y., 1955.

  (2) *Huck Towel Patterns* (books 1–5), Mildred V. Krieg, Riverside, Ill., 1940.

e. Metallic thread. Used for embellishing projects such as evening bags.

f. Pins. Used to pin hems, for example, and to mark the center of a piece to be embroidered.

g. Scissors.

h. Thimble.

i. Thread. Used for sewing hems and for garment constructions.

j. Yarn. Used to embroider articles that are not laundered, such as knitting bags and purses.

10-3. Processes

a. The item to be decorated should be well planned in order to center the design on the piece. It is sometimes advisable to complete the hems on the smaller articles in order to determine the correct size; however, skirts and purses can be completed better after they are decorated.

b. Selection of a pattern is an interesting and important part of the work. The pattern must be suited to the piece it will decorate.

(1) A large project, such as a skirt, an apron, draperies, or curtains, is suited to the larger pattern, which can be repeated several times in the project.

(2) Smaller patterns are better for small articles such as guest towels, bibs, and place mats.

(3) Exceptions to these generalities can sometimes produce rather dramatic effects. One large motif on a guest towel can be most effective. Small, border patterns combined with a large pattern can look very nice on a skirt.

(4) Interesting effects can be obtained by using two, three, or four colors of floss or yarn, by using metallic threads with colored thread; or by using different colors of huck.

c. Because it is advisable to avoid splicing the strands of embroidery floss, each strand should be sufficiently long to be embroidered across the piece once. Some patterns indicate the necessary length of each strand. *For example,* No. 2, T 3 1/2, means that the second row of embroidery needs a strand 3 1/2 times the width of the material to be embroidered. The length of each strand in the pattern varies according to the number and size of the offsets in the pattern. For instance, in figure 10-2, thread No. 3, which goes straight across will need to be just slightly longer than the width of the piece being embroidered, while strands 1, 2, 4, and 5 need to be more than two times the width of the piece or T 2 1/2.

d. Centering the pattern is a very essential step, especially in smaller pieces where the entire pattern can be seen at a glance.

(1) Find the center pair of threads in the width of the material by folding the piece in half or by counting the pairs of threads across the row. Mark the center pair with a pin.

(2) Locate the center of the design in the pattern and mark it.

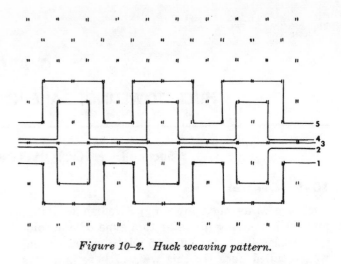

Figure 10-2. Huck weaving pattern.

(3) Locate the center of the embroidery floss or yarn and pull it half of its length under the center pair of threads.

e. Strand 1 in the selected pattern is worked first on one side of the center, then on the other, by drawing the strand under the pairs of threads indicated in the pattern. Extreme care must be taken with this first strand of the design to insure accuracy in following the design because the placement of all subsequent strands are based on the first one. A guide string of a color other than the pattern can be run straight across the piece and under each pair of threads. This can be helpful in starting the first strand of the pattern. Only the first strand needs to be centered, so others can be started at the right as is customarily done in sewing.

f. Reading patterns can be done in two ways; the method used depends upon the way in which the pattern is "written."

(1) Some patterns are shown by means of a diagramatic drawing, as has been done herein. In such cases, the diagrams are followed by counting the pairs of threads diagramed.

(2) Another method of recording patterns, which is more difficult but more accurate for complex patterns, is to follow written directions. These directions are usually illustrated with photographs of the pattern; however, these photographs frequently do not show detail clearly. The code of the written directions is as follows:

(*a*) Symbols such as 1 over 2 are used to indicate offsets. This means to count one pair of threads ahead (1 over) and 2 pairs up or down (fig. 10-3).

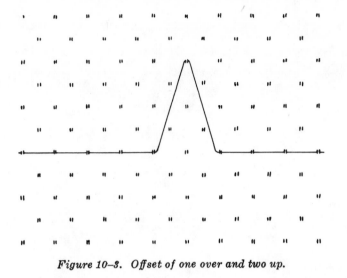

Figure 10–3. Offset of one over and two up.

(*b*) Open loops are indicated by 1/2 (meaning 1/2 over) by 1 1/2 (one and one-half rows up). So 1/2/1 1/2 is as shown in figure 10–4, as is 1/2/2 1/2 and 1/2/1/2.

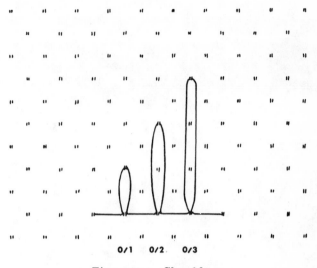

Figure 10–5. Closed loops.

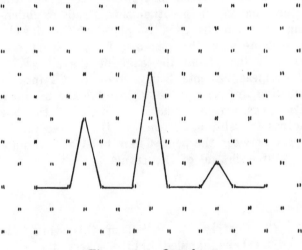

Figure 10–4. Open loops.

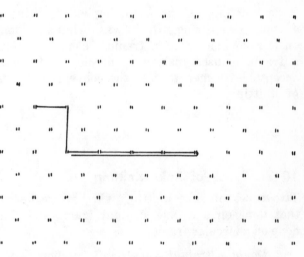

Figure 10–6. One method of ending huck weaving.

(*c*) Closed loops are written as 0/1, 0/2, and 0/3 (fig. 10–5). A loop of 0/4 is rarely used.

g. Ending the work is done in several ways; the method selected depends upon the project and the design.

(1) The end can be stitched into the edge of the huck and hidden in the hem.

(2) The strand can be woven back on itself for several pairs of threads (fig. 10–6).

10–6. General

Rake knitting, as the name implies, is actually a type of knitting which was originally done on a rake instead of a frame. Perhaps because a frame is used instead of needles, it is more acceptable to men than is the conventional type of knitting.

10–7. Types of Rake Knitting

Two types of rake knitting will be considered: that done on a double straight frame and that done on a circular frame.

a. Double Straight Rake Knitting. This is the most frequently used type of rake knitting.

(1) *Using the frame.* Knitting is done on a frame with a double row of pegs.
The longer the frame, the wider the knitted piece can be; the farther apart the pegs, the larger the stitches and the lacier the piece. The frame pictured is used for making a stole. It is made of 1/4-inch dressed pine and is 30 inches long and 3 inches wide. The 53 pegs are made of 1/4-inch doweling and placed with 26 on one side of the 1/2-inch slit in the center of the frame and 27 on the other side. Brads or finishing nails can be used in place of the dowels. The centers of the pgs are 1 inch apart and are 1/4 inch from the edge of the slit. With these measurements, 3 pegs give about 1 inch of knitting and 4 rows of knitting make an inch. The pegs are not placed opposite to the one across the slit, but rather in the center of the space between the pegs. There must be a thumbtack at each end of the frame.

(2) *Casting on.* In all of this work, the yarn must be handled lightly—"keep the yarn loose." Two stitches or ways to wrap will be considered. Variations of these can be worked out as skill is developed.

NOTE

In the directions for this, it is assumed that the worker is right handed.

(a) *Plain stitch.* To cast on the plain stitch, make a loop just large enough to fit over the first peg and then slip it over. Pass the yarn across the slit and around the far side of the first peg in the far row, cross the slit again, and take the yarn around the near side of the second peg on the near row of pegs (A, fig. 10–8). Continue to the end of the rows of pegs. Pass the yarn around the last peg and back, *retracing the way it came*, but have the yarn of

the return wrap lie above that of the first wrap (B, fig. 10–8). Continue wrapping to include the peg with the original loop of yarn, then twist the yarn around the thumbtack at the end of the frame.

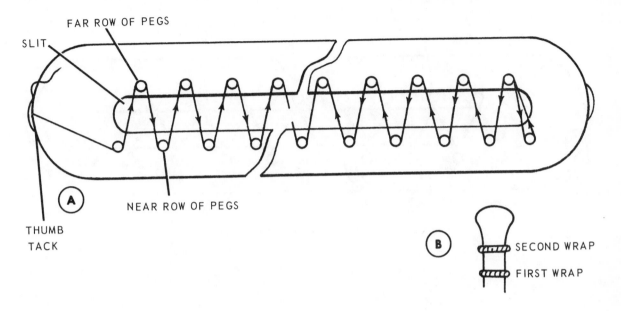

Figure 10–8. Wrapping for plain stitch.

(b) *Figure 8 stitch*. To cast on the figure 8 stitches, make a loop just large enough to fit, and slip it over the first peg. Pass the yarn across the slit and counterclockwise around the far side of the first peg across the slit. Bring it back across the slit again and pass it clockwise around the second peg on the near row of pegs. Continue to the end of the rows of pegs. Pass the yarn around the last peg as shown in figure 10–10 (this last peg will have just one loop around it and no twist) and back, retracing the path of the yarn, but not in the same direction. To keep the yarn of the return wrap above that of the first, push the first loops down before wrapping the second. Continue wrapping, to include the peg with the original loop of yarn, then twist the yarn around the thumbtack at the end of the frame.

(3) *Knitting*. Either the plain stitch or the figure 8 stitch leaves each peg with two wraps of yarn; yarn from the first wrap is below that from the second or return wrap. With a crochet hook, No. 1 leather modeling tool, bent paper clips, or the fingers, *lift the strand of yarn from the first wrap past the strand from the second, up over the peg, and then let go of it as it gets

to the center between the two rows of pegs. Do this with the yarn on all of the pegs (to include the first one with the tied loop) except for the last peg which had just one wrap. Each peg will now have just one wrap of yarn which becomes the first wrap. Unwind the end of yarn from the thumbtack and retrace the path followed by the yarn around the pegs. At the end of the row, wrap the yarn around the thumbtack and repeat from*. Continue with the wrapping and taking off sequence. As the knitting forms, it goes down through the slit in the frame. Work until the piece is the desired length.

(4) *Double and triple stitching*. Either the double or triple stitch may be employed to give more firmness or more warmth to the garment. The following directions apply to knitting on either the straight or the round frame:

(a) *Double stitch*. Wrap the pegs one additional time to have three strands on each peg. To knit, lift the lowest strand over the upper two strands and on off of the nails.

(b) *Triple stitch*. Wrap the pegs so that there are four strands on each. Lift the lowest

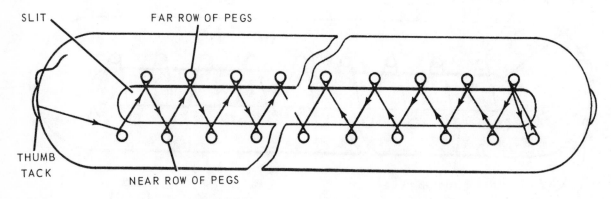

SLIT

FAR ROW OF PEGS

THUMB
TACK

NEAR ROW OF PEGS

Figure 10–10. Wrapping for figure 8 stitch.

strand over the upper three strands and on off of the nail.

(c) *Stitch change.* To change from single to double or from double to triple stitch, wrap one strand on the peg and proceed as for the desired stitch. To change back from triple to double or from double to single stitch, lift the lower *two* strands up and over the nails, leaving the desired number on the peg.

(5) *Shaping.* Stitches can be added and taken off to shape the pieces much in the same way as in conventional knitting.

(a) *Adding stitches.* When the end of the row of stitches is reached, wind the yarn on one or more of the empty nails adjacent to the knitting according to directions. Then wind these

stitches back across the rake knitting in the same way as the other stitches.

(b) *Casting off stitches.* Lift the last stitch to be knitted onto the peg of the next to the last stitch to be knitted (this will be in the outer row). Then lift the stitch which was already on the peg up over the new stitch and off of the nail.

(6) *Taking work off.* Taking the work off the frame is done in essentially the same way as in knitting. It is the same for both the plain and the figure 8 stitches. Ending is done after the knitting step when there is but one strand on the peg. A crochet hook is the best tool to use. Starting at the end away from the long end of yarn, take the loop of yarn off of the first peg,

keep it on the hook and take the yarn off of the second peg, or number 2 (fig. 10–12). Slip the first loop over the second loop and off of the hook. *Now there remains only one loop on the hook. Take the yarn off of the next peg and onto the crochet hook. Slip the second loop over the third loop and off of the hook. **Take the yarn off of the fourth hook and repeat between * and **. To determine which peg is next, follow them back, using the same sequence in which they were wrapped the last time. Continue in this manner until the last loop is the only one remaining on the crochet hook. Tie the remaining end of yarn through the last loop in order to keep it from slipping back through the next loop.

(7) *Fringing.* If a scarf or stole is the project, a fringe is usually tied to each end. This is not difficult to do, especially if certain short cuts are followed. To measure the yarn, *loosely* wrap it around a book. The book selected should be of a size to make a strand of yarn 12 to 16 inches long as it is wrapped around the book once. Wrap the yarn over the entire surface of the book so as to avoid pile up of yarn, which influences the length of each strand. Count as the wraps are made, to avoid making too many and thereby wasting yarn. Two or three of these double strands looped into each stitch at each end of the scarf is about right. When the desired number of strands are on the book, cut the yarn in the space between the pages of the book (fig. 10–13). Finally, double two or three strands of yarn in half, insert the doubled end through the stitch of the scarf or stole just far enough for the ends of the fringe to be drawn up through the doubled end, and thereby fix the fringe into the stitch (fig. 10–14).

b. Circular Rake Knitting. On this round rake knitting frame, circular articles such as caps are made. Frames are commercially available in several different sizes in order to make caps for dolls and children as well as for adults. The caps can be made of double thickness for more warmth, and the long skating caps which are so attractive in bright colors can be done on this round frame.

(1) *Selecting the frame.* Circular rake knitting frames can be purchased in the following sizes:

15-inch diameter with 43 pegs
13-inch diameter with 36 pegs
10 1/2-inch diameter with 41 pegs
8-inch diameter with 26 pegs
5 1/2-inch diameter with 19 pegs

These frames are made of plywood about 5/8 inch thick. The pegs are 1/4 inch in diameter with a 5/8-inch knob at the lap. The centers of the pegs are about 3/4 inch apart. It is felt that in this frame finishing nails or brads cannot be substituted for the 1/4-inch pegs, as the smaller diameter of the nails would make knitting very difficult and the product less attractive.

(2) *Casting on.* To cast on the circular frame, make a loop and slip it over a peg. Pass the yarn around the next peg, putting the yarn from peg to peg, on the inside of the circle of pegs (fig. 10–16). The yarn must be kept loose at all times. Continue this process, wrapping each peg in succession, until each has a wrap of yarn around it.

(3) *Knitting.* When all of the pegs have a loop on them, *start with the next peg and wrap a second loop *above* the first loop. As this is done on each peg, lift the first loop past the second loop, up over the peg, and then let go of it behind the peg. Carry the yarn to the second peg and repeat from *. Continue until the cap is the desired length. Tie on new colors or new skeins of yarn with a light, well-made square knot, and continue knitting. It is possible to make the piece heavier by wrapping the frame two or three times around, resulting in two or three wraps

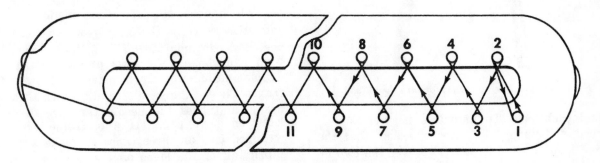

Figure 10–12. Removing the work from the frame.

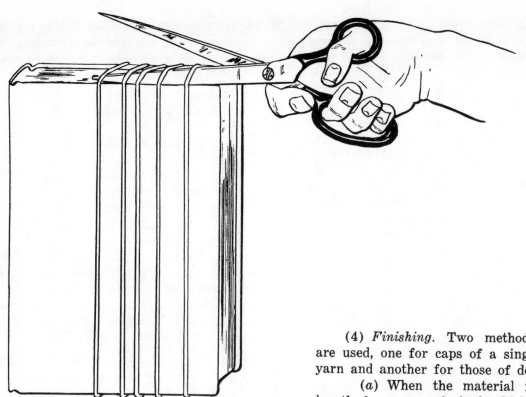

Figure 10-13. Measuring and cutting yarn for fringe.

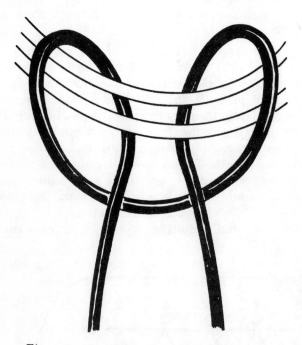

Figure 10-14. Fixing the fringe into the stitch.

around each peg. To knit this heavier fabric, proceed, following * to * above, except that the bottom loop of yarn is pulled up over the two or three loops on the peg instead of just one loop.

(4) *Finishing.* Two methods of finishing are used, one for caps of a single thickness of yarn and another for those of double thickness.

(*a*) When the material is of sufficient length for a cap of single thickness, break off the yarn about a yard from the last stitch. Thread a large needle onto the far end of this yarn and pass it through the loops of yarn on the pegs, in succession. When the yarn has passed through all of the loops, remove the loops from the frame and draw them together on the strand of yarn. Pull the loops together firmly and sew them up with the strand of yarn and needle so that they are flat and firm and will not pull out.

(*b*) For a cap of double thickness, the piece must be twice as long as the finished cap is to be. When it is of sufficient length, cut the yarn so as to leave about a yard of yarn from the last peg used. To double the material, follow the row from the last stitch made, down to the bottom edge of the piece. At the bottom, there will be two loose stitches. Bring them up through *the center* of the frame and loop them over the peg which holds the last stitch made. Loop the end stitches from the next row over the next peg, and continue until all of the stitches have been looped over the pegs and the knitting is double and hanging down inside the center of the frame. Thread the yard strand of yarn through a needle and pass the needle through all of the loops on each peg. (If the frame has been wrapped two or three times to make a heavier fabric, all of the loops on the peg are threaded onto the needle.) Tie and sew as for single fabric.

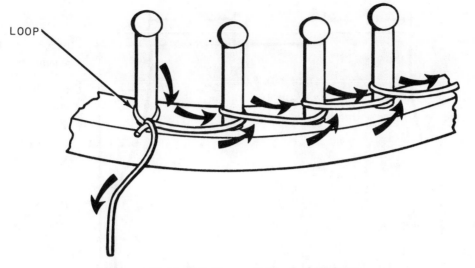

LOOP

Figure 10–16. Winding a round rake knit frame.

10–8. Types of Projects

Although rake knitting is not nearly as versatile as the conventional type of knitting, many interesting and useful projects can be made in this manner.

a. On the straight frame, it is possible to make squares and stripes for an afghan or baby blanket, stoles, and scarves. A size between a stole and a scarf can be folded over, sewed or crocheted up the back, and a ribbon put through to make a hood. It is also possible to make sweaters on these frames. Directions for a boy's slipover sweater are listed below.

(1) Boy's slipover sweater (without collar).

(*a*) Quantity of yarn required: 10–11 ounces of four-ply yarn.

(*b*) Gauge: Three pegs = 1 inch of knitting, 4 rows of knitting per inch.

(*c*) Rake: No. 2 (3/8 inch–3/4 inch) makes a very good sweater. No. 3 (3/8 inch–5/8 inch) makes a closer sweater.

(2) Study figures 10–17 and 10–18 carefully and consult them as you follow the directions given here. The back and front of the sweater are knitted in one piece. Triple stitch is used for the bands at the bottom of the sweater and double stitch for the body part.

(3) To knit the back of the sweater (fig. 10–17)—

(*a*) Cast stitches on about 36 pegs to make it 12 inches wide.

(*b*) Knit 2 1/2 inches of triple stitch.

(*c*) Change from triple stitch to double stitch by winding rake and lifting the two lower threads over the upper thread and off the rake.

(*d*) Knit 10 1/2 inches double stitch.

(*e*) Cast stitches off four pegs at both ends of knitting (A–A, fig. 10–17).

(*f*) Knit 1 1/4 inches.

(*g*) Cast stitches off two pegs at each end of knitting (B–B, fig. 10–17).

(*h*) Knit 1 1/4 inches.

(*i*) Cast stitches off two more pegs at each end (C–C, fig. 10–17).

(*j*) Knit 2 inches.

(*k*) Cast stitches off 9 pegs directly in the center of the knitting to make the back of the neck (fig. 10–20).

(4) To knit the front of sweater (fig. 10–18)—

(*a*) Knit both shoulders straight for 3 inches, using a separate ball of yarn for each shoulder.

(*b*) Then, to make the V neck, every time the yarn is wound toward the center, add one peg on each shoulder piece until the two parts of the knitting meet in the center at E.

(*c*) Add two pegs at C and B, figure 10–18, on both armholes.

(*d*) Add four pegs at A, figure 10–18, on both armholes.

(*e*) If the sweater is to be left open down the front for a few inches and laced with a cord, continue using the two balls of yarn, winding each from the side of the sweater to the center only and back to the side. If the sweater is to

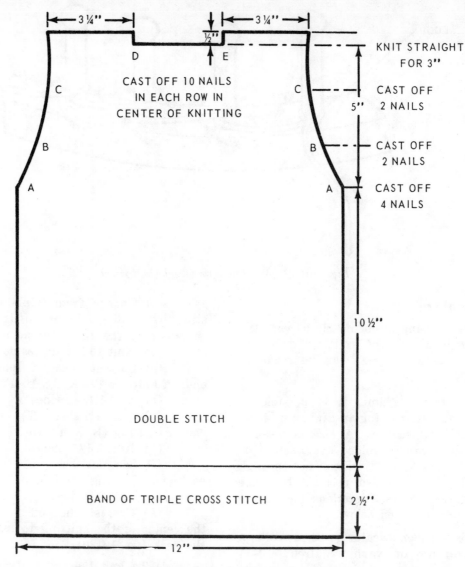

Figure 10–17. Pattern for back of boy's slipover sweater.

be closed from point E, figure 10–18, down, cut off one ball when the last winding brings it to the armhole at A, figure 10–18. Continue knitting the full width of the front with the other ball.

(f) Knit 10 1/2 inches.

(g) Change from double stitch to triple stitch for the band by winding once across the rake and back to make three threads around each peg before lifting the lowest thread over the upper two and off.

(h) Knit 2 1/2 inches triple stitch to correspond to the band at the bottom of the back of the sweater.

(i) Cast knitting from the rake.

(j) Take up the loose stitches at the be-

ginning of the knitting at the lower edge of the back.

(k) Sew up the underarm seams.

(l) If sweater is to be sleeveless, crochet around the armholes and the neck with a single crochet stitch. If the neck has been left open down the front for a few inches, crochet around this opening, making loops for the cord lacing.

(5) To knit the sleeves (fig. 10–19)—

(a) Begin to knit the sleeve at the top. Cast stitches on 16 pegs in the center of the rake, 8 pegs in each row.

(b) Using the single stitch, add 2 pegs in each winding until about 30 pegs are in use,

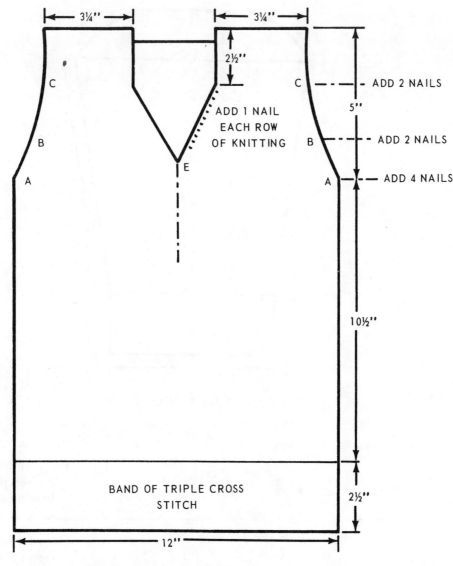

3¼"

3¼"

2½"

C

ADD 2 NAILS

5"

C

B

ADD 2 NAILS

ADD 1 NAIL
EACH ROW
OF KNITTING

B

A

ADD 4 NAILS

A

E

10½"

BAND OF TRIPLE CROSS
STITCH

2½"

12"

*Figure 10–18. Pattern for front of boy's slipover
sweater.*

15 pegs in each row. The sleeve should measure about 10 inches at E–F, figure 10–19.

(c) Knit five rows, then cast a stitch off one peg on one side of the sleeve.

(d) Knit five rows, then cast a stitch off one peg on the other side.

(e) Knit four rows, cast a stitch off one peg on the first side of the sleeve.

(f) Knit four rows, cast a stitch off one peg on the other side.

(g) Repeat (e) and (f) and (e) again.

(h) Knit three rows, then drop one peg on each side.

(i) When the sleeve measures 12 inches from D to F, figure 10–20, change to a double stitch on the next winding. Knit 2 1/2 inches double stitch for the cuff.

(j) Cast the knitting from the rake.

(6) The details for decreasing at neck and armholes are shown in figure 10–20.

b. The circular frame is less versatile than the straight one; however, interesting and colorful caps and tubular scarves can be made in various sizes for different members of the family.

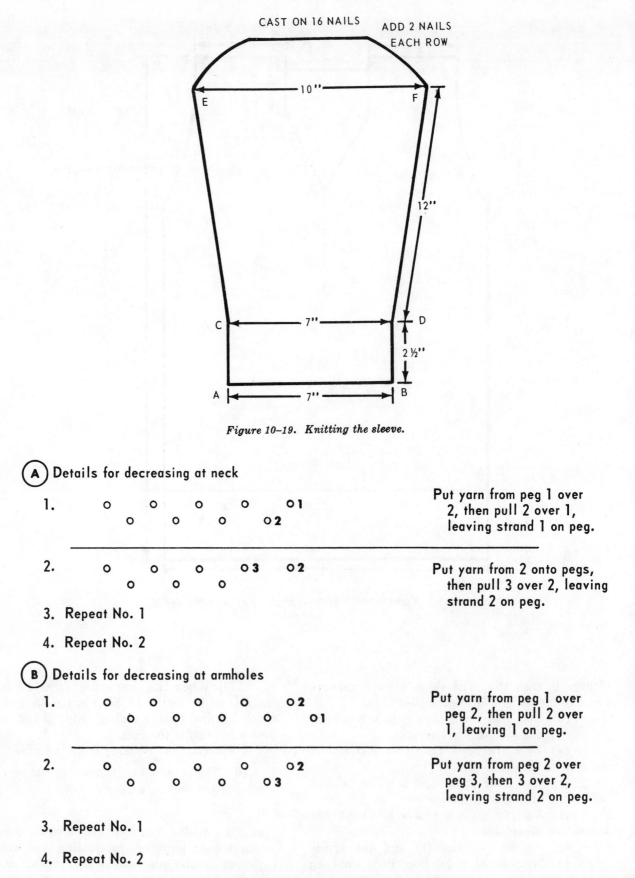

CAST ON 16 NAILS   ADD 2 NAILS
EACH ROW

10"

E   F

12"

C   7"   D

2½"

A   7"   B

Figure 10–19. Knitting the sleeve.

(A) Details for decreasing at neck

1.   ○   ○   ○   ○   ○1
       ○   ○   ○   ○2

Put yarn from peg 1 over
2, then pull 2 over 1,
leaving strand 1 on peg.

2.   ○   ○   ○   ○3   ○2
       ○   ○   ○

Put yarn from 2 onto pegs,
then pull 3 over 2, leaving
strand 2 on peg.

3.   Repeat No. 1

4.   Repeat No. 2

(B) Details for decreasing at armholes

1.   ○   ○   ○   ○   ○2
       ○   ○   ○   ○   ○1

Put yarn from peg 1 over
peg 2, then pull 2 over
1, leaving 1 on peg.

2.   ○   ○   ○   ○   ○2
       ○   ○   ○   ○3

Put yarn from peg 2 over
peg 3, then 3 over 2,
leaving strand 2 on peg.

3.   Repeat No. 1

4.   Repeat No. 2

*Figure 10–20. Details for decreasing (a) neck and (b)
armholes.*

Section III. NEEDLEWORK

10–11. Crocheting

Crocheting is done with a single needle which has a hook on the end. The stitches used in crocheting are based on variations of a loop pulled through another loop. A partial list of articles which can be crocheted follows:

Afghans
*Baby clothes
*Bags
 Bedspreads
*Belts
*Collars

*Gloves
*Hats
*House slippers
*Lace trim
*Mittens

*Rugs and
    bathmats
*Stoles
*Sweaters
  Tablecloths

*Shorter projects that are usually more practical for use in occupational therapy.

a. Equipment. A crochet hook is the only equipment needed to crochet. These hooks come in various sizes and in several materials.

(1) Steel crochet hooks are the smallest of the three kinds. They are usually 5 inches long and range in size from No. 15, which is the smallest, to No. 00, which is the largest of this type. The steel hooks are used mainly with cotton crochet thread of various sizes, although the larger ones can be used with wool.

(2) Bone hooks are usually 4 1/2 to 5 inches long and range in size from No. 1 to No. 6. They are made to be used with wool.

(3) Plastic and aluminum hooks can be 5 1/2, 6, 9, or 10 inches in length. Size is con-fusing as it is indicated in different ways by different manufacturers. Some manufacturers use letters, some numbers, and some use both. Usually, the number system runs from 0, the smallest, to 9, the largest.

(4) Wooden crochet hooks are 9 to 10 inches long and are sized from No. 7, the smallest, to No. 16. These large hooks are designed to use for crocheting with rug yarn, rags, and roving, usually to make rugs and bathmats.

(5) Afghan hooks are made for work in afghan stitch. They may be of plastic, aluminum, or steel. They are from 9 to 12 inches long.

b. Supplies. Crochet cotton is available in 6 ply, 4 ply, and 3 ply. It is a high-twist, cotton material, ranging in size from No. 250, the smallest and not commonly available, to No. 1 for rather coarse work. Heavier cotton is marked "heavy." Table 10–1 indicates in general the size of crochet cotton to use for various projects and the size of needle recommended for the size of cotton.

Table 10–1. Size of Crochet Cotton Thread and Hook

	Texture of work	Cotton thread	Size thread	Size hook
FINE:	Lace, insertions, church lace, edgings.	Mercerized crochet cotton.	60 70 80	12–13 13–14 15–16
MEDIUM:	Edgings, insertions, doilies, tablecloths, bedspreads, chair sets, church laces.	Six-cord mercerized crochet cotton.	10 20 30 40 50	6–8 9 10–12 10–12 12
COARSE:	Hats, bags, pot holders, luncheon sets.	"Heavy cotton"	One size only.	1–4

10–12. Embroidery Work

Beautifying household accessories and cloths with embroidery work is a satisfying and transforming art. It can be as simple as following lines marked on a piece of cloth, or it can be an all-absorbing creation of a work of art. Different cultures and ages have contributed to our present knowledge and skills so that embroidery work can be primitive in design and texture or it can be quite sophisticated. Because of the wide variety of selection, the decorating reflects the personality of the decorator and can greatly influence or even establish a decor. Everything from dish towels to wall hangings can be decorated.

a. A partial list of some of the items that can be enhanced with different types of embroidery is given below.

(1) *Applique.* This is the old art of cutting out one piece of material and sewing it onto another piece. A variety of techniques and materials can be used to enhance the beauty of articles such as children's clothes, place mats, quilts, skirts, sweaters, tablecloths, and towels.

(2) *Crewel embroidery.* Crewel is a series of bold, simple stitches embroidered in colorful wool yarn on linen. It, too, is an old art used in some simple patterns as well as in making elaborate wall hangings. At present, it is employed largely in decorating chair covers, handbags, knitting bags, pictures, and pillow tops.

(3) *Cross-stitch.* One of the easiest and most versatile embroidery stitches is the cross-stitch. It can be done on stamped patterns or made from a chart on gingham, monk's cloth, embroidery linen, or needlepoint tapestry. Either embroidery floss or wool yarn can be used, according to the item that is to be decorated. This type of work lends itself effectively to a small simple or complex motif, as well as to an allover tapestry or sampler-type pattern.

(4) *Cutwork.* The fabric, usually linen, is embroidered in buttonhole stitch according to the pattern, then certain areas of the fabric are cut away. This is work to challenge the skilled person. Pieces such as dresser scarves, pillowcases, and tablecloths decorated with cutwork have an elegance and delicacy that are never out of style.

(5) *Monograming.* Initials or a monogram may be put on towels, sheets, pillowcases, scarves, and tablecloths to personalizes them. The satin stitch is perhaps the nicest way to embroider a monogram, but this is a comparatively slow process and a certain degree of skill is required. The project may be shortened and suited to the skill of the worker by using some other stitch such as chain stitch, outline stitch, or cross-stitch.

(6) *Transfer pattern embroidery.* In all probability this is the most frequently used method of decorating common household items. Many items such as dish towels, dresser scarves, guest towels, place mats, pillowcases, tablecloths, and toaster covers may be purchased stamped and ready to embroider. It is also possible to buy iron-on transfer patterns which are pressed with an iron onto the fabric to be decorated. Directions for the stitches used and suggested colors are usually avaialable with the patterns. The work is not complicated, it works up rapidly, and the use of different colors is interesting. This is a good way to learn to embroider; then, if the person is so inclined, he may advance to more difficult techniques and more creative work as his skill develops.

(7) *Needlepoint.* This is one of the old methods of embroidery and it is still very popular. It can be a very simple filling in of a small, ready-marked picture or it can be a very involved design worked on plain needlepoint canvas. Needlepoint is not complicated, as it is most commonly done by purchasing the piece with the design part worked. Filling in the background then becomes a repetitive, relaxing project which can be done while conversing or watching tele-vision. Because needlepoint wears well, it is used for chair seats, footstool covers, glass cases, handbags, pictures, pillows, and even rugs. It is done with a special needlepoint or tapestry wool and with a blunt pointed needle.

b. A needle of the appropriate size is the only equipment essential to doing embroidery work, but some of the aids on the market are helpful.

(1) There are a number of types of needles. In selecting the appropriate one, consideration must be given to the size of the material to be used in relation to the size of the eye through which the material must be threaded. Another consideration is the point of the needle. If it is to go through cloth, it must be sharp; if it is to go betweeen threads as in huck toweling and needlepoint, it should be blunt so as to push the threads aside.

(2) Embroidery hoops are 6- to 8-inch metal or wooden rings made so that one fits over the other. The smaller ring is put under the cloth and the larger ring pushed down over it so that the cloth is held firmly and taut. This assist usually facilitates straighter and more even work.

c. Supplies vary according to what is to be decorated. It is, of course, necessary to have the basic fabric and either cotton or wool floss to use as decoration.

(1) There are three kinds of cotton floss commonly used in embroidery work, and each comes in many colors and shades. These are washable.

(a) Six strand is made up of six untwisted strands which are easily separated for finer work.

(b) Pearl cotton is a loose twist, heavier thread which does not separate.

(c) Rayon, floss, which is a shiny floss, makes the embroidery work stand out more than work in cotton floss, but it tends to be less durable.

(2) Crewel work and needlepoint which are not laundered are usually worked in wool. There is a wool specifically made for needlepoint and a finer one for crewel work.

(3) Transfer patterns can be purchased and the design transferred to the piece to be embroidered, or the piece with the design stamped on it can be purchased.

d. Each type of embroidery work has a set of stitches peculiar to that work. The stitches are not difficult and can usually be figured out from a diagram. As in most other types of needle-work, the skill is in making neat, even stitches and in using colors well.

10–13. Knitting

Knitting is a series of loops or interlocking stitches made with two straight needles. Following is a list of some of the articles which can be knitted:

Afgans
Baby blankets
*Baby clothes
Bedspereads
*Caps
Coats
Dresses
*Gloves
*Hats
*Mittens
*Scarves
*Socks
*Stoles
*Sweaters
*Denotes small projects.

a. *Equipment*. A pair of knitting needles is the only equipment needed for knitting. Knitting needles are made of steel, plastic, aluminum, nylon, or wood and may be single-pointed, double-pointed, or circular. Smaller needles are usually used with finer yarns and larger needles with heavy yarns. Interesting textures such as lacy stoles can be obtained by varying this general rule and using, for instance, a large No. 12 wooden needle with a fine yarn. The knitting pattern will suggest a size of needle and the type of yarn to use, but if the garment is to fit, each knitter must adjust the size of the needle in order to be knitting the number of stitches per inch called for in the pattern gauge.

(1) Single-pointed needles are used in pairs to knit back and forth in rows. Steel needles are made in the smaller sizes of 0, 1, 2, and 3. Aluminum and plastic needles are made in 7-, 10-, 12-, and 14-inch lengths in sizes varying from 0–5 in the shorter lengths and from 0–8 in the longer lengths. Both wooden and plastic needles are avaliable in the large sizes 10–15 in the 14-inch length.

(2) Double-pointed or sock needles are used in sets of four for making the small tubular pieces needed for mittens, socks, and gloves. They are made in 5, 7, 10, and 14 inches; the 5 and 7 inches are the most commonly used. They can be of steel, plastic, or aluminum, and are sized to match the single-pointed needles.

(3) Circular needles are for knitting large tubular pieces such as skirts and some sweaters. They are made of a piece of needle 3 to 5 inches fixed on each end of a plyable nylon or plastic cord. The needle part is sized as are other needles, and the entire length of the circular needle ranges from 9 inches in the smaller sizes to 36 inches in the larger sizes, with 29 inches the most frequently used. It is possible to use these circular needles as single-pointed needles and to knit back and forth in rows with them.

(4) Some of the many available knitting accessories are helpful to have.

(a) Rubber or metal point protectors are used to keep the knitting on the needles when they are not in use.

(b) Small bobbins are useful for holding different colors of yarn while knitting argyles.

(c) Counters are an aid when increasing or decreasing stitches.

(d) Stitch holders are available for holding stitches to be knitted as a later time. A large safety pin is a good substitute.

b. *Supplies*. Wool yarns of innumerable types and textures are most commonly used in knitting, although cottons can also be used. The general types are considered here, with no attempt to go into the many variations within each type.

(1) Knitting worsted is a 4-ply, sturdy wool yarn used for heavy ski-type sweaters, accessories, and afghans. Because of its size, knitting with worsted is faster and less tedious.

(2) Germantown yarn is a 4-ply wool yarn, similar to worsted in thickness, but softer. It is used for carriage covers, afghans, and babies' and children's outer garments.

(3) Fingering yarn is usually 3-ply wool, smooth, lightweight, and soft. It wears well, so men's, women's, and children's socks and light-weight sweaters are made from it.

(4) Sock and sweater yarns are available in both 3-ply and 4-ply wool. Both have a firm, tight twist for firmness and strength, as well as long wear and warmth in socks, gloves, mitttens, and medium-weight sweaters.

(5) Baby yarns, usually 3-ply, may be of wool, nylon, or a mixture. Wool is warmer and more resilient, but it requires more care in laundering than nylon.

(6) Cotton yarns can also be knitted. They are less expensive than wool, cooler to wear, and easier to launder. Because cotton fibers are not

as elastic as wool, the yarn does not stretch, which makes it more difficult to knit than wool. Cotton yarns are used to knit bedspreads, tablecloths, and clothes.

(7) Many other yarns are available for special textures. These include mohair, boucle, angora, bulky knits, and novelty yarns with rayon or metallic threads in the twist.

10–14. Stuffed Toys

These dolls or animals can be made from many types of materials. They can be simple in design or they can be quite complex. What is made depends not only upon the age and size of the recipient, but also upon the finances and the capabilities of the person making the toy.

a. Equipment. All the equipment that is needed is a sewing neeedle, a pattern, and scissors.

b. Supplies. To make stuffed animals, there needs to be material for the outside of the animal, sewing thread, stuffing, and materials to make a face or features.

(1) Material for the outside of the toy can be stockings, socks, gingham, felt, wool, Indianhead, or claico. The material can be new or used, and almost any color can be used.

(2) The pieces can be stitched together with contrasting or matching pearl cotton. six-strand warp thread, or heavy sewing thread.

(3) Materials for stuffing varies almost as much as does material for the outside.
   (*a*) Foam rubber is expensive, heavy, and messy.
   (*b*) Cotton is expensive and it tends to become lumpy, especially if the animal is very large or if it is played with a great deal.
   (*c*) Nylon hose are very good for stuffing as they are light, washable, do not bunch up, and are quite inexpensive. A big problem is getting enough of them.
   (*d*) Lint collected in the dryers of a laundry has been used successfully. It is light, it does not lump, and it is not expensive.

(4) The face can be embroidered, appliqued, or stenciled. Some people like buttons for eyes

and bits of felt for the tongue. These look nice and are recommended unless the child is of the age at which he might pull them off and swallow them.

c. Process. Making a stuffed toy is as much a construction problem as a sewing problem. To make a stuffed toy, this procedure should be followed:

(1) Cut the outside material, using the pattern. Plan the pieces to conserve material and take care to make the right number of pieces for each part of the pattern.

(2) Pin all of the pieces together to be sure that they fit and that there are the correct number of parts.

(3) Sew the pieces together, making sure to have an opening through which to put the stuffing, using one of the following stitches:
   (*a*) Running stitch (fig. 10–21).

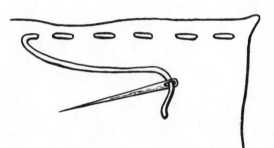

Figure 10–21. Running stitch.

   (*b*) Whipstitch (fig. 10–22).

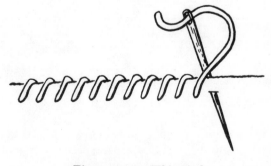

Figure 10–22. Whipstitch.

   (*c*) Buttonhole stitch (fig. 10–23).

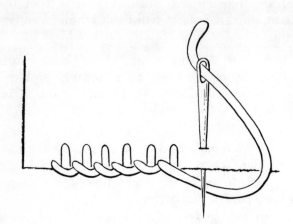

Figure 10-23. Buttonholde stitch.

(4) Put the stuffing in the pieces and sew up the hole. The toy should be soft, so do not put so much stuffing in that it is hard.

(5) Assemble the pieces if so indicated. This is done by sewing them to the appropriate spot at the right angle.

(6) Embroider or applique the face.

CHAPTER 11

LEATHER

11-1. General

Leather has been used as an aid to further man's progress since the time he learned to tie leather around his feet to protect them from injury and to carry water in skin bags so that he could roam farther from the rivers and springs. Early tribes used skins for making tents, beds, armor, harnesses, shoes, and bow strings, and for fastening arrowheads on shafts. The beginnings of recorded history are on skin rolls which go as far back as 1500 B.C. The tanning process was known in Roman times, as Romans made clothing of leather. During the thirteenth century, tanning was developed sufficiently that bed coverings and clothes were made from highly colored and decorated leathers. Because natural and synthetic materials have been developed with properties designed to do a specific job, leather is now considered to be a luxury item rather than as one of the basic materials used for protection from cold and injury. The feeling of luxury, plus the basic satisfaction derived from working to enhance a fine natural product, makes leatherwork a pleasurable and satisfying activity for the craftsman.

11-2. Leathers

Many types of leather are available on the market, so it is important to know how to select the best leather for the intended purpose.

a. Tanning. Skins must be cleaned, cured, and tanned before they become leather. Cleaning removes all of the flesh, hair, and unwanted particles that might cause the skin to decay before it is tanned. Curing preserves the skin until it is tanned. Tanning is the process through which the cured skins are made into durable, lasting leather. The agents used in tanning are mainly vegetable, chrome (chemical), or oil.

(1) In vegetable tanning, which produces the only skins satisfactory for tooling, the pelts are immersed in vats containing water and bark, nuts, and leaves from various plants. The liquid is made stronger each day by the addition of more of the plant materials until every fiber of the leather is permeated. The hides are left in the solution from 2 to 6 months, after which time they are thoroughly worked to clean them of sediment and bark. Vegetable tanned leather absorbs water more readily than do other leathers. The fresh cut is cream tan or light brown in color and, when this leather burns, it becomes black. Perhaps the best and easiest test when purchasing leather is to dampen a bit and make a mark with a tool or with the thumbnail to see how well it takes the mark.

(2) In chrome or chemical tanning, the pelts are immersed in solutions of water, common salt, and acids to open the pores of the skins. Then the chrome salts, when added, can penetrate rapidly and completely, thus producing chrome-tanned skins within a few hours. Because of this, chrome-tanned leather is less expensive than vegetable-tanned leather. It can be used for projects that will not be decorated since chrome-tanned leathers resist water and cannot be tooled or carved. A freshly cut piece of chrome-tanned leather shows a gray-green edge and retains that color when it is burned. Once again, one of the best tests is to dampen a bit if it and make a small mark with a tool or the thumbnail to see if the mark stays in the leather.

(3) Some leather is oil- or chamois-tanned. This process is used for flexible soft leathers such as chamois skins.

b. Types of Leather. There are many types of leather, each with characteristics which make it appropriate for certain uses.

(1) *Carving and tooling leathers.*
(a) *Calfskin.* Calf is a fine-grained, lightweight, close-textured leather used commercially for the upper parts of shoes, for purses, for bookbindings, and for other fine leather articles. It is available in many colors and can be embossed to imitate other types of leather. Tooling calf has an especially soft surface which can be decorated by a number of different processes. Wal-

lets, writing secretaries, picture frames, and key cases are most commonly made from tooling calf. The skins range in size from 10 to 14 square feet.

(b) *Cowhide.* This is a heavy coarse-grained leather. Since it can be processed into several types of leather, it has many uses. Saddles and shoe soles are made from the heavy thicknesses, or the hide may be thinned and used in the making of handbags and billfold backs. In thinning, it is sometimes split into different thicknesses which are used for moccasin soles and shoe linings. The split can be buffed and made into suede or velvet splits which are strong and durable. Since these hides are large, they are usually cut and sold by the side, which is 20–25 square feet.

(c) *Morocco.* Actually goat leather, this is available in many colors. Frequently, it is embossed for commercial use. It is is not embossed, it can be tooled and used for billfolds, book bindings, and linings. It is usually 2 1/2-ounce weight, and the skins vary in size up to 10 square feet.

(d) *Pigskin.* This is a coarse-grained, very strong, durable leather. It can be tooled, but not easily. Letter cases, purses, and wallets are made of this leather. It varies a great deal in thickness, and the hides are from 9 to 16 square feet in size.

(e) *Sheepskin.* This leather is less expensive but is not as strong or as durable as calf. It can be tooled, however, and is available in a number of colors. The skins are medium in weight and vary from 7 to 12 square feet.

(f) *Steerhide.* Steer is a pebbly-grained pliable leather. It tools well and can be used for any project appropriate to its 2 1/2- to 5-ounce weight. Because the hide is large, it is sold by the side, which ranges from 20 to 28 square feet.

(2) *Lining leathers.*

(a) *Chrome calf.* Because of the tanning process, this leather cannot be tooled. Lightweight chrome calf, available in several colors, makes a smooth, fine lining. The skins are from 7 to 12 square feet in size.

(b) *Skiver.* This is a very thin sheepskin which is good for lining when little additional thickness is desired. Because it is so thin, it is not strong so it should be cemented solidly to the piece being lined. Available in several colors, the skins are from 6 to 12 square feet.

(c) *Suede.* This is a type of leather finish, rather than a type of leather. Lining suede is usually made from sheep and is dyed in a wide range of colors. Skins are from 5 to 9 square feet.

(3) *Miscellaneous leathers.* The following leathers cannot be tooled, but they are interesting to work with because of the texture of the leather itself. With these leathers, the design of the project and the skillful use of the leather makes the project interesting. Of course, all chrome-tanned cowhide, steer, and calf belong in this group of leathers. Others are as follows:

(a) *Alligator.* Genuine alligator is a beautifully grained leather which comes in shades of mahogany and brown. It is used commercially for shoes, billfolds, keycases, belts, and handbags. Some of these articles can be made in occupational therapy. The leather is sold by the inch and the skins are from 6 to 14 inches wide.

(b) *Alligator calf.* Calf which is embossed to look like alligator but is much less expensive. It comes in a variety of colors and the skins may be as large as 14 square feet.

(c) *Embossed cow or steerhide.* This heavy durable leather is used for briefcases, notebooks, handbags, and other large projects. Usually black or brown, it is sold by the side, which comes as large as 28 square feet.

(d) *Lizard.* In general, this leather is used in the same way as alligator. The grain is finer, however, and the skins are smaller, ranging from 8 to 11 inches wide.

(e) *Ostrich.* Genuine ostrich is identified by the quill holes. It is a beautifully grained leather for handbags, wallets, key cases, and belts. This grain pattern is frequently embossed on less expensive leathers. True ostrich skins range in size up to 14 square feet.

(f) *Slunk or unborn calf.* Because of its source, this leather is soft and pliable and is tanned with the very flat short hair of the calf still on the leather. It comes in brown or black with white and is used to make handbags, wallets, belts and other small projects. The hides are small, 4 to 5 square feet, and quite expensive. The shorter the hair, the higher the price. Baby calf may be substituted for slunk, but the leather is not as soft and the hair is longer. In some substitutes for slunk, the hair is clipped to make it shorter.

c. *Purchasing Leather.* Much of the effectiveness of leatherwork depends upon the selection of quality leathers, so the expert craftsman needs to be particular about the type of leather he uses.

Because the better grades of leather are expensive, it is important to buy and to use the leather wisely. In ordering, the type, grade, amount, thickness, and color desired must be designated.

(1) *Type.* The use to which the leather will be put, as well as individual preference, dictates the type.

(2) *Grade.* Some tanneries indicate the grades of leather with letters; others, with numbers. The grade refers to the range markings in the finished sides rather than to the processing or to the wearing qualities. Because there is a limited amount of "A" or "1" grades, this grade is considerably more expensive than the others.

(3) *Amount.*

(a) *Hide or whole skin.* Leather from smaller animals, such as calf, pig, lamb, and goat, are sold by the skin. There are parts of the skin such as the neck, legs, belly, and flank that are not too desirable for carving. Since the price is less for a skin than for a choice cut, it is usually more economical to buy an entire skin where quantities are used and where objects of different shapes are made. The less desirable areas can be used for gussets or for inside pockets.

(b) *Side.* Leather from larger animals, such as cowhide, comes by the side or half hide and is sold by the square foot. One side is usually 22 to 26 square feet. Included in the footage are the less desirable areas such as the neck, leg, belly, and flank areas (fig. 11–1).

(c) *Back.* A back of leather is a side with the belly part cut off. It is usually 15 to 18 square feet.

(d) *The square foot.* This method is generally used when a rather small quantity (1 to 3 square feet) is desired for one project. The price is somewhat higher than for a whole or half skin, but there is no waste.

(e) *Leather cut to the exact size of the patterns.* All waste is eliminated in this way, but the price is higher than for either of the two other methods. For most projects, the price will be specified per square inch.

(f) *Cutout project kit.* Many leather items may be bought already cut and put up in kits. Leather is quite expensive when purchased in this way unless only one item is to be made.

(g) *The pound.* Many companies have assortments of small pieces of leather suitable for making small projects. These pieces of leather are sold at a specified price per pound and are inexpensive; however, they are sometimes crushed or creased.

(4) *Thickness.* Getting the right thickness of the leather is also important to the finished product. The thicker leathers are more expensive, of course. Tanners are now grading the thickness by the weight; an ounce represents 1/64 inch of leather in thickness. Table 11–1 compares the thickness, the ounces, and the recommended uses.

d. Leather Storage. Leather must be stored in a clean, dry place to keep mildew from forming and out of direct sunlight so that it will not change color. It must also be stored so as to prevent wrinkles and folds. Ideally, skins should be stored flat in a drawer or on a table. Because so much space is required for this arrangement, substitutes have been devised. Leather can be hung, grain side up, over a round-topped sawhorse or pole. The round top prevents creasing. If such an arrangement is not practical, several hides of leather can be rolled, *grain side out* to prevent wrinkles, over a corrugated paper core, then covered with paper to protect them from scratches. Rolls of leather must be stored flat, rather than on end, to keep the ends from creasing.

11–3. Leather Tools, Findings, and Supplies

Much of the leather, tools, findings, and supplies are more economical if purchased in quantity.

a. Tools. Although almost any number of leather tools can be purchased, it is possible to do nice leatherwork with only a leather punch, ruler, knife, modeler, needles, swivel knife, the seven basic carving tools, a snap set, and a mallet. Other tools are designed to do a specific job with more facility. Some of the leather tools are chrome plated and therefore rustproof, but the

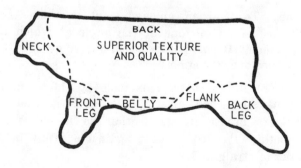

Figure 11–1. Portions of a side of leather.

Table 11-1. Thicknesses and Uses of Leather.

Thickness	Ounces	Inches	Recommended Project	Comments
	3 or 4	3/64 or 4/64	Billfold backs Zipper gussets Pocket secretary backs	Carving jobs where leather needs more body than calf.
	4 or 5	4/64 or 5/64	Heavy wallet backs Light clutch bags	Versatile. Makes heavier articles than thickness above, lighter than thickness below.
	5 or 6	5/64 or 6/64	Small bags Light bag straps	
	6 or 7	6/64 or 7/64	Carved handbags Contour belts Straps	Most popular weight.
	7 or 8	7/64 or 8/64	Large handbags Carved narrow belts Briefcase backs Small pistol holsters	
	8 or 9	8/64 or 9/64	Wider belts Rifle holsters Pistol holsters Saddlebags	Heft and substance.
	9 or 10	9/64 or 10/64	Wide belts Heavy pistol holsters	Heavy-duty articles.
	10 or 11	10/64 or 11/64	Lineman's belts	Strength and body. Easy to carve.

steel tools must be kept free from rust by rubbing them with steel wool occasionally and coating them lightly with oil if they are to be stored for any length of time. However, the oil must be removed from the tool before it is used. The sharp edges of tools need special care to prevent nicks and to keep them sharp enough to cut leather smoothly.

(1) *Awl.* Awls (fig. 11–2) are available in several sizes and are used to punch holes for saddle stitching. They are also used to enlarge holes. To sharpen an awl, pull it along the surface of an oilstone at the angle at which it is ground. Revolve it between the fingers as it is pulled over the stone.

(2) *Bone folder.* This tool (fig. 11–3) may be made of wood, plastic, or bone. It is used to make a crease in the leather so it will fold smoothly. It must be used against a firmly held ruler or straightedge.

(3) *Cement jar.* These jars for rubber ce-

Figure 11-2. Saddler's awl.

Figure 11-3. Bone folder.

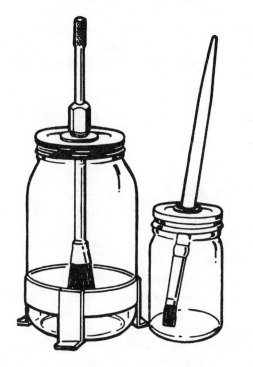

Figure 11-4. Cement jars.

Figure 11-5. Dividers.

ment are made with a brush permanently inserted (fig. 11-4), which saves both time and cement. The larger jar holds 6 1/2 ounces of cement and has a metal bracket with which it can be fastened to the workbench. The smaller jar holds 4 ounces and has a smaller brush. Unless many people are doing leatherwork, there are important advantages to using the smaller jar. It holds less cement so if the cement dries, less is lost;

the brush is smaller so it is easier to control than the larger brush in the larger jar; and there is a convenience in having several small jars rather than one large one.

(4) *Dividers.* Dividers (fig. 11-5) are used to space stitches and holes, as well as to lay out circles.

(5) *Draw gauge.* A draw gauge (fig. 11-6) is an efficient and time-saving device for cutting straight pieces of heavy leather such as are used in belts and bag straps. The blade can be replaced when it becomes dull. The tool can be adjusted to cut strips from 1/4 inch to 3 1/2 inches.

(*a*) Loosen the wingnut at the far end of the handle, then set the handle the desired distance from the blade, and tighten the wingnut.

NOTE

Before cutting the strap with this tool, one edge of the leather must be straight, as the part above the handle of the tool follows the contour of the leather.

(*b*) With a knife, make a 1/4- to 1/2-inch starting cut at the end of the leather.

(*c*) Slip the blade into this cut and have the cut edge of the leather against the flat part of the tool above the handle. Carefully pull the handle, thereby forcing the blade through the leather, to cut it. Take care to keep the cut edge of the leather firmly against the tool.

NOTE

It is sometimes easier to hold the draw gauge in a vise and pull the leather along the blade.

(6) *Edge beveler.* This is a knife-like tool (fig. 11-7) shaped to bevel and round off the cut edges of leather. Edge bevelers are available

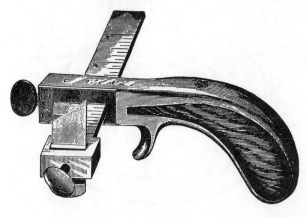

Figure 11-6. Draw gauge.

227

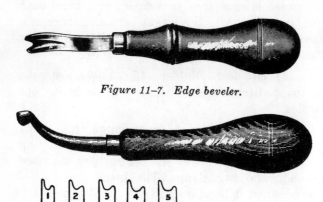

Figure 11-7. Edge beveler.

Figure 11-8. Edge creaser.

Figure 11-9. Using a lignum vitae edge creaser.

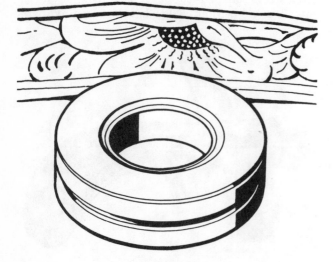

Figure 11-10. Edge slicker.

in several sizes to accommodate different thicknesses of leather. For the best results, cutting should be done with the grain of the leather, and the tool must be kept sharp. It is sharpened by wrapping a piece of emery cloth around a round object of a diameter to fit the curvature of the edger and then moving the tool back and forth over the emery cloth.

(7) *Edge creaser.* A creaser is used to make a line parallel with the edge of a piece of leather. The line provides a finishing touch to raw edges and is especially good for edging straps and belts. At least two types of tools are made to do this, and they come in several sizes in order to make lines of different distances from the edge of the leather.

(a) *Metal edge creaser.* The metal end of the creaser (fig. 11-8) marks the leather. For a different size of line, a different tool is needed. There are, however, creasers which can be adjusted to any desired size.

(b) *Lignum vitae creaser.* According to some craftsmen, the wood on a lignum vitae creaser (fig. 11-9) makes a line of better color on the leather than does metal. The tool is grooved on both sides and on both ends so that lines of four different sizes are readily available.

(8) *Edge slicker.* This slicker (fig. 11-10) is made of lignum vitae and is used to burnish the raw edges of heavy leather such as straps. The leather is dampened and the slicker is rubbed vigorously back and forth along the edge to produce a brown burnished color. If a slicker is not available, identical results may be obtained by using heavy, clean, brown wrapping paper in the same way.

(9) *Embossing wheel and carriage.* This tool, used for decorating borders of leather, consists of one or more cylindrical stamps on which there is a negative design. As the cylinder is rolled over damp leather, the design is pressed into the leather. Different stamps may be purchased for a variety of designs (fig. 11-11).

(10) *Eyelet setters.* These tools are made to spread the underside of eyelets and thereby set them in the leather. Several types of setters are available.

(a) *Punch-type eyelet setter.* For best results, holes are punched with a punch, then the eyelets are set with this tool (fig. 11-12).

(b) *Eyelet setter.* With this setter (fig. 11-13), a mallet must be used to drive the setter into the eyelet.

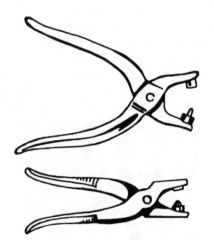

Figure 11-11. Embossing wheel and designs.

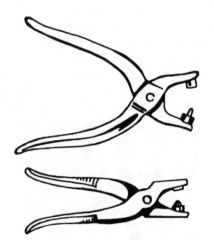

Figure 11-12. Puch-type eyelet setter.

Figure 11-13. Eyelet setter.

Figure 11-14. Fid.

(11) *Fid.* This awl-like tool with a somewhat rounded point (fig. 11-14) is used for enlarging holes, for stippling, and for tightening lacing.

(12) *Golka pliers.* These special pliers (fig.

11-15) are designed with one, sometimes two, notches in the jaw for shaping the golka tips around leather lacing to form a lacing needle.

(13) *Golka tip.* Lacing needles are made by pinching these metal tips (fig. 11-16) around the end of a piece of lacing with golka pliers. They are available in 1- and 2-inch lengths.

(14) *Gouger.* This is an adjustable tool (fig. 11-17) for cutting grooves of different depths in heavy leather to aid in making a place for the leather to fold.

(15) *Grommet setter.* The grommet setter (fig. 11-18) works on the same principle as the eyelet setter but sets large grommets, which usually have washers. The setters are made in several sizes in order to accommodate gormmets of different sizes.

(16) *Knives.* Several different types of knives are used in leatherwork, for different purposes. All of them must be kept sharp in order to work efficiently.

(a) *Cutting knives.* There are several kinds of cutting knives, and the choice is usually the preference of the user. The knives in A and B, figure 11-19 must be sharpened like chisels, but C, figure 11-19 has a heavy-duty replaceable blade. This blade is also retractable and can be pulled completely back into the handle or extended to three different lengths.

(b) *Skiving knives.* Figure 11-20 illustrates three types of skiving knives. The first one (A, fig. 11-20), a skife, is a curved holder for Schick injector blades which are easily replaced

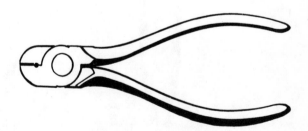

Figure 11-15. Golka pliers.

Figure 11-16. Gokla tip.

Figure 11-17. Gouger.

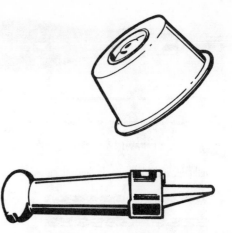

Figure 11-18. Grommet setter.

when they become dull. This type of skiver is perhaps the easiest to use. The knife in B, figure 11-20, a skiving knife, is good for skiving into hard-to-reach places. To work effectively, this knife must be kept very sharp and well honed. The head knife (C, fig. 11-20) is for cutting

heavy leather; it is used more by skilled leather craftsmen than by amateurs. It is especially good for cutting around corners and also doubles as a skiver. Both sides of this knife blade need to be sharpened. To do this, start with one point of the blade on the oilstone and use a circular motion and at the same time gradually turn the handle around to the other point. Then, turn the blade over and repeat the process on the other side.

(c) *Swivel knife.* This is the knife (fig. 11-21) used to cut the design and the decorative cuts in leather carving. It is called a swivel knife because the lower part swivels. Some swivel knives are adjustable to any size of hand; others

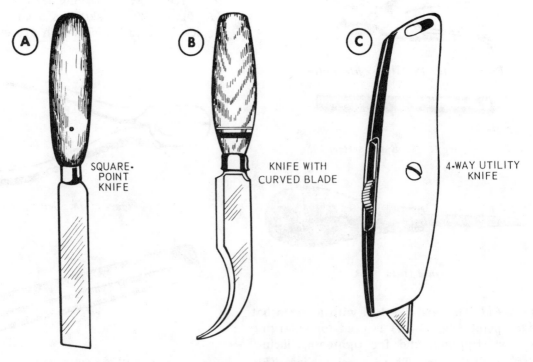

A SQUARE-POINT KNIFE

B KNIFE WITH CURVED BLADE

C 4-WAY UTILITY KNIFE

Figure 11-19. Cutting knives.

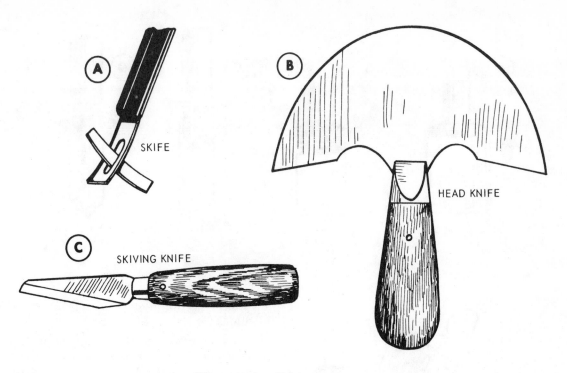

Figure 11-20. Skiving knives.

do not adjust. Some are made so that the blades are easily removable and a blade, especially ground for a specific work, can be slipped into the shaft. Blades can be hollow ground (A, fig. 11–22), straight (B, fig. 11–22), angled (C, fig. 11–22), and even double pointed (D, fig. 11–22). The blade of the swivel knife must be kept very sharp for best results. The principle of sharpening the blade is the same as it is for chisels. Figure 11–23 illustrates a swivel knife sharpener. This guide is designed to hold the swivel knife blade at the right angle to assist the beginner in maintaining the correct bevel as it is stroked on the sharpening stone. Another great help in keeping the swivel knife blade in top condition is to keep a strop handy so that the blade can be stropped frequently. This strop can be made by gluing the smooth side of a piece of leather to a board. The flesh side of the leather should be rubbed well with jeweler's rouge. Whenever the blade begins to pull as it cuts through the leather, it should be stropped on the leather. This extra care of the blade will pay off well in better and more pleasurable carving.

(17) *Lacing pliers.* These pliers (A, fig. 11–24) are not an essential tool, but they come in handy when the lacing is hard to pull and for reaching up through layers of leather to reach the needle.

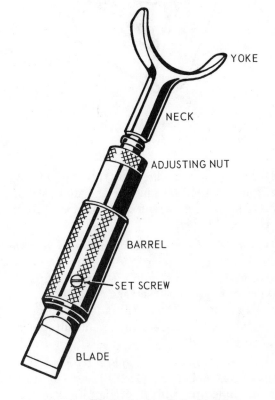

Figure 11-21. Swivel knife.

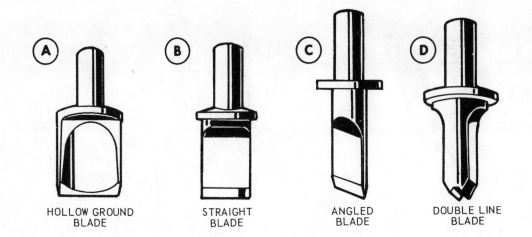

Figure 11–22. Swivel knife blades.

HOLLOW GROUND BLADE   STRAIGHT BLADE   ANGLED BLADE   DOUBLE LINE BLADE

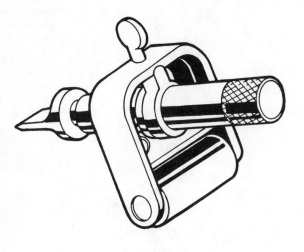

Figure 11–23. Swivel knife sharpener.

(18) *Lacing pony.* The pony (B, fig. 11–24) was designed to facilitate lacing or saddle stitching by enabling the person to work with both hands (C, fig. 11–24).

(19) *Mallet.* Mallets may be made of lignum vitae, hickory, rawhide (fig. 11–25), or fiber. They are used to strike saddle stamps, snap setters, eyelet and grommet setters, etc. These nonmetal tools are used rather than a metal hammer, so the metal leather tools will not mushroom on the end being tapped.

(20) *Marking gauge or space marker.* This is a spur-like tool (fig. 11–26) used to mark leather for punching with a single punch or awl. The points on the spur are spaced to mark a certain number of markings per inch. The gauges come in different sizes, or they have interchangeable wheels which make 5, 6, or 7 marks per inch. To use the marker, push it along the leather,

using a straightedge or a marked line for a guide.

(21) *Modeling tools.* Modeling tools are designed to press on dampened leather to make a permanent mark. A number of modeling tools in various sizes and shapes are available on the market, but only these types are needed to do all but the most specialized type of work. These tools must be kept smooth and free from nicks or burrs, as any defect in the tool will mark or even cut the leather. *Fine* steel wool or crocus cloth and the rouge board can be used to keep modeling tools smooth.

(a) *Modeler.* A, Figure 11–27 illustrates the most used of the three modeling tools. One end is elongated and curved so it is useful for tracing, stippling, and lining, and for modeling in small places. It is also handy for ripping out or tightening lacing and for reaching a lacing end in an otherwise inaccessible place. The opposite end is flattened and curved into a spoon-shaped end for modeling. Most modeling can be done with this tool. It is often called a number one modeler.

(b) *Deerfoot.* This tool (B, fig. 11–27) is so named because the shape of the ends resembles a deer's foot. The ends are the same shape, but one is smaller than the other. The deerfoot is used in places which are too small for the modeler. It is also good for beveling and for depressing outlines. Because of the sharpness of its end, even a slight bump may cause a rough spot in the tool, so it should be checked for rough spots before it is used.

(c) *Ball tool.* A sphere at each end makes this tool (C, fig. 11–27) ideal for embossing leather and for stippling. One sphere is larger than the other.

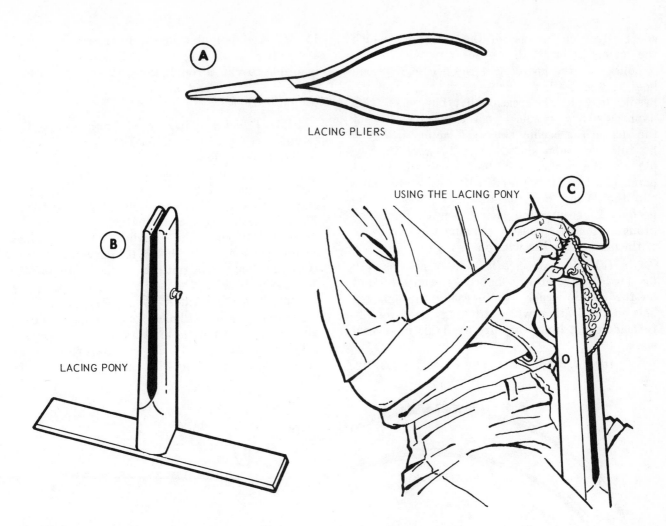

Figure 11-24. Use of lacing pliers and lacing pony.

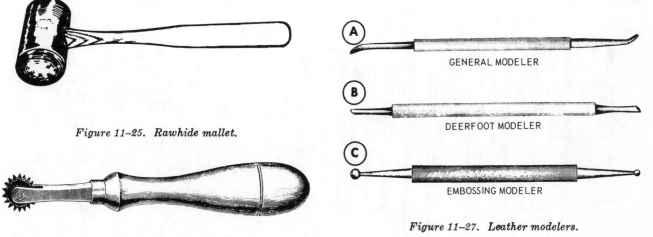

Figure 11-25. Rawhide mallet.

Figure 11-26. Marking gauge.

Figure 11-27. Leather modelers.

(22) *Leather needles.* There are several types of leather needles, each specific for the type of work to be done.

(a) *Curved needle.* These needles (A, fig. 11-28) can sew in places where a straight needle would be hard to manage.

(b) *Two-prong lacing needle.* Although there are other needles designed for leather lacing, this type (B and C, fig. 11-28) is the most commonly used because of the ease with which the lacing is inserted, the security with which it holds, and the low cost of the needle. The end holding the leather may get "sprung," or the needle may break occasionally, but when this happens a new needle is not expensive. To put the lace in the needle, skive the lacing so that it fits into the wedge-shaped space between the two parts of the needle. Open the needle with the left hand (F, fig. 11–28) and with the right hand slip the lacing between the two parts of the needle. To secure the lacing, gently force the prongs into the lacing by pushing the two parts of the needle together with pliers.

(c) *Harness needle*. These needles (D, fig. 11–28) have an egg-shaped eye and are blunt on the end in order to slip easily through the hole in the leather when stitching. Used mainly for saddle stitching, they are available in several sizes.

(d) *Glovers needle*. These needles (E, fig.

11–28) are triangular shaped in cross section and are sharp on the edges, as well as at the point, in order to cut through the leather. They come in several sizes and are used in sewing light-weight leather.

(23) *Punches*. There are a number of different types of punches, each designed to do a certain type of job.

(a) *Grip punches*. Punches with handles that are squeezed together are frequently called grip punches. They are used in occupational therapy frequently to strengthen grasp of the hand. To overcome the drawback of having just a limited number of holes to punch, a saddle stamping tool can be put into a tube of the punch. The grasp is strengthened then, as the design is pressed into the leather. Some grip punches are made to punch round holes, some punch slit holes, and some punch both kinds. The *rotary or revolving punch* (fig. 11–29) is one of the most versatile of the round hole punches because six

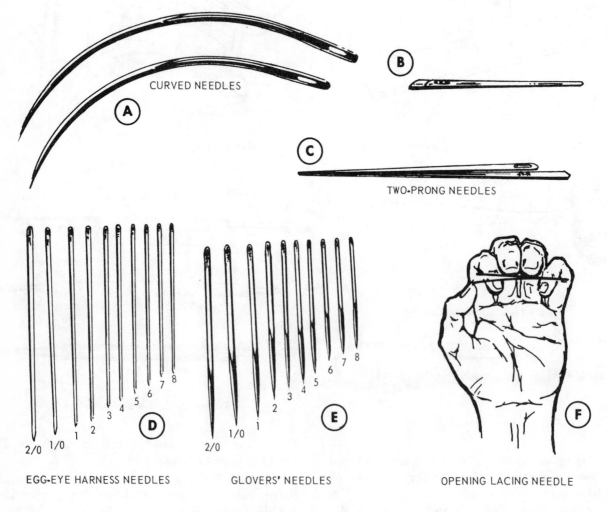

Figure 11–28. Leather needles.

sizes of holes are available by just turning the revolving head. It is particularly handy when setting snaps which need two sizes of holes. Tubes can be replaced or sharpened when they become dull. To sharpen them, place the punch in a vise. Pull a strip of medium abrasive cloth back and forth along the shank and cutting edge of the tube as the cloth is moved around the tube. If the anvil becomes rough, file it smooth or replace it with a commercial anvil or a large copper rivet. The *single-prong punch*, which has one tube, is available at a lower price than that of the rotary punches. They do the same job, but with a choice of usually just two sizes of tubes, which are not easily interchangeable. This punch is very satisfactory if the craftsman uses the same size of hole quite consistently. The *slit punch* (fig. 11–30) is a grip-type punch which makes slit holes like those made by a thonging chisel. (Slitters are available in 1/8- or 3/32-inch sizes and with a single or a triple prong.) This punch is designed for punching slit holes in places which are hard to reach with a thonging chisel. In occupational therapy, it is used by patients who need the exercise provided by the punching but who want slits instead of round holes in the leather. The *combination punch* (fig. 11–31) has two gauges; the depth gauge, which determines the distance of the hole from the edge of the leather, and the distance gauge, which gauges the distance between stitches. This punch has removable tubes and can be fitted with tubes from 00 to 7 in size; it also has a three-prong

slit punch attachment with anvil, a one-prong slit punch, and eyelet-setting dies.

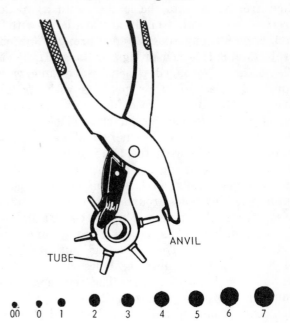

Figure 11–29. Rotary punch and available tube sizes.

Figure 11–30. Grip punch for slits.

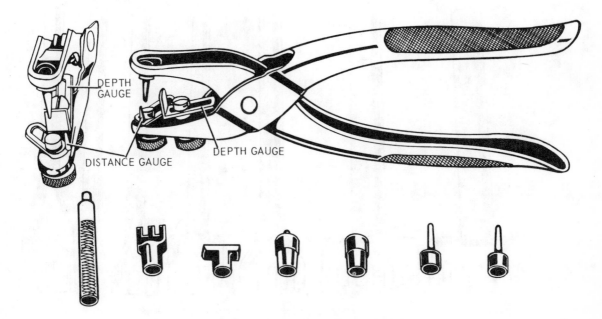

Figure 11–31. Combination punch and gauges and accessories.

(*b*) *Thonging chisels*. These chisels (fig. 11–32) or leather punches make slit holes when they are driven into the leather with a wooden or rawhide mallet. Chisels are available with 1, 3, 4, 6, or 8 prongs in 3/32-inch prongs for small projects and 1/8-inch prongs for larger projects. The 8- and 6-pronged punches save time when punching holes for larger projects with straight lines, but they are not good for rounding corners. The 4-prong size does not punch as efficiently, but it is a better size for corners and general use. It may be made with the tines slanted, on the theory that the lacing lies smoother if the slit is at an angle (4, fig. 11–32). The 1-prong punch is for punching holes around corners and in otherwise inaccessible places. The most versatile section of punches seems to be a 4-prong punch and a 1-prong punch. The 8-pronged punch (7, fig. 11–32) will make uniform holes in soft, thin leather for hand stitching. The tempered steel punch is more durable than the cast metal. To sharpen a thonging chisel, whet the chisel on an oilstone, holding it at the angle at which the prongs are ground. Stropping is done on the roughed leather stropping board.

(*c*) *Drive punches*. There are tubular drive punches with one end sharpened for cutting and the other end solid for being struck with a mallet. In addition to the conventional round ones which come in graduated sizes (A, fig. 11–33), drive punches are made in special shapes to do a specific job. Oblongs of different sizes are used to make slots for D-rings and belt buckles. One is made to cut the point of a strap (B, fig. 11–33). It is also possible to use the principle of the drive punch to cut such items as links for belts, wallet parts, and picture frames. To sharpen a drive punch, hold it almost parallel with the oilstone and rotate it as it is pulled across the stone.

(24) *Ruler*. It is important to make accurate measurements in leatherwork, so a ruler is an important tool. The ruler should have a metal edge.

(25) *Saddle stamps*. Saddle stamps (A, fig. 11–34) are steel tools which are patterned at one end so that when the tool is lightly struck with a mallet (B, fig. 11–34), the pattern is pressed into the leather. Over 300 tools with different patterns are available, but the 7 tools in A, figure 11–34 are considered to be the ones necessary to complete a basic leather design. In addition to many variations of the seven basic tools which are stamped many times to contribute to a large pattern, some stamping tools have a pattern which can be repeated to make a design such as the basket weave in A, figure 11–35 and the floral design in B, figure 11–35, and some are complete units within themselves (C, fig. 11–35). It is also interesting, as well as quite economical, to make saddle stamps by carving on the head or a cross section of a nail with files and a drill.

(26) *Shears*. Although leather should be cut with a knife for a good clean edge, it is handy

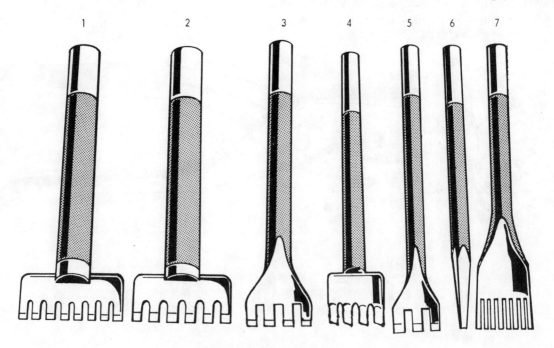

Figure 11–32. Thonging chisels.

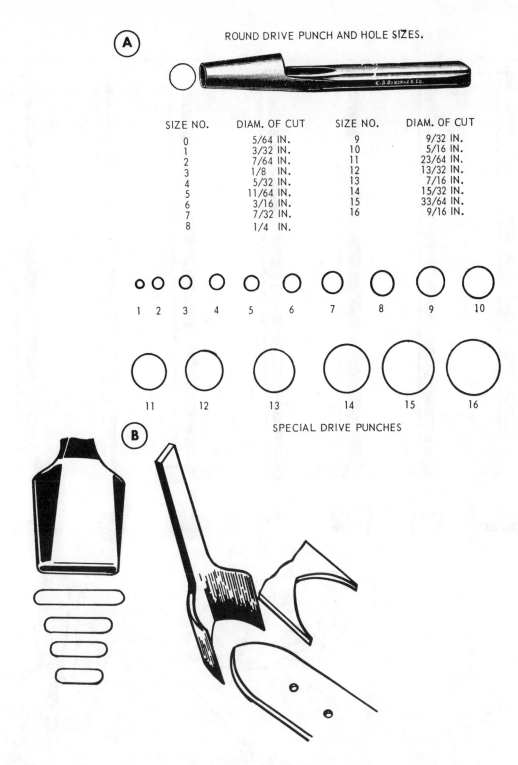

ROUND DRIVE PUNCH AND HOLE SIZES.

SIZE NO.	DIAM. OF CUT	SIZE NO.	DIAM. OF CUT
0	5/64 IN.	9	9/32 IN.
1	3/32 IN.	10	5/16 IN.
2	7/64 IN.	11	23/64 IN.
3	1/8 IN.	12	13/32 IN.
4	5/32 IN.	13	7/16 IN.
5	11/64 IN.	14	15/32 IN.
6	3/16 IN.	15	33/64 IN.
7	7/32 IN.	16	9/16 IN.
8	1/4 IN.		

SPECIAL DRIVE PUNCHES

Figure 11–33. Drive punches.

to have heavy-duty scissors to trim the leather or to make rough cuts. Leather shears (fig. 11–36) with a serrated blade to keep the leather from slipping are available, and some will cut up to 7 or 8 ounces of leather.

(27) *Snap sets.* Because there are two dif-ferent types of snaps, there are two different types of snap setters.

(a) *Round snap setters.* The sets in A, figure 11–37 (round and anvils) are presently available and are the same except for size and versatility. The round set is made for setting 16

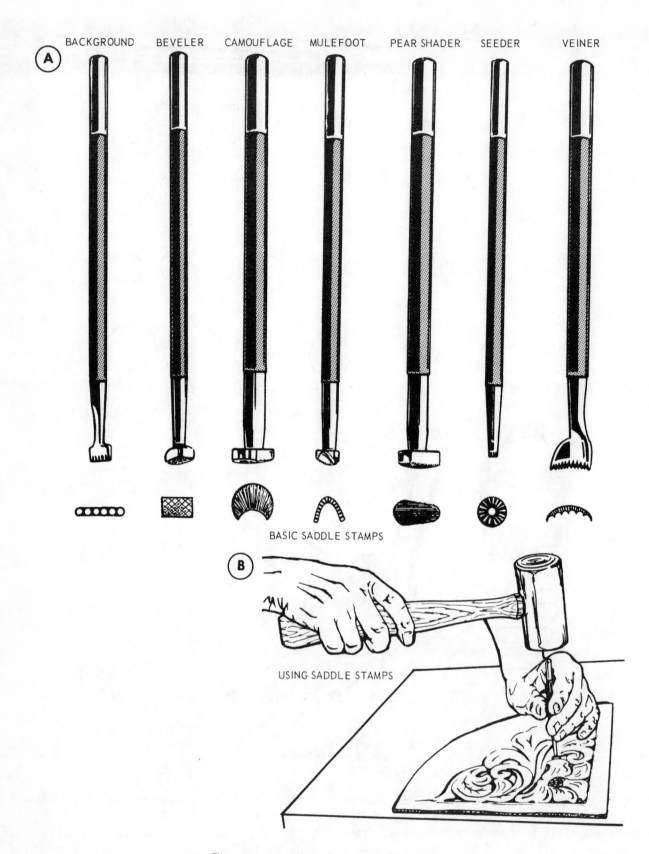

BACKGROUND BEVELER CAMOUFLAGE MULEFOOT PEAR SHADER SEEDER VEINER

BASIC SADDLE STAMPS

USING SADDLE STAMPS

Figure 11-34. Saddle stamps and their use.

238

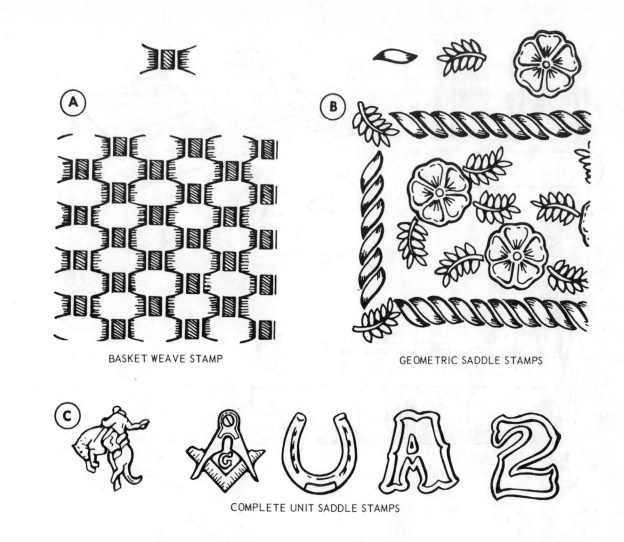

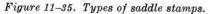

BASKET WEAVE STAMP

GEOMETRIC SADDLE STAMPS

COMPLETE UNIT SADDLE STAMPS

Figure 11–35. Types of saddle stamps.

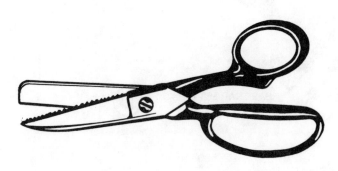

Figure 11–36. Leather shears.

line belt and glove snaps, while the anvil will set 18 and 20 line birdcage snaps; 10, 14, 16 line glove snaps; and 16 line belt snaps (B, fig. 11–37). The cap and spring setter in C, figure 11–37 is an older snap setter than are the others illustrated, but it is being used in many places.

(b) *Bar snap setter.* This set (fig. 11–37) is for setting bar snaps. It is used on such items as billfolds, coin purses, key cases, and pass cases.

(28) *Square.* A 12-inch square (fig. 11–38) is a useful tool for measuring and squaring leather.

CAUTION

A steel square leaves a permanent dark mark on damp, natural leather.

(29) *Stippler.* This is an efficient tool for stippling backgrounds (fig. 11–39).

(30) *Templates.* Some of the most frequently used designs for belts, wallets, etc., have been reproduced on plastic templates which facilitate putting the design on the leather. The lines of the design protrude on the underside of the template.

(31) *Tracing tool.* This slightly pointed tool (fig. 11–40) is used for tracing designs on leath-

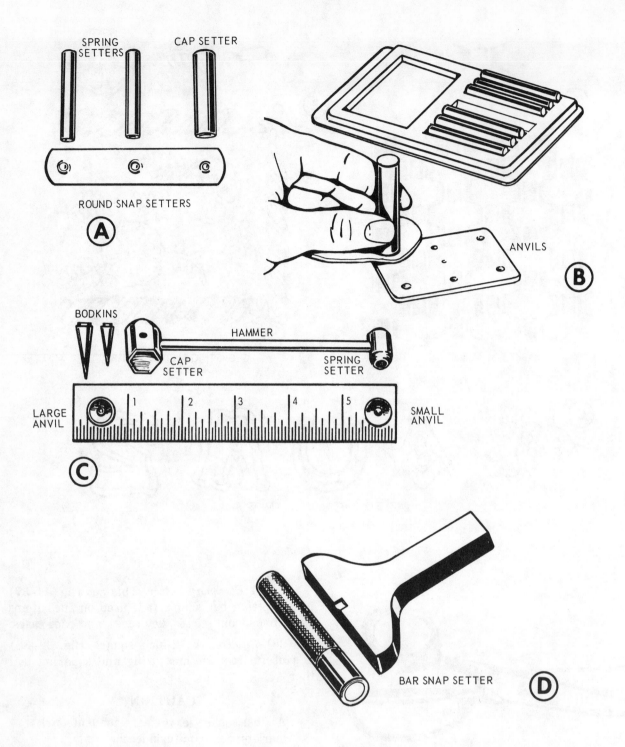

Figure 11-37. Snap setters.

er. The pointed end of a modeler is a good substitute for a tracing tool.

b. Findings. The purchase of good findings and their skilled and well-planned application can enhance the appearance and increase the usefulness of a leather project. Many findings are available in either nickel or brass finish. It is desirable to use the same color of findings throughout a project.

(1) *Bag clasps.* There are a number of different types and sizes of bag clasps (fig. 11-41) for a variety of prices. The size and shape of the clasp should harmonize with the design of the purse. It is not always necessary to buy a clasp.

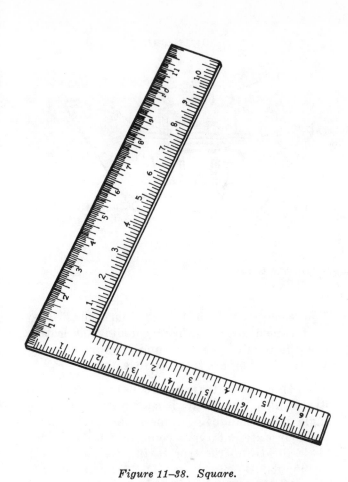

Figure 11-38. Square.

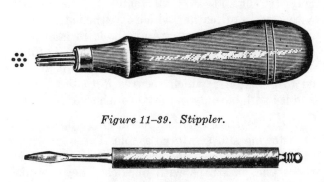

Figure 11-39. Stippler.

Figure 11-40. Tracing tool.

With a bit of ingenuity, some interesting, decorative, and safe clasps can be made entirely of leather. Any clasp must be applied with accuracy, however, for errors are frequently irreparable. There are four parts to a turn lock clasp (fig. 11-42), for example, and the following sequence of application is important for best results.

NOTE

The clasp is added after the tooling is completed and the leather finish has been applied.

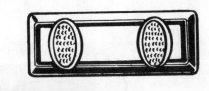
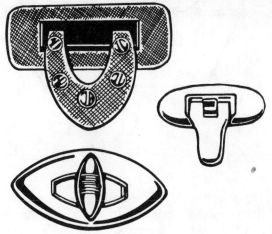

Figure 11-41. Bag clasps.

(*a*) Fold the purse to shape and locate the site for the lock. (Remember to make allowance for the purse to have things in it.)

(*b*) Recheck the site of the clasp to be sure that it is centered; then cut a hole in the flap the exact size of the opening of the plate.

(*c*) Again fold the purse to shape and put the prongs of the turn lock through the hole just cut in the flap. Mark where the turn lock is to be set by pressing the prongs against the body of the purse.

(*d*) Cut *slits,* where marked, with a single-pronged thonging chisel and insert the prongs of the turn lock into the slits just made.

(*e*) Place the backplate (B, fig. 11-42) over the prongs on the flesh side of the leather and bend the prongs over the plate.

(*f*) Cement the lining to the cover of the bag, thereby covering the prongs and backplate of the turn lock. If the purse is not to be lined, cement a thin piece of leather over the prongs.

(*g*) Since the lining has covered the hole cut for the plate in (*b*) above, cut the lining to the shape of the hole.

(*h*) Put the end projections of the top part of the clasp (A, fig. 11-42) down through the hole in the flap from the grain (smooth) side of the leather.

(*i*) Place the plate for this part over the end projections on the lining side and bend the projections down over the plate.

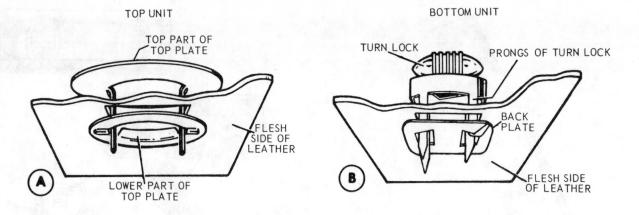

TOP UNIT

TOP PART OF
TOP PLATE

FLESH
SIDE OF
LEATHER

LOWER PART OF
TOP PLATE

BOTTOM UNIT

TURN LOCK

PRONGS OF TURN LOCK

BACK
PLATE

FLESH SIDE
OF LEATHER

A

B

Figure 11–42. Application of a turn-lock bag clasp.

(2) *Buckles.* There are many types and sizes of buckles, each designed to do a specific job. Even in the field of leatherwork, there is a range of types and sizes. Among belt buckles of the same general construction, there is a great difference in the design of the buckle and in the worth (fig. 11–43). Buckles differ both in construction and in the way in which they fasten. Each type of buckle has a certain range of size. For instance, the size of the plain belt buckle is 1/2, 5/8, 3/4, 1, and 1 1/4 inch. Western buckles are made for belts 1 1/2 to 2 inches wide, and the buckle for the watch band comes in 3/8-, 1/2-, 3/4-, and 5/8-inch size. The size of the buckle is determined by the inside length of the part of the frame on which the tongue swivels; it indicates the width of leather that can be fastened. It is wise, therefore, to select the buckle before cutting the leather for a belt. To fasten a buckle to a leather belt, first skive the buckle end of the leather (A, fig. 11–44) so that, when the leather is turned back on itself, it fits together without a bump. Second, determine where the buckle will be located. If a keeper is to be used, the end of the belt should extend far eonugh back to go over the keeper. If it is to hold only the buckle, it needs to fold only far enough to be stitched or riveted to hold the buckle. Third, cut a slot parallel with the edge of the belt (B, fig. 11–44) for the tongue to go through at the place where leather folds over the base of the frame. This is best cut with a special drive punch or, if this is not available, a punch and a knife can be used. Rivet or saddle stitch the leather to hold the buckle and keeper (C, fig. 11–44).

(3) *Chap snap.* These snaps (fig. 11–45) are designed to hold chaps in place, but they have other uses such as hooks for leashes and straps.

They come in 1/2-, 3/4-, and 1-inch sizes. They are fastened to the leather by folding the leather over the base of the snap and riveting it in the way that buckles are fastened to leather.

(4) D-*rings.* D-rings are used in fastening straps when the strap is supposed to slide or angle as on handbags, camera cases, etc. There are four different types commonly used. Figure 11–46 illustrates the true D-ring (A, fig. 11–46), rectangular D-ring (B, fig. 11–46), and round D-ring (C, fig. 11–46); all fasten to the project with a strip of leather which is either stitched or riveted in place. They are available in gold color or nickel and in 1/2-, 5/8-, 3/4-, 1-, and 1 1/4-inch sizes. The last D-ring in D, figure 11–46 is attached to a fastener which secures it to the leather and is available only in the 3/4-inch size.

(5) *Eyelet.* This is a metal ring (fig. 11–47) used to line and reinforce a hole. These rings are used for places which get hard use, such as on shoes and on straps with buckles. They are also used to fasten key plates onto the leather. They are available in large (1/4 inch), medium, and small sizes and in black, brown, nickel, or brass. To set an eyelet, punch a hole the size of the eyelet in the leather. Put the eyelet on some scrap hardwood or on an anvil made for the purpose; slip the leather, flesh side up, over the eyelet, hold the setter over the eyelet and strike the setter with a mallet. (The punch-type setter employs the same principle.) The smooth, round part of the eyelet fits into the groove made for it and the end with the nib is pushed down into the sharp part of the eyelet and spreads it out against the leather. When setting eyelets, remember that the smooth, round part of the eyelet should be on the side of the leather which is seen.

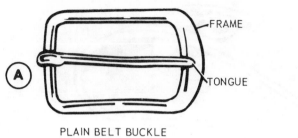
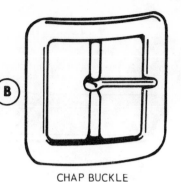

FRAME

TONGUE

A

PLAIN BELT BUCKLE

B

CHAP BUCKLE

C

WATCH BAND BUCKLE

D

FANCY BELT BUCKLE

E

WESTERN BUCKLE

Figure 11-43. Types of buckles.

(6) *Gormmet.* A grommet (fig. 11–48) is used in much the same way as an eyelet, but it is usually larger and has two parts that fit together. It is normally made of brass and is in 1/4- or 5/16-inch size for leatherwork. To set a grommet, use a grommet setter. Punch a hole in the leather slightly smaller than the grommet; put a grommet on the base of the die; place the leather, grain side up, over the grommet; then put the washer, convex side up, on top of the leather. Place the tapered point of the punch into the gommet and die, hold it vertically and strike it two or three sharp blows with a mallet (fig. 11–49).

(7) *Keepers.* Keepers (fig. 11–50) are rectangular loops which keep the tip of the strap in place. They are available in leather or metal. The metal ones correspond to buckle sizes and designs. A leather keeper is easy to make and there is the advantage of the leather matching the belt.

They are held in place in the way that metal keepers are held ((2) above).

(8) *Key plates.* Key plates have either 4 or 6 metal hooks (fig. 11–51) for holding keys. They are fastened to a piece of leather with eyelets. The plate should be fixed in the position shown in figure 11–52 with the origin of the loops up so that the loops fall down over the plate. When it is in the right position, mark the spots where the holes should be, then punch them, and proceed as for setting eyelets in (5) above.

(9) *Key post.* One part of the post fits into the other part (fig. 11–53) and the keys slide on the shank of the larger part. The parts are threaded together so that they hold quite well. To insert this post, fold the leather, then punch it a little more than half the width of the top of a key from this fold. Insert the larger part of the post into one layer of leather from the grain side; then put the keys on the post. Put the second

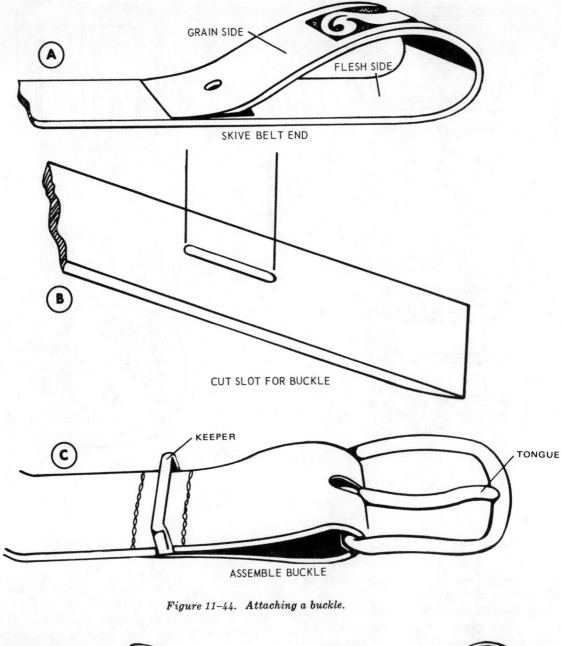

Figure 11–44. Attaching a buckle.

Figure 11–45. Chap snap.

part of the leather over the keys and turn the smaller part of the post into the larger part.

(10) *Lacing.* Leather lacing is available mainly in calf and goat in black, dark brown, medium brown, and tan. Lacing is made 3/32 and 1/8 inch wide; the 3/32 inch is the most frequently

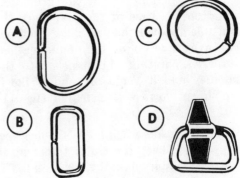

Figure 11–46. D-*rings.*

Figure 11-47. Eyelet.

Figure 11-48. Grommet.

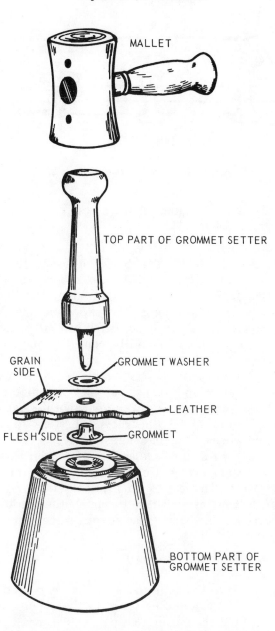

MALLET

TOP PART OF GROMMET SETTER

GRAIN
SIDE

GROMMET WASHER

LEATHER

FLESH SIDE

GROMMET

BOTTOM PART OF
GROMMET SETTER

Figure 11-49. Setting a grommet.

used. Florentine lacing is 1/4 inch or 3/8 inch wide. Plastic and vinyl lacing is available in a

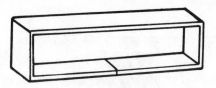

Figure 11-50. Metal keeper.

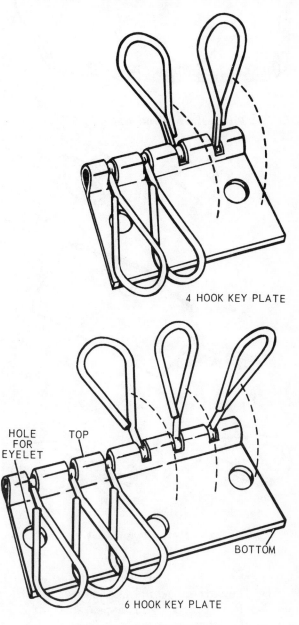

4 HOOK KEY PLATE

HOLE
FOR
EYELET

TOP

BOTTOM

6 HOOK KEY PLATE

Figure 11-51. Key plates.

variety of colors. It is less expensive than leather lacing and more colorful, but many people feel that it is not as rich looking.

(11) *Lanyard hooks.* These are small hooks for lightweight use, mainly for lanyards. Some hooks do not swivel (fig. 11-54) and some do.

(12) *Rivets.* Rivets are used as a method of

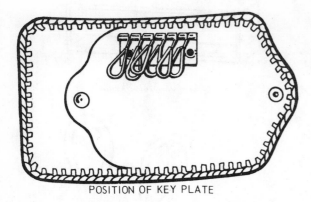

POSITION OF KEY PLATE

Figure 11–52. Position of key plate.

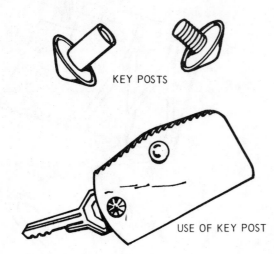

KEY POSTS

USE OF KEY POST

Figure 11–53. Key posts and their use.

PLAIN

SWIVEL

Figure 11–54. Lanyard hooks.

fastening two pieces of leather together (fig. 11–55). They are quick and easy to use, and they hold fairly securely. The appearance of this method of fastening is not as pleasing as some of the other methods, however. Rivets are available in different sizes and lengths for different thicknesses of leather. To set a rivet, punch a hole through the thickness of leather. The hole should be just a little larger than the shank of the rivet. Insert the base of the rivet up through the hole and the top of the rivet over the base. With the rivet and the leather on some scrap hardwood, strike the top of the rivet

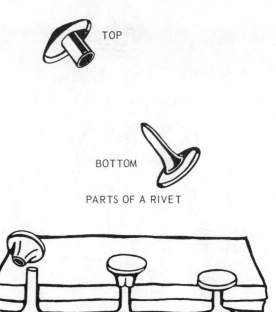

TOP

BOTTOM

PARTS OF A RIVET

SETTING A RIVET

Figure 11–55. Fastening with a rivet.

sharply with a mallet. Always test to see that the rivet is secure.

(13) *Snaps.* A number of different types of snaps are available. The birdcage seems to be most successful type for the work done in occupational therapy. Snaps are sized by the line, which is 1/40 inch long. The cap of a line 20 snap would be 1/2 inch across. When snaps are ordered, the catalog should be consulted for correct sizes.

(a) *Bar snaps.* Bar snaps are more expensive than round snaps, but they are nice on small leather projects for a more professional finish. Figure 11–56 illustrates the steps to be followed when setting bar snaps.

(b) *Birdcage snaps.* Line 18 birdcage snaps are a good all-around size snap for most light work. The caps are available in several colors to contrast with or to match the leather. With reasonable care, these snaps can be applied quite successfully.

PROCEDURE
(fig. 11–57)

Step 1. Have the four parts of the snap ready. The cap and eyelet form the upper unit and the spring and post the lower.

Step 2. Locate the exact spot where the cap is to be and punch a hole in the leather the size of the eyelet. It is wise to determine the correct size first on scrap leather.

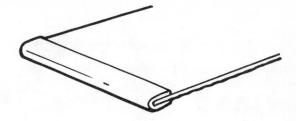

Step 1. Place the bar stud on the edge of the leather, as it will go with the bar part on the grain side of the leather and the stud part on the flesh side. To keep the bar from slipping, use a bit of rubber cement.

Step 2. Put the bar part of the snap and the grain side of the leather on a piece of scrap leather stud side up on the table. Place the hole in the setter over the stud and the sides of the setter over the bar. Tap the end of the setter sharply but lightly with a rawhide mallet to clamp the bar securely to the leather.

Step 3. To locate the spot where the lower button should be placed, aline the parts of the project as they should be, then push the bar down firmly. The stud will mark the spot where the center of the button should be set.

Step 4. Set the button by first placing the prongs on the flesh side of the leather and pressing hard enough for them to make an impression in the leather. With an awl, punch holes where marked and insert the prongs of the button through the leather from the flesh side to the grain side.

Step 5. Put the leather on the bench, flesh side down and with the prongs sticking up. Place the socket on top of the prongs, making sure that it is alined evenly.

Step 6. Aline the tubular part of the snap setter with the prongs and the socket, then tap it in place gently with a rawhide mallet.

Figure 11–56. Steps in setting a bar snap.

Step 3. Place the eyelet over the largest anvil of the snap setter and push the leather, *grain* (or smooth) side up, down over the eylet; then put the cap over the eyelet.

Step 4. Put the concave part of the snap setter

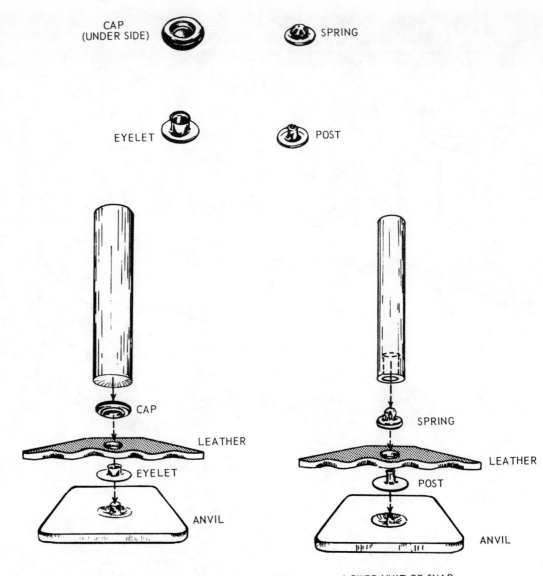

CAP
(UNDER SIDE)

SPRING

EYELET

POST

CAP

LEATHER

EYELET

ANVIL

UPPER UNIT OF SNAP

SPRING

LEATHER

POST

ANVIL

LOWER UNIT OF SNAP

Figure 11–57. Setting birdcage snaps.

over the cap, keep it perpendicular, and strike the tool a sharp (but not hard) blow with a mallet to set the cap and the eyelet.

Step 5. To locate the correct spot for the spring and post unit, aline the parts of the project as they should be; then push the cap down firmly. The eyelet will leave an impression at the spot where the post should be.

Step 6. Punch a hole in the leather the right size for the post.

NOTE

Since the post is smaller than the eyelet, the hole for the post must be smaller.

Step 7. Place the post over the smaller anvil of the snap setter; then put the leather *grain* (or smooth) side up over the post and the spring on the post.

Step 8. Next place the part of the setter tool with a hole large enough to fit over the spring, and strike it with a sharp (but not hard) blow with a mallet to set the spring and the post.

Step 9. Test the snap. If it is too loose to hold well into the cap, tap the spring *lightly* until it fits. If the cap will not fit over the spring, compress the spring all around *gently* with a pair of pliers and test again.

(*c*) *Dot fasteners.* Dot fasteners (fig. 11–58) are larger and stronger and they hold better than other snaps, but they are not as decorative. They are set in the same way as birdcage snaps, but a larger snap set is needed.

(*d*) *Glove snaps.* Glove snaps (fig. 11–59) are used and installed in the same manner as birdcage snaps. The stud is less adjustable, however, than it is in the birdcage snap.

(14) *Zippers.* Medium and heavy zippers are used in leatherwork. They are available in certain lengths and in a continuous length with pulls and stops to attach. They are machine-sewed or saddle-stitched to the leather.

(*a*) Cut an opening in the leather the length of the zipper and about 3/8 to 1/2 inch wider than the metal part of the zipper.

(*b*) Apply cement to the flesh side of the leather just along the edges of the opening cut for the zipper and to the tape, but only where it will be in contact with the leather.

(*c*) With the zipper on the table, cement the leather to the tape, starting at the pull end of the zipper. Take care to keep the width of the opening uniform for a neat appearance.

(*d*) Mark and either machine-sew or saddle-stitch the zipper in place.

Figure 11–58. Parts of a dot fastener.

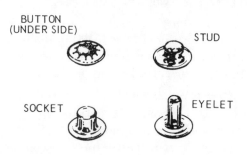

BUTTON (UNDER SIDE)

STUD

SOCKET

EYELET

Figure 11–59. Parts of a glove snap.

c. Supplies.

(1) *Barge cement* This is a heavy type of cement that is water- and oilproof and has excellent permanent holding properties, plus flexibility. Although this cement holds too securely and is too flammable for general use in leatherwork, it is good to have some on hand for gluing pieces of leather that must hold for some time.

(2) *Dye.* A number of different leather dyes are on the market in many different colors. Care must be taken when applying them as it is almost impossible to remove dye that has been put on in error or that has been spilled.

(3) *Finishes.* A number of coatings are on the market to preserve the leather and to make it shine. The selection of the one to use is based on personal choice. Care must be taken to follow the directions for application, as each type is applied a little differently.

(4) *Oxalic acid.* A teaspoonful of oxalic acid dissolved in a pint of warm water is an excellent cleaning solution for leather. The solution is applied with a cloth or a cellulose sponge and is wiped off with a sponge wrung out of clear water. It is not used on dyed leathers.

(5) *Rubber cement.* This is a quick-drying elastic cement which is used to hold pieces of leather together *temporarily* to facilitate lacing. This cement is not designed to hold over a long period of time. It is available by the 1 1/2-ounce tube, 1/4-pint jar, and quart and gallon cans. Because it dries so rapidly, the container must be kept closed when it is not being used.

(6) *Saddle soap.* This is excellent for cleaning and polishing the finished leather project.

(7) *Wax.* A good grade of paste wax provides protection and gives a nice gloss to the leather.

11–4. Laying Out and Cutting Leather

Skillful laying out and cutting the leather is the foundation of a good project. Decorating is more successful if the best part of the leather is used, and the pieces will fit together better if they are cut accurately.

a. Placement of Pattern. The best leather is in the center of the hide. If the hide has been cut into a side, the best part is along the cut edge because the cut is made down the center from front to back. Ideally, all outside pieces of a project should be from the center of the back. That, of course, is not possible. However, if this goal is kept in mind, pieces nearer the center can be saved for the parts of the project that will show the most. If wallets are to be cut from the hide such as is illustrated in figure 11–60, so far as possible, backs should be cut from the A area and the inside pieces from the B areas. If this is not practical, cut the backs from A and B areas, the pockets from B and C areas, and the inside pieces from C areas. When making large purses, cut the main part of the purse from A and B areas and save the C areas for gussets. (The pliability of these softer parts is better for gussets than the stiffer area.) The C areas are also good for projects such as key cases and coin purses, in which softer leather is better.

b. Cutting. There are several ways to facilitate cutting so that a better job can be done.

(1) Probably the most important part of good leather cutting is to have *sharp tools.* If the tool is sharp, less pressure will have to be used and so more accurate cutting can be done. A sharp tool also leaves a clean, smooth edge. It helps to hone the sharpened tools before using them.

(2) It is important to use the correct cutting tool for the leather being cut.

(*a*) Knives are best for cutting straight edges and for cutting all 4- through 11-ounce leathers.

(*b*) Scissors made especially for cutting leather can be used successfully on 3- or 4-ounce leather, on alligator or lizard, and on curved lines which are hard to cut with a knife.

(*c*) Straight edges such as those on for belts are best cut with a draw knife if the guiding edge of the leather can be made straight.

(3) When a template, ruler, or a square is used when cutting with a knife, the guide must

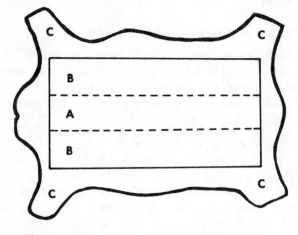

Figure 11–60. Parts of a hide-guide for cutting.

be held down *firmly* on the leather. Enough pressure should be exerted on the knife to cut the leather with one stroke. Cutting must not go past a corner and extend past the end of the pattern, as this practice wastes a great deal of leather. Instead, cutting should stop about 1/16 inch from the corner and the cut should be finished with the knife pointing in the opposite direction.

c. Standard Measurements. One of the pleasures of doing handwork is having the finished piece exactly the way the craftsman wants it. Although deviations from the standard are frequently to be encouraged to foster originality and to stimulate interest, a standard supplies a point of reference.

(1) Standard sizes for four of the most popular projects are as follows:

(*a*) *Women's billfold.*

Outside piece 7¼ x 3⅛ inch cut 1
*Inside piece 7 x 2⅞ inch   cut 1
**Small pockets 2 x 2⅞ inch   cut 2
**Large pockets 3 x 2⅞ inch   cut 2

(*b*) *Men's billfold.*

Outside piece 8½ x 3½ inch cut 1
*Inside piece 8¼ x 3¼ inch cut 1
**Small pockets 2½ x 3¼ inch cut 2
**Large pockets 3¾ x 3¼ inch cut 2

(*c*) *Keycase.*

Outside piece 5 x 3⅜ inch cut 1
Inside keypiece 1½ x 3⅜ inch cut 1

(*d*) *English wallet.*

Outside piece 7½ x 6¾ inch cut 1
Inside pieces 3¼ x 6¾ inch cut 2

*The inside piece is cut ¼ inch shorter than the outside piece so that the wallet will be smoother when it is folded.

**Pockets can be cut to almost any size *under* 3¼ inches, according to the size of the piece of leather.

(2) The process of carving, especially with heavy leather, stretches the piece out of shape sufficiently to keep them from fitting together well. There are two ways to correct for this—

(*a*) If the piece is to be lined, glue it to cardboard before it is tooled. After tooling, turn the leather side down and *peel* the *cardboard* from the leather. (If the leather is peeled from the cardboard, it will wrinkle.)

(*b*) If the piece is not to be lined, cut the leather about an inch larger than the finished piece will be, then after the piece is carved, cut it to the exact size.

11–5. Decorating Leather

There are a number of ways in which leather can be decorated. Some methods, such as tooling, are appropriate to thinner leathers because cutting into the leather is not a part of the process; carving which entails cutting is appropriate to heavier leathers; and stamping can be done on either weight. Dyeing is an embellishment which can be used to enhance either tooling or carving. Before leather will take the impression of a pattern, it must be dampened in a certain way and then the pattern must be transferred to the leather. The following methods of dampening and transferring the pattern are essentially the same for all types of decorating:

a. *Dampening.* Lightweight leather, such as tooling calf, is dampened in a different way from heavier leather, such as cowhide.

(1) Lightweight leather. The flesh side of the leather is moistened with a fairly damp sponge or cloth. Brown or black leather should feel cool to the touch, but water should not be visible when the modeling tool is pushed along the leather. Natural color leather should feel cool, but it should be *permitted to dry until it returns to its natural color.* If it is done correctly, the modeling tool will burnish the leather and bring out rich brown shadings which stay in the leather.

(2) Heavy leather is dampened by casing or by wetting it with a sponge.

(a) *Casing.* At least 24 hours before the cowhide is to be used, it is immersed in a sink of water until bubbles no longer form. It is drained and then wrapped in clean cloth and put in a cool, airy place. As soon as the leather returns to natural color, it is ready to carve. If it dries out too much (no longer feels cool), it is dampened a little with a damp, not wet, sponge. If the leather cannot be worked on after about 24 hours, it should be unwrapped and permitted to dry in order to prevent mildrew. To begin work again after it has dried, it need only be dampened again with a sponge and allowed to return to its natural color. This is the most effective method of dampening leather because it opens the pores and makes the leather "plump," but the time involved and the forethought needed to case the leather can create a problem.

(b) *Dampening with a sponge.* This is done in the same way as for thinner leathers. It takes longer to dampen, however, and longer for the leather to return to natural color.

b. *Transferring the Design to the Leather.* When the leather has dried to its natural color, the design can be transferred to the leather. There are several ways to do this—

(1) *Tracing design.* Trace the design from the original on to tracing paper. Lay the tracing paper on the grain side of the damp leather, fasten it to the underside of the leather with masking or cellophane tape, and go over the lines with the small end of a modeler or with a tracing tool. Hold the tool in the same way as a pencil and use about the same amount of pressure. Be sure to put the tape on the flesh side as it will leave a mark on the grain side of the leather.

(2) *Use of template.* If the desired design is on a template, place the template on the leather with the raised design side of the template down on the leather. Push the lines into the leather gently with the spoon-like end of the modeler (fig. 11–61). In this way, the design is transferred easily and accurately to the leather.

c. *Tooling.* Tooling is decorating leather without cutting into it. Outline tooling, modeling, stippling, and embossing are all variations of the tooling process. They are appropriate to thinner leathers such as calf. All tooling except some steps of embossing are done with the leather flesh side down on a hard surface such as is offered by marble, Masonite, Formica, or special material made for this purpose and sold at leathercraft stores.

(1) *Outline tooling.* With this method, only the outline of the design is pressed down (fig. 11–62). It is one of the simplest methods of decorating leather. Line designs, initials, and

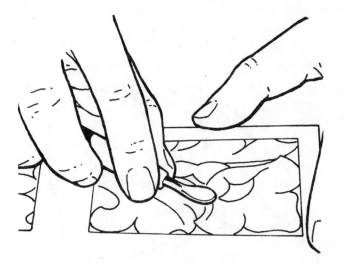

Figure 11–61. Using a template.

names are frequently put onto leather with this method. Dampen the leather and transfer the design to it. Use the more pointed end of a modeler and press down the design, using a ruler as a guide. For wider lines, use a deerfoot modeler. If there are a number of lines, stretching of the leather may be prevented by starting the line at the outer edge and then working toward the center. Accuracy is especially important in outline tooling because errors cannot be corrected in leatherwork and when straight lines are used, they are almost impossible to hide.

(2) *Modeling.* The background is depressed and the design is left to stand out above the background in modeling (fig. 11–63). Dampen the leather and transfer the design onto it. With the spoon end of a modeling tool, start at the edge of the design and push the background down with short, circular strokes. For small areas, use the deerfoot modeler. The area which is pushed down should be smooth and should not show toolmarks. Always move the tool away from (rather than toward) the part of the design which is to be left raised so that if it slips the design will not be marked. Take care to have the tool smooth and to keep the fingernails and jewelry from marking the leather; damp leather retains all marks.

(3) *Stippling.* Basically, stippling (fig. 11–64) is decorating with small dot-like depressions in the leather. With this process there is more contrast between the raised design and the background than there is with tooling. First, dampen the leather and transfer the design. With one of several tools—the "pointed" end of a modeler, a ball-end modeler, or a stippler—make small, dot-like depressions in the background.

(4) *Embossing.* Embossing (fig. 11–65) is raising a part of the design above the surface of the leather by working from the flesh side. This process is combined with modeling, for as

Figure 11–62. Outline tooling.

Figure 11–64. Stippling.

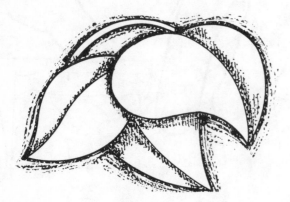

Figure 11–63. Modeling.

Figure 11–65. Embossing.

252

the design is raised, the background is pushed down.

(a) Dampen the leather and transfer the design.

(b) Hold the dampened leather in one hand and stretch the part of the design which is to be raised by forcing it with a ball-end modeler.

(c) Put the leather, flesh side down, on a piece of marble and push the background down with the spoon part of a modeler.

(d) Work steps (b) and (c) above alternately until the design is raised higher than is possible in modeling.

(e) After the leather has dried, fill in the raised part of the design to keep it from pushing in. This may be done in one of two ways: One, mix cotton with flour and water and, on the flesh side, fill in the raised part of the design. Two, cover both sides of small bits of newspaper or tissue paper with rubber cement and place them in layers into the raised part of the design.

(f) After the filling material is thoroughly dry, cement a lining to the flesh side of the leather to hold the filling in place.

d. Carving. Carving is cutting the design into leather, then using various saddle stamps to put down the background and to decorate the design. Carving (fig. 11–66) is usually done on leather of 5- or 6-ounce weight or more. If carving is done on thinner leather, it is best to carve with cardboard between the leather and the hard surface. Proficiency in carving requires practice and the work is time-consuming. It is frequently ad-

visable for a student to carve a small article before he begins a larger piece in order to familiarize him with the tools and to give him some understanding of what is involved in making a large piece. The fundamental principles of leather carving are standard among craftsmen, but the sequence of application varies. The following sequence has been found helpful when working with unskilled students who have difficulty distinguishing between design and background:

(1) *Dampening and transferring design.* Dampen the leather and transfer the design onto it.

(2) *Cutting.* Cut the design to one-half the thickness of the leather with a sharp swivel knife. To cut, hold the knife with the index finger over the yoke of the knife, the knurled barrel between the thumb and the long finger, with the ring and little fingers held along the side of the blade (fig. 11–67).

NOTE

The knife is tipped back with the yoke away from the operator so that the cut is made with the back part of the blade as it is *pulled* toward the operator along the traced design. The direction of the blade is changed by rotating the barrel between the thumb and index finger. *Care must be taken to keep the knife from tipping to the right or to the left,* as the cut must be at right angles to the surface of the leather.

Finish each cut by gradually lifting the knife from the leather, thereby making a cut that is shallow at the end. Make straight cuts with the aid of a straightedge. It is suggested that the parts of the design be cut in the following order: border lines, flowers, stems, and then leaves. Do not try to recut a line, cross another cut, undercut, or make the cuts too deep. Always have the leather damp and always use a sharp knife. Using a swivel knife requires skill which is developed through practice, so practice on a piece of scrap leather until some degree of skill is developed.

(3) *Beveling.* Bevel the design with one of the several types of bevelers. Hold the tool between the thumb and the index and long fingers of the left hand, with the thick part of the tool in the knife cut. It is easier to see the work if the thicker part of the tool and the knife cut are placed so that they are in full view, rather than if they are on the side away from you. To

Figure 11–66. Leather carving.

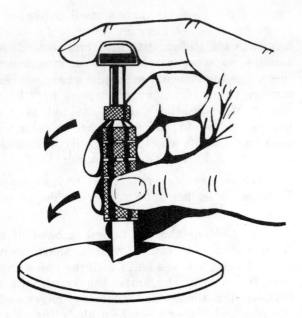

Figure 11–67. Using a swivel knife.

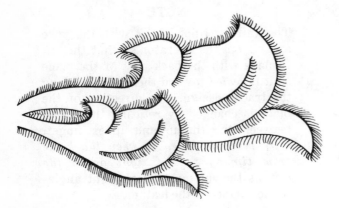

Figure 11–68. Design showing beveling.

make a smooth, deep bevel, move the tool along the cut as it is struck a sharp (but not hard) blow with the mallet, making certain to overlap the prior mark. The design indicates where to bevel. *Always bevel away from the part of the design that is to stand out.* If one leaf, for instance, overlaps another, bevel down the one that is overlapped (fig. 11–68) to make the carving look three-dimensional. It is not necessary to bevel around the background areas, as the background tools will put this leather down.

(4) *Backgrounding.* There are several types of tools for putting down the background, and each provides a little different texture of background. The selection of the one to use is a matter of personal taste; they are all used in the same manner. The surface of the leather must be almost dry in order to obtain good tex-

ture and rich color when backgrounding. Hold the tool between the thumb and the index and long fingers of the left hand. Strike the tool with a sharp (but not hard) blow to make an impression that is deep, but do not cut through the surface of the leather. If the leather has the right amount of moisture, the tool mark on natural-color leather will be a rich brown. Move the tool around as it is struck and try not to overlap impressions. Get into small places by tilting the tool so that just a small part impresses the leather. The art of good background work is to maintain even depth of depressions so that the background looks even and regular.

(5) *Decorating.* Beveling and putting down the background make the design stand out sufficiently to give it meaning for most patients. It is therefore often easier for them to decorate after the beveling and background are complete. If a commercial pattern is being followed, the suggested tool to use is shown by the catalog number of that tool indicated on the drawing. The pattern may be followed if the tools are available, or the craftsman may interpret the design as he sees it. Some of the more frequently used decorating tools (fig. 11–34) follow, along with suggestions on how and where to use them:

(a) *Camouflage.* This stamp is available in several sizes and shapes. Use it to decorate flowers, leaves, and stems. Space the impressions uniformly, beginning at the base of the part with strong, sharp blows and gradually lessening the striking force as the tip of the part is approached.

(b) *Mulefoot.* This is a "v" or "u" shaped tool used mainly to touch up flowers or stems. It is often used to accent the juncture of petals and leaves.

(c) *Pear shader.* The shader is available in different sizes, and the face may be smooth, checked, or ribbed to produce different effects. Use it to produce shaded effects on leaves and petals. If the leather has the right moisture content, the area depressed by this tool will turn dark. Move the shader along as it is struck, thereby producing a smooth, tapered depression.

(d) *Seeder.* Seeders vary in design, size, and shape. They are used principally for flower centers or swirls. Take care when striking this tool, as it is small and sharp, and will cut the leather if the blow is too hard. Stamp the outer circle of the seeds first, then fill in the remainder of the seeded area, but do not overlap impressions.

(e) *Veiner.* Veiners vary greatly in size

and pattern. Use them to decorate plane surfaces on leaves, stems, and flowers. Space these impressions uniformly and tip the tool toward one end, as indicated to conform to the contour of the design.

(f) *Decorative cuts.* The last step in decorating a carving is to make a few well-made dress cuts with a swivel knife. To make these cuts, start the cut deep (one-half the thickness of the leather) and rotate the swivel knife as it is pulled toward the body in a tapered cut.

e. Inverted Leather Carving. Inverted carving can provide an interesting change from the conventional type of carving. In this type, the design is depressed with the tools and the background areas remain untouched. There are three types of inverted carving.

(1) *Silhouette stamping.* This is probably the easiest type, as it entails cutting only the outlines of the design, beveling into the design, then matting down within the lines (fig. 11–69). Lacy designs, rather than solid, should be selected for this method. It is suggested that to prevent narrow slivers of leather from curling up, lines be cut at the points of areas not to be joined (fig. 11–70).

(2) *Inverted carving.* In this type, beveling is done toward the inside; then the design is decorated as in the conventional type of carving (fig. 11–71).

(3) *Rough-out carving.* This is the same as inverted carving (fig. 11–72), but it is done on the flesh side of the leather. After carving and stamping, the leather is sanded with coarse sandpaper to produce a suede-like finish.

f. Stamping Leather. In this method of decorating, stamping tools are used without first cutting the leather with a swivel knife. The method is adaptable to simple primitive designs as well as to complex allover geometric designs or to ingenious, meaningful designs. The stamps are used just as they are in leather carving,

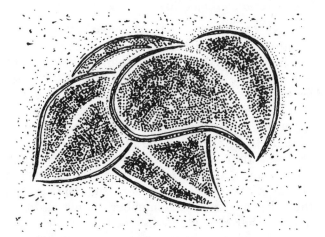

Figure 11–69. Silhouette inverted carving.

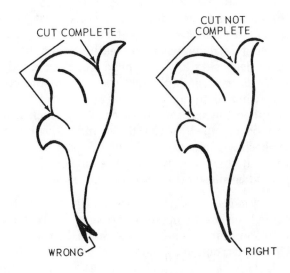

Figure 11–70. Technique of cutting with a swivel knife on silhouette carving.

Figure 11–71. Inverted carving.

Figure 11–72. Rough-out inverted carving.

and care must be taken not to cut through the leather with the tool. The skill in this work lies in the even placement of the stamping tool and in the use of the same striking force.

g. Dyeing Leather. Dyes are used to give color to leather. They can be used over entire surfaces to change the color or they can be used to color certain areas of the design. Using dye can be tricky because different leathers and even different areas of the same piece will not have the same reaction to dyes. The directions on the dye container should be followed and the dye tested on a scrap piece of the same leather before using it on the project. Dyes are applied after the decorating is done. If the dye is to be applied all over, a sponge or clean cloth is used as an applicator. The hands should be protected with rubber or plastic gloves. If only certain areas are to be dyed, a soft brush is used as an applicator. After the dye has dried thoroughly, the excess dye is removed with sheep wool or a soft cloth, and a finishing coat is applied to the leather (para 11–8*b*).

11–6. Construction Processes

After the leather has been decorated, the project must be assembled. The various processes which are a part of assembling are quite standard, but the sequence in which they are employed depends upon the project. The sequence of steps must be carefully planned. For instance, the lining of a purse is put on *after* the findings that must be *covered* are applied and *before* the findings that are *not covered* are applied. Good planning and careful execution of the plan can serve to enhance the decorating and to give the project a professional look.

a. Edge Finishing. Careful finishing of an edge that is not to be laced does a great deal toward making the piece look finished. Good edge finishing is particularly important for straps of bags, cases, and watches. Before any of the actual finishing processes are started, the edge must be made as smooth as possible with a sharp knife and an edge beveler, or with fine sandpaper rubbed in one direction. It is often desirable to make a line along each edge with the edge creaser. There are several ways to finish raw edges of leather—

(1) *Dyeing edges.* Edges that will receive little wear can be dyed to match or to contrast with the color of the leather. Dye is applied with a small brush. Care must be taken to not get dye on the finished side of the leather.

(2) *Burnishing.* The edge is dampened and then burnished with a bone folder, an edge slicker, the edge of a lignum vitae edge creaser, the spoon part of a modeler, or with brown wrapping paper.

(3) *Casing compound.* An edge casing compound or a gum tragacanth solution applied to the edge and then rubbed with a coarse cloth in one direction gives protection to edges that will get wear. After the fibers are set by this process, they should be burnished.

(4) *Edge enamel.* There is a waterproof edge enamel, available for the edges of watch bands and belts, that retards discoloration from perspiration. After the enamel is applied, the fibers are smoothed and set by stroking them in one direction with a coarse cloth.

b. Skiving. This is the process of reducing the thickness of leather. It is done in the areas of the leather that are to fold or bend; with less bulk, the leather is more pliable. Care must be taken to not weaken the leather. Skiving is also done on edges that are to be laced or sewed, in order to reduce the bulk of the layers of leather. In determining the amount of leather to remove, the assembled edges, after skiving, should equal, if practical, the original thickness of one of the pieces of leather. The depth of cut then depends upon the number of pieces to be put together. If two pieces are to be laced, each piece should be skived to one-half of its original thickness; if three pieces are to be laced together, each should be skived to one-third of its original thickness, and so on. Skiving tools must be very sharp so that they will cut smoothly and easily. Skiving is done with the leather on a flat surface, flesh side up. If a head knife or a skiving knife is used, it is pushed away from the operator to make the cut. The skife or safety beveler is pulled toward the operator. Very thick leather can be clamped to the table and skived with a spokeshave. No attempt should be made to cut the full thickness at once, but rather the leather should be sliced off in thin, smooth layers.

c. Folding. Leather frequently needs to be folded, either to make a stronger, more finished edge on thin leather or to shape heavy leather. These instructions should be followed:

(1) *Thin leather.* First, skive the leather to about one-half of its original thickness at the place where it is to fold. Dampen the flesh side

of the leather and make a line where the fold is to be, using a straightedge and the small end of the modeler. When the leather has dried, apply cement to each side of the fold, let the cement set, then fold the leather over and smooth it down gently with a mallet or bone folder. If the folded area is not long, use cement (especially barge cement) which will hold quite well; stitch the fold if it is long or if there is to be much wear.

(2) *Thick leather.* Sharp folds on heavy leather are difficult, but folds of 80°–90° or wider are done in the following manner: Mark the location of the fold on the flesh side of the leather with a straightedge and an awl. With a gouger or with a knife, cut a V-groove along the marked line, always on the flesh side. (The groove should be not more than one-half the thickness of the leather.) Moisten the leather along the groove and fold the leather to the desired angle. If the leather is strong and firm, a mallet may be used to stretch the damp leather. Allow the leather to dry in the desired position.

d. Forming Leather. There are occasions when it is expedient to form leather so as to have it fit over the nose piece of a camera or some other such protrusion.

(1) Construct a die for forming leather (fig. 11–73) from a smooth-grained wood. The outside dimensions of the insert piece will be the inside dimensions of the formed leather. Slightly round the edges of the forming die or mold. Allow for the thickness of the leather between the two parts of the die.

(2) Cut the cowhide (about 4 ounces) 1 inch to 1 1/2 inch larger than the formed piece.

(3) Case the leather (para 11–5a(2)(a)) and, while it is still wet, place the leather over the opening of the die, grain side down.

(4) Tack the edge of the leather to the die (fig. 11–73).

(5) Place the insert part of the die over the leather and the opening in the bottom piece of the wood. Apply gentle but steady pressure on the insert, forcing it and the leather into the open space in the wood below. An extra large piece of wood over the insert may insure more even pressure. Pressure may also be applied with a clamp such as a C-clamp (fig. 11–73) which can hold the insert in place until the leather has dried.

(6) After the leather is dry, remove it from the mold; trim off the excess flanged edge (fig. 11–73), and line the formed piece if it is so indicated.

(7) Attach the molded piece to the article by stitching the flanged part to the project being made.

e. Cementing. In occupational therapy, cementing is used to hold the leather in place until it is sewed, which then holds it permanently. The principles of cementing are the same for small areas such as edges and for large surfaces such as linings, but the techniques are somewhat different. Leather cement should be kept in an airtight can or jar to prevent drying. If the cement dries out, lacquer thinner or Zyol may be used to restore the consistency. It is convenient and it saves on cement to have a brush in the jar (fig. 11–4).

(1) *Cementing edges.*

(a) Apply a 1/4-inch strip of cement along *both* surfaces which are to be held together. If one surface is grain side, rough it up a little with a knife or with sandpaper before applying the cement.

(b) Let the cement dry on *both* surfaces until the shine of the cement is gone.

(c) Press the two parts together and tap them lightly with a mallet to make a stronger union.

(d) If a wallet is being cemented, press the outside and inside pieces together on one half of the wallet; then fold it in the center and press them together on the other half. This procedure results in a smoother fold.

(2) *Cementing linings.*

(a) Spread the rubber cement evenly over the flesh side of the lining and the heavier leather. If the area is large, such as might be found in a handbag, pour the cement and smooth it evenly with a piece of cardboard or a tongue depressor. For a piece the size of a keycase or a wallet, spread the cement evenly with a brush.

(b) Let the cement dry on *both* surfaces until the shine is gone.

(c) If the piece is not designed to fold, aline the two pieces and press one end of the lining to the heavier leather, while holding the other end up. Work up from the cemented end, pressing and smoothing the lining to the heavier leather; then, with a knife or scissors, trim the lining even with the heavier leather.

(d) For small projects which will be fold-

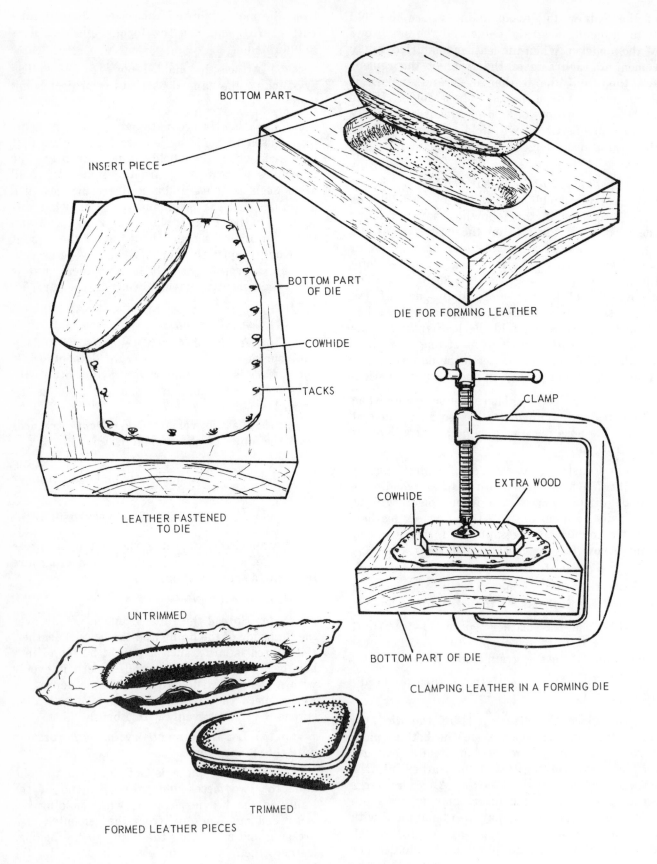

BOTTOM PART

INSERT PIECE

BOTTOM PART
OF DIE

COWHIDE

TACKS

LEATHER FASTENED
TO DIE

DIE FOR FORMING LEATHER

CLAMP

COWHIDE

EXTRA WOOD

BOTTOM PART OF DIE

CLAMPING LEATHER IN A FORMING DIE

UNTRIMMED

TRIMMED

FORMED LEATHER PIECES

Figure 11–73. Forming leather.

ed, such as wallets and key cases, smooth the lining up to where the piece is to fold. Fold the heavier piece and smooth the lining well into the fold. Continue to smooth the lining from the fold to the other edges. Trim the lining as in (c) above.

(e) When cementing a lining to a large project, use the same method but put sheets of paper, if needed, between the lining and the heavier leather to keep the two pieces from sticking together until the area being worked with is smooth.

- When doing a notebook, center the lining with the binder metal upon the heavier leather and firmly press the two surfaces together where the cover folds. The sheets of paper at the side of each fold will keep the lining from sticking while the folds are being smoothed.

- When lining a purse, start cementing the lining to the heavier leather at the front (not the flap) of the purse. Center the lining accurately so that the pockets will be in the right position. Slip paper between the layers of leather to hold them apart while working on the pockets and the first fold. Slip the paper out and work on the back and second fold. When the lining is in, trim it to fit the heavy leather.

NOTE

If the leather (whether a large or a small project) is not folded when the lining is put on, the lining will wrinkle when it is folded. If the lining is not pushed up well into the fold, it will tear when the piece is opened.

11–7. Lacing

The quality and attractiveness of leather articles is judged, at least in part, by the appropriateness and neatness of the lacing. Some types of lacing cover the raw edges of the leather while others leave them exposed. Lacing can be quite decorative, or it can be unobtrusive so that the design of the leather dominates. The selection of the type of lacing and the lacing material is up to the craftsman, who considers the use and the desired results in his choice.

a. *Marking and Punching.* To look its best, lacing must be uniform; the first step toward this is to have the holes evenly spaced. Spacing is not difficult if gauges and markings are used correctly. Three types of holes are made to accomodate the different types of leather lacing—

(1) *Round holes.* This hole is made with a rotary punch; a combination punch; or, rarely, with a drive punch. To facilitate punching with any round hole punch, hold a piece of scrap leather under the piece to be punched and punch through both pieces. There is a selection of the size of hole (fig. 11–29). Size 00 is nice looking because it comes up close to the lacing; however, it is so small that it offers resistance as the lacing is pulled through. This might make it prohibitive for a person with weak pinch or for use with wide florentine lacing. Size 0 or 1 are probably the most used sizes. The larger sizes are used to help people with poor sight or with a weak pinch. There are two ways to mark round holes—

(a) *Marking for revolving punch.* Mark a line 3/16 inch from the edge of the leather. This can be done with a ruler and the small end of a modeler, or perhaps more easily with dividers (fig. 11–74). Set the dividers, then pull them along the leather with one prong over the edge of the leather and the other prong lightly marking the leather 3/16 inch from the edge (A, fig. 11–74). This method is particularly good if the edges are curved. Next mark the distance between holes with a marking gauge. To use the marker, push it along the leather using the line just marked or a straightedge as a guide. As the marker is pushed, press it gently, just enough to have a + mark where each hole is to be punched (B and C, fig. 11–74).

(b) *Setting a combination punch.* It is not necessary to mark the leather when a combination punch with a depth and a distance gauge is used. Set the depth gauge so that the holes will be punched at the desired distance from the edge. This is usually 3/16 of an inch. To use the distance gauge, punch three or four holes at the selected distance apart (usually 3/16 inch). Hold the tube of the punch in the last hole made and slip the distance gauge into next to the last hole made and secure it with the nut. To gauge the next hole, slip the distance gauge in the last hole. This will put the tube of the punch at the correct distance from it.

(2) *Slit holes.* These holes are made with thonging chisels, which are available in different sizes and shapes. Slit holes are nice looking because the leather fits up close to the lacing. However, it is sometimes difficult to pull the needle and the leather through these holes if the hands are not strong, and there is a tendency for a long piece of lacing to wear as it is pulled through the slit.

(a) *Marking for slit hole.* Mark a line 3/16

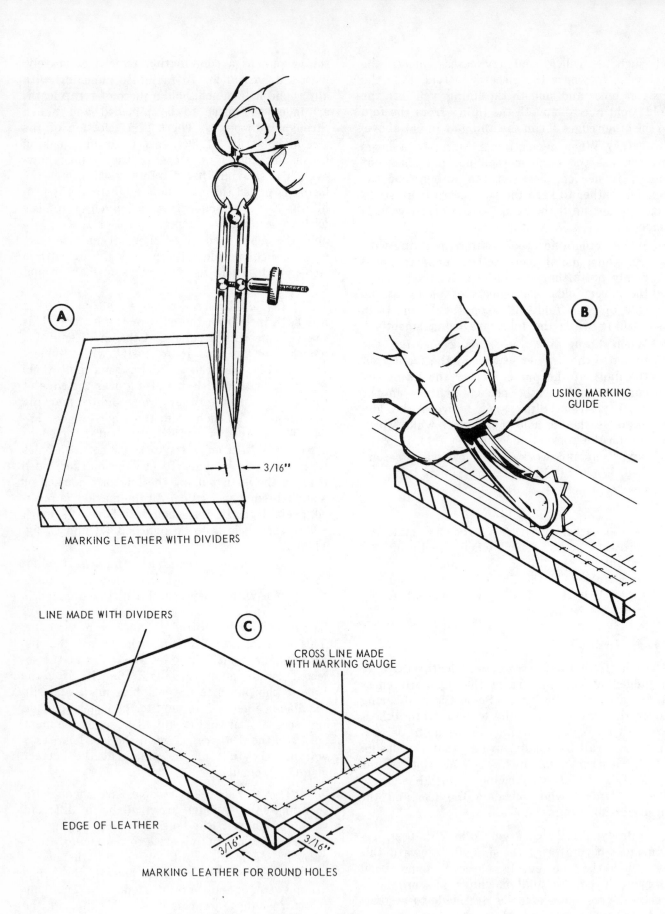

MARKING LEATHER WITH DIVIDERS

USING MARKING GUIDE

LINE MADE WITH DIVIDERS

CROSS LINE MADE WITH MARKING GAUGE

EDGE OF LEATHER

MARKING LEATHER FOR ROUND HOLES

Figure 11-74. Marking leather.

inch from the edge of the leather. Do this just as for round holes, with a ruler and the small end of a modeler or, more easily, with dividers. Pull the dividers along the leather with one prong over the edge of the leather and the other prong lightly marking the leather.

(b) *Punching.* Put the leather to be punched on scrap lumber or leather so that the chisel does not mar a good surface as it is driven through the leather and so that the chisel is not dulled by striking a surface that is too hard. Place the chisel with the prongs along the marked line. Hold the chisel perpendicular to the leather and strike the end a sharp tap with a mallet until the prongs just cut through the leather. Do not drive the punch into the leather so far that the leather is split. Do not attempt to use a slit punch on leather that is too thick for the prongs of the punch (fig. 11–75). For thick leather, round holes can be made with a rotary or combination punch. After the chisel has cut the first set of holes, pull it out and reposition it along the line but with the last prong in the last slit previously made, thus maintaining even spacing.

NOTE

At the end of the line to be punched, it is sometimes desirable to have just one or two more holes instead of three. If so, put the last two or three prongs in the punched holes, thereby making the desired number of holes. A single pronged punch can also be used to punch a single hole where needed, as well as to

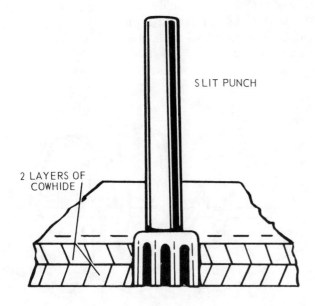

Figure 11–75. Leather too thick for slit punch.

SLIT PUNCH

2 LAYERS OF COWHIDE

punch around curved areas. It is sometimes easier to use a round hole punch for the corner hole where two or three stitches are put in the same hole.

(3) *Holes for stitching.* Holes for stitching are usually made with an awl. If the leather is lightweight, the awl can be forced through the leather by hand or an 8-pronged drive punch may be used. Heavier leather may require the use of a mallet or if the leather is extremely heavy, the holes can be drilled with a drill press.

(a) *Marking for stitching.* Mark for these holes in much the same way as for holes to be punched with a revolving or combination punch. Mark a line with dividers. This line may be as much as 1/4 inch from the edge for heavy leather. If the stitches will receive heavy wear as at the bottom of the soles of slippers, make a groove for the thread along this line with a gouger. Mark the stitching holes with a marking gauge, either along the line or in the groove. The spacing of the holes varies from 14 per inch to 4 or less per inch. The thickness of the leather and the type of thread used determines the distance between holes.

(b) *Punching.* Make the holes then with the awl or drill at the spot indicated by the markings.

b. Basting. It is wise to baste the pieces of the project together to see if they fit as they should. To do this with either round or slit holes, fasten the first holes on each side together with cord or with a safety pin. Then count down five or ten holes on both pieces and tie or pin again. When a corner is rounded, it is sometimes helpful to ease the leather around by putting two stitches in the larger part which meet in one hole in the smaller part (fig. 11–76), thus pivoting around the corner. This can also be done if there is a discrepancy between the number of holes in each piece. When the piece is basted, check to see if everything fits together as it should and if so, start the lacing, removing the bastings only as the lacing nears them.

c. Types and Methods of Lacing. There are a number of different styles of leather lacing, but only those most frequently used in occupational therapy clinics are described. Directions for additional types may be obtained from books on leather. Measurements given are valid only if the holes are 3/16 inch from the edge of the leather and are 3/16 inch apart.

(1) *Hints for lacing.* There is more to doing

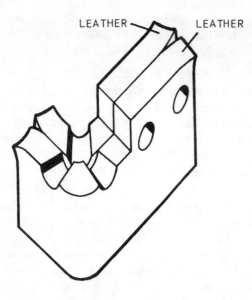

Figure 11–76. Pivoting lacing around a corner.

good lacing than just mastering the mechanics of each type. Some suggestions, common to most types, that should serve to improve the quality of work are as follows:

(a) It is necessary to develop the feel of how tightly to pull the leather and then keep this tightness throughout an entire project. The lacing should be pulled so that it fits snugly against the leather, but not so tight that it will pull the leather.

(b) When the lacing must go around a corner, extra stitches are necessary to allow the lacing to pivot. This is done in several ways; for example, three stitches can be put in the corner hole, or two stitches each can be put in the hole before the corner hole, the corner hole, and the hole following the corner.

(c) After any lacing or stitching is completed, it should be flattened to give it a more professional appearance. To do this, dampen the lacing *slightly*, then protect it by placing it between two scrap pieces of leather or between layers of paper, and tap it lightly with a rawhide mallet.

(d) Anyone working with a number of people should be able to do lacing with either the right or left hand. This skill is developed by actually doing lacing with the nondominant hand.

(e) For best results, the length of lacing for any project should be cut into pieces of not more than a yard in length. If too long a piece of lacing is used, it becomes worn and stretched

as it is pulled through the holes so that it will not be uniform in appearance.

(f) Lacing must always be done in the same direction on the same project. When the lacing runs out, the new piece must be started at the point where the old one ran out. If this is not done, it is almost impossible to end the lacing smoothly.

(g) Keeping the lacing from twisting is one of the most important and perhaps one of the most difficult parts of lacing. This can be done in several ways: Perhaps the easiest method is not to let go of the needle until it is brought around and "parked" (fig. 11–77) in one of the holes. When this is done, the needle must be turned over so the lacing will not be twisted. Another very similar method is to bring the needle around and turn it over, then slip it under the thumb of the hand holding the leather. This method requires a little more coordination, but some people prefer it because it eliminates the danger of the needle slipping out of the hole. More skilled people are able to keep the lacing from twisting by holding the needle between the fingers of the right hand even while pulling the lacing through the hole. The least efficient method is to straighten the lacing each time the needle is inserted.

(h) There is a right side and a wrong side to all lacing except whipstitch and saddle stitching. The stitches slant more on the right side than they do on the wrong side, and the edge of the leather is usually better covered on the right side (fig. 11–78). To get the right side of the lacing on the outside of the project, the right side of the project is held toward the person doing the lacing and the lacing is done with the needle going from front to back, away from the person who is lacing.

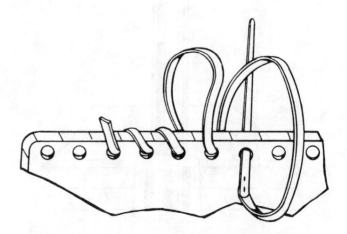

Figure 11–77. Parking the needle.

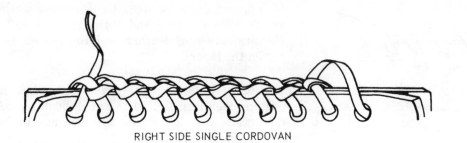

RIGHT SIDE SINGLE CORDOVAN

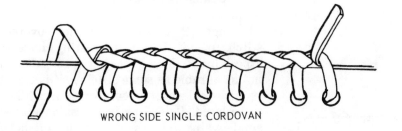

WRONG SIDE SINGLE CORDOVAN

RIGHT SIDE DOUBLE CORDOVAN

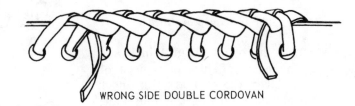

WRONG SIDE DOUBLE CORDOVAN

Figure 11–78. Right and wrong sides of lacing.

(2) *Whipstitching.* Several variations of the whipstitch will be considered because of the nice appearance of these stitches and the ease with which they are accomplished.

Single whipstitch
The single whipstitch (fig. 11–79) type of lacing does not give good edge covering, it is not as decorative as some of the other types of lacing, and it does not wear well. It is easy to do, however, and it requires a length of lace only three times the distance to be laced.

- *Lacing single whipstitch.* To accomplish the whipstitch, start by putting the needle through a hole from front to back and pull the lacing through the hole until almost to the end. Hold about 1 inch of the end under the thumb before it is pulled through. Put the needle through the next hole (do not twist the lacing) and pull the lacing through and continue.

- *Splicing single whipstitch.* If two thicknesses of leather are being laced, put the needle through the hole in the first layer of leather, then down between the layers. Start the new lace by putting the needle between the two layers, then through the hole of the second layer of leather toward the back (fig. 11–80), then continue lacing. The two ends between

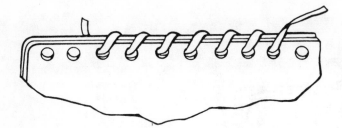

Figure 11–79. Single whipstitch.

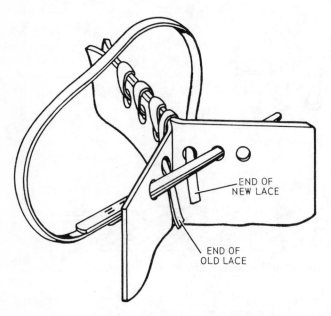

END OF
NEW LACE

END OF
OLD LACE

Figure 11–80. Splicing single whipstitch.

the layers can be cut off at about 1 inch and glued along the edge. If just one piece of leather is being laced, the ends are run under the lacing for about an inch on the underside, or each piece to be joined can be skived, then glued together with barge-type cement (fig. 11–81).

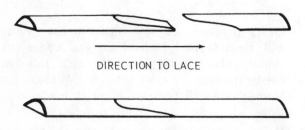

DIRECTION TO LACE

Figure 11–81. One method of splicing lace.

• *Ending single whipstitch.* Continue lacing until all of the holes are laced. This will bring the working end right up to the 1 inch end left at the beginning. Pull the beginning end down, out of the hole in the first layer of

lacing, and down between the layers of leather. Put the working end through the hole in the first layer of leather and then down between the layers.

Double whipstitch

This stitch (A, fig. 11–82) covers the edge, is decorative, wears well, and is not difficult to do. It requires a lace six times the distance to be laced. To get the effect shown, do the whipstitch twice in each hole. The mechanics of the stitch are the same as for whipstitch.

Alternate whipstitch

The edge (B, fig. 11–82) is not covered in this stitch, but it is an interesting novelty stitch, especially if done in two colors. Although it is not as durable as some stitches, it is easy to do. It requires a lace of about four times the distance to be laced. It is done in the same way as is the single whipstitch except for punching holes.

Cross whipstitch

This stitch (C, fig. 11–82) does not cover the edge of the leather, but it is very attractive, especially so if done in two colors of lacing. It is similar to single whipstitch, so it does not wear well; but it is easy to do. The lacing for this stitch is measured six times the distance to be laced.

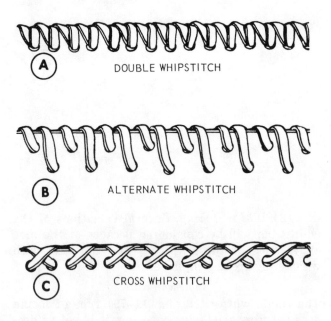

A DOUBLE WHIPSTITCH

B ALTERNATE WHIPSTITCH

C CROSS WHIPSTITCH

Figure 11–82. Types of whipstitching.

(3) *Florentine lacing.* This lacing (fig. 11–83) is sufficiently wide to cover the edges of the leather. Although it is plain, it is quite decorative and nice looking, and it wears fairly well. Lacing is done in the same way as for the single whipstitch, but more care must be taken to insure

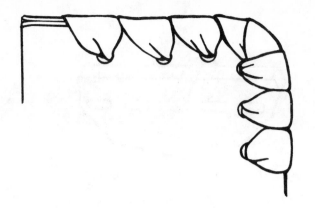

Figure 11-83. Florentine lacing.

that each stitch is well in place. Florentine lacing requires a length about four times the distance to be laced. If the holes are 5/16 inch from the edge of the leather, more lacing will be needed than if they are 3/16 inch from the edge. The method of lacing Florentine is the same as for single whipstitch, but measuring and punching is different because of the width of the lacing. For lacing 1/4 inch wide, a No. 0 round hole is used and for 3/8 inch, a No. 1 hole. The holes can be 3/16 inch to 5/16 inch from the edge of the leather and are spaced the width of the lace. Splicing and ending the lacing are the same as for single whipstitch.

(4) *Single cordovan or buttonhole.* This stitch does not completely cover the edge of the leather, but it is rather decorative. It wears well and requires less time and less coordination than the double cordovan. For this stitch, a length of five times the distance to be laced is used.

(*a*) *Lacing single cordovan.* With the outside of the project toward you, start the lacing at a point where the inside of the project can be easily reached or at a part of the project where the leather is double and not near a corner. Figure 11-84 illustrates the steps.

(*b*) *Splicing single cordovan.* When lacing two thicknesses of leather and splicing (fig. 11-85) is necessary, end with the lacing going through the loop (step 2, fig. 11-84). Figure 11-85 illustrates the rest of the procedure. If single leather is being used, either skive both sides and glue the pieces together with barge-type cement or run the ends under the lacing or the back side of the piece.

(*c*) *Ending single cordovan* (fig. 11-86).

(5) *Double cordovan or buttonhole.* This type of lacing is probably the most frequently used. It covers the edge of the leather completely, is decorative, and wears well. It requires a length seven and one-half times the distance to be laced.

(*a*) *Lacing double cordovan.* With the outside of the piece toward you, start the lacing where the leather is double and where the layers of leather are accessible but not near a corner (fig. 11-87).

(*b*) *Splicing double cordovan.* When lacing two thicknesses of leather and splicing is necessary, end with the lacing going under the cross (steps 3, fig. 11-87). Then bring the working end of the lace from the back to the front, insert it through the hole of the top layer of leather, then down between the two layers. Start the new piece by putting it up between the layers of leather, through the hole in the bottom piece of leather, then around front, and under the cross. Continue lacing (fig. 11-88). If the splice should need to be made on single thickness leather, figure 11-89 illustrates a good splice, which can also be used if the leather is double.

(*c*) *Ending double cordovan.* Ending a double cordovan appears complex at first glance, but it is not difficult when the steps are mastered. Work until the last stitch is completed in the hole next to the starting hole. Figure 11-90 illustrates the procedure.

(6) *Saddle stitch.* This is actually hand sewing. Because it does not cover the edges of the leather, the edges must be well finished when this stitch is used. Saddle stitching can be quite decorative if a contrasting color of thread is used to stitch plain leather, or it can be made to blend unnoticeably on a decorated piece if the thread blends with the color of the leather. Saddle stitching will wear very well if the stitches are recessed into a groove of the leather. Wearing qualities are increased too, if the thread or cord is strong and if it is pulled over a cake of beeswax several times before it is used. Saddle stitching is not at all complicated to do; in fact, it is perhaps the most simple form of lacing. There are two types of saddle stitching in popular use—

Double or true saddle stitch

This is the true saddle stitch used to secure two pieces of leather together. Holes are punched for this stitching as indicated in *a*(3) above. After the thread is waxed, thread a needle on each end of the thread.

• *Stitching double saddle stitch.* Start the stitching by passing one needle through the first

Step 1. To start the lacing, insert the working end of the lacing into the starting hole from front to back. Pull it through the hole except for about 1 inch, which is held down on the back so it forms a loop.

Step 2. Take the working end of the lacing from the back of the piece, bring it toward the front and put it under the loop.

Step 3. Bring the working end of the lacing from the back to the front and insert it into the second hole and pull the lacing through.

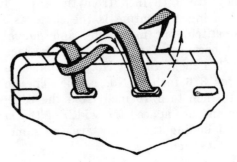

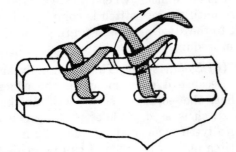

Step 4. Next bring the working end from the back to the front and insert it under the single strand of the loop made by the lacing in Step 3.

Step 5. Repeat Steps 3 and 4 through the hole and under the loop until the last stitch is completed in the hole next to the starting hole.

Figure 11–84. Single cordovan.

hole. Be sure to have an equal length of thread on each side of the leather. Pass both needles through the second hole but in opposite directions (fig. 11–91). Draw the stitches tightly by pulling one thread in each hand at the same time.

NOTE

The work should be held securely in a clamp or vise so that the hands may be free to use the two needles.

- *Splicing the saddle stitch.* To splice the most secure way, tie to a square knot down between the layers of leather.
- *Ending the saddle stitch.* Secure the threads by sewing back over two or three stitches, or tie a knot between the two layers of leather as in splicing.

Single saddle stitch

This type of saddle stitching is often used as decoration, as well as a method of holding two

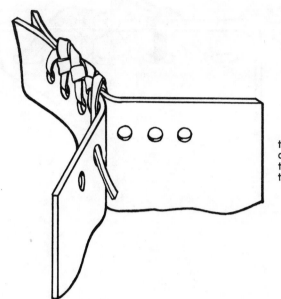

Step 1. Bring the working end of the lacing from the back to the front and insert it through the hole of the top layer of leather, then down between the two leathers.

Step 2. Start the new piece by putting it up between the layers of leather, through the hole in the bottom piece of leather and then around the front and under the loop made by the last piece of lacing. Continue lacing.

END OF OLD LACE

END OF NEW LACE

Figure 11–85. Splicing single cordovan, double thickness.

Step 1. Lace up to the starting hole as illustrated.

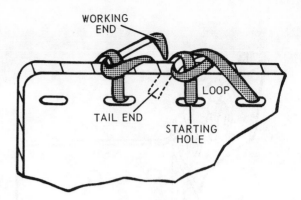

Step 2. Pull the 1-inch tail out of the loop at the first starting hole, and insert the working end of the lacing through this loop. Be sure to maintain the original position of the loop.

Step 3. Pull the tail end of the lacing out of the hole in the top layer of leather and down between the two layers.

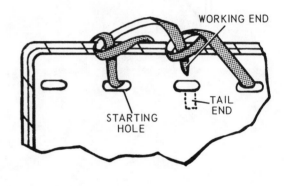

Step 4. Complete by putting the working end through the hole in the top layer of leather and down between the two layers of leather. Cut the ends to about 1 inch and glue down.

Figure 11–86. Ending single cordovan.

pieces of leather together. It is accomplished in a manner similar to that of the double, except that it is easier and somewhat faster. Because the stitch is single, it is not as strong as the double stitch.

- *Stitching single saddle stitch.* Use a single blunt needle and put it down through the first hole, leaving a 3-inch tail. Put the needle up through the second hole, down through the third, in a manner similar to sewing, until the lacing is completed (fig. 11–92).
- *Splicing.* This is the same as in double saddle stitching.
- *Ending.* If the lacing ends where there is a double layer of leather, as it should on a key case or wallet, tie the end to the 3-inch piece left at the beginning. Tuck the knot down between the layers of leather. If the ends do not meet where the leather is double, bring the thread around to the back or flesh side of the leather and tie.

   (7) *Machine sewing.* Machine sewing has

little place in hand leatherwork because hand sewing is better looking and stronger. It can be used to advantage in special jobs such as sewing zippers to leather and pockets to linings. Some suggestions for machine sewing on leather are given below:

   (*a*) Use the conventional home sewing machines only on light- and perhaps medium-weight leather. A heavy-duty machine is needed for heavier leathers.

   (*b*) Set the machine to make 8 to 12 stitches per inch in light leather and 5 to 8 stitches per inch in heavy leather.

   (*c*) If the feed dogs of the machine mark the leather, slip a piece of paper under the leather and over the feed dogs. Sew through the leather and the paper, then tear the paper away after the sewing is completed.

11–8. Finishing and Care of Leather

   a. Cleaning Leather. Leather frequently becomes soiled as it is handled in processing. It

Step 1. Insert the working end of the lace through the starting hole. Leave about a 1" tail. Bend this tail over so it forms a loop and hold it in place with the hand that is holding the project.

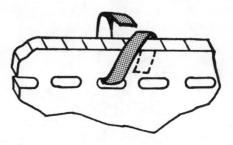

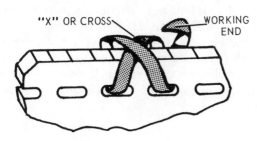

"X" OR CROSS

WORKING END

Step 2. Bring the working end of the lace over this loop and through the next hole. The loops cross over one another forming the X.

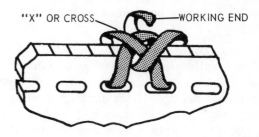

"X" OR CROSS

WORKING END

Step 3. Bring the working end of the lace over and back under this X. Tighten this stitch by pulling the lace.

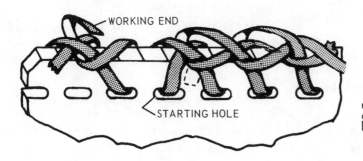

WORKING END

STARTING HOLE

Step 4. Repeat through the hole and under the cross until the last stitch is completed in the hole next to the starting hole.

Figure 11–87. Double cordovan.

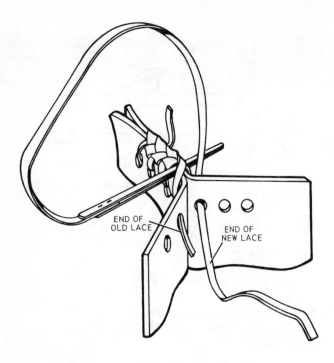

Figure 11–88. Splicing double cordovan on two thicknesses of leather.

should therefore be cleaned before a finish is applied.

(1) *Oxalic acid.* A solution of one teaspoonful of oxalic acid dissolved in a pint of warm water is used to clean leather. It is applied with a cellulose sponge. If the first application is not sufficient, another one may be in order. It is wise to rinse the solution with clear water after the application. Allow the leather to dry thoroughly before any other preparation is used.

(2) *Saddle soap.* This old standard is good for cleaning leather that is not too dirty. It has the added feature of softening the leather and restoring the natural oils. A lather of the soap is made with a sponge dipped in water, which is then rubbed on the leather. After the saddle soap has dried, the leather can be polished with a soft cloth or with the hand.

(3) *Special commercial cleaners.* These are available on the market. The instructions for using them will be on the container and should be followed for best results.

b. *Finishing Leather.* A protective coating should be applied to the leather to protect it against perspiration, finger marks, and dirt. There are several types of coatings:

(1) *Lacquers.* A number of preparations on the market provide basically a lacquer finish to the leather. They give the leather a good protective finish and a high luster. The choice of which to use seems to be a matter of individual preference. Directions for use are on the container.

(2) *Oils.* Most oils (like neatsfoot oil) protect, waterproof, and soften leather. They are used mainly to prolong the life of boots, saddles, and straps.

(3) *Resins.* These give a soft, satiny appearance to the leather.

(4) *Wax.* Wax helps to preserve the leather, provides a protective coating, and gives a nice, soft shine.

(a) *Liquid wax.* This is applied more quickly than paste wax. Just rub it over the surface of the leather, let it dry, and polish it.

(b) *Paste wax.* A good paste wax provides a hard but not brittle protective coating and a nice soft shine. If a small lump of wax is put between several layers of soft cloth and then the cloth is rubbed over the surface of the leather, it is possible to wax over carving and lacing with less danger of pieces of wax sticking to the rough parts.

11–9. Leather Design

Some understanding of and skill in working with leather is recommended as a background for designing projects and making original designs. It is both satisfying and convenient, however, to be able to design and execute a custom-made case for a favorite tool, camera equipment, or toilet articles. Some suggestions to use as a guide follow.

a. *Making a Pattern.* Designing original projects can be interesting as well as practical. Ideas can be obtained from articles about leather; from pictures; or, perhaps most often, from a specific need. Design the project first and actually construct it from heavy paper.

(1) Make each part of the project out of heavy paper.

(a) For each bend, add the thickness of the leather to the length of the piece.

(b) In places where the leather overlaps, add the thickness of the leather in the overlap.

(c) Add twice the thickness of the leather to the length for each fold that is made.

(d) Add 1/4 inch (fig. 11–93) to the piece for each area to be sewed or laced.

(2) Construct the project from the paper pattern, making the folds and bends where they

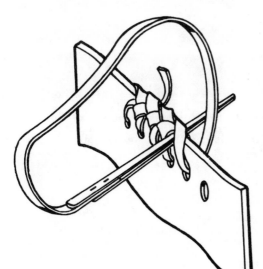

Step 1. Stop the lacing after putting the needle under the cross and drawing the lace through.

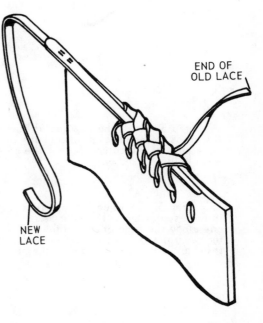

END OF
OLD LACE

NEW
LACE

Step 2. Start the new piece by drawing the needle and lacing between the edge of the leather and about four stitches of lacing. The new lacing should be grain-side up. The end of the new lace is then completely hidden under the stitches of the old lacing.

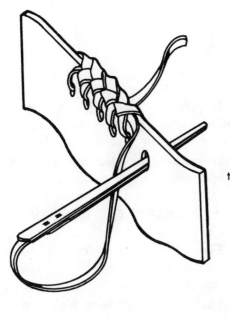

Step 3. Draw the needle and the lacing through the next hole.

Figure 11-89①. Splicing double cordovan on one thickness of leather (sheet 1 of 2).

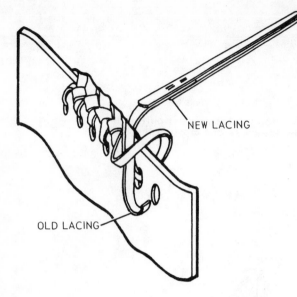

NEW LACING

OLD LACING

Step 4. Bring the remaining end of the old lacing across the top of the lacing at an angle and hold it on top of the new piece as it angles down to enter the hole.

Step 5. Next, the new lacing is put under the cross in the usual manner, but with the old lace held as indicated above. The new lace holds the old one.

Step 6. Continue lacing with the new lace in the usual manner, but hold the end of the old one along the edge of the leather and lace over it for several stitches to secure it well, then cut it off and continue lacing with the new lace.

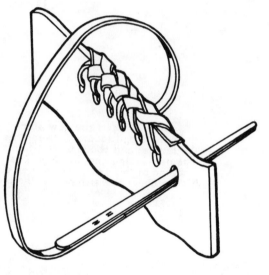

Figure 11–89②. Splicing double cordovan on one thickness of leather (sheet 2 of 2).

will be in the finished project. Fasten corners and gussets with tape, paper clips, or pins, or sew them.

(3) Mark the locations for clasps, fasteners, D-rings, etc.

(4) Correct errors in the paper model so that the pattern will be correct.

(5) Proceed then as in paragraph 11–4 to place and cut the pattern.

b. Making a Design. After making an original pattern, the craftsman may have difficulty finding a design to fit into the area of the pattern. He may wish to adapt an existing design or perhaps make one of his own.

(1) Inspiration for the design may come from other designs, tapestries, designs in fabrics, from rugs, or even directly from nature.

(2) In leather, consideration must be given to the background spaces to make them varied and interesting but not so large that putting down the background stretches the leather out of shape.

(3) Flowing lines that are not too precise are more easily corrected if the tool should slip than are geometric designs.

(4) The principles of good design in chapter 1 apply to designing in leather but must include the considerations of (1) through (3) above.

Step 1. Pull the tail completely out of the starting stitch and hole.

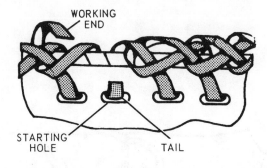

Step 2. Pull the tail out of the loop, leaving the loop free and the tail hanging loosely. Make sure the loop maintains the same position as it did in the stitch.

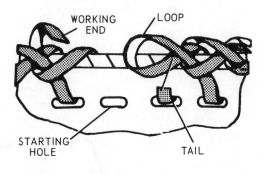

Step 3. Bring the working end of the lacing through the starting hole which is free.

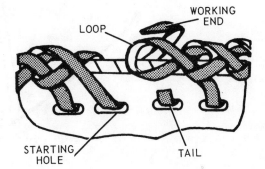

Figure 11–90①. Ending double cordovan (sheet 1 of 2).

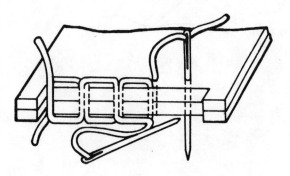

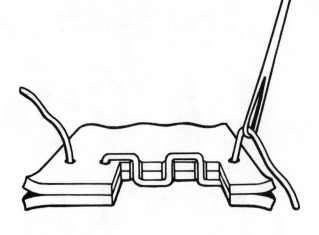

Figure 11–91. Schematic drawing of saddle stitching.

Figure 11–92. Schematic drawing of single saddle stitch.

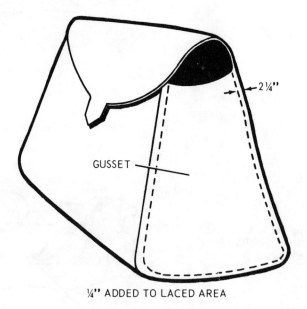

2¼"

GUSSET

¼" ADDED TO LACED AREA

Figure 11–93. One-fourth inch added to laced area.

Step 4. Bring the working end of the lacing up through the loop, from the back.

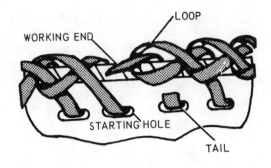

Step 5. Now bring this working end under the cross, or X.

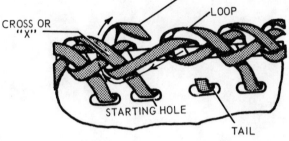

Step 6. Now cross the working end over itself and then down through the loop toward the front.

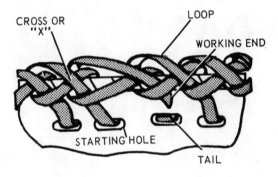

Step 7. Pull the tail out of the hole in the top layer of leather and down between the layers.

Step 8. Put the working end through the hole in the top layer of leather and down between the layers.

Step 9. Adjust this ending stitch to look like the others. Cut the ends, leaving about ½ inch and tuck or glue them to the sides of the leather.

Remember! To end double cordovan, put the lacing through the hole, up through the loop, under the X or cross, and down through loop toward the front and through the hole. Slip the ends between the layers of leather.

Figure 11–90②. Ending double cordovan (sheet 2 of 2).

CHAPTER 12

TYPES OF PRINTING

Section I. PRINTING

12–1. Introduction

a. Since prehistoric times, man has sought methods of communication and of recording important events. Sign language was probably the earliest method of communication. Important events and religious traditions were handed down by word of mouth from generation to generation. Men with unusual memories were chosen to learn and to pass on these tribal legends and traditions. With the passage of time came picture writing on stone; *for example,* those done by the American Indians. Gradually, there was a change from pictures to symbols. Symbols came to mean sounds rather than thoughts, and phonetic writing came into being. These can be seen in ancient Mexican scripts, as well as in the phonetic characters of the Phoenicians. The ancient Assyrians, Chaldeans, and Egyptians carved their symbolic characters on tablets of stone, as in the Egyptain hieroglyphics. The Chaldeans replaced the heavy stones with clay tablets and developed cuneiform writing with punches.

b. China used clay tablets and stamps much earlier. Also their imperial seals and inked rubbings were taken from stone inscriptions. Wood-block printing and later even paper money was widely known throughout the empire.

c. Japan also used woodblock printing. The world's oldest known printed book is a collection of Buddhist scriptures printed from woodblocks.

d. Our present alphabet came from the Phoenicians, Greeks, Romans, and Anglo-Saxons; our numerals from the Romans and Arabs.

e. The Egyptians manufactured a crude kind of paper called papyrus and later parchment and vellum were introduced. But long before this, the Chinese and Japanese made paper from rags and bamboo.

f. The early books were laboriously hand written with quill pens. These books were scarce and so expensive that only the very wealthy owned them. Men in various countries tried to find more rapid methods for producing books. Johann Gutenberg, famous for the Gutenberg Bible, is credited with inventing movable metal type in Germany during the 15th century.

g. The next problem was that of reproducing pictures. From the wood block or wood engraving, line engraving spread to metal. Copper was found to be less expensive than gold and silver, as it was soft and easily worked. Armor makers had put designs in metal with acid, and from this arose, early in the 16th century, the art of etching.

h. As soon as printing made books available to the common man, learning took a tremendous spurt. Printing, with its international origins, justifiably claims to be one of the leading factors in man's progress and development.

12–2. Glossary

a. General. It is necessary to know printing terms in order to follow the instructions for the various printing processes.

b. Terms.

(1) *Body.* The piece of metal on which type is cast.

(2) *Brayer.* A hand roller device used for inking a form.

(3) *California job case.* A type case in general use which has compartments for both capitals and lower case letters, as well as for figures and punctuation marks.

(4) *Case.* A drawer for type, with compart-

ments for each letter, figure, and punctuation mark, or for leads and slugs.

(5) *Chase.* A cast iron or steel frame in which type is locked up for placing in the press.

(6) *Composing stick.* A small metal frame in which the pieces of type are assembled into words and lines.

(7) *Distribution.* Replacement of the type in the correct compartments in the case after the printing is completed.

(8) *Dumping.* The process of moving the type from the composing stick to the galley.

(9) *Em.* The square of the height of any size type. Thus the em of any 12-point type is 12 points square.

(10) *En.* One-half the width of an em body in type measurement.

(11) *Feeding the press.* The process of placing the paper that is to be printed in the press and removing it from the press.

(12) *Font.* A complete assortment of type of one face and size, to include capitals, small letters, numerals, and punctuation marks.

(13) *Format.* The general makeup of the item to be printed.

(14) *Furniture.* Wooden spacing material, sized by picas, which fills the space between the type and the chase.

(15) *Galley.* A 3-sided shallow metal tray used for transporting and storing type.

(16) *Gauge pins.* Metal guides placed in the tympan paper to hold the paper to be printed.

(17) *Gravure.* The intaglio process of printing, such as etching and engraving, where the printing areas are depressed. The plate is loaded with ink and wiped, with the ink remaining in the depressions in proportion to their depth. It has the unusual ability to print all the way from delicate detail to dense solids.

(18) *Inking press.* The process of applying ink to the printing press.

(19) *Justification.* Spacing the lines of type out to a uniform width so that the alinement will be even on the right side.

(20) *Layout.* A working diagram for the printer to follow, marked to show such things as placement and spacing of text, margins, and size and kinds of type to be used.

(21) *Leads.* Thin strips of lead, usually 2 points (1/36 inch) thick, less than type height, used as spacing material between lines of type.

(22) *Letter press.* Common method of printing in which the printing areas of the type stand in relief above the nonprinting areas so the ink can be rolled on and transferred by pressure to the paper.

(23) *Line gauge.* A printer's rule, usually divided into both picas and inches.

(24) *Lock up.* Fastening the type tightly in a chase so that it may be inserted in the press for printing.

(25) *Lower case.* Small letters of a type font, as distinguished from capitals.

(26) *Margins.* The part of a page outside the main part of the printed matter.

(27) *Offset.* Photo offset lithography. A lithographic plate is moistened, inked, and printed on a rubber cylinder. The wet ink on the cylinder is then pressed against the paper and "offset" onto it.

(28) *Pica.* The printer's standard of measurement. It is equal to 12 points (about 1/6 inch).

(29) *Pie or pi.* Type which has been spilled or mixed up.

(30) *Planer.* A block of wood which is placed on the type and tapped before final lockup to insure that the type faces are all even.

(31) *Point.* A unit of measurement used to size type, 1/2 of a pica, or .01384 of an inch, about 1/72 of an inch.

(32) *Press.*

(*a*) *Cylinder.* A printing press with a rotating cylinder with a flat bed underneath which holds the type and which moves back and forth.

(*b*) *Platen.* A printing press on which the paper rests on a flat surface and is pressed against the type which is also held flat.

(*c*) *Rotary.* A printing press which prints from curved plates on a cylinder. The paper is usually in a roll but may be in sheets.

(33) *Proof.* A trial printing of the type or plate.

(34) *Proofreading.* Reading the proof to correct such errors as type, spelling, and punctuation.

(35) *Quad.* Metal space used in printing. An em quad is the size of a capital M and an en quad is half that width.

(36) *Quoins.* Metal wedges used to lock up type in the chase.

(37) *Reglets.* Thin wooden strips used for a space between lines of type.

(38) *Rollers.* The composition cylinders on a press which transfer the ink from the ink disc to the type.

(39) *Rules.* Strips of lead or brass used to print lines.

(40) *Slugs.* Thin strips of lead, usually 6 points thick, less than type height, used as spacing material between lines of type.

(41) *Solvents.* Various liquid agents which will dissolve printer's ink and which can thus be used to wash the press and the type.

(42) *Spaces.* Blank pieces of lead (quads) used between words.

(43) *Tying up.* Placing string firmly around the prepared type so that it may be moved (dumped) more easily before it is placed in the chase and locked up.

(44) *Tympan.* A hard paper which is placed on the platen of the press to provide a base for the paper to be printed.

(45) *Type.* A rectangle, usually of head, with a face shaped to produce a letter, figure, or some other character when pressed against the surface to be printed.

(46) *Type face.* The style of type, or the end of the type on which the character is produced.

(47) *Type foot.* The opposite end of type from the face.

(48) *Upper case.* Capital letters of a type font.

12–3. Equipment, Tools, and Materials

a. Equipment.

(1) *Printing presses.* Two types of platen presses are commonly used in Army occupational therapy clinics: the hand press and the foot press. The size of the press is determined by the inside measurements of the chase. Hence, an 8 x 12 press means the inside measurements of the chase are 8 x 12 inches. Most of the foot presses resemble the Chandler and Price 8 x 12 platen press (fig. 12–1). The hand presses usually resemble the Chandler and Price pilot press pictured in figure 12–2. The inside measurements of the chase are usually 6 1/2 by 10 inches.

(a) *Oiling.* The press should be oiled weekly with a good grade of machine oil, less frequently if it is not in regular use. When oiling the press, start at a certain point, go all around the machine, and end up where you started oiling. First, wipe off all the dirt and grease and be sure that the oilholes are not stopped up. The floor press has about 30 oilholes and oilcups; the hand press has considerably fewer. In addition, all the joints of the throw off, the rocker lock, and the cam roller and stud in the raceway of the large gear cam wheel on the foot press (fig. 12–1) should be oiled. The side arms, roller saddles, and roller stocks require special attention and should be oiled more frequently than once a week if the press is in daily use. Lack of oiling and cleaning cause a press to wear out more quickly than anything else. Do not oil too heavily, and wipe up excess with a rag. Do not oil any part of the press while it is running, but turn it over by hand after oiling to permit the oil to soak between the moving parts. A beginner should look at the oiling diagram of the press until he learns the location of all of the oilholes.

(b) *Care of rollers.* Rollers come in summer and winter grades. Summer rollers are harder in order to withstand the heat and humidity. Winter rollers are softer in order to keep them from drying out and hardening. There are also all-season rollers on the market which can be used year round and are not affected by normal temperature and moisture changes. If a roller is in good condition, it will feel slightly sticky to the touch and have a shiny surface. Take special care of these rollers, which are made of a composition material formed around the metal core. When the composition of the rollers becomes damaged, they should not be discarded but should be sent to a commercial concern where new composition can be placed on the original metal core. This is usually more economical than purchasing new rollers. If two of the materials in the composition roller come in contact with water, they will swell and even blister. In humid weather, the rollers should be covered with a thin coating of machine oil to keep them from getting waterlogged and unusable. To care for the rollers properly, remove all ink from them and from the ink disc daily, or oftener if the ink starts to dry. When the press is stopped, roll the rollers all the way down. *Never* leave them standing on the ink disc or on the type. The ink disc will make a flat place on the rollers within just a few minutes, and the type will make deep indentations or cuts in the rollers. When the press is not in use, thoroughly clean the rollers with a good type wash and remove from the press. Most hand press cabinets have a drawer with special notches

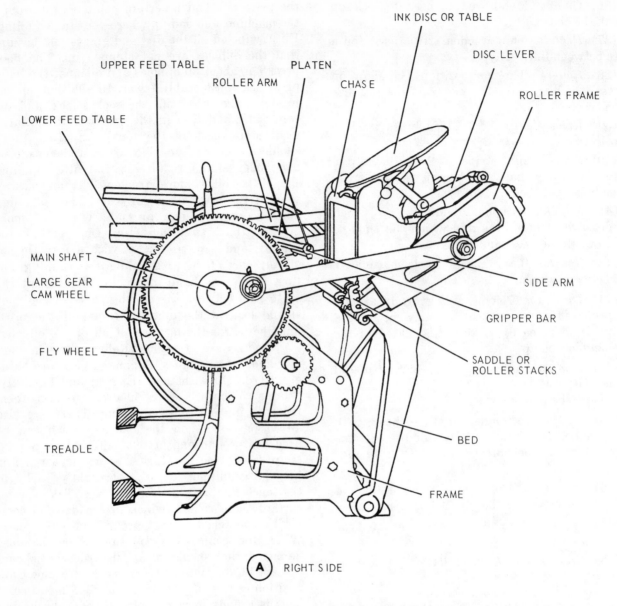

INK DISC OR TABLE

DISC LEVER

ROLLER FRAME

UPPER FEED TABLE

PLATEN

ROLLER ARM

CHASE

LOWER FEED TABLE

MAIN SHAFT

LARGE GEAR
CAM WHEEL

SIDE ARM

GRIPPER BAR

FLY WHEEL

SADDLE OR
ROLLER STACKS

BED

TREADLE

FRAME

(A) RIGHT SIDE

Figure 12–1①. Foot press (sheet 1 of 4).

just to hold these rollers so that they do not touch any surface.

(c) *Storage.* If the press is to be stored, apply a thin coating of oil to the ink disc, the fly wheel, and any other metal area that is not painted. This is done to prevent rust. If the rollers are also to be stored, put in a cool, dry place. Be sure that the composition part does not touch any surface. In very dry or very humid areas, the rollers may also be coated with a thin covering of oil.

(2) *Type cabinet.*

(a) *Use.* The type cabinet (fig. 12–3) is usually of wood construction, with approximately 16 drawers. These drawers are divided into

many compartments and are made to hold type, leads, and slugs. The cabinet top is slanted on two sides so that two drawers of type may be placed there for convenience while type is being set or distributed. When full of type, these drawers are extremely heavy. If a drawer is to be used without removing it from the cabinet, the drawer directly below should be pulled out 3 or 4 inches in order to help support the weight of the drawer in use.

(b) *Care.* The cabinet should be dusted and occasionally given a protective coat of wax or furniture polish. Type should *never* be cleaned on this cabinet as the type wash will remove its finish.

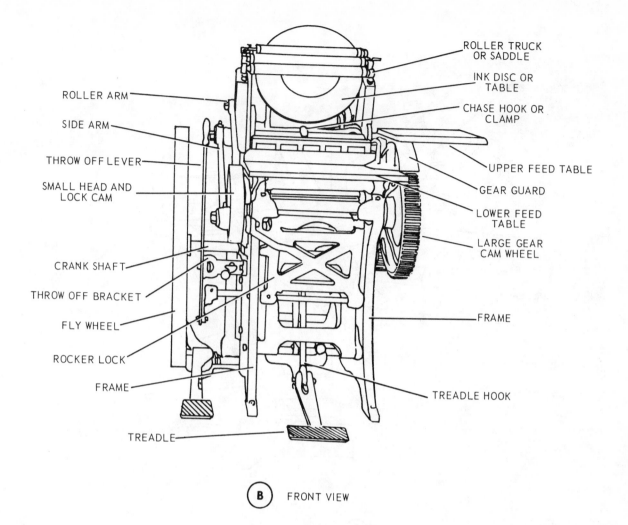

ROLLER ARM

SIDE ARM

THROW OFF LEVER

SMALL HEAD AND
LOCK CAM

CRANK SHAFT

THROW OFF BRACKET

FLY WHEEL

ROCKER LOCK

FRAME

TREADLE

ROLLER TRUCK
OR SADDLE

INK DISC OR
TABLE

CHASE HOOK OR
CLAMP

UPPER FEED TABLE

GEAR GUARD

LOWER FEED
TABLE

LARGE GEAR
CAM WHEEL

FRAME

TREADLE HOOK

B FRONT VIEW

Figure 12–1②. Foot press (sheet 2 of 4).

(3) *Handpress cabinet.*

(*a*) *Use.* This is the cabinet (fig. 12–4) upon which the handpress is usually mounted. Those most commonly in use contain a chase rack for five chases, shelves for twelve galleys, and two drawers, one of which contains notches to hold the press rollers.

(*b*) *Care.* The cabinet should be dusted, especially the shelves for the galleys, so that they will slide in and out smoothly. Occasionally the cabinet should be given a protective coat of wax or furniture polish. Type should *never* be cleaned on this cabinet as the type wash will remove its finish.

(4) *Lockup cabinet.*

(*a*) *Use.* This small cabinet (fig. 12–5) has a slab of marble 12 by 18 inches set into the top. Type is locked up on this marble. It is the only safe surface on which to clean type. The front of the cabinet is divided into approxi-

mately eight large sections. These sections vary in depth from 10 to 50 picas and are meant to hold the furniture and reglets when they are not in use.

(*b*) *Care.* The cabinet should be dusted and occasionally given a protective coat of wax or furniture polish. The marble slab should be kept clean and free from ink and the furniture and reglets should be placed in the correct sections.

(5) *Rule case.*

(*a*) *Use.* This is a small wooden case (fig. 12–6) which is divided into compartments varying in size from 1 to 36 picas. It is used to hold the rules when they are not in use.

(*b*) *Care.* Since this case is small, it is usually kept in a drawer. The drawer should not be one which is apt to be slammed as the rules will come out of the case easily. This would not only mix the sizes up, but would also damage

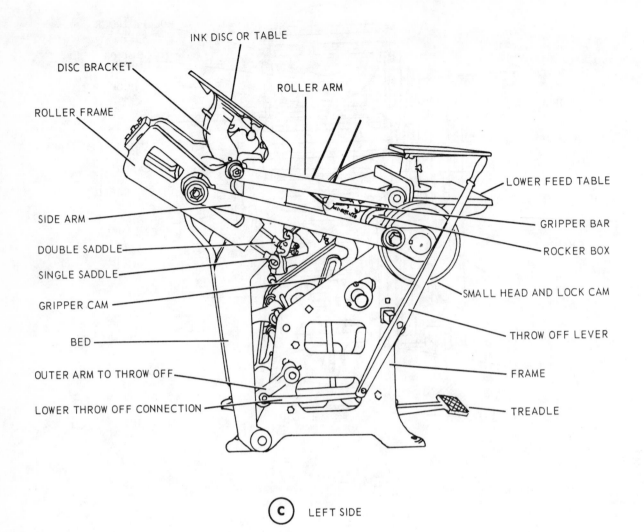

INK DISC OR TABLE

DISC BRACKET

ROLLER ARM

ROLLER FRAME

LOWER FEED TABLE

SIDE ARM

GRIPPER BAR

DOUBLE SADDLE

ROCKER BOX

SINGLE SADDLE

GRIPPER CAM

SMALL HEAD AND LOCK CAM

BED

THROW OFF LEVER

OUTER ARM TO THROW OFF

FRAME

LOWER THROW OFF CONNECTION

TREADLE

Ⓒ LEFT SIDE

Figure 12–1③. Foot press (sheet 3 of 4).

the rules, which are very thin lead. Even in a drawer, this case collects dust and needs to be cleaned out from time to time.

(6) *Paper cutter.*

(*a*) *Use.* The paper cutter (fig. 12–7) is used to cut paper and lightweight cardboard into the desired size. If the cardboard is too thick or there are too many layers of paper, the paper will not be cut smoothly and the spring of the cutter may be damaged. The paper cutter is not to be used to cut materials other than paper as they will quickly dull the blade.

(*b*) *Care.* Care should be taken that type cleaner is not spilled on the paper cutter. This will not only remove the finish, but also the guide lines.

(*c*) *Storage.* If the paper cutter is to be stored, a light coat of oil should be applied to all

metal parts which are not painted. This is done to prevent rust.

(7) *Lead and slug cutter.*

(*a*) *Use.* Leads and slugs are usually purchased in 2-foot strips. This cutter is used to cut them to the desired length.

(*b*) *Care.* This cutter (fig. 12–8) is constructed to cut the lead from which leads and slugs are made, and other items should not be cut on this piece of equipment. A thin coating of oil should be applied to all unpainted metal parts to prevent rust.

(8) *Type.*

(*a*) *Foundry type.* There are various kinds of type, among them Monotype, European foundry types, and American foundry type. They can be distinguished by their feet or lack of them (fig. 12–9). Monotype has no feet, the bottom

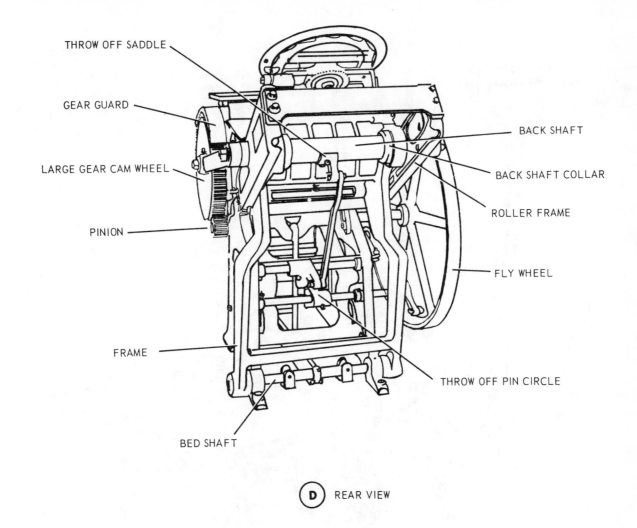

THROW OFF SADDLE

GEAR GUARD

LARGE GEAR CAM WHEEL

PINION

FRAME

BED SHAFT

BACK SHAFT

BACK SHAFT COLLAR

ROLLER FRAME

FLY WHEEL

THROW OFF PIN CIRCLE

D REAR VIEW

Figure 12–1④. Foot press (sheet 4 of 4).

being cast flat. European types are higher than the American standard of .918 of an inch and must be milled down to this height if they are used in an American printing press. Hence the feet are removed. American foundry type has feet. Foundry type can be obtained in sizes up to 144 points. However, due to the weight of the type and the difficulty of casting, wood is preferred for the larger sizes of type. Wood type can be obtained in sizes varying from less than 1 inch (48 points) to 10 inches high.

(*b*) *Type metal.* The same three elements are used in casting the various kinds of type, leads, and slugs; only the proportions change. Type from different companies may vary a little, but the following proportions seem to be representative for American foundry type:

Lead _____ 50%
Antimony _____ 25%
Tin _____ 25%

Lead alone makes too soft a printing surface. Antimony makes the alloy harder when the metal is cold. It also makes it more fluid when molten and a better face can be cast. Tin adds to the fluidity and allows casting to be done at a lower temperature. It also adds to the toughness of the metal.

(*c*) *Font.* The font, or package of type, varies considerably, so care should be taken when ordering. A complete font contains caps (capitals), lower case, figures, and points (punctuation marks). Cap fonts contain caps and points. Lower case fonts contain smaller letters and points. Figure fonts contain the figures, commas, periods, hyphens, and dollar signs. In some styles of type, the fonts are composed of only caps, figures, and points while others have only caps and points. Spaces and quads are sold in separate fonts. If the size of the type is too large, the font may have to be split into thirds. A font does

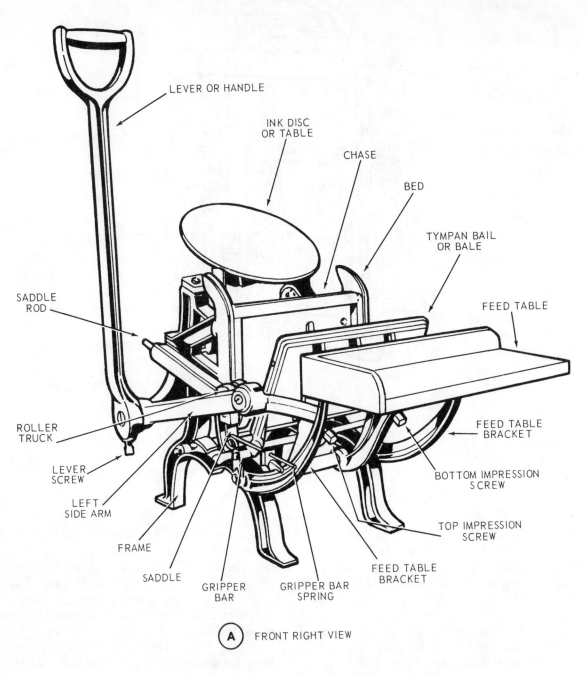

LEVER OR HANDLE

INK DISC
OR TABLE

CHASE

BED

TYMPAN BAIL
OR BALE

FEED TABLE

SADDLE
ROD

ROLLER
TRUCK

LEVER
SCREW

LEFT
SIDE ARM

FRAME

SADDLE

GRIPPER
BAR

GRIPPER BAR
SPRING

FEED TABLE
BRACKET

FEED TABLE
BRACKET

BOTTOM IMPRESSION
SCREW

TOP IMPRESSION
SCREW

A FRONT RIGHT VIEW

Figure 12–2①. Chandler and Price pilot press (sheet 1 of 2).

not contain the same number of each letter. The assortment varies with the frequency of use. Thus, there will be many of the letters "a, e, i, s, t," fewer of the letters "b, g, p, q," and even fewer of the letters "j, q, z."

(*d*) *Classification of type faces.* There are hundreds of different styles of type face. The styles below are distinctive and are used in conjunction with the rest of the style names such as Bodoni, Century Schoolbook, Goudy, and Wedding. Thus, there is Bodoni Bold, Century Schoolbook Italic, and Wedding Text, as well as two types of Alpha Blocks which are interesting because they stimulate creativity.

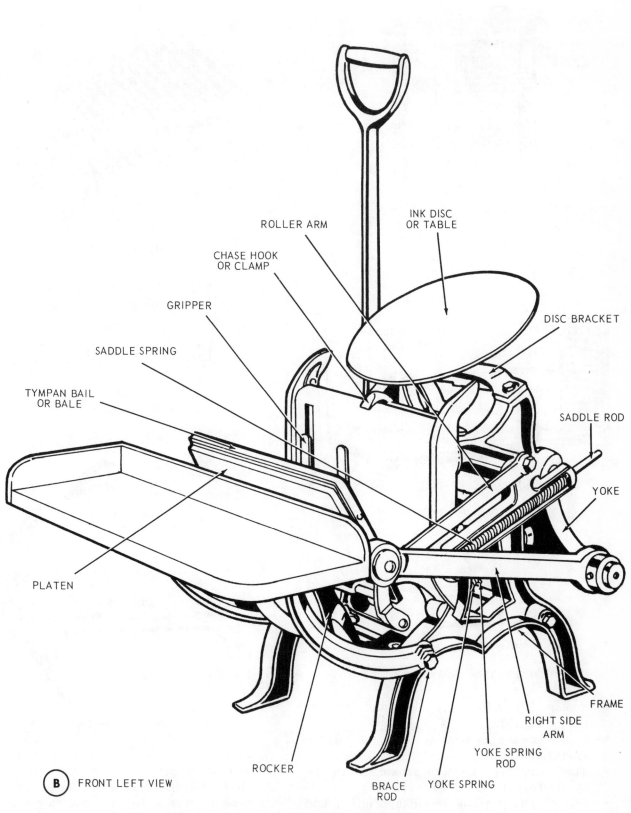

ROLLER ARM

INK DISC
OR TABLE

CHASE HOOK
OR CLAMP

DISC BRACKET

GRIPPER

SADDLE SPRING

SADDLE ROD

TYMPAN BAIL
OR BALE

YOKE

PLATEN

FRAME

RIGHT SIDE
ARM

ROCKER

YOKE SPRING
ROD

BRACE
ROD

YOKE SPRING

B FRONT LEFT VIEW

Figure 12–2②. Chandler and Price pilot press (sheet 2 of 2).

TYPE CABINET

Figure 12-3. Type cabinet.

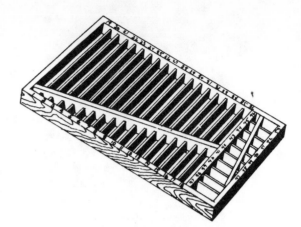

Figure 12-6. Rule case.

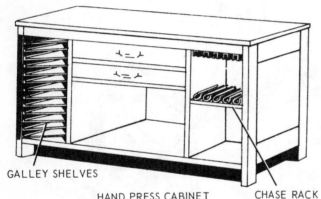

GALLEY SHELVES

HAND PRESS CABINET   CHASE RACK

Figure 12-4. Handpress cabinet.

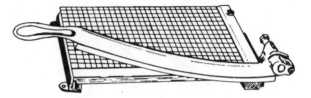

Figure 12-7. Paper cutter.

MARBLE TOP

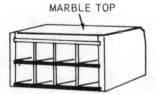

Figure 12-5. Lockup cabinet.

- *Roman.* The letters are plain and straight (A, fig, 12–10).
- *Italic.* The letters slant to the right (B, fig. 12–10).
- *Text.* This type is more ornate, as in the Goudy Text (C, fig. 12–10).
- *Script.* This type is less like printing and more like writing, as in Stylescript (D, fig. 12–10).
- *Bold.* The letters are thicker and heavier in

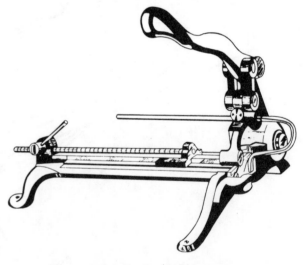

Figure 12-8. Lead and slug cutter.

appearance. This shows in comparing Bodoni and Bodoni Bold (C and F, fig. 12–10).
- *Alpha blocks.* These are types on whose surface appears a variety of straight sections, curves, and angles. They are set like blocks to form letters, monograms, figures, borders, backgrounds, and designs of various kinds.

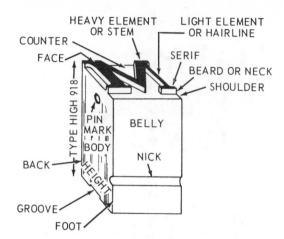

Figure 12–9. Parts of a piece of type.

They are available in two styles, linear and reverse (G, fig. 12–10), which may be used separately or combined. There are 19 linear characters and 23 reverse characters in 12-, 24-, and 36-point sizes which can be arranged by the setter into seemingly endless combinations.

(e) *Care.* When not in use, type should be kept correctly sorted in well-labeled drawers in the type cabinet. The label should show the type size and the name of the type face. Type should be thoroughly cleaned after each use, as old ink becomes hard and difficult to remove. The type is soft and easily damaged, so it should not be dropped, nor should anything be placed directly on the face. If tweezers are being used to pick up the type, care must be taken that they do not slip, as they can easily scratch the type face. Damaged type should not be returned to the drawer.

(9) *Spacing materials.*

(a) *Leads and slugs.*

NOTE

The use of these items will be discussed in paragraph 12–5 on printing processes.

Since leads and slugs are thin as well as soft, they are easily damaged. They should not be dropped nor should anything be directly on top of them. If it is necessary to cut them, the lead and slug cutter should always be used, and extreme care must be used to see that they are placed squarely on the cutter and that the number setting is exact. If the cutting is not done very accurately, the leads and slugs will not fit snugly in the composing stick as they should. When not in use, they should be kept in the type

cabinet in the drawer designed to hold them. The leads and slugs should not be intermixed and should be sorted according to length.

(b) *Spaces and quads.* The use of these items will be discussed in paragraph 12–5 on printing processes. Some spaces, 3-em and smaller, will vary slightly from the proportions shown in figure 12–11.

(c) *Furniture and reglets.* These items are used to fill the spaces between the type and the chase and will be discussed further in paragraph 12–5. When not in use these items should be kept in the lockup cabinet, correctly sorted as to length. Any ink which may be on them should be removed with type wash before they are put away.

b. *Tools.*

NOTE

The use of these tools will be discussed in paragraph 12–5.

(1) *Brayer.*

(a) *Use.* Brayers (fig. 12–12) are used to spread ink smoothly over a surface that is to be used for printing, either type or a linoleum block. When a proof needs to be taken or only a few copies made from a linoleum block print, the brayer is used instead of placing the material in the press. It is much quicker and easier for a short job.

(b) *Care.* The same care should be used with the brayer as with the press rollers. It should be thoroughly cleaned after being used and the roller part should not be left resting on any surface. Most brayers have two or three metal legs upon which the brayer can rest with the roller off the table. The brayer can also be hung up if care is taken that the roller does not touch anything. Brayers, like press rollers, can be purchased in varying degrees of softness, depending upon the purpose for which they are to be used. Like the press rollers, the brayer is also affected by heat, humidity, and dryness.

(c) *Storage.* If the brayer is to be stored, the roller should be given a light coat of oil. It should be stored in a cool, dry place and the roller should not touch any surface.

(2) *Brush.* When type cleaner and a rag are not sufficient to remove the ink from type or from a linoleum block, then a brush (fig. 12–13) is used in place of a rag.

(3) *Chase.*

(a) *Use.* The chase (fig. 12–14) is a metal frame built to fit snugly in the press. The type

Figure 12–10. Selected specimens of type faces.

is locked into this chase and then put in the press ready for printing.

    (b) *Care.* The chase is of a semisteel construction, but if too much force is exerted during the lockup process, the chase will bow and even break, usually at a corner. It can be mended by welding, but this is often not satisfactory. When not in use, it should be kept in the chase rack in the hand press cabinet. Th printing job should not be stored in the chase.

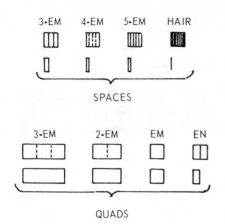

SPACES

QUADS

Figure 12–11. *Quads and spaces.*

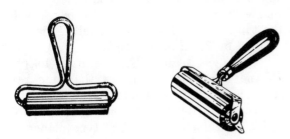

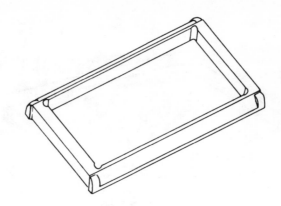

Figure 12–14. *Chase.*

Figure 12–12. *Two styles of brayers.*

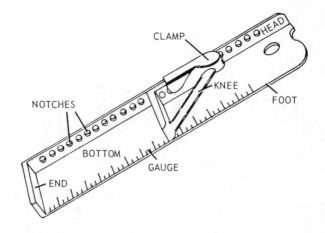

Figure 12–15. *Composing stick.*

Figure 12–13. *Brush.*

(4) *Composing stick.*

(a) *Use.* The composing stick (fig. 12–15) is the frame, usually of stainless steel, into which the type is placed and made ready for printing (para 12–5).

(b) *Care.* The projections in the knee must be fitted firmly into the rectangular slots in the head of the stick before the knee is clamped down. Otherwise, the knee will be crooked and may jam.

(5) *Galley.* These metal trays (fig. 12–16) are handy for many things in printing. If the

text to be printed is fairly long and the composing stick will have to be emptied more than once, the type can be assembled here as it comes out of the composing stick. If the material which has been set up is to be used again or if it is something which is used regularly, it can be tied up and stored in the galley on a galley shelf in the hand press cabinet. This will eliminate setting up and distributing the same text repeatedly. Since the number of chases per press is limited, the type should not be left locked up in the chase unless it is going to be used daily. The galley is also useful for sorting pied type. When the printing is finished, the type is taken out of the chase and placed in the galley for distribution.

(6) *Gauge pins.*

(a) *General.* There are two or three other kinds of gauge pins, from simple curved wire to more complicated pins. The pin in figure 12–17 is most commonly used in occupational therapy.

(b) *Use.* These pins are placed in the

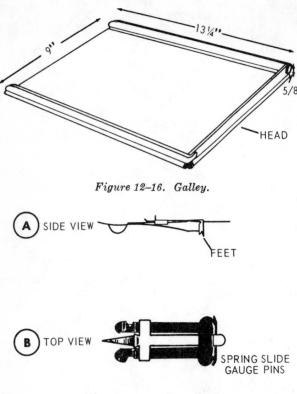

Figure 12–16. Galley.

A SIDE VIEW — FEET

B TOP VIEW — SPRING SLIDE GAUGE PINS

Figure 12–17. Gauge pins.

tympan paper to hold the paper to be printed. Placement of these pins is very exacting.

(c) *Care*. If the brass tongue of the gauge pin is bent repeatedly, it will break off. The tongue should not protrude too far beyond the pin when it is in place, as it may come in contact with the type and damage both type and pin.

(7) *Ink knife*.

(a) *Use*. The ink knife (fig. 12–18) is used to apply the ink to the ink disc. If colors of ink are to be mixed, the knife is used to mix them.

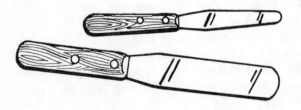

Figure 12–18. Types of ink knife.

(b) *Care*. The knife should be cleaned after use and kept free from rust. It is not for use in prying covers off of ink cans.

(8) *Line gauge*.

(a) *Use*. These rulers (fig. 12–19) are used for all measurements in printing. They come in two styles, brass and wood, and are marked off in picas and inches.

(b) *Care*. They should be kept clean and readable. Care should be taken that type wash is not spilled on the wooden ones, as it will remove the markings.

(9) *Mallet*. This may be either rawhide or all wood. The wooden ones are preferred as they are easier to clean if ink gets on them. The mallet is used with the planer to plane the type.

(10) *Planer*.

(a) *Proof planer*. This is used to take proofs. The planer (fig. 12–20) is usually a block of maple with a small piece of leather attached to the top and faced with thick felt. It is about 3 1/4 by 8 by 2 1/2 inches high.

(b) *Type planer*. This is used to plane down the type and is smaller than the proof planer. There are two sizes of these commonly in use, 3 1/4 by 6 by 2 1/2 inches high and 1 3/4 by 3 by 1 1/2 inches high. The type planer may have leather on the top, but it has no felt on the face.

(11) *Quoins*. There are two or three different styles of quoins. Those in A, figure 12-21 are the most commonly used. These metal wedges come in pairs. They may be obtained in three sizes: Number 0 (dwarf), Number 1 (small), and Number 2 (large). Another type which is not uncommon is pictured in B, figure 12-21.

(12) *Quoin key*. Each style or size of quoins needs a special key to lock and unlock it. These keys look alike except for the end which is inserted into the quoins. This end may be square (B, fig. 12–21) or have gear-like notches, as in figure 12–22.

(13) *Safety can*. Type wash is kept in safety cans because it is inflammable and also because it evaporates quickly. Usually one or both of the safety cans shown in A and B, figure 12–23 are used. The smaller can is generally called a benzine can, after one of the popular type washes.

(14) *Step-on waste container*. For safety reasons, the dirty cleaning rags and inky papers are kept in a metal waste can. The container in figure 12–24 is preferred to the regular can with a lid, due to its ease of use, especially with full or dirty hands. These containers should be emptied daily.

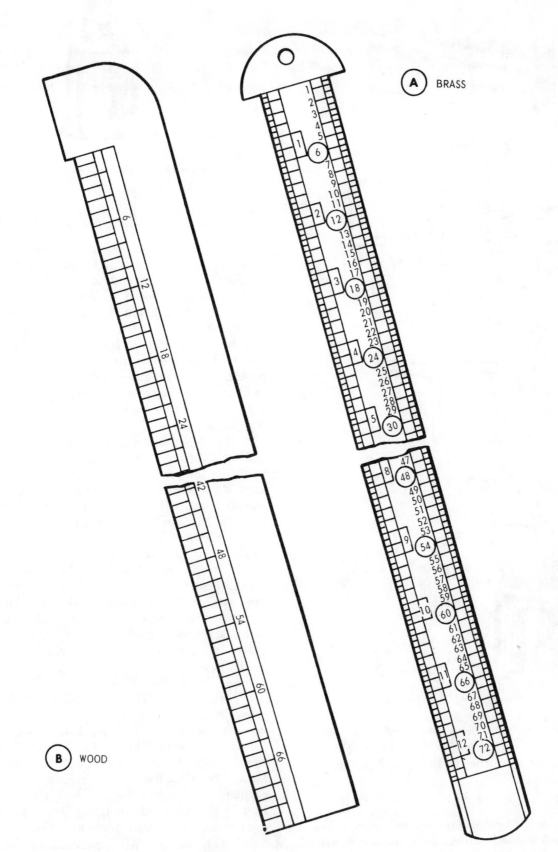

Figure 12–19. Line gauge.

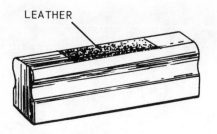

LEATHER

Figure 12-20. Planer.

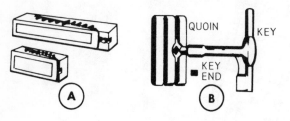

QUOIN

KEY

KEY END

A

B

Figure 12-21. Quoins.

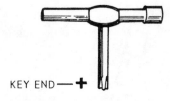

KEY END —

Figure 12-22. Quoin key.

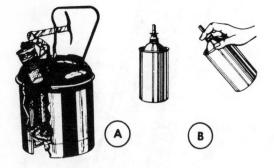

A

B

Figure 12-23. Safety cans.

Figure 12-24. Step-on waste container.

(15) *Tweezers.* These are most useful in replacing damaged or incorrect type once the text has been set up, either in the composing stick or in the chase.

c. Materials.

(1) *Ink.* For the professional printer there are as many kinds of ink as there are kinds of paper and he will therefore choose the ink best suited to the paper he is to use. The many-purpose lithographic ink comes in ¼-pound tubes and 1-pound cans in a variety of colors. Ink oxidizes rapidly when exposed to air. If the user digs down into the ink and leaves air pockets, scum forms quickly and the ink soon hardens. For this reason, a tube of ink is better. So little of the ink is exposed to air that hardening is not a problem. Even a tube must be used carefully, as it can split open at the bottom. Lithographic ink has an oil base, so it needs a solvent for cleaning purposes.

(2) *Paper.* The variety of paper is nearly endless. The user must make his choice based upon the purpose for which it is to be used and upon its availability. He should try the ink on a sample piece of paper if he is uncertain about how the paper will take the ink.

(3) *Powder.* A can of powder is very handy in the printing area. Talcum or foot powder will do. It is used to sprinkle on the tympan paper when, through error or in setting the gauge pins, the text has been printed in the tympan paper. If powder is rubbed or sprinkled lightly over the wet ink imprint on the tympan paper and then blown off, the ink will not reprint on the back of the paper.

(4) *Type cleaner.*

(a) *Kinds.* There are numerous kinds of type cleaner, or type wash, on the market. Care needs to be taken when ordering, however. Two things must be kept in mind: fire hazards and patient health. If at all possible, the type cleaner should be a nonflammable solvent. Many of the cleaners are highly volatile and must be used in a well-ventilated area, for their fumes are dangerous to breathe for any length of time.

(b) *Storage.* All type cleaners evaporate quickly and should be kept in tightly closed containers. The benzine can and safety can are best for this use.

12–4. Printing Measurements

a. *Point System.* Since common measuring devices were not accurate enough to use in printing because of the hundreds of very small pieces to be assembled, the printers developed their own system of linear measurement, which is known as the point system. This system is based on the point and the pica. For absolute accuracy, one point equals .013837 of an inch. However, for most work, the following table is generally used and considered accurate enough:

12 points equal 1 pica
6 picas equal 1 inch
72 points equal 1 inch
72 picas equal 1 foot.

All type, leads, slugs, and rules are measured by the point system.

b. *Pica.* One pica has the width of 12 points. All items of composing material except type are measured in picas. This includes furniture and reglets.

c. *Line Gauge.* The printer's ruler is called by various names: line gauge, line measure, type gauge, type rule, and pica stick. The line gauge commonly in use is 1 foot long marked off in inches on one edge and picas on the other. Wooden line gauges with the graduation printed on them are given out by manufacturers, but the brass or steel gauges with the graduations etched in are more accurate.

d. *Type Measurement.* Type is measured by its height and its size.

(1) *Type height.* Type height varies, depending upon the country where it is made. The American standard for printing material such as type, rules, and engravings is .918 of an inch. This measurement is from the foot, or base, of the type to the face, or printing surface.

(2) *Type size.* Type size is measured in points, and the body size of the type is measured from the back to the belly. The sizes in a series of type will range from 6 to 72 points.

12–5. Printing Processes

a. *Setting Type.*

(1) *Using the composing stick.* The material which is to be printed should be typed or printed (rather than written) on a piece of paper with all of the correct punctuation marks and spacing. The length of type line to be used must be determined from this, taking into consideration the purpose and amount. If the material is already printed, it is only necessary to measure the printed matter with the line gauge to determine the length of the type line. If the material is typed or printed (as opposed to written), then the length will have to be estimated, taking into consideration the size of type to be used. It is better to estimate too long a type line than too short a line. You should set the composing stick for the determined length. Be sure that the knee is firmly in place before seating the clamp. Place a slug of that length in the stick, at the head. The slug should fit well but not bind. Always use a slug here rather than a lead, as a slug is more rigid and gives better support to the type when it is removed from the stick. Find the case, or drawer, holding the desired type and place it on one of the slanting top portions of the type cabinet. If only a small amount of type is to be set, the case may be left in the cabinet. Be sure the case directly below it is pulled out nearly halfway to help support the weight of the case to be used. Hold the composing stick in the left hand with the end and foot away from you and the head and clamp toward you (fig. 12–25). Tilt the stick slightly so that if water were poured in it, the water would run toward the head and left toward the knee. Now everything is ready to set the type.

(2) *Setting the type.* To set type, take the letters from the case (fig. 12–26), one at a time, with the right hand. As the type is picked up, turn it between the thumb and index finger so that the face is up and the nick away from you. Place one letter of the type in the composing stick against the slug and the knee with the face up and the nick showing. Place the next letter to the right of this one (and so on), holding it in place with light pressure of the left thumb. After the first word is set, insert a space and then set the second word. Use 3-em spaces commonly between words. Continue in this manner until the entire line is finished. Read and correct the line before justifying it. This is very important, for if corrections are made last, then the line will have to be justified again if errors are found. The line of type will be upside down and

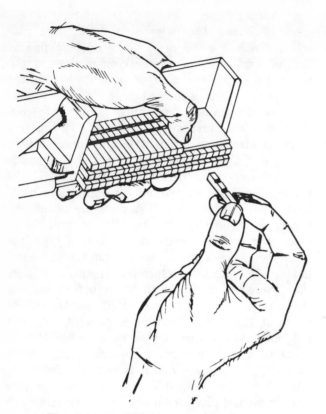

Figure 12-25. Holding the composing stick.

should always be read this way from left to right, never turned around. This will be difficult at first, but practice will soon speed up reading ability. (If this should prove too difficult for an individual student, a mirror may be used.) When correcting the line, look for broken type, misspelled words, different type faces and especially for the following problem characters: d b p q u n i j / I 1 l 9 6 2 5 o ◯ 0, ' and ". If the type does not fill the line and needs to be centered, do this now. Insert quads in pairs, one at the beginning and one at the end of the type line until there is no longer room for a pair of them. Fill the remaining space in the same manner with pairs of spaces. Place these smaller spaces next to the type rather than on the outside edge where they will slip out of place when the type is moved or tied up. After the line of type has been corrected, it is ready to be justified.

(3) *Justifying type.* Justification is the spacing out of type lines so that each will be firm in the stick and all lines will be exactly the same width. Test the justification of the type line by tilting the top of the line forward away from the head and see if the pressure of the stick (end and knee) will hold it in place. If the line

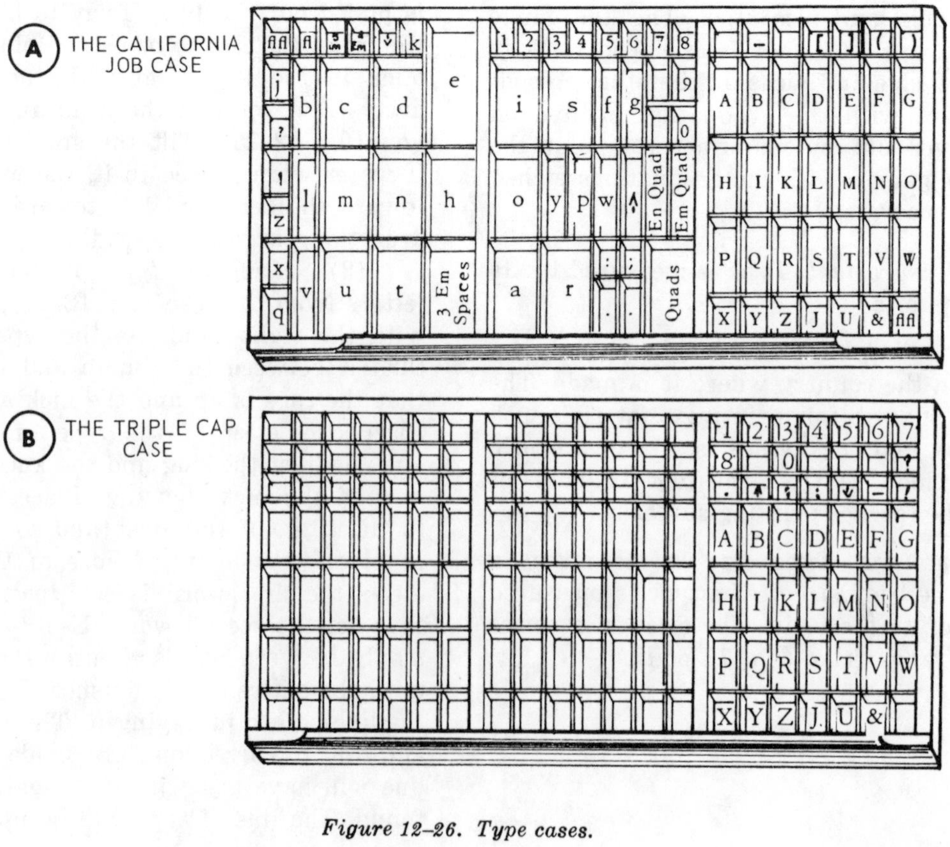

Ⓐ THE CALIFORNIA JOB CASE

Ⓑ THE TRIPLE CAP CASE

Figure 12-26. Type cases.

falls, it is too loose and needs more spacing material. If it must be forced forward, it is too tight and some spacing material must be removed. Justification is a very exacting process. If the line is forced, the knee of the stick will be sprung. This will cause type lines to be wider near the foot of the stick then those near the head of the stick. Sometimes, when justifying type, a letter or space will go part way into the line and then bind. This could be caused by the type being "off its feet" (which means that the type line is slanting and touches the top of the knee but the bottom of the type line does not fit squarely against the knee). To correct this, take out the last character in the type line. If this is a thin character, take out the first character in the line also. With the thumb, push the type to the right firmly against the end of the stick. Straightening a few characters at a time, work all the way across the type line. Replace the character that was removed from the front of the line and push the entire line to the left back against the knee and push the end character into place. If the line is badly off its feet, this process will have to be repeated more than once before the end character will go all the way down into the line. If the line is too loose, problems will be experienced when all of the lines are locked up in the chase. Do not force thin spaces into a line, as they will probably bend. Remove a quad from the end of the line, insert the thin space, and replace the quad. Spacing and justification go hand in hand.

(4) *Spacing.* Spacing of type is the selection and insertion of spaces to meet a certain specification, to make the lines flow smoothly, or to give a desired effect on the page. Lines may be perfectly justified but badly spaced. You probably have noticed that lines of typewritten material are even at the left edge and uneven at the right because the spaces between the letters and between the words are uniform. The lines on a page of printed material are even on both sides due to the use of spaces of different widths between words and in some cases between letters. Spacing is slow, exacting work.

(*a*) Unevenly spaced lines do not look good; they are hard to read; and they mark the word as inferior. A properly spaced page of type composition has spacing which appears uniform and will not have lines of spacing that continue down through several lines of type. Uniform spacing does not necessarily mean that the same size spaces are used between all the words. The

space sizes are adjusted to make the white areas appear uniform.

(*b*) Not enough space between the words is also poor, as it causes them to run together, which is difficult to read. The ideal space to use between words is determined by the type face. The lower case character "o" has been chosen as the ideal width for the spaces. If 3-em spaces are used between words and the last word does not come out flush at the end of the line, other larger spaces or combinations of spaces are put in place of the 3-em spaces until the line is firm. Do not use a space wider than an en quad. This is called "spacing out" a line.

(*c*) Sometimes there is not enough room for the last word in the line and it must be divided. This division must be done correctly between syllables, with a hyphen placed after the first section of the word. If there is not room enough for the next word or a full syllable, then the line must be "spaced in." To do this, exchange the 3-em spaces for other smaller spaces or combinations thereof, so that the necessary letters will fit in the line. If the spacing must be further changed between some words to justify the line correctly, look at the shapes of the end letters of the words. Slanting letters like "k, v, w, y"; open letters like "c, j, r, t"; and periods and commas and space; so do some of the capitals like "A, L, T." Space can be decreased between combinations of these and also between combinations of short and tall letters like "l" and "e." Two other places where space can be decreased are commas and periods, especially between a period and the capital of the next sentence.

(*d*) Indentations for the paragraphs are usually 1-em quad. Generally, the same size space is used between sentences as between words. No space is placed between a word and a period or comma. A hair space is placed between a word and a colon, semicolon, exclamation point, or question mark. A hair space is also placed between a word and quotation marks, both at the beginning and end of the quotation. If there is an exclamation mark or question mark after the word, no space is placed between it and the quotation marks. Space between the lines varies with the size of type and the purpose for which it is to be used. For straight composition, a lead is used in the stick between the lines. If more space is desired, a slug may be used. The next row of type is then set, spaced, and justified. The compositor continues in this manner unitl the type is all set or until the composing stick is about half full. Place a slug after the last type line and the type form is now ready to be "dumped."

b. Handling Type Forms.

(1) Transferring type from composing stick to galley. Emptying a stick of type successfully takes considerable dexterity. If a beginner, practice a few lines at a time until skill is acquired.

(*a*) Place the galley on the slanting top portion of the type cabinet with the open end to the left and the lower edge firmly against the raised edge of the cabinet top.

(*b*) Place the stick of type in the galley, resting against its lower edge, with the open side (foot) of the stick away from the body. Check to be sure that there is a slug supporting both the head and foot of the type form.

(*c*) Grip the type form firmly with thumbs at its head, index fingers at its foot, and middle fingers pressed against the open edge of the composing stick as in figure 12–27.

Figure 12–27. Dumping the type.

(*d*) Push the form forward along the bottom of the stick with a slight rolling motion. Do not lift the type and never unclamp the knee of the composing stick. When there is room enough, slide the thumbs down to the bottom of the stick to get a firmer grip on the type form. Continue to push the type lines out of the stick with a firm grip. Keep the middle fingers pressed against the stick to hold it against the galley and, at the same time, let the sides of these fingers act as extensions to the end and knee and press against the ends of the type lines as they slide out of the stick. Never try to lift the type lines, for unless the lines have been perfectly justified, the type will pi. (Only an experienced compositor should lift the type form into the galley.)

(*e*) Keeping the type form firmly pressed on all four sides, slide it along the bottom of the galley, turning it counterclockwise until the left ends of the type lines rest against the lower side of the galley. As this is done, it will be necessary to lift the left middle finger slightly to clear the side of the galley. Be sure only the finger lifts and not the type.

(*f*) When the ends of the type lines are against the galley, remove the left hand and push the lines to the right until the head of the type form is against the head of the galley (fig. 12–27). Be sure that it is firmly in place with the type square on its feet. The slant of the galley will keep the characters at the open ends of the type lines from falling down.

(*g*) If more sticks of type are to be added before the type form is complete, be sure that one of the slugs between the two sticks of type is removed. Otherwise, two slugs will be side by side, making a double row of space. If leads have been used in setting the type, then replace both of these slugs with one lead.

(*h*) To keep the type from being pied in the galley, tie up the type form.

(2) *Tying up type form.* A piece of string, strong but not bulky and long enough to go around the type form five or six times, is needed.

(*a*) Place slugs at the head and foot of the type forms but not at the sides.

(*b*) Hold one end of the string in the left hand and with the right hand, wind the string clockwise around the form, beginning at the upper left-hand corner. Let the first turn lap over the end of the string at the beginning corner. The left hand is now free to steady the type form, pressing it toward the lower right-hand corner of the galley. Wind the string smoothly with each turn just above the previous one. Draw the string tight just before turning each corner and the form will be tightly and securely tied.

(*c*) After the last corner is reached, hold the string in place with the left hand, and with the right hand, push a loop between the string and the form, using the ear on the line gauge. Do not use a lead for this, as it will bend. Now catch the loop of string below the windings and pull it tightly against the corner as in figure 12–28.

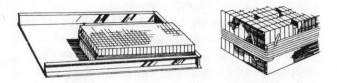

Figure 12–28. A job properly tied up on the galley.

(*d*) Cut off the excess string, leaving a short end sticking out so that it can be easily untied. Keep the loop and string ends short so that they will not get under the type in the form. Push the string down on all corners to the middle of the slugs to keep the type from buckling.

CAUTION

Type should never be tied up in the composing stick, but always in the galley in the correct position as shown in figure 12–28. Tied forms must be handled carefully, as they are easily pied even though well tied.

(3) *Emptying galley*. If a large form, it is easier to place the galley on the stone (marble top of the lockup cabinet), slide the type to the end of the galley, and draw the galley out from under the form. If a small form, place the open end of the galley flat on the stone and slide the form out onto the stone.

c. Proofing Forms.

(1) *Stone proofing*. After the type is tied up, a printed impression, called a proof, is taken for the purposes of correction. In modern printing plants, proofs are taken on proof presses. For this process, the type form may be left in the galley and the galley placed on the stone. This process is called "pulling a proof" and must be done carefully so that a clean, sharp print of the entire form will be made. (A messy proof cannot be read to find damaged type and typographical errors.)

(*a*) A brayer is used to ink a type form for proofing (fig. 12–29). The ink used should be a bit sticky. Either the ink disc on the printing press or a clean piece of plastic should be used to ink the brayer. A few small spots of ink should be put across the disc or plastic. Too little ink is preferred, rather than too much, as more can be added if needed and too much ink will make a smeary proof. (The cover on the ink container must be replaced to prevent a skim from forming on the ink.) The brayer is rolled back and forth and from side to side across the disc or plastic, with gentle pressure until the inked area in each direction is a little wider than the brayer. At the end of each stroke, the brayer is lifted and the roller is permitted to spin. This will make the ink spread more quickly. (If the roller is not lifted, the same areas will come in contact with the ink each time, and it will not spread evenly). The brayer is rested on its legs or supports while the type form is checked. One hand should be

run over the form to see that no type or other matter is sticking above the surface of the form. A check should be made to see that the string ends are not under the form, the form is firmly against the head and one side of the galley, and all of the type is squarely on its feet. The brayer is held with the handle straight up so that the legs will not hit the type; it is run across the ink a few times and then the type form is inked. The brayer is rolled across it from the open corner to the closed corner and from the open edge to the closed edge. It should never be rolled toward the open edges, as the type may be pushed off its feet because there is less support on the open edges. While the form is being inked, a very light, even pressure should be used, just enough to make the roller turn as it is rolled across the form. Special care must be taken with the edges. If there is too much pressure on the starting edge, the ink will pile up and print darker. Too much pressure on the finishing edge will wipe off the ink and make a streaky print. One way to eliminate edge problems is to place furniture or several layers of leads and slugs on each side of the form to act as bearers. The problem here is that these bearers must be exactly type high (.918 inch). They will then support the roller as it comes in contact with the type and as it leaves the type. The bearers may be removed before the proof is pulled or may be left in place. The form must be checked to be sure that careless inking has not pushed any of the type off its feet.

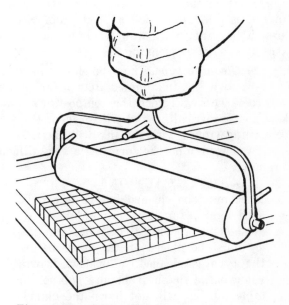

Figure 12–29. Inking the type form for proofing.

(*b*) Usually a thin piece of paper is used for proofing. Some people recommend moistening one side of the paper with a damp sponge. The dry side is then placed on the type. The paper is held at both ends and it is permitted to dip slightly in the center. It is positioned so that it centers over the form and is carefully brought in contact with the type. The ends are released gently as soon as the center touches the type. Do not move the paper after it touches the form, as this will cause the print to slur.

(*c*) The impression is now taken with a proof planer and mallet. The planer is held firmly in place on the type and paper with the left hand while it is tapped with the mallet. If the form is larger than the planer, the planer will have to be moved progressively across the form to make a complete impression. Care must be taken that the paper does not move, too. The force of the mallet should be straight down on the center of the planer and only as strong as necessary to get a clear impression on the paper. A slanted blow will cause a slur on the proof. Usually, the planer is struck with the end of the handle rather than the head of the mallet. The mallet is held in a perpendicular position with the head up, as a steadier blow can be delivered this way with less danger of slurring. Damage can be done by careless handling of the planer or by hitting too hard with the mallet. Special care must be used with small groups of type and of type with delicate letters. Characters at the ends of the lines are also easily damaged.

(*d*) After the impression has been made, the paper is lifted at one corner or one end, and stripped from the type with a slow, steady pull. Since it is difficult to pull a good proof without slurs, a beginner may want to pull one or two extra proofs before cleaning the type.

(2) *Cleaning type.* The type should be washed to remove the ink immediately after pulling the proof. This will keep the compositor's hands clean for proofreading and will prevent the type from being stored with the ink still on it. If ink is allowed to dry on the form, it is very difficult to remove.

CAUTION
Type must be cleaned before it can be used again, for it is impossible to do good printing with dirty type. The galley must be placed on the stone before the type is cleaned. (Type wash will remove the finish from any cabinet or table top but will not harm the marble top of the lockup cabinet.)

A small rag is checked to be sure that it is free from anything that might scratch the type. Then, it is wadded up in the hand and its exposed surface dampened with a little type cleaner. Any good type cleaner may be used. The form is washed by wiping the dampened rag across it. The wiping must always be toward the closed corner of the form and never along the lines of type, as this will throw the type off of its feet. Only a light pressure is necessary so rubbing should be gentle. If this is not sufficient, a type brush may be used to clean the shoulder of the type. Only a little cleaner is used on the brush. A brush must never be used first, as it will drive the ink from the type faces down into the body of the form. Too much type wash will do the same thing. The ink must be cleaned from the top of the spacing material in the blank areas of the type form. Then, the rag should be shaken out and the form wiped dry with a dry portion of it. Lastly, the ink spots and excess cleaner are wiped up from the galley and stone. The proof is now ready to be corrected.

WARNING
Dirty cleaning rags are a fire hazard and must be kept in a closed metal container to prevent spontaneous combustion.

(3) *Proofreading.* In commercial printing plants, trained proofreaders read the proofs and use standard proof marks to show the changes to be made. The printed copy should be perfect, so the proofreader must be very accurate in finding and correcting every error. Words about which there is doubt as to the spelling or as to the use of hyphens must be looked up in a good dictionary. The proof should actually be read twice with these things in mind. First, it should be scanned for typographical errors. Second, it should be compared with the original copy, checking every word, space, and punctuation mark. The mechanical defects and errors most commonly found are—

Broken type
Wrong fonts
Bad spacing
Inverted letters
Omitted letters
Transpositions
Protruding spaces
Bad word divisions
Misspelled words

Wrong paragraphing
Improper capitalization
Bad punctuation
Faulty grammer
Inconsistent spelling
Crooked lines
Bad makeup
Wrong indentations
When an error has been found, it should be marked in such a way that the proper correction can be made, but the error itself should not be covered up. It is always well to have a second person check the proof, too, as it is easy, especiallly for the beginner, to miss an error or defect.

d. Correcting the form.

(1) Once all of the errors have been found, the form must be untied so that the necessary corrections may be made. The galley is placed back on the slanted top of the type cabinet and one hand is used to hold the form down and against the corner of the galley. The other hand is used to grasp the end of the string that was left when the form was tied up, and the loop is pulled out. (The string may then be unwound counterclockwise with no difficulty.) Corrections should be made systematically, starting with those in the first line and working down the type form until they have all been done. As a general rule, all corrections should be made in the composing stick.

(2) There are a few corrections which do not affect the justification and which can be made in the galley without returning the line to the stick; these include such things as turning over an upside-down letter, replacing a damaged character with a good one, or exchanging a comma for a period, as they are all the same widths. Any character may be inserted that is exactly the same width as the one taken out. If the two characters appear to be the same width, this may be easily checked by taking two characters that are *exactly* the same out of the correct case and placing them side by side on the bottom of the galley. They must be placed on their *sides*, not on their back or belly. Now, a finger should be run over the exposed sides, and any difference in width will be immediately felt.

(3) For all other corrections, each line to be corrected must be put back in the stick so that it can be rejustified after the corrections are made. The same stick that was used to set the type is used to make corrections. The line setting must be the same length as that used in the type

form. If the knee has been moved or a different stick must be used, a line must be placed from the form in the stick and the knee set up against it to obtain the correct setting.

(*a*) The first line to be corrected is found and the thumbs and index fingers are put against the ends of the line. With firm pressure, the line of type to be removed and all type that is toward the open end of the galley is pushed down the galley a half inch or so. Two slugs are inserted in this open space, one against the portion of the type that is not being moved and the other against the type line that is being removed. This line is tipped back and two slugs are inserted in this space, also. There should now be a slug on each side of the line to be removed, as well as a slug against each of the two portions of the type form that will remain in the galley (fig. 12–30). Thus, if one of these lines should fall, it is easy to stand it up again. If there is room in the galley, the composing stick is placed in it; if not, the stick is placed firmly against the upper edge of the galley.

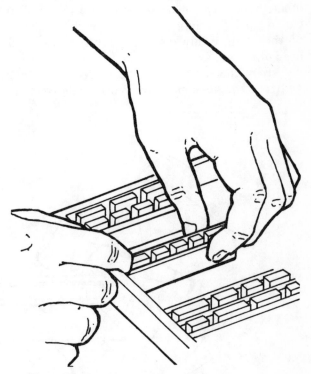

Figure 12–30. Placing slugs at open ends of type groups.

(*b*) The line to be corrected is grasped firmly between the thumbs and index fingers, with the middle fingers pressing against both ends of the line (fig. 12–31), as was done when the type was "dumped." The line of type is slid out into the open section of the galley. Lifting it is avoided, if possible, but if it must be lifted out of the galley it should be squeezed firmly with all fingers and thumbs and lifted quickly, turning the faces toward the printer and the feet away. The feet must be quickly turned down in front of the stick and "walked" into place against the head of the stick. This is done with a gentle forward and backward motion. If the stick is in the galley, then the line only has to be slid to the foot of the stick and worked into place in the same manner. If it is difficult to get the line into place, the end character is removed but the knee is not unclamped. The slug that covers the notches of the type line is removed. Now the necessary corrections may be made in the line.

(c) When this is completed, the line must be carefully justified. The slug is now replaced against the type line. The line is moved from the stick to its original place in the type form on the galley, using the "dumping" method. The extra slugs are removed by putting the index finger against the open end and pushing up and to the left until they can be grasped and removed by the other hand. The spaces between the lines are closed up by sliding the form together. The top of the form is always kept tightly against the head of the galley.

(d) The next line to be corrected is found and treated the same way. Working is continued on down the type form until all the corrections have been made.

(4) If words must be added or taken out, the type must be reset. This is called overrunning or rerunning. To overrun type, the type form must be placed in the galley the other way around with the foot of the form against the head of the galley. The beginning of the composition will then be at the open end and open side of the galley. The lines are spread and the slugs inserted, as in removing one line for correction. The composing stick is set for the correct length of type line. Now, from the line to be overrun, as many characters as can easily be picked up are transferred to the stick. Type is transferred until the place to be corrected is reached. The correction is made and type is again transferred from the galley until the line is filled. This line must be justified carefully and setting type from the galley to the stick must be continued until all of the type form has been reset. The reason why the type form must be turned around in the galley is obvious now. If it had been left in its normal position, the type would have fallen over, due to the slant of the cabinet top, as soon as the front characters in the line were removed.

(5) Using tweezers. There are places where it is difficult to remove the type with the fingers. In these spots, tweezers are a great help. It is also often necessary to use tweezers to remove damaged or incorrect characters from the type

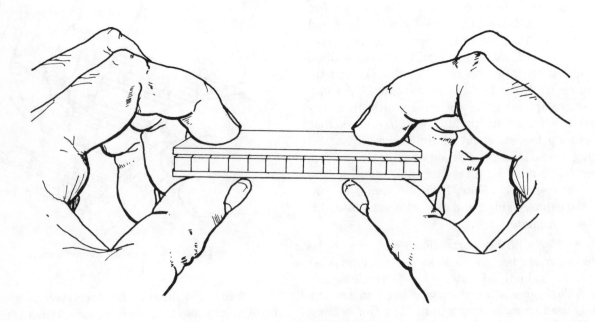

Figure 12–31. Lifting a line of type.

form when the corrections are being made in the galley. However, tweezers should never be used on type in the stick, type in a form that is tightly tied, or in any other place where the type is not loose. If carefully used, tweezers are handy tools, but careless use can damage the type. The tweezers points should be eased down onto the type body.

CAUTION

Tweezers must never be used if the fingers can·be used. If the character is held firmly in place and not loose, the tweezer points will usually slip over the type shoulder and ruin the face.

e. Looking Up Forms.

(1) *Imposing stone.* After the type form has been proofed, corrected, and tied up again, it is ready for printing and must be locked up. This is done on the imposing stone (called a stone because of the flat marble or sandstone slab on top of the imposing table). In most occupational therapy clinics, the imposing stone is the marble slab set in the top of the lockup cabinet. This stone must be perfectly clean before placing the type form on it. Even if it looks clean, it must be wiped off with a brush or clean rag before using it. A tiny piece of grit at the base of a letter will damage it when the type is planed down or will cause that letter to cut into the paper when an impression is taken.

(2) *Positioning form in chase.* The type form is slid from the galley onto the stone. A large form is easier to remove if the form is held steady and the galley is quickly pulled from under it. The string is left in place and the type form turned so that the head is toward the printer. The chase is placed around the form with one of the longest sides toward the printer and the ends to right and left. (The side nearest the printer will be the lowest side when the chase is in the press.) The chase is slid about until the type form is located a little above and slightly to the left of center.

(a) If the type form is wider than it is long, the head of the form goes toward the printer and the bottom of the chase. If the form is longer than it is wide, the head of the form goes toward the left end of the chase. Normally, the sheet of paper will fall to the left of, and above, center on the platen. In this way, the printer can read the printed piece for poor inking or for any other problems that may develop in the printing process, without interrupting the feeding process.

(b) Since the bottom of the platen will have two gauge pins and the left side only one, the bottom is the best place for the head, as the form will always be parallel with the top edge of the paper. If the head is placed to the left and the paper has been cut squarely, the form will print parallel with the head only.

(c) If the printing is not be placed in the center of the sheet of paper, the type form is placed so that the sheet of paper will be centered on the chase when in the press. Two good examples of this are stationery and envelopes. If a letterhead is to be printed, the form will be located well toward the bottom of the chase. The same is true of envelopes, if they are to be printed on the back. If the return address is to be placed in the front upper left-hand corner, then the type form will be placed low in the chase and over toward the left-hand side—how far over depends upon the length of the envelope being used. If the sheet of paper to be printed is very long, it will feed into the press better if held horizontally, so the form should be placed accordingly.

(d) Large, heavy forms should be placed slightly below center, as the impressional strength of the press is greatest at that point. Once the form has been placed in the best position in the chase, the furniture must be added.

(3) *Placing furniture.* There are several kinds of furniture. There are several methods of placing furniture around the form.

(a) *"Chaser" method.* The "chaser" method (A, fig. 12–32) is the simplest and most frequently used method. The pieces of furniture used at each of the four sides of the type form are longer than the sides and overlap in such a way that they do not bind at the corners. This is done by placing the piece of furniture at the top of the form, the side furthest from the printer, even with the type form at the left-hand side and extending beyond the form at the right. The piece of furniture on the right-hand side butts up against the top piece and extends below the type form. The piece of furniture at the bottom of the form, the side nearest the printer, butts up against the furniture on the right and extends beyond the form at the left. The piece of furniture on the left side of the type form butts against the furniture on the bottom and extends beyond the furniture at the top. The top piece should butt up against the left one. There should now be pieces of furniture overlapping clockwise all around the type form.

(b) *Exact-width method.* This method (B, fig. 12–32) is used when the width of the form is exactly the same as a standard furniture length. Two lengths of furniture as long as the form width are placed, one at the top and one at the bottom, and two pieces of suitable length are placed one on each side. This method should only be used by an expert printer, for if the furniture lengths at the top and bottom of the form are even so much as a fraction longer than the width of the form, they will receive the pressure, and not the form, when it is locked up.

(c) *Built-out method.* In this method (C, fig. 12–32), when neither side of the form fits any standard length of furniture, then the form itself may be built out, usually with metal furniture, to fit a standard length of furniture. The furniture is placed around the type form, as in the ordinary method (D, fig. 12–32). Once a frame of furniture has been placed around the type form, then the remaining space is filled in between the type form and the bottom edge of the chase, that nearest the printer, with furniture which is slightly longer than the form. Now the same thing is done on the left side. On each of the two remaining sides, a space about four picas wide is left for the quoins and the remaining space is filled with furniture, as was done on the other two sides. The lockup is now ready for the quoins.

(4) *Using quoins.* Quoins, pronounced "coins," are used to lock up the form in the chase. The quoins are placed in the spaces left for them at the top and right-hand side of the chase. These spaces were left close to the form for a reason. If they are placed too far from the type form, the firmness and rigidity of the lockup is lost to a great degree. Unless the form is very small, two pairs of quoins are placed at the top and one or two at the right, depending upon the size of the form. Additional quoins will be needed for larger forms. When wedge-shaped quoins are used, the inside quoins, those nearest the form, must always be placed pointing toward the solid sides of the lockup. The solid sides are those which contain just furniture and no quoins. Thus, the thrust of the quoins when they are tightened will press the form against a solid side of the lockup. If the quoins are turned the wrong way, they defeat their purpose as they press the form away from the solid sides. It is impossible to lock up a form securely if the quoins are turn-

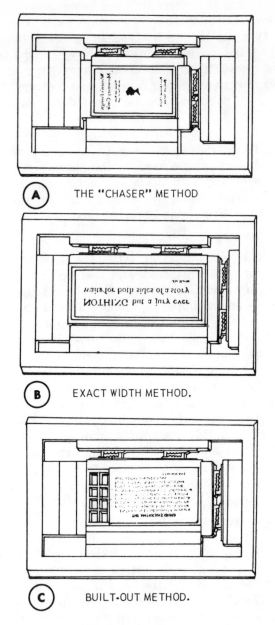

A — THE "CHASER" METHOD

B — EXACT WIDTH METHOD.

C — BUILT-OUT METHOD.

Figure 12–32. Placing furniture around the form.

ed the wrong way. After the outside quoins are in place, the string may be removed from around the form. Six-point reglets may be inserted between the sides of each pair of quoins and the furniture next to them. This not only takes up the space left by the string, but also protects the furniture from being damaged by the quoins. The form is now ready to be planed.

(5) *Locking up process.* If wedge-shaped quoins have been used, they should be pushed together with the fingers. If the other type quoins have been used, they should be opened until they are no longer loose in the chase. This is done by giving the quoins a slight twist with the quoin

key. If any of the material appears to be out of line, now is the time to make adjustments.

(a) A locked form should never be planed. The quoins should be loosened, the planer placed on the face of the type, and its back tapped lightly with the quoin key. If two sizes of planer are available, the smaller or midget one should be used. The tapping brings all of the pieces of type to the same plane. The quoins should be tightened slightly and the form planed again. It is possible to tell, by listening to the sound made while planing, whether the type has remained down on the stone or not. If the form has sprung, there will be a hollow sound. Any spring must be eliminated before the form is put in the press, for it is impossible to do good printing with a form that does not lie flat against the press bed. This is done by unlocking the form, deciding on the cause of the spring, and correcting it. The following things can cause the form to be sprung: too tight lockup, warped furniture, binds, excess pressure on some areas due to inaccurate material, or poor makeup. Careful, even locking up takes patience, but it is essential. A strong turn on one of the quoins when the others are loose will throw the material out of line and cause improper pressure on the quoins. One quoin should be given a slight turn and then the next one. This rotation should be repeated until all the quoins along the side and end of the form are locked evenly and firmly. Only enough pressure should be applied to the quoins to make the form secure. The chase can be sprung, or even broken, if too much pressure is applied.

(b) The form must be tested to see that everything is tight in the chase: one corner of the chase is raised and rested on the quoin key. Any pieces loose enough to fall will stay in the form if the chase has not been lifted too high. All of the furniture is pressed down on in order to see if it is firmly in place. The type faces are pressed with a finger to see if any can be pushed down. The quoin key is removed from under the chase; any loose parts will go back into position. The form is unlocked and the faults corrected. Loose lines must be rejustified. When all the faults are corrected, the type is planed against and relocked correctly.

f. Making Ready and Feeding.

(1) *Placing tympan paper and packing.* Before the first impression can be made, clean tympan paper and fresh packing need to be placed on the platen. The packing will have to be adjusted later after the first impression has been made, but the printer's hands will stay cleaner if as much of this as possible is done now before the rollers are inked. Four sheets are often about the right amount of packing. Hard paper, pressboard, or tagboard is better than soft packing, as it gives a sharp, strong impression and causes less wear on the type. Soft packing will cause the type to punch into the paper. The estimated amount of packing paper is cut to size, slightly smaller than the platen, and lain on the platen. The tympan paper, or drawsheet, is cut next and put over the packing, or tympan, to hold it in place. The tympan paper should be cut the same width as the platen, but about three inches longer so that it will reach well under the bails when they are clamped down. The bails are clamped down after insuring that the tympan paper is flat, firm, and uniformly tight. If there is much excess paper sticking out from under the bails, it should be trimmed off as it will interfere with the printing process. The press is ready to ink.

(2) *Inking the press.* The press should be inked before the form is placed in it. This prevents lumps of ink from getting on the form and filling up the type.

(a) A clean, dry rag should be used and the ink disc wiped off to be sure that it is free of dust. The rollers are rolled up where they can be reached and gently wiped also.

(b) If the ink comes in a can, a paper usually covers the ink under the lid. This paper should be removed and saved so that it can be replaced when the can is closed. Any skim or hard lumps from the ink surface are removed with the ink knife and a little ink is kept on the knife. The ink surface is kept level and is not dug down into, as this will cause the ink to oxidize and dry out more quickly. If the ink comes in a tube, both hands are used to squeeze out the ink. One hand is placed around the bottom and one at the top. Equal pressure is applied with both hands when squeezing out the ink. The hand at the bottom of the tube should prevent the tube from splitting there, which is a fairly common problem. Only a little ink is squeezed out.

(c) With the ink knife, a small amount of ink is applied in tiny dabs, well spaced over the ink disc. A very small amount of ink is needed. The beginner will invariably use too much ink, which will result in smudged copies. If too much ink has been applied, it is necessary to clean the press and start over. More ink can always be added during the printing if it is needed. This is done by putting a very small amount of ink on the lower left side of the ink disc, out of line with the form so that the rollers cannot carry it to the type before it is evenly distributed.

(*d*) The tympan bails must be checked to be sure that they are clamped securely in place and the press run through one complete cycle by hand.

(*e*) If everything seems all right, the press is pumped by hand or foot,. depending upon the model, until all of the ink is evenly distributed over the ink disc.

(*f*) The disc is checked carefullly to see that there are no specks of ink or foreign material. If there are any, they are removed with the ink knife and the press run through one more cycle. If the ink is now even and smoothly spread, it is time to put the chase in the press.

CAUTION

The lid on the ink container must be replaced in order to keep the ink from drying out.

(3) *Positioning the chase.* The rollers must be rolled down to their lowest position in the press. Both the press bed and the back of the type form are wiped off. The chase is held so that the type faces are toward the printer and the quoins are at the top and the right-hand side. The person doing the work stands at the right side of the press and carefully lifts the chase into the press. The bottom edge of the chase will be behind the two lugs at the bottom of the press bed. With the left hand and the right hand holding the chase, the top chase clamp is lifted. The chase is pushed back against the bed and the clamp is sprung securely down over the top edge of the chase. The chase is pushed over against the left side of the press bed; then, if the chase has to be removed before the job is completed, it can be replaced in the same position. During this process, neither the grippers nor any other part of the press must. hit the type faces, as they will be damaged. Also the chase must not be dragged on the rollers as they, too, will be damaged. The chase must be held until it is securely clamped in place. The printer should stand in front of the press and sight across the trippers to see if they will clear the form. If they will not, he should move them safely out of the way, as they will smash the type. They can be correctly positioned after the gauge pins are placed. Any gauge pins that may have been left in the tympan paper are removed. The press is now ready to make the first impression.

(4) *Setting gauge pins and grippers.* An impression is made on the tympan paper by pumping one complete cycle on the press. If the press is a foot press, the throwoff lever must not be pushed forward in order that an impression can be made. If there is too much packing while making this impression, the pressure can be felt and the press backed up before the type form is damaged.

(*a*) A clean rag is used to wipe the ink from the tympan paper and a little talcum powder is sprinkled over the damp area, then the excess powder is wiped off with a rag.

(*b*) If the printing is to be centered on the paper, the margins may be laid out in the following manner: Using scrap paper cut the same size as that to be printed, the sheet of paper is placed on the printed impression with the top edge of the paper at the top edge of the printed impression, the edge furthest from the printer. The paper will cover about half of this impression. A pencil mark is made on the paper in line with the bottom of the printed impression, the side nearest the printer (A, fig. 12–33). All of the paper from this line toward the printer represents the combined width of the top and bottom margins.. The center of this combined width is found by folding it in half and making a pinch mark on the edge at the center point. The pinch mark is placed in line with the bottom of the printed impression, where the pencil mark was previously made. A pencil mark is made on the tympan paper at the top edge of the sheet of paper near the left side of the sheet. The edge of the sheet of paper is lined up even with the left side of the printed impression and the top is in line with the pencil mark just made on the tympan. Now another pencil mark is made on the tympan paper at the top edge of the sheet of paper, but near the right-hand side (B, fig. 12–33). The same method is used to find the width of the side margins, using a pinch mark as before. With the top edge of the sheet of paper parallel to a type line (C, fig. 12–33), the pinch mark is placed just at the edge of the printed impression. A pencil mark is made on the tympan paper at the left-hand edge of the sheet of paper and about 2 inches up from the other marks.

(*c*) If the printing is not to be centered, the margins can be drawn directly on the tympan paper, using a ruler to figure out the desired width of the margins.

(*d*) There are several types of gauge pins. The spring tongue gauge pin is most commonly used and its placement is described here. (Some printers glue quads to the tympan and do not use

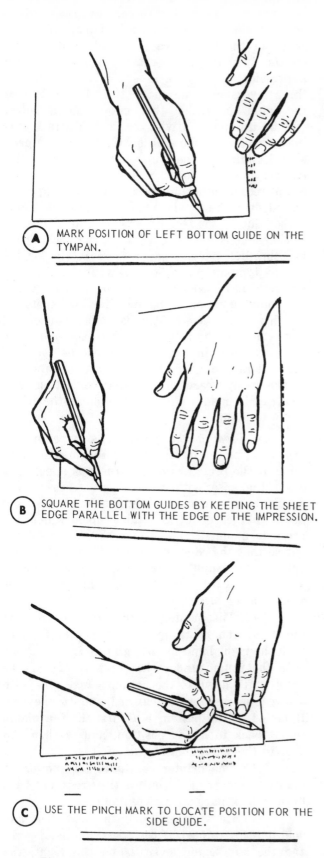

A — MARK POSITION OF LEFT BOTTOM GUIDE ON THE TYMPAN.

B — SQUARE THE BOTTOM GUIDES BY KEEPING THE SHEET EDGE PARALLEL WITH THE EDGE OF THE IMPRESSION.

C — USE THE PINCH MARK TO LOCATE POSITION FOR THE SIDE GUIDE.

Figure 12–33. Centering printing on the paper.

any pins.) Three gauge pins are placed in the tympan paper. Two are placed on the lines just drawn at the top of the sheet and one on the line at the left side. The lower right pin should be placed near the right corner of the sheet of paper; the lower left pin should be placed in a little way from the left corner; and the pin at the left side should be placed a little below the center of the sheet. These are the positions which allow for the most convenience in feeding paper into the press. Each pin should be placed with the feet right on the pencil line and the body of the pin away from the sheet of paper. If the margins are narrow, the pins are placed where the tongues will not hit any of the type, as this will damage the type faces. The pins should only go through the tympan paper, or draw sheets, as the packing should be free for any further adjustments that may be needed.

(e) A sheet of scrap paper of the correct size is placed in the gauge pins and an impression is printed on it. The margins are measured and the positions of the gauge pins are adjusted as needed.

(f) When the margins are all correct, the feet of the pins are fastened into the tympan paper by tapping the pins lightly with a press wrench. The points on these feet should now be pressed into the tympan paper. This will prevent the pins from slipping. If a long or heavy run of printing is expected, the gauge pins should be fastened with sealing or candle wax to keep them from moving.

(g) After the gauge pins are in place, the grippers must be set. The grippers hold the paper flat against the tympan paper and prevent it from sticking to the type form, thus preventing slurred print. A sheet of scrap paper is placed in the pins; the grippers are loosened and moved into position. This position is over the right and left margins. Care must be taken that they do not touch the type form or the gauge pins, as the grippers will smash both of them. The grippers are pulled down by hand and are watched to see exactly where they will fall. They must be clear of the printed area on the paper by about one pica. If the margin is very narrow, the left-hand gripper cannot be used. It should then be placed over to the left far enough to clear the gauge pins. In this case, a string or rubber band can be stretched between the two grippers to help hold the paper. The string must clear all printed areas. Now the gripper nuts are tightened so that they will stay in place. The next step is to adjust the impression.

(5) *Regulating the impression*. Regulating the impression so that all parts of the form print a firm, even impression is called "make ready." On a platen press, two things cause "make ready" to be needed: First, type, rules, and linoleum blocks often vary in height, making an uneven surface; and, second, the platen press is constructed so that, ever when the form is perfectly level, more pressure is exerted on the edges of the form. This causes a light impression in the center and dark impressions around the edge. As recommended in the discussion on placement of the tympan paper, it is better to place the packing, or tympan, on the platen before inking the press, but adjustments will have to be made later. Most printers also recommend that these adjustments be made before the gauge pins are set, as placing packing under the tympan paper after the pins are set may change their position. However, the adjustments can be done after the pins are set if care is taken and only the top tympan bail is released.

(*a*) The imprint can be darkened by adding more sheets of paper to the packing under the tympan paper, or drawsheet, and it can be tightened by removing sheets from the packing. The impression should be very light to start with and darkened by adding a sheet at a time to obtain the correct impression. The back of the sheet of paper being printed must be checked. If the imprint of the type shows through, there is too much packing. If so, the packing is removed a little at a time until, when the impression is printed on a fresh sheet of paper, the back remains perfectly smooth and the print is still dark enough on the front. The larger the form, the more packing is needed to print it correctly. If only a line or two is to be printed, less than half the packing used for a large form will be needed.

(*b*) The corners of the form will not print evenly if the platen is out of line. The platen can be lined up by adjusting the four big screws underneath it. This adjustment requires endless patience, skill, and considerable time. It should not be attempted by a beginner except under the supervision of an experienced printer. Some forms need very little "make ready" while others, especially old type and linoleum blocks, need more "make ready" than merely adjusting the impression. The "make ready" then becomes an intricate process which is best learned by practical experience under the supervision of an experienced printer.

(*c*) An impression of the type form is made on a sheet of paper of the exact thickness and texture as that to be printed. If the impression needs to be darker in certain areas, this is done by tearing out onionskin paper to fit the shape of the light area and pasting it directly on the tympan paper exactly under the faint impression. It may be necessary to add two or three layers in some spots. It is better to tear the onionskin, rather than cut it, as the edges will be thinner and will not leave distinct edge lines which may show up on the printed impression. Building up the tympan, or packing, in this manner is called "overlay." After the overlay is completed, another sheet of tympan paper is placed over the "make ready" to keep it undisturbed during the feeding process. Paper of equal thickness must be removed from the packing below the first tympan paper to make up for the second tympan paper, or draw sheet. The impression may also be built up by pasting paper in a similar manner behind the low spots on the type form itself. This is called "underlay" and is used if the rollers are shrunken or if they do not deposit ink on all parts of the form. If the rollers are good, the platen true, and the "make ready" carefully done, a perfect impression can be made. When this is done, the job is ready to print.

(6) *Feeding the press*. The paper to be printed is placed in a pile on the right-hand feed table, if the press has one. If there is none, as is often the case with a hand press, the paper should be placed on the right side of the hand press cabinet or of the table upon which the press is mounted. The paper should be fanned out so that the edges nearest the printer's right-hand project slightly over each other and incline a little forward (fig. 12–34). This makes the sheets easier to pick up.

(*a*) The printer stands erect in front of the press and picks up the top sheet of paper with the right hand by dragging it from the pile with the thumb under the sheet of paper. The sheet is fed down to the bottom gauge pins with a sweeping motion, downward and to the left. It is fed to the bottom pins first, as the platen comes back to a flat position, and is then slid over to the side guide on the left.

(*b*) The printer continues the motion of his hand and brings it out of the press and back to the pile of paper in a sweeping curve.

(*c*) He will then grasp the next sheet and hold it ready to feed. If the press is a hand press and the handle, or lever, is on the right, the printer will not pick up the next sheet of paper

Figure 12–34. Paper ready for printing.

with his right hand, but will instead grasp the handle and pull it all the way forward, causing an impression to be made on the sheet of paper. He must not release the handle but must push it back into its upright position. If the handle is on the left, this is done by the left hand.

(*d*) Once the sheet of paper has been printed, the left hand removes it by dragging it over the edge of the platen and placing it on the delivery board, the top of the cabinet, or the table, depending upon the size of the sheets of paper. Care must be taken not to touch the printed area when removing the paper from the press. The paper is gripped by the margin; if the margin is too narrow, the end of the index or middle finger is covered with a cap of sandpaper. This finger is used to remove the paper, so the ink will not be smeared. It is best to spread the paper out and not pile it up, as the fresh ink will smear. It needs a little time to dry before being stacked together.

(*e*) The next sheet of paper is fed to the guides as soon as the printed one is out of the way.

(*f*) If the press is a foot press, much more coordination is required and the beginner should do a few dry runs before attempting to print. First, he should practice pumping the press with the throwoff lever pushed forward. He should get used to the rhythm of pumping the press, as a beginner has a tendency to start pushing down with his foot before the treadle has gone all the way to the top of its cycle. Once this is mastered, he should make a dry run with the paper. He should pump slowly and leave the throwoff lever pushed forward. When the rhythm and the coordination of hands and foot have been mastered and the printer feels relaxed

and at ease, then the throwoff lever is pulled back and printing is started. A printer must always stay alert even when relaxed. As accuracy and rhythm improve, the press may be pumped more rapidly. If the paper misses the guides, he must not attempt to reach for it, but continue the rhythmic motion of the right hand and at the same time push the throwoff lever forward with the left hand. This will prevent an impression from being made on the paper. Any attempt to correct the error by the right hand will cause it to be caught in the closing press. If there is not time enough to use the throwoff lever, he should step on the brake. This will instantly stop the press.

(*g*) If an impression is accidentally made upon the tympan paper, the press is stopped and cleaned off. This may be done either by wiping the tympan paper with a rag dampened with type wash or by dusting it with talcum powder. If the tympan paper is not cleaned off, the ink on it will offset on the back of the next few sheets of paper printed.

(*h*) The printer must stay alert, not only to see that each sheet is fed squarely into the gauge pins, but to watch for any problems that may develop during the printing process. The gauge pins must not slip, the grippers must not work loose, and the shade or color of the ink must not change. The press must be stopped at intervals and the ink compared with one of the first sheets printed. If it looks grey rather than black, more ink needs to be added, as described in the discussion on inking the press. If the ink is smudged and offste on the back of the printed sheets of paper, there is too much ink and some needs to be removed, as described in the same discussion.

(*i*) After the printing job is completed, the type form is removed from the press, the type and press are cleaned, and the printed sheets are picked up after the ink has dried.

12–6. Cleaning the Press

The press is cleaned with the same good-quality type wash and with rags that are free from hard objects which will scratch, just like those used to clean the type. There are different methods of cleaning the press, but the following seems to be the most commonly used:

a. A few drops of type wash are put on the ink disc and it is wiped clean with a used rag.

b. Now a clean rag is moistened with the type wash.

c. The flywheel of the foot press is turned by hand or the handle of the hand press is pulled forward, and the rollers are moved slowly up to the disc.

d. As the top roller is about a quarter inch below the disc, it is cleaned with the damp rag as the roller continues to roll upward. The same thing is done with the second and third rollers. They are cleaned by rubbing them gently from side to side. Too brisk rubbing will remove the surface of the roller and ruin it.

e. When the rollers are up at the top of the disc, a clean place on the rag is selected and cleaning is continued as the rollers move down the disc. By the time they have cleared the disc, they should all be clean.

f. The flywheel must continue to be turned by hand or the handle of the hand press pushed back until the rollers have reached their lowest point. The rollers must never be left standing on the ink disc or type form, as they will become flattened.

g. With a clean rag, the disc is wiped off again. The disc and rollers should now be thoroughly clean. The printer must not let the inky type wash run down on the press bed or on the platen. If this should happen, it must be cleaned off at once. All dirty rags are placed in a closed metal container since spontaneous combustion can take place in the damp rags. The type must also be put away.

12–7. Distributing the Type

a. Identifying Type. When the chase is removed from the press, it is placed on the marble slab and the type is properly cleaned. If the chase is small enough, it is placed in a galley and the quoins are unclamped and removed, the furniture is removed, and so is the chase. The quoins are put where they belong, the furniture is replaced in the lockup cabinet correctly according to length, and the chase is returned to the chase rack in the hand press cabinet. The type form is positioned in the galley with the top firmly against the head of the galley. If the chase is too large to place in the galley, the type form is tied up, and then the quoins, furniture, and chase are removed. The type form is slid into the galley with the top firmly against the head and the string is then removed. The

type is now ready to be returned to the proper sections of the correct case. This is called "distribution."

(1) The correct case in which the type belongs must be found and used. Although there is a 3-way check system by which the size, face, and nicks are compared, this is not foolproof and the 5-way check is better. From the type form, a wide letter such as a capital "H" is removed. From the case to be tested, a similar letter is removed. The two are placed together and the following compared: the size, the face, the nicks, the feet, and the width of the characters. If all of them are the same, the two test pieces are returned to their respective places, and a lower case letter is taken from the form and a like one from the case. The same five points are checked and, if they, too, are all similar, then the case is the correct one.

(2) If more than one size or style of type has been used, each kind must be sorted out and placed together. This not only saves time and effort but also reduces the possibility of error. Accuracy is more important than speed. If the type is incorrectly distributed, a great deal of time will be wasted by the next person looking for correct letters and spaces. Likewise, if the letters taken from the case to be used in comparison checks have been put in the wrong case, then the entire type form to be distributed will be erroneously placed in the wrong case.

b. Distributing Letters. Although an experienced printer will pick up several lines of type at a time to distribute, the beginner should only pick up one. He should always start at the foot of the type form and gradually work to the head. This reduces the possibility of pi-ing the type.

(1) The line of type is picked up as illustrated in figure 12–27. It is then moved to the left hand by taking a firm grip with the right hand and shifting the left hand into a new position as shown in figure 12–35. The palm is up, the left thumb is against the left end of the line, the left middle finger against the right end of the line, and the left index finger backing up the line. The line must be held level or the type will slide off the slug.

(2) The top slug is removed and, if the line is held correctly, the nicks will be showing and the line reading from left to right, with the letters upside down.

(3) The beginner will, of course, find it easier to distribute the type one word at a time

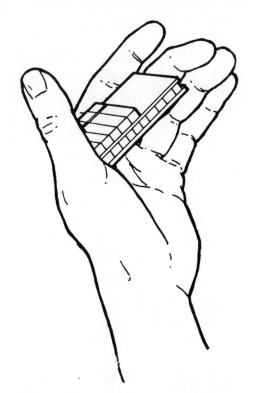

Figure 12–35. Holding type for distribution.

directly from the galley. In this way, he will neither increase his skill nor his speed; therefore, the practice must be discouraged. As the beginner practices and acquires more skill, he will be able to pick up several lines at a time. He should always begin at the right side of each line and, with the right hand, pick up a word or so at a time.

(4) The letters are held, with the nicks up and the faces toward the printer, between the thumb and index finger. A slight rolling motion of the thumb and index finger, with the help of the middle finger, will separate the type and, by relaxing the pinch of the thumb and index finger slightly, the type may be dropped one at a time.

(5) As each letter is separated, it must be dropped into the correct compartment of the case. The letters must not be thrown into the case or dropped from a distance, as either practice will damage the type. They are released as close to their compartments as possible.

(6) The quads may be distributed with the letters. However, if the printer is uncertain of the sizes, they should be put aside in the galley and distributed separately.

(7) Type from other fonts, such as letters in italics, should be put in a stick or galley to distribute after everything that belongs in the case in use has been distributed.

c. Distributing Spacing Material. After all of the type of one size has been distributed, the spaces can be accurately and quickly sorted for thickness by spreading them out in the galley side by side. The finger can quickly detect the variations in thickness (fig. 12–36). When they are all sorted by thickness, three that are thought to be 3-em spaces are removed and placed side by side, nicks up. Then a fourth space is turned on its side. It should be equal to the width of the other three if they are 3-em spaces (fig. 12–37). The sizes of the other groups can be determined in the same manner. The leads and slugs are sorted (fig. 12–38) by placing them upright in the galley parallel to and against the head. They must be shaken down against one edge. The longest ones are picked out and placed against the other side and the next longest ones next to them. This is continued, picking out successively shorter lengths until all of the leads and slugs are lined up by lengths in a series of steps. The leads and slugs are picked out separately and are ready to be put away in the case. The correct compartment may be found either by measuring the length with the line gauge or by comparison with the leads and slugs already in the compartment. If any odd lengths are found, they should be carefully cut to the nearest even pica measure on the lead and slug cutter. The galley is returned to its shelf in the hand press cabinet. A check is made to see that everything has been cleaned and returned to its proper place. As soon as the ink on the printed sheets is dry enough to stack the sheets, the printing job has been completed.

12–8. Safety Measures in Printing

a. Printing Presses. The handpress does not require safety guards by the very nature of its operation, since the handle is operated by the printer and he can stop it at any time. The foot press is a different matter. The operation of this press requires a steady, coordinated rhythm of pumping by foot. It is difficult for a printer to interrupt this rhythm quickly and, even if he did, the press would still roll on for a bit from its own momentum. The platen comes into contact with the type with tremendous pressure to make the impression. Therefore, it is imperative that the printer not have his hand on the platen after it has started to move. Even pushing the

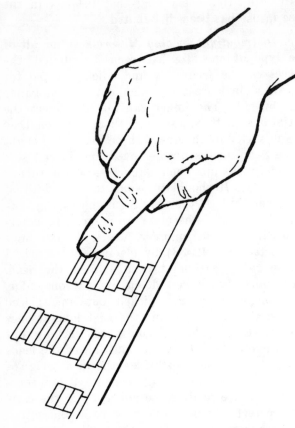

Figure 12-36. Sorting spaces for distribution.

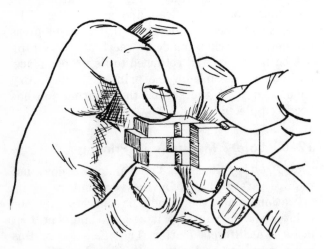

Figure 12-37. Determining size of spaces.

throwoff lever forward will not prevent curshed fingers or hands, as the space thus provided is not as thick as a person's fingers. Consequently, all foot presses should be provided with a brake for instant stopping and with a platen guard that will push the hand away from the type. No printer should ever reach for a sheet of paper

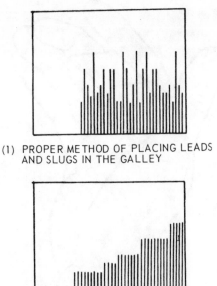

(1) PROPER METHOD OF PLACING LEADS AND SLUGS IN THE GALLEY

(2) LEADS AND SLUGS SORTED IN READINESS FOR THE CASE

Figure 12-38. Sorting leads and slugs.

that has slipped. This is probably one of the chief reasons for fingers being crushed in a press. The foot press should also be equipped with a flywheel guard and a gear guard to keep fingers and clothing from being caught. A press must never be oiled while it is in motion. It is oiled and then the oil worked in by operating it by hand for a few minutes. The printer should do some dry runs on the foot press and not print until he has learned the rhythm of the press and the coordination of the feeding process. No matter how many guards are on the press, carelessness will cause some accidents. Therefore, the printer must give his undivided attention to his work. Any adjustments of paper, ink, or press parts must not be done while the press is in motion. If an accident does occur, it should be reported to the supervisor at once.

b. Cutters. Both the paper cutter and the lead and slug cutter, although hand operated, are potentially dangerous, as they can remove portions of the fingers or hand. The user should watch what he is doing and keep his fingers away from the blade. The paper cutter should always be left with the blade all the way down.

c. Type Wash. Most type washes are inflammable and volatile. Some are more so than others. All type washes should be kept in closed metal containers. Some printing plants use unleaded gasoline for cleaning type and kerosene for cleaning rollers. Benzene and naphtha are also in common use.

d. Oily Rags. All oily rags and those with type wash should be kept in a closed metal container. The step-on waste can is the best for this purpose. Even papers that are covered with ink, oil, or type wash should be discarded in this can. Since spontaneous combustion can occur in damp rags stored in a warm place, the can must be emptied at least each evening. Smoking should not be permitted in the printing area at any time.

12–11. Introduction

Printing from a design cut into wood is an old art. Linoleum block printing stemmed from this age-old craft after the development of linoleum. Because linoleum can be cut with more facility than wood, this craft is more appealing to the amateur craftsman and more versatile work can be done. Block printing is used for a wide variety of items, such as greeting cards, stationery, monograms, programs, book plates, banners, drapes, luncheon sets, and place mats. The choice of the design to be used depends upon the purpose for which it is to be used. Section I, chapter 2, on design will be helpful to the printer in choosing his design.

12–12. Tools, Equipment, and Materials

Materials for block printing are not elaborate or expensive.

a. Block Printing Ink. Block printing ink comes in 1 1/2- or 4-ounce tubes with either a water base or an oil base and in a variety of colors. The oil base ink is more permanent, but must be cleaned off of such items as tools with turpentine or some other solvent. The water base ink does not dry out in the tube, even though prints made with it dry rapidly. Water can be used for removing water base block printing ink.

b. Brayer. (Para 12–3*b*(1)).

c. Bursh. (Para 12–3*b*(2)).

d. Cutters.

(1) *Push type.* Linoleum cutters are normally pushed away from the user while carving linoleum blocks. There are several sizes of cutters. The smaller ones are called veiners; the larger ones, gougers. Normally, a set consists of six cutters (A. fig. 12–39), but there are larger sets containing as many as ten cutters (B, fig. 12–39). Most of these cutters are made like pens and fit the same handle. After they are placed in the handle, they are tightened in place with a knurled locking screw. The handle should be of sturdy construction and feel comfortable in the hand. Figure C, 12–39 shows this handle. In addition, there are cutters which are permanently fixed in individual handles (fig. 12–40). These cutters may also be used for carving wood.

(2) *Pull type.* These are tools which are drawn toward the user when cutting. They are also pen-like and fit into the same handle as the

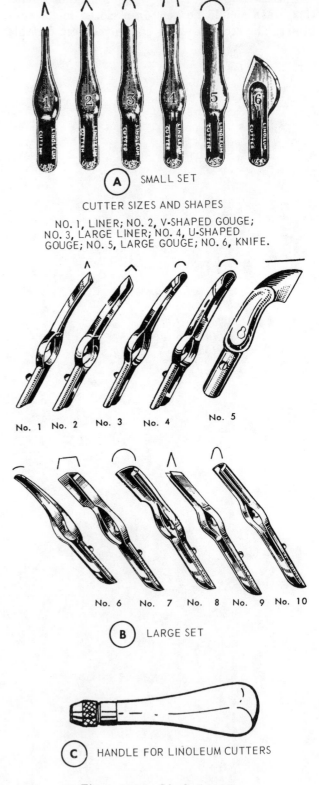

A SMALL SET

CUTTER SIZES AND SHAPES

NO. 1, LINER; NO. 2, V-SHAPED GOUGE;
NO. 3, LARGE LINER; NO. 4, U-SHAPED
GOUGE; NO. 5, LARGE GOUGE; NO. 6, KNIFE.

No. 1   No. 2   No. 3   No. 4   No. 5

No. 6   No. 7   No. 8   No. 9   No. 10

B LARGE SET

C HANDLE FOR LINOLEUM CUTTERS

Figure 12–39. Linoleum cutters.

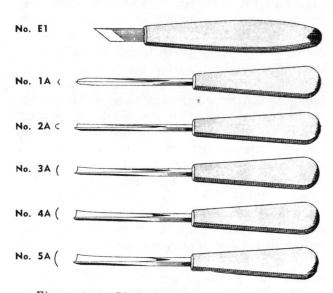

No. E1

No. 1A

No. 2A

No. 3A

No. 4A

No. 5A

Figure 12–40. Block cutting tools with permanently fixed handles.

push type. Called linozip (fig. 12–41), they come in four sizes, similar to the conventional-type cutters. However, these are safer to use, as the tool is not being pushed toward the free hand. Since this tool is held like a pencil, it is also much easier and more accurate to use than the push cutter.

NOTE
All of these cutters may be kept sharpened with a small handstone.

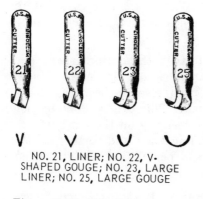

NO. 21, LINER; NO. 22, V-SHAPED GOUGE; NO. 23, LARGE LINER; NO. 25, LARGE GOUGE

Figure 12–41. Linozip cutters.

e. Linoleum Blocks. The linoleum used for block printing is called battleship linoleum. It comes in many thicknesses up to 1/4 inch, which is best for block printing. Usually it is a natural brown, but it can be obtained in a variety of colors. Cork carpet is similar but coarser and

softer, so care should be taken not to confuse the two.

(1) *Mounted.* Linoleum blocks (fig. 12–42) come in precut sizes which vary from 1 1/2 inch by 1 1/2 inch to 9 inches by 12 inches. The linoleum is often white, which makes for easier drawing. It is mounted on 5-ply plywood. The linoleum itself is 3/8 inch thick, which with the plywood, gives it a type height of 31/32 of an inch. The mounted linoleum is used in the printing press or for printing on paper.

Figure 12–42. Linoleum blocks.

(2) *Unmounted.* The unmounted linoleum has no backing and is used when printing by hand or on cloth. If bought in bulk, it must be cut to the desired size. After the linoleum has attained room temperature, place it on a table and mark out the desired size with a square. First, go over the lines with a small veiner, then cut with a stencil knife. Cut from one side of the piece to the other with a steady pressure, making a cut of uniform depth. Then grasp the whole piece with both hands and break it on the cut. The burlap on the back will still hold the pieces together, but this may be cut with scissors or a knife.

12–13. Processes

a. Putting a Design on the Block. Once the design has been decided upon, it should be drawn out on good, fairly tough, white paper. (Some people draw it directly on the linoleum block.) If the design has a definite right and left side, as with lettering, the drawing will have to be reversed before it is put onto the block. This can be done either by placing the reversed drawing in a window and tracing it or by putting the drawing on a sheet of carbon paper with the carbon coated side against the back of the drawing and tracing it. If strong, transparent paper is available for the original drawing, it will not have to be traced at all, merely turned over. Now, the design is ready to put on the block.

b. Preparing the Block for Carving. If the linoleum has been waxed, the wax should be removed with turpentine or heat and the surface then cleaned with an art gum eraser. If the surface of the linoleum is not perfectly smooth, it can be sanded down with very fine sandpaper. Cold weather affects linoleum, making it hard and easily cracked; if the linoleum is cold, it should be warmed before using. If the block does not have a white surface, it may be painted with either white poster paint or flat, white oil paint. This makes the traced design easier to see. To prepare the block, place the drawing on a piece of linoleum about one inch larger than the design. Now, put a piece of carbon paper on the block under the drawing and fasten both papers to the block with tape or thumbtacks. (If thumbtacks are used, be sure that they are placed outside of the drawing or in parts which will be left white in the print, as holes made by the tacks will be noticeable.) Use a hard, sharp pencil or a mimeograph stylus to trace the lines of the drawing. If the design is to be one of simple repeat patterns, measure the parts of the design that will be the connecting units very carefully so that they will match.

NOTE

Some people fill in the portion of the design that is to remain with ink. This increases clarity and helps avoid errors in copying and cutting. It also gives an accurate picture of the finished design.

c. Carving the Block. All parts to be printed must be left the original height; only the unprinted areas are cut away. The block may be put in a vise or clamped to the table for carving, but then it cannot be turned freely as the carver works. Care must be taken that the cutting tool does not slip and go into the hand that holds the block. This can be prevented by always keeping the block-holding hand back of the area being carved. For cutting fine lines and for all detail work, the push-type cutter is held like a pencil. For heavy lines and gouging (routing) out large areas, the push-type cutter is held under the palm with the forefinger on top to guide it (fig. 12–43). The pull-type cutters are all held like a pencil. These have one advantage over the push-type as they can be used like a pencil to sketch right on the block. The first tool used

should be the U-shaped or V-shaped veiner, depending upon the nature of the print to be carved. In the first cutting, outline the entire design with one of these tools. Do not cut on the line itself, but just outside of it. The thickness of a line must be preserved to carry out the design. After all the outlining is done, gouge out the large areas that are not to be printed. Again, the gouge to be used depends upon the size and type of work being done. After the area that is not to be printed has all been cut away, add the details with a U-shaped or V-shaped veiner. (There are many ways of carving, as each person has his own favorite method. An etched line can be made by holding a veiner upside down and scratching the surface of the linoleum. A stippled surface can be made by using the side of the cutting edge or the point of a knife. By practice and experimentation, new techniques may be learned.) The following things must be kept in mind while carving:

(1) Cut the wide spaces deeply so that the paper or cloth will not pick up any excess ink that may be in the background areas.

(2) Make shallow cuts in the narrow spaces.

(3) Do not dig in over the cutting edge of the tool, as this will leave ragged lines.

(4) Do not make deep vertical cuts or undercuts. The edges should be slanting (fig. 12–44), not vertical.

(5) Do not cut through to the burlap backing.

(6) When cutting a straight line, do it all in one steady thrust, as each stopping place will show.

(7) Keep the cutters sharp all the time to get clear edges on the design. Make tests as the cutting progresses to be sure that no errors are being made. This can be done by holding a piece of paper securely on the cut surface of the block and rubbing back and forth over the block with a soft lead pencil. The design will show up very well.

d. Printing With the Block. There are numerous ways in which to print with the block.

(1) One method is to lock the block up in a chase, like a type form, and print it in either the hand or foot press. All of the other methods require the use of a brayer and a piece of marble, plastic, or glass. The cloth or paper to be printed must be free of wrinkles or folds. On it, indicate with pencil dots (not lines) the guidelines where

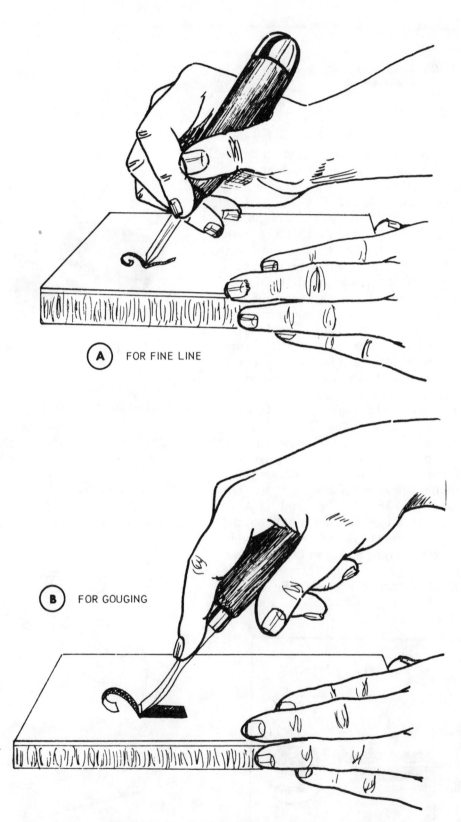

A   FOR FINE LINE

B   FOR GOUGING

Figure 12-43. Holding linoleum cutter.

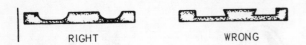

Figure 12–44. Right and wrong cuts in carving the linoleum block.

the corners of the block are to be placed. Spread the material out over a smooth pad of newspapers or tack it down to a flat surface. Squeeze a small amount of block printing ink on the slab and roll it out with the brayer until it is evenly distributed on the brayer (fig. 12–45). The surface of the ink should look velvety and not shiny. Place the linoleum block on a flat surface with the carved side up. Roll the brayer back and forth and across over the design, with special attention to the corners and edges, until the design is completely covered with a thin coat of ink (fig. 12–46). However, do not use too much ink; it makes a messy print. Next, take a proof of the block on a piece of scrap material. (Be sure that it is the same material as that to be printed.) Do this by placing the block, ink side down, on the scrap of material and applying pressure. The amount of pressure to be applied depends upon the amount of solid area in the design. A great deal of solid area requires a lot of pressure; fine lines and a lot of white background require less pressure. If the proof is not clear, either there was not enough pressure on the block or not enough ink on the block. If the print appears blotchy, there was either too much ink on the block or the design was not carved deeply enough. Correct whatever is wrong and keep taking proofs until everything is perfect. Since there are many ways in which to print the block (the variety of ways in which the pressure may be applied to the block), take care that the inked block is placed exactly within the guidelines made upon the material.

Figure 12–46. Inking the block.

(2) Besides the printing press, pressure may be applied to the block by the following methods:

(*a*) Use an old book press (fig. 12–47). One can often be found around the clinic and is excellent for printing linoleum blocks. Fit it with a sliding workboard of plywood to make the printing easier.

(*b*) Use one of the many small presses on the market made just for block printing.

Figure 12–45. Inking the brayer.

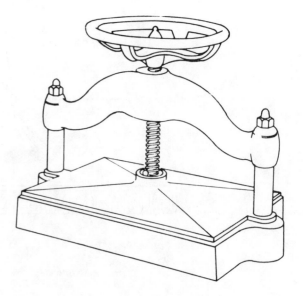

Figure 12–47. Book press.

(c) Use an old clothes wringer in this manner: place the inked block face up, with the material to be printed placed on the inked surface, and cover it all with a sheet of heavy cardboard or newspaper. Then, run all of this through the clothes wringer.

(d) Place the inked block face down on the material to be printed and press a cold electric iron over the back of the entire block.

(e) With the ink block placed face down on the material to be printed, pound the block over the entire back surface with a mallet.

(f) Place the material on the floor with the inked block face down on top of it and step on the block several times, facing a different direction each time in order to distribute the pressure evenly.

(g) If the block is very small, place it inked side down on the material to be printed and press down on the block with the thumbs.

(h) Place the block with the inked surface up. Carefully put the material to be printed on the inked surface. Cover the whole thing with newspaper and, with an even amount of pressure, run a rolling pin over the newspaper.

(i) Place the block with the inked surface up; then carefully put the material to be printed on the inked surface and rub the entire surface gently with the bowl of a teaspoon or a glass doorknob. Be careful that nothing slips.

NOTE
Blockprinting can be done either with the linoleum mounted on wood blocks or unmounted. Unmounted linoleum is better for printing textiles, although several of the other methods can also be used.

e. Block Printing on Textiles. The linoleum block is carved in the same manner as that for paper. Instead of printer's ink or block printing ink, use one of the several good textile paints now on the market. Do not use a cloth of too coarse texture, or the ink will print only on the upper threads, which will destroy the effect of the design. Linen, percale, pongee, or similar fabrics are recommended. If a simple repeat design is to be used, sometimes it is easier to cut the entire block in the shape of the design instead of the usual rectangle. For the actual printing, use the mallet, foot, cold electric iron, rolling pin, teaspoon, or glass doorknob to apply the pressure.

f. Block Printing With Several Colors. This process is much the same as single color printing except that a separate block must be cut for each color. Color register is the term applied to the cutting and printing of two or more blocks in color. The trick with color printing is to place the blocks in exactly the right place on the material to be printed. In order to have as near a foolproof method as possible, use jigs in the carving and often in the printing. The jig used in registering the colors while carving the blocks is called a register jig. It is made by building a right angle of wood and attaching it to a plywood base. The right angle of wood, after it is attached to the base, must be the same height as the blocks to be carved (fig. 12–48).

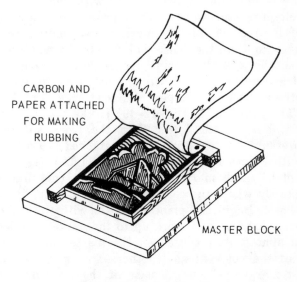

CARBON AND PAPER ATTACHED FOR MAKING RUBBING

MASTER BLOCK

Figure 12–48. Register jig.

(1) Carve out the entire design on the first block. This will then be called the master block.

(2) Place the master jig snuggly in the exact corner of the jig.

(3) Tack to the jig a piece of carbon paper, face down on the carved master block, and, on top of it, a few sheets of paper.

(4) With a soft lead pencil, make a rubbing of the carved master block. This rubbing registers the original cut, which is called the master cut.

(5) Remove the carved master block and place an uncut block in the jig in the exact position occupied by the master block. The register of the master block, backed with carbon paper, stays in place. On this rubbing, with a sharp pencil or stylus, trace out all the areas to be printed in one of the colors of the original design. Make the color areas slightly larger than

those on the master block so that they will overlap just enough to avoid white lines showing around the different color areas.

(6) Replace this block with as many blocks as there are colors in the design.

(7) After each block is carved, return it to the register jig and make a rubbing with a crayon or pencil of the correct color.

(8) Prove each of the color blocks after it is carved. Now there should be a block carved for each color to be used. The raised area is for one color only; all other parts should be cut away.

(9) Print a proof of the blocks to see how the colors will register. Start with the lightest color first and work to the darkest. On the back of each block, plainly mark corresponding corners so that the back will not be turned accidentally and thus print upside down. Some articles can be printed with the help of a jig while others, such as drapes, are too large for this. (The printing jig (fig. 12–49) is like the register jig, but a little lower than the block so that pressure can be applied. It is attached to its base with hinges for ease of operation.) If a jig cannot be used, mark with pencil dots (not lines) exactly where the corners of the blocks are to be placed. Begin the printing. Start with the lightest color first and work up to the darkest, which is almost always used on the master block and ties the color areas together. The margins can be marked off on the base of the printing jig. Use a different brayer and piece of marble for each color of textile paint. Use any of the methods mentioned in subparagraph *d*(2) above to apply the necessary pressure.

NOTE

In some prints, one color can be applied right after the other and the whole print completed at once. In other prints, it may be desirable to let one color dry before applying the next one. Experience is a great help in color printing. As experience is gained, you will want to go from simple 2- or 3-color prints to more complicated prints.

12–14. Safety Precautions

Use great care when cutting the block to prevent cutting the hands.

a. Have the linoleum warm enough to cut easily.

b. Cut away from the body unless pull cutting tools are used.

c. Do not have the holding hand in front of the tool. Holding the block against a bench dog or holding it down with a C-clamp may help.

NOTE

The clamp must be put on so that it will not mar the block.

d. Keep the tools sharp so that less pressure and more control can be used in cutting.

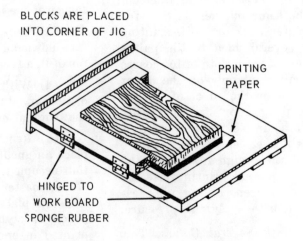

BLOCKS ARE PLACED
INTO CORNER OF JIG

PRINTING
PAPER

HINGED TO
WORK BOARD
SPONGE RUBBER

Figure 12–49. Printing jig.

CHAPTER 13

WOODWORKING

Section I-II. ABRASIVES AND WOOD PREPARATION

13–6. General

One of the most important steps in woodworking is the careful preparation of the wood for finishing. Most of the sanding and smoothing should be done before the work is assembled. It is this part of the work that brings out the beauty of the wood and produces the fine smooth surface so admired in good woodworking. Too often, woodworkers, especially amateurs, get in a hurry and take short cuts in preparing the wood. This practice frequently results in a disappointing piece of work rather than in one to be admired.

13–7. Preparation of Wood

In order to decide how to prepare the project for finishing, it must be carefully examined to determine the nature of the defects. Some of the more common ones are listed, along with methods of correction.

a. Mill marks may be wavy unevenness across the surface of the lumber caused by the planer or jointer, marks from the saw blade, or circular marks from the disc sander. If they are deep, removal may be started with a belt sander. In order to finish the job (or to remove the mill marks if they are not deep), a cabinet scraper or sandpaper of different grades is used.

b. Scratches along the grain are less noticeable than scratches across the grain. The amount and depth of scratching determines the method of removal. If scratches are deep, sanding may be started with a belt sander, then finished with hand sanding. Light scratches may be removed with only hand sanding. In order to prevent wavy areas in the surface of the wood, the scratch must not only be sanded, but also the area around it.

c. Dents that have only crushed the wood and not broken its surface can often be raised by wetting the affected area with a few drops of water. If this does not raise the dent, steam may be more effective. This may be created by placing a few drops of water on the area, then touching them with a hot instrument. A soldering iron and a damp cloth may be used; even holding a steam iron over the area may bring up the dent.

d. Dents which do not respond to the treatment in *c* above, may be filled with a material that will adhere to the wood, not shrink when dry, take stain well, and yet not fill the pores of the wood around it. Materials which can be used include plastic water putty, wood compound paste, plastic wood, a glue and sawdust mixture, and melted stick shellac. Regardless of the choice, a great deal of knowledge and skill is required to prevent an unsightly blemish, especially if the piece is to be stained. In fact, if this is to be the finish, it is better to be careful in selecting and handling the wood so that patching will not be necessary. However, if the surface is to be painted, all that is required is careful sanding to insure a smooth surface since the paint covers the color of the wood and the patch.

13–8. Sanding

After dents have been raised or filled, the unassembled pieces are sanded. At best, sanding tends to be somewhat tedious. Selection of the best type of sandpaper, the correct grit, and employment of the best working methods can speed up this part of the work to some extent and, at the same time, not sacrifice the desired results.

a. There are three types of abrasive papers most commonly used in woodworking—

(1) Flint paper is grayish-tan in color and is the most commonly used because it does the job and is the least expensive. It is less durable than other papers as it dulls quite rapidly.

(2) Garnet paper is reddish in color and is more expensive than the flint. Because it becomes dull less rapidly, it seems to cut faster and it can be used longer than flint paper. It is especially good when sanding plastic.

(3) Aluminum oxide paper is dark gray, almost black in color, and can be used either wet

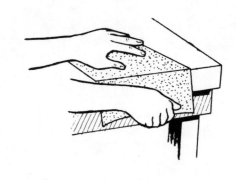

Ⓐ OVER THE EDGE OF A BENCH

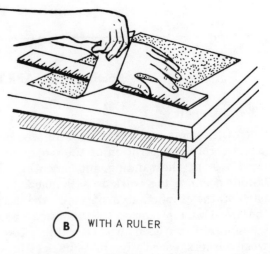

Ⓑ WITH A RULER

Figure 13–1. Tearing sandpaper.

or dry. When wet, it is used on varnished or lacquered surfaces only.

b. All three types of abrasive papers are available with different sizes of grits ranging from very fine to very coarse. Table 13–1 indicates the mesh size and the comparable marking on each type of paper. Flint and garnet papers are usually marked very fine, fine, medium, or coarse, rather than with a number. Authorities seem to differ on the exact number grades included in the descriptive term; however, the variance is not sufficient to warrant concern. Selecting the best grit of sandpaper for the job to be done is a matter of judgment sharpened by experience. The rougher the flaws in the wood, the coarser the sandpaper should be to take them out. Finer sandpaper is used to remove the scratches left by the coarse paper, and so on. In table 13–1, the column entitled "Use" is a guide to aid in the selection of the best grit to use.

c. Suggestions for more effective use of abrasive papers are listed below:

(1) Sandpaper is usually purchased in sheets that are 9 by 11 inches in size. For ease of handling and for economy, it should be torn, usually into 4 or 6 parts. There are several ways to tear sandpaper; but two of the most effective are described below. (No matter which method is used, tearing is helped by first working the smooth side of the paper over the rounded edge of the bench to limber the paper and to prevent cracking when it is torn or wrapped around the sandblock.)

(a) Fold the sandpaper with the sand side inward and crease with the fingers. Repeat, but with the sanded side out. Hold one part in each hand and then tear quickly with a sharp movement.

(b) Tear with the fold held over a straight edge, such as the side of the bench (A, fig. 13–1). Or tear it with a ruler held firmly along the fold and the free part of the sandpaper pulled up to tear along the fold and the straight edge of the ruler (B, fig. 13–1).

Table 13–1. Grits of Abrasive Papers

Mesh No.	Flint	Garnet	Aluminum oxide	Marking	Use
400	- - - - - -	- - - - - -	10/0	Very fine	
320	7/0	- - - - - -	9/0	Very fine	
280	6/0	8/0	8/0	Very fine	
240	5/0	7/0	7/0	Very fine	
220	4/0	6/0	6/0	Very fine	Finish sanding or sanding shellacked or varnished surfaces.
180	3/0	5/0	5/0	Fine	
150	2/0	4/0	4/0	Fine	
120	1/0	3/0	3/0	Fine	Finish sanding.
100	1/2	2/0	2/0	Medium	Intermediate sanding.
80	1	1/0	1/0	Medium	
60	1 1/2	1/2	1/2	Coarse	Rough sanding.
50	2	1	1	Coarse	
40	2 1/2	1 1/2	1 1/2	Coarse	
36	3	2	2	Very coarse	
30		2 1/2	2 1/2	Very coarse	
24	- - - -	3	3	Very coarse	
20		3 1/2	3 1/2	Very coarse	
16	- - - - -	- - - -	4	Very coarse	

(2) Most sanding should be done with the sandpaper wrapped around a sandblock. The block can be made of scrapwood. It should be a size comfortable to hold and also fit the pieces of sandpaper. A good size is about 3/4 by 2 1/2 by 4 inches. A cushioning substance such as cork, rubber, felt, or leather should be glued to the bottom of the block. This cushion prolongs the life of the sandpaper and makes the sanding smoother.

(3) Different types of surfaces require different techniques of sanding:

(a) Flat surfaces are always sanded with the grain of the wood, never across it or with a circular motion (A, fig. 13–2).

(b) End grain should be sanded in one direction, rather than with a back-and-forth motion (B, fig. 13–2).

(c) When rounding corners or when

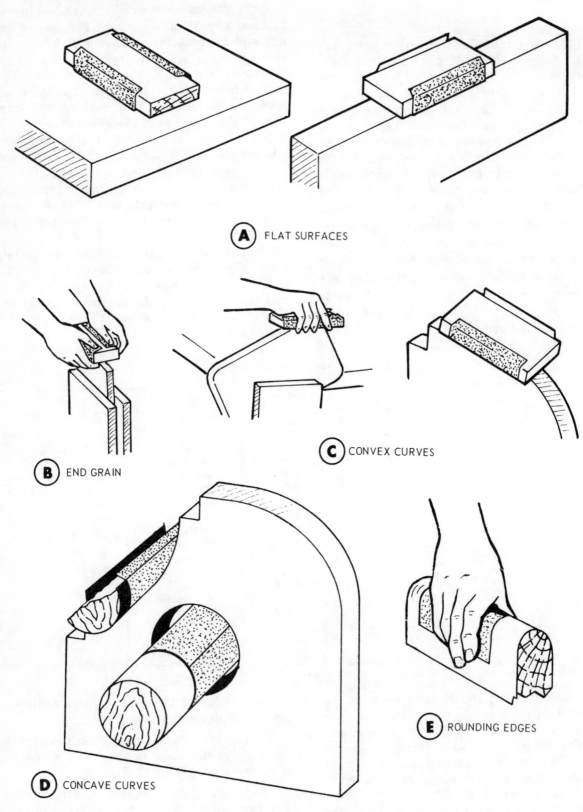

A FLAT SURFACES

B END GRAIN

C CONVEX CURVES

D CONCAVE CURVES

E ROUNDING EDGES

Figure 13-2. Sanding.

sanding a curve, sanding should be done in one direction (not back and forth) and with the grain of the wood (C, fig. 13–2).

(d) Concave surfaces and the edges of holes are sanded with the sandpaper wrapped around a dowel or broom handle (D, fig. 13–2). Once again, sanding will be better if there is padding on the surface of the sander.

(e) Edges may be rounded or rounded edges may be sanded by holding the paper in the palm of the hand while sanding (E, fig. 13–2).

(4) An extra smooth finish may be obtained by sponging the wood after sanding to raise the small wood fiber. After the wood has dried, the raised fibers are smoothed off by using 3/0 sandpaper held in the hand. For an *extra* fine surface, this sponging process is repeated several times.

(5) On the final sanding after the piece has been assembled, the glue which is not removed with sandpaper should be removed with a knife.

(6) Just before a finish is applied, the sanded piece is cleaned of dust and sandpaper residue, either with a clean brush with fairly stiff bristles or with a clean cloth dampened *slightly* in turpentine.

13–9. Steel Wool

Steel wool is another form of abrasive that is used in woodworking. It is not used in the preparation of wood for finishing but rather for rubbing down between coats of finish. It is frequently used with a lubricant such as linseed oil to prevent scratching. It, too, is available in grades of coarseness.

Coarse	No. 3	Very fine	No. 00
Medium coarse	No. 2	Extra fine	No. 000
Medium	No. 1		No. 0000
Fine	No. 0	Finest	No. 00000

13–10. Final Polishing

Pumice and rottenstone are both fine powders that are used with an oil in the final polishing of shellac, varnish, and lacquer finishes.

a. Pumice is a spongy, light, porous volcanic rock that is ground to different degrees of fineness for the polishing of wood finishes, ivory, marble, and fine metals. There are a number of colors and types of pumice stone but that most commonly used in woodworking is grayish in color; FF and FFF indicate the amount of coarseness used. Pumice is mixed with fine motor oil, paraffin oil, linseed oil, or lemon oil to form a paste; then it is rubbed on the final coat of shellac, varnish, or lacquer to make the surface highly polished and smooth.

b. Rottenstone is a limestone that is decomposed to a friable state. It is dark brown in color and is a finer powder than pumice. It is used in the same way as pumice; however, because it is finer, it produces an even higher polish than pumice.

Section III. DESIGN, LAYOUT, AND PLANNING

13–11. General

Ideas for projects come from a number of sources. The patient may wish to copy something that he has seen or he may look through books and magazines to find ideas to copy or adopt. A number of magazines, newspaper, or books contain plans for projects that are attractive and practical to make. Frequently, however, the idea for a project stems from a recognized need for a table, step stool, a chest, or perhaps something for a child. Any project must have good design and it must be well planned in order for it to give the pleasure and use anticipated by the maker.

13–12. Design

There are three elements of good design: the usefulness of the project for its purpose, its durability, and the proportions of the design that make it pleasing to look at.

a. The object that is made and the size depends in part upon the use to which it will be put and where it is to be used. A piece is useful if it fulfills the use for which it was intended. There are rather standard heights for such things as chairs, tables, coffee tables, and lamps. These standard measurements should be used unless there is a good reason to deviate. For instance, if a table is to be made of a size to fit into a certain space in the kitchen, it should be of the standard table height so that it will fit with the chairs and the other furniture. An invaluable source for standard measurements of many everyday articles is a large mail order catalog.

b. Durability of a project is obtained by good

construction of well-planned joints and by the proper use of suitable material.

c. Proportion is the size relationship of the parts of a project to the whole. A good proportion relation is two to three; that is, a table would be in good proportion if it were two units wide and three units long. Deviations from this basic rule can be interesting and pleasing, however. Some suggestions for the division of space are as follows:

(1) A vertical line that divides the whole space should divide it into two equal areas or into the two-to-three relationship.

(2) When the vertical line divides the whole space into three parts, the center part should be larger than the two side parts, which should be of equal size.

(3) When an area is divided into three parts by horizontal lines, the middle part should usually be larger than the upper and lower parts.

13–13. Putting Ideas on Paper

When planning a project, it is often helpful to make a number of small sketches to determine the general style and proportions. After the general idea is formulated, the dimensions can be determined and the piece drawn to scale.

a. In working drawings, an object may be represented by several views; two or three are usually used. The front-view drawing is usually done in the lower part of the paper with the side view to one side of it. If there is to be a top

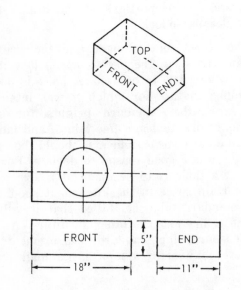

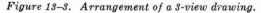

Figure 13–3. Arrangement of a 3-view drawing.

Border Line

Object Line

Hidden Object Line

Center Line

Extension Line

2"

Dimension Line

Figure 13–4. Line code.

view, it is customarily put above the front view (fig. 13–3). These drawings are usually made to scale and certain lines mean certain things. This code (fig. 13–4) is good to know in order to communicate accurately.

(1) The object line is heavy to show the exact shape of an object more clearly.

(2) Parts that cannot be seen are represented by a line of 1/8-inch dashes, called the hidden object line.

(3) The dimensions of the object are shown by means of the dimension line, which is a fine line with an arrowhead at the end and a break in the center for the number.

(4) The extension line is placed at the end of the dimension line and refers to the part of the object being dimensioned.

(5) Centerlines are for locating holes.

b. Pieces with irregular lines are laid out by means of squares (fig. 13-5). An inch square on the pattern may equal 3 inches on the actual piece. This is not difficult to reproduce if these steps are followed:

(1) Fold a large sheet of brown paper in half and measure it off into squares. With the example used above, it would be measured into 3-inch squares.

(2) Mark on the brown paper where the

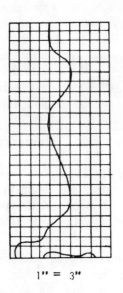

$1'' = 3''$

Figure 13–5. Transferring irregular lines.

curve crosses the lines of each of the squares, following the pattern.

(3) Draw in the curves freehand.

(4) Check the larger drawing with the pattern and make corrections.

(5) Cut out the pattern as drawn on the folded brown paper. Place this full-sized drawing on the lumber and trace around it.

c. Blueprints are photographic reproductions of drawings. Their lines and numbers are white on a blue background.

13–14. Step-by-Step Planning

Proper planning of a project pays off, both in

time and in the quality of the finished product. The operations must be done in the proper sequence, each joint must be planned, and the proper tools must be used for each operation. Planning is particularly important when working with students, for it gives tham a plan to follow that allows for more independence and prevents constant questions and reliance on the technician. To expedite the planning, list each step to be taken in the order in which it is to be done and also list the tools needed for that operation.

13–15. Layout

Laying out the pattern on the lumber is the important first step. Errors in measuring made here are almost impossible to correct later.

a. Examine the lumber for cracks, checks, and knots. Plan the pattern so that these flaws are not incorporated in the work or so that they will not show in the completed project.

b. Check to see that the lumber is of the required thickness.

c. Lay out the pattern so that there is as little waste as possible.

d. Use squares when marking lines so that the pieces will be square with the edge.

e. Check the measurements before starting to saw.

Table 13–2. Sample Planning Table

Step No.	Operation	Tools	Estimated completion time
1	Lay out pattern on lumber	Pattern, try square pencil	14 Sep
2	Saw lumber	Circ. saw	14 Sep
3	Make joints—Blocked rabbet on bottom and top	Circ. saw	
	Blocked butt on sides	Chisel	15–15 Sep
4			

Section IV. FASTENERS

13–16. General

There are innumerable types of wood fasteners on the market. To get the desired results in a finished product, the most suitable size and type of fastener must be used. Proper selection, of course, is dependent upon an adequate knowledge and understanding of the selection.

13–17. Nails

Nails provide the simplest and quickest way of fastening two pieces of wood together. They are used a great deal on rough or inexpensive work such as house framing, packing boxes, crates, and wood construction where a well-finished surface is of minor importance.

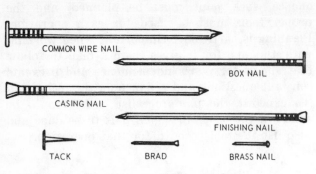

Figure 13–6. Types of nails.

penny system. Penny as applied to nails stands for "pound," and refers to the weight of 1,000 nails. *For example,* nails weighing 6 pounds per 1,000 are called six-penny (6d) nails (the letter "d" following the numeral is an abbreviation of "denarius" which is the Latin word for penny). The larger of these common nails are called spikes.

(2) *Finishing nails.* These are small headed nails of the same diameter as penny nails or of comparable length. They are used for medium fine work where it is not desirable for the head to show. They are sized by the penny and purchased in the same way as common nails (table 13–3).

(3) *Box nails.* These nails have a heavy head but a smaller gauge than common nails and are used when there is danger of splitting the wood with the larger gauge nail. They are made plain, barbed, coated with resin, or coated with cement. The latter three are more difficult to pull out than the plain ones, so they have better holding power. Both nails are a little thinner than common nails.

a. Because nails are used for numerous purposes, they are manufactured in many different sizes and of different materials (fig. 13–6).

(1) *Common wire nails.* Common nails are made with a large flat head. They are made in different lengths, and each length is made heavier than that of the finishing or box nail. They are also sold in a larger variety of sizes than any other nail. They are sized by the old English

Table 13–3. Size, Length, and Gauge of Nails

Size	Length in inches	Gauge	Common nails No/lb	Finishing nails No/lb
2d	1	15	876	1158
3d	1 1/4	14	568	884
4d	1 1/2	12 1/2	316	767
5d	1 3/4	12 1/2	271	491
6d	2	11 1/2	181	359
7d	2 1/4	11 1/2	161	
8d	2 1/2	10 1/4	106	214
9d	2 3/4	10 1/4	96	
10d	3	9	69	134
12d	3 1/4	9	63	120
16d	3 1/2	8	49	91
20d	4	6	31	61
30d	4 1/2	5	24	
40d	5	4	18	
50d	5 1/2	3	14	
60d	6	2	11	

(4) *Casing nails.* Casing nails are small-headed nails of the same diameter as box nails. They are used for such things as blindnailing flooring, since they can be countersunk into the wood because of their small heads. They resemble brads but are of the same gauge as box nails.

(5) *Brads.* Brads are used for fine work such as interior trim and small projects. They are made in lengths of from 3/8 inch to 3 inches in different gauges and are sold in 1-pound cardboard boxes that are labeled as to length and gauge. The higher the number, the smaller the

diameter of the wire. One of the most commonly used is the 1-inch long, 18-gauge size. Brads should be countersunk into the wood with a nail set and, for finer work, the hole should be covered with plastic wood or putty.

(6) *Tacks.* Carpet or upholsterers' tacks are made of iron and have a sharp point and a large head. They are made in lengths from 3/16 inch to 18/16 inch (1 1/8 inch) and are sold by the pound or 1/4 pound in cardboard boxes.

(7) *Brass nails or escutcheon pins.* These nails are made of either brass or copper and

have a small round head. They may be from 1/4 inch to 1 1/2 inch long and can be obtained in various thicknesses.

(8) *Shingle nails, felt roofing nails, and plaster board nails.* These are short and have very large heads to prevent the material from pulling out over the nail.

b. Driving and Pulling Nails.

(1) *Driving.* In order to drive a nail with the claw or carpenter's hammer, grip the handle firmly with one hand near the end of the handle; hold the nail near the point with the thumb and forefinger of the other hand. Place the point of the nail on the work at the exact spot where it is to be driven and tap it squarely but lightly until it has penetrated the wood to a depth sufficient to hold securely. Remove the fingers and drive the nail into the work. The face of the hammer should hit flat against the head of the nail (fig. 13–7). Rest the hammer on the work before striking to get the "feel" or "aim" so that your blows will be more sure and accurate.

(2) *Pulling.* To pull nails, slide the claw of the hammer under the head of the nail, making certain that the head is caught securely in the slot of the claw. Pull back until the handle of the hammer is nearly vertical, then slip a block of wood under the head of the hammer (fig. 13–8) and pull the nail completely free. The block of wood will prevent marring the work, increase leverage, and prevent the nail from pulling out sideways, which would make a large hole.

c. Suggestions for using nails.

(1) Several nails should not be driven close together in a line following the grain since they will act as wedges and split the wood.

(2) If a nail bends while it is being ham-

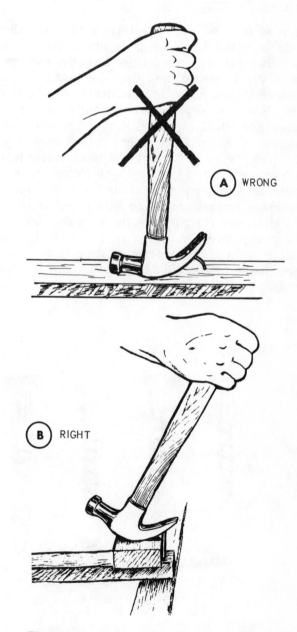

Figure 13–8. *Pulling nails with a clawhammer.*

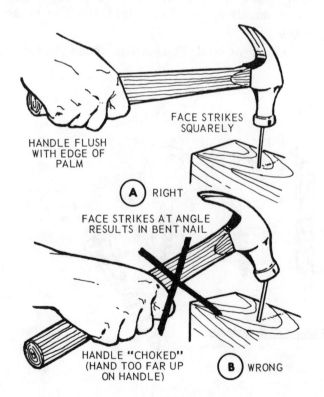

Figure 13–7. *Using the hammer.*

mered, it should be removed and another nail driven in the same hole.

(3) If a nail does not go into the wood straight, it must be taken out and another driven into the wood in a different place.

(4) Nails have a tendency to follow the grain of the wood. If the nail does not go in the desired direction because of this, blunt the point a little with a hammer.

(5) In hardwoods, it is well to bore a hole for a nail by using an awl or a hand drill. To do this, cut off the head of the nail and use it in the drill instead of a twist drill.

13–18. Screws

Screws have several advantages over nails: they may be withdrawn without injury to the material, they hold the wood more securely, they can be easily tightened, and they are neater in appearance than nails. The disadvantages are that they are more expensive and require more care, time, and effort to insert. Parts of a screw are shown in figure 13–9. There are a number of different types of screws, the most common of which are shown in figure 13–10. Screws may be purchased that are made of steel, copper, bronze, or brass, or that are plated with nickel or brass. Steel screws (bright) are the strongest and the least expensive, but they rust if they become damp or wet. To prevent rusting, screws are sometimes blued. (Bluing material can be purchased commercially.)

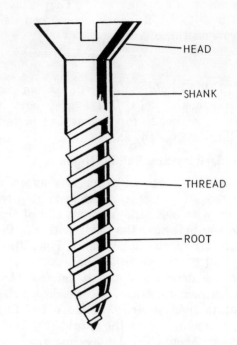

Figure 13–9. Parts of a wood screw.

a. *Classification of Screws.* Screws are classified mainly according to the shape of the head.

(1) *Flathead.* These screws are used where they will not show on the finished surface. They should be countersunk and they may be covered with plastic wood or with wood doweling. They are commonly made with a bright, blued, or brass finish.

(2) *Oval head.* These are designed primarily

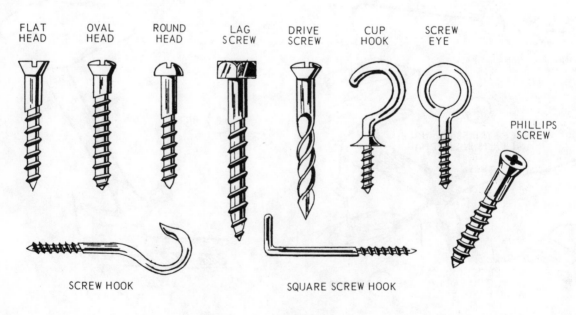

Figure 13–10. Types of screws.

for fastening hinges and other hardware to wood. When inserted, they should be countersunk to the oval part. They usually come in blued or brass finish.

(3) *Roundhead*. These screws should not be countersunk but should be used where the head is supposed to show. They are commonly made of brass or are blued or plated.

(4) *Lag*. These screws have a square head like a bolt and are driven in place with a wrench. They are used in heavy timber construction and come in diameters of 1/4 inch to 1 inch and in lengths from 1 inch to 16 inches.

(5) *Drive*. Drive screws are half nail and half screw and are driven into wood like a nail. However, because of the partial threading, they have better holding power than nails.

(6) *Phillips*. Instead of the usual groove in the head, this screw has a cross-shaped recess. It is easier to start than a standard screw because the driver point centers itself and the screwdriver is less likely to slip. A special Phillips screwdriver is used with these screws.

(7) *Screw hooks, cup hooks, and screw eyes*. These may be obtained in different sizes and are made of steel, brass, or galvanized iron. They have many uses in an occupational therapy clinic; for instance, hanging tools and paint brushes, starting belts, and hanging pictures.

b. *Sizes of Screws*. Wood screws are made in lengths from 1/4 inch to 5 inches. The diameter or gauge is indicated by numbers running from 0 to 24. Screw gauges and wire gauges are not the same. The higher the gauge number, the greater the diameter of the screw. The most common sizes of screws run from No. 5 to No. 12; that is, from 1/8 inch to nearly 1/4 inch.

c. *Ordering or Purchasing Screws*. When purchasing screws, the desired length, gauge, shape of the head, and finish must be specified. *For*

example, a 1 1/4-inch No. 7, flathead, brass screw is designated as "1 1/4"—No. 8, FHB," and a roundhead screw of the same size is "1 1/4"— No. 8, RHB." Small and medium sized screws are packed in boxes containing one gross. Larger screws come in boxes containing half a gross. It is also possible to purchase them at a certain price per screw or per dozen.

d. *Selecting Type and Size*. The selection of the type and size of screw depends upon the job. About two-thirds of the screw should enter the wood. Thus, if the stock is thin, a thin screw should be used. One with a small gauge number would be the desired length. For a heavy screw that gives extra strength, one with a high gauge number is selected for its length. Table 13–4 gives the gauge number available for each length of screw.

Table 13–4. Gauges Obtainable in Various Lengths of Screws

Gauge	Length in inches	Gauge	Length in inches
0–4	1/4	6–20	2
0–8	3/8	6–20	2 1/4
1–10	1/2	6–20	2 1/2
2–12	5/8	8–20	2 3/4
2–14	3/4	8–24	3
3–14	7/8	10–24	3 1/2
3–16	1	12–24	4
4–18	1 1/4	14–24	4 1/2
6–20	1 3/4	14–24	5

e. *Applying Screws*. Two holes of different diameters must be bored in the wood when screws are to be used. The first, or shank hole should be equal to the diameter of the shank; the second, or pilot hole, should be equal to the diameter of the root. In hard woods, the second hole should be bored as deeply as the screw enters the wood; in soft woods it should be bored about half this distance. When flathead or oval head screws are used, the upper end of the first hole is widened with a countersink. Table 13–5 indicates the size

Table 13–5. Diameter of Shank and Pilot Holes for Various Gauges of Screws

Gauge No. of screw	Shank hole	Pilot hole, soft wood	Pilot hole, hard wood	Diameter of screw
2	3/32	- - - - - -	1/16	.086
3	7/64	1/16	5/64	.099
4	1/8	5/64	3/34	.112
5	1/8	5/64	3/32	.125
6	9/64	3/32	7/64	.138
7	5/32	7/64	1/8	.151
8	11/64	1/8	9/64	.164
9	13/64	9/64	11/64	.198
10	15/64	5/32	3/16	.216
12	1/4	11/64	13/64	.242
16	9/32	13/64	15/64	.268
18	5/16	15/64	17/64	.294

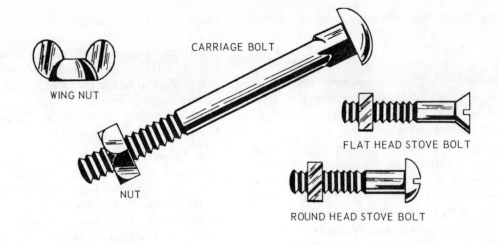

WING NUT

CARRIAGE BOLT

FLAT HEAD STOVE BOLT

NUT

ROUND HEAD STOVE BOLT

Figure 13–11. Types of bolts.

drills that should be used in drilling both the shank hole and the pilot hole in soft and hard woods. When applying screws, the correct size and type of screwdriver must be used for ease in application and preservation of the screw. If the screw is difficult to insert, rubbing it across a piece of dry soap sometimes makes it go into the wood more easily. The screw should be turned so that the screwhead is parallel to the grain of the wood.

13–19. Bolts

Bolts differ from screws because they have the same diameter from end to end, rather than tapering. The bolt projects through the pieces being held together and a square or hexagonal piece of metal, called a nut, is screwed on the projecting threaded end. When it is desired that the piece be easily removable, a winged nut is used instead of a bolt. Bolts are used for heavy work in woodworking where great strength is required or where wood is fastened to metal or masonry.

a. Types of Bolts. As in other types of hardware, there are a number of different kinds of bolts, but only the most common woodworking bolts will be considered here (fig. 13–11).

(1) *Stove bolts.* These inexpensive bolts are made from 3/8 inch to 6 inches long and from 1/8 inch to 1/2 inch in diameter. They may have a flathead, which should be countersunk, or a round one, which should not. They are slotted for a screwdriver.

(2) *Carriage bolts.* Carriage bolts are made especially for wood. They come in sizes from 1 inch to 12 inches long, and from 3/16 inch to 3/4 inch in diameter. The head is round, but not

slotted, and a square section just below the head prevents them from turning in the hole when they are driven home.

b. Applying Bolts. A hole of the same diameter as the bolt is drilled through both of the pieces that are to be held together. A metal washer is placed between the nut and the wood (usually between the head and the wood). These washers distribute the pressure of the bolt over a larger area, thus preventing the head and nut from digging into the wood. Washers are sized by the size of the hole in the center.

13–20. Miscellaneous Fasteners

In addition to nails, brads, and bolts, other types of hardware are used in woodworking.

a. Corrugated Fasteners. These fasteners (fig. 13–12) provide one of the many means by which joints and splices are fastened in small timbers and boards. They do not provide a secure joint but, in places where there will be strain such as a mitered picture frame, they are a quick and satisfactory method of joining two pieces of wood. These fasteners are made of 18- to 22-gauge sheet metal with alternate ridges and grooves. The ridges vary from 3/16 inch to 5/16 inch. The top is cut square and the bottom is sharpened, with beveled edges. They are made with the ridges running parallel or running at a slight angle to one another. The latter type has a tendency to compress the material, as the ridges are closer at the top than at the bottom. Corrugated fasteners are made in several lengths and widths. The width varies from 5/8 inch to 1 1/8 inch and the length from 1/4 inch to 3/4 inch. The number

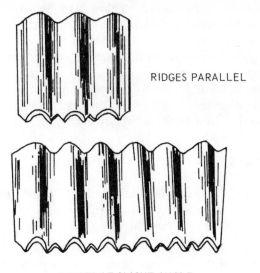

RIDGES PARALLEL

RIDGES AT SLIGHT ANGLE

Figure 13–12. Corrugated fasteners.

of ridges range from 3 to 6 per fastener. (Figure 13–147 shows how these fasteners may be used.)

b. Hinges. A hinge provides the easiest way to make a movable joint between two pieces of wood. Hinges are made in many different forms and of different materials such as brass, iron, galvanized iron, brass-plated iron, and nickel. Hinges are sized according to the length and width of each leaf.

(1) *Types of hinges.* Some of the common forms of hinges are shown in figure 13–13. The butt hinge is used for many items—from doors to jewel boxes. Continuous hinges can be obtained in any length and are used for pianos, boxes, and cabinet doors. Both the strap and the T-hinge are used on garage and cellar doors, gates, and toolboxes. Hinges are also used in places where some minor decoration is desired.

(2) *Fastening hinges.* Hinges may be set flush, or a little below the surface of the wood, in a groove called a "gain." Strap, surface, spring, hasp, and T-hinges are screwed to the surface of the wood without cutting any recess, while butt and continuous hinges are recessed. For greater security, hasps should be attached in such a way that the screws are hidden or covered so that they cannot be removed. When hinges are used for the lid of a box or chest, they should be placed so that the distance from the hinge to the edge of the box is equal to the length of the hinge. The exact position is determined by placing the lid in position on the box and marking the length of the leaves on both pieces. Lines are

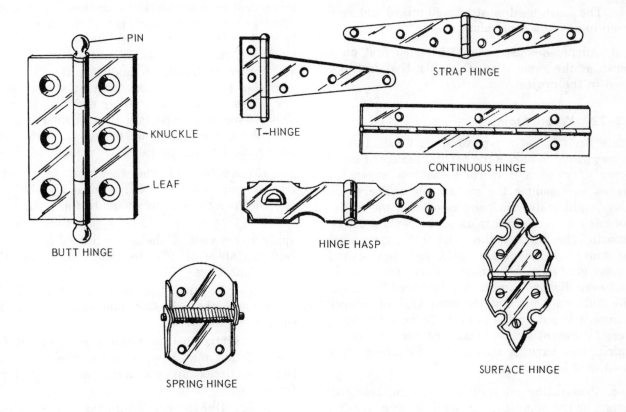

Figure 13–13. Types of hinges.

then squared across these points. The recess must be carefully made to the same depth or the thickness of the hinge with a chisel or a knife. The hinges are placed in position and the wood is marked for boring. Only the pilot hole is made, as the shank hole is in the hinge. The screws are inserted and if parts have been accurately measured and made, the hinges will fit.

c. Other Hardware. There are innumerable kinds of locks, fastenings, and door handles on the market which can be applied to wood. Some are quite simple to install; others are rather complicated. When the occasion arrives to use any of these, it is advisable to follow the directions that come with them or to look up the method of installation in a book on woodworking.

Section V. FINISHES

13–21. General

The choice of a finish is the responsibility of the craftsman. It is guided not only by personal choice and ability, but also by the type of lumber used, the final condition of the wood before finishing, the use the piece will get, the time it is to be used, and the way it will blend in with its surroundings. Combined with a wise selection of finishes are several physical considerations which are essential in obtaining a good finish.

a. Finishing should be done in a room apart and it should be made as clean and dust free as possible to keep the wet surface of the newly finished piece free from dust particles.

b. Brushes should be of good quality and clean.

c. The finish used must be well mixed and free from lumps and contamination.

d. All finishes used should be tried first on a scrap of the same type of lumber that is to be used in the project.

13–22. Wood Stains

Stain itself is not a type of wood finish. It is a color applied to enrich the natural beauty of some types of wood and to color the less expensive woods to resemble the costlier ones. There are also bright stains that add color to a piece. Before any type of stain is used, the wood must be smooth; the final sanding with 3/0 paper must be done; and all grease spots, tool marks, and excess glue must be removed. Time, extra work, and even disappointment may be saved by trying the stain on a piece of the same type of lumber before it is put on the project. There are a number of different kinds of stain but only oil, water, spirit, and varnish stains, the most frequently used, will be considered.

a. Penetrating oil stain is prepared, ready to apply, by the manufacturer. Coal-tar dyes are dissolved into a base of naphtha, benzine, or turpentine. The stain is available in different quantities in a number of shades that are made to resemble different types of wood.

(1) *Advantages.* Penetrating oil stains are more costly to purchase than are some of the other types but, in the final analysis, they may be less costly, especially as they are used in an occupational therapy clinic. They require less mixing and preparation, and colors are constant if purchased from the same manufacturer. They are more easily applied by an amateur because they do not streak or raise the grain of the wood. They can be applied with a brush or with a clean cloth.

(2) *Disadvantages.* These stains are more expensive, which is a consideration only if a great deal of staining is to be done. A greater disadvantage in clinic work is that they are slower to work with than the other stains. It takes 24 hours for them to dry sufficiently for application of another material. In addition, it is always advisable to apply a work coat of shellac over dry oil stain before any other material is used. This is especially important if paste filler is used. The color of the stain tends to seep through varnish or shellac, which causes a change of color.

(3) *Application.* The wood must be smooth, free of glue, dust, and oil; it must also be well sanded. Then these steps should be followed:

(*a*) If there is any exposed end grain, apply a thin coat of shellac or linseed oil to prevent the absorption of too much stain and too much darkening.

(*b*) Be sure that there is sufficient stain to complete the job. One pint covers about 25 square feet of surface.

(*c*) Mix the stain thoroughly. Check for pigment that may have settled to the bottom of the can. Break up any lumps that may have formed.

(*d*) Dip the brush into the stain to about one-fourth of its length and remove excess stain by pressing the brush lightly against the side of the can. The brush should not drip or splash.

(e) Apply the stain by brushing evenly and rapidly with log even strokes *with* the grain of the wood. It is advisable to start on the under surfaces or the back of a project. Continue brushing until the section is covered with stain.

(f) Remove the excess stain with a soft clean cloth, wiping *with* the *grain*. Allow an equal amount of time for each section before wiping to assure uniform color. If some areas are too light, restain them, wiping off only enough stain to make the surface match the rest of the work. If an area is darker than the rest, try to wipe off more stain with a cloth dampened in benzine or turpentine.

(g) Allow 24 hours for the stain to dry before adding another coat of material.

b. Water stain is available only in powder form, which is mixed into hot water and is allowed to cool at the time that the stain is to be used. Because other powdered stains are available to be dissolved into other solvents, care must be taken to get the right combination of stain and solvent.

(1) *Advantages*. Water stain is the choice of the professional wood finisher because it is inexpensive and is available in a large variety of colors, which can be used as is or can be combined to make any desired shade. These colors penetrate the wood deeply so that they do not fade, even when subjected to strong light for a period of time. Since they are transparent, they add a clear brilliant color to the wood and do not cover the beauty of the grain. Because of their water base, they dry fast enough that another coat can be applied within a few hours. In addition, a work coat of shellac is not necessary before wood filler is used.

(2) *Disadvantages*. Water stain is more difficult to apply than other stains partly because some skill is required to prevent streaks and lap marks. Practice on scrap wood is suggested in order to learn to handle the stain before actual staining is begun. Second, it is also necessary to raise the grain of the wood first with clear water, allow it to dry, and then sand the surface with 3/0 or 5/0 garnet paper to remove the resulting fuzzy surface. If this is not done, the water in the stain will raise the grain and then any sanding to remove the fuzzy surface will remove some of the stain of the wood. The third objection to water stain is that it will not penetrate wood that has been previously finished, even after seemingly every trace of the old finish has been removed.

(3) *Application*. Water stain is applied as follows:

(a) To prepare the wood, sponge with clear water and allow it to dry *completely*, then sand with 3/0–5/0 garnet sandpaper.

(b) Mix the stain according to the directions on the package.

(c) To assure better, more even staining, position the pieces so that they will be in a horizontal position while being stained.

(d) Start with the under, back, and side parts, leaving the parts that show the most for the last.

(e) Use a wide, stiff-haired brush and fill it with stain, but not so full that it is dripping.

(f) Stain one section at a time, *with* the *grain*, using full strokes. On a large area, it is advisable to start at the center and work toward the ends of the piece. If the section cannot be completed with one brushful, refill the brush and, instead of starting where the staining stopped, start about 2 inches away from it and work toward the line and away from it.

(g) If the wood is not dark enough, brush on a second coat. It is better to use two coats of light stain than one coat of dark stain.

(h) To pick up excess stain in a corner or molding, dry out the brush on the edge of the stain container and go over the spot with the "dry" brush.

(i) Allow at least 4 hours drying time before applying the next coat.

c. Spirit (alcohol) stain, like water stain, is available in powder form to mix into alcohol, but it can also be purchased ready-mixed. While these stains do not come in the variety of colors that water stains do, they can be combined in different ways to produce almost any color or shade desired. Once again, experimenting on a scrap of lumber is advisable.

(1) *Advantages*. These stains are transparent, so they leave a clear color on the wood and enhance the appearance of the grain. Because of the nature of the alcohol base, spirit stains will dry within a matter of minutes. They do not raise the grain of the wood as water stains do so the need for the extra wetting and sanding of the wood is eliminated. They have the added advantage of penetrating a shellacked, varnished, or lacquered surface to color the wood underneath.

(2) *Disadvantages*. Rapid drying of alcohol stain may be an advantage in saving time, but this same rapid drying makes it almost impossible for even an experienced person to apply this type of stain to a large area without lap or streak marks. However, it can be used quite successfully to stain pieces on which a surface can be covered with one brush stroke. This stain does not penetrate the wood deep enough to prevent fading so it is not fast to light.

(3) *Application*. The secret of successful staining when using alcohol stain is to cover the area as quickly as possible. The stain dries so rapidly that an area cannot be reworked. Each time the brush goes over an area, it leaves another coat of color, so these steps should be followed:

(*a*) Prepare the wood in the usual manner.

(*b*) Use as large a brush as is convenient to handle in the area to be stained, have the work horizontal if possible, and start in the not-too-well-seen areas.

(*c*) Fill the brush to capacity, but do not let it drip.

(*d*) Work with the grain; work with long strokes and rapidly.

(*e*) When the brush runs dry, quickly refill it and continue working rapidly.

d. Varnish stain is a mixture of varnish and penetrating oil stain combined to produce a colored varnish that is designed both to color the wood and to varnish it in one operation. The properties of the varnish prevent the stain from being clear and from penetrating the wood; the pigment of the stain keeps the varnish from being clear. As a result, varnishes tend to leave a streaky, muddy finish on the wood.

(1) *Advantages*. This combination of varnish and stain saves time and gives a dark protective coating in areas such as interiors of cabinets or closet shelves where the fine grain of the wood cannot be seen.

(2) *Disadvantages*. A muddy, streaked finish is almost unavoidable with this combination of ingredients.

(3) *Application*. The best results are obtained if these procedures are followed:

(*a*) Prepare the wood in the usual manner.

(*b*) Fill the brush to capacity and, following the grain, start at the center and brush toward each end.

(*c*) Do not go over an area already done, as an additional coat of color will be deposited.

(*d*) If there is an area with too much stain, some of it can be removed by "drying" the brush against the edge of the can and going over the dark area with the dry brush.

(*e*) Follow the drying-time suggestions on the can.

13–23. Wood Fillers

Good commercial wood products have a fine smooth finish. In fact, as the finish gets finer, the price of the piece becomes higher. Pinpoint holes in the surface and the lack of gloss and smoothness of finish so often found in amateur work usually result because the hollow cells of the wood soaked up the finish. To prevent this, filler is used after staining. Paste filler is used on open-grained wood; liquid filler, on close-grained wood.

a. Open-grained woods, such as oak, mahogany, and walnut, need to have a paste wood filler applied to fill the pores so that a smooth finish is possible.

(1) *Selection of a filler*. A good filler must adhere to the wood, not shrink or crumble when dry, and must dry hard in a reasonable period of time. The following ingredients are recommended and should be listed on the container:

- Silex powder—to provide the solid base material.
- Linseed oil—to keep the silex in paste form.
- Oil color—to color the filler the desired shade.
- Japan dryer—to hasten drying.

Fillers are obtainable readymade in almost any color of stained wood surfaces. They may also be purchased without stain and can be colored as desired with an appropriate oil color. The color of the filler should be close to the color of the stained wood rather than to the color of the natural wood. Because the filler becomes a little lighter when it dries, it should be slightly darker than the stained wood.

(2) *Preparation for filling*. Since the filler in the can is too heavy to enter the pores of the wood, it must be thinned with benzine or turpentine until it is the consistency of cream. Then it will spread easily with a brush. If the wood has been stained with water or alcohol stain, the filler can be applied directly, as soon as the stain is thoroughly dry. If oil stain has been used, a work coat of shellac must be applied and allowed to dry before the filler is applied. This may also

be done over other stains to prevent darkening of the stain by the filler.

(3) *Application of filler.* A brush wide enough to cover a manageable section of the work easily is used to apply the filler. The filler can be applied in any direction, but the coating must be even and it should be brushed into the pores of the wood. When the filler is applied, it is lustrous but, as it dries, it becomes dull. When it picks up on the finger and leaves the wood clean, it is ready to be removed.

(*a*) Pushing hard, rub *across* the *grain* with a rough material such as burlap or excelsior. In this way the filler is pushed into the pores of the wood as it is removed from the surface.

(*b*) Next, use a soft, clean wiping rag *with* the *grain* to clean off all of the remains of the filler on the surface of the wood. Continue this wiping process until the clean rags no longer pick up any filler.

WARNING

Filler not wiped off of the surface will become more noticeable when other finishes are applied.

(*c*) To remove the filler from curves, corners, and other hard-to-reach places, use a sharpened dowel with cloth over the end.

(*d*) Stir the filler to mix it before doing the next area.

(*e*) Let stand for at least 24 hours in order for the filler to dry sufficiently to apply any other type of finish.

b. Close-grained woods such as birch, cedar, cherry, fir, gum, pine, and spruce need liquid fillers to seal the pores of the wood. Some of the liquid fillers and notes on their use are listed below.

(1) *Shellac.* As it comes from the can, shellac is diluted by adding one part alcohol to one part shellac for use as a filler. Two hours are allowed for drying. It is then sanded lightly with 4/0 garnet paper. White shellac is used to fill surfaces that have a light color stain or that are to have a clear varnish or light paint finish. Orange shellac can be used on dark stains or with dark paints.

(2) *Varnish.* The use of varnish as a liquid sealer is less popular than shellac, perhaps because 24 hours must be allowed for it to dry. It can then be sanded and covered with more varnish or paint, but not with shellac or lacquer.

(3) *Lacquer.* Lacquer is a good sealer but only if more lacquer is to be applied. It dries in about an hour and can then be sanded.

(4) *Dilute paste filler.* The proper shade of paste filler is diluted with benzine or turpentine to the consistency of varnish. It is brushed on as in *a*(3) above, and when it begins to show signs of dullness, it is removed.

13–24. Clear Finishes

There are several types of finishes that are clear and colorless so that the color and beauty of the grain of the wood can show through. Woods with natural beauty such as oak, mahogany, walnut, birch cherry, and maple are usually finished with a clear finish that enhances the grain and color. Clear finishes are applied after the wood is stained and filled.

a. Shellac has been used as a finish since the fifteenth or sixteenth century and it is still considered to be a fine finish for wood. It is made from the residue deposited on the branches of trees by a small red insect of Ceylon and India called the lac bug. The residue is collected, processed, and sold in flakes to the dealer. It is made into orange and white shellac, which are both shellac but cannot be used interchangeably. Orange is the unbleached natural shellac. It gets its name because it is transparent orange in color. It is less expensive and more durable than the bleached or white shellac and can be used very nicely on dark-stained surfaces where the orange color will not affect the color of the surface. A bleaching agent is added to orange shellac to produce "white" shellac, which remains transparent and is actually rather eggshell in color. White shellac is used on light surfaces that would have too much color if orange shellac were used. The bleaching process leaves white shellac more susceptible to moisture; when exposed, the shellac becomes milky white instead of clear. The rapid drying quality is also lost if white shellac is stored over a period of months. Because of this, it is advisable to purchase shellac in quantities that can be used within a few months.

(1) *Advantages of shellac finish.* Under certain circumstances, shellac produces a strong, yet smooth, durable finish. It is sufficiently flexible to resist marring, so it is used on floors, bowling alleys, and certain pieces of furniture. It dires so rapidly that it becomes dustproof within a few minutes, and other coats of material can be applied within hours. It is also an excellent sealer

when thinned with alcohol to the correct consistency. It can be covered with filler, varnish, more shellac, paint, enamel, and lacquer.

(2) *Disadvantages of shellac finish.* Shellac is not waterproof nor is it alcohol proof. It turns white when it becomes moist so it is not a good finish for outdoor furniture or for kitchen tables which are apt to get wet. It should not be used where it will be in contact with heat as it will become soft and then blister and crack. Shellac is also a poor finish for bars or coffee tables as the alcohol in liquor will act as a solvent and destroy the finish. It will not adhere to lacquered, waxed, or enameled surfaces. White shellac, in particular, must be carefully stored away from strong light and kept at room temperature. Glass containers are preferred for storage, as in time the shellac will become discolored in metal. After shellac has been stored for several months, its drying qualities are affected and it cannot be used.

(3) *Application.* Shellac can be applied in several ways.

Using a Brush

Applying the shellac with a brush is an effective, controllable method to use on most projects. The surface of the wood must be made smooth and clean and if stain is used, it must be applied first. The shellac should be thinned to the correct consistency. Because shellac dries so fast, all material must be ready so that the work can progress as rapidly as possible. The piece to be shellacked should be in the horizontal position.

1. Start at the middle of the area usually, then with full, even strokes in the direction of the grain, work toward each end and then toward the edge.
2. If the brush must be refilled, start again about 2 inches from the line where it ran out and work over toward that line, then away from it.
3. If a spot has been missed, rather than rebrushing, let it go but be sure to get it on the second coat.
4. Pick up excess shellac with a "dry" brush.
5. Do not be concerned with the small air bubbles that appear on the surface, as they will disappear as the shellac sets.
6. Let it dry. Shellac dries so that it will not pick up dust within a few minutes, but at least 3 hours should elapse before it is sanded.
7. Sand with 5/0 garnet sandpaper and take care not to remove the thin coat of shellac with

the sandpaper. If the smooth side of the sandpaper is dampened with a wet sponge, the paper will become more pliable and will be less likely to scratch. This is particularly important if the piece has been stained.
8. Apply the second coat the same way as the first coat.
9. Decide how many coats to use. This decision is up to you and varies with the type of wood, the use to be made of the piece, and the amount of time available for finishing. It is agreed, however, that two thin coats are better than one thick one.
10. After the last coat of shellac has dried for at least 24 hours, rub it. The fineness of the finish depends, in part, upon the material used in this rubbing. For a semigloss finish, use 2/0 steel wool and rub in the direction of the grain, using long straight strokes. No. 3/0 powdered pumice and oil rubbed with the grain will produce a fine, smooth, semigloss surface.
11. Clean and wax the piece.

Using Padding

Another method of applying shellac is called padding. While it is possible to use this method on flat surfaces, it is usually used, in occupational therapy clinics, on turned pieces while they are still in the lathe. The piece must be sanded, then it is usually smoothed with steel wool. It can then be stained if so desired and filler applied in the usual manner. After the filler has been cleaned off, apply shellac (which can be thinned with denatured alcohol) while the piece is turning on the lathe.

1. Put some shellac into a shallow dish and some boiled linseed oil into another.
2. Arrange a lint free, clean cloth into an oval pad and dip it first into the linseed oil.
3. After working the linseed oil into the pad, dip it into the shellac and work the shellac into the pad.
4. While the piece is turning on the lathe at medium or slow speed, press the saturated pad against the piece and, at the same time, keep the pad moving back and forth to distribute the shellac and linseed oil evenly over the surface.
5. When the pad becomes dry, dip it again into the linseed oil and shellac and repeat the process for five or six applications, or until the

desired amount of shellac has been applied and the desired gloss attained.

6. After 24 hours of drying time, rub the turning piece with a pad saturated in linseed oil to increase the richness of tone and luster.

b. Varnish is another transparent finishing material that has been used for thousands of years. It was used by the early Greeks to protect the wood of their ships from the elements of the seas. It was originally made of copal gum resins combined in varying proportion of oil and turpentine and a dryer. A high percentage of gum, sometimes referred to as short oil, produces a varnish that dries with a hard finish which can be rubbed to a high gloss suitable for fine cabinet work. As the percentage of gum is lessened, a long oil varnish is produced, drying time is increased, and the varnish remains flexible and durable. This surface will not take the high polish that a short oil varnish will take but it is more durable for marine and exterior finishes as it is not as affected by moisture and temperature. A big disadvantage to these natural varnishes is the slow drying time. This has been overcome in recent years with the discovery of synthetic resins. It is now possible to produce varnish with qualities similar to the natural ones, but which dry more rapidly.

(1) *Fast-drying varnish.* These synthetic, fast-drying varnishes have so superseded the natural varnishes that they are the ones handled by paint dealers. Like the natural varnishes, different proportions produce different qualities of surface, so there are several types of varnish available on the market, each with a different purpose. They dry dustproof in less than 4 hours and an additional cost can be applied, usually in 6 hours.

(*a*) Cabinet varnish is a short oil varnish so it dries with a hard surface which can be rubbed to a high gloss. It is a good versatile finish for all types of interior work and is recommended for general indoor work, such as is done in occupational therapy.

(*b*) Flat varnish is a short oil synthetic varnish which dries with a dull finish so that it does not have to be rubbed. It, however, does not have the richness and beauty of a hand-rubbed piece. It can be applied as a final coat over several coats of cabinet varnish or one coat can be applied to a prepared surface which needs little protection.

(*c*) Interior spar (bar) varnish contains more oil and is recommended for interior use, but on places which are subject to some abuse. It is recommended for coffee tables, bars, and cabinets, or any place where alcohol or water may be spilled or scratching may occur. It can be rubbed to a satin gloss but it does not take as high a polish as cabinet varnish. It is also referred to as bar varnish because of its use.

(*d*) Exterior spar varnish is a long oil varnish that is waterproof and so is designed to protect wood that will be used outdoors. It flows easily and sets within several hours. However, it takes longer to dry completely than varnishes used for interior work. It cannot be rubbed to a luster. When this varnish is used, no other type of material should be applied under it. If spar varnish is not used directly on the raw wood and from the first coat to the last, the finish will blister and crack. Shellac cannot be used, even as a sealer.

(2) *Advantages.* These varied varnishes on the market provide a suitable type for almost any finishing work, indoors or outdoors. They are slightly amber in color and are transparent so they do not color the wood. They can therefore be used on either a natural or stained surface. They flow easily, go on smoothly, and dry with a surface sufficiently hard to protect the wood and to be polished to a high luster. They can be water-, alcohol-, and scratch-resistant and can even be resistant to heat.

(3) *Disadvantages.* The greatest disadvantage to using varnish as a finish on wood is the length of time required for drying, even with synthetic quick-drying types. A varnished surface does not become dustproof for 2 hours and at least 6 hours of drying are required before another coat can be applied. Not only is time a factor to consider but, in order to have a smooth coat, the wet piece must be in a dust free environment with a temperature of 70° to 80° F, each time a coat of varnish is applied. Many people do not have such facilities so they are forced to use another finish.

(4) *Application.* All aspects of applying varnish must be carefully worked out in order to obtain the desired clear, hard, shiny finish. The room in which the varnishing is done must be free from dust and traffic. It must also be above 65° F and below 85° F, preferably between 70° and 80° F during the time that the piece is drying.

(*a*) Clean the surface of the wood with benzine to remove all traces of dirt, dust, grease, and oil. This is necessary, not only before the first coat has been applied, but also between coats. It is advisable to handle the piece as little as possible between coats, because the fingers carry oil. To remove the dust from sandpapering between coats, wipe the piece with a tack rag. (A tack rag is made by sprinkling a few drops of varnish on a clean, lint free cloth. Then the varnish is worked into the cloth until it becomes tacky. It is then ready to pick up traces of dust and dirt as it is rubbed along the varnished surface. It can be stored in a closed container to keep it moist and ready for use again.)

(*b*) Choose the brushes used for varnishing so that they are of an appropriate size for the job to be done and clean them carefully. It is advisable to use a new brush, if at all possible, and even if it needs to be cleaned before using it to varnish. To clean it, first shake out any dust or loose bristles by hitting the bristles gently with the hand. After that, wash the brush in turpentine or benzine and dry it off before dipping it into the varnish.

NOTE
A brush that has been used to apply a coat of varnish need not be cleaned and stored between coats. It should be suspended in a container (fig. 13–14) so that the bristles do not touch the bottom, and the container should contain sufficient brush-keeper varnish or turpentine to cover the bristles of the brush.

(*c*) Usually, start varnishing the most inconspicuous parts of the project first and leave the areas that show the most until last. If possible, the area being varnished should be hori-

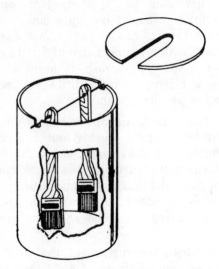

Figure 13–14. Brush container.

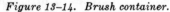

zontal. Do not stir the varnish as this causes air bubbles to form. If the varnish is not going to be used from the can, pour it so as to prevent air bubbles from forming. Some authors suggest thinning the first coat of varnish with a little turpentine, while others feel that it should be used as it comes from the can. If the varnish seems a little thick, warm it in the can slightly in hot water to make it thinner and easier to handle. (Never put the can of varnish directly over the heat.) If it still seems thick, then adding a little turpentine might be indicated.

(*d*) Next, dip the brush into the varnish, filling it to capacity but not to overflowing. Work the brush in the varnish until the trapped air bubbles have been worked out. Work from the center of the area, brushing with the grain, using full, long strokes toward the edges of the area. Continue until the area is covered.

(*e*) To cross-brush, a process that picks up any excess varnish left by the first application and helps to spread the varnish more uniformly, dry the brush by stroking the bristles against the edge of the container. Slant the brush slightly toward the direction of the stroking and go over the surface just varnished, stroking lightly *across* the grain of the wood. Continue the cross-brushing until the area just varnished has been covered.

(*f*) Use "tipping" to smooth out the cross strokes left by the cross-brushing. Dry the brush and again go over the surface, this time *with* the grain. Hold the brush in an almost vertical position and so that just the tip of the brush touches as it is moved from end to end. Tipping must be done while the varnish is wet.

(*g*) After the varnish is completely dry, lightly sand with 3/0 garnet or 500 wet-dry sandpaper before the next coat of varnish is applied. To test for dryness, push the thumbnail into the coating of varnish. If no mark is left, it is ready for the sanding. Remove the dust from the sanding with a tack rag before applying any other coats.

(*h*) For the final coat, "flow on" the varnish. That is, apply it more heavily and work it very little.

(*i*) Rub the final coat to obtain a semigloss luster. This can be done with 2/0 powdered pumice stone with oil or water for a lubricant. The use of water leaves a smoother surface but, because it allows the pumice to cut faster, take care not to rub too much of the varnish off.

c. Lacquer is a synthetic liquid made of a combination of resin gums dissolved in a solvent made up of nitiated cotton, banana oil, alcohol, benzol, and solvent naphtha. Because it is synthetic, the qualities can be controlled to some extent. Modern lacquer is water- and alcohol-resistant; it is also heat-resistant to some extent. Because of these qualities and its rapid drying time, it has become one of the most frequently used finishes in the industrial world. In this capacity, it is applied with a spray gun. However, a slower drying lacquer has been developed that can be applied with a brush.

(1) *Advantages.* The short drying time required for lacquer not only makes it possible to apply several coats in 1 day but this also means that the piece dries before much dust settles and sticks to the surface. Clear lacquer is very transparent and, with this finish, the beauty of the grain of the wood can be enjoyed. It dries sufficiently hard to produce a satin-smooth, very fine surface. Lacquer also comes in colors that are opaque. These are called lacquer enamels.

(2) *Disadvantages.* The fast drying qualities of lacquer make its application with a brush very difficult even when it is brushing lacquer. A smoother surface is obtained by spraying. If the amount or type of woodworking does not justify the purchase and setting up of spraying equipment (to include adequate exhaust, ventilation, and spark-resistant machine), it may be advisable to select another type of finish. Because of its composition, lacquer cannot be applied over varnish, paint, or penetrating oil stain. This incompatibility with turpentine means that a special sealer and solvent must be used with lacquer.

(3) *Application.* Lacquer is made by a number of manufacturers. Although it is all lacquer, the composition differs sufficiently so that each type has a specific thinner, method of application, way of cleaning brushes, and so on. It is therefore necessary to follow the directions on the can of the lacquer being used. If the object is large, the lacquer is sprayed in order to obtain a smooth surface. Brushing lacquer is available clear or in a limited variety of colors. It is the same as spraying lacquer except that it contains an ingredient to slow its drying time. It can be used on such things as small picture frames, boxes, and decorative pins. The surface of the wood and the brush must be free of dirt, dust, oil, and any turpentine-based product. A few general suggestions, applicable to most types of lacquer, are given here for small objects.

(*a*) Use water stain first, as a recommended practice for use under lacquer.

(*b*) After 24 hours, apply a work coat of shellac to seal the stain. After the shellac has dried, paste filler may be used, but it must be sealed with a coat of work shellac before lacquer is applied. Or a lacquer sanding sealer may be applied, instead of the paste filler, directly after a 24-hour drying period.

(*c*) Apply lacquer with a well-filled brush because it dries too quickly to allow for rebrushing.

(*d*) When the first coat is completely dry, apply another coat directly, without sanding. (If the first coat has picked up dust, it may be sanded with 8/0 garnet paper before the second coat.) A third coat may also be indicated.

(*e*) Dry the final coat for 48 hours, after which time it can be polished with rottenstone and oil.

(4) *Safety.* Lacquer is a highly volatile substance which can be exploded by a spark. Because of this, great care must be taken to provide good ventilation during its use and to dispose of rags and remaining lacquer and solvent in a safe manner. Unless a specially equipped area can be provided, spraying should not be done. Even the use of pressurized cans is discouraged because of the possibility of their being ignited by a cigarette.

d. An oil finish gives a good initial appearance and it certainly brings out the richness of the wood. It must be renewed rather frequently, however, as it does not hold up over a period of time. For this finish, apply a small amount of hot, boiled linseed oil to the wood, either with a brush or with a clean cloth. Then rub it with the hand, first across the grain, then parallel to it. After two or three such coats each day for a week, the polish begins to appear. If desired, use a very thin coat of shellac after the first two applications of oil as a shortcut. Sand it with 2/0 or 3/0 *used* sandpaper before more applications of oil are made. A coat or two of wax applied after the desired gloss has been obtained will help to preserve the finish.

e. A number of coats of wax also provide a

finish which brings out the beauty of the wood. To prevent lumps of wax from getting into corners, wrap the wax in two or three thicknesses of cheesecloth and apply it evenly over the surface. Let the wax dry for a few minutes, then polish it with a soft brush or a textured cloth (terrycloth, for instance), first across the grain and then parallel to it. After the wax has dried thoroughly, apply a second coat. Apply other coats as needed to obtain the desired luster.

f. An increasing number of very fine clear wood finishes are being put on the market. They are synthetic products which have properties peculiar to their composition. It is suggested that these be used when and where indicated and that the accompanying directions be closely followed. Be alert for toxic and fire contraindications, however.

13–25. Opaque Finishes

Opaque finishes are used for protection of the wood and as a phasing cover for the less expensive woods that have poor grain or flaws. The most commonly used opaque finishes are paint and enamel. Colored lacquers also fall in this category but are less frequently used. Both paint and enamel can be washed with soap and water so either is appropriate to use as a finish in kitchens, laundries, nurseries, and children's rooms. Although these finishes are opaque, they do not cover defects in the texture of the wood. Before any of these finishes are applied, the wood must be carefully sanded, dents must be raised, holes filled, and a sealer of some type must be used to fill the pores of the wood.

a. Paint is composed of pigment; oil, usually linseed or varnish oil, is the vehicle in which the color is dispersed. In addition, a dryer to hasten oxidation and thereby shorten drying time and turpentine to thin the paint so that it can be brushed easily are used. Paints are available in a great variety of colors and, if the desired shade is not available, blending can produce it. Flat paint is made to dry with a flat dull finish and is sometimes preferred for walls to decrease the glare; however, it is more difficult to wash because of the texture. Glossy paints dry with a gloss finish and, because they can be washed so easily, are used for such things as furniture, window frames, and door frames. If the gloss is too much, they can be rubbed with pumice or rottenstone to dull the luster.

b. Enamels are colored varnishes. The pigment is ground into varnish, dryer is added to hasten drying, and turpentine is used to facilitate spreading. Like varnishes, enamels can be slow drying or can dry in 4 hours. They are made to dry with a very shiny gloss finish, semigloss, or flat finish.

c. Lacquer enamels, their characteristics, and application were discussed in paragraph 13–24*c*.

d. Applying paint and enamel should be done according to the directions on the container, but a few general suggestions are offered.

(1) Prepare the wood by sanding, scraping, raising, or filling dents, so that it is smooth.

(2) If the directions call for a primer coat, shellac that is cut with alcohol is good to use.

(3) Stir the paint or enamel until it is smooth and well blended. Straining the paint through a nylon stocking will remove small bits of scum if they present a problem.

(4) If the paint or enamel needs to be thinned, use the recommended thinner; if none is suggested, use linseed oil or turpentine.

(5) Apply the paint or enamel with a brush that is full, but not dripping, in long even strokes. The surface should be well covered, but too much paint or enamel will "run."

(6) Allow the surface to dry thoroughly, using the directions as a guide, then sand it smooth with fine sandpaper, and clean it with a cloth to remove the dust.

(7) Apply a second and perhaps a third coat in the same manner, but do not sand the final coat.

13–26. Care and Cleaning of Paintbrushes

a. Purchasing Brushes. In theory, the purchase of the best brushes that one can afford is a wise investment in view of lasting qualities and the results obtainable. This theory should certainly be followed in a personal purchase.

There should be a variety in the width of brushes commensurate with the size of the projects being done. Most students several 1-, 1 1/2-, and 2-inch brushes and one or two 3-inch brushes. Because more small projects are made, more small brushes will be needed.

b. Cleaning Brushes. This is a very important part of the finishing process, for if it is not done well, the next coat will be defective.

(1) The first step to good cleaning is to select the correct solvent for the finish used. The correct solvent will usually be indicated on the can, especially if it deviates from the usual. Table 13–6 can be used as a guide. It is often helpful to have such a guide near the paint cabinet.

(2) If the painting job is not complete and the brush will be used within a day or two, the brush may be hung in the solvent of the material being used, which will keep if soft until it is used again. Before use, wipe as much solvent from the brush as possible so that the first strokes of the finish will not be thinned.

(3) When the brush will not be used for more than a day or two, it must be cleaned well in order to keep it in good shape and ready for the next job. To do this, follow these steps:

(*a*) Wipe as much paint off of the brush as is possible by brushing it back and forth on newspaper. When doing this, brush so that the bristles remain straight.

(*b*) With the bristles straight, slosh the brush up and down in the proper solvent.

(*c*) Brush more paint and solvent off on newspapers.

(*d*) Repeat (*b*).

(*e*) Repeat (*c*).

(*f*) Repeat (*b*) but with clean solvent.

(*g*) Repeat (*c*).

(*h*) Stroke the brush across a bar of mild soap, using warm water and getting the suds into the bristles, yet keeping the bristles straight.

(*i*) Rinse the soap and paint out of the brush.

(*j*) Repeat (*h*).

(*k*) Repeat (*i*).

(*l*) Shake as much water out of the brush as possible.

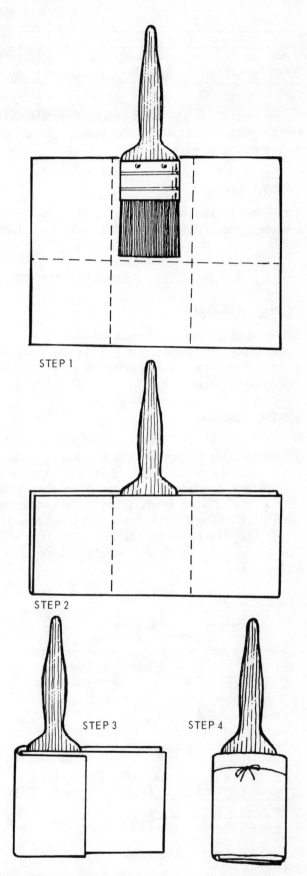

Figure 13–15. Steps in wrapping a paintbrush.

Table 13–6. Selecting Correct Solvent

Water	Alcohol	Turpentine	Acetone	Lacquer thinner
Water stain ⎯⎯⎯⎯⎯	Alcohol stain ⎯⎯⎯	Oil stain, filler, var-	Dope ⎯⎯⎯⎯⎯	Lacquer; lacquer enamel.
Water base paints ⎯⎯	Shellac ⎯⎯⎯⎯⎯	nish, paint enamel.		

(*m*) Wrap the brush, making certain that the bristles are straight, and secure the paper with a string or with a rubber band (fig. 13–15).

13–27. Safety

The solvents and paints used in finishing wood are very flammable. Rags and papers should be taken out immediately after use or stored in a covered can which is emptied at the end of each day. Smoking must be prohibited in the area in which finishing is done.

Section VI. HANDTOOLS: CHISELS AND GOUGES

13–28. General

Chisels and gouges are simple tools, each with a single blade that is used for the careful removal of small areas of wood, often from otherwise inaccessible places.

13–29. Chisels

Wood chisels (fig. 13–16) are used for accurate cutting and for fitting and shaping as, for example, in making wood joints. They are also used for surface decorating. The chisel consists of a single beveled steel blade fitted with a wooden handle. Chisels are divided into two types according to the way in which the handle is attached. The blades are of different weights, thicknesses, and shapes.

a. Tang Chisel. The upper end of a tang chisel blade is shaped into a tapering point which is driven into the wooden handle. A ring, called a ferrule, is fitted around the lower end of the handle to prevent the wood in the handle from splitting. Because of its design and light construction, the tang chisel will not withstand heavy blows.

b. Socket Chisel. The upper part of a socket chisel blade is shaped like a hollow cone. The handle of the tool is fitted into it. The construction is heavy so that the chisel will withstand the blow of a mallet when heavy work is being done. Chisel handles used for heavy or medium work are usually tipped with leather to prevent

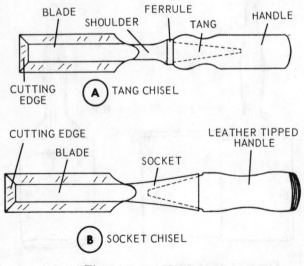

Figure 13–16. Wood chisels.

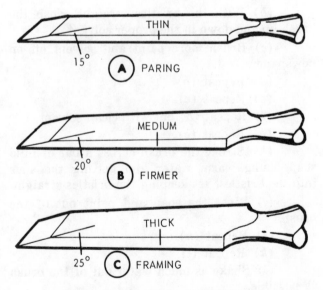

Figure 13–17. Types of chisel blades.

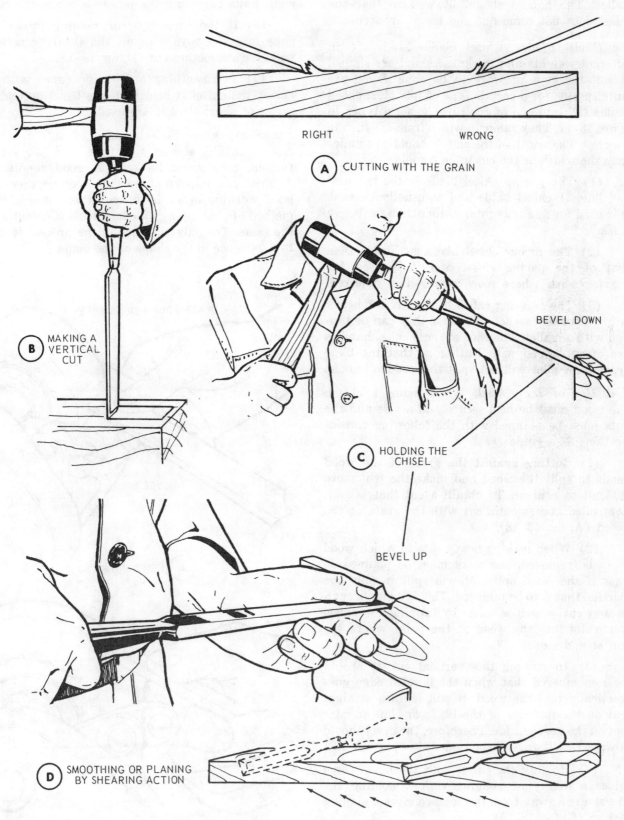

A   CUTTING WITH THE GRAIN

RIGHT   WRONG

B   MAKING A VERTICAL CUT

C   HOLDING THE CHISEL

BEVEL DOWN

BEVEL UP

D   SMOOTHING OR PLANING BY SHEARING ACTION

Figure 13–18. Using the chisel.

the handle from splitting under the blows of the mallet. The handle should fit well so that the chisel does not come out and cause an accident.

c. Chisel Blades. Chisel blades are made in different weights and thicknesses and are shaped to suit the type of work to be done. Some are quite specific for a certain type of job. Most chisel blades fall into one of the three general types in figure 13–17. They range in width from 1/8 inch to 2 inches. The width of the chisel should be smaller than the width of the cut to be made.

(1) The paring chisel blade is the thinnest and longest chisel balde and is usually beveled. It is used for fine smoothing rather than for heavy work.

(2) The firmer chisel blade is thicker than that of the paring chisel and it is used for heavier work where more strength is required.

(3) The framing chisel blades are for heavy work. They are socket chisels, so they can be tapped with a mallet. The ends of these chisel handles are often capped with leather so that the blow from the mallet will not split the wooden handle.

d. Use of the Chisel. When using a chisel, the wood must be held securely in a vise and the cuts must be planned with the following considerations as a guide:

(1) Cutting against the grain of the wood tends to split the wood and make the tool more difficult to control. To obtain a cut that is well controlled and smooth, cut with the grain of the wood (A, fig. 13–18).

(2) When making heavy cuts in which wood is to be removed, the work must be planned so that if the wood splits, it will split in only the portion that is to be removed. This is done through a stop cut, which is made by tapping the chisel vertically into the wood at the point where the cut should stop.

(3) In making this vertical cut, it should be remembered that when the beveled edge goes vertically into the wood, it will leave a straight cut on the flat side of the blade and an angular cut on the beveled side. Therefore, the bevel should always face the area to be removed (B, fig. 13–18).

(4) Holding the chisel with the bevel down gives a lifting or gouging action; holding the bevel up or away from the surface gives a planing action (C, fig. 13–18).

(5) For smoothing cuts, the chisel should be held with the left hand close to the cutting edge so as to guide the chisel accurately. The right hand furnishes the power to make the cut.

(6) If the smoothing or planing stroke is done in a sideways manner, the shearing action will give a smoother cut (D, fig. 13–18).

(7) In smoothing an outside curve with a chisel, the chisel is held with the bevel up and a series of short strokes are used.

e. Sharpening. For the sake of safety, good craftsmanship, economy of time, and job satisfaction, tools must be kept in good condition. A large and important part of keeping them in good working order is to keep them sharp. The method of sharpening all edged tools is essentially the same. The only variance in the process is due to a variance in the shape of the blade.

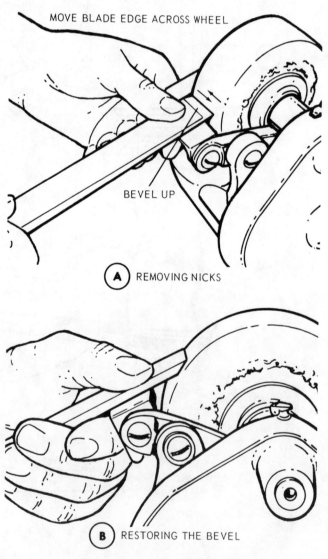

MOVE BLADE EDGE ACROSS WHEEL

BEVEL UP

(A) REMOVING NICKS

(B) RESTORING THE BEVEL

Figure 13–19. Grinding the blade.

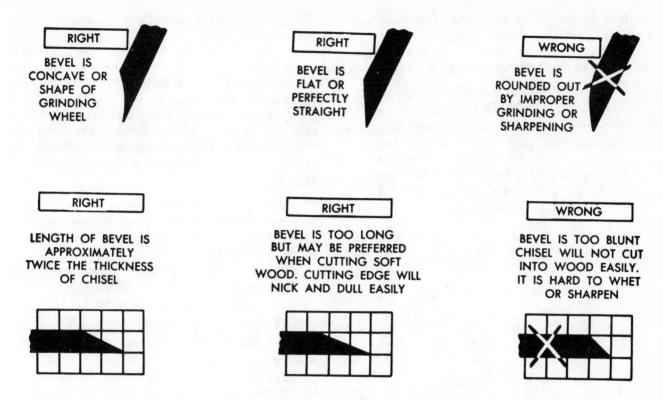

Figure 13-20. Chisel bevels.

(1) *Grinding.* The grinding machine should be used *only* when the cutting edge has been nicked or when the proper bevel cannot be restored by using the oilstone. This is the way to grind properly—

(*a*) Square the cutting edges and remove nicks by holding the blade with the bevel up and moving it across the face of the grinding wheel from side to side. Hold the blade so that the edge will be ground at the proper angle to the side of the blade (fig. 13-19). Keep the blade cool by dipping it frequently in water or light oil to prevent loss of temper or hardness.

(*b*) Restore the proper bevel by adjusting the toolrest on the grinding machine so that the bevel of the blade rests on the grinding surface of the wheel at such an angle as to give the proper bevel to the blade (A and B, fig. 13-19). Continue careful grinding until all nicks have been removed from the cutting edge, and the correct bevel is obtained. For chisels, the cutting edge is at right angles to the side of the blade and the bevel is 25° (fig. 13-20).

(2) *Honing.* When the nicks have been removed and the proper bevel restored, the blade is sharpened or whetted (fig. 13-21) on a clean oilstone lubricated with a light film of oil. To do this properly, hold the beveled edge of the blade at a slightly steeper angle than the angle at which it was ground and move the blade back and forth, lengthwise on the oilstone. Use a circular motion in order to cover the whole surface of the stone. Hone first on the coarse side of the oilstone, then on the fine side. After the bevel has been sharpened, remove the burr or wire edge by turning the blade over and taking a few strokes on the stone with the blade flat against the stone. Do not bevel the flat side.

(3) *Stropping.* An extra sharp edge may be

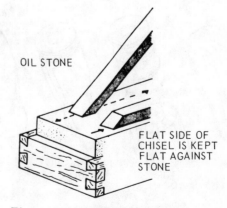

Figure 13-21. Whetting or honing.

obtained by stropping the blade (fig. 13–22). A good strop to have handy is made by gluing a piece of heavy cowhide, skin side up, to a flat even board. To improve stropping, rub a little jeweler's rouge into the leather from time to time.

NOTE

If a strop is not only kept in the woodworking area, but also in the leather section, the swivel knives and leather cutting tools can be stropped for that extra fine edge which is so important for professional-type work.

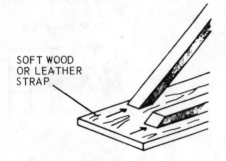

Figure 13–22. Stropping.

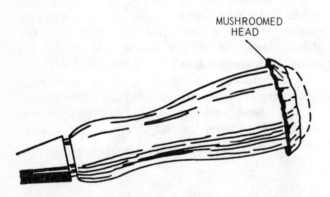

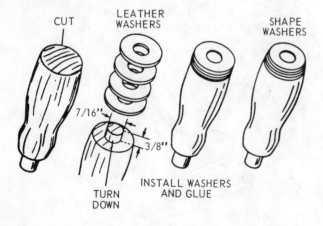

Figure 13–23. Repairing mushroomed heads.

f. Care of the Chisel. Care of chisels is important, as they are easily dulled or even chipped. When they are not in use, they should be kept in racks to prevent damage to the blade. As with all tools, the chisel should be used for only its intended purpose. Because the blade is made of steel, it must be kept clean and covered with a thin film of oil to prevent rust. If the handle of the chisel should become mushroomed from use, the leather can be replaced with leather washers (fig. 13–23).

g. Safety. Safety precautions are important to observe when using chisels. Because of their shape, sharpness, and manner of use, they are potentially dangerous tools.

(1) When using a chisel, always keep both hands in back of the cutting edge.

(2) Always cut away from the body.

(3) Do not carry chisels in a pocket.

(4) Clamp the wood firmly so that it does not move.

(5) See that the chisel is put down so that it will not roll or be brushed off of the bench and fall on someone's foot.

13–30. Gouges

These tools are very similar to chisels except for the shape of the cutting end. The different shapes, or sweeps, vary from a wide arc to a V-shape. There are two kinds of gouges: outside ground with the bevel on the convex surface or outside of the blade (fig. 13–24) and the inside

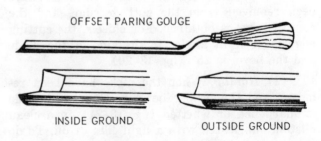

Figure 13–24. Gouges.

ground with the bevel on the concave surface or inside of the blade. Some gouges are made with an offset shank to give room for the hand when the bevel is being held parallel to the cutting surface.

a. Use. Gouges are used for wood carving, for decorating, and for shaping wood as in modeling. Special gouges are made to be used with the wood lathe to "turn" wood. Gouges are handled in the same manner as chisels. Their care and maintenance are the same except for sharpening. This process is different because of the shape of the blade.

b. Sharpening Gouges.

(1) Grinding is done only on the bevel side of the gouge. An outside bevel is ground on a regular grinding wheel but, for an inside bevel, the wheel must be fitted with a conical wheel. When grinding, the gouge is rolled both left and right so that it will be evenly ground along the bevel.

(2) Honing of an outside ground gouge is done on an oilstone. In addition to moving it around on the stone, it must be rolled again so as to whet the entire bevel. A slip stone is used on the concave side to remove the wire or burr. (Slip stones (fig. 13–25) are oilstones made in a

INDIA GOUGE SLIP

CARBORUNDUM SLIP STONE

CARVING TOOL SLIP STONES

Figure 13–25. Slip stones.

variety of sizes, shapes, and coarsenesses to fit into the hard-to-reach concave surfaces of gouges and carving tools.)

c. Stropping Gouges. Gouges are stropped in the same way as chisels.

Section VII. HANDTOOLS: CLAMPS AND VISES

13–31. General

Holding tools, to include C-clamps, hand screws, bar clamps, miter clamps, and vises are very important when assembling finished parts of a project or when holding pieces to be shaped. Knowledge of these tools and skill in their use make work easier and help to make possible a better finished product.

13–32. Clamps

As considered here, clamps are holding devices made with two parts which are brought together, usually with screws. Only those most commonly used in woodworking are included. These clamps are not fixed to a bench or a worktable.

a. C-clamp. This clamp is shaped like the letter "c" (fig. 13–26). Because of its shape, it is well adapted to clamping small pieces of wood, for applying pressure at points inaccessible to other clamps, for holding work onto the bench, and so on. It consists of a steel frame, threaded to receive an operating screw with a swivel head. C-clamps are sized according to the distance they

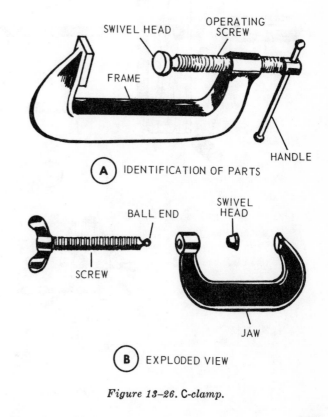

Figure 13–26. C-clamp.

will open, and this size is marked on the body of the clamp. They are available in light, medium, and heavy service.

(1) *Use.* These clamps can be used with any material. Small pieces of soft wood or heavy leather should be placed between the clamp and the work to protect the surface of the wood from clamp marks.

(2) *Care.* A well-cared-for C-clamp is clean, free from dust, and properly oiled. The swivel head must be kept clean, smooth, and grit free. If the swivel head becomes damaged, replace it in the following manner: Pry open the crimped portion of the head and remove the head from the ball end of the screw. Replace it with a new head and crimp it in place.

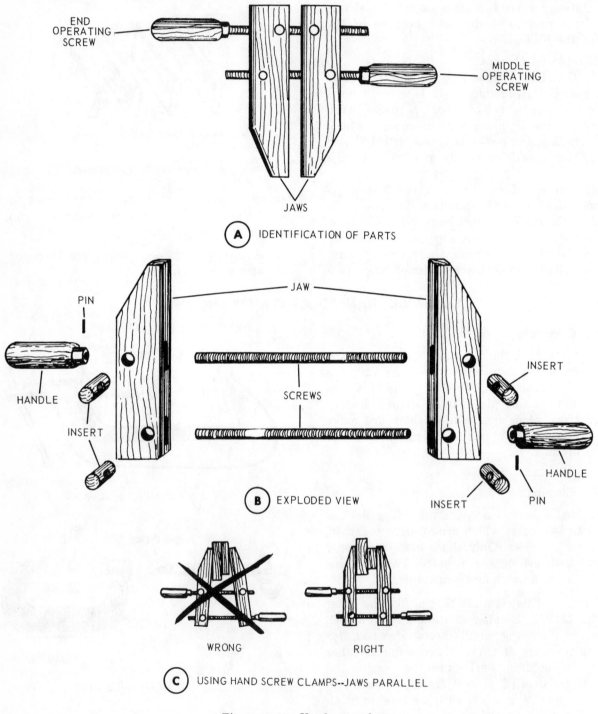

Figure 13–27. Hand screw clamp.

b. Hand Screw Clamps. This clamp (fig. 13–27) consists of two hard maple jaws with two operating screws. Each jaw has two metal inserts into which the screws are threaded. Although made only to hold wood, they are some of the most versatile of all holding tools. The jaws may be adjusted to hold a wide variety of irregularly shaped objects, as well as holding flat blocks together. They come in sizes ranging from 4-inch jaws, with a 2-inch opening to 18-inch jaws with a 14-inch opening.

(1) *Use.* It is important to have the jaws parallel to the surfaces of the work so that even pressure may be applied to all parts of the piece being clamped. To adjust the hand screw to fit, grasp a handle in each hand and revolve the operating screws together until the opening is about as large as desired. Adjust the jaws to the stock and screw the middle operating screw firmly. Adjust the end operating spindle next so that the jaws are parallel and press evenly on the stock. To remove the hand screw, release the end operating screw first, as this forces the jaws apart.

(2) *Care.* Hand pressure, rather than a wrench, should be used to tighten these hand screws. To care for the screws, keep them lightly oiled, to include a light coat of linseed oil on the jaws. If the finish of the wooden jaws is worn so that bare wood is exposed, clean and sand the jaws and coat them with varnish. Hang the clamps on racks or pins, or keep them carefully in a toolbox. The screws may become damaged, the inserts may be worn, or the wooden jaws may split or warp. When it becomes necessary to replace any of these parts, disassemble the clamp. Remove the handles from screws by filing off peened ends of attaching pins. Drive out pins. Turn both screws from the inserts and remove the inserts from the jaws. Replace damaged screws, inserts, and handles. Install inserts in jaws and turn the screws into position in the to jaws. Turn new screw into handle or old screw into new handle, depending on which part is being replaced; aline holes; and tap in a new pin. Peen end of pin to secure the screw in the handle.

c. Bar Clamps. Bar clamps (fig. 13–28) are used to glue stock which is too wide to be spanned by other clamping devices. They are used chiefly to glue edge joints in wide pieces such as table tops. They are made of steel and are available from a 2-foot to a 6-foot opening. Usually several clamps are used at one time.

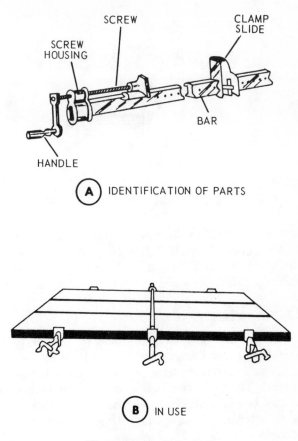

A — IDENTIFICATION OF PARTS

B — IN USE

Figure 13–28. Bar clamp.

(1) *Use.* When these clamps are used, it is wise to plan their placement before applying the glue and to protect the wood being glued with a piece of scrap wood. There is also a tendency for the boards to buckle in the clamps. This danger may be lessened by using hand screws at the end of the boards being glued as close to the screw housing as is possible.

(2) *Care.* These clamps are heavy so they tend to be thrown around and thereby damaged. They should be cleaned of matter such as glue, lightly oiled, and carefully stored where they will not fall or stick out and trip a passerby.

d. Miter and Corner Clamp. These clamps (fig. 13–29) facilitate the holding of mitered corners such as are found on picture frames. They open to 3 inches so they will accommodate most sizes of molding.

(1) *Use.* Lumber cut at a 45-degree angle is put in one clamp against another piece of lumber with a similar cut. It is advisable to work with four clamps. Each clamp holds one corner so as to speed up the gluing process.

(2) *Care.* Because these clamps are precis-

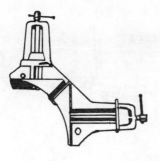

Figure 13–29. Miter clamp.

ion-cast from high-strength aluminum alloy, with plated screw threads, little care in the way of coating with oil is required. They must be kept clean of glue, however, and handled with care.

13–33. Vises

These are holding devices made to fasten to a workbench and designed to hold objects by means of two jaws which open and close as a screw is turned. The most common true woodworking vise is the bench vise. Because the machinist's vise is so often used in woodworking, it also will be considered.

a. Woodworker's Bench Vise. The woodworker's bench vise (fig. 13–30) holds lumber to be worked. It is attached to the bench so that the two top edges of the vise are flush with the top of the bench. The movable jaws may be adjusted entirely by turning the handle; or, in a more rapid method found in some vises, by setting the handle, pushing the movable jaw to approximately the correct position, and then firming it against the mark by turning the handle. These vises vary in size and weight and usually open from 9 to 12 inches.

(1) *Use.* Material to be worked on may be held between the jaws of this vise. It is wise, however, to protect it with pieces of wood from being damaged by the vise. Lumber too large to be held in the vise may be held between the vise dog (the part of the vise that can be pulled higher than the top of the bench) and the bench dog (the metal T-shaped piece that fits into holes in the bench).

(2) *Care.* The screws of the bench vise must be kept clean, free from rust, and lightly oiled.

b. Machinist's Bench Vise. This is a heavy-duty, versatile, large steel vise, with rough jaws to prevent work from slipping (fig. 13–31). The vise is bolted to the bench, where it swivels and stands about 9 inches above the bench.

(1) *Use.* Work must be flanked with wood so as to prevent marking from the rough jaws. Because of the additional height, this vise is sometimes used to hold work for patients with a shoulder injury.

(2) *Care.* This vise must be kept clean and lightly oiled after use. The screws and slide should be oiled frequently but not the swivel base of the swivel jaw joint. When the vise is not in use, the jaws should be left so that they nearly touch and the handle should be in a vertical position.

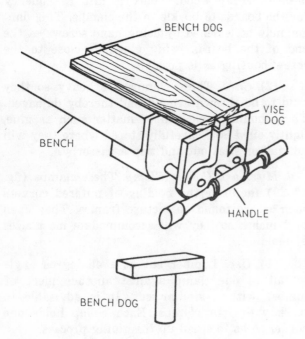

Figure 13–30. Woodworker's bench vise.

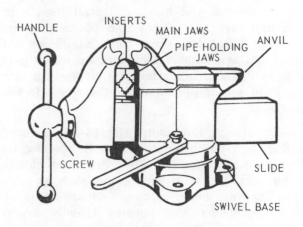

Figure 13–31. Machinist's bench vise.

13–34. General

Frequently, it becomes necessary to drill holes when working with wood. They may be pilot holes for screws, holes for insertion of saw blades, holes drilled as a part of making a joint, or holes needed for any number of reasons. Several kinds of drills and bits, each designed for a certain type of job, are used.

13–35. Types of Drills

a. Hand Drill. This is a relatively small drill (fig. 13–32) used to bore holes with a diameter of 1/4 inch or less in either wood or metal. It consists of a shaft with a handle at one end and a chuck for holding twist drills at the other. Near the middle of the shaft is a ratchet wheel with a crank handle. Turning this handle causes the shaft and the chuck to turn. Straight shank twist bits from 1/32 to 1/4 inch may be used in this drill.

(1) *Use of the chuck.* The chuck has several V-grooved fingers or jaws that hold the tang in the bit. The shank of the bit is first inserted into the chuck of the drill. To do this, open the chuck by grasping the shell and turning it to the left until the jaws are open wide enough to hold the shank of the bit. Close the chuck by turning it

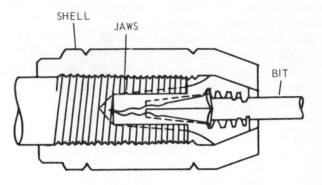

Figure 13–33. Bit inserted in chuck, cross section.

to the right until the bit is held firmly (fig. 13–33).

(2) *Use of depth gauge.* It is frequently desirable to have holes to a measured depth or to make several holes of uniform depth. This can be done by making a depth gauge to slip over a twist bit (fig. 13–34). Cut a piece of wood to a length so that the twist drill will project the desire distance when the piece of wood is bored and slipped over the drill. The piece of wood should be exactly equal to the length of the part of the drill that should not bore into the lumber.

(3) *Safety precautions.* Too much force should not be put on the head of the drill when boring with any drill. The bit might break, or it might unexpectedly go completely through the lumber and throw the operator off balance, thus causing an injury.

b. Brace. The brace is used for larger holes than can be drilled with the hand drill. It is made to take bits with round or square straight shanks up to 1/2-inch diameter, to include the screwdriver bit, twist drill, expansive bit, auger bit, and the countersink bit. It consists of a head that is fastened to the crank by a bearing that

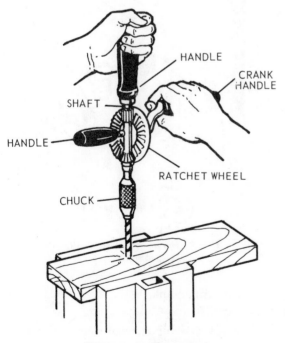

Figure 13–32. Hand drill.

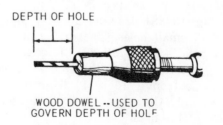

Figure 13–34. Using a twist bit and a wood dowel.

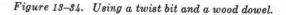

351

permits the crank to turn. The crank is a steel shaft and provides leverage. The ratchet brace (fig. 13–35) controls whether the chuck turns or not when the crank is turned. It may be set to permit the chuck to turn either forward or backward while remaining stationary as the crank is turned in the other direction. This permits holes to be bored or screws driven in places where complete turns of the crank cannot be made. It is possile to drill either vertically or horizontally with this brace (fig. 13–36).

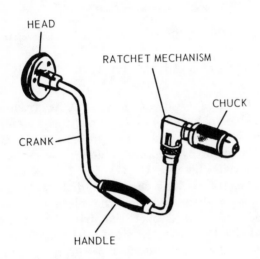

Figure 13–35. Ratchet brace.

c. Breast Drill. The breast drill (fig. 13–37) is used to drill holes in either metal or wood. It will take bits with square or straight round shanks up to 1/2 inch. This drill has a speed shift lever that can change the speed of the drill or bit at any time from high (a 3-to-1 ratio) for small holes to low (1-to-1 ratio for large holes. The center position of this speed shift lever locks the gears so that the chuck can be opened or closed. The breast plate is adjustable for greater comfort. As the operator leans against this plate, more pressure can be applied as the drill is turned. This drill can be used in either a vertical or horizontal position.

d. Automatic or Yankee Drill. The automatic drill (A, fig. 13–38) provides an easy and quick way to drill small holes. The drill can be used with one hand (B, fig. 13–38). It takes special bits which are inserted in the chuck. These bits range in size from 1/16 to 11/64 inch (C, fig. 13–38). Usually these special bits are stored in the handle of the drill.

e. Care and Maintenance of Drills. The follow-

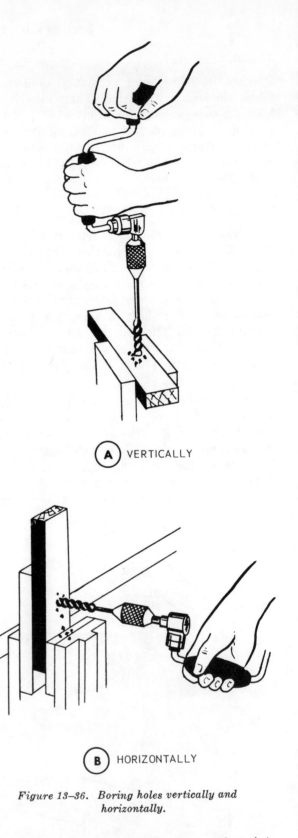

Ⓐ VERTICALLY

Ⓑ HORIZONTALLY

Figure 13–36. Boring holes vertically and horizontally.

ing rules are important in the care and maintenance of a drill:

(1) Insert the bit carefully into the chuck so that it is straight. Tighten it firmly so there

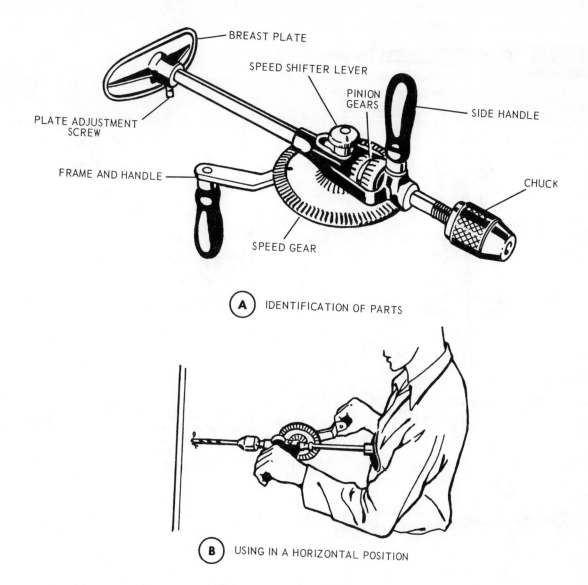

BREAST PLATE

SPEED SHIFTER LEVER

PINION GEARS

SIDE HANDLE

PLATE ADJUSTMENT SCREW

FRAME AND HANDLE

CHUCK

SPEED GEAR

A IDENTIFICATION OF PARTS

B USING IN A HORIZONTAL POSITION

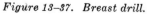

Figure 13–37. Breast drill.

is no "play" to strain the jaws or to break the bit.

(2) Keep the drill lubricated at all times. Apply light oil to the handle bearings, ratchet mechanism, and the shell and jaw mechanism of the ratchet. Use a general purpose grease to lubricate the head bearings. Use light oil on the gear and pinion teeth of the breast drill.

(3) Insure that assembly screws are tight at all times.

(4) For short periods of storage, apply a film of light oil to all metal surfaces and store the drill in a safe, dry place.

13–36. Types of Bits

a. *Twist Bit and Drill.* Twist bits or drills

(fig. 13–39) are boring tools used for boring smaller holes than are possible with any other bit. They range from 1/32 inch to 1/2 inch in diameter and are sized by thirty-seconds and sixty-fourths of an inch. The size of the bit is stamped on the shank. They can be used to bore either wood or metal. Twist bits with a straight shank (A, fig. 13–39) are used in the hand drill or in th drill press. (In the drill press, it is advisable to use high speed drills rather than the carbon drills.) The twist bits with the square shank (B, fig. 13–39) are designed to be used only with the brace or the breast drills. Both types of twist bits or drills may be purchased singly or in sets of the most commonly used sizes.

(1) *Use.* To use, first insert the shank of the

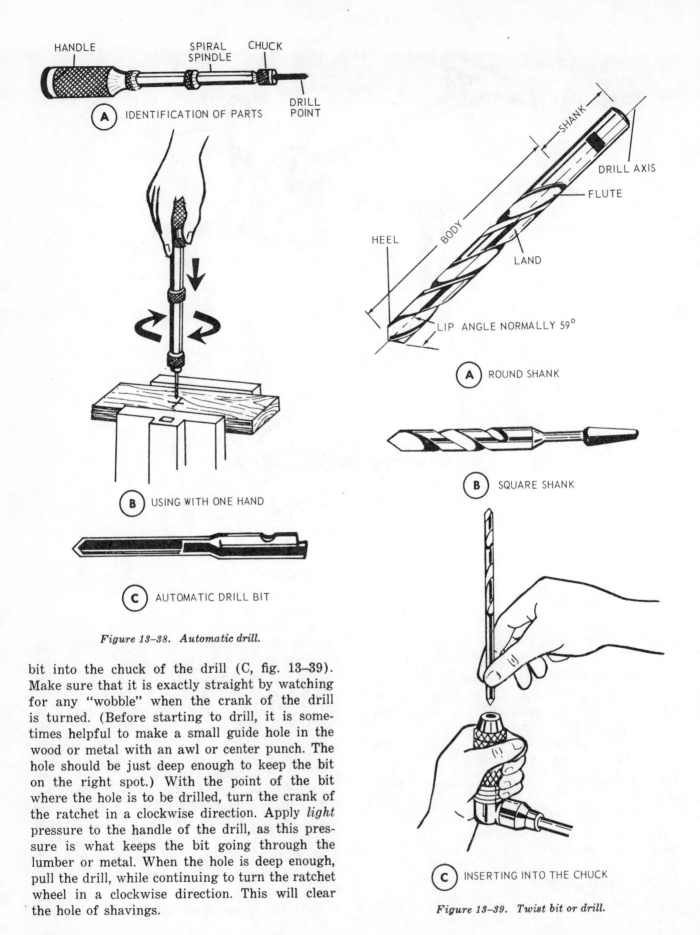

A IDENTIFICATION OF PARTS

HANDLE SPIRAL SPINDLE CHUCK

DRILL POINT

B USING WITH ONE HAND

C AUTOMATIC DRILL BIT

Figure 13-38. Automatic drill.

SHANK

DRILL AXIS

FLUTE

HEEL BODY LAND

LIP ANGLE NORMALLY 59°

A ROUND SHANK

B SQUARE SHANK

C INSERTING INTO THE CHUCK

Figure 13-39. Twist bit or drill.

bit into the chuck of the drill (C, fig. 13-39). Make sure that it is exactly straight by watching for any "wobble" when the crank of the drill is turned. (Before starting to drill, it is sometimes helpful to make a small guide hole in the wood or metal with an awl or center punch. The hole should be just deep enough to keep the bit on the right spot.) With the point of the bit where the hole is to be drilled, turn the crank of the ratchet in a clockwise direction. Apply *light* pressure to the handle of the drill, as this pressure is what keeps the bit going through the lumber or metal. When the hole is deep enough, pull the drill, while continuing to turn the ratchet wheel in a clockwise direction. This will clear the hole of shavings.

(2) *Care and maintenance.* Keep bits oiled and protected from striking any metal object. This is done by keeping them wrapped in a piece of cloth or by standing them in a block of wood or in a drill index (fig. 13–40). These drills can also be sharpened, a worthwhile procedure especially with larger bits, on the grinding wheel (fig. 13–41). First, grind the tip to the proper angle. Both cutting edges must make the same angle with the axis and both must be of the same length. The angle of the heel and that of the lip differ, and the angle changes gradually along the point between the heel and the lip. To obtain this gradual angle, start grinding with the heel of the drill bit against the wheel and gradually raise the shank end of the bit as it is twisted in a clockwise direction toward the lip. Use only enough pressure to hold the bit against the wheel without overheating, which will cause loss of temper. Dipping the drill frequently into cold water while grinding will also avoid overheating.

b. Auger Bits. An auger bit (fig. 13–42) has a square tang and is used in a brace or a breast drill. These bits are exclusively for boring holes in wood. They vary in length from 7 to 10 inches

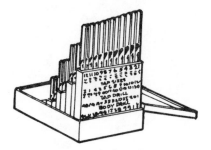

Figure 13–40. Drill index with drills.

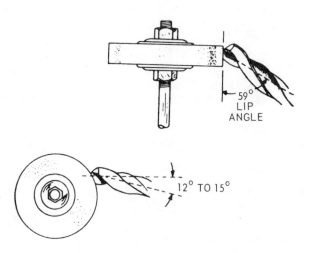

Figure 13–41. Sharpening a twist drill.

and graduate from 1/8 inch to 1 1/8 inch in diameter by sixteenths of an inch. The size of the diameter of the bit is indicated on the square tang by a single number. This number indicates the sixteenth of an inch. For instance, No. 4 is 4/16 or 1/8 inch, No. 5 is 5/16 inch, and No. 6 is 6/16 or 3/8 inch.

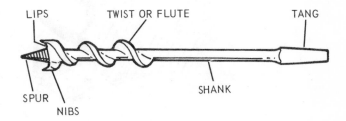

Figure 13–42. Auger bit.

(1) *Use.* Insert the tang of the bit into the chuck of the brace as far as possible. Put the point of the spur at the exact center of the spot where the hole is to be bored. Turn the crank of the brace or the handle of the breast drill and apply only enough pressure to assist the spur in drawing the bit into the wood. (As the spur draws the bit down, first the nibs cut the fibers of wood at the side of the hole, then the lips chip the wood out to make a hole.) When the hole is the desired depth, back the bit out by turning the crank or handle in the opposite direction until the spur is free from the bottom of the hole. Withdraw the bit the rest of the way, turning it in the direction that it entered in order to remove the shavings from the hole. When a hole is bored completely through a board with an auger bit, the board will split on the side away from the bit when the bit is forced all the way through (A, fig. 13–43). There are two ways to prevent this splitting—

(*a*) Pull the bit out of the wood when the tip of the spur begins to show through the board. Insert the spur on the opposite side at the spot where it began to come through the board and complete the hole (B, fig. 13–43).

(*b*) Clamp a piece of scrap wood very tightly to the under side of the piece being bored. Take care to prevent the good lumber from being marked by the clamps. This method of preventing the wood from spiltting when boring through a piece of wood with an auger bit is shown in C, figure 13–43.

(2) *Maintenance and care of auger bits.* Be sure that the bit will not hit any dirt or metal

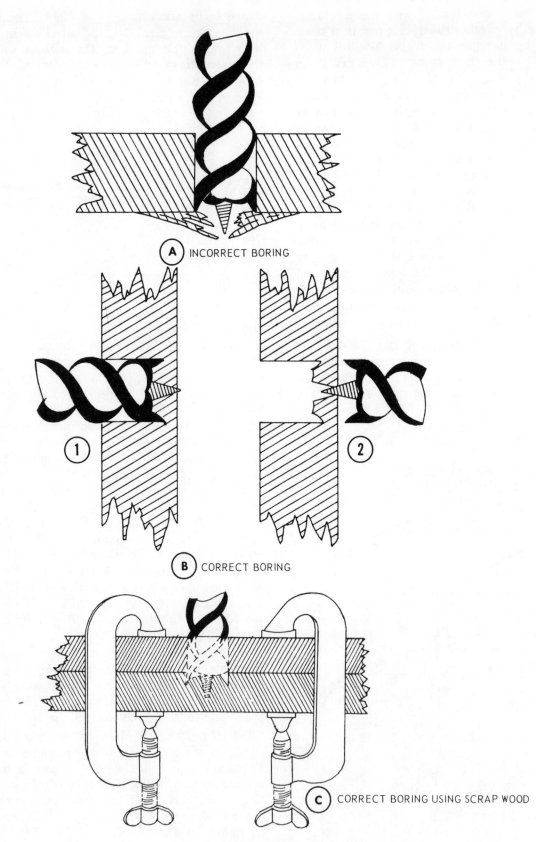

A INCORRECT BORING

1

2

B CORRECT BORING

C CORRECT BORING USING SCRAP WOOD

Figure 13–43. Use of an auger bit.

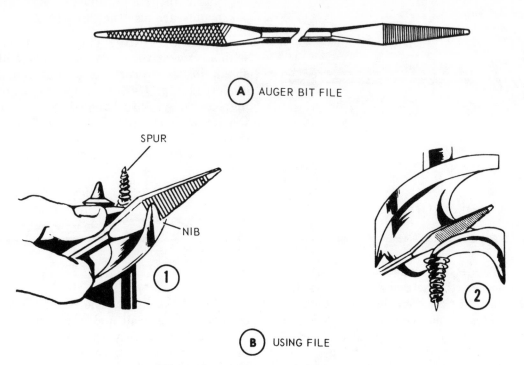

A AUGER BIT FILE

SPUR

NIB

1

2

B USING FILE

Figure 13-44. Sharpening the auger bit.

such as nails as it goes through the wood. Keep the bits cleaned, oiled, and stored so that they do not rub against each other. Use an auger bit file to sharpen the auger bit (A, fig. 13-44). Place the bit with the spur end up against the side of the bench. File the inside of the nib, carefully keeping the original bend. File lightly until a fine burr shows on the outside of the nib, then carefully remove this with a light stroke of the file. Never sharpen the outside of the nib. Be sure that both nibs are the same length (B①, fig. 13-44). Sharpen the top side of the lips by placing the bit, spur side down, on the edge of the bench. Do not file the underside of the lips (B②, fig. 13-44). If the spur needs sharpening, which is rare, carefully file the threads to restore their original shape.

c. Forstner Bit. The forstner bit (fig. 13-45) is used to bore holes nearly all the way through a piece of wood without splitting the other side. It can be used to clean out the rough bottom of a hole made by an auger bit or to bore a large hole where a small one was. It cuts end grain and knots very well and is used to make a hole in thin stock. The average set of forstner bits ranges from 1/4 to 1 inch in diameter. The forstner is very similar to the auger bit in several ways. It may have a square shank so that it can

be used in a brace or in a breast drill; it is used exclusively in wood; and it is marked in the same way as auger bits. Its difference lies in the fact that it is made with a 1/2-inch straight round shank to be used in a drill press. There is no spur, so the rim is used for centering. To center with the rim, make a circle on the wood with the dividers for guiding the lips of the bit. Cut the wood then by these lips.

d. Expansion Bit. This is an auger-type bit (fig. 13-46). Because of the adjustable cutting blades, it takes the place of several large auger bits. There are usually two interchangeable cutting blades. The smaller cuts holes from 7/8 inch to 1 1/2 inch and the larger from 1 1/2 to 3 inches

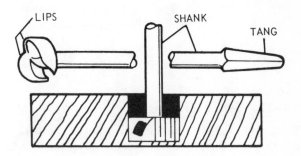

LIPS   SHANK   TANG

Figure 13-45. Forstner bit.

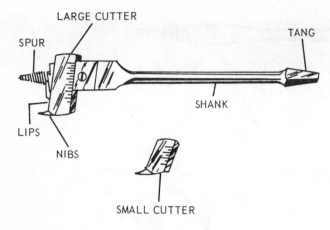

Figure 13–46. Expansion bit and extra cutter.

in diameter. To set the expansion bit with a screwdriver, loosen the setscrew and slide the cutter to the desired size, then tighten the screw. Read the diameter of the hole from the marked scale on the balde. By moving the cutter 1/32 of an inch, the diameter of the hole is changed 1/16 inch. It is always advisable to test the size of the hole by boring a test hole in a piece of waste wood. Splitting the wood when using this bit can be prevented in the same way as when using

the auger bit (*b*(1) above). Maintenance and sharpening are also the same (*b*(2) above).

e. Screwdriver Bit. This is a specialized bit with a screwdriver blade on one end and a square shank to fit a brace or a breast drill on the other end (fig. 13–47). Use it to facilitate driving screws. As with handled screwdrivers, select the bit with the blade tip that fills the slot of the screw.

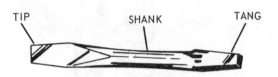

Figure 13–47. Screwdriver bit.

f. Countersink Bit. The countersink bit has a conical cutting head and a square shank. Use it in a brace or a breast drill to form the top of the pilot hole for a screw so that the flathead of the screw will be flush with the surface of the wood. The rose type (fig. 13–48) is the most commonly used and may be used on both wood and soft metals.

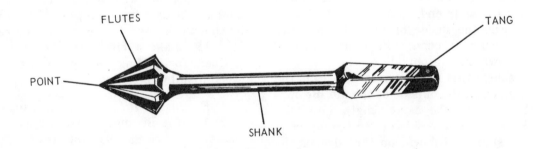

Figure 13–48. Countersink bit.

Section IX. HANDTOOLS: FILES

13–38. Types of Files

Files (fig. 13–49) are classified and named according to their length, shape, cut, and coarseness.

a. Length. Files range from 4 to 14 inches

in length, which is measured from the point to the heel. The tang is not included.

b. Shape. Most files fall into one of the four following shapes, which can be either tapered or blunt in overall shape (fig. 13–50).

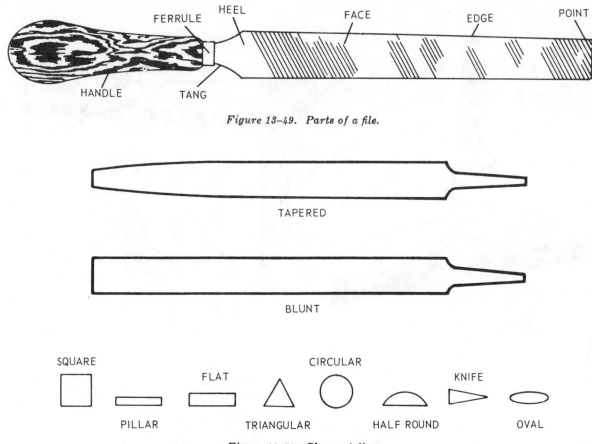

Figure 13-49. Parts of a file.

TAPERED

BLUNT

Figure 13-50. Shape of files.

(1) *Quadrangular.*

(*a*) *Square.* Used mainly for filing slots and keyways.

(*b*) *Pillar.* Used for filing where one side of the work is not to be filed. Usually has one smooth edge.

(*c*) *Flat.* Used for general purposes.

(2) *Triangular or three-square.* Used for filing internal angles and for cleaning out square corners.

(3) *Circular.*

(*a*) *Round.* Used for circular openings and curved surfaces.

(*b*) *Half-round.* May be used for filing

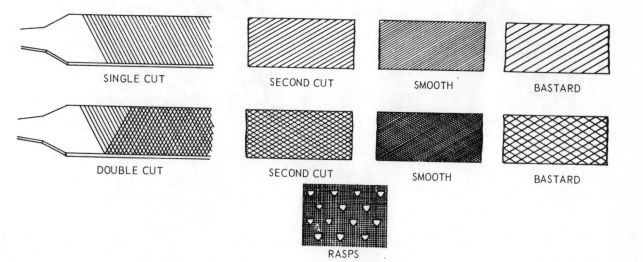

Figure 13-51. Cut of files.

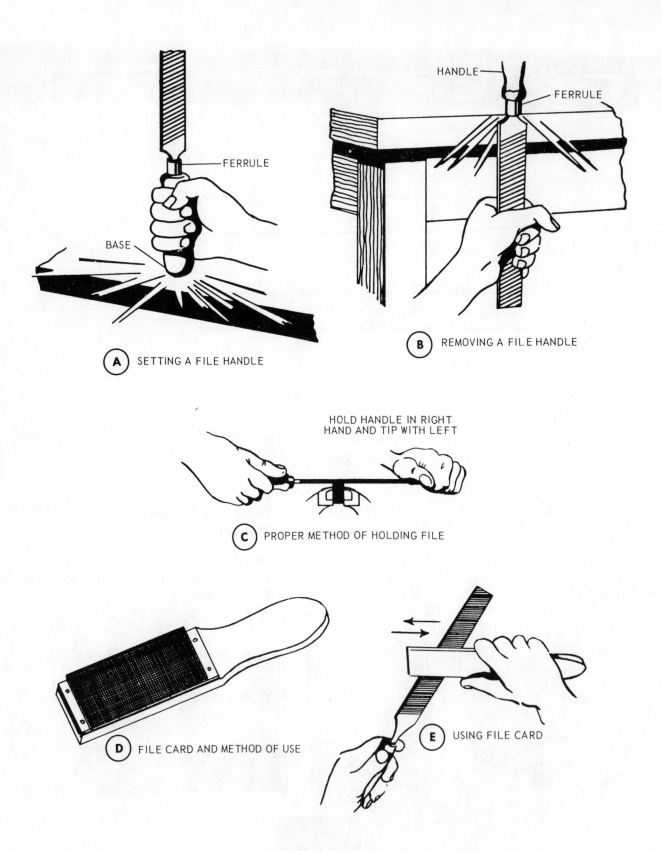

A — SETTING A FILE HANDLE

FERRULE

BASE

HANDLE

FERRULE

B — REMOVING A FILE HANDLE

HOLD HANDLE IN RIGHT
HAND AND TIP WITH LEFT

C — PROPER METHOD OF HOLDING FILE

D — FILE CARD AND METHOD OF USE

E — USING FILE CARD

Figure 13–52. Use and care of file.

either flat or curved surfaces. Also a good general purpose file.

    (4) *Miscellaneous.*

        (a) *Knife.* Used for work on acute angles.

        (b) *Oval.* Used for filing curved surfaces.

    c. Cut. Cut refers to the characteristics of the file teeth or to the way the file is cut (fig. 13–51). There are three common types—

    (1) Single-cut files are used where a smooth surface is desired.

    (2) Double-cut files are used for faster removal of material than is obtained from the single file. However, it does not leave as smooth a surface.

    (3) Rasps are used on wood and soft substances for the fast removal and shaping of the material.

    d. Coarseness. Coarseness is graded as follows:

    (1) Smooth.

    (2) Second cut.

    (3) Bastard cut.

13–39. Use of Files

In woodworking, files are used only if some other cutting tool cannot be used to better advantage.

    a. Selection of the file to use is made with consideration of the amount of material to be removed and the desired condition of the surface. It is sometimes expedient to start the work with a coarse, double-cut file and then remove the resulting roughness with a smoother single-cut file.

    b. It is important to protect the hand from the tang of the file with a handle. To put the handle on, slip the handle over the tang of the file, hold the file up, then strike the base of the handle sharply to set the tang. To remove the file from the handle, hold the file with one hand and the handle with the other. Pull the file from the handle while striking the ferrule end of the handle against the edge of a bench (A and B, fig. 13–52).

    c. The work to be filed must be held securely either in a vise or by some other means, for the file is held in both hands, the handle in the right hand and the point end in the left (C, fig. 13–52).

    d. The file is pushed at a slight angle, then lifted from the work, and brought back to the starting position.

    e. Files are made to cut only on the forward stroke. Pulling the file while it is on the work only dulls the teeth.

    f. The person using the file should stand over the work to prevent vibration, which causes excess noise and cuts efficiency.

    g. To counteract the tendency of the file to ride down on the corners, the pressure on the file must be lightened at the beginning and at the end of each stroke.

    h. The file must be held level in order to get a level edge.

13–40. Maintenance and Care of Files

    a. New files should be broken in by first using them on a soft material such as wood.

    b. To prevent the teeth from becoming clogged or "pinned," chalk can be rubbed on the file or the angle of filing can be changed after each 10 or 15 strokes. When the teeth do become clogged, a wire brush, called a file card (D and E, fig. 13–52), is used to clean them. Small pieces that cannot be removed with the file card should be picked out of the teeth with a pin or a sharp nail.

    c. Files should be kept in racks or placed upright in a row of holes bored into the tool rack. If they are kept where they can rub or bump against other tools, they will become dull.

    d. Despite the fact that files are made of steel, they must be kept clean of oils and lubricants.

13–41. Safety Precautions

    a. Always use a handle on all files except Swiss, needle, and auger bit files. If a commercial handle is not available, protect the hand from the point of the tang by driving the tang into a block of soft wood or similar material.

    b. Use a file card to clean the file, rather than striking it against a hard object to knock the material from between the teeth. Files are brittle and may break.

    c. Do not use too much pressure when filing as the brittle files may break and cause injury.

13–42. General

Hammers are some of the most used and perhaps some of the most misused tools of all handtools. An understanding of the types and the uses for which they were designed will increase the effectiveness of the hammer. Two types of hammers are most commonly used in woodworking.

13–43. Carpenter's Hammer

Hammers are sized by the weight of the head; the most common are 12, 16, and 20 ounces. While the 16 ounce is the best for general use, the purchase of other weights may be indicated for an occupational therapy clinic in order to grade the amount of resistance for the patient. The carpenter's hammer or claw hammer (fig. 13–53) is the most commonly used tool for driving nails. It has a steel head with a wooden handle. The face of the head is used to drive nails and the claw is used to pull nails out of the wood. There are two types of carpenter's hammers—

a. The plain-faced claw hammer has a flat face. It is easier for the beginner to learn to drive nails with this hammer, but it is more difficult to drive the head of the nail flush with the surface of the wood without leaving hammer marks.

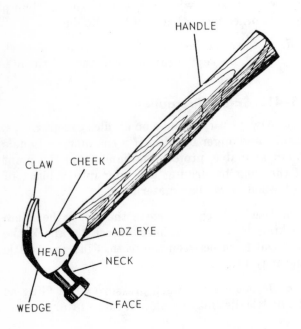

Figure 13–53. Carpenter's hammer.

b. The face of the ball-faced hammer is slightly rounded or convex. It is generally used in rough work. An expert can use it to drive a nail flush with the surface of the work without damaging the wood.

(1) *Driving nails.* For information on driving nails, see paragraph 13–17*b.*

(2) *Care of the hammer.*

(*a*) *Replacement of a handle.* For safety and efficiency, the hammer handle (A, fig. 13–54) should be replaced or tightened immediately when it becomes loose. When it loosens, set it by striking the end of the handle with a mallet, thereby driving the wedges back into the handle (B, fig. 13–54). These wedges may be of metal or of straight-grained soft wood.

CAUTION

Nails or screws should not be used in place of wedges.

If the handle is broken, remove it from the head, seat a new handle, and replace the old wedges. If it is difficult to remove the old handle, saw it off close to the head and drive it through the larger end of the eye.

(*b*) *Care of the face.* The face of a hammer should be kept clean and smooth. This usually can be done by rubbing it with emery cloth. If it becomes necessary to grind the surface to restore it, take notice if it is a ball or plain face and grind it to the proper shape. Dip the hammer head in water often, in order to prevent burning and loss of temper while grinding. Do not grind the face oftener, or remove more material, than is necessary to restore the surface.

(3) *Safety precautions.* As with other tools, hammers must also be used in a safe way. Before using a hammer, see that the handle is secure to the head, lest the head fly off during use. In addition, always get the fingers of the other hand out of the way before striking with force.

13–44. Tack Hammer

Tack hammers are available in 5- and 7-ounce sizes. The 7-ounce, double-faced hammer, with one face magnetic, is preferred for upholstering work. Usually one end of the tack hammer (fig. 13-55) is magnetized, which helps pick up a tack. With the head of the tack against

WOODEN WEDGE METAL WEDGE

SAWING OFF PROJECTING
END OF HANDLE

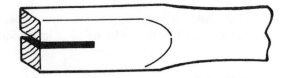

MAKE SAW CUT IN END OF HANDLE
FOR WOODEN WEDGE

WEDGE

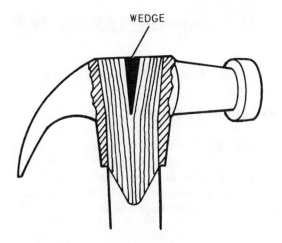

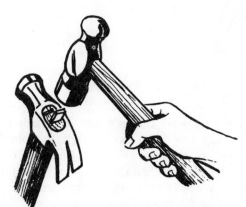

DRIVING WEDGE

WEDGE EXPANDS
HANDLE IN HEAD

(A) HAMMER HANDLE

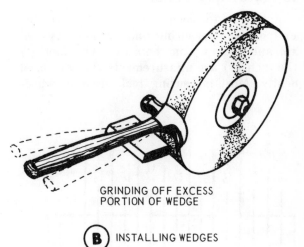 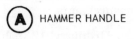

GRINDING OFF EXCESS
PORTION OF WEDGE

(B) INSTALLING WEDGES

Figure 13-54. Wedges.

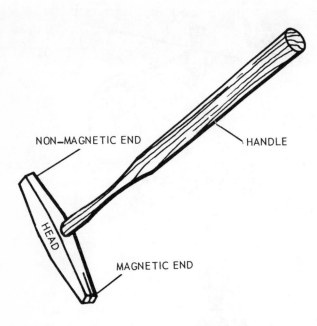

HEAD

MAGNETIC END

Figure 13-55. Tack hammer.

the magnetic face of the hammer, the tack can be tapped into the wood far enough to hold it. The hammer is then turned over and the non-magnetic side of the hammer is used to pound the tack in place. Care and safety precautions are the same as for the carpenter's hammers.

13–45. Nail Set

In finer work, it is often desirable to have the head of the nail below the surface of the wood. Sinking a brad or a finishing nail is done with a nail set. It is a round knurled steel shaft 4 to 5 inches long and about 1/4 inch in diameter, with a tapered point. The point is cup-shaped to keep it from slipping off the nailhead. The points vary in size from 1/32 to 1/8 inch across the cup and should not be larger than the diameter of the nail being set. The nail set is placed on the nailhead, held in a line with the nail, and rapped with a hammer until the nail is the desired distance below the surface of the wood (fig. 13–56).

NOTE
The holes where the nails have been can be filled with putty or plastic wood.

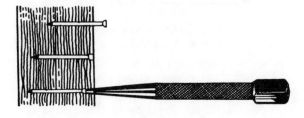

Figure 13-56. Using a nail set.

Section XI. HANDTOOLS: MEASURING DEVICES

13–46. Measuring Device

Important aids to good woodworking are the proper tools for measuring and marking as well as skill and accuracy in their use. The foot (') and the inch (") are measurements that are used frequently. Most measuring tools used in wood-

working are divided into inches and halves, quarters, eights, and sixteenths of an inch (fig. 13–57). If the finished product is to turn out as planned, measurements must be accurately made, then checked against errors.

13–47. Types of Measuring Devices

Use of the correct measuring device for the job to be done will be of great help in making accurate measurements.

    a. Ruler. Ordinary 12-inch, 18-inch, or 2-foot rulers are used for measuring small projects, as they are more manageable than the larger rules. These may be made of wood, plastic, or steel.

    b. Folding or Zigzag Rule. This rule unfolds to 6 feet in length. It is made of wood or lightweight metal and folds so that it can be easily carried or stored. This rule is used in measuring long distances where slight variations in measurement are not important. It is easily bent or

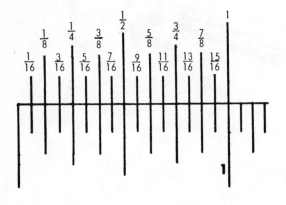

Figure 13-57. Divisions of an inch.

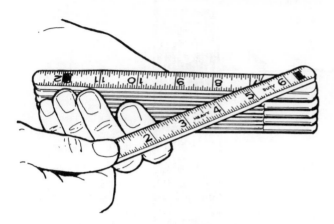

Figure 13-58. Folding rule.

broken, particularly when it is being opened. Figure 13-58 shows the proper method of opening it. When not in use, it should be folded up and put away to prevent damage to it.

c. *Steel Tape.* The steel tape (fig. 13-59) is a ribbon of steel 3/8 inch wide and graduated in feet, inches, and fractions of an inch. These tapes are available in 6-, 8-, 10-, 12-, 50-, and 100-foot lengths and are used for measuring longer distances than is convenient with a folding rule. The tape is fixed to a reel and is housed in a case into which it retracts either automatically by a spring or by manually winding it back with a folding handle on the case. A small ring or chip of metal is attached to the end of the tape so that it can be easily held or made fast to a stationary object. This makes it unnecessary to have someone hold the end in position while a measurement is being taken. The tape should be returned to its housing immediately after use in order to prevent kinking. Care must also be taken to keep the tape from kinking when measuring around corners or when it becomes twisted. If the tape is of uncoated steel, care must be exercised to prevent rust. If it is used in damp or wet areas, it must be thoroughly dried and lightly oiled before reeling it back into its housing.

d. *Steel or Carpenter's Square.* This is an all-steel, L-shaped tool consisting of two arms: the longer one, the blade, and the shorter, the tongue. These blades meet at a right angle, called the heel. The blade and tongue are marked into inches and fractions thereof. Squares come in different sizes for marking on different sizes of stock. To use the square, the blade is held along the edge of the board with the tongue across the face of the board, then a line is made along the tongue (fig. 13-60). If this is done correctly, the line will be at a right angle with the edge of the board. The square can be used to measure, to test for squareness, and to check for warping of the board. Squares are usually made of steel, so they must be kept lightly oiled to prevent rusting. However, they will sometimes rust from the humidity in the air; when this happens, the markings become hard to read. It may be

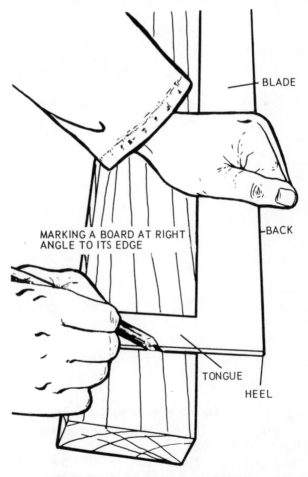

BLADE

BACK

MARKING A BOARD AT RIGHT ANGLE TO ITS EDGE

TONGUE

HEEL

Figure 13-60. Using a carpenter's square.

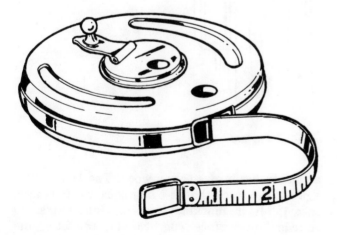

Figure 13-59. Steel tape.

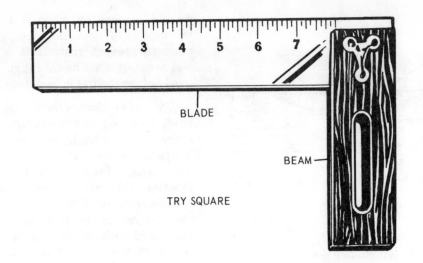

BLADE

BEAM

TRY SQUARE

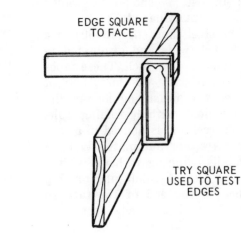

TRY SQUARE
USED AS A GUIDE
FOR MARKING ACROSS
SMALL LUMBER

EDGE SQUARE
TO FACE

TRY SQUARE
USED TO TEST
EDGES

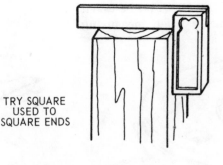

TRY SQUARE
USED TO
SQUARE ENDS

Figure 13–61. The try square and its use.

cleaned by rubbing it lightly with fine steel wool or emery cloth. It must then be protected with a light coating of oil.

e. Try Square. The try square is composed of a steel graduated blade set at a right angle in a thicker beam of steel or wood. The beam butts against the stock that is being squared. It is used as a guide in marking lines at right angles to an edge or surface (fig. 13–61), to determine if a board is the same thickness throughout its length, and to test an edge or surface for squareness. Both the blade and the handle should be kept lightly oiled to prevent rusting. Oil on the wooden handle will keep it from drying out. The handle and blade may work loose from one another and thereby lose squareness. To test for this, place the handle against the edge of a straight board and make a mark along the blade. Turn the square over and see if the blade rests on the same mark. If it does not, the angle between the two marks made by the blade is twice the amount the square is in error. To correct, loosen the screws by which the handle is fastened to

the blade and adjust the blade until it tests correctly.

f. Sliding T-bevel. The bevel square (A, fig. 13–62), as it is sometimes called, is composed of a steel blade from 6 to 12 inches long with a 45-degree bevel point at one end. The other end is fitted into a slotted wooden or metal beam or handle and is held in place by means of a thumbscrew. With this thumbscrew, it can be set at any desired angle (B, fig. 13–62). It can be used to transfer angles from one piece of lumber to another (C, fig. 13–62) or to test bevels (D, fig. 13–62). The T-bevel is cared for in the

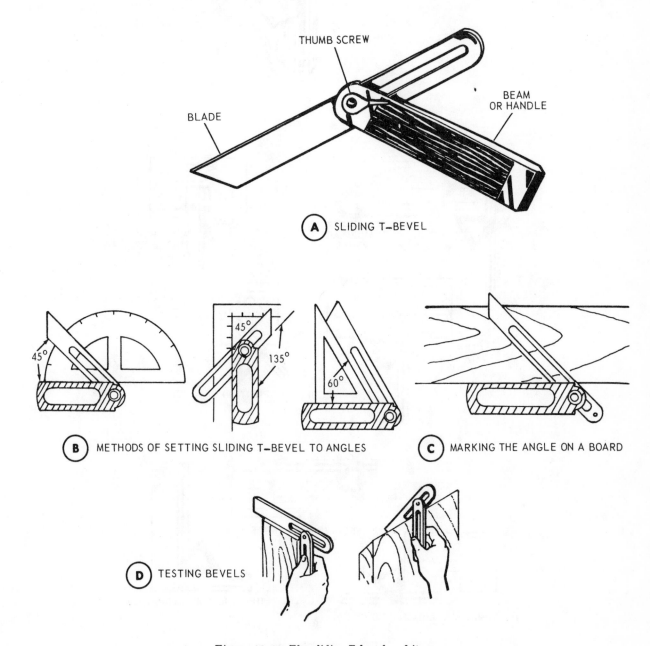

Figure 13–62. The sliding T-bevel and its uses.

same way as the try square. When not in use, the blade should be fixed into the handle with the thumbscrew.

g. *Combination Square.* The combination square (fig. 13–63) is a steel graduated blade from 6 to 24 inches long. It is grooved along the entire length of one side. The blade is fitted to a metal head, which can be clamped at any distance along the blade. This head has machined edges which are at 90-degree and at 45-degree angles to the blade. The head is fitted with a level vial and a steel scriber is set into the end of the head opposite to the blade. The head is clamped securely in any position along the blade with the

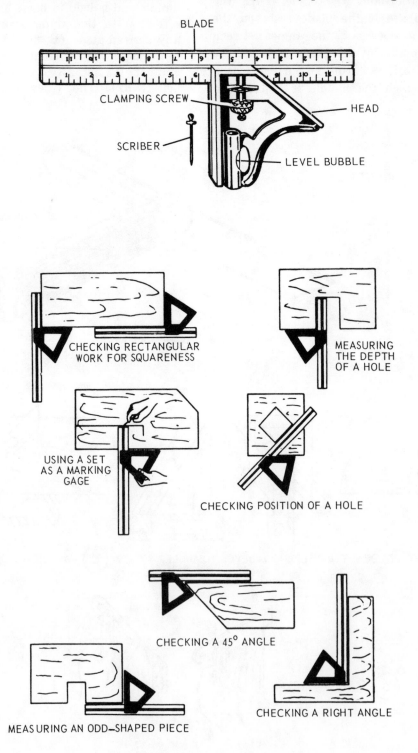

Figure 13–63. The combination square and its uses.

clamping screw. It can be used as a try square, as a depth gauge, or as a marking gauge. It can also be used to check 45-degree angles and to test for level. The combination square is cared for in the same way as the carpenter's square. However, it is a more precise instrument which must be handled with care.

h. Marking Guage. The marking gauge is used to mark a line parallel to an edge or end of a piece of wood. (A light line is preferable to a deep one. If the line is not plain, a light pencil mark is put on the gauge line.) It is made of wood or metal and it may have a roller instead of the pin indicated in A, figure 13–64. The beam is graduated but, for accurate marking, it is best to measure with a ruler the distance from the pin or spur to the head and then set the head, by means of the thumbscrew, at the desired distance from the pin (B, fig. 13–64). When the marking gauge is used, the pin should project 1/16 inch.

i. Dividers. Dividers (A, fig. 13–65) consist of

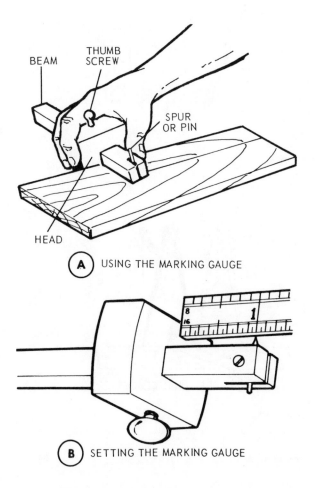

A USING THE MARKING GAUGE

B SETTING THE MARKING GAUGE

Figure 13–64. Using the marking gauge.

a pair of pointed legs, joined together at or near the top. The wing in a wing divider is an arc used to hold the legs apart at any desired distance by means of a setscrew. At one end of the wing is an adjusting screw and spring that permits fine setting of the legs. Dividers are used to describe circles or arcs; to transfer measurements from the work to the rule, or from the rule to the work; or to mark lengths into equal parts (B, fig. 13–65). Dividers must be treated like any other sharp instrument. They must not be left lying around where they might be brushed off and fall on someone or where someone might brush against the sharp points. They must not be carried in the pocket but should be placed flat in the toolbox or hung on a toolboard when not in use. The points of dividers may be kept sharp by rotating them against an oilstone. If they are badly dulled or bent, they may be ground by rotating them against a grinding machine. If this is done, care must be taken to prevent loss of temper of the metal and to keep the legs of even length. Because they are made of steel, they should be kept lightly oiled. When not in use, the setscrew should be set lightly to prevent damage to the arc or to the legs of the dividers if they should fall.

j. Carpenter's Level. The carpenter's level (fig. 13–66) is a 24-inch woodblock with true surface edges. It is used to determine whether a surface is level or if an upright is plumb. It has two bubble tubes. The one in the middle of one of the long edges indicates levelness of a surface. It is level if the bubble comes to rest exactly between the two scratch marks on the bubble tube. The other bubble tube is at right angle to the first one and indicates vertical level or "plumb." The level should be handled with care, as the bubble tubes break easily. It should also be rubbed with a light rubbing oil to prevent drying of the wood.

k. Contour Gauge. The contour gauge (fig. 13–67) or template former outlines any shape. To use it, press the steel teeth against an irregular surface, slip it away, and trace either the male or female template of the irregular contour onto paper, tile linoleum, or any surface. The gauge is 6 inches long but two or three can be joined to make a 12- or 18-inch tool for wider areas.

NOTE

Contour gauges are not available through normal supply channels at present.

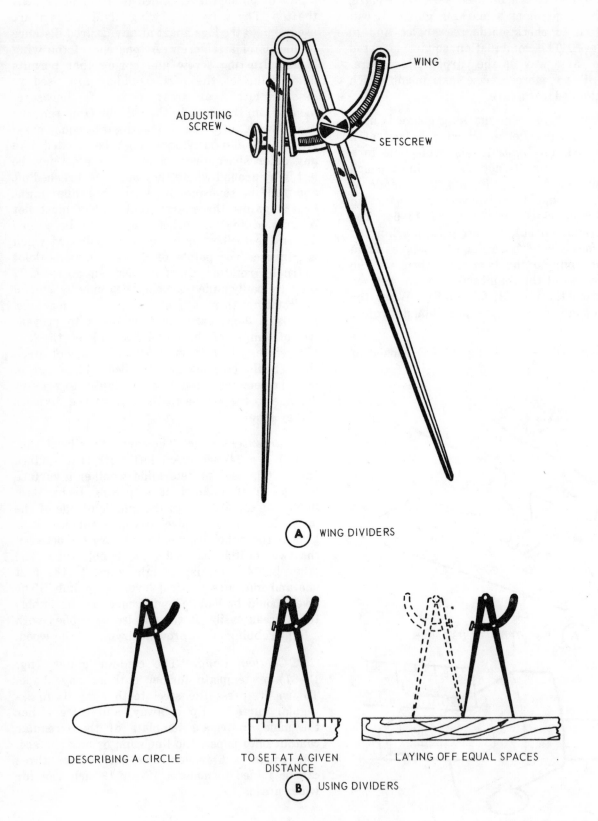

WING

ADJUSTING
SCREW

SETSCREW

A WING DIVIDERS

DESCRIBING A CIRCLE

TO SET AT A GIVEN
DISTANCE

LAYING OFF EQUAL SPACES

B USING DIVIDERS

Figure 13–65. Dividers and uses.

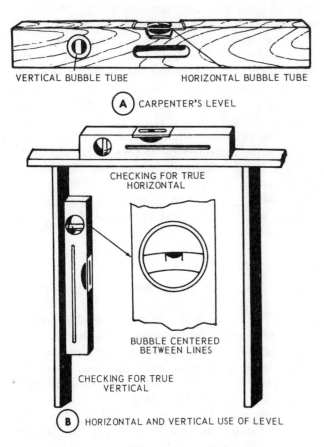

Figure 13–66. Carpenter's level and its uses.

VERTICAL BUBBLE TUBE   HORIZONTAL BUBBLE TUBE

A CARPENTER'S LEVEL

CHECKING FOR TRUE
HORIZONTAL

BUBBLE CENTERED
BETWEEN LINES

CHECKING FOR TRUE
VERTICAL

B HORIZONTAL AND VERTICAL USE OF LEVEL

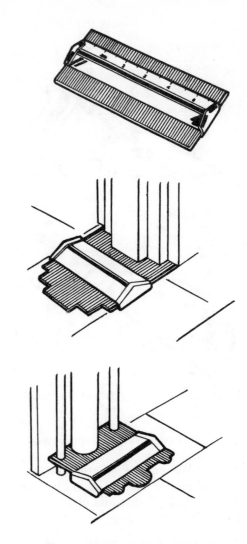

Figure 13–67. Contour gauge.

Section XII. HANDTOOLS: PLANES

13–48. General

A plane is used to smooth boards; to remove relatively small amounts of wood from the surface or edge of a board, thereby obtaining the desired thickness or width; or to "true" or square a board. There are a number of different kinds of planes which fall mainly into two general types: bench planes and block planes (fig. 13–68). These two types are similar in general construction, method of operation, and care. However, because each is designed for a specific job, the size, shape of blade, and finer points of construction vary (table 13–7).

13–49. Bench Plane

The bench plane (fig. 13–68) is designed, as its

name implies, for use while the work is held on the workbench. It is used primarily for shaving and smoothing with the grain of the wood. For this purpose, the bevel of the cutting edge of the blade is turned down. There are four sizes of bench planes—

a. Jointer Plane. The largest bench plane, 18 to 24 inches long, with blades 2 3/8 to 2 5/8 inches wide. Because of its length, it rides across small hollows or depressions in the work without cutting. It is therefore used to "true" edges or surfaces of boards.

b. Jack Plane. Similar to the jointer, 11 1/2 to 15 inches long, with blades 1 3/4 to 2 3/8 inches wide. It can be used for the same type of work as the jointer plane, but on narrower lumber. Be-

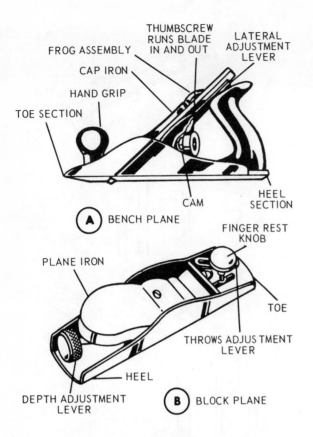

FROG ASSEMBLY

THUMBSCREW
RUNS BLADE
IN AND OUT

LATERAL
ADJUSTMENT
LEVER

CAP IRON

HAND GRIP

TOE SECTION

CAM

HEEL
SECTION

Ⓐ BENCH PLANE

PLANE IRON

FINGER REST
KNOB

TOE

THROWS ADJUSTMENT
LEVER

HEEL

DEPTH ADJUSTMENT
LEVER

Ⓑ BLOCK PLANE

Figure 13–68. Bench and block planes.

cause it is between the jointer plane and the smoothing plane in size, it may be used as a substitute for both if just one plane is to be purchased.

c. Junior Jack Plane. Smaller than the jack plane, 10 to 11 1/2 inches long, with blades about 1 3/4 inch wide. It is lighter in weight and therefore easier to handle than the jack plane.

d. Smoothing Plane. The smallest of the bench planes, 5 1/2 to 10 inches long, with blades 1 1/4 to 2 3/8 inches wide, Unlike the other bench planes, it is not used to true a board, but rather to smooth rough surfaces. Because of this, the cutting edge of the blade is shaped like that of the block plane.

13–50. Use of the Bench Plane

To plane a piece of wood with a bench plane, clamp the piece of wood securely, then grasp the plane with the left hand on the knob and the right hand on the handle (fig. 13–69). To keep the board even while planing, bear down firmly on the knob when starting the stroke; bear evenly on both knob and handle in the middle of the stroke; and, at the end of the stroke, lighten the

pressure on the knob and bear down on the handle. Keep the body well over the work to facilitate the control of the pressure. On the return stroke, raise the cutting edge of the plane so that it will not drag on the wood. For rough cuts, angle the plane at about 30 degrees (fig. 13–70) and for smooth, about 10 to 15 degrees. When planing sides and edges, work from the outside toward the middle and, as much as possible, with the grain of the wood. If the grain is torn or roughened by the plane, reverse the direction in which the plane is pushed. A common cause of this difficulty is having the plane adjusted to take too deep a cut; the shavings should be thin and should come up through the mouth to be deflected by the cap iron. To avoid splits in the wood, bevel waste edges (fig. 13–71) of excess stock areas and then work toward the bevel. To keep the edges true while planing, hold a block of wood against the side of the work and under part of the plane (fig. 13–72).

13–51. Block Plane

This is a smaller plane than the bench plane, from 4 to 8 inches long, with a blade from 1 inch to 1 5/8 inch wide. It is designed to smooth across end grain or to make close joints. It is also used for many small smoothing jobs. Although it is made somewhat different from the bench planes, it is adjusted in the same manner as they are. The blade is shaped like that of the smoothing plane but it is used with the bevel up, instead of down, and the blade is held in place by a lever lock, instead of a cap iron. The block plane is held in one hand while being used. To smooth cross grain, adjust the plane to take light cuts, not deep ones, and make the strokes short and at an angle. Always cut toward the center of the board since, if the blade runs over the edge of the lumber (fig. 13–73), a corner of the wood may split off. Here, too, a slight bevel on the waste side of the lumber may prevent a split.

13–52. Adjustments of Planes

Ordinarily, the bench plane is disassembled only to the extent of removing the cap iron, blade, and level cap (fig. 13–68). The steps in reassembling and adjusting the plane are listed below.

a. Lay the cap iron crosswise on the flat side of the blade and insert the cap iron screw into the enlarged end of the blade slot. Slide the cap (still crosswise) along the slot until the cap can be turned parallel to the blade without having

Table 13-7. Characteristics and Uses of Planes

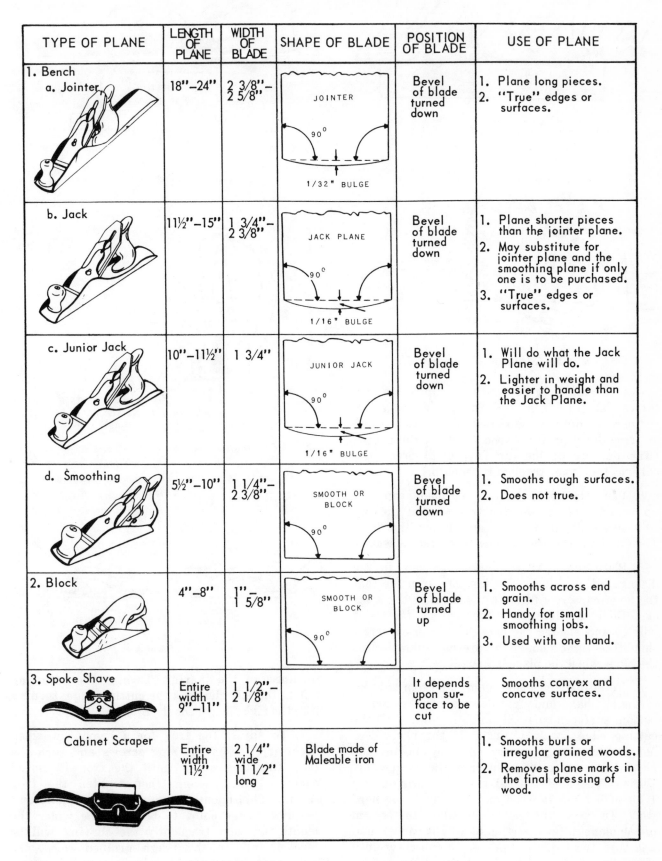

TYPE OF PLANE	LENGTH OF PLANE	WIDTH OF BLADE	SHAPE OF BLADE	POSITION OF BLADE	USE OF PLANE
1. Bench a. Jointer	18"–24"	2 3/8"–2 5/8"	JOINTER 90° 1/32" BULGE	Bevel of blade turned down	1. Plane long pieces. 2. "True" edges or surfaces.
b. Jack	11½"–15"	1 3/4"–2 3/8"	JACK PLANE 90° 1/16" BULGE	Bevel of blade turned down	1. Plane shorter pieces than the jointer plane. 2. May substitute for jointer plane and the smoothing plane if only one is to be purchased. 3. "True" edges or surfaces.
c. Junior Jack	10"–11½"	1 3/4"	JUNIOR JACK 90° 1/16" BULGE	Bevel of blade turned down	1. Will do what the Jack Plane will do. 2. Lighter in weight and easier to handle than the Jack Plane.
d. Smoothing	5½"–10"	1 1/4"–2 3/8"	SMOOTH OR BLOCK 90°	Bevel of blade turned down	1. Smooths rough surfaces. 2. Does not true.
2. Block	4"–8"	1"–1 5/8"	SMOOTH OR BLOCK 90°	Bevel of blade turned up	1. Smooths across end grain. 2. Handy for small smoothing jobs. 3. Used with one hand.
3. Spoke Shave	Entire width 9"–11"	1 1/2"–2 1/8"		It depends upon surface to be cut	Smooths convex and concave surfaces.
Cabinet Scraper	Entire width 11½"	2 1/4" wide 11 1/2" long	Blade made of Maleable iron		1. Smooths burls or irregular grained woods. 2. Removes plane marks in the final dressing of wood.

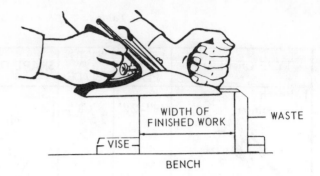

Figure 13-69. Pressure control on a plane.

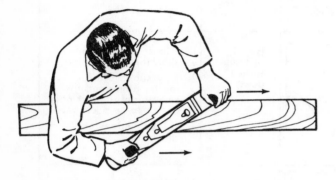

WIDTH OF FINISHED WORK — WASTE

VISE

BENCH

Figure 13-71. Beveling waste edges.

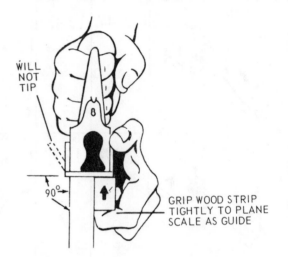

Figure 13-70. Slanting for rough cutting.

WILL NOT TIP

90°

GRIP WOOD STRIP TIGHTLY TO PLANE SCALE AS GUIDE

Figure 13-72. Using a block to keep sides square (end view).

the cap spring drag across the cutting edge. Set the cap at 1/16 inch from the cutting edge for ordinary planing; at 1/32 inch, for cross-grained or irregularly grained wood. Tighten the screw. (The purpose of the cap iron is to break the chips as they come through the mouth.)

b. Place the assembled cap and blade, cap iron up, into the plane over the frog so that the cap iron screw fits into the round slot in the frog. The cap and iron should now be correctly seated.

c. Place the lever cap, with the cam in the disengaged position, over the cap iron so that the lever-capscrew fits into the holes in the lever cap. Slide the lever cap forward as far as it will go and engage the cam. The lever-capscrew should be tight enough to prevent vibration of the blade when the plane is in use.

d. To adjust the plane, hold it bottom side up in the left hand and sight down along the smooth bottom surface. Turn the adjusting nut until the cutting edge barely projects. If the blade does not project evenly, straighten it by moving the adjusting lever to the right or to the left (A, fig. 13-74). The blade should extend approximately 1/10 inch for soft wood and 1/32 inch for hard wood. To extend the blade, sight along the bottom of the plane in the direction of a light background and turn the adjusting nut or thumbscrew until the cutter edge projects enough to cut the desired

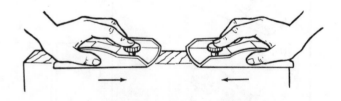

Figure 13-73. Planing end grain.

thickness of the shaving. Turning the adjusting nut to the left shortens the cutting edge, turning it to the right lengthens it (B, fig. 13-74).

e. To adjust the frog for a heavy cut when necessary, loosen the frog screws and turn the frog adjusting screw until the frog is moved backward far enough, then tighten the frog screws. This opens the mouth of the plane and permits larger chips to be cut. The wider the mouth, the less frequently the shaving will be broken and, in the tough grained wood, the rougher the work will be.

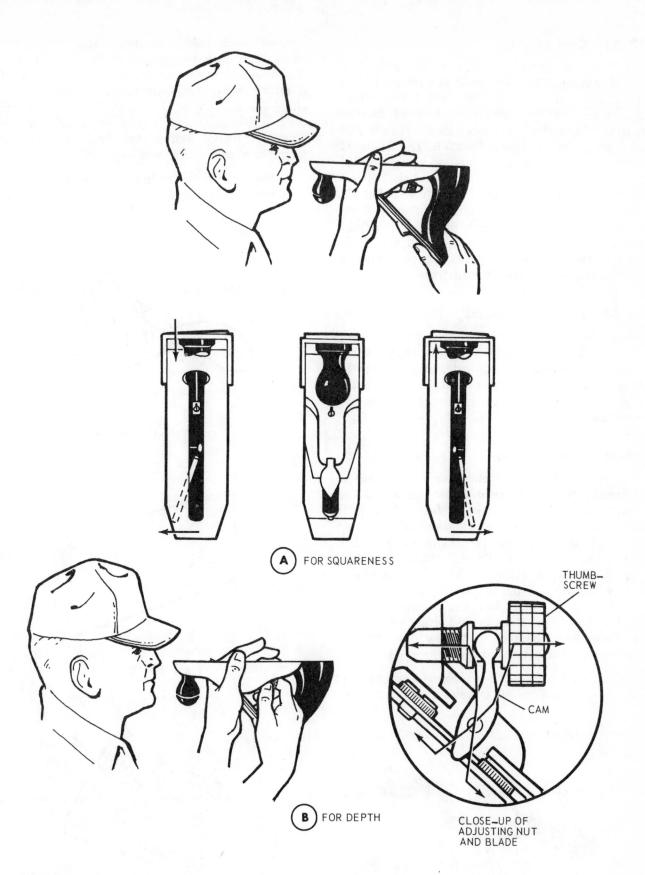

THUMB-SCREW

CAM

B FOR DEPTH

CLOSE-UP OF
ADJUSTING NUT
AND BLADE

Figure 13-74. Adjusting a plane.

13–53. Care of Planes

Good care of the plane pays off in better and easier planing. The blade must be protected from being dulled or chipped. The wood being planed should be free of nails, dirt, and all foreign matter. If the blade becomes dull, sharpen it just like wood chisels (para 13–29e). The angle of bevel is 25 degrees. The shape and angle of the cutting edge must be maintained and the corners of the blade should be very slightly rounded off. Always lay the plane on its edge; putting it down with the blade on the bench will dull the blade. Before putting the plane away, pull the blade up into the body of the plane. Cover it with a thin coating of oil to prevent rusting.

13–54. Safety Precautions

Since plane blades or irons are sharp, do not rub the fingers on them or carry them in the pocket. When planing against the grain of the wood, watch for splinters that can injure the fingers. Always finish the job so as to leave the work smooth.

13–55. Related Tools

a. *Spokeshave.* The spokeshave (fig. 13–75) is a greatly modified plane used for smoothing and shaping convex and concave surfaces of wood. It has a short bottom which makes it adaptable for shaping. The blade is held in place with a screw and a clamp and the adjustments are similar to that of a plane. To use the spokeshave, clamp the work firmly in a vise, grasp the tool by the handles, and place the thumbs near the center of the tool. Make the cut either by pushing or by pulling the tool. It is best to cut with, rather than against, the grain of the wood.

b. *Cabinet Scraper.* The cabinet scraper (fig. 13–76) is made up of a metal frame with two handles which hold a scraper blade. Adjust the blade for depth by means of the thumbscrew. It should produce a fine, thin, even shaving as it is pushed with the grain. Use long even strokes along the surface of the wood. The scraper will remove irregularities in the wood left by the plane. It works well in the final dressings of burrel or woods with irregular grain.

c. *Hand Scraper.* The hand scraper (fig. 13–77) is a rectangular piece of steel. The sharp edge

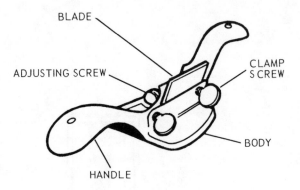

Figure 13–76. Cabinet scraper.

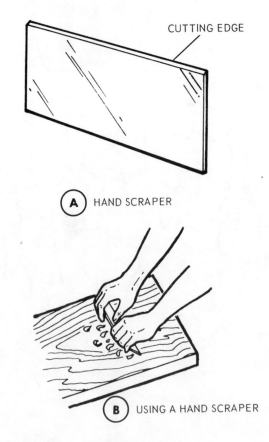

Figure 13–77. Hand scraper and its use.

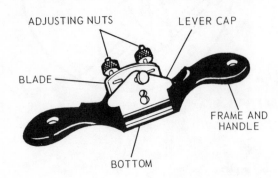

Figure 13–75. Spokeshave.

of the steel is used, rather than an actual blade. Use it to remove mill marks and scratches before the piece is sanded. To use, hold the scraper firmly in both hands and angle it toward the wood in the direction it is being pushed or pulled. When removing the wavy mill marks left from a power plane, hold it about a 30-degree angle to the edge of the wood. Because the scraper is made of steel, it will rust, so the surface must be covered with a light coat of oil before storing.

d. Other Planes. Other planes adapted for specific use include the rabbet plane, on which the plane blade extends through both sides of the plane, making it possible to plane along a corner or to shape tenons which will fit into mortises; and the router plane, which is used for cutting grooves or dadoes.

Section XIII. HANDTOOLS: PLIERS

13–56. General

Pliers are holding or gripping tools used to hold material, grasp objects that are hard to reach with the fingers, bend wire, and do a variety of things specific to the various crafts in which they are used. They are not considered to be woodworking tools but are used mainly for first echelon maintenance work.

13–57. Common Pliers or Combination Slip Joint

These are perhaps the most commonly used pliers (fig. 13–78). The better ones are made of drop-forged steel so they can withstand hard usage. The slip joint permits a wider opening of the jaws and the jaws have serrations, or teeth, for gripping. They are made in a variety of shapes and sizes. The angle nose (fig. 13–79) is a common and useful variation. The size of pliers is determined by the overall length, which ranges from 5 to 10 inches. Some combination pliers have a side cutter for cutting soft wire.

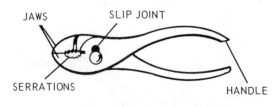

Figure 13–78. Common pliers.

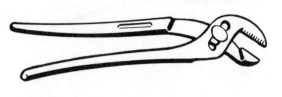

Figure 13–79. Angle nose pliers.

a. Use of Common Pliers. To spread the jaws of slip-joint pliers, first spread the ends of the handles apart as far as possible. Give the handles a little tug which moves the slip joint or pivot to the open position. To close, spread the handles as far as possible, then push the joint back into the closed or smaller position by pushing the ends of the handle. Tempting as it is, do not use pliers instead of a wrench to turn bolts or nuts because they will damage and round the corners of the bolt or nut on which they are used.

b. Maintenance and Care of Common Pliers.

(1) Keep the serrations on the jaws of the pliers sharp. When they become dull, hold the plier open in a vise and recut the serrations with a triangular file (fig. 13–80).

(2) Keep pliers clean and covered with a light coating of oil when not in use. Store them with the jaws closed and so that they will not be damaged by striking hard objects.

(3) Do not use pliers on hard metal as this will damage the serrations of the jaws.

(4) Keep the pin or bolt at the hinge just tight enough to hold the two parts of the pliers in contact.

c. Safety Precautions. Keep the fingers away from the jaws of the pliers and keep the hand well back on the handles to prevent it from being pinched in the hinges.

13–58. Side-Cutting Pliers

The jaws of these pliers (fig. 13–81) do not open as far as the slip-joint. They also have two sharp edges between the nose and the joint. Although these pliers are designed to cut and to peel wire, they are used in occupational therapy sections only for cutting wire. They, too, come in a number of different shapes and sizes.

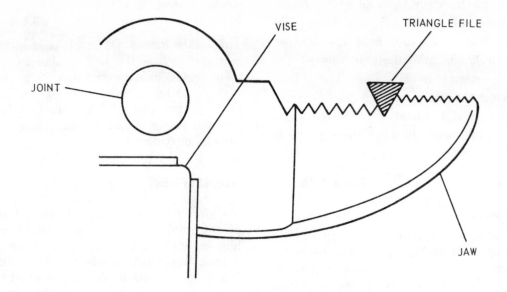

Figure 13–80. Sharpening jaw face serrations.

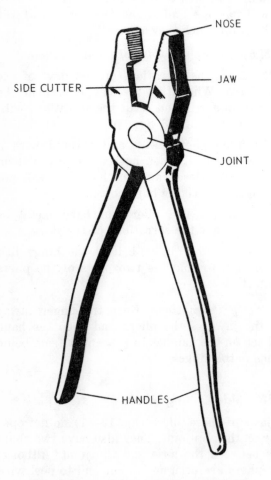

Figure 13–81. Lineman's side-cutting pliers.

a. Use of Side-Cutting Pliers. When cutting wire, keep the wire as near the joint as possible to increase the leverage and prevent misalinement of the jaws. If the pliers need too much force to cut wire, either the wire is too heavy or the cutters are dull.

b. Care of Side-Cutting Pliers. Check carefully to see if the cutting edges will close properly if they are sharpened. (Some side-cutting pliers are designed so they can be sharpened.) Keep these pliers cleaned and oiled. The joint must also have a drop of oil from time to time. When not in use, they should be kept closed to protect the cutting edge.

c. Safety. Safety precautions are the same as for the slip-joint pliers (para 13–57*c.*).

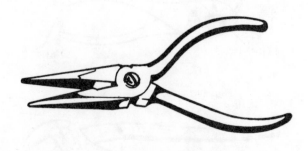

Figure 13–82. Long-nose side cutter.

13–59. General

Woodworkers' saws are the crosscut, ripsaw, backsaw, miter, keyhole, compass, plumber's, and coping. Although each type of saw has a specific use, they have certain similarities. The cutting edge of each saw is a line of sharp teeth. These teeth act as two rows of cutting instruments running close together in parallel grooves. To prevent the saw from binding as it is pushed through the wood, the teeth are set, one to the right and one to the left, alternately (fig. 13–83), in order to cut a groove wider than the thickness of the saw. This groove is known as the kerf (fig. 13–84). The amount of set or width of kerf necessary is determined largely by the type of lumber which the saw is designed to cut. Green or soft lumber requires more set than hard or dry lumber. A coarse saw is better for doing fast work and for cutting green (undried) wood, while a fine saw does smoother, more accurate cutting on seasoned lumber. The teeth of woodworking saws are designed to cut as the saw is being pushed away from the operator. Saws are sized by the number of tooth points to the inch. There is always one more point per inch than there are teeth (fig. 13–85).

13–60. Types of Saws

a. *Crosscut Saw.* The teeth of this saw (fig. 13–86) are designed to cut *across* the *grain* of the wood. The cutting edge of each tooth is on the side, with the sharp point on the outside and the bevel on the inside of each tooth (fig. 13–84). Eight to ten points per inch is a good-size crosscut saw for general work. The number stamped near the handle indicates the number of points per inch. The blade of this saw (fig. 13–86) is 18 to 20 inches long and tapered in width.

(1) To saw, grasp the handle with the index finger extended toward the point, curl the other fingers around the grip of the handle and curl the thumb in the direction opposite to the fingers (fig. 13–87). The extended index finger tends to give better accuracy in sawing.

(2) In starting the cut, place the saw on the piece of wood so that the heel of the saw rests with the inside edge just touching the line to be sawed. Use the thumb of the opposite hand to guide the blade and the fingers and palm to hold the lumber (fig. 13–88). Pull the saw, exerting no pressure but allowing the weight of the saw to rest on the lumber. In this manner, a small groove is made in which the saw can be run.

(3) To cut the wood, hold the saw perpendicular to the wood at about a 45-degree angle to the lumber and push the saw forward with just enough pressure to make a cut, guiding the saw with the forefinger of the moving hand and with

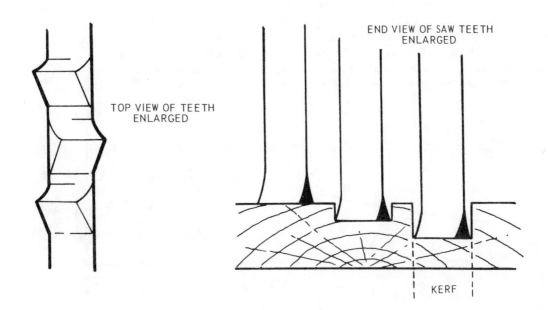

TOP VIEW OF TEETH ENLARGED

END VIEW OF SAW TEETH ENLARGED

KERF

Figure 13–83. Saw teeth.

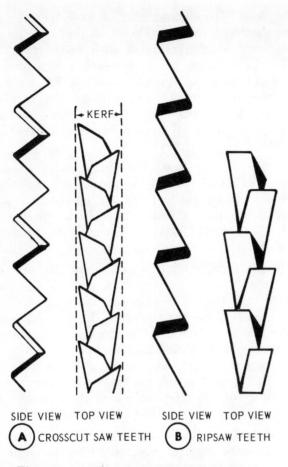

Figure 13–84. Comparison between crosscut saw teeth and ripsaw teeth.

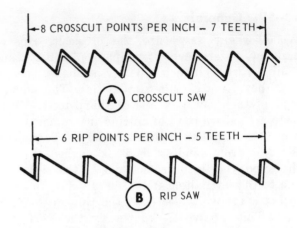

Figure 13–85. Tooth points per inch on a crosscut and on a ripsaw.

the thumb of the holding hand. Do not force the saw, as this may cause it to bend or to jump out of the groove and thereby scar the face of the lumber. Continue this backward and forward motion until the saw has cut through the lumber. Exert pressure only on the push stroke, as it is on this stroke that the cutting is done.

(4) When the saw is nearly through the lumber, support the part which might fall, until the saw has cut all of the fibers. This prevents splitting the last piece of wood.

b. *Ripsaw.* The parts of the ripsaw are the same as the parts of the crosscut (fig. 13–86). The teeth, however, are designed to cut *with* the *grain* of the wood. They are sharpened straight across the front edge, making the cutting edge like two rows of chisels cutting into the wood (B, fig. 13–84). Five to seven points per inch is a good size for a ripsaw. It is used in the same manner as the crosscut except that the blade is held at a 60-degree angle to the lumber.

c. *Backsaw.* The teeth of a backsaw (fig. 13–89) are similar to those of a crosscut saw but, since there are about fourteen per inch, they are smaller and finer. The average length of the blade is about 12 inches. It is thin, but is stiffened with a heavy metal back. Because of the construction, the backsaw makes a finer cut than the crosscut.

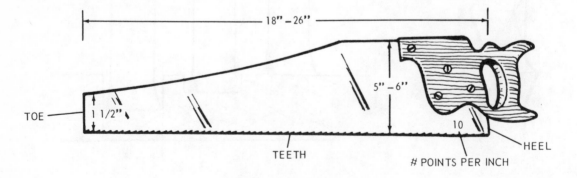

Figure 13–86. Crosscut or ripsaw.

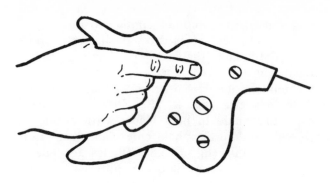

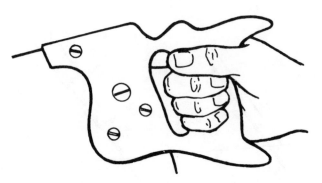

Figure 13–87. Proper grasp of crosscut or ripsaw.

Figure 13–88. Using the crosscut handsaw.

It is used in fine wood such as in making joints where accurate fitting is necessary. It may be used to cut either with or across the grain and is used in the same manner as the crosscut and ripsaws.

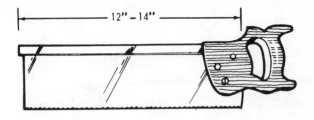

Figure 13–89. Backsaw.

d. Miter Saw. The miter saw looks like a long backsaw, different only in length and with a miter box (fig. 13–90). With this saw, lumber can be cut accurately at any angle. This is helpful in making accurate joints. The commercial miter box can be set to cut at almost any angle. A small wooden miter box can be made to use for frequently used angles (fig. 13–91).

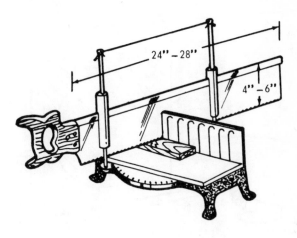

Figure 13–90. Miter saw and box.

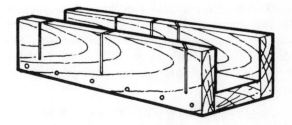

Figure 13–91. Hardwood miter box.

e. Keyhole Saw. This saw is made for smaller types of work, such as cutting keyholes and fitting locks in doors, hence the name. It is narrow enough to enter a 1/4-inch hole and cuts a wide kerf so that the blade may turn in making curved cuts. It frequently comes nested (fig. 13–92) with

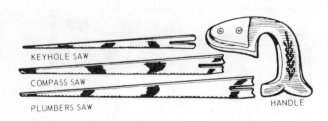

Figure 13–92. Nested saws.

a compass saw and a plumber's saw with a common, easily removable pistol-grip handle.

f. Compass Saw. The blade of the compass saw is also designed to cut a wide kerf for sawing curves. It is used for starting interior cuts to be completed by other saws and may be used for either crosscutting or for ripping (fig. 13–93).

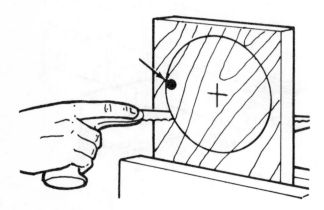

Figure 13–93. Using a compass saw.

g. Plumber's Saw. This saw has a heavy blade with fine teeth and is designed to cut through nails or soft metal encountered in sawing. The blade is thick enough to permit a woodcutting saw to pass freely through the kerf it makes in the nail.

h. Coping saw. The coping saw (fig. 13–94) is a versatile saw for cutting thin woods and plastic. It consists of a steel frame, a handle, and a replaceable blade. The blade is held under tension by the spring in the frame. In some saws, this is accomplished by bending the frame together while inserting the blades; in others, by turning the handle or the adjustment screw until the desired amount of tension is obtained. In most frames, this blade is adjustable so that it can be used at any angle. The blade can be inserted with

the teeth pointing away from the handle and the saw used in a manner similar to the way a ripsaw or crosscut is used or, if the teeth point toward the handle, the saw is used as a jeweler's saw. In the latter case, the thin material being cut should be supported on a "V" board which is held in a vice (fig. 13–95). Some coping saw frames are made to hold blades with a pin in each end, while others hold only blades bent into loops or a kink (fig. 13–96). Blades for either wood or metal are available in different widths and in a variety of number of teeth per inch.

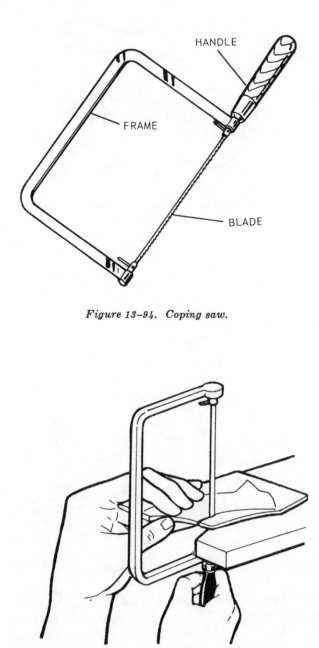

Figure 13–94. Coping saw.

Figure 13–95. Using a coping saw and a "V" board.

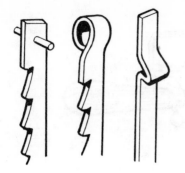

Figure 13–96. Types of coping saw blades.

13–61. Maintaining Saws

a. Care of Saws.

(1) Do not kink or bend the blade of a handsaw, as such distortions prevent the blade from sliding through the kerf. If the saw kinks in the cut and then pressure is applied to force it through the wood, the blade will bend and a kink will usually result. Another rather common practice which results in a bent saw blade is to lay the saw down on an uneven surface and then perhaps put other tools on it.

(2) Do not saw through metal objects in the wood with a saw designed to cut wood. Either remove the object or cut it with a plumber's saw.

(3) When not in use, oil saws and put away. Saws rust easily and a rusty saw will bend in the cut.

(4) Break off pieces of waste with the hand or a mallet. Twisting it off will distort the blade.

(5) Raise the work to a height sufficient to keep the blade from striking the floor. If the work cannot be raised, limit the strokes to prevent kinking.

(6) Keep the saw sharp to facilitate cutting. It is possible to sharpen a saw, but to do a satisfactory job requires so much skill and time that it is usually considered to be inadvisable. From a supply-economy angle, it is less expensive to take good care of saws so that they will last as long as possible; then order replacements when indicated.

b. Sharpening Hand Saws. Material on sharpening saws is included only so that the technician will have it available in case the saws cannot be sent to a professional sharpener. Limited skill and time make professional sharpening expedient.

(1) *Saw-sharpening equipment.*

(a) *Saw vise.* The saw vise (fig. 13–97) is a special vise or clamp with long jaws. It has a handle on the front which can be pulled away from the vise to open the jaws. Closing the handle puts pressure on the jaws of the vise by means of a cam, so that the blade of the saw being filed will be held securely.

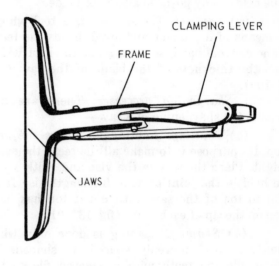

Figure 13–97. Saw vise.

(b) *Clamping assembly.* The vise is held to the workbench by means of a clamp, which has a turnscrew to hold it securely to the bench, and a wing nut, which will permit the vise to be set at various angles to the clamp (fig. 13–98).

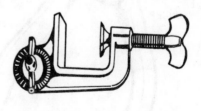

Figure 13–98. Clamping assembly.

(c) *File holder.* The file holder (fig. 13–99) consists of a wooden handle to which is attached an adjustable frame for holding a triangular file. A pair of clamping screws on the file holder fastens the frame to the jaws of the vise.

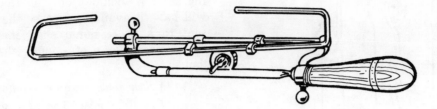

Figure 13–99. File holder.

It can be adjusted so as to hold the file at any desired angle to the teeth being filed. In addition, a clamp on the top of the frame permits the file to be held at any position along the blade.

(d) *Saw set*. The saw set is a tool which, by means of a plunger and anvil, bends the teeth of the saw outward, so as to make the kerf wider than the thickness of the blade of the saw (fig. 13–100).

(2) *Sharpening processes*. There are five steps in the sharpening of a saw—

(a) *Jointing*. Jointing is always the first step. Its purpose is to make all the teeth the same height. Place the saw in the vise and, with a flat file held in the jointing tool, file lengthwise from heel to toe of the saw until a flat top has been filed on the tip of each tooth (fig. 13–101).

(b) *Shaping*. Shaping is done only when the teeth are unevenly spaced or shaped. To shape, file the teeth with a tapered file to the correct uniform size and shape. The gullets must

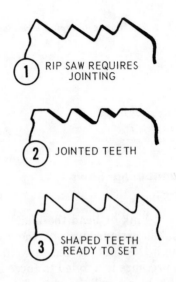

Figure 13–101. Jointing a saw.

be of equal depth. For the crosscut handsaw, the front of the tooth should be filed with an angle of 15 degrees from the vertical, while the back slope should be 45 degrees with the vertical. Disregard the bevel of the teeth and file straight across at right angles to the blade, with the file well down in the gullet while shaping. If the teeth are of unequal size, press the file against the teeth with the largest flat tops until the center of the flat tops made by jointing is reached. Then move the file to the next gullet and file until the rest of the flat top disappears and the tooth has been brought to a point. Do not bevel the teeth while jointing. The teeth are now ready for setting.

(c) *Setting*. In setting, particular care must be taken to see that the set is regular. It must be the same width for the entire length of the blade and the same width on both sides of the blade. The depth should never be more than half the depth of the tooth; if the set is made deeper, it may spring, crimp, crack the blade, or break out the teeth. To set the handsaw, place the saw set over the blade so that the guides are over the teeth with the anvil behind the tooth to

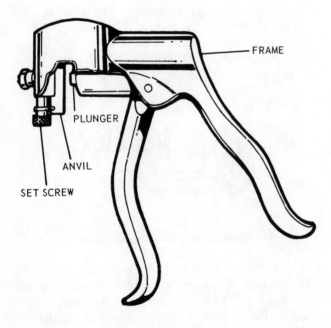

Figure 13–100. Saw set.

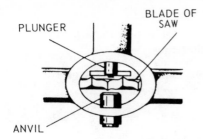

Figure 13-102. Setting saw teeth.

be set (fig. 13–102). The anvil, with its bevel at the top, is held in the frame by means of the set screw. Press the handles together now. The plunger will press the tooth against the anvil and bend it to the angle of the bevel of the anvil. Each tooth is set in this manner, alternating to either side of the blade.

(d) *Filing*. In filing the handsaw (fig. 13–103), the saw is put in the vise with the handle to the left. Begin to file at the heel. Adjust the file holder so that the file is held at the proper angle and the file is between two teeth. File both teeth at once with one or more strokes of the file. Work down the whole saw, shifting the file by means of the clamp on the top of the file holder. Then turn the saw around so that the handle is to the right, readjust the file holder, and work down the entire length of the saw again. In filing the ripsaw (in addition to adjust-

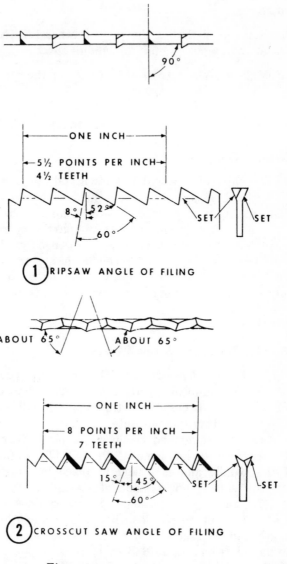

Figure 13-104. Angles of saw teeth.

ing the saw for the angles shown in figure 13–104), lower the file handle about 2 inches to give a bevel on the top of the teeth which lean away.

(e) *Dressing*. Dressing of the saw is necessary only when there are burrs left on the side of the tooth by filing. These burrs cause the saw to work in a ragged fashion. Remove them from both the handsaw and the large crosscut saw by laying the saw on a flat surface and running an oilstone or a fine file lightly across the side of the tooth.

13–62. Safety Precautions

a. Make sure that, if the saw slips from the work, it will not cut the hands or legs.

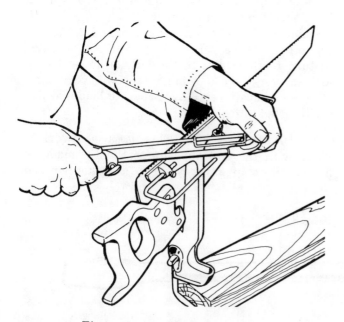

Figure 13-103. Filing the handsaw.

b. Always lay the saw down carefully in such a position that no one can brush against the teeth and be cut.

c. Remember that a sharp, well-cared-for tool is safer than a poorly maintained dull one.

d. Make sure both rows of teeth are of the same length. If they are not, the saw will curve as it cuts.

e. Set the teeth before filing to avoid injury to the cutting edges.

f. Never make the depth of the set more than half that of the tooth itself.

Section XV. HANDTOOLS: SCREWDRIVERS

13–63. General

The screwdriver is a widely known and frequently used tool. A joint or fixture held with screws is more secure and more durable than one held with nails, and it can be taken apart and reassembled. As with most commonly used tools, there are many types of screwdrivers, some of which are adapted for highly specialized jobs. Only the most frequently used will be considered here.

13–64. Types of Screwdrivers

a. Common Screwdriver. This tool (fig. 13–105) has a round or square steel blade anchored firmly in a hardwood or plastic handle. For heavy duty work, there is an integral handle screwdriver. It is so named because the blade forms an integral part of some of the outside surface of the handle and is locked in place by rivets. The tip is flat and is made of steel, hot-forged to size and heat-treated. Screwdrivers are sized according to the length of the blade. This length ranged from 1 1/4 to 12 inches with the tip range from 1/8 to 3/8 inch. It is important for the tip to fit the screw. The width of the tip should equal the length of the screw slot and the tip should fit securely into the slot (fig. 13–106).

b. Phillips or Cross-Tip Screwdriver. The tip of the Phillips is shaped like a cross so as to fit the Phillip screw (fig. 13–107). The blade ranges from 1 inch to 3 inches in length, and the tips are made in four sizes to fit the various sizes of Phillips screws:

Screwdriver size		Phillips screw size
1	fits	4 and smaller
2		5 through 9
3		10 through 16
4		18 and larger

c. Clutch Head. These screwdrivers (fig. 13–108) are made to fit the recessed heads of clutch bit screws, more commonly called butterfly or figure-8 screws. These, too, come in various sizes according to the size of the screw.

d. Offset Screwdriver. Screws that are located in tight corners and are inaccessible to other screwdrivers can sometimes be reached with an offset screwdriver (fig. 13–109). These screwdrivers are made in a variety of sizes and tip widths. They are also made with Phillips tips and with four blades, called the double tip.

e. Ratchet Screwdriver. With this screwdriver, it is possible to drive and remove screws more rapidly than with the common screwdriver. It has a ratchet arrangement which makes it possible to drive in one direction and release in the other. These screwdrivers can be adjusted to turn to the right, to the left, or to be locked and so work like a common screwdriver. Some of these screwdrivers have separate blades which are inserted into a chuck.

f. Screwdriver Bits. This is a screwdriver blade with the end opposite to the tip made to fit the chuck of a breast drill, a socket wrench

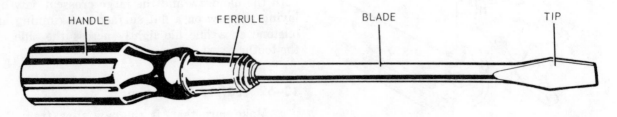

HANDLE   FERRULE   BLADE   TIP

Figure 13–105. Standard screwdriver.

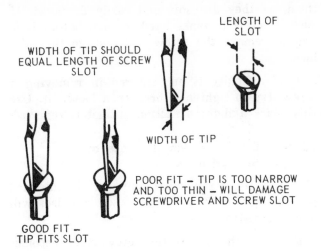

WIDTH OF TIP SHOULD
EQUAL LENGTH OF SCREW
SLOT

LENGTH OF
SLOT

WIDTH OF TIP

POOR FIT — TIP IS TOO NARROW
AND TOO THIN — WILL DAMAGE
SCREWDRIVER AND SCREW SLOT

GOOD FIT —
TIP FITS SLOT

Figure 13–106. Proper blade for specific screw.

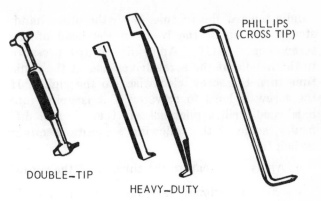

PHILLIPS
(CROSS TIP)

DOUBLE–TIP

HEAVY–DUTY

Figure 13–109. Offset screwdriver.

13–65. Use of the Screwdriver

Before driving a screw, select the screwdriver with the largest tip that will fit into the head of the screw. Hold the screwdriver in the palm of one hand, with the forefinger extending down the

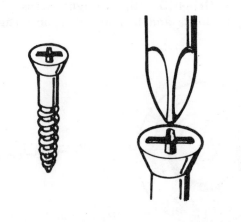

Figure 13–107. Phillips screw and screwdriver.

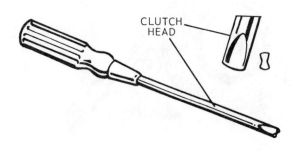

CLUTCH
HEAD

Figure 13–108. Clutch-head screwdriver.

handle, or perhaps a spiral ratchet. This speeds up and reduces the mark of driving screws. As with common screwdrivers, the bit should be selected to fit the screw.

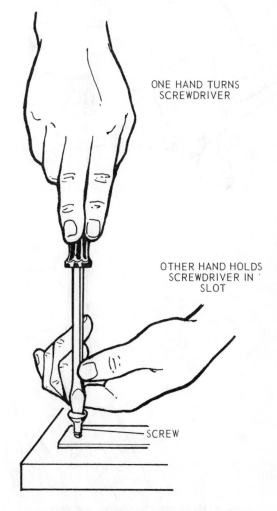

ONE HAND TURNS
SCREWDRIVER

OTHER HAND HOLDS
SCREWDRIVER IN
SLOT

SCREW

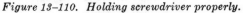

Figure 13–110. Holding screwdriver properly.

handle toward the ferrule. With the other hand, steady the tip of the blade in the head of the screw (fig. 13–110). Apply downward pressure to the handle of the screwdriver and at the same time turn the screw clockwise (to the right). If the screw is hard to drive or if it is going into hardwood, drill a pilot hole. If there is still difficulty, some of the following suggestions might be helpful:

a. Apply soft soap to the threads of the screw.

b. For additional leverage, use a wrench, either at the flared tip or on a screwdriver with a square blade (fig. 13–111).

c. When driving brass screws, do not force

them, as they are soft and easily damaged. If such a screw becomes hard to turn before it is seated, remove the screw and enlarge the pilot hole.

d. If difficulty is encountered in removing a screw, try to tighten it first, then loosen it. Use this "back and forth" action until it is removed.

13–66. Care and Maintenance of Screwdrivers

a. Use the screwdriver only for its intended purpose. Using it for a lever or a chisel will damage the tip.

b. When the tip of the screwdriver becomes nicked or if the edges become rounded and no longer fit a screw slot properly, file or regrind to the proper shape.

(1) Grind the tip straight across to remove the nicks and to make it square (fig. 13–112).

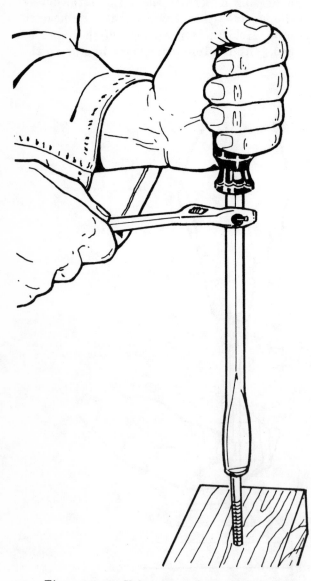

Figure 13–111. Using a wrench on a square shank screwdriver.

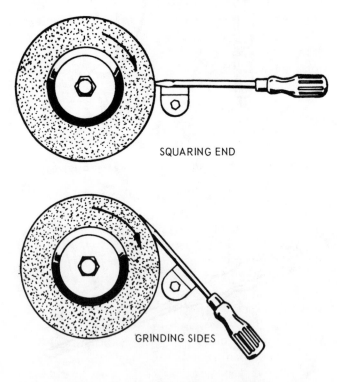

SQUARING END

GRINDING SIDES

Figure 13–112. Grinding a screwdriver.

(2) Adjust the tool rest to hold the screwdriver against the wheel at the proper angle to make the sides of the tip nearly parallel or a bit concave. Grind the sides (fig. 13–113) until the tip is just thick enough to completely fill the slot in the head of the screw.

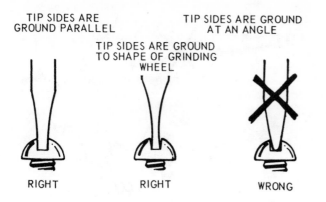

TIP SIDES ARE
GROUND PARALLEL

TIP SIDES ARE GROUND
TO SHAPE OF GRINDING
WHEEL

TIP SIDES ARE GROUND
AT AN ANGLE

RIGHT   RIGHT   WRONG

Figure 13–113. Grinding screwdriver blade tip.

(3) Dip the tip of the screwdriver in water frequently to prevent loss of temper. If the tem-per is lost, retemper it by heating about 1/2 inch of the blade to a cherry red. Dip about 3/4 inch of the end of the blade into clean cold water. Quickly rub the hardened end with an emery cloth to brighten it. The color will begin to creep back into the tip. When the tip becomes light blue, quench it in cold water.

13–67. Safety Precautions

a. Keep the screwdriver clean of grease and dirt to prevent slipping.

b. Do not use more force when driving a screw than is necessary.

c. Keep the blade properly shaped.

d. Do not carry a screwdriver in the pocket.

Section XVI. HANDTOOLS: WRENCHES

13–68. General

Wrenches are used to tighten or to loosen nuts, bolts, or parts that are held together by threads. There are many wrenches designed for specific jobs. They can be divided into fixed end and ad-justable wrenches.

13–69. Fixed-End Wrenches

As the name implies, these wrenches are not adjustable but instead are made in different sizes and are frequently purchased in sets. Three types will be considered—

a. Open-End Wrench. These tools are forged from chrome vanadium steel and are heat-treat-ed. They usually have a double end and are made with the ends at an angle of 10 to 23 degrees to the body of the wrench (fig. 13–114). This en-ables the user to work more effectively in close quarters. The jaws may also be offset to facili-tate turning a nut or bolt that is recessed. The size of the opening between the jaws determines the size of the wrench. If it is a double-end wrench with a 1/2-inch opening in one end and a 9/16-inch opening in the other end, it is called a 1/2 by 9/16-wrench. The size of the opening is usually stamped on the side of the wrench. Wrenches with larger openings are made longer and heavier to increase leverage strength.

(1) *Use of open-end wrenches.* It is impor-tant for a wrench to fit squarely on the nut or

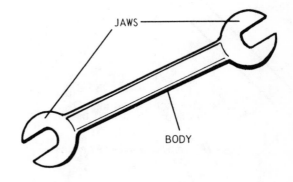

JAWS

BODY

Figure 13–114. Open-end wrenches.

bolthead (fig. 13–115). If it is too loose, the wrench will slip and round the corners of the bolt. The angle is there to give more leverage in close quarters. The wrench is turned over after each turn of the nut or bolt, and the angle of the wrench opening is reversed (fig. 13–116). If a nut or bolt is hard to start, a little penetrating oil should be put around it so that the oils run into the threads.

(2) *Care and maintenance of open-end wrenches.* Open-end wrenches with damaged jaws can be made serviceable again by grinding and/or filing the jaws to the next larger standard size. The jaw faces should be flat and parallel. The jaws need to be dipped in water frequently as they are being ground in order to preserve the temper, which can be lost because of over-heating. All wrenches must be kept clean and be

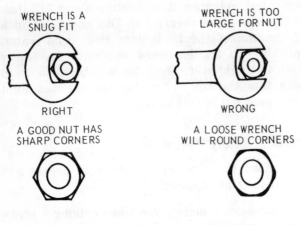

WRENCH IS A
SNUG FIT

WRENCH IS TOO
LARGE FOR NUT

RIGHT

WRONG

A GOOD NUT HAS
SHARP CORNERS

A LOOSE WRENCH
WILL ROUND CORNERS

Figure 13–115. Fitting open-end wrench.

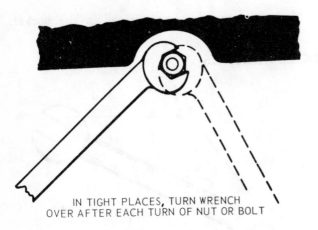

IN TIGHT PLACES, TURN WRENCH
OVER AFTER EACH TURN OF NUT OR BOLT

Figure 13–116. Use of open-end wrench.

carefully put away after use. They can be broken with improper handling.

(3) *Safety precautions.* It is possible to strike the hand a nasty blow and even be thrown off balance while using a wrench. This can be prevented by planning the operation so that the wrench is pulled, rather than pushed. However, there may be times when the wrench must be pushed. In this event, rather than wrapping the fingers around the handle, the base of the palm should be used against the handle of the wrench and pushing done with the hand open. The handle must not be extended in order to increase the leverage on a wrench (fig. 13–117).

b. *Box Wrenches.* Box-end wrenches (fig. 13–118) are so named because they completely surround the head of the bolt or nut. They usually have a double end, have either 6 or 12 points arranged in the circle, and are available in the same sizes as open-end wrenches. Some have the heads set at an angle to provide clearance for the

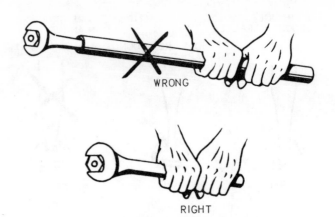

WRONG

RIGHT

Figure 13–117. Do not increase leverage on wrench.

hand; these are available with a ratchet. The ratchet is convenient because, with it, the wrench does not need to be removed from the bolt or nut to start a new stroke.

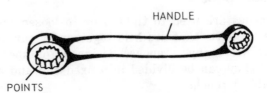

HANDLE

POINTS

Figure 13–118. Box-end wrench.

(1) *Use of box wrenches.* Compared with the open-end wrench, the box wrench has some advantages and at least one disadvantage.

(*a*) Because of the 12 points in the circle, it can be used with a 15-degree swing of the handle, which makes it best when working in close quarters.

(*b*) The sides of its opening are thin so that it will fit into tight places where the open-end wrench will not because of its thicker jaws.

(*c*) It will not slip off the nut.

(*d*) A disadvantage is that it is slow to use because it must be lifted off of the nut at the end of one stroke, then placed back onto the nut in a different position for the beginning of the next stroke. (This disadvantage does not apply to the ratchet box wrench.)

(2) *Care and safety of box wrenches.* Care of and safety precautions are the same for box wrenches as for crescent wrenches (para 13–70a).

c. *Combination Box and Open-End Wrench.*

Combination wrenches with one open end and a box wrench at the other end (fig. 13–119) are made with almost any combination of sizes, offsets, and angles. The advantage of this wrench is that after a tight nut or bolt is "broken loose" with the box end of the wrench, it can be completely and quickly unscrewed with the open end.

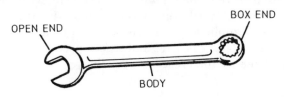

Figure 13–119. Combination box and open end.

d. Allen Wrench. This is a special bar of tool steel, usually 6-sided and L-shaped, that is made to fit hollow-set screws (fig. 13–120), which are found in equipment throughout an occupational therapy clinic. They come in sets which are sized to fit most set screws. The short end of this wrench is used to give a final tightening or to "break loose" tight screws. The long end is used to turn screws rapidly when little leverage is needed.

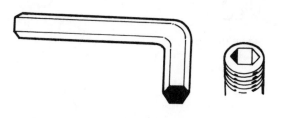

Figure 13–120. Allen wrench and setscrew.

13–70. Adjustable Wrenches

These wrenches are for turning nuts and bolts and various parts that have threads. Because they are adjustable, the same wrench fits a number of different sizes of nuts and bolts.

a. Crescent or Single Open-End Wrench. The crescent (fig. 13–121) is a handy wrench because it is light and easy to handle, and it adjusts to many sizes of nuts and bolts. It is made of forged alloy steel and is often crome plated so it requires little care. Crescent wrenches come in various

sizes and, as the maximum jaw capacity increases, the handle of the wrench is made longer for greater leverage.

Maximum jaw capacity (in inches)	Length of wrench (in inches)
1/2	4
3/4	6
7/8	8
1 1/8	10
1 5/16	12
2 1/16	16

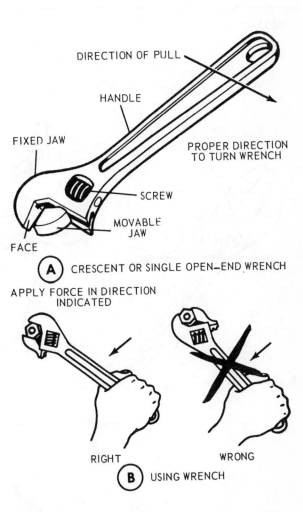

Figure 13–121. Crescent or single open-end wrench and its use.

(1) *Use of crescent wrenches.* The wrench is placed on a nut or bolt so that the force used to turn it is applied to the stationary jaw side of the wrench (fig. 13–121). After the wrench is in position, tighten the knurled screw until the wrench fits the nut or bolt head as tightly as is possible. If the wrench is not adjusted correctly, it will slip, which may cause both an injury to the hand and damage to the corners of the nut or bolt.

(2) *Care of the crescent wrench.* The movable jaw on these wrenches may not remain parallel to the stationary jaw after prolonged use. The trouble may be due to wear and weakening of the worm spring. To increase the resiliency of this spring, remove the axle screw from the wrench and separate the adjustable jaw, worm screw, and worm-screw spring from the handle (fig. 13–122). If the worm-screw spring is in good condition, stretch it to increase the tension and thus help to keep the adjustable jaw from tipping.

(3) *Safety in use of crescent wrench.* The safety precautions for crescent wrenches are essentially the same as for other wrenches. An added precaution is to see that the pulling force is applied to the fixed jaw and not to the adjustable jaw.

b. Monkey Wrench. This wrench (fig. 13-123) is used in the same manner as crescent wrenches (*a* above). With this wrench, too, the turning force is applied on the right side of the handle (fig. 13-124). The care and safety precautions are the same as for crescent wrenches.

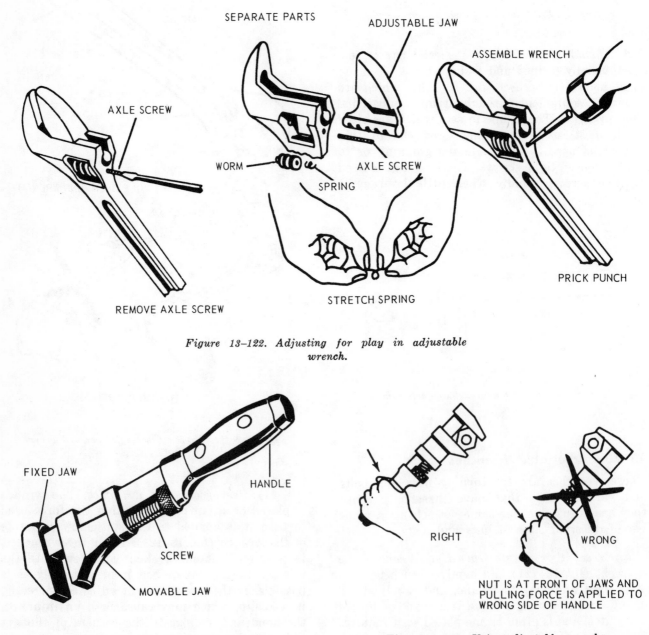

Figure 13–122. Adjusting for play in adjustable wrench.

Figure 13–123. Monkey wrench.

Figure 13–124. Using adjustable wrenches.

13–71. General

The strength, durability, and worth of a piece of furniture or equipment depend a great deal upon the proper selection of joints used throughout the piece, the skill of workmanship employed in making these joints, and the appropriate choice of glues and fasteners that are used to reinforce joints.

13–72. Types of Joints

A piece of furniture or equipment usually includes one or more types of joints. It is necessary to plan in advance the type of joint to be ued for each purpose. In order to make a wise selection, you must know the kinds of joints, as well as the purpose for which they were designed.

a. Butt Joint. This is a simple joint to make and one of the most commonly used. While it does not require the degree of skill of some of the more complex joints, it is important that the ends and surfaces where the two pieces meet be as square as possible. The butt joint (fig. 13–125) is not as good looking or as strong as other joints. To increase the strength, it should be glued, then held together with dowels, nails, screws, or corrugated fasteners (fig. 13–126). A stronger butt joint is made by "blocking" the joint (fig. 13–127). The block can be square or triangular, large or small. If it is small, it is glued into the angle of the joints. If it is large, it can be glued but it can also be nailed or screwed. If screws are used and if it is not glued, it is impossible to disassemble the joint.

b. Dado Joint. The dado joint is used to support shelves, bookcases, cabinets or drawers. It

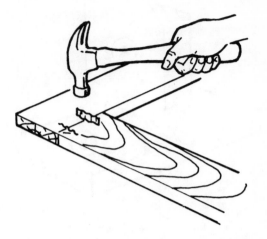

Figure 13–126. Corrugated fasteners used with a butt joint.

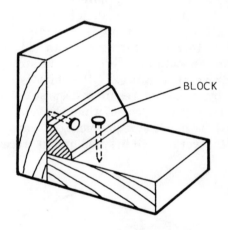

Figure 13–127. Blocked butt.

is also used in the construction of doors and windows. The joint consists of a recess cut across a board, from one edge to the other, into which the other piece of the joint just fits. To make this joint, mark the piece into which the recess is to be cut (B, fig. 13–128), by holding it at the desired spot and making a line on it the exact width of the recess (A, fig. 13–128). Continue the two lines down both edges with a try square. The marking gauge, set to the desired depth of the recess, is used to mark the depth. The saw cuts should be made along the inside of the lines (B, fig. 13–128) to the depth indicated. A miter saw is preferred for these cuts. The wood between the two cuts then can be removed with a router plane or with a chisel. The joint should fit snugly but not be tight. The joint can then be

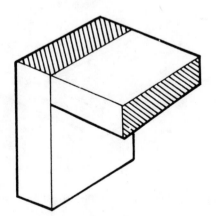

Figure 13–125. Butt joint.

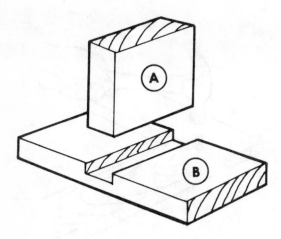

Figure 13–128. Dado joint.

glued, nailed, screwed, or doweled to secure it.

c. Dovetail Joint. The dovetail (fig. 13–129) is one of the strongest of all joints because of its design. If well made, there is strength, even without glue. In better furniture, both old and new, the joint appears in a series to give strength and to improve appearance. If the joint is made entirely by hand, it requires accurate workmanship and a great deal of time. Dovetail jigs, to be used with power equipment, are available to assist the worker and to speed up the process.

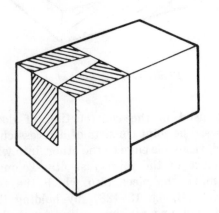

Figure 13–129. Dovetail joint.

d. Lap Joints. There are several different kinds of lap joints, each for a different purpose. Lap joints tend to be stronger than many other joints because of their shape and because they offer more gluing surface. These joints are neat and nice looking, as half of the thickness of both boards is cut away so that when they are joined the surfaces of the wood are flush. They are

made with a saw and chisel in essentially the same manner as the dado joint. Care, patience, and accuracy must be exercised in measuring and in cutting these joints in order to insure a good fit. As with other joints, they can be reinforced with glue, dowels, nails, or screws.

(1) *Cross-lap joint.* The cross-lap joint (fig. 13–130) is used when two pieces of lumber cross as for the base of stands for signs and Christmas tree stands.

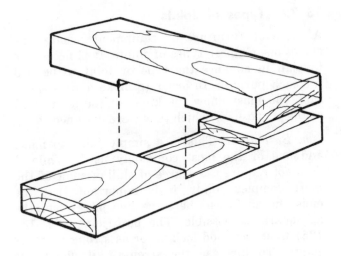

Figure 13–130. Cross-lap joint.

(2) *End-lap joint.* The end-lap joint (fig. 13–131) is very useful for work in an occupational therapy clinic. It provides a neat, secure, and strong way to join the parts of rug and braid-weaving frames. If the frames are to be permanent, glue and screws may be used to hold the joint. If they are to be broken down and reassembled, perhaps for storage, two bolts with washers and wing nuts in each joint will hold the joint securely.

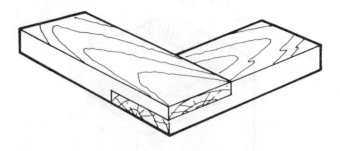

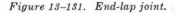

Figure 13–131. End-lap joint.

(3) *Half-lap joint.* The half-lap joint (fig. 13–132) is mainly used for joining lengths of pieces together. If it is well done, it is neat and strong.

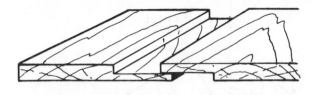

Figure 13–132. Half-lap joint.

(4) *Middle-lap joint.* The middle-lap joint (fig. 13–133) is used in making such items as toys, doors, and furniture.

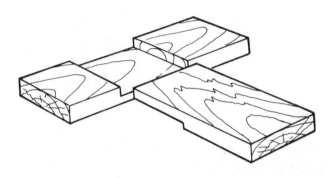

Figure 13–133. Middle-lap joint.

e. *Miter Joint.* The miter joint (fig. 13–134) is one of the more extensively used joints. It is good where symmetry of appearance is desired and in places where it is important to avoid showing end grain, such as in picture frames. Miter joints are usually made at a 45-degree angle, which can be cut with an accurate miter box or measured with a tug square, combination square, or T-bevel. It is a rather difficult joint to make well, especially in a picture frame where each side of all four joints must be very accurate in order to have a square frame with well-fitted joints. When a picture frame is measured, it is the *inside* part of the frame that must be the right size for the picture. The outside measurements of the frame will be the length of the side of the picture plus twice the width of the part of the molding that does not slip over the picture. Figure 13–135 illustrates the calculations for a picture with a 12-inch side. Miter joints may be held after gluing in a miter vise. Because of its design, the joint must be reinforced. Nails and corrugated fasteners are adequate for picture frames, but where more strength is needed, the joint should be screwed, doweled, splined (B, fig. 13–134), or lapped (C, fig. 13–134).

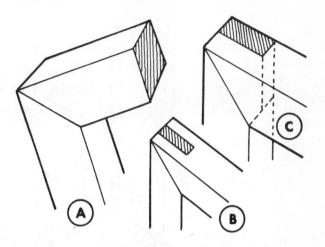

Figure 13–134. Miter joint.

f. *Mortise-and-Tenon Joint.* This is one joint, with the tenon being one-half and the mortise the other half. Because this joint is one of the strongest and best looking, it is extensively used in tables, chairs, desks, window sashes, and other articles where both strength and looks are important. There are a number of variations of the basic joint, three of which are shown (fig. 13–136). They are all made, however, in essentially the same manner. The pieces in which the joint is to be made must be square. Knife lines are marked around the tenon member at the desired length of the tenon. The thickness and width of the tenon is then marked on the end and on the two sides of the piece. A backsaw is used to cut the tenon to shape but the sawing must be on the outside of the tenon line and the inside of the shoulder line. The tenon can then be trimmed carefully with a chisel (fig. 13–137). The location and size of the mortise are marked on the mortise member. With a brace and bit, upon which a depth gauge has been fastened, a series of holes are bored in the place where the tenon is to fit (fig. 13–138). Then with chisels of the right size, the hole must be carefully cleaned out until the tenon fits well. If this joint is well made, it is strong enough when glued and does not need to be reinforced with nails or screws. If the fit of the joint is exceptionally well, chamfer the tenon a little to provide space for more glue.

g. *Rabbet Joint.* The rabbet joint (fig. 13–139) is very similar to the dado joint, except that with the rabbet, the pieces are joined at the end. This joint is extensively used in making such things as drawers, window and door frames, book shelves, and furniture. The pieces into which the

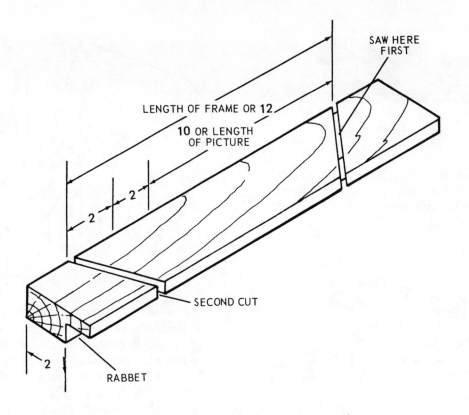

SAW HERE FIRST

LENGTH OF FRAME OR **12**

10 OR LENGTH OF PICTURE

2

2

SECOND CUT

2

RABBET

Figure 13-135. Cutting a picture frame.

oint is to be put must be square. The joint is marked, cut, chiseled, and reinforced in the same manner as the dado joint. If, however, the rabbet point is made with the grain, it can be done with a power saw or with a rabbet plane

h. Tongue-and-Groove Joint. This joint (fig. 13-140) is similar to the mortise-and-tenon joint; however, both the mortise and the tenon are continuous. The tongue-and-groove joint is usually machine made. Lumber for flooring can be purchased already tongued and grooved.

13-73. Joint Reinforcements

Only a few joints are so made that some type of reinforcement is unnecessary. Selection of the reinforcement depends upon how strong the joint needs to be and upon the appearance desired.

a. Spline. This is a thin piece of wood that fits into a groove made across the two parts of a joint. As it is glued into place, it strengthens the joint. Splines are often used to reinforce miter joints (fig. 13-141). It is also possible to use a long one to spline a long board. The spline can be hidden if the groove for the spline is made

with the circular saw in such a way that the cut does not run the full length of the board.

b. Dowels. These may be put into almost any type of joint (fig. 13-142) to give it strength. Although it takes some time and skill to dowel a joint, it is well worth the extra effort in a nice piece because, although there is strength, no fasteners are visible. Dowels are round pieces of wood, usually birch or maple, that come in 36-inch length and range from 1/4 to 1 inch in diameter. Dowels grooved to hold more glue are also available. In making a doweled joint, the pieces must be alined just as they are to be glued; the part that is to be joined is opened up and a line marked across the edge where the dowel is to enter (fig. 13-143). A line is made that intersects the first line at the exact spot where the center of the dowel should be. This usually bisects the cross line that was made originally. If several dowels are to be set, a marking gauge set to make the cross line will be helpful. With a nail or awl, a starter hole is made to guide the bit. Drilling must be accurate, so a depth gauge is used and care must be taken, either through the use of a doweling jig or a tug square, to have the hole at a 90-degree angle to the edge of the board. Another similar hole

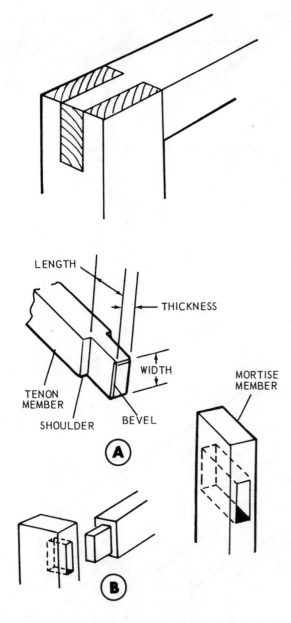

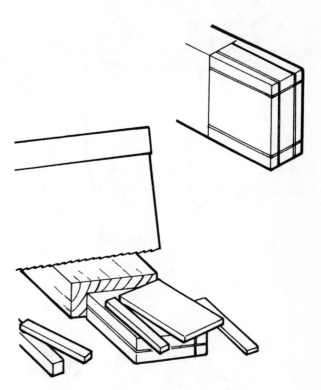

Figure 13–137. Cutting a tenon.

Figure 13–136. Mortise-and-tenon joint.

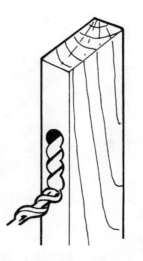

Figure 13–138. Starting a mortise.

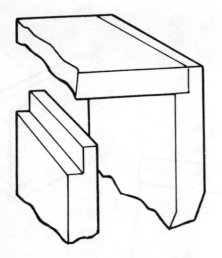

Figure 13–139. Rabbet joint.

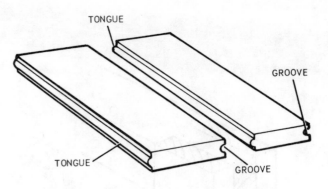

Figure 13–140. Tongue-and groove joint.

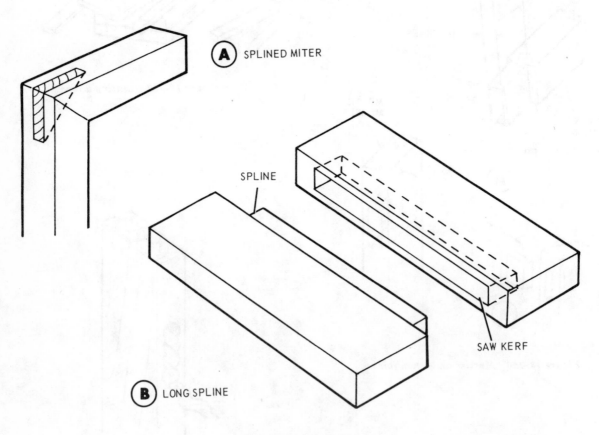

Figure 13–141. Spline.

is made in the other side of the joint. Next, the dowel is cut about 1/8 inch shorter than the combined length of the two holes just made and is sharpened down a bit on the edge with a dowel sharpener (fig. 13–144). The joint, holes, and dowels are coated with glue and the joint assembled and held with a clamp. The dowel may show on one or both sides; if so, it is a through dowel (A, fig. 13–145). If it does not show, it is a blind dowel (B, fig. 13–145).

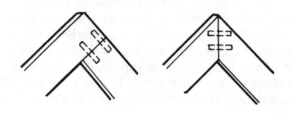

Figure 13–142. Doweled joints.

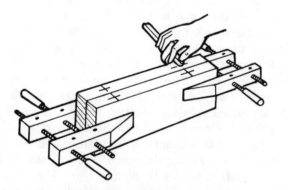

Figure 13–143. Measuring for dowels.

Figure 13–144. Dowel sharpener.

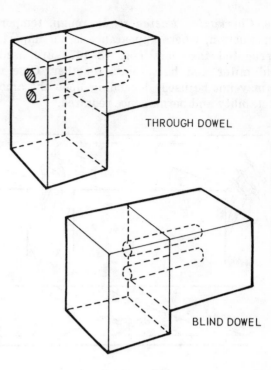

THROUGH DOWEL

BLIND DOWEL

Figure 13–145. Types of dowels.

c. Screws. A joint that is held with glue and screws is solid and durable; even a butt or miter joint reinforced in this manner is quite stable. If a joint is to be taken apart and reassembled, it is held with screws but is not glued.

d. Nails. Nails are used to hold joints in rougher work. If nails are driven at an angle, called "toenailing," they have greater holding power (fig. 13–146). The addition of glue greatly strengthens a nailed joint.

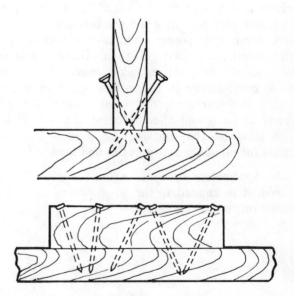

Figure 13–146. Toenailing.

e. Corrugated Fasteners. In rough, temporary construction, where appearance is not important, corrugated fasteners (fig. 13–147) are used to hold miter and butt joints together. Glue may or may not be used, depending upon the amount of stability and permanence required.

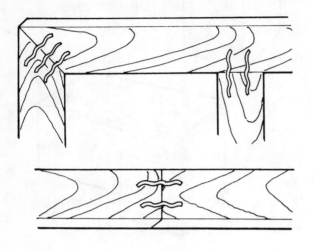

Figure 13–147. Use of corrugated fasteners.

13–74. Gluing

Gluing is said to be the oldest, neatest, strongest, and most durable method of fastening wood joints together. It is usually used in combination with various types of fasteners because of the added strength it provides. It will not, however, fill in and compensate for a poorly fitting joint.

a. Selection of Glue. Selection of the best glue to use depends upon the object itself, as well as where and how it will be used. Some glues, such as casein and plastic, are more resistant to water and dampness; some, such as hot animal glue and plastic, are stronger than others; some set in a short time, others take longer; the newer glues come ready to use, others must be mixed. Table 3–8 contains the most commonly used types of glue and their general characteristics. The label on the container of glue is the best guide for all of these properties and uses.

b. Application of Glue. After the glue is prepared, it is applied to the wood according to the directions on the container.

(1) *Glue sizing.* The open pores of end grain tend to absorb the glue and take it away from the joint. It is therefore advisable to size the end grain if there is to be an appreciable amount of glue within the joint, such as would be found in a butt or dado joint. To do this, a thinned coat of glue is applied to the end grain which will be in the joint. Much of the glue will absorb into the grain but any that remains on the surface should be removed when it sets.

(2) *Amount of glue.* The glue is applied to the joint, using a sufficient amount to hold the joint well, yet little enough so that the pieces will not slide or become too messy when they are clamped together and most of the glue is forced out of the joint. After clamping, the glue should be cleaned off of the wood. It can be wiped off immediately or allowed to become rubbery, then removed.

(3) *Gluing stained pieces.* Glue is absorbed into the pores of the wood even if it is on the wood for just a short time. If glue is in the pores, stain will not be absorbed at the same rate as it will be where there has not been any glue. Therefore, it is advisable, especially for unskilled workers, to stain the pieces before they are glued. This does not apply when paint is used.

13–75. Clamping

Glued joints must be put under pressure until the glue sets. The joint can be held with nails or screws if they are to be used, but frequently it is clamped for better application. There are many clamps made expressly for keeping glued work under pressure. These can be used as described in section VII. Frequently, however, the right number, size, or type of clamp is not available for a particular piece. It then becomes necessary to improvise methods that will be effective (fig. 13–148). It is important to plan the clamping in detail and to place the wood in the clamps with the protective blocks in place *before* glue is applied to the wood. This is particularly important, of course, when using a fast-drying glue, but it also prevents making errors and having to work them out with the wet glue smearing up the wood.

Table 13–8. Properties of Some Common Types of Wood Glue

Type of glue	Source	Mixing	Apply	Drying time	Strength	Shop uses	Water resistance
Animal	Animal or fish	Soak in cold water, then heat in glue pot to 140° F; takes all day.	Hot	Sets rapidly	Very strong	Joint work not exposed to water.	Low.
Cold liquid animal	Animal or fish	Ready-mixed	Cold or warm	Varies with type	Medium	Repair work	Low.
Casein, powdered	Milk	Water soluble; takes 20 min to mix for each use.	Cold	4–5 hrs	Good on oily woods. Works when cool, too.	For semi-water-resistant joint work and as a filler.	Good.
Plastic	Plastic resin	Mix in cold water; ready immediately.	Cold	Sets up hard enough to work within 5–6 hrs. Clamping is necessary.	Very strong	Joint work	Very high.
Epoxy	Resin	Resin and hardener, easily mixed.	Cold	Clamping not necessary. Hardens overnight.	Strong. Resists heat.	Wood, masonry, metal, china, glass.	Waterproof.
Resorcinol glue	Liquid resin and powdered catalyst to be mixed.	Cold	8–10 hrs. Clamping necessary.	Strong at any temperature.	Outdoor furniture, boats, etc., where dark color does not matter.	100% waterproof.
Powdered resin	Resin	Mix for each use	Cold	Clamping necessary.	Strong if joint fits well.	Not good for poor joints or oily surfaces.	Good.
Contact cement		Liquid ready-mixed for use.	Cold	Bends on contact when dry.	Light duty	Leather. Good for large surfaces like wall paneling.	High.
White glue		Liquid ready-mixed for use.	Cold	Sets in 20–30 min with moderate pressure.	Moderate strength.	Paper, fabric, canvas, felt, and cork to wood.	Moderate.

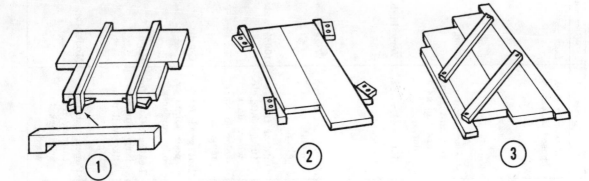

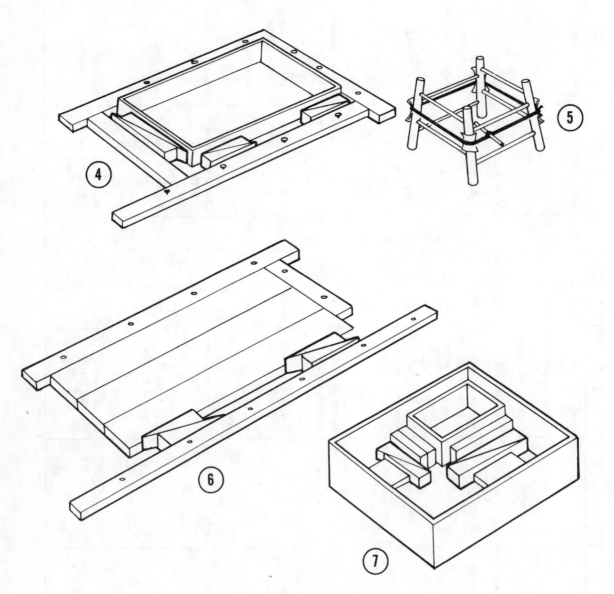

Figure 13-148. Improvised clamping.

13–76. General

There are innumerable kinds of lumber that are used in woodworking. Each type has certain qualities which make it more or less adaptable for certain kinds of work. It is therefore necessary to be able to select the most appropriate type of lumber for a project and to be able to order lumber of the right kind, size, grade, and finish for the work.

13–77. Categories of Wood

There are two main categories of wood—hardwood and softwood.

NOTE
This is rather misleading as it has nothing to do with the hardness or softness of the wood.

a. *Hardwood.* This is cut from deciduous (broadleaf) trees. Both maple and basswood are considered to be hardwoods, although maple is hard and basswood is soft. The more common hardwoods include maple, basswood, birch, oak, yellow poplar, chestnut, mahogany, cherry, walnut, ash, and elm.

b. *Softwood.* Conifers (trees with needle-shaped leaves) furnish the type of lumber classed as softwood. Georgia yellow pine is heavy and hard, while northern white pine is light and soft, yet both are considered to be softwoods. Yellow pine, Douglas fir western pine, hemlock, white pine, redwood, cedar, cypress, and spruce are some of the most common softwoods.

13–78. Types and Qualities of Wood

From the different species of trees, the qualities of woods vary a great deal. Some of the more common types of woods, with information on quality and appropriate uses, are listed below.

a. *Balsa.* A light, very soft wood that is commonly used in model building.

b. *Basswood.* A soft, even-textured, and light-colored wood that is excellent for chip carving. Selected grades are used for drafting boards, cutting boards, and furniture. Basswood is also used in the manufacture of toys.

c. *Birch.* Heavy, strong, fine-grained, and hard. Birch is easily turned on the lathe and will

d. *Cedar.* Soft, very light in weight, close-grained, but not strong. The heartwood is light brown in color with a rose tinge and the sapwood is almost white. It has a strong, unique odor that makes it insect-repellent. For this reason, it is used for closet and trunk linings. Care must be taken when working with cedar, as it splinters easily.

e. *Fir, Douglas.* A close, straight-grained wood that is strong and heavy. It is used in heavy construction work.

f. *Mahogany.* A strong, open-pored, and durable wood. It is red-brown in color, takes a good finish, and works easily. It is the choice of the craftsman and is used in the manufacture of boats and fine furniture. There are a number of species which vary somewhat in quality. The Honduras is the most commonly used.

g. *Maple.* One of the hardest and strongest woods that grow in the United States. It is light in color with a reddish brown cast and has very close pores. It is rather difficult to work because it is so hard, but it takes an excellent finish. It is used for making high-grade furniture and for flooring. Bird's eye maple has a variation in grain that is somewhat spotty and wavy. It is quite beautiful and is used in veneers for the most part. Other types of wood may also have this bird's eye quality in the grain.

h. *Oak.* Coarse-grained and open-pored in texture and yellowish to red-brown in color. It is heavy, hard, and strong so it is used for heavy furniture, interior trim, and flooring.

i. *Pine, Sugar.* A soft, straight-grain wood with uniform density. It is relatively free from knots, is easy to work, and requires a minimum of sanding. It is suitable for whittling or carving either large or small projects.

j. *Pine, White.* Light in weight, soft, and not strong. The grain is fine, straight, and even. The heartwood is light brown and the sapwood is nearly white.

k. *Pine, Yellow.* A tough, reddish, coarse wood that is suitable for heavy construction. It is sometimes used for carving where the pattern of grain is desired.

l. Plywood. Thin sheets of wood glued together. While plywood, in the true sense, is not a kind of wood, it is included in this list because it is used a great deal and has individual characteristics that distinguish it. In each layer, the grain runs in a different direction, which gives the wood unusual strength for its thickness. The 1/4-inch plywood usually is 3-ply, while the 5-ply is either 1/2 or 3/4 inch thick. It is possible to purchase plywood in which the top layer has been sandblasted or scraped to provide interesting texture. Plywood is also made with the top layer of a hardwood veneer. If carefully worked, these fancy plywoods can be made into attractive articles. When plywood is worked it should be treated as cross-grain lumber. If it is not handled correctly, the layers of wood will split, or pieces will split off. This wood also warps quite readily if it becomes damp, because the dampness decreases the strength of the glue. To prevent warping, plywood should be used indoors and should be kept well finished.

m. Poplar. A light, soft wood, of uniform texture. It is worked easily so it is used in model making and in the manufacture of toys.

n. Spruce. Light-weight and strong; used primarily in the manufacture of wood pulp. The density and grain vary so much that certain parts are suitable only for heavy, coarse construction, while other parts are suitable for chip carving and whittling.

o. Walnut. Heavy, hard, strong, durable, open-pored, and easily worked. This is said to be the outstanding American furniture hardwood. It takes an excellent finish, to include just wax or oil over its natural color. It is used commercially for furniture, trim, veneers, and gun stocks. In occupational therapy, it is used in carving and small projects, and in combination with plastic and lighter woods.

13–79. Purchasing Lumber

a. Grades of Wood. Lumber is graded by the number of flaws it contains. In relation to these, the following terminology is used: A *blemish* is a small knot in the wood that mars the appearance but does not alter the soundness of the

Table 13–9. Wood Qualities

Explanation of abbreviations used below:

HARDNESS	WORKABLENESS	WARPING	SPLITTING & GLUING
1—Very soft	E—Easy	-:- Readily	E—Easy
2—Soft	ME—Moderately easy	— Not readily	MD—More difficult
3—Medium	MD—More difficult		D—Difficult
4—Hard	D—Difficult		H—Hard
5—Very hard			

	Hardness	Workableness	Warping	Splitting	Gluing	Grain
Ash	5	E	—	MD	MD	Med-Close
Balsa	1	E	—	MD	E	Close
Basswood	1	E	—	MD	E	Close
Birch	3	ME	—	H	D	Very Close
Cedar	2	E	—	E	E	Close
Cherry	3	MD	—	H	E	Close
Douglas Fir	3	ME	—	MD	E	Close
Elm	3		-:-	H	E	Med-Close
Fir	2	ME	-:-	H	E	Close
Gum	4	ME	-:-	H	E	Close
Mahogany	4	ME	—	MD	E	Med-Close
Maple	5	ME	—	H	MD	Very Close
Oak	5	MD	Varies	MD-H	Varies	Coarse
Pine	2	E	—	MD	E	Varies
Poplar	2	E	—	MD	E	Close
Redwood	3	E	—		E	Close
Spruce	2	ME	—	E	E	Close
Teak, India	5	ME	—	H	E	Medium
Walnut	4	ME	—	MD	E	Med-Close

wood. A *defect* mars the soundness of the wood. A knot of more than 1 1/4 inch in diameter is considered a defect.

(1) Yard lumber is the term applied to most softwoods that may be purchased for shop use. It may be cut as ordinary boards, flooring or moldings, and is divided into two main groups: select and common lumber.

(*a*) Select lumber, as the name indicates, is the better of the two. It is subdivided into grades—
- Grade A is practically free from defects.
- Grade B may have minor defects or blemishes.
- Grade C has more defects or blemishes.
- Grade D has still more defects or blemishes.

(*b*) Common lumber is not as free from imperfections as select lumber, but it is adequate for some purposes and it is less expensive. It is subdivided as follows:
- No. 1 Common—is sound, although it may have small knots.
- No. 2 Common—has large, coarse defects.
- No. 3 Common—contains a greater number of defects.
- No. 4 Common—contains still more defects.
- No. 5 Common—is considered poor lumber and is unusable for shop work.

(2) Hardwood grading differs from that of softwood. It is graded as First, Second, Third, and so on. First, of course, is the best grade and indicates that there are no defects in a board of 4 to 9 board feet, or but one defect in a board of 10 to 15 board feet.

b. Measurement of Lumber. The price of lumber is based on the cost per board foot. A board foot is 1 inch thick, 12 inches wide, and 1 foot long. The measurements are given in the following order: thickness, width, then length. Thickness and width are given in inches; length is given in feet.

Example: How many board feet are there in four pieces of lumber 2" x 6" x 5'?
Answer: 2 time 6/12, times 5, times 4 = 20 board feet.

Even though lumber is purchased by the board foot, it is cut in lengths of even multiples of two. Care must be taken to see that the lumber purchased will fit the storage space. Lumber is also cut in even numbered widths such as 2 inches, 4 inches, and 6 inches. To obtain a board 3 inches wide, it must be cut from a 4-inch piece and the purchase price therefore will be that of the 4-inch piece. In softwoods, 1 inch is the minimum thickness that can be purchased. If thinner stock is desired, it must be planed down. The minimum thickness when purchasing hardwoods is 5/8 of an inch.

(1) The measurements in *b* above are made on rough lumber that is furry and splintery. Therefore, planing not only smoothes the surface, but also decreases the size of the piece. A board that is sold as 1 inch thick is actually only 13/16 of an inch thick. This must be taken into account when ordering. Other standard dimensions are as follows:

1/2 inch is 5/16 inch
5/8 inch is 7/16 inch
3/4 inch is 9/16 inch
1 inch is 13/16 inch
1 1/4 inch is 1 1/16 inch
1 1/2 inches is 1 5/16 inch
2 inches is 1 3/4 inch
3 inches is 2 3/4 inches
4 inches is 3 3/4 inches

(2) The width of lumber is also based on the size of the piece in the rough. Standard dimensions for width variations are as follows:

1 inch is 13/16 inch
3 inches is 2 5/8 inches
12 inches is 11 1/4 inches

(3) Random lengths and/or widths of lumber may be ordered. Random lengths will be 8, 10, or 12 feet long. Random widths will be 3 1/2, 5 1/2, 7 1/2, 9 1/2, or 11 1/2 inches wide. The cost of lumber purchased this way is the same price per linear foot as is lumber cut to specified lengths and widths. There is no monetary savings, and the random sizes may prove to be less than desirable in planning projects.

c. Surfacing Lumber. When lumber is purchased, a request must be made to have it surfaced. It may be surfaced in any combination desired; the following symbols are used on the order to designate what should be done:

S1S—surface on one side
S2S—surface on two sides
S1E—surface one edge
S2E—surface two edges
S1S2E—surface one side and two edges
S4S—surface four sides (this is the usual request)

d. Plywood. Plywood is made 4 feet wide and the desired number of feet may be purchased. For quantity buying, sheets 4 by 8 feet are quite convenient. It is also necessary to indicate whether the plywood should be clear on both sides or on just one side.

13–80. Introduction

a. Power tools make some woodworking and plastic operations easier, quicker, and more accurate than hand methods.

b. Power tools should be in a separate room that can be locked, or they should be fitted with individual locks so that they can be kept completely out of the treatment picture if it is so desired. Directions for operation and care of each tool should be kept with the tool. If no directions are available, write to the manufacturer and request this information, or refer to a book in which it is given.

13–81. Band Saw

A band saw consists of an endless saw blade that is tracked over two or three rubber-tired pulley wheels (fig. 13–149). It is good for cutting a variety of materials other than wood, but it cannot perform as many different operations as the circular saw. The band saw requires a floor space of 6 by 6 feet and the table should be from 42 to 44 inches from the floor.

a. Sizes of Band Saws and Blades. Band saws are sized by the width that can be cut between the blade and the upright support. They range from 14 to 26 inches. The amount of vertical clearance between the table and the blade guide can be regulated to take 1/8 inch to 6 or 6 1/2 inches. Blades for band saws are purchased according to the width and the number of teeth per inch. They come in 1/8- to 1-inch widths. For ordinary work, a 1/4- or 3/8-inch blade is used; the 1/8-inch blades are for cutting sharp curves. Blades with 10 to 24 small teeth per inch are for cutting plastic and metal. Blades with 8 to 10 teeth per inch are for cutting wood. Blades may be purchased prewelded to the correct size, or they may be bought by the foot, to be welded as needed.

b. Band Saw Blades. To do good and pleasurable work with a band saw, the blade must be welded properly, it must set on the saw correctly, and it must be sharp. Such care will do much to prevent drifting of the blade, frequent breakage, and burning of the wood.

(1) *Broken or unwelded band saw blades.*

When a blade breaks, it can be rewelded and used again if it is in good condition. Band saw blades should be brazed (which is a lower temperature process than welding), unless they are welded electrically for a stronger joint. The joint is more durable if the blade is cut at an angle from 3/4 to 1 inch long (fig. 13–150), rather than if it is cut straight across. Blades break from prolonged usage or they may break because of one of the following:

• Improper alining and adjusting of guides.
• Dullness.
• Loss of set
• Feeding work in too fast.
• Twisting.
• Too much tension.
• Improper welding.
• Using the wrong blade for the job.
• Sawing nails or screws.

(2) *Changing band saw blade.* Because blades break rather frequently, anyone in the woodworking area should be skilled at changing blades. To do this properly, these steps should be followed:

(*a*) Disconnect the machine.

(*b*) Open upper and lower guard doors, remove pin in table slot, and loosen vertical adjustment screw.

(*c*) Remove the old blade. If it has been broken, pull it off very carefully as it is "springy" and may flip around and cause an injury. If the blade is in one piece, pull the steel pin out of the slot in the table and lower the upper wheel by turning the vertical adjustment wheel. Grasp the saw blade with both hands, lift it off of the upper and lower wheels, and coil it into three loops ((3) below).

(*d*) Slip the new blade onto the upper and lower wheels with the teeth pointing downward. The guides (fig. 13–151) should be back out of position. Tighten the vertical adjustment screw and revolve the wheels by hand to see how the blade "rides." If the blade does not run in the center of the wheels, tilt the upper wheel with the tilt adjustment screw. The rear edge of the saw blade should be perpendicular to the table. (Figure 13–152 illustrates excessive tilt of the wheel.)

(*e*) Adjust the tension of the saw with the vertical adjustment screw. If the saw does not have a tensioning spring, the blade should bend 1/8 to 1/4 inch when pushed lightly on the side of the saw blade.

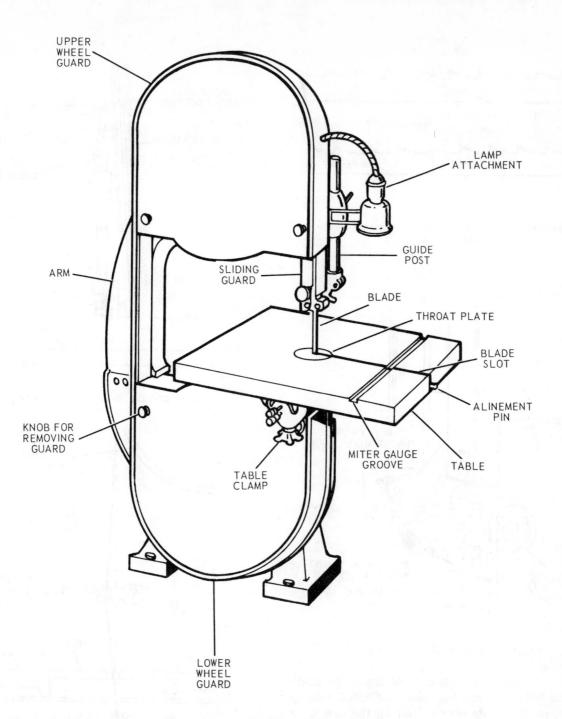

UPPER
WHEEL
GUARD

LAMP
ATTACHMENT

ARM

SLIDING
GUARD

GUIDE
POST

BLADE

THROAT PLATE

BLADE
SLOT

ALINEMENT
PIN

KNOB FOR
REMOVING
GUARD

TABLE
CLAMP

MITER GAUGE
GROOVE

TABLE

LOWER
WHEEL
GUARD

Figure 13-149. Band saw (table model).

(*f*) Bring the blade guides forward and tighten the jaws to allow the saw blade to run freely between them. Be sure that the jaws of one blade guide are directly below those of the other and not out of line (fig. 13–153).

(*g*) Move the roller or thrust wheels so that they are within 1/32 inch of the rear edge of the saw. The saw blade should touch the guide wheels only when sawing is being done.

(3) *Coiling a band saw blade.* An uncoiled blade is an unmanageable and therefore a dan-

gerous thing to have around, especially in an area where there are a number of people. Figure 13–154 illustrates how to coil a band saw blade properly.

(4) *Sharpening band saw blades.* It is less expensive and better to replace a dull blade than to have a technician sharpen it. The following directions for sharpening are to be used *only* if new blades or professional sharpeners are not available.

(*a*) To hold the blade in place for sharp-

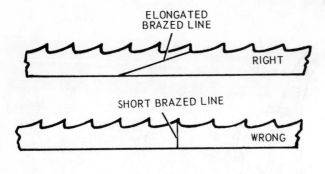

Figure 13–150. Methods of cutting brazing line in band saw blades.

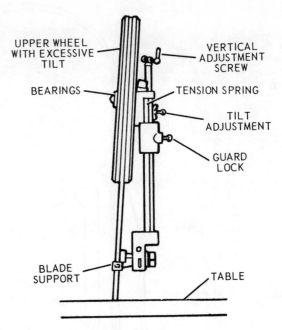

Figure 13–152. Excessive tilt of wheel.

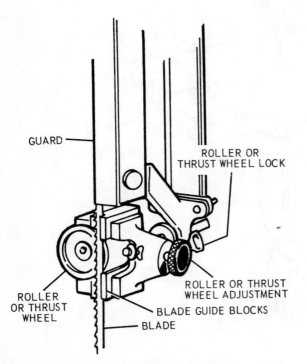

Figure 13–151. Band saw blade guide.

ening, a special saw vise may be used, the blade may be held between two pieces of wood held in a vise, or the blade may be put on the saw with the teeth in reversed direction, pointing up.

(*b*) The teeth must be set just as with a hand saw. The top half of the teeth is set with the bending line parallel to the back of the blade (fig. 13–155). Because the teeth are set in pairs, one to the right and one to the left, it is important that the blade have an even number of teeth in order to maintain this pattern.

(*c*) To file, use an extra slim, tapered triangular file about 7 inches long. Place the file in the gullet of the tooth and roll it slightly to the right to provide an 8- to 15-degree hook (fig. 13–156). The angle between the front of one

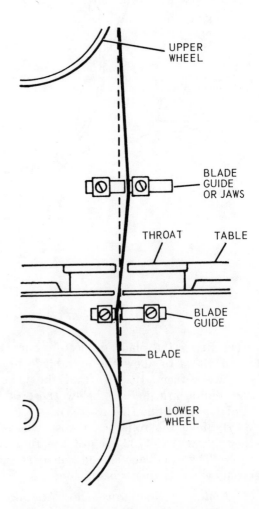

Figure 13–153. Blade guides out of line.

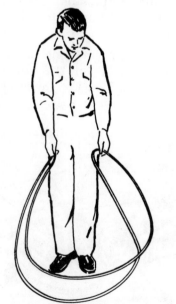

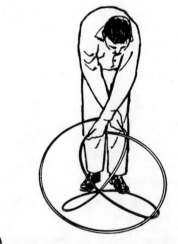

A Hold the saw blade vertically grasped at each side at about the middle with the teeth pointing away from the body.

B Press with the thumbs on the side of the saw at the back, so that the cutting edge is bent and the part of the saw above the fingers bends down.

C Without changing the grasp on the saw blade, place the upper loop inside the lower loop on the floor.

D Then move the hands together, with one crossing the other. This will partly form three loops, so that when the blade is released, it will coil on the floor.

Figure 13–154. Coiling a band saw blade.

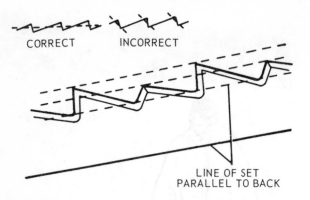

Figure 13–155. Line of set of a band saw blade.

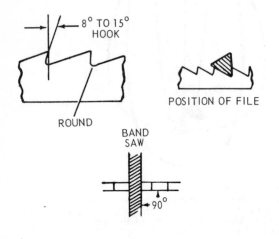

Figure 13–156. Filing the hook on the band saw blade.

tooth and the back of an adjacent tooth is 60 degrees and the gullet is round. The teeth of band saw blades are filed square across. To keep the teeth uniform in shape, try to apply uniform pressure to the same number of strokes on each tooth.

(d) If, after the blade is touched up, it has a tendency to drift from the guide line, there is inequality of sharpness or set of the teeth, and the job needs to be redone.

c. Using a Band Saw.

(1) Cutting should be done only when the saw is running at full speed.

(2) The stock is fed into the blade with light pressure of the right hand and with the left hand used to help guide the work. Both hands must be kept well away from the blade.

(3) The narrower the blade, the smaller the circle that can be cut. Trying to cut too small a circle can result in a pinched or broken blade. To prevent this, several cuts can be made to the

edge of the curve to break it into smaller parts (fig. 13–157). A change in the sound of the saw often indicates when the blade is being pinched.

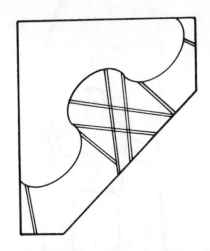

Figure 13–157. Kerfs made for freeing band saw blade on sharp curves.

(4) Holes may be bored in square corners and the stock sawed away to square the corner.

(5) Although stock is usually fed into the band saw manually, it is possible to use a fence for straight cuts or a miter gauge for miter cuts.

(6) Several pieces of lumber can be sawed in the same way at the same time. One way is to drive nails or brads into the waste part of the several layers. Care must be taken then to avoid sawing through the nails.

(7) Sawing at an angle (fig. 13–158) is done by tilting the table of the saw to the desired angle as indicated on the gauge under the table.

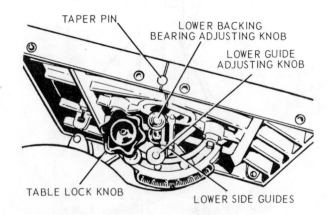

Figure 13–158. Sawing at an angle with a band saw.

d. Care of the Band Saw. The band saw requires relatively little care.

(1) Clean the sawdust from inside by removing the wheel guards and vacuuming or brushing the dirt away.

(2) Brush sawdust from the saw.

(3) Apply a thin coating of oil on the table to prevent rust.

(4) Release blade tension of the saw when it will not be used over a period of time.

(5) If the saw is used frequently, oil the bearings every month with SAE 10 machine oil. Oil the following points each month if the saw is used frequently or every 6 months if it is used infrequently:

• Upper and lower wheel bearings.
• Table tilt supports or guide.
• Upper wheel tilt and tension screws.
• Blade guide blocks.

e. Safety Precautions. The band saw is considered to be less dangerous than the circular saw, but safety precautions are important to prevent accidents.

(1) Set the clamp and guide post 1/4 inch above the stock to protect the hands.

(2) Keep the floor and the saw free from scraps of wood and obstructions

(3) Roll up sleeves before using the saw.

(4) Do not wear ragged clothing, gloves, or a long loose tie while sawing.

(5) Listen for a change in the hum of the saw, as it may indicate trouble.

(6) Replace the throat plate when it becomes worn lest pieces of wood drop down and cause the blade to break.

(7) Do not back the saw blade out of a cut unless necessary, then do it slowly and with care.

(8) Do not allow anyone to stand to the right of the saw while the saw is in use, as the blade might break and cause injury.

(9) Wait for the blade to stop moving before removing scraps from the saw table.

(10) Disconnect the saw before changing the blade or making repairs.

13–82. Jigsaw

The jigsaw (fig. 13–159) is regarded by some as an auxiliary to the band saw. It can be used for operations such as sawing curved outlines and inside sawing or pierced work that cannot be done on a band saw. The jigsaw blade moves up and down rapidly through a 1/8- to 3/4-inch stroke; it saws on the downward part of the stroke. Jigsaws are made in small bench types as well as in large production machines. They require a floor space area of 6 by 6 feet, and the table of the saw should be 37 inches from the floor.

a. Sizes of Jigsaws and Blades. The size of a jigsaw is determined by the distance between the blade and the upright arm of the frame. The general range in size is 18, 24, and 26 inches, with 24 inches being the most commonly used. The guide assembly can be raised to about 2 inches above the throat plate, but the jigsaw will not easily cut 2-inch material unless it is quite soft. Jigsaw blades may be 4, 5, or 6 inches in length, with 6 inches being the most frequently used. They come with the end kinked or plain, or with a pin, so care must be taken to purchase the right blade for the saw. These blades vary in width from .040 to .187 inch. The narrower blades are not as sturdy as the wider ones, but it is possible to cut sharper curves with them. The blades are usually 6 inches long and the number of teeth per inch range from 7 to 32. The larger teeth are for cutting wood and plastic, the smaller ones for wood and plywood, and the 32 per inch for metal. The best blade for general use has 10 teeth per inch. Because jigsaw blades are inexpensive, they are not rewelded if they break, and they are not worth sharpening.

b. Changing a Jigsaw Blade. Before starting, disconnect the machine. The blade is held in the saw between the flat jaws of the upper and lower chucks, where it is secured with wingnuts. The teeth point downward.

(1) First secure the blade in the lower chuck, then in the upper chuck leg, pushing the spring casing and the upper chuck down enough before the blade is secured, to put some tension on the blade (fig. 13–160).

(2) Fasten the front edge of the guide block in line with the gullets of the teeth. Then bring the roller, which moves independently, forward and tighten in the position where it just touches the blade (fig. 13–161).

(3) To remove a broken blade, loosen the wingnuts of the upper and lower chucks and remove the blade or blade pieces.

c. Using a Jigsaw. The jigsaw is easy to operate and is relatively safe if ordinary precautions and good judgment are used. The saw must have

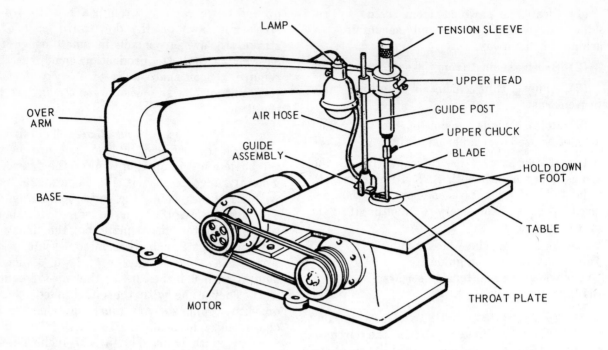

Figure 13–159. Jigsaw.

the right blade correctly mounted, and it must be adjusted to the best speed for the operation being done.

(1) *Adjusting the speed*. The speed of the jigsaw can be adjusted between 600 and 1750 rpm. The faster the speed, the smoother the cut—but the harder the direction of the cut is to control. Because of this, beginners should keep the speed down until they become skilled at guiding the saw. The average speed maintained is about 1200 rpm. The speed of the saw is changed by the placement of the belt on the pulley (fig. 13–162).

(2) *Lowering the jigfoot*. The jigsaw blade moves up and down, so there is a tendency for the stock being cut to move up with the blade. This is overcome by lowering the guidepost until the jigfoot rests lightly on the material to be sawed (fig. 13–163).

(3) *Feeding the stock carefully*. All of the adjustments must be checked to insure that they are correct, then the motor is started. The stock is fed into the blades slowly, evenly, and directly into the teeth. Cutting is done on the waste edge of the guideline so as to have sufficient amount of stock for the finishing process.

(4) *Blowing sawdust away*. Most jigsaws are equipped with a blower attachment that delivers a stream of air through an airbase which blows sawdust away from the area being sawed.

(5) *Backing from a kerf*. Care must be taken when pulling the blade back through the kerf lest the blade be pulled from the chuck and broken.

(6) *Doing inside cuts*. To do pierced work or inside cuts, a hole larger than the blade width must be bored. The blade is removed from the top chuck, slipped through the bored hole, and replaced into the chuck. When sawing in that area is completed, the top part of the blade is again taken out of the chuck and the piece is removed.

(7) *Doing angle cuts*. The table of the jigsaw tips in the same way as the table of the band saw. The pressure foot can be adjusted to hold the work in all but the greatest angles.

(8) *Using sanding and filing attachments*. Special sanding and filing attachments (fig. 13–164) are available that fit into the sanders and the file jaws in the lower chuck. The sanders and the files come in various shapes for special jobs. The saw must be set on slow speed when the sanding attachment is being used.

(9) *Sawing plastic*. Plastic over 1/4 inch thick is difficult to saw on a jigsaw because the rapid motion of the blade creates sufficient heat to melt the plastic and trap the blade. Oil and water slow this process to some degree, but not enough to make it satisfactory.

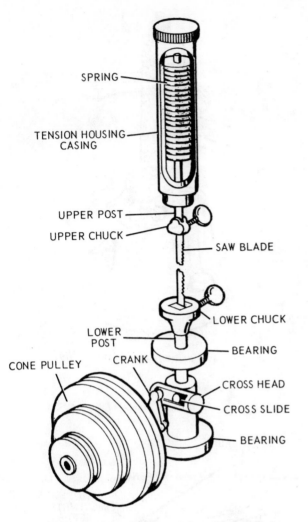

Figure 13–160. Mechanism of the spring-loaded jigsaw.

d. Care of the Jigsaw. The jigsaw must be kept free from sawdust and the table needs an occasional light coating of oil to prevent rust. The mechanism is splash lubricated so there is an oil cup into which SAE 30 machine oil is put. There is also a drain for removing the oil when it is changed. This should be done every 3 to 6 months, depending upon the amount of use. The guide shaft, the blade guide, the upper shaft bearing, the blade tension housing, and the lower drive assembly are lubricated.

13–83. Table or Circular Saw

The table saw (fig. 13–165) is considered by some to be the most useful of the power tools. A motor-driven circular saw blade is adjusted by a hand wheel until it projects through a slot in the top of the flat cast iron table (called the "throat") a little further than the thickness of

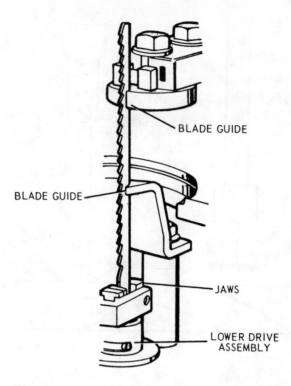

Figure 13–161. Guide plate, roller, and lower guide for saber plate.

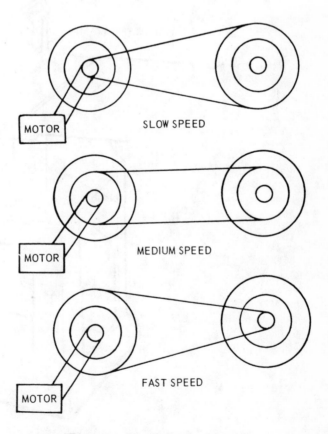

Figure 13–162. Pulley arrangement.

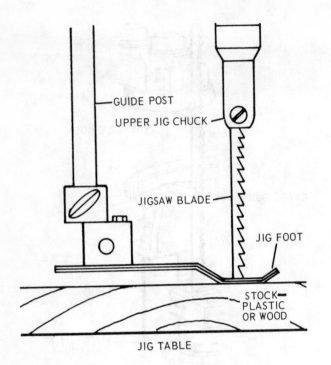

Figure 13–163. Stabilizing the stock.

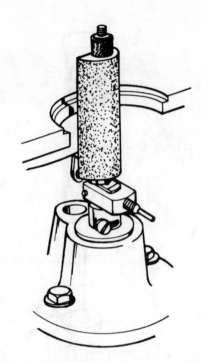

Figure 13–164. Sanding attachment for jigsaw.

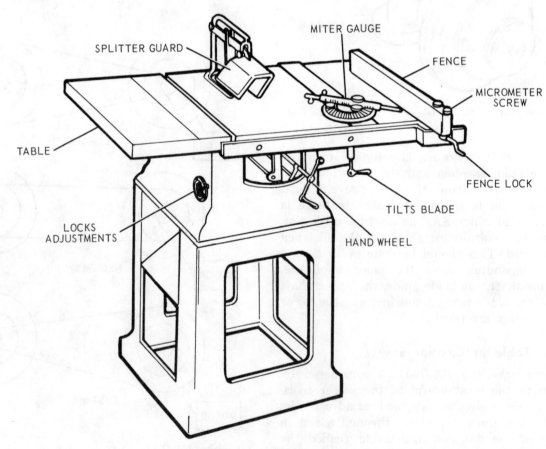

Figure 13–165. Table saw.

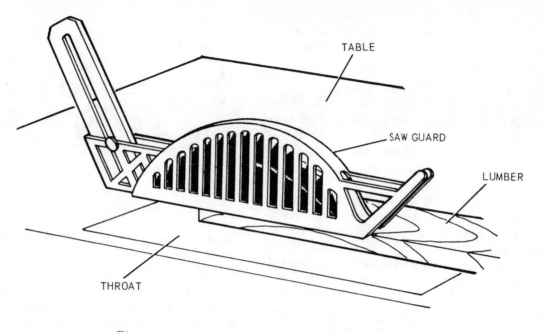

Figure 13–166. Combination guard and splitter for circular saw.

the board to be sawed. The guide or "fence" is set as far from the blade as the lumber should be cut, and the wood is fed into the saw by holding it against the guide with a push stick. It is possible to do various operations such as grooving and mitering by adjusting the saw in different ways or by changing to a different type of blade. Floor space needed is 8 by 6 feet.

a. Saw Guards. A saw guard should be used on all cuts whenever possible. There are several types of guards on the market.

(1) *Combination guard and splitter.* A combination saw guard and splitter (fig. 13–166) is useful. The saw guard part covers the blade and is made so that it automatically lifts at the beginning of the cut, rides on the wood being cut, then drops in place on the saw table when the wood gets past the blade. It is combined with a splittering or spreading guard (fig. 13–167) which consists of a beveled, shaped piece of steel which fastens behind the blade with bolts. The back of the splitter is a little thicker than the saw blade, so it keeps the kerf from closing and pinching the blade.

(2) *Plastic guard.* Another efficient guard available on the market is made of heavy-duty plastic so that the operator can see the blade through the plastic. This guard (fig. 13–168) is extremely adjustable so it can be used for protection while making all but a very few cuts.

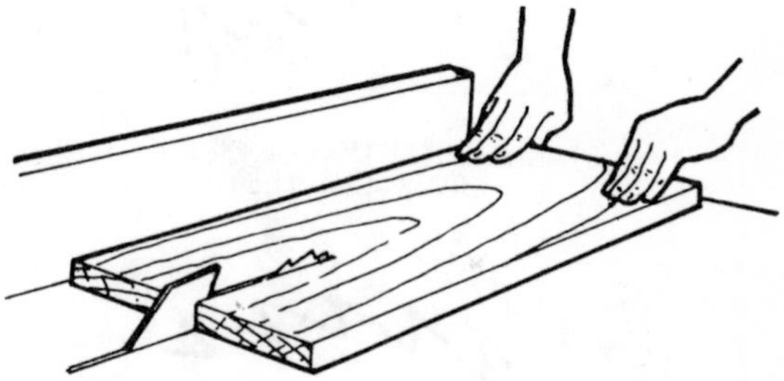

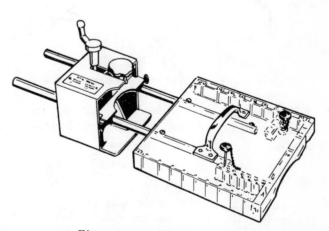

Figure 13–167. Splitter.

Figure 13–168. Plastic saw guard.

b. Saw Sizes. Circular saw sizes are determined by the maximum diameter of the saw blade which can be used with the machine, such as a 7-, 8-, or 10-inch blade.

c. Types of Blades. Three types of circular saw blades are used for all ordinary work. These are the rip blade, crosscut blade, and the combination blade. The rip blade has teeth that resemble those of a hand ripsaw; that is, a series of chisel points. The teeth of the crosscut blade also resemble those of a hand crosscut saw; that is, they are filed to knife points. The combination saw blade (fig. 13–169) has some crosscut teeth and some ripsaw teeth, and can therefore be used for both ripping and crosscutting. This blade is the most frequently used for general shop work. To cut grooves, two saws that resemble a combination saw are placed side by side on the arbor. For wider grooves, one or more inside cutters are placed between the saws. This assembly of saws and cutters is called a dado head (fig. 13–170).

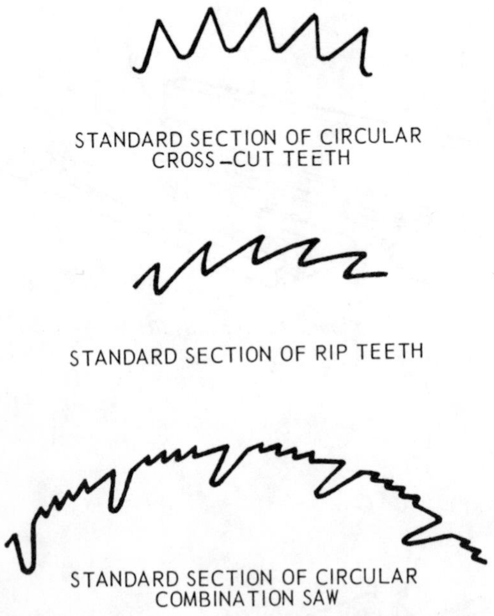

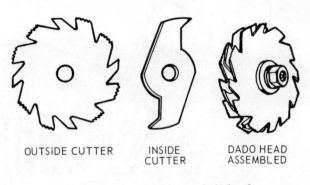

OUTSIDE CUTTER   INSIDE CUTTER   DADO HEAD ASSEMBLED

Figure 13–170. Parts of a dado head.

with a solid table, remove the throat plate. In both cases, it is now possible to get at the nut which holds the saw blade.

(3) Remove the nut that holds the saw blade. To do this, stand in front of the saw, wedge a piece of wood between the saw blade and the frame, and hold the wood with the left hand. Slip the wrench furnished with the machine over the nut and pull toward you with the right hand (fig. 13–171). Remove the nut, collar, and saw blade.

STANDARD SECTION OF CIRCULAR CROSS–CUT TEETH

STANDARD SECTION OF RIP TEETH

STANDARD SECTION OF CIRCULAR COMBINATION SAW

Figure 13–169. Teeth of standard circular saws.

d. Changing of Circular Saw Blades. These steps should be followed in changing a circular saw blade.

(1) Always unplug the saw before starting to change the blade.

(2) On a saw with a movable table, pull the framework on which the movable table slides sideways, away from the saw blade. On a saw

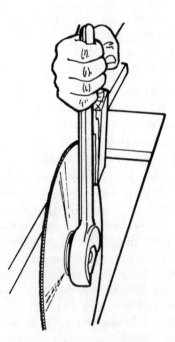

Figure 13–171. Loosening nut preparatory to removing saw blade.

(4) Note that the end of the arbor has a left-hand thread. This means that when the nut is turned to the right, or clockwise, it is loosened; when turned to the left, or counterclockwise,

it is tightened. The reason for this is that the nut will tend to tighten itself more as the saw is running.

(5) Hold the blade to be used so that the manufacturer's name is toward you and slip it over the arbor. When the manufacturer's name is visible, the teeth of the saw always point in the right direction.

(6) Replace the collar and nut. Wedge the saw blade as before and tighten the nut by pushing the wrench away from you. Only a moderate pressure of the wrench is necessary.

(7) Push the table back in place or replace the throat plate. Drop the saw guard over the saw.

e. Sharpening of Circular Saw Blades. It is not recommended that the amateur sharpen a circular saw blade. The sharpening should be done commercially by a professional. If the sharpening process is not done properly, the blade will vibrate and have a lateral motion, causing it to bind and increase the chances of a kickback. Using a dull blade can also cause a kickback. Rather than use a dull blade, sawing can be accomplished by hand saws which can be sharpened.

f. Sawing Operations. Many operations are possible on a circular saw. Only the basic cuts are considered, however.

(1) *Ripping operation.*

(a) Set the ripping fence to the desired width either by measuring from one of the teeth set or bent toward the ripping fence, or by using the scale engraved on the table of many machines. Clamp the fence in position and make final adjustment with the micrometer screw.

(b) Place the stock on the table and raise or lower the saw blade until it projects 1/8 inch above the stock.

(c) Insure that the stock lies flat on the table and has one straight edge that is held against the ripping fence.

(d) See that the splitting guard is in place and lower the saw guard over the saw.

(e) Start the machine, stand a little to one side, and hold the stock near its end. Hold the stock against the ripping fence and push it toward the saw with a firm, even motion. It is advisable for a beginner to work slowly.

(f) Let the sawed-off stock fall to the floor or have a helper at the rear of the saw remove it.

(2) *Cutting short pieces to length (less than 12 inches).*

(a) Use the ripping fence as a stop to obtain the correct length of the pieces to be cut. To prevent these pieces from being pinched between the saw and fence, which would result in a dangerous kickback, use a clearance block, which is a small iron plate screwed to the end of the ripping fence nearest the operator.

(b) To set the fence, hold the block against it at the place where the scale is marked on the table, or measure to one of the teeth set toward the fence. Then clamp the fence in position and screw the block to its end.

(c) Use a crosscut or combination saw and place both splitter and saw guard in position. Start the machine and hold the jointed edge of the stock against the miter gauge with both hands. Push both the stock and the gauge past the saw and cut a small piece off the end to square it.

(d) Push the squared end of the stock against the clearance block, hold it firmly against the miter gauge, and cut off the first piece (fig. 13–172), which will lie on the table between the saw and the ripping fence.

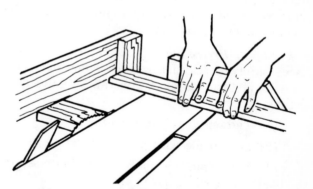

Figure 13–172. Cutting short pieces of stock to length, using clearance block. (Saw guard was deleted for illustrative purposes only.)

(3) *Cutting longer pieces of stock to length (more than 12 inches).*

(a) Cut the pieces roughly to length by hand.

(b) Check for a steel stop rod. Some miter and cutoff gauges are equipped with this rod which can be clamped in a slot in the face of the gauge. Use it if available (fig. 13–173).

(c) If a stop rod is not available, screw a strip of wood to the gauge and nail or clamp a stopblock to it at the desired length.

(d) Place the squared end of each piece

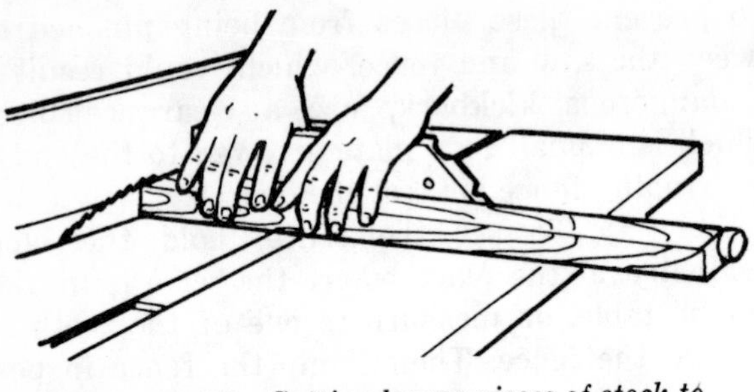

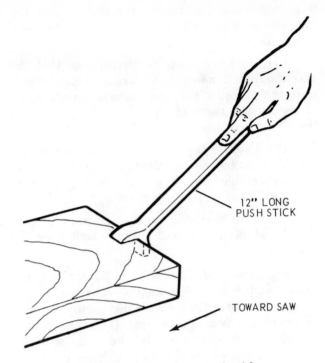

Figure 13–173. *Cutting longer pieces of stock to length using stop rod. (Saw guard was deleted for illustrative purposes only.)*

of stock against the stopback and hold it firmly to the face of the gauge. Move the piece forward and, when it passes the saw, the other end is cut to exact length and squared. Cut one piece at a time.

g. Care and Maintenance of the Circular Saw. The circular saw should be kept clean and free from dust. The table must have a light coating of oil to prevent rust. Most table saws provide for oiling of the bearings, whether they are sleeve or ball bearings. Most ball bearing types are dust-sealed, but they will have to be taken apart and oiled or greased on occasion. Inject oil in all oil-cups on the saw at intervals appropriate for the amount of use of the saw.

h. Safety Precautions. It is important to observe safety precautions while using this saw, as without them its operation can be quite dangerous.

(1) Tighten guard on machine before using.

(2) Lock blade with a wrench before using.

(3) Never place a guard guide too close to the blade, as it will rub the arm.

(4) Use a wooden push stick (fig. 13–174) on all narrow pieces of wood; never use a metal push stick because it will dull or break the saw blade or be flipped out of the hand.

(5) Turn off the saw after completing the cutting of one piece.

(6) When working, stand to one side of the saw and do not allow any other person to stand in line with saw.

(7) Do not reach over the saw; have someone take away the stock after it has been run through the saw.

(8) Never put strain against the blade when sawing.

12" LONG PUSH STICK

TOWARD SAW

Figure 13–174. *Using a push stick.*

(9) Adjust the blade so that it appears just above the material being cut.

(10) Do not do any freehand cutting or try to cut curves on the table saw.

(11) Do not wear loose or ragged clothes or gloves.

(12) Roll up sleeves before starting the saw.

(13) Talk to no one while using the saw.

(14) Keep the saw blade sharp; a dull blade is dangerous.

(15) Check the blade for cracks by tapping it before each use.

13–84. Sanders

a. Disk Sander. A disk sander (fig. 13–175) consists of a sandpaper-covered metal disk which is rotated rapidly by a motor. There is an adjustable table fastened to the sander (fig. 13–176) which can be tilted to hold the stock at an angle for a bevel. The table is usually equipped with a miter gauge so that end wood can be sanded square to the sides and so that miters can be sanded. Floor space needed is 6 by 4 feet.

(1) *Using the sander and safety precautions.* Care must be taken to keep the hands away from the disk. There is also danger of the work being thrown by the wheel. This can be prevented to a great degree by holding the work on the

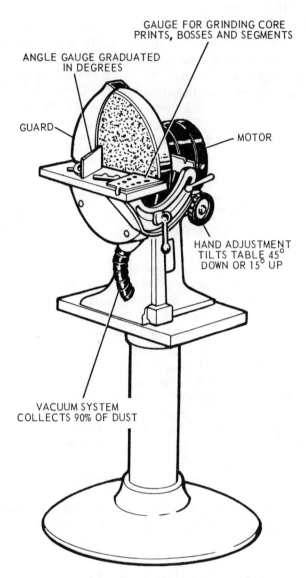

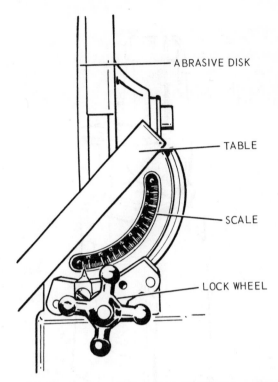

GAUGE FOR GRINDING CORE
PRINTS, BOSSES AND SEGMENTS

ANGLE GAUGE GRADUATED
IN DEGREES

GUARD

MOTOR

HAND ADJUSTMENT
TILTS TABLE 45°
DOWN OR 15° UP

VACUUM SYSTEM
COLLECTS 90% OF DUST

Figure 13–175. Disk sander.

ABRASIVE DISK

TABLE

SCALE

LOCK WHEEL

Figure 13–176. Adjustable table for disk sander.

side of the wheel that is going down toward the table. It is also helpful to remember that the outside of the wheel sands more rapidly than the inside. When sanding hardwood, the piece must be kept moving so that burning of the wood does not occur. As a safety precaution, operators must always wear goggles or a face mask when operating the sander. Dust collectors of various kinds are available for the disk sander.

(2) *Changing the sanding disk.* Sanding disks are available on the market from 10 to 16 inches in diameter. They are usually of garnet paper in 00 to 2 1/2 grit for different types of work. Grit 1 or 1 1/2 is good for general work.

When the disk becomes worn, it must be changed. (Before the sandpaper is changed, the sander should be disconnected.) The disk of sandpaper is adhered to the metal disk of the sander with a resin-like compound called distic or with rubber cement. The metal plate must be completely cleaned of old distic, then the new distic is applied to the metal disk and the sandpaper is put on the disk. If rubber cement is used, the old cement is cleaned off the plate, then both the disk and sandpaper are coated again with rubber cement. After the rubber cement dries, the sandpaper is pressed onto the disk.

b. Belt Sander. Belt sanders are used to sand flat as well as curved surfaces. This is done by pressing the work against an endless abrasive belt. There are several types of belt sanders. The vertical (fig. 13–177), the horizontal (fig. 13–178), and the combination of disk and belt sanders (fig. 13–179). A sander is also made that can be used either in the vertical or in the horizontal position.

(1) *Using the sander and safety precautions.* Most of these sanders have a backplate to use as a guide in sanding flat work. They also have an adjustable and removable table slotted for a graduated gauge to use when sanding angles. Sanding can be done on the curve of the

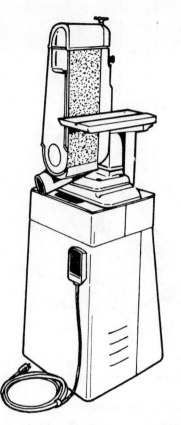

Figure 13–177. Vertical belt sander.

wheels, which are usually two sizes just for that purpose. All of this makes the belt sander quite versatile. Care must be taken to prevent injury from the moving belt. The dust collector reduces irritation from dust in the air and cuts down on cleaning.

(2) *Changing and adjusting the sanding belt.* The grits most commonly used are No. 1 to 3/0, and they are usually garnet. When the belt becomes worn, it must be replaced with a new one. To do this, loosen the two inside nuts, thereby releasing all tension. Slip the belt over the pulleys so that the arrow on the inside of the belt points toward the guide fence. Tighten both adjustments so that there is sufficient tension for the belt to move when the power pulley is moved by hand. Turn the power pulley over several times to see if the belt is tracking properly. If the belt shifts to the right, loosen the right outside nut and tighten the right inside one. This will throw the belt to the left; but if not sufficiently to the left, slightly loosen the left inside nut and tighten the left outside nut. Continue to adjust until the belt is tracking. If the belt is tracking to the left, reverse the above procedure. Do not start

the machine until the belt is tracking in the *center* of the pulleys.

(3) *Care of the belt sander.* The sander must be kept clean and free from dust. To do this, keep the steel parts free from rust and apply a thin coating of oil occasionally. Put a few drops of oil on each end of the drive shaft. Every 4 to 6 months, remove the belt and take out the screw in the center of the idler pulley. Place a few drops of SAE 30 or 40 oil in the hole and replace the screw and belt.

c. *Portable Belt Sander.* The portable belt sander (fig. 13–180) consists of an endless sanding belt. The belt runs over two rubber-covered pulleys with a flat surface between then called a shoe or backing plate.

(1) *Using the portable belt sander.* The belt sander is used mainly for sanding flat surfaces, but it can be used for round surfaces by using sanding surface over a pulley. It smooths, levels, and edges. It removes tool and cutter marks and will chamfer, round, or bevel. Paint and varnish may be removed rapidly with the use of open grit belts. This machine may also be used in any position: horizontally, vertically, overhead, or on its side. It can be used on wood, metal, glass, or composition materials. When clamped in a vise or fastened in a special stand, it becomes a stationary bench sander for use on flat or curved surfaces. A boom and a counterbalance to hold the machine makes sanding vertical surfaces a much easier chore. Final polishing is speeded and made less tedious by substituting a felt belt for the sanding belt and then machine-rubbing the article to a glistening finish.

(2) *Changing the belt.* The belt is put on by bringing the pulleys closer together. Then the belt is slipped over the pulleys so that it will run in the direction of the arrow stamped on its smooth side. There is an adjustment to keep the belt centered on the pulleys. The sander must never be plugged in unless the switch is in the "off" position; otherwise; the sander will run off the table and fall to the floor, causing serious damage to the machine. The machine must always be disconnected before changing the belt.

d. *Care and Maintenance of Sanders.* Sanders must be kept free from dirt and sawdust. The dust collectors must be emptied frequently for efficient operation. All moving parts must be kept lubricated. Oil must be put in the cups and the chart furnished with each tool must be checked for additional places needing oil. The table of the

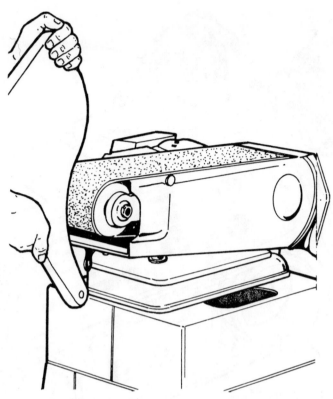

Figure 13–178. Horizontal belt sander.

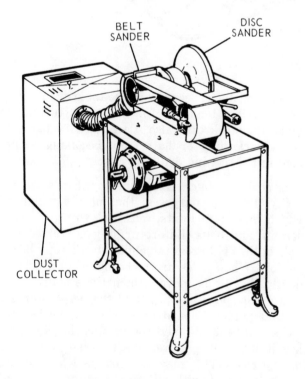

BELT
SANDER

DISC
SANDER

DUST
COLLECTOR

Figure 13–179. Combination sander.

disk and belt sander should have a light coating of oil to prevent rust.

13–85. Drill Press

A drill press (fig. 13–181) consists of a vertical column set in a bench or floor base. On the upper end of the column is the motor which drives the drill. Both the column and the drill are moved down to the work by means of either a hand-operated or foot-operated lever. The press is equipped with a depth-gauge mechanism. The table can be raised, lowered, or tilted 45 degrees to both sides. Floor space needed is 6 by 5 feet.

a. Sizes of Drill Presses. The size of the drill press is figured according to the largest diameter stock that can be held on the table and drilled through the center. In other words, if the distance from the column to the center of the table is 8 inches, a 16-inch disk can be drilled through its center and the size of the drill press is therefore 16 inches.

b. Changing the Speed. The speed of most such

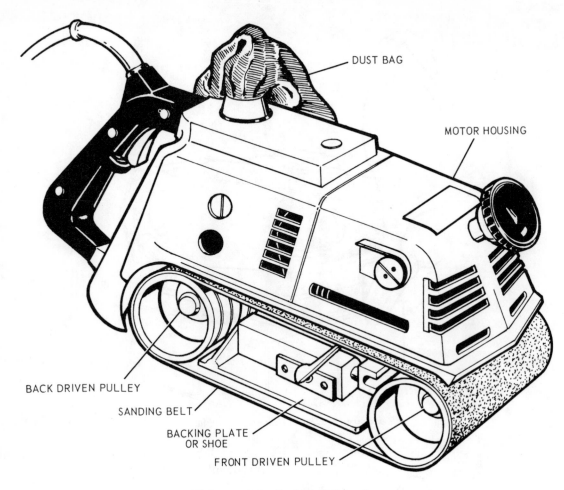

DUST BAG

MOTOR HOUSING

BACK DRIVEN PULLEY

SANDING BELT

BACKING PLATE
OR SHOE

FRONT DRIVEN PULLEY

Figure 13–180. Portable belt sander.

machines can be varied by changing the position of the belt; thus, the drill can be used at high speed for wood or low speed for metal. The speed is faster if the diameter of the power-driven pulley is larger than the other pulley. A slower speed is obtained by the reverse, when the diameter of the power-driven pulley is larger than the other pulley. A slower speed is obtained by the reverse, when the diameter of the power-driven pulley is smaller than the other pulley. A slower speed is needed for drilling metal.

c. Changing Bits. The chuck in which the drill is held is made to hold all types of drills and bits. The drill is secured in the chuck with a key. Care must be taken to secure the drill and to remove the key before turning on the power. It is also necessary to see that the drill is adjusted so that it will not drill into the table of the press when the lever is lowered. The material being drilled

must be fastened securely to the table or in a vise, as there is a tendency for the drill's turning to make the stock turn also. Care must be taken to prevent clothing or hair from becoming entangled in the turning drill and chuck.

d. Drilling Holes. Holes are bored in wood for many different purposes, the most common of which are for joints, electric wires, dowels, screws, and bolts. Before drilling is started, the hole in the drill press table must be directly below the bit. When holes are to be bored to a certain depth, the bit is moved down the required distance alongside the stock and the depth stop set at that point. When drilling plastic, the heavier stock will heat and melt the palstic, thereby making it impossible to remove the drill when the plastic cools. This may be prevented by keeping the hole coated with oil and by pulling the drill out as often as is necessary to keep it cool.

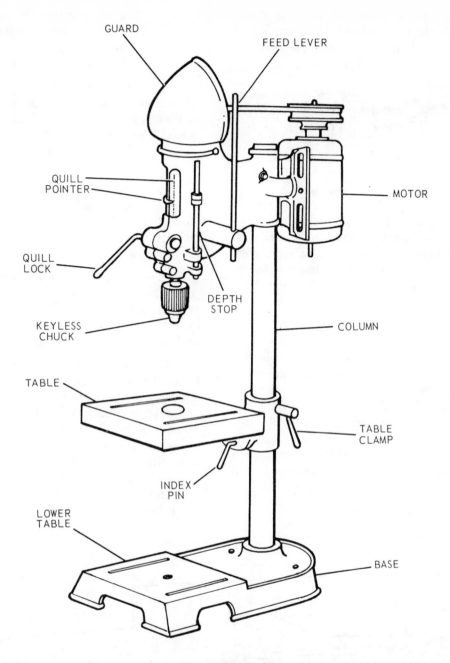

GUARD

FEED LEVER

QUILL
POINTER

QUILL
LOCK

KEYLESS
CHUCK

DEPTH
STOP

TABLE

INDEX
PIN

LOWER
TABLE

MOTOR

COLUMN

TABLE
CLAMP

BASE

Figure 13–181. Drill press.

e. Sanding. Edge sanding can be done with sanding drums up to 3 inches in diameter. To wear the sandpaper down evenly, an auxiliary table with a hole drilled in its center is clamped to the table and raised with wooden blocks of various thicknesses between it and the drill press table.

f. Care and Maintenance of the Drill Press. The drill press must be kept clean and the table, lower table, and columns should have a light coating of oil to prevent rust. The ball bearings are sealed so they need no attention. The outer shell

of the drill should be lubricated occasionally when in the lowered position. The splined end of the spindle shaft should have a few drops of oil at regular intervals, depending on the frequency of use.

g. Safety Precautions. Following are some precautions to prevent injury while using the drill press:

(1) *Secure material to be drilled.* There is a tendency for the drill to grab and either spin the piece off of the table or to spin it in the drill. To prevent this, large pieces are clamped to the

table or assistance is requested to hold them. Small pieces should be secured in the drill press vise (fig. 13–182), then the vise held securely.

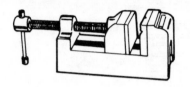

Figure 13–182. Drill press vise.

(2) *Secure loose clothing.* Loose clothing such as sleeves, ties, and scarves should be secured before using the press. There is also danger, with certain hair styles, of the hair getting tangled in the chuck. A hair net or cap should be worn with such styles.

13–86. Jointer

The jointer (fig. 13–183) is essentially an electric plane. It differs from an electric planer, however, in that it is designed to plane the edges of wood (so that they may be joined together), while the planer smoothes the surfaces of wood. Jointer sizes are measured by the maximum width of the stock that can be passed through it, such as 4 inches, 6 inches, etc. Floor space required is 8 by 5 feet.

a. Description of the Jointer.

(1) Two rectangular tables that slide on inclined ways are mounted on the casting, one on each side of the cutter head. The tables are raised or lowered by screws operated by hand wheels.

(2) Two to six knives are set in a tubular head that revolves at high speed. The wood to be planed is supported on the tables and is pushed across the revolving cutter head. All machine planing is based on this principle of rotary cutting.

(3) Instead of cutting off long shavings as a hand plane would, the knives make a series of short hollow cuts. As the wood is moved across the cutter head, a small ridge is formed between each hollow knife cut.

(4) The jointer is equipped with a fence, somewhat resembling that of a circular saw. It is fastened to the rear table, but also extends over the front table. It can be moved crosswise and usually can be tilted to an angle of 45 degrees.

(5) A guard automatically covers the cutter head. Several types are made. One of the most common types swings on a pivot and is held against the fence with a spring. Stock being planed pushes the guard aside, but the spring holds the guard against the side of the stock so that the part of the cutter head between the operator and the stock or fence is always covered. Another type of guard rides on top of the work being planed.

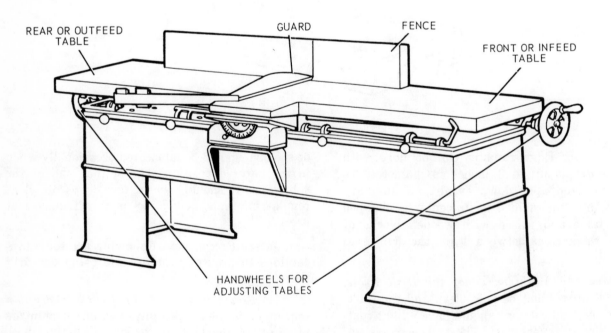

Figure 13–183. Jointer.

b. Adjusting the Outfeed Table.

(1) The jointer has two rectangular iron tables called the infeed or front table and the outfeed or rear table.

(2) The infeed table is the one toward which the cutter head revolves. On this table, stock to be planed is held before it is pushed over the cutter head to the outfeed table.

(3) The outfeed table must be exactly level, with the knives at their highest point of revolution. The infeed table must be lowered to produce a cut; its distance below the outfeed table is equal to the thickness of the cut.

(4) If the outfeed table is too low, it will be noticed that, as the stock leaves the infeed table, it will drop down over the cutter head (fig. 13–184).

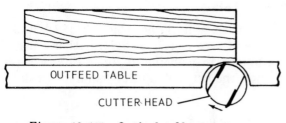

Figure 13–184. Outfeed table to low.

(5) If the outfeed table is too high, a tapering cut is made; more is planed off at the beginning of the cut and hardly anything at the end (fig. 13–185). It is possible to feel at the beginning of the cut that the end of the stock butts against the lip or edge of the outfeed table.

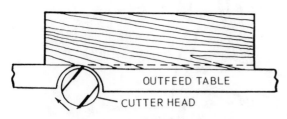

Figure 13–185. Outfeed table too high.

(6) The outfeed table should be set so that it is too low, then the stock run part way over the knives, and the machine stopped. The stock over the outfeed table will not touch it at all. To remedy this, the outfeed table is raised until it supports the stock.

c. Changing Knives in the Cutter Head. To change the knives in the cutter head, these steps should be followed:

(1) Disconnect the machine.

(2) Check the outfeed table and be sure it is at the correct height.

(3) Pull the tables away from the cutter head for more working room.

(4) Cover one of the knives with a piece of wood or leather belting to protect the hands when loosening or tightening the screws that hold it in the cutter head. Different manufacturers use different means to secure the knives and usually furnish a special wrench.

(5) See that the new knives are properly sharpened and of the same weight. Insert one sharp knife in the slot. Set it a little above the correct height and tighten the screws very lightly.

(6) Place a level on the outfeed table so that one end of it projects over the cutter head (fig. 13–186). If the knife lifts the level when the cutter head is revolved with the hands, it is too high. Tap lightly with a mallet to lower.

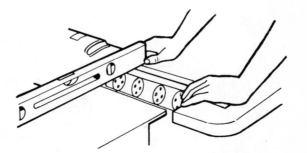

Figure 13–186. Adjusting knife to height, using straightedge or level.

(7) After all knives are replaced, move the tables back to their original position and see that the cutter head has enough clearance before turning on the power.

(8) Now joint the knives with a fine cutting oilstone (fig. 13–187). Place the stone on the outfeed table with one end projecting over the cutter head. Wrap a piece of paper around the part of the stone that rests on the table. When the jointer is running, the knives will touch the stone at their highest point of revolution.

(9) Clamp a stopblock for the oilstone to the infeed table, start the machine, and move the oilstone from side to side until the knives are all ground down to the same height.

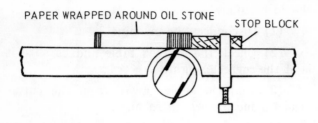

PAPER WRAPPED AROUND OIL STONE   STOP BLOCK

Figure 13–187. Jointing knives with an oilstone.

d. Care and Maintenance of the Jointer. The jointer should be kept clean and the table, frame ways, and adjusting screws kept covered with a light coating of oil. To oil the bearings, remove the pulley and the collar next to the bearings. Use SAE 20 machine oil on these and in oilcups on the machine. The frequency of oiling depends upon the amount of use.

e. Safety Precautions. The jointer is one of the more dangerous of the power tools; therefore, safety precautions must be well understood and observed.

(1) Use only sharp knives of equal weight and make certain that they are set accurately.

(2) Use a push block to push the wood over the slit.

(3) Do not hold the hands over the end of the stock.

(4) Always use the guard.

(5) Do not take too heavy a cut, as this might cause the wood to kick back. A correct cut is when the outfeed table supports the wood on a straight line as it is passing over the cutter heads.

(6) Always stop the machine before cleaning off shavings or moving the fence.

(7) Keep the floor around the machine clean and in good condition.

(8) See that the tables and fence are properly set and locked before starting the machine.

(9) Do not wear loose clothing or gloves while using the machine.

13–87. Lathe

The wood-turning lathe (fig. 13–188) was invented and used centuries before other machines. It is unique in principle of operation because it combines the art and skill of handtool work with

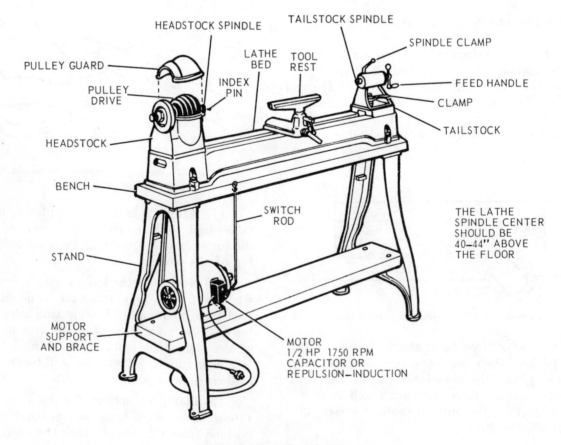

Figure 13–188. Wood lathe.

the mechanical movement of a machine and is used for shaping round work. The lathe is sized by the distance between the headstock and the lathe bed. A 6-inch lathe will turn a 12-inch bowl. Floor space needed is 8 by 5 feet.

a. Description of a Lathe. The essential parts of a lathe are the headstock, or live center, to which are attached faceplates, chucks, and grinding arbors; the tailstock or dead center, which supports the opposite end of the work; and the metal bed which keeps the centers alined. If the piece is to be shaped like a table leg, the work is rotated rapidly between the headstock and tailstock centers. If the piece is to be shaped on one end like a bowl, it is put on the faceplate. With turning tools supported on the tool rest, the rotating wood can be shaped. The turning tools are similar to ordinary chisels and gouges and are sharpened in the same way (sec. VI), but lathe tools are somewhat longer.

b. Wood Turning Tools.

(1) *Gouges.* Wood turning gouges and chisels (fig. 13–189) usually are long and are made of thicker steel than similar bench tools. They are made in different widths and are provided with long and thick handles. Since they are not driven into wood like ordinary chisels, they have no shoulder. There are several types, each with a different purpose.

(*a*) The gouge is beveled on the outside or convex side, and the length of the bevel is about twice the thickness of the steel. The cutting end of a wood-turning gouge also is rounded. Gouges are used to round off square stock and to make concave cuts.

(*b*) The skew chisel is beveled on both sides. Its cutting edge forms an angle of 60 degrees with one side of the chisel. Skew chisels are used to smooth straight, cylindrical stock, to make V-cuts, and to round beads and other convex surfaces.

(*c*) The left and right skew chisels are scraping tools and are beveled on one side only. They are used to smooth straight cylindrical surfaces and to do faceplate work.

(*d*) The parting or cutoff tool is thicker in the center of the blade than at the edges so that it will not bind or overheat when a cut is made with it. It has two bevels that meet at the ridge or high point. The parting tool is used to make narrow cuts to a given depth or diameter. It is often used in conjunction with the outside calipers.

(*e*) The square-nose chisel is like an ordinary chisel, but has a longer and heavier blade. It has only one bevel and is a scraping tool. It is used to smooth straight, cylindrical surfaces, as well as for faceplate work.

(*f*) The round nose chisel is also a scraping tool. It has only one bevel and a rounded cutting edge. It is used to form concave surfaces, as well as for faceplate work.

(*g*) The diamond or spear point is a right and left skew chisel combined in one tool. It is beveled on one side only and is used like other scraping tools.

(2) *Measuring tools.* Different types of calipers are used to measure the piece and to compose the piece being made with the pattern.

(*a*) The dividers have two sharp steel points. They are used to step off measurements and to make circles on faceplate work (A, fig. 13–190).

(*b*) The inside calipers are used to measure the inside diameters of turned boxes, bowls, rings, etc. (B, fig. 13–190).

(*c*) The outside calipers are used to measure outside diameters of turned work, (C, fig. 13–190).

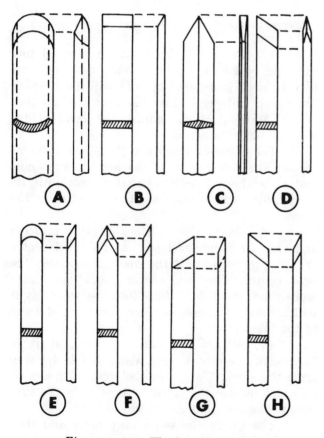

Figure 13–189. Wood-turning chisels.

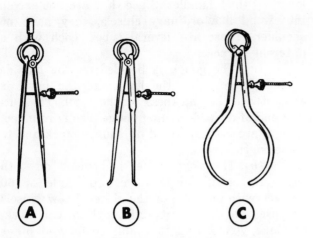

Figure 13–190. Dividers and inside and outside calipers.

c. *Spindle Turning.* This covers all operations on stock that is held between the headstock (line center) and the tailstock (dead center).

(1) *Centering stock.* Stock must be centered and mounted in the lathe well to keep it from flying out of the lathe during the turning process.

(*a*) Square the stock to dimensions and allow at least 1/4 inch more than the largest diameter of the turning. It is also well to square the ends before mounting the stock in the lathe. In some cases, it is necessary to allow an inch or more on the length; in other cases where the marks of the centers will not show, it is better to cut them to exact length.

(*b*) Draw the diagonals on both ends of the stock to locate the exact center. When using hard lumber, make shallow saw cuts along the diagonals on one end of the stock (fig. 13–191). On the other end, bore or punch a small hole in the center.

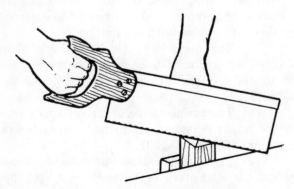

Figure 13–191. Sawing on diagonals.

(*c*) Remove the live center from the lathe and drive it into the end on which the diagonals were sawed so that its prongs enter the saw cuts (fig. 13–192). Use a mallet because the blows from a steel hammer will eventually widen the end of the live center so that is will no longer fit the spindle.

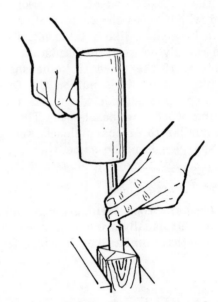

Figure 13–192. Driving line center into end of stock.

(*d*) Put a few drops of machine oil into the hole bored in the other end. Soap or wax may be used instead of oil and will not discolor the wood. This end must be lubricated so that the constant friction against the dead center will not burn the wood.

(*e*) Without removing the stock from it, replace the live center in the headstock spindle and slide the tailstock along the bed until its dead center enters the hole bored for it in the wood.

(*f*) Clamp the tailstock in this position and turn its handwheel so that the dead center exerts pressure against the wood; then clamp the dead center. The cone center should not enter more than about 3/16 inch into the wood, as it will otherwise cause excessive friction in spite of the lubrication.

(*g*) Adjust the tool rest so that it is level with the centers and about 1/8 inch away from the stock. Clamp the tool rest in this position and revolve the stock by hand to make sure that it has sufficient clearance.

(*h*) Check the setup once more and then start the lathe.

(2) *Turning a plain cylinder.* The stock is fastened in the lathe as described in (1) above and then these steps should be followed:

(*a*) Use the gouge for rounding the square stock. Grasp the handle at the end with the right hand and hold the blade about 1 inch from the cutting edge with the left hand. Have the palm of the left hand in contact with the tool rest to act as a guide for the tool. Roll the gouge a little toward the right, lift the handle slowly, and begin the cut a few inches from the dead center, pushing the gouge away from you or toward the right (fig. 13–193).

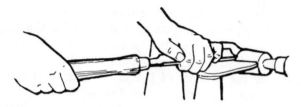

Figure 13–193. Cutting with a gouge.

(*b*) Make another cut in the same direction, but begin it nearer the center of the stock. Make two or three cuts more until most of the stock appears round.

(*c*) Then roll the gouge toward the left and pull it toward you or to the left, rounding the left end of the stock. Move the tool from one end of the stock to the other until a uniform surface of sufficient diameter is produced. Do not begin the cuts at the ends of the stock, because the gouge may catch in the wood and cause it to be thrown from the lathe. If too long a cut is taken while rounding off the corners, large splinters are likely to fly off and may injure the operator.

(*d*) Stop the lathe to see if the stock is nearly round. If wide flat sides are still visible, further rounding with the gouge is necessary.

(*e*) When round, stop the lathe and move the tool rest closer to the work. Then set the calipers to about 1/16 inch more than the finished diameter is to be. Hold the calipers loosely in the left hand and a parting tool in the right hand.

(*f*) Make a cut with the parting tool (fig. 13–194) near one end and at the same time hold the calipers in the groove formed. When the correct depth is reached, the calipers slip over the stock. Make similar cuts about 2 inches apart throughout the length of the cylinder in order to obtain the correct diameter (fig. 13–195).

(*g*) Using the scraping method, smooth

Figure 13–194. Cutting to size with a parting tool.

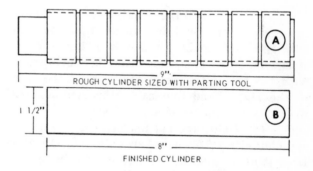

ROUGH CYLINDER SIZED WITH PARTING TOOL

FINISHED CYLINDER

Figure 13–195. Method of turning a plain cylinder.

the cylinder with a square-nose chisel (fig, 13–196). Run the lathe at its maximum speed, hold the chisel flat on the tool rest, and move it back and forth until the grooves made by the parting tool have disappeared and the cylinder is smooth and of uniform diameter.

Figure 13–196. Smoothing with square-nose chisel (scraping method).

(*h*) Square the end that runs on the dead center with the parting tool or with the point of the skew chisel held so that its side is flat on the tool rest (fig. 13–197).

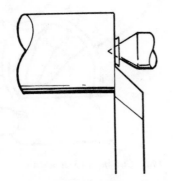

Figure 13–197. *Squaring end with skew chisel (scraping method).*

(*i*) Measure the length of the cylinder from the squared end and cut down at this point with the parting tool until only 1/4 inch of the stock remains. This may then be cut through with the toe of the skew chisel. Hold the chisel in the right hand and catch the cylinder with the left when the wood separates.

(*j*) Using the cutting method, smooth the cylinder with a 3/4-inch skew chisel (fig. 13–198). Hold it at an angle of 60 degrees to the surface and cut with the middle of the bevel. The chisel may be moved in either direction, but the cut should never be started at the end. The end which runs on the dead center is squared with the point or toe of the skew chisel when its edge is held on the tool rest. The bevel of the chisel must be parallel to the end in order to make a square cut (fig. 13–199).

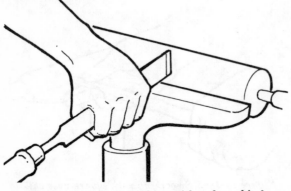

Figure 13–198. *Smoothing with a skew chisel.*

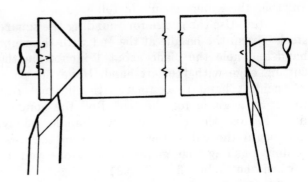

Figure 13–199. *Squaring one end of stock and cutting the other to length (cutting method).*

(*k*) Measure the length of the cylinder from the squared end and cut down with the toe of the skew chisel at this point. Hold the chisel so that this cut will be square to the cylinder. With the toe or heel of the skew chisel, make a series of sloping cuts against this square surface. Make the cut deeper gradually until only 1/4 inch of the stock remains. Finish the cut with the point of the skew chisel, holding it in the right hand only, and catch the cylinder with the left as the wood separates.

d. Faceplate Turning. Faceplate work means that the stock is fastened to a faceplate or screw chuck which screws onto the end of the live spindle and is supported entirely on that.

(1) *Fastening work to faceplate.*

(*a*) Use only stock with a flat, smooth surface and mark a circle on it a little larger in diameter than the finished dimension. To center the faceplate accurately on the stock, mark a circle also on it that is equal in diameter to that of the faceplate, using a compass or a pair of dividers.

(*b*) Saw the dish to size on a band saw, place the faceplate on the small circle marked, and fasten it with screws.

(*c*) If the wood is hard, first mark and bore the screw holes. The screws will enter the wood more easily if soap is applied to their threads.

(*d*) Place a leather or cardboard washer on the live spindle and screw the faceplate onto it. (The washer prevents the faceplate from jamming against the shoulder of the live spindle.)

(2) *Turning with a faceplate.* Scraping tools generally are used for faceplate work. The tool operations involved are facing off, squaring an edge, and cutting a hole or recess.

(*a*) After mounting the stock, place the tool rest parallel to the disk to be turned and a little below its center. The cutting is to be done only on that half of the disk nearest the operator.

(*b*) Face off. This means turning the face of the disk so that it is flat and even. If much stock has to be taken off, use a roundnose chisel first and work it back and forth across the disk from its left edge to its center.

(*c*) Smooth with a square-nose chisel (fig. 13–200) and test for flatness with the edge of a square held along the diameter of the disk (fig. 13–201).

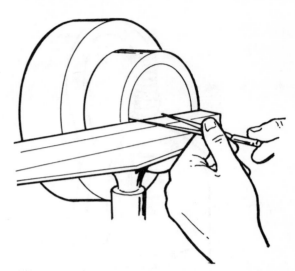

Figure 13–202. *Marking circle with the dividers set to the radius.*

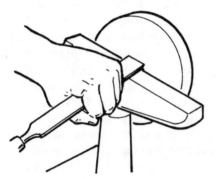

Figure 13–200. *Smoothing face of disk with square-nose chisel.*

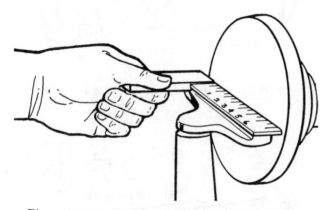

Figure 13–201. *Testing for flatness with a try square.*

(*d*) To square the edge, first mark the diameter of the disk with a pair of dividers. Set the dividers to a little more than the radius (fig. 13–202), place both legs on the tool rest in a horizontal position, stick one point into the exact center of the revolving disk and bring the other one gradually in contact with its surface.

(*e*) Hold a skew chisel flat on the tool rest and at right angles to the disk. Cut with its toe outside the line marked with the dividers. Take several light cuts and test for squareness after each one, until the disk is of the correct diameter.

(*f*) Do not stand directly in front of the edge when squaring or shaping the disk, because it may split and come apart. When shaping the edge, take only very light cuts and have the tools very sharp.

(*g*) Cut a hole or a recess with a skew chisel. (Recesses are simply large and shallow holes which are cut with round-nose and skew chisels.) Use the roundnose chisel, which cuts more rapidly, if it is to be a large or deep hole, but make the finishing cuts with a skew chisel.

e. Care and Maintenance of the Lathe. The lathe must be kept clean and the lathe bed covered with a light coating of oil to prevent rust. Lubrication is specific for the exact tool so read the directions that come with the lathe. When the chisels are not in use, they should be coated with oil to prevent rust.

f. Safety Precautions. Safety precautions for the lathe are similar to those for other tools, with a few additional ones.

(1) Have the lathe turning slowly when the wood is rough.

(2) Have no loose clothing or bathrobe cords where they will get into the turning parts. Roll up sleeves.

(3) Wear goggles, when operating the lathe.

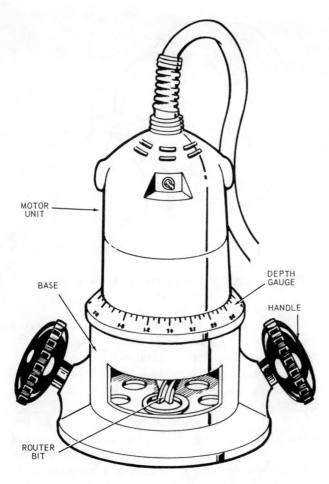

Figure 13-203. Portable router.

(4) Clear the space around the lathe and be sure the floor is clean.

(5) Do not talk while operating the lathe.

(6) Do not lay chisels on the lathe or lathe table, as the vibration of the motor jars the tools enough to make them fall.

13-88. Portable Router

A portable router (fig. 13-203) is a high-speed motor that is held in the hand while it is guided over the stock. The motor screws into a base which is fitted with two handles and a guide for both

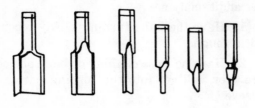

Figure 13-204. Router and veining bits.

straight and curved edges. The depth of the cut is determined by the distance the motor is screwed into the base.

a. Using the Router.

(1) *Veining.* To vein and flute means to cut shallow grooves. Veined lines are narrow; flutes are somewhat larger. These grooves are used to decorate a wood surface. Viened lines are usually left open, but may be filled with a paste of contrasting color. Veining and fluting bits have rounded ends, while router bits have flat ends (fig. 13-204).

(2) *Shaping.* Shaping work may be done with special bits that have a round shank below the cutting edges. The shank is called a "pilot" and regulates the depth of the cut. It follows all edges, both straight and curved (fig. 13-205).

(3) *Miscellaneous work.* Small holes, mortises, grooves, dadoes, and rabbets may be easily and quickly made on a router. The holes and mortises are limited in depth by the length of the router bits. Mortising (fig. 13-206) is making a closed groove in wood for making a joint. A groove (fig. 13-207) is a channel that usually runs the length of the wood, whereas a dado is a channel that runs across the width of the wood.

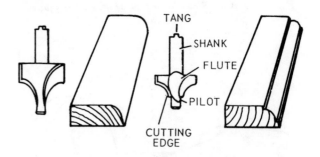

Figure 13-205. Beading and rounding over bits.

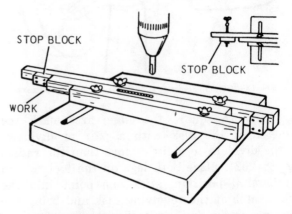

Figure 13-206. Mortising with a router bit.

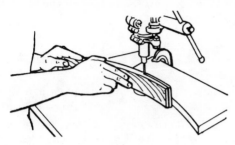

Figure 13–207. Grooving curved stock.

A rabbet (fig. 13–208) is a rectangular groove cut on the adjoining edge and face of a board. It is used on pictures, mirrors, and window and door frames.

b. Care and Maintenance of the Router. The only maintenance needed on the router is to keep it clean. The ball bearings of the router are grease-sealed and do not need to be lubricated.

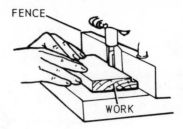

Figure 13–208. Rabbeting on a router.

c. Safety Precautions.

(1) Always wear goggles when using the router.

(2) Keep the bits sharp at all times.

(3) Disconnect the router when changing bits.

(4) Always turn the router off before setting it down, as the drill will drill the table or bench.